Graffiti Scratched, Scrawled, Sprayed

Studies in Manuscript Cultures

Edited by
Imre Galambos, Konrad Hirschler, Caroline Macé,
Cécile Michel, Jörg B. Quenzer and Eva Wilden

Volume 35

Graffiti Scratched, Scrawled, Sprayed

Towards a Cross-Cultural Understanding

Edited by
Ondřej Škrabal, Leah Mascia,
Ann Lauren Osthof and Malena Ratzke

DE GRUYTER

The publication of this volume was funded by the Deutsche Forschungsgemeinschaft (DFG, German Research Foundation) under Germany's Excellence Strategy – EXC 2176 'Understanding Written Artefacts: Material, Interaction and Transmission in Manuscript Cultures' – project no. 390893796.

ISBN 978-3-11-221547-0
e-ISBN (PDF) 978-3-11-132630-6
e-ISBN (EPUB) 978-3-11-132631-3
ISSN 2365-9696
DOI https://doi.org/10.1515/9783111326306

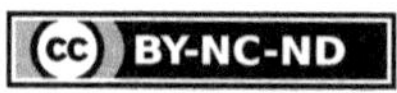

Library of Congress Control Number: 2023947844

Bibliographic information published by the Deutsche Nationalbibliothek
The Deutsche Nationalbibliothek lists this publication in the Deutsche Nationalbibliografie; detailed bibliographic data are available on the internet at http://dnb.dnb.de.

This volume is text- and page-identical with the hardback published in 2023.
This book is published with open access at www.degruyter.com.

Printing and binding: CPI books GmbH, Leck

www.degruyter.com

Contents

Ondřej Škrabal, Leah Mascia, Ann Lauren Osthof and Malena Ratzke
Towards a Cross-Cultural Understanding of Graffiti: Terminology, Context, Semiotics, Documentation —— 1

Africa

Ursula Verhoeven
Writing Wherever Possible and Meaningful: Graffiti Culture in Ancient Egypt. Context, Terminology, Documentation —— 47

Seth M. Markle
'Spray It Loud': Hip Hop Graffiti Culture and Politics in Dar es Salaam, 2003–2018 —— 77

America

Jarosław Źrałka
Incised Images among the Palaces and Temples: The Content and Meaning of Pre-Columbian Maya Graffiti —— 109

Alexander Araya López
Graffiti and the Media: Between Politics, Art and Vandalism —— 143

Central and East Asia

Matsui Dai
Old Uyghur Graffiti Inscriptions from Central Asia —— 173

Nadine Bregler
Chinese Graffiti in Dunhuang? —— 215

Minna Valjakka
Transcribed Flows and Arrhythmias: 'Graffiti' in Relation to Epigraphic and Artistic Trajectories in Today's Mainland China —— 233

Intermezzo

Sanja Ewald in conversation with Mirko Reisser
The Spray Can as an Attitude to Life between Illegal Action and Commercial Art: A Conversation on the Emergence of a Modern Graffiti Form with the Artist Mirko Reisser alias DAIM — 267

South and West Asia

Ingo Strauch
Graffiti in Ancient India: Towards the Definition of a Genre of Indian Epigraphy — 287

Carlo G. Cereti
Graffiti in Middle Iranian: Some Preliminary Notes — 327

Michael C.A. Macdonald
Voices in the Wilderness: Some Unexpected Uses of Graffiti — 355

Mia Trentin
Medieval and Early Modern Graffiti in Eastern Mediterranean: A New Methodological Approach — 383

Europe

Rebecca R. Benefiel, Holly M. Sypniewski
Documenting Ancient Graffiti: Text, Image, Support and Access — 425

Anne Vieth
Curating Graffiti: The Exhibition *Wände* | *Walls* in the Kunstmuseum Stuttgart — 467

Contributors — 487

Index — 491

Ondřej Škrabal, Leah Mascia,
Ann Lauren Osthof and Malena Ratzke

Towards a Cross-Cultural Understanding of Graffiti: Terminology, Context, Semiotics, Documentation

In early May 2013, a teenager from Nanjing defaced a 3,500-year-old wall relief in the Luxor Temple with a clumsily executed graffito: 'Ding Jinhao visited this place' (*Ding Jinhao dao ci yi you* 丁錦昊到此一游, Fig. 1). The photograph from the scene soon went viral and instantly elicited outright denunciation worldwide. Critical voices were particularly strong in China, where netizens, media and officials condemned the uncivilized comport of Chinese sightseers at both domestic and overseas tourist attractions, airing a general frustration over the growing number of similar reports. Nevertheless, while disapproving of such vandalistic behaviour, historically-minded writers were quick to note that, from the perspective of the *longue durée*, Ding was really just following the practice of many earlier predecessors: European explorers, Arabic merchants, Greek colonizers and even ancient Egyptians themselves all left written marks on the walls of the temple.[1] In the same vein, the editors of a recent volume on graffiti pointed out that, by noting his presence on the temple wall, the fifteen-year-old Ding was 'enacting an ancient Egyptian behaviour'.[2]

Even more so, Ding was enacting an ancient *Chinese* behaviour. The formula he scrawled over the torso and *shendyt* of Amun-Ra is identical to one the cheeky Monkey King once inked on what he took to be a massive pink pillar at the edge of the world. In this fantastic story from *Journey to the West*, first published in China towards the close of the sixteenth century CE and still going strong, the almighty Buddha challenges the Monkey King to escape from the palm of his hand. Rather than reaching the edge of the world, the Monkey King reaches only the edge of the Buddha's expanding palm, mistaking the fingers for monumental pillars. The inscription 'The Great Sage, Equal to Heaven, visited this place' (*Qitian*

1 Murphy 2013; Perrottet 2016; Baird and Taylor 2016, 23; Dirven and van Gelder 2018, 1. See Trentin in this volume on early modern Europeans' Grand Tour graffiti.

2 Ragazzoli, Harmanşah and Salvador 2018, 3.

https://doi.org/10.1515/9783111326306-001

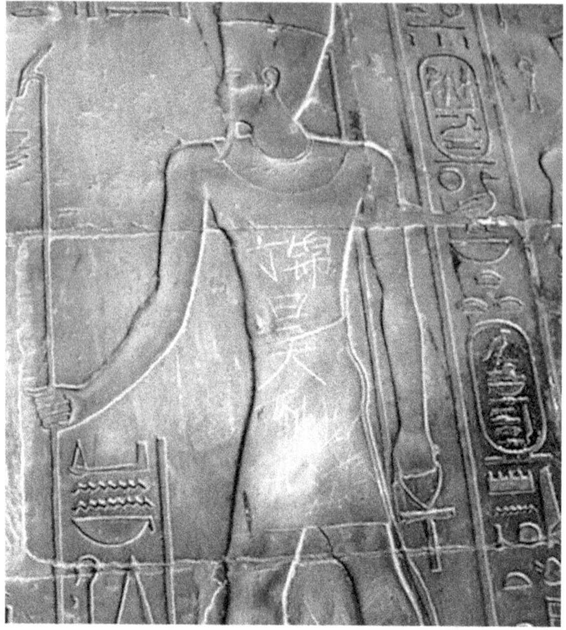

Fig. 1: Ding Jinhao's scrawl inside the Luxor Temple, with the surrounding hieroglyphic inscriptions. Photograph © "Kong you wu yi" 空游无依, <weibo.com/u/1440641483>.

Dasheng dao ci yi you 齊天大聖到此一游) was supposed to attest to Monkey's achievement; instead, however, it served as proof of his failure, along with the odour of monkey urine, with which the brazen protagonist desecrated the rightmost of the 'pillars'.[3] To be sure, rather than being a product of the author's imagination, the formula '[such and such] visited this place' (*dao ci yi you*) was borrowed into the novel from contemporaneous traveller practice.[4] Four hundred

3 For an English translation of this famous story, see Wu Cheng'en 2012, 194–195.

4 The first part of the formula, literally 'arrived here' (*dao ci* 到此), first appears in the ninth century CE at the latest, when Chinese pilgrims used to note their presence at Buddhist sites across the country. Some of the grotto temple sites in Gansu Province still preserve these formulas inked or engraved along with the name and/or the date of arrival at the site, such as Maijishan grotto no. 213 ('arrived here on the fifth day of the fourth month of the ninth year of the Kaibao [era]' 開寶九年四月五日到此), corresponding to the year 976 CE; see Tianshui Maijishan shiku yishu yanjiusuo 1998, 286. The formula engraved in 1329 CE in Mogao grotto no. 126 differs slightly from the one used by Monkey but conveys the very same idea: 'On the twenty-fifth day of the fifth month of the second year of the Tianli [era], Suo Zhong, the resident of Andao quarter of the Jining circuit, arrived here to visit' 天曆二年五月廿五日晉寧路安道坊住人索中到此遊耳;

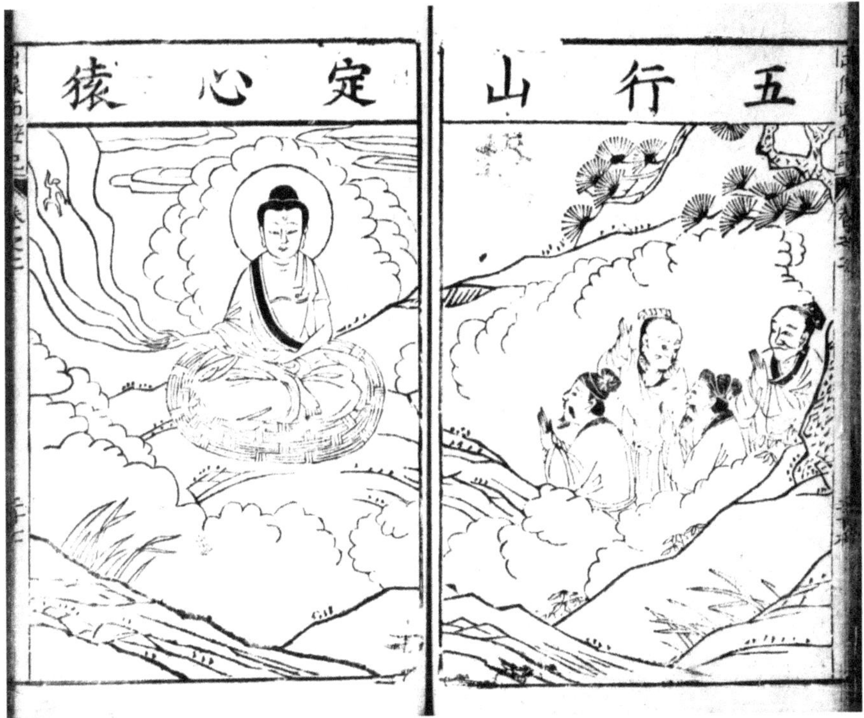

Fig. 2: The Monkey King's vain attempt to escape from the palm of the Buddha's right hand as depicted in the Hall of Transgenerational Virtue 世德堂 woodblock print edition of *Journey to the West*, 1592 CE, *juan* 2, fols 26b–27a.

years later, it remains ubiquitous at tourism sites in China and beyond,[5] inspiring the Dings of this world to perpetuate this contagious habit.

What this case highlights are two basic tenets of the present volume: first, that historical and contemporary graffiti practices are inextricable and must be studied together; second, to fully understand graffiti practices, we need to place them not only in historical, but also in truly global perspective.

---

see Matsui and Arakawa 2017, 370–371. Compare the Latin *hic fuit* ('was here'), used throughout Europe from antiquity to the early modern period.

5 Reportedly spotted on various landmarks worldwide, including the Statue of Liberty; see 'Guangzhou Renda daibiao faxian "dao ci yi you" keshang Ziyou nüshen xiang" 廣州人大代表發現 "到此一游" 刻上自由女神像, *Sohu News*, 29 November 2007, <http://news.sohu.com/20071129/n253683008.shtml> (accessed on 11 March 2023).

1 Why take a cross-cultural approach to graffiti?

There is little doubt that coupling the Monkey King's inscription with a scent mark in the above story was a satirical analogy, voicing the sixteenth-century author's disdain of travellers' graffiti; yet, knowingly or not, it clearly involved some profound anthropological premises. The constantly increasing number of graffiti documented through fieldwork and research indicates that wherever people learned how to write, the writing (and non-writing) sooner or later spilled over to places and surfaces that were originally not conceived to receive writing, as though leaving a graphic mark was a deeply ingrained instinct. In other words, humans' urge to claim their voice in the surrounding visual landscape seems to be one of the universals of literate societies past and present.

The language, script, content, style and writing tools will differ from place to place and person to person; yet some of what people actually *do* through graffiti may well share common ground regardless of time and space. Thus, while always embedded in specific socio-cultural contexts, graffiti not only constitute sources for the study of particular communities and cultures; when considered globally, they may also offer general insights into the anthropology and sociology of writing.

Travellers' graffiti may just be a perfect example of this. Why is it that visitors, pilgrims or travellers tend to leave a graphic footprint at the destination site? The likes of the Monkey King write their monikers to prove an achievement, either to their contemporaries, posterity or future self, while a pilgrim's scrawl at a cultic site can often embody an act of devotion;[6] Ding's own motives are unknown, but most likely fall into the 'me too' category so prominent in adolescents. What other categories can be established, and how do they correlate with different demographics and cultural traits? What are the prerequisites for a society to develop this specific type of 'epigraphic habit'?[7] And what are the common behavioural alternatives to writing and drawing in this context? To explore these questions, we need to engage with the broadest possible range of materials, including not only cultures that are geographically and culturally adjacent, but also those remote in both time and space, considering evidence as diverse as the various layers (including modern ones) of visitors' graffiti on the above-mentioned ancient Egyptian

6 See, for instance, Naveh 1979; Felle and Ward-Perkins 2021b.
7 For the notion of 'epigraphic habit', see MacMullen 1982.

sites, medieval Viking ship graffiti in Hagia Sofia, and the votive ink inscriptions left behind by seventeenth-century Japanese travellers in Angkor Wat.[8]

Over the last two decades, the study of graffiti has emerged as a bustling field, propelled by ambitious documentation and research projects and the realisation of the historical, sociological, linguistic and anthropological value of this special form of graphic expression. While locally or regionally rooted projects remain the driving force, ever more talks, articles, workshops, edited collections, monographs and even handbooks evince a growing interest in situating graffiti and graffiti practices in broader territorial, historical or cultural contexts. Edited collections in particular represent crucial venues for the promotion of comparative and cross-cultural research, as they offer the opportunity to introduce less visible fields and topics to the larger community of researchers from unrelated disciplines.[9]

A few recent volumes offer a diverse array of case studies spanning from Mesoamerica to East Asia, but it is ancient Mediterranean, medieval European and modern Euro-American spaces, with their shared, intertwined epigraphic cultures, that have predominantly been in focus. This is certainly not out of neglect; rather, it is an understandable result of the auspicious confluence of several historical and socio-economic factors: material preservation of the actual (historical) graffiti *in situ*, scholars and scholarly traditions appreciating the value of these materials, and often also the availability of public funds for such undertakings. Consequently, scholars in these fields have been able to fruitfully relate their individual case studies to a more general 'North Atlantic' context of graffiti creation and reception and herald the potential of future cross-cultural research.

Aside from the flourishing fields that have burst forth to show the way, there are also fields that have just started to sprout, as well as latent fields to which the concept of 'graffiti' has yet to be introduced. In some of these fields, conspicuously overlapping with areas of the Global South, the presence of 'graffiti'-like inscriptions has been acknowledged and documented yet disregarded and never

8 For the former, see Thomov 2014; for the latter, see Shimizu 1965 or the English summary in Ishizawa 2015, 48–53.

9 It is impossible to provide the exhaustive list here; the most consequential volumes include Baird and Taylor 2011; Keegan 2015; Lovata and Olton 2015; Youkhana and Förster 2015; Ross 2016; Avramidis and Tsilimpounidi 2017; Ragazzoli et al. 2018; Lohmann 2018c; *Sur les murs: histoire(s) de graffitis* 2018; Emberling and Davis 2019; van Belle and Brun 2020 and Felle and Ward-Perkins 2021b. See also the special issues of *Tijdschrift voor Geschiedenis* 1/2018 and *Journal of Early Modern Studies* 9/2020 ('Stone, Castles and Palaces to Be Read: Graffiti and Wall Writings in Medieval and Early Modern Europe'). Probably the first monograph on graffiti with a comparative angle is Reisner 1971. Good research overviews can be found in Lohmann 2020 and Sarti 2020 (historical graffiti) and Rodriguez 2015 (contemporary graffiti).

appreciated by scholarly traditions; in other fields, both old and new discoveries await funds for researchers to even begin an inquiry; and in still others, inscriptions have been studied but never related to the phenomenon of graffiti.[10] Nevertheless, all these fields are of equal and critical importance for the truly comprehensive study of graffiti.

Thus, the goal of this volume is to complement these recent efforts to showcase the diversity in the creation, reception and curation of graffiti around the globe throughout history and up to the present day, and in so doing, to raise the topic of a cross-cultural approach to the study of graffiti. Inviting hitherto less internationally visible fields to partake in the comparative feast is essential to this undertaking, as they can enrich and diversify the current understanding of graffiti. At the same time, we are delighted that many 'established' fields can be represented here, too, to reflect on their long-standing research traditions and share their abundant fieldwork, documenting and publishing experience. In this regard, the contributions by Ursula Verhoeven, Mia Trentin, Rebecca Benefiel and Holly Sypniewski offer invaluable sources of inspiration and practical knowledge for anyone developing documentation projects in previously unexplored fields, but also an interesting point of reference and reflection for seasoned archaeologists seeking more food for thought.

2 Graffiti and the 'written artefact' approach

In recent years, researchers have identified several key topics in the study of graffiti. This volume lays emphasis on four of them: the terminology and definition of graffiti; their spatial context and relation to other inscribed objects; their multigraphic property of involving both script and images; and their methods of documentation. In exploring these, we propose to approach graffiti through the prism of written artefacts,[11] taking the material object as a point of departure: a wall, a rock face, a commuter train, a toilet door. In this approach, the material carrier of graffiti can be perceived as equivalent to manuscript media such as

10 The best examples of these fields are graffiti studies on sub-Saharan Africa and Central, Southeast and East Asia, most of which are only in their infancy, especially for historical periods; see for instance Griffiths 2021 and Kirichenko 2021.

11 This approach builds on the advances of both archaeology and 'new' or 'material philology', and lies at the heart of the Cluster of Excellence 'Understanding Written Artefacts: Material, Interaction and Transmission in Manuscript Cultures' at the Centre for the Study of Manuscript Cultures, University of Hamburg.

scrolls, codices or notebooks. A wall hosting graffiti by a range of individuals, then, can be likened to a codex containing a plethora of texts copied by different scribes or other so-called multiple-text manuscripts.[12]

On the one hand, this broad perspective helps us live up to the key commitment of the study of graffiti – to consider the subject in its spatial context.[13] Not only does it compel us to consider the spatial setting of individual graffiti, but also their mutual relation in places where they cluster and form assemblages, or, as Michael Macdonald aptly calls it in his contribution to this volume, 'graffiti companionships'. On the other hand, the focus on the material medium helps us better appreciate the often unexpected affordances of man-made artefacts and the creativity they spark. For instance, equipping communal latrines with screens and doors not only marked a watershed in the human perception of privacy, but also gave rise to the new genre of *latrinalia*.

Generally speaking, erecting walls prompts separation, yet it also provides new avenues for graphic expression. But is it useful to construe, for instance, the thousands of kilometres of the Great Wall of China as a single written artefact? It would surely be a composite one, consisting of countless formally inscribed slabs, official plaques and unauthorized graffiti accumulated across centuries. Yet it still seems legitimate to ask how the construction of the Great Wall ushered literacy into previously inconceivable spaces; how its presence reshaped patterns of writing production in those locales; how graffiti contribute to its unique 'sense of place';[14] or what role it plays in inspiring travellers to record their names at other tourist sites. And, conceptually speaking, what agency does the Great Wall have in the public discourse about graffiti, the preservation of cultural heritage and related policies? All these questions demonstrate that, as far-fetched as it may seem today,[15] applying the concept of a written artefact to large man-made structures may well be a productive approach.

---

12 On multiple-text manuscripts, see Friedrich and Schwarke 2016 and Bausi, Friedrich and Maniaci 2020.

13 Benefiel 2010; Baird and Taylor 2011; Lohmann 2018b. Compare also Matsumoto 2022, 293.

14 For the notion of 'sense of place', see Tuan 1974; Relph 1976; Tuan 1977.

15 The trends in the advancement of documentation technologies show that the holistic approach will be increasingly feasible even for artefacts that could previously not be considered in their entirety. Fifty years from now, a 3D scan of the entire Great Wall will surely sound less 'science fiction' than it does today. In fact, as discussed below, the traditional textual focus in documentation reflects not only the scholarly interest in texts, but also the historical limitations of documentation techniques. The digital age does away with these limitations to a large extent and shifts the paradigm in the study of written artefacts.

The particular locales of a (larger) written artefact where graffiti occur, either singly or in assemblages ('companionships'), can thus be approached as 'graffiti sites'. Probing into the spatial and temporal relations between individual graffiti sites and the multilayered, multigraphic and multilingual features of those consisting of graffiti assemblages will shed further light on the dynamics of their production and underlying socio-cultural factors.

3 On terminology: Why 'graffiti'? And what is it anyway?

Standardized terminology is the sine qua non of comparative and cross-cultural research. In this regard, the term 'graffiti' is a powerful conceptual weapon, yet it is a kind of double-edged sword. On the one hand, as a marketing label, it has done outstanding service in increasing the salience of this type of long-neglected material,[16] which, as a result, has achieved acceptance as a fully fledged member of the 'historical source' family in many (but still not all) disciplines. Moreover, unlike labels such as 'informal inscriptions' or 'secondary epigraphy', 'graffiti' is succinct and inclusive: it can encompass writing as well as non-linguistic signs, drawings and doodles, and it does not unjustly imply the primacy of other, 'more important' kinds of writing. It is an invaluable keyword that facilitates interdisciplinary communication; it is also a chic concept that ignites interest far beyond the ivory towers of the academic community.

Yet, on the other hand, the word 'graffiti' lives a fully unbridled linguistic life, lending itself to all (im)possible semantic permutations by way of interpretation, reinterpretation and misinterpretation on the part of scholars, curators, the general public, media and policymakers. Even within the academic sphere, the use of the term remains extremely fluid, utterly subjective and thus notoriously problematic, as it commonly denotes a heterogenous range of epigraphic phenomena across disciplines and scholarly traditions. In the opening essay of this volume, for instance, Ursula Verhoeven discusses no less than seven general approaches to the definition of 'graffiti' that have emerged solely within the Egyptological tradition. While this demonstrates the field's awareness of the issue of definition, it also underscores the difficulties of resolving it.

The question of how to define 'graffiti' has been broached time and again over the last two decades and constituted one of the main incentives for several

16 Baird and Taylor 2011, 5; Baird and Taylor 2016, 22.

publications.[17] Our incentive was no different – and in line with previous collections, we too have steered clear of enforcing a single, uniform definition throughout the entire multi-author volume. Instead, we have invited the contributors to elaborate on issues of definition and terminology in their respective essays. Yet, unwilling to shy away from the issue completely, and in the hope of stimulating further discussion, we offer here our deliberations on the tangle of issues surrounding the use and disputed definition of the term 'graffiti'.

The crux of the discord around the issue of definition seems to lie in the different expectations regarding the purpose of the term 'graffiti'. One camp of scholars assumes a strictly 'documentary' attitude, seeking to find a convenient catch-all label encompassing a variety of informal inscription types sharing some common traits.[18] Many of these scholars engage in archaeological surveys and the documentation of graffiti *in situ*, and they are thus justifiably reluctant to employ tentative hypotheses as the guiding principle for classification; they prefer to record and classify their material in the most objective way possible. As archaeologist and social historian Mia Trentin argues in this volume, this kind of descriptive approach is the indispensable first step for any subsequent attempts at definition.

The 'interpretive' camp, on the other hand, has a different agenda. They maintain that among that great variety of informal inscriptions, there is one particular type that stands out for its distinct, transgressive character: being inscribed in places without the consent of their owners or custodians, however nominal they be. For this latter camp, the term 'graffiti' is charged with implications: by the sheer act of designating an inscription as a 'graffito', they deliberately make a series of claims and assumptions about its creation, purpose and reception.

The key notion in the interpretive approach is *not* the medium (wall or street furniture), technique (scratching or painting), space (indoor or outdoor, public or domestic) or style (formal or informal); it is the *relation* between the graffitist and the surface.[19] It is a fleeting romance rather than a sanctified marriage; an unsolicited making instead of a sponsored undertaking; an arbitrary appropriation, not an official intervention. It is the creator taking possession of the surface, not the surface (via its owner) taking possession of the creator, as is the case, for instance, in commissioned street art.[20]

---

17 See especially Ragazzoli et al. 2018.

18 Such as being scratched or incised on walls in an informal hand.

19 Compare Béatrice Fraenkel's notion of graffiti as a type of 'writing act' (Fraenkel 2010).

20 Interestingly, both camps do agree that once 'graffiti' are commissioned, they lose their 'graffiti' status – they cease to be informal, not to say illegal; they become official inscriptions or graffiti-style art. In our understanding, graffiti may but need not be street art, and street art is

Clearly, the two camps – the 'documenters' and the 'interpreters' – can never agree on a definition of 'graffiti'. Even within individual camps, the search for consensus is not without controversy. Every scholar's judgement is entrenched in their individual epistemological frameworks and informed by research experience, on the one hand, and the placement, style, material properties, content and context of the inscription on the other, typically taking official (usually commissioned) inscriptions as a benchmark. However, it is only when there is a shared understanding of the ultimate purpose of the term 'graffiti' that hopes for consensus are not in vain.

It is up to the scholars and their respective fields to decide which of the two purposes is better served by the term 'graffiti'. One would not, however, go too far in observing that the overwhelming majority of people today, including funding bodies, associate the word 'graffiti' with inscribing practices that are unauthorized and unsanctioned if not illicit and illegal. In current public discourse, the word 'graffiti' is simply not a neutral one, nor is the phenomenon it designates, and it may appear unjustifiable if not hypocritical to disregard this, no matter what the etymology suggests.[21] On the other hand, the 'interpretive' definition would no doubt warrant laborious stocktaking and narrowing down the corpora of actual 'graffiti', a factor rendering it less attractive to many. But Ingo Strauch's contribution in this volume is a superb example of how useful such terminological retrospection can be: reviewing all materials previously dubbed 'graffiti' in Indological scholarship has allowed him to identify typological incongruities and in turn to define a much more homogenous and elastic corpus of graffiti.

To add to the complexity, if we insist that it is vital for comparative research that both historical and modern graffiti practices are studied side by side, we necessarily face another terminological issue. Unlike the term 'contemporary art', which is commonly used both in the broad sense of any art produced during our

not limited to graffiti. For an in-depth discussion on the definition of street art and its relation to graffiti, see Young 2014, 3–10.

21 For a good overview of the criminal connotations graffiti have today, see Bloch and Phillips 2021. The English word 'graffiti' is derived from Italian *graffiare*, 'to scratch'/*graffiato* 'scratched', and was first used by nineteenth-century archaeologists to refer to informal inscriptions engraved in walls; see also Benefiel and Sypniewski, this volume. In many disciplines dealing with historical graffiti, the singular 'graffito' vs. plural 'graffiti' distinction is usually maintained; in the study of contemporary graffiti, it is not uncommon to use 'graffiti' as a collective noun denoting both singular and plural, or to use 'graffiti' as the singular form and 'graffitis' as the plural. Throughout this essay, we adhere to the former convention, and use the words 'graffito' and 'graffiti' to denote graphic expressions regardless of the production technique, be they engraved, chiselled, sprayed, inked, chalked, pencilled, cut or produced in any other way.

lifetime and in the narrow sense of a specific art style, the term 'contemporary graffiti' (as well as 'modern graffiti') is typically reserved only for a particular graffiti style – 'tags', 'bombs', 'throw-ups' and 'pieces' – that has its roots in the cityscapes of 1960s to 1970s Philadelphia and New York. While this is beyond doubt the most visually salient and culturally influential type of graffiti in most countries of the Global North today, by no means does it represent the only type of graffiti practice thriving in the contemporary world. There is a host of diverse graffiti practices in the present-day world that lack any genetic link to North American urban subcultures: political graffiti, for instance, have been populating city streets throughout the second half of the twentieth century and up to the present day,[22] and elaborate *latrinalia* have been disseminating wisdom and humour across age groups and social strata for generations.[23] Lovers and travellers globally surrender to the temptation to eternalize their affectional commitments or touristic achievements with the help of chalk, charcoal, stone, pencil or any other pointed object, with particularly strong traditions in India and, as mentioned above, in China.[24] Small entrepreneurs worldwide make use of graffiti to advertise their services, be it the omnipresent 'Plumber King' of Hong Kong (Fig. 3)[25] or the Bedouin camel-owners at the Wadi Rum Reserve, Jordan, including the rock face just steps away from the ancient Nabatean petroglyph site at Lawrence's Spring. And while some of these heterogenous practices boast an ancient pedigree, some may well be products of modernity and thus 'modern' or 'contemporary' even in the narrow sense.

---

22 European tradition is particulary prominent here, with an abundance of turbulent events such as the 1952 'Ridgway – Go Home' campaign in Paris, the May 1968 protests Europe-wide, the 1977 anti-prison movement in Barcelona and, most recently, Brexit, the Covid-19 pandemic and the Russian invasion of Ukraine; the iconic graffiti sites of the Berlin Wall or the Lennon Wall in Prague both have a respectable history going back to at least 1970s.

23 Compare the opinion by the two-time Pulitzer Prize winner Norman Mailer: 'Some of the best prose in America is graffiti found on men's-room walls' (Mailer 1966, 116). For studies on *latrinalia*, see for instance Dundes 1966; Reisner 1971, 107–118; Hentschel 1987; Cole 1991; Ferem 2006; Stumpf 2013; Meade 2015; Trahan 2016.

24 Lovers' graffiti seem to be especially prominent in India; see Karkoon 2023. For a case indicative of a Myanmar lovers' graffiti tradition, see Htun Khaing 2018. Trees are popular media for these types of graffiti; for studies on *arboglyphs*, see Mallea-Olaetxe 2000; Kruschwitz 2010; Summerfield 2012; Lovata 2015; Kobiałka 2019.

25 Billy Potts, 'Meet the Plumber King, Hong Kong's Unexpected Graffiti Icon', *Zolima City Mag*, 29 January 2021, <https://zolimacitymag.com/meet-plumber-king-hong-kong-unexpected-graffiti-icon/> (accessed on 20 May 2023).

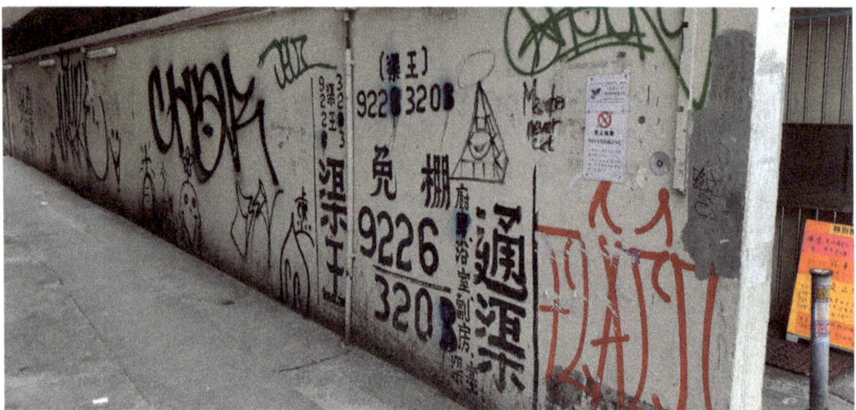

Fig. 3: The 'Plumber King' ad repeated three times amidst other graffiti in a nameless alley near 432 Des Veux Rd W, Hong Kong, May 2023: 'The Plumber King: no scaffolding, 9226 3203, sewers cleared: kitchens, bathrooms, subdivided flats, clogged sewers' 渠王 免棚 9226 3203 通渠 厨房 浴室 劏房 渠塞 (the largest graphs at bottom); '9226 The Plumber King 3203' 9226 渠王 3203 (small graphs at top left); '(The Plumber King) 9226 3203' 〔渠王〕 92263203 (top). Photograph © Ondřej Škrabal.

Yet whether or not political graffiti, guerilla advertisements or any other specific type of graffiti represent practices that first emerged only during the twentieth century are questions that remain for future research; what we can say today is that such research will be impossible without placing them in diachronic and global perspectives. And to close the circle, the lack of clear-cut terminology will greatly hamper such endeavours. If both the terms 'contemporary graffiti' and 'modern graffiti' remain monopolized by New York-inspired tags and pieces, what solution can there be?[26] We either need another label to refer to the overall set of graffiti produced in the contemporary world, or to simply repurpose the label and inject it with a broader, less Eurocentric meaning.[27] While the former would only add to the general confusion, insisting on the latter may in fact bring about the desired conceptual hygiene: reserving 'contemporary graffiti' as a general term for

26 'New York-inspired' or 'New York style' are terms used by both the scene and academics to refer to graffiti style deriving from the 1970s New York graffiti, i.e. tags, bombs, throw-ups and pieces; this style is sometimes also dubbed 'hip hop graffiti', but the connection of graffiti and hip hop music is only a 1980s development. In a German-speaking context, the term 'style writing' is often used to refer to this type of graffiti.

27 The same is true for the label 'modern graffiti', which, by analogy with 'modern art', would ideally subsume all the new graffiti types that emerged in the wake of the transition to modernity.

any graffiti produced today, and using more specific labels for particular styles or genres (e.g. 'New York-style' graffiti, 'anti-style' graffiti, *pixação*, love tags etc.). As the first step towards this ideal, speaking of 'contemporary graffiti practices' rather than just 'contemporary graffiti' may help to realize the desired disambiguation and highlight the plurality of present-day practices.

All in all, despite this unfavourable terminological reality, the comparative dialogue remains viable. The indispensable precondition is, however, that authors make an explicit statement of their position, clarifying and justifying their terminological choices. This will still not make comparisons easy, but at least possible.

4 Spatial context: Graffiti on portable and mobile artefacts?

Generally speaking, most scholarship past and present has identified walls and other architectonic structures as the main type of written artefact bearing graffiti. However, there are also scholarly traditions that go beyond this traditional understanding and employ the term 'graffiti' for inscriptions preserved on portable or mobile objects. For instance, this approach is widely adopted by scholars dealing with Sasanian numismatic material, such as Alexander B. Nikitin, who classifies as 'graffiti' the Middle Persian inscriptions added onto Sasanian and Arab-Sasanian coins dating predominantly from the sixth to the seventh century CE.[28] These writings fulfilled the need of private individuals, probably the owners of the coins, to prove the piece's quality.[29] Of a different opinion is Carlo Giovanni Cereti, who questions the use of the label 'graffiti' when applied to specific typologies of portable objects. As discussed by him in his contribution to the present volume, despite the formal aspects characterising inscriptions on silver vessels dating to the Sasanian period (224-651 CE), which might lead to their classification as graffiti, writings on precious objects should instead be considered a specific 'subgroup of texts'.[30] Also in this volume, Michael Macdonald discusses how the term 'graffiti', while predominantly confined to the realm of 'rock writings',

28 Nikitin 1993; see also Daryaee 2017.

29 However, the prevention of forgery was not the only motivation behind the practice of scribbling on coins. We frequently witness the practice of scribbling the owner's name on coins or adding notes associated with financial calculations; see Nikitin 1993, 99.

30 These texts are generally votive inscriptions or dedications to the Sasanian kings.

might occasionally be applied to North Arabian epigraphic studies for the classification of inscriptions on mobile limestone objects.[31]

In Anatolian studies, a similar classification has been proposed for doodles that are nowadays generally categorized as other types of epigraphic artefacts.[32] Even in Classical studies, where the term 'graffito' is infrequently applied to inscriptions on portable materials, this label is occasionally used to classify less formal writings on various supports, like roof tiles, marble slabs and ceramic containers.[33] On the other hand, in this volume, Ingo Strauch rejects the use of the term 'graffiti' for inscriptions on Indian pottery and other portable artefacts; instead, he proposes a classification of inscriptions based on their specific function.

Outside the field of epigraphy, Janine Rogers extends this definition even to notes written in manuscripts. She shows that apart from names and drawings, the margins of medieval manuscripts often contain pictorial and verbal riddles, a practice that finds parallels on medieval walls.[34] These 'poetic graffiti' seem to establish a dialogue between the authors of these marginalia and the manuscript readers.[35] Dai Matsui discusses a similar phenomenon in his contribution to this volume. Among other evidence, he considers the Old Uyghur scribbles on the margins or back sides of Buddhist manuscripts discovered in the cave temples in Turfan and Dunhuang, China. These 'manuscript inscriptions', as labelled by Tibor Porció,[36] can easily be seen to parallel the visitors' graffiti, dating mainly between the tenth and the fourteenth century CE, recorded in the same cultic spaces. Similar scribbles and doodles appear also in Chinese manuscripts from Dunhuang, as analysed in the chapter by Nadine Bregler, who shows that some of them likewise 'made it' onto the temple walls. The transfer from manuscripts to walls is even more prominent in the chapter by Ursula Verhoeven, who shows how texts of the school curriculum found their way onto the walls of rock tombs at Asyut, Egypt. On the very same note – just in the opposite direction – Sabine

31 These inscriptions indeed seem to share similarities in their graphic features and content with those commonly found on rock surfaces.

32 Ünal 1989.

33 On the classification of writings on roof tiles and marble slabs as graffiti, see Bîrzescu 2006, 172. For an overview of the use of the label 'graffiti' applied to inscriptions on ceramic containers in Classical archaeology, see Bakker and Galsterer-Kröll 1975; Kütter 2008; Weiß-König 2010; Lohmann 2018a.

34 Rogers 2018, 180.

35 A description of the 'graffiti' identified in the Findern Manuscript (Cambridge University Library Ff.1.6.) may be found in Rogers 2018, 180–182.

36 See Porció 2014, 161, 164–167.

Kienitz has recently argued that intercession books emerged in German churches in order to direct the visitors' writing from church walls onto the pages of a codex.[37]

As these examples suggest, differences in the classification of writing as 'inscriptions' and 'graffiti' reflect specific terminological choices in different fields of research. This is even more true for the use of the word 'graffiti' to refer to scribblings in and on manuscripts and book covers. Establishing the boundary between graffiti and other forms of writing remains a matter of debate; at the very least, however, it appears that the interconnectedness of graffitiing with other inscription and manuscript practices is a noteworthy phenomenon that deserves further inquiry.

5 Cultural context: Divergent perceptions of graffiti in time and space

Dealing with graffiti implies the need to reflect on their interaction with the surrounding space.[38] As all the contributions to this volume underline, the social, political and religious context determines specific choices in the performance of graffitiing practices. This form of 'space appropriation' through graffiti,[39] regardless of whether it is dictated by religious and/or political needs, can be observed in various societies from antiquity to modern times. At the same time, this general context shapes the audience's perceptions and attitudes towards graffiti.

To address just one cultural domain, the importance of graffiti in cultic practices is demonstrated by their recurrent discoveries in sacred spaces. In diverse cultures and territories, writing in religious contexts was considered an essential medium in the dialogue between gods and devotees. In some places, such as the Christian religious complexes of the Nubian lands in modern Sudan, the abundant presence of graffiti has been interpreted as witness to a 'graffiti industry',[40] which might have involved religious personnel writing on behalf of devotees. The recurrent involvement of the authorities in charge of cultic spaces in graffiti-

37 Kienitz 2022, 184.

38 Understanding the importance of inscriptions in shaping natural and urban landscapes from antiquity to modern times is at the core of the investigations of the Research Field 'Inscribing Spaces' at the Cluster of Excellence 'Understanding Written Artefacts' at the University of Hamburg <https://www.csmc.uni-hamburg.de/written-artefacts/research-fields/field-b.html> (accessed on 29 June 2023).

39 On this aspect, see also Ragazzoli, Harmanşah and Salvador 2018, 9.

40 Łajtar 2021, 165.

making and/or their consent thereto are attested in Egypt as well as in medieval and early modern Europe, which has led various scholars to the conclusion that graffitiing practices were more commonly seen as legitimate gestures of piety rather than illicit acts in the past.[41]

Here, too, it is important to note that the discussion of the status of graffiti will remain unsettled without elaborating a terminological stance. There is no doubt that under the 'documentary' definition, there will be plentitudes of informal inscriptions that show no trace of illicitness or transgression; on the other hand, precisely those features will be required by the 'interpreters' to justify the use of the label 'graffiti'. Regardless of label, however, this debate is extremely important, as it makes us reflect upon our preconceptions, skewed by contemporary notions of legal systems, aesthetics and protection of cultural heritage. The abundant presence of informal inscriptions in some of the interior spaces of the past – be they cultic or domestic – can strike us as rather unexpected today. Yet as Matthew Champion points out, prior to the nineteenth century, the notion of preservation of cultural heritage or at least historical architecture sites was not particularly well articulated,[42] and the attitude that people of the past assumed towards scribblings at such sites would at times differ from our own. This realisation impels the 'interpreters' to seek actual evidence of voices that disapproved, criticized or complained about graffiti.

Recent years have seen increased attention to this kind of evidence, especially from early and late modern Western Europe.[43] In her contribution to this volume, Nadine Bregler brings to the fore the negative attitudes of medieval contemporaries towards scribbles written on walls in the Buddhist cave shrine complex in Dunhuang. Based on the similarity in content between the scribbles and manuscripts recovered from the site, she argues that some of the graffiti may have been produced by students who dwelled in the complex while acquiring a Buddhist education. To be sure, informal writing on walls as such was not outlawed in medieval China (as long as the content was not heretical or messianic), yet the disapproving attitude shows that it was at times considered irritating and transgressive.[44] This and similar cases can serve as a reminder that just like today, the abundance of graffiti in the past is not always indicative of its legality or acceptability, but rather of the cost-benefit analysis not turning out in favour of

41 Champion 2015, 5–7; Felle 2021, 178.
42 Champion 2021.
43 Ritsema van Eck 2018; Castillo Gómez 2020, 73–75; Kienitz 2022, 182–184.
44 See Bregler's paper for more references to complaints about graffiti in China, going back as early as the second century CE.

prevention, prosecution or removal. Overall, different communities in different periods and regions undoubtedly developed different attitudes towards graffiti, which should always be studied individually, without modernist preconceptions or overgeneralising inferences.

Aside from places of religious import, graffiti stand as tangible testimonies of engagement with spaces and monuments of the past that have recurrently had a specific political significance. In his contribution to this volume, Carlo Giovanni Cereti examines various examples of graffiti from Persepolis dating mainly to the Sasanian period and earlier (*c.* 180–651 CE). He shows how many of the pictorial and script-based[45] graffiti recorded at this site reflect the need of the sub-Arsacid kings of Fars to mark their role as heirs of the Achaemenians. Graffitiing practices were likely seen by the sub-Arsacid kings of Fars as a suitable medium by which to legitimate their reign through the reappropriation of Achaemenid spaces of political relevance, hundreds of years after the end of the First Persian Empire (559–330 BCE). The appropriation of historical sites by later rulers through graffitiing practices in different cultures and times reflects how graffiti establish an ideological identification and symbolize the continuity of temporal power.

Writing on walls in domestic spaces seems to have been a widespread practice also in antiquity, as it somehow still is today. While from the contemporary perspective, children could be considered the most obvious agents behind this particular form of 'domestic art', the examination of graffiti in private spaces from antiquity up to modern times in fact reveals a whole gamut of authors as well as needs that graffiti were called to answer. Pompeii certainly offers the richest corpus of evidence for understanding how people engaged in graffiti practices inside

45 In the study of graffiti, as in all interdisciplinary research, there is a range of terminological possibilities that have often seen a long history of discussion and are thus rooted deeply within the respective traditions. This is reflected in the terminological use of the contributors to this volume (e.g. Verhoeven, Cereti, Matsui), as well as in the co-existence of terms among contributions to recent volumes in the field (e.g. Felle and Ward-Perkins 2021b). In this introduction, we distinguish between 'script-based' or 'written' graffiti, on the one hand, and 'pictorial' graffiti on the other, and we describe 'script' and 'pictorial elements' rather than 'text' and 'image'. This decision reflects the terminological tradition of the Centre for the Study of Manuscript Cultures, with the aim of facilitating discourse on written artefacts from all eras of human history and all cultural areas (Wimmer et al. 2015). The terminological choice is informed in particular by discussions on multigraphic written artefacts. Speaking of 'script-based' and 'pictorial' graffiti enables us to conceptually distinguish between the physical or visual features of a written artefact and its content. This content can be texts, encoded in script, or pictorial elements. Against the background of semiotics, the term 'pictorial' has an advantage over 'figural' in being very descriptive – thus, for instance, leaving space for the many geometric and symbolic signs we observe in graffitiing practices around the globe.

private buildings. For instance, they might witness the visit of guests who left their names, perhaps a short motto or a prayer as a tangible memento of their presence in these spaces.[46] In his contribution to this volume, Jarosław Źrałka shows how in the pre-Columbian Mayan civilisation, graffiti are recurrently found in elite residential buildings, not only scribbled on the walls but framing the entire architectural space. The recurrent representation of game boards on the floor or benches, used to play a game known as *patolli*, exemplifies the social – and in this case ludic – dimension that is so frequently embodied in graffiti practices.[47] However, graffiti in private contexts could also have fulfilled more practical functions. In the so-called House of Nebuchelus at Dura-Europos, sometime in the third century CE, an unknown graffitist copied on a wall a receipt recording the shipment of various items.[48] For unknown reasons, the author found it more convenient to use the surrounding architectural space as a writing surface, instead of the papyrus sheets or potsherds on which similar types of documents were customarily written.[49]

6 Graffiti in a written environment

A number of contributions in this volume showcase how graffiti interact with various types of written artefacts. They frame royal inscriptions, votive and funerary

---

46 For an overview of graffiti in Pompeian domestic contexts, see Benefiel 2014.

47 Inscribed game boards are a cross cultural phenomenon enjoying a growing interest not only among historians and archaeologists but also scholars of economics, computer science, cognitive science, psychology, linguistics, anthropology and art history. Out of this consideration, from the early beginnings, publications such as the *Board Games Studies* journal or the volume *Ancient Board Games in Perspective* (Finkel 2007) were designed as cross-cultural and cross-temporal. Focal points of previous studies are the Egyptian (Mulvin and Sidebotham 2003; Jacquet-Gordon 2003, 12–13; de Voogt, Nilsson and Ward 2020), Ethiopian and Eritrean cultures (Manzo 2020) and Greco-Roman traditions (Purcell 1995; Roueché 2014; Widura 2015; Schädler 1994, 1998, 2008; Talloen 2018; Gabel et al. 2022; Carè 2022). According to several studies, game boards can serve as indicators of intercultural contact (de Voogt 1995, 2012 and de Voogt, Dunn-Vaturi and Eerkens 2013; Crist, Dunn-Vaturi and de Voogt 2016; Hall 2019).

48 Baird 2015. Similar evidence has been recorded at the archaeological site of Ephesus. Several 'shopping lists' dating mainly from the third century CE have been found incised on the walls of the houses of Hanghaus 2 (Chaniotis et al. 2007, 1291–1293), testifying to various domestic activities such as the purchase of food or payment of taxes and to individuals serving the household members (for instance the 'preceptor' σχολαστικός). For an overview, see Chaniotis et al. 2007.

49 Compare, for example, an account of money found probably in the nomos Arsinoites and dating to the second century CE, now kept in the papyrological collection of the University of Michigan (*P.Mich.* inv. 306Vo).

stelae, and modern advertisement posters and traffic signs. The interaction takes the shape of a spatial interplay between graffiti and other written or pictorial expressions. This phenomenon may originate from different social needs; for instance, the identification of specific written monuments as places of historical memory, ethnic and political identity, or religious significance. Graffiti may appear in an urban or natural space before it becomes monumentalized,[50] while in other instances, they emerge soon after the creation of the written monument (e.g., temple relief, stela, votive inscription) as an expression of religious devotion or reverence for temporal power. The Luwian culture provides an interesting example of how graffiti might have interacted with a pre-existing monument. Near Manisa in modern Türkiye, a monument dedicated to Tarkasnawa, king of Mira (*c.* 1350 BCE),[51] is surrounded by three graffiti sites mentioning rulers of the Land of Mira.[52] As this example shows, graffiti may reflect a practice that occurred long after a space of cultural memory has been created and socially recognized.

Graffiti often betray the cultic or religious significance of a specific space throughout the centuries. The graffiti discovered in the Catacomb of Commodilla near the via Ostiense in Rome demonstrate the reappropriation of this cultic space by the *viatores ad martyres* (i.e. 'travellers to the martyrs').[53] In this context, numerous graffiti largely attributed to Anglo-Saxon visitors of the early Middle Ages, dating predominantly between the seventh and eighth century CE, are scribbled near pre-existing inscriptions.[54]

In other instances, graffiti reflect the phase of abandonment or change in function of a specific natural landscape or architectural space. At the site of Athribis in Middle Egypt, the Coptic graffiti (*c.* sixth to seventh century CE)[55] recorded in the area of the temple of Ptolemy XII – which was transformed into a nunnery at the beginning of the late antique period – mark the transformation of spaces originally devoted to the cult of the divine triad Repit, Min-Re, Kolanthes. This

---

50 Evidence from Pharaonic Egypt is discussed, for instance, in Ragazzoli 2018, 24.

51 As identified by its subsidiary Luwian inscription (Karabel A); see Hawkins 1998, 1–2.

52 Harmanşah 2018, 52–57.

53 Carletti 2021, 78.

54 Such as the devotional texts associated with the fresco of St. Luke the Physician, framing an epigraph dated to the reign of emperor Constantine IV Pogonatus (668–685 CE); see Carletti 2021, 78, 87.

55 The chronology is based on the date 594/595 CE (AM 311) preserved in a graffito in the Refectory and on the study of the ceramic material discovered in this area of the religious complex. For a discussion of the dated graffito [REF-10 (E-05)], written by a female monastic named Antinoe, see Davis 2020, 265. For an overview of results of the study of the pottery discovered in the Refectory and Six-Pillared Hall, see Pyke 2019a and 2019b.

conversion is underlined by the Christian graffiti framing the hieroglyphic inscriptions on the columns of the so-called Six-Pillared Hall,[56] where their closeness to the temple's hieroglyphic inscriptions seems, in truth, to be motivated solely by the spot's suitability for writing.

This last example raises an important question about the graffitists' reception of spaces and monumental inscriptions. It remains challenging to trace clear connections between pre-existing inscriptions and historical graffiti, since in most of the previously mentioned cases, the proximity between graffiti and other forms of writing seems dictated mainly by the significance of the space itself, as a place of cultural memory and/or political importance, rather than by the physical presence of other forms of writing.[57] Only on rare occasions is it possible to ascertain the existence of a real dialogue between graffiti and other written artefacts. This is of course much easier to grasp in modern times, for instance in subvertising graffiti that engage explicitly with the text of commercial or political advertisements.

Aside from sharing their space, graffiti sometimes inherit graphic features particular to other written artefacts. For instance, the format and layout of some of the graffiti discovered in the Upper Church of Banganarti, as well as in the tombs at Dongola in modern Sudan (ancient Nubia), recall the layout of manuscripts produced throughout the region during that period.[58] As Rebecca Benefiel and Holly Sypniewski discuss in their contribution to this volume, graffiti might also emulate the form of written artefacts customarily made of metal, bone, stone and other materials. Take the example of the so-called 'Sator Square', an early Latin palindromic word puzzle or cryptogram found scratched onto the walls of a house in Pompeii.[59] Stone amulets, stelae, bronze bells and even human skulls featuring this lettered magic square are widely attested throughout the Mediterranean from antiquity to medieval times. Indeed, not rarely does the outline of a graffito clearly recall an inscribed object such as a *tabula ansata*, stela or codex. The practice occurs especially in religious contexts, where graffiti assume shapes

---

56 Numerous graffiti have also been recorded in the nearby refectory. A discussion of the Coptic graffiti associated with the female monastics inhabiting this religious complex can be found in Davis 2020.

57 This might lead to the attribution of the status of *patina* to graffiti; on this concept, see Dawdy 2016.

58 On the graffiti discovered in Banganarti and Dongola, see Łajtar and van der Vliet 2009; Łajtar 2020. For an introduction to medieval manuscripts from Christian Nubia, see Tsakos 2019. On the discovery of fragments of manuscripts in Faras and other sites, see Łajtar 2018, 42–43.

59 For details on the Sator square (also known as Rotas square), see Benefiel and Sypniewski in this volume and O'Donald 2018. For the various attestations of the square, see <https://www.britannica.com/topic/SATOR-square> (accessed on 29 August 2023).

typical of memorial or monumental inscriptions, serving as a cheaper substitute. In Egypt, this phenomenon is well known in cultic spaces, where priests and lay people used graffiti as a means of leaving behind tangible traces of their imperishable religious observance.[60]

Graffiti meant to substitute votive objects and cultic equipment in general are attested from Mesoamerica[61] to the Mediterranean,[62] all the way to the extreme borders of the Egyptian lands.[63] An outstanding example is the widespread practice of enclosing graffiti in *tabulae ansatae*, which can be found in such diverse contexts as Egyptian settlements from Greco-Roman times[64] to the religious complexes of the Byzantine era,[65] the domestic structures of Dura-Europos,[66] the tower tombs of Palmyra,[67] the Cave of Elijah in Israel[68] and the rock faces of the Syros Island in the Aegean Sea.[69] The *tabula ansata* was a favourite form, especially for votive tablets produced in a variety of materials in Imperial Rome, suddenly appearing across the lands of the Roman Empire. The practice of enclosing a graffito in a shape that unmistakably recalled recognisable writing supports was not only broadly diffused throughout the ancient Mediterranean, but continued from the Byzantine period up to the early modern age.[70] Abundant evidence is yielded by the Church of the Holy Sepulchre in Jerusalem, where throughout the centuries various pilgrims have left their names, often followed by short prayers, enclosed in representations of a stela (Fig. 4).[71] Extensive parallels for this practice exist, from the representations of stelae in Pharaonic Egypt[72] to grave-

60 Jacquet-Gordon 2003.

61 Patrois 2013, 439, 443.

62 On the graffiti *tabulae ansatae* preserved in Pompeii, see Kruschwitz and Campbell 2009, 59–70.

63 For the evidence from the Philae Island, see Pope 2019, 74–75. For further evidence from the Egyptian territory, see Marciniak 1981 and Ragazzoli 2017.

64 Nilsson 2015, 157.

65 Subías Pascual 2003, 30–42.

66 Baird 2015, 25–26.

67 As'ad and Yon 2001, 104.

68 Di Segni 2021, 34.

69 Nowakowski 2021, 113.

70 See the practice – especially widespread between the First and the Second World Wars – of enclosing short prayers dedicated to the Holy Virgin in heart-shaped graffiti mimicking silver and golden amulets, recorded, for instance, in several churches in the province of Perugia, Italy during a survey by Leah Mascia in August 2021.

71 For an introduction to graffiti recorded in this religious complex, see Stern 2018a, 35–39. An overview of graffiti resembling funerary stelae and other written artefacts found in the ancient tombs surrounding Jerusalem can be found in Stern 2018b, 154.

72 Ragazzoli 2018, 30.

stones in the medieval churches of the United Kingdom.[73] Cases like these show that even where an individual graffito appears all by itself, our understanding of it will be greatly enhanced should we view it from a multigraphic perspective.

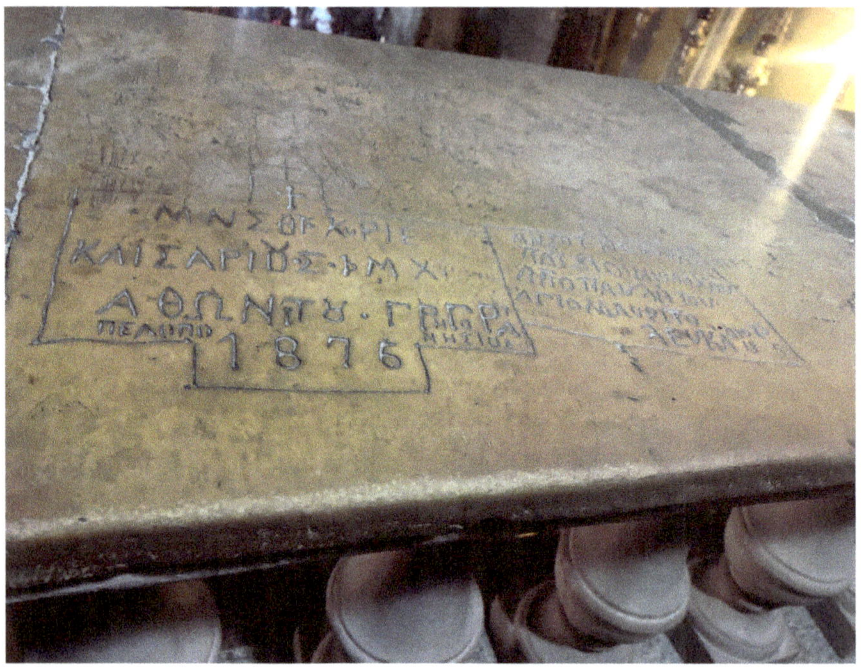

Fig. 4: Votive graffiti enclosed in representations of stelae engraved on the balcony of the Calvary (Golgotha) by pilgrims visiting the Church of the Holy Sepulchre in Jerusalem, October 2022. Photograph © Leah Mascia.

7 Semiotics: Script, image, diagrammatic signs and the multigraphic aspect of graffiti

Graffiti as an object of cross-cultural research are a multigraphic phenomenon. Especially when viewed from a global perspective, we see graffiti sites that do not exclusively or primarily employ script. Graffiti undogmatically use different semiotic modes: pictorial, symbolic and diagrammatic signs share space with written

73 Champion 2015, 202–203.

graffiti across the globe. The co-occurrence of graffiti in more than one script adds to this variety. By highlighting the juxtaposition of these modes of presentation and studying their relation to each other, we aim at overcoming the separate treatment or lack of attention that has resulted from a division of labour among the 'textual' and 'visual' disciplines.

In the context of our volume, the term 'multigraphic' functions as an umbrella term for the phenomena studied in fields of research that have become known as word-and-image-studies, intermediality or multimodality, among others.[74] The term 'multigraphic' denotes the combination of more than one graphic system or convention of using graphic signs: the combination of script and image or symbol is the most obvious option; another would be script embellished or used in ways that draw attention to the 'iconicity' of script,[75] as we find in various traditions of contemporary graffiti writing. Within this volume, this sense of iconicity comes to the fore in several contributions. In a conversation between cultural historian Sanja Ewald and graffiti artist Mirko Reisser, they concur that in 'New York-inspired' graffiti, 'writing and image merge into a pictoriality and are perceived as a whole'.[76] The iconicity of script is also evoked by forms of 'public calligraphy' (*tizi*) or 'water calligraphy' (*dishu*) in China, which are among the forms of writing investigated by Minna Valjakka. Emphasising both the interrelatedness and fluidity of the concepts of 'calligraphy', 'art' and 'graffiti', she explores the interplay between the three and proposes a nuanced approach to the disentanglement of their multifaceted relations.

A multigraphic perspective can inform research on script-based graffiti that evoke conventions of older script systems or traditions of handwriting, e.g. graffiti that merge Arabic calligraphy or cuneiform script with modern graffiti styles.[77] Artist Osama Sadiq from Baghdad, Iraq, makes frequent use of cuneiform script that emerged in the Ancient Near East as early as the fourth millennium BCE. In his work, Sadiq either employs the cuneiform signs themselves or stylizes Arabic script to appear like cuneiform writing (Fig. 5).[78] Multigraphic stylized script like

74 Robert 2014, 86–87; Rippl 2015; Bateman, Wildfeuer and Hiipala 2017.

75 Hamburger 2011, 250–251.

76 Compare also Strehle 2008, 16.

77 See the 2021 interview series 'Writing on the Wall: Artists in Conversation' by the J. Paul Getty Museum for a recent collaboration between a research institution and contemporary graffiti artists from the US and beyond; <https://www.getty.edu/museum/programs/courses/the_writing_on_the_wall/index.html> (accessed on 19 June 2023).

78 See for instance his Instagram profile: 'osama sadiq #cuneiform_art (@osama_sadiq1)', <https://www.instagram.com/osama_sadiq1/> (accessed on 19 June 2023). Sadiq is among the artists portrayed in the Getty Museum interview series 'Writing on the Wall'.

that in Sadiq's work often features under the name 'calligraffiti', a term that has gained recent popularity in Arabic and European cities, to the extent that the Museum of Islamic Art in Berlin has started incorporating classes on calligraffiti into its educational programmes.[79]

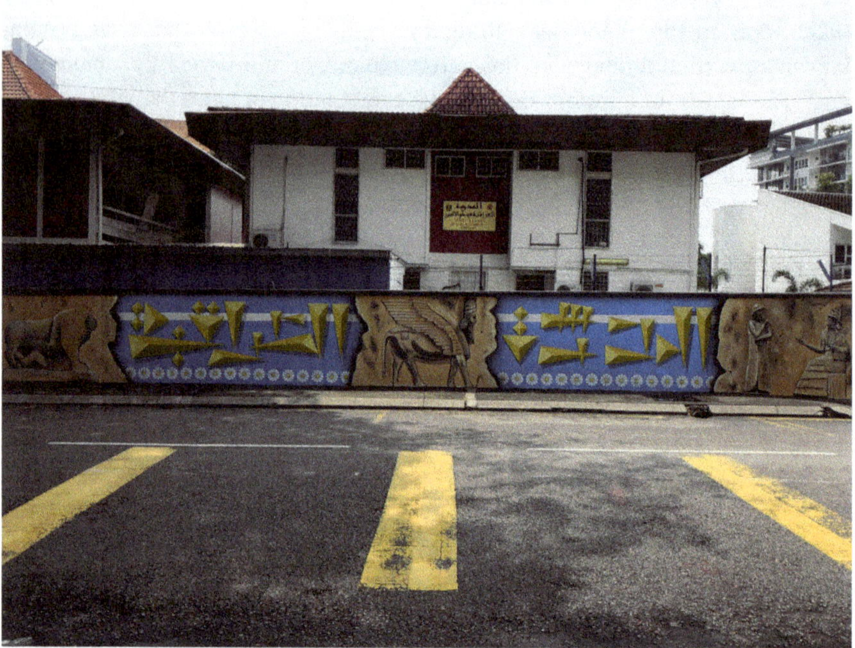

Fig. 5: Artwork by Osama Sadiq on a wall at the Iraqi school in Kuala Lumpur, with the word 'Iraqi School' written in stylized Arabic script which is made to look like cuneiform script. Kuala Lumpur, Malaysia, 2019. © Osama Sadiq, reproduced with permission.

In corpora studied by scholars of classical history and archaeology, such as the Ancient Greek, Roman and Egyptian cultures, what has been studied as graffiti – while not exclusively script-based by far – is often addressed from the viewpoint of epigraphy, and thus primarily as text.[80] Consequently, scholars have treated

79 See the museum website at <https://islamic-art.smb.museum/e-learning/old-new/?lang=en> (accessed on 19 June 2023).

80 'Text' is intended here in the narrower sense of 'script-based'. Some of the papers presented during our 2021 workshop series 'Scratched, Scrawled, Sprayed' made use of a broader understanding of the term, referring to 'intertextuality' in the tradition of Julia Kristeva or to the concept

these graffiti as a 'sub-category of epigraphy'.[81] While recent surveys, databases and publications usually include pictorial or diagrammatic graffiti in their general scope of interest, they are not always treated equally but rather as exceptions to the rule: 'If textual graffiti are the second-class citizens of the epigraphic tradition, in Classics, Ancient Near Eastern Studies and Egyptology at least, then pictorial graffiti are the third class'.[82]

At times, pictorial graffiti are left out of the analysis for very pragmatic reasons. In a recent volume edited by Antonio E. Felle and Bryan Ward-Perkins, graffiti are considered to be 'informal and personal texts placed secondarily on existing structures or on living rock'.[83] Felle and Ward-Perkins explicitly state that this definition is meant to encompass pictorial graffiti, but they inform the reader of the volume's emphasis on script-based graffiti due to a lack of data on pictorial material – 'to say anything meaningful about these images requires detailed topographical analysis of their distribution across cities and natural sites, a work that is only just beginning'.[84]

Yet in other areas, as geographically and culturally distant as medieval England and pre-Columbian America, pictorial, heraldic and diagrammatic graffiti are on par with script or even dominate the scene. Scholars of these objects of research have adopted a different emphasis and developed other approaches. The Norfolk Medieval Graffiti Survey in England, directed by archaeologist Matthew Champion, uses a typology in which 'text' is one category among twenty, ranging from 'apotropaic' to 'dot patterns'.[85] Among the contributors of this volume, Jarosław Źrałka asserts that in Mayan graffiti from the pre-Columbian era – mostly, but not exclusively, from 250 to 950 CE – hieroglyphic script makes up only a small fraction of the recorded graffiti. It is pictorial representations of human or animal figures, deities and architecture that dominate the corpus, and they therefore constitute the majority of categories in the respective classification

---

of 'culture as text', prominent in the humanities of recent years. Cf. Lea 2006; Bachmann-Medick 2012, 99 and passim. Sven Ouzman explicitly discussed and problematized the idea of 'graffiti as material culture' and 'material culture as text' in his presentation at the abovementioned workshop series, exploring, among others, San rock art, graffiti by European settlers in South Africa and prison cell graffiti from Western Australia; see Ouzman 2021.

81 Lohmann 2020, 39; see also Lohmann 2018b, 12–15, with regard to the archaeological standard *Corpus Inscriptionum Latinarum*.

82 Ragazzoli, Harmanşah and Salvador 2018, 6. That volume can be applauded for a programmatic inclusion of a wide spectrum of pictorial graffiti.

83 Felle and Ward-Perkins 2021a, xvii.

84 Felle and Ward-Perkins 2021a, xviii.

85 Norfolk Medieval Graffiti Survey 2017, 7; see also Champion 2012, 106.

system and database. Carlo Giovanni Cereti proposes an initial framework for the study of graffiti in Middle Iranian languages. He discusses multigraphic corpora of graffiti on rock surfaces, likely dating between the third and seventh century CE, where script-based graffiti co-exist alongside pictorial ones at sites in Southern Khorasan, Iran and the Upper Indus region in today's Pakistan. Mia Trentin specifically sets out to change the logo- or script-centric tradition of graffiti research by adapting ontologies established in cultural studies and museology, with the aim of producing object descriptions rather than text classifications. Trentin's project focuses on multigraphic graffiti from the medieval and early modern era, i.e. before the seventeenth century CE, in the Eastern Mediterranean.

In theory, the term 'written artefact' can be applied quite freely both to the individual graffito and the object on which it is situated. Although we may not ordinarily perceive the latter as being defined by their providing a surface for graffiti, a change of perspective can inspire us to re-evaluate our heuristics: the idea of multigraphic written artefacts or, for larger objects, multigraphic graffiti assemblages has the potential to encompass this wide range of observable phenomena without restricting the analysis to specific modes, materials or combinations.

Thus, we invited contributors to deliberate on both the multigraphic aspect and the idea of written artefacts, exploring the prospects for comparative research questions on graffiti and beyond. They reflect on the kinds of dialogue in which different cultures have engaged different modes of graphic expression. While adopting and developing digital humanities methods for the study of graffiti is already underway, combining experience in epigraphy and iconography appears to be a path less travelled in some of the disciplines present in this volume, yet marks a desirable future project. As will be visible from the contributions, the potential of and the need for trans- and interdisciplinarity, and of researchers from traditionally different fields working together to reach a better understanding of graffiti, cannot be overemphasized.

8 On documentation: Digital technologies in working with graffiti

Although the development of methods for documentation follows diverse paths in different fields, it is notably the new technologies and databases that promote and encourage interdisciplinary standards in the recording of graffiti. The concept of a written artefact could be a key to a unifying perspective regarding documentation, regardless from which camp – 'documentary' or 'interpretive' –

scholars descend; yet, as a matter of fact, the 'documentary' approach to the definition of graffiti is naturally much more prominent among scholars who actually record graffiti *in situ*, at least in the case of historical graffiti.

At first, interdisciplinarity may appear as a challenge due to the diverse nature of graffiti. In fact, it is an opportunity, as Ursula Frederick has proven with her research on modern graffiti in Australian cities. Using archaeological documentation methods, she convincingly demonstrates how the socio-cultural dispositions of cities are deeply interwoven with their 'graffiti habit'.[86] Moreover, unlike in historical graffiti, the field of contemporary graffiti has a multitude of readily available sources. In his 1991 book, contemporary artist Stephen Powers focused on the (at the time) sparsely documented contemporary graffiti, which primarily assumed the form of unorganized piles of photographs stored in a shoe box.[87] Powers justly emphasizes the oral dimension of recording graffiti, especially that of storytelling:

> Graffiti is about doing it, being it, and getting it. Proper documentation has, until recently, been the furthest thing from the writers' minds. And, ironically, the most dedicated archivists of the expression are not even writers. So true graffiti lives in the moment, and while every mark a writer makes will probably get buffed or fall into the hands of someone who's missing a lot of details, at least we've got the stories. [...] The real story of graffiti is necessarily an oral history. [...] The story gets darker and more visible with each retelling and it can't be painted over.[88]

As Powers highlights, what we document and call a 'graffito' is a snapshot of the cultural practice of graffiti writing. Prior to the creation of the actual artefact, there is often an occasion or intent (however short it may have been).[89] For example, a graffiti artist would design his 'piece' in a sketchbook, and the actual sprayed version of it can later appear as a video on YouTube.[90] Or two friends meet to debate how to spread rumours by writing them secretly at night in charcoal on the wall of a public street, as Lucian imagined for Athens in the second century CE.[91] Further, the history of a graffito does not necessarily end with being

---

86 Frederick 2009, 2014.

87 Powers 1999, 6.

88 Powers 1999, 6.

89 Chaniotis 2011, 194; Lohmann 2018b, 25 and 28.

90 For examples in this volume, see contributions by Ewald and Reisser, Araya-López and Markle.

91 This refers to a passage from the ancient author Lucian, who narrates a dialogue between the two friends, Chelidonion and the *hetaira* Drosis, who plot against the puritan teacher of Drosis' former client; see Lucian, *Dialogi Meretricii*, 10.4; see also Chaniotis 2011, 194 on this passage.

sprayed, scrawled or drawn; it may be commented on,[92] 'crossed' or catalogued by the police or a researcher,[93] and removed by the cleansing department of the city.[94] Therefore, when recording graffiti, we mainly document just one stage of its existence.

Traditionally, the documenting begins with the question: what belongs to a particular graffito and what does not?[95] The challenges this question entails – especially for historical graffiti – are numerous: their extremely small size, fragility and textual brevity, yet presence in large numbers, with graffiti clustering and overlapping one another.[96] Here, taking the written artefact as the point of departure can help overcome many of these issues: we no longer concentrate on a single graffito or a graffiti cluster and its boundaries, which are often ambiguous; rather, we can document the entire written artefact or graffiti site with digital photography, 3D devices and programmes for photographic enhancement (Fig. 6).[97] Then, deciding what constitutes a single graffito is a matter of analysis and not of documentation; this renders documentation more objective and available for possible reinterpretation. In other words, previously, the verdict of what belongs to a graffito had direct bearing on what was recorded; it often had to be delivered in limited time at the site, and it commonly depended on the personal experience of a single researcher.[98] With the holistic 'written artefact' approach, the ramifications of subjective choice are reduced to a minimum. Recording the entire artefact does justice to the context of the graffiti it contains, a feature most welcome by both 'documenters' and 'interpreters'.

Traditional text-focused techniques of documentation are vestiges of the technological limitations of paper-based past. With the robust digital technologies of today and tomorrow, these historical limitations are obsolete and should not dictate the way documentation operates today. And even if the idea of documenting some written artefacts in their entirety – such as the Great Wall of China – appears unrealistic today, it should be regarded as a beacon pointing in the direction of further work.

---

92 Lohmann 2018b, 279–290, 361.

93 Frederick 2009, 217; Ewald and Reisser in this volume.

94 Historic England 2021, 13, argue in their guide *Graffiti on Historic Buildings: Removal and Prevention* that '[s]cratches or inscriptions that have gained historic importance should be distinguished from modern ones, so that they can be preserved.'

95 Keegan 2015, xiii; Baird and Taylor 2016, 18.

96 Valente et al. 2019, 731; Trentin in this volume.

97 Cosentino et al. 2015; Valente et al. 2019; Valente and Barazzetti 2020, 5 on the development of different techniques; Schröer-Werner 2022, 197–198 on the possible bias of photography.

98 Valente and Barazetti 2020, 2 Fig. 1.

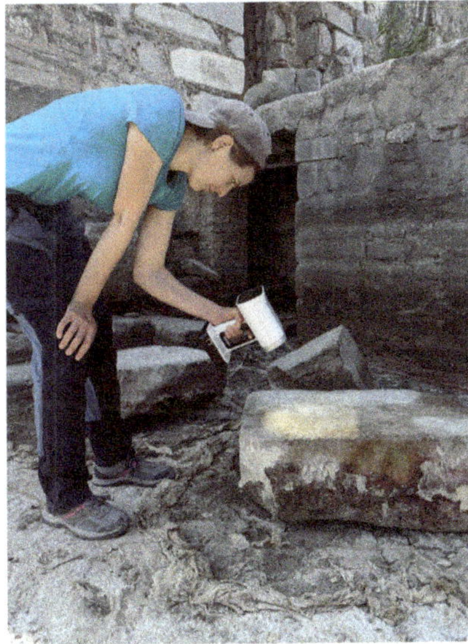
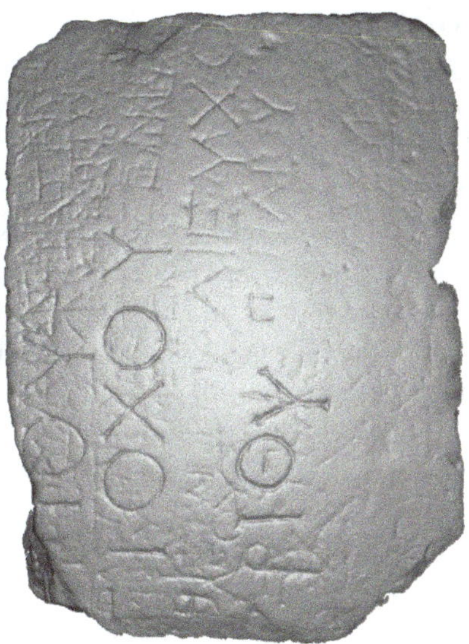

Fig. 6: Ann Lauren Osthof testing the wireless 3D scanner Artec Leo on graffiti (I.Milet 316) at the ancient harbour city Miletus, Türkiye, July 2022 (left) and the scanning data processed with Artec Studio 16 (right). Photograph © Jenny Gabel, scan © Ann Lauren Osthof, reproduced with the kind permission of the Miletus Excavation / Milet Kazısı <https://www.miletgrabung.uni-hamburg.de/>.

Furthermore, the new documentation methods enable researchers to measure the object without touching it. With a 3D scan, the graffiti can be reproduced multiple times and therefore reread or reinterpreted.[99] Moreover, immersive technologies allow researchers to revisit the graffiti site in virtual reality after the fieldwork. With less effort, equipment, time and training, an orthophotography creates the ideal setting (in terms of light and size) to study small objects in a larger context and to analyse the graffiti site in a spatial context.[100] However, the wide array of possible documenting technologies introduces the issue of choices and settings to ensure transparency and reproducibility.[101]

With these new technologies in mind, one needs a solid methodology that handles and makes sense of the newly available data and its digital storage and

99 Valente and Oreni 2017.

100 Valente and Barazzetti 2020; Wild et al. 2022 on AUTOGRAF, a freely available orthorectification tool; cf. Trentin, Benefiel and Sypniewski in this volume.

101 Valente et. al. 2019, 733. Further factors are the accessibility of the site, availability of electricity, cost of the devices, the time it takes to document, and the participation of trained scholars.

preservation. All data should ideally be publicly accessible and sustainable, that is, updatable.[102] As has already been remarked, graffiti can be numerous. With careful documentation, which includes text and object qualities, materiality and spatial context, databases are constantly growing. These principles are forged by a general understanding of how fragmented or incomplete the remains of the previous cultures are. Hence, archaeologists of the twenty-first century tend to document everything.[103] As we turn to contemporary graffiti, the amount of data increases exponentially and grows continuously. From a long-term perspective, it will not be possible to document all graffiti, so it would seem more fruitful to record representative graffiti sites with a thorough ontology for metadata and thus make them accessible for future research questions.

Sustainability implies not only manageable data but also consistent terminology, which makes comparisons possible in the first place. Two established descriptive toolkits could provide the basis for interdisciplinary research. Originating from historical European script-based graffiti, the Leiden Conventions are a system of punctuation marks that presents the state of preservation and reading variants of a text according to the researcher's interpretation.[104] This papyrological initiative goes back to the thirties of the nineteenth century and is nowadays employed by the EpiDoc encoding guidelines.[105] A broader range of scholarly fields uses the Getty Art & Architecture Thesaurus (AAT) for pictorial graffiti and the description of materiality.[106] Still, there are also graffiti that we can document although we may not be able to decode them in further analysis. To facilitate future comparative studies, glossaries could integrate the cultural and temporal connotations of each term in various disciplinary contexts.

Regarding databases, various solutions have emerged in graffiti studies in the past decade: the Norfolk Medieval Graffiti Survey (NMGS), headed by Matthew Champion, largely relies on volunteers to record 'graffiti inscriptions' in churches

---

102 See <https://www.go-fair.org/fair-principles/> (accessed on 26 June 2023) and Trentin in this volume.

103 Fleming 2001, 13; Baird and Taylor 2011, 7: 'Given that graffiti are increasingly studied both as a category of evidence and as part of broader archaeological and textual toolkits, it is now necessary to treat it with further methodological rigour despite the slippery problem of definition.'

104 Wilken 1932; <https://scholarlyeditions.brill.com/sego/standards/> (accessed on 5 April 2023); cf. Trentin, Benefiel and Sypniewski in this volume.

105 The EpiDoc schema was developed to encode texts in XML with the help of TEI (Text Encoding Initiative), see Elliott et al. 2006-2022.

106 <https://www.getty.edu/research/tools/vocabularies/aat/> (accessed on 13 March 2023). On ancient and medieval graffiti, see Trentin, Benefiel and Sypniewski in this volume; for contemporary graffiti, see Graf 2019 and 2020.

across the United Kingdom.[107] In contrast, in most other projects, graffiti are recorded by specialists; however, some projects, such as the Ancient Graffiti Project (AGP), have developed databases that are designed to be accessible to as many non-specialists as possible who are interested in graffiti.[108] As showcased by Rebecca Benefiel and Holly Sypniewski in their contribution to the present volume, this includes, for example, translations, re-drawings and comments as an easy gateway. Moreover, the Informationssystem Graffiti in Deutschland (INGRID) is a database specifically customized for researchers, taking into account image rights and developed for further research using metadata and a special annotation style.[109] These different types of databases highlight the multifaceted options in the research on graffiti. For cross-cultural research, the key point is that databases and the data they contain must be compatible. In this volume, Mia Trentin develops a workflow towards a comparable methodological ontology. Furthermore, Ann Graf has worked on a search engine connecting existing databases.[110] This enables research within the discipline as well as on a comparative and cross-cultural scale.

Yet – and this is especially important for contemporary graffiti – truly interdisciplinary documentation is not purely a task for researchers; it involves artists, curators, media, law and the broader public who shape, create and reflect on discourse and practice. Dialogue with practitioners and non-experts is vital to this,[111] which is why this volume features an interview with Hamburg's foremost graffiti artist. As a long-term insider and eyewitness to the Hamburg graffiti scene's development, Mirko Reisser tells and thereby records his own graffiti stories. Other contributions in this volume dealing with contemporary graffiti practices hearken back to Powers's point on the crucial role of oral narratives in the study of graffiti: Seth Markle's study stems from fifteen years of interviews, photographs and videos of the Tanzanian Wachata Crew. Anne Vieth's article voices the curatorial perspective, understanding graffiti as artistic expression. Her exhibition *WÄNDE | WALLS* displayed how graffiti has influenced public places over the last three decades with the help of two thousand photographs. By transforming a part of Stuttgart Central Station into a growing art gallery, she also visualized the

107 Norfolk Medieval Graffiti Survey, <http://www.medieval-graffiti.co.uk/> (accessed on 5 April 2023).

108 Benefiel 2017; <ancientgraffiti.org/Graffiti/> (accessed on 10 April 2023).

109 Niemann 2022; <https://www.uni-paderborn.de/forschungsprojekte/ingrid/> (accessed on 10 April 2023).

110 Graf 2018 and Graf 2020.

111 Holler 2014 on GraffDok; Burghardt et al. 2015. On scientific literature creating a dialogue between science and artist(s), see Eisewicht and Lintzen 2022.

production of graffiti and forcefully entered the public discourse.[112] Finally, Alexander Araya López's study explores these public discourses through narratives in media in Latin America, closing the circle that leads back to storytelling.

This section ends on an optimistic note, as a number of innovative thoughts and steps towards comparative and sustainable documentation have already been undertaken. Amidst the growing number of databases, descriptive terminology has become increasingly standardized, yet text-based toolkits remain largely Eurocentric. The vast range of technologies available enables recordings adapted to the specific circumstances of each site, and their affordability opens up unprecedented potential for crowdsourcing. We can document large areas quickly and, concerning contemporary graffiti, frequently. Making metadata openly accessible promotes transparency and the reproducibility of analysis. Both the 'documentary' and 'interpretive' camps of scholars can agree on shifting the scope and documenting written artefacts in their entirety, as this meets both the former's requirements to 'document everything' as well as the latter's imperative to separate documentation and analysis.

9 Concluding remarks

As discussed earlier in this introduction, the 'written artefact' approach has bearing on several issues in the study of graffiti, especially its definition, documentation and considerations of its multigraphic aspect. Yet it is important to note that this approach does not stop with the analysis of the material aspect of the artefact, but quite the contrary: it is simply the prism through which we view our materials while placing them in their historical, socio-cultural or political contexts.

The range of possible approaches can be glimpsed from just a few contributions in this volume. Matsui Dai, for instance, demonstrates the value of graffiti written in Old Uyghur on the walls of medieval Buddhist caves in present-day Turfan and Dunhuang as key sources for an alternative history of religious practice. Unlike the official canons and sutras, they offer insights into the lived experiences of pilgrimage and devotion, but also the boredom of prolonged stays in the cave monastery. Foregrounding the issues of (non-)literacy and audience, Michael Macdonald explores the incentives behind the production of Safaitic graffiti in the basalt deserts of ancient North Arabia. While doing so, he points out the

112 For essays on an exhibition of historical graffiti, see Marraccini 2020 and Rachiele 2020.

common pain of graffiti studies: a highly heterogenous corpus with referents scattered across the most diverse fields and genres in the external reality.

In an ethnographic vein, Seth Markle's essay traces the 'coming of age' of the Tanzanian Wachata Crew and their turn to entrepreneurialism amidst the dilemma of sustainability and cultural responsibility, a dilemma well known to most contemporary graffiti artists. To offer even more subjective insights from within the graffiti scene, Sanja Ewald interviewed the Hamburg graffiti artist Mirko Reisser. In their conversation, Reisser reveals much insider knowledge about graffiti writing, his own motivations and aesthetic preferences as well as the challenges of preserving one's own work despite its ephemeral nature.

These personal voices can be contrasted with the perspective of media sociology. How outsiders perceive and appraise graffiti depends on the discourses they encounter in society and media. While the media can reflect the attitude of general society to a certain extent, it can also amplify the views of particular stakeholders and influence public opinion. Alexander Araya López identifies several narrative frames employed by Latin American newspapers and shows how strikingly different they can be depending on which practices are actually labelled as 'graffiti'. Finally, from a different perspective still, the art historian and curator Anne Vieth addresses the conflict between two discursively salient aspects of graffiti – its aesthetic and its illegality – as they pertain to a set of successful graffiti art exhibitions in Stuttgart, Germany.

Undoubtedly, these approaches are far from being exhaustive. Arranged geographically from Africa to America and Asia to Europe, the essays in this volume seek to kindle further discussion and inspire new endeavours along the unbeaten path – towards a cross-cultural understanding of graffiti.

Acknowledgements

This volume grew out of a series of online workshops organized by this volume's editors during the second pandemic summer semester in 2021.[113] We would like to thank all the participants of these events for sharing insights and ideas that have led to an interesting cross-pollination among various disciplines, and also for their support of the virtual format, which was back then still largely uncharted territory

113 This was the workshop 'Scratched, Scrawled, Sprayed: Towards a Cross-Cultural Research on Graffiti', held in three instalments on 26 February, 5 and 12 March 2021, and the follow-up workshop 'Scratched, Scrawled, Sprayed ... and Drawn: Multigraphic Graffiti across Times and Cultures' on 2 July 2021, all under the virtual aegis of the Centre for the Study of Manuscript Cultures, University of Hamburg.

for many of us. We are grateful to those speakers who could not contribute to the publication but offered much food for thought and discussion in their inspiring presentations: Matthew Champion, Jitse H. F. Dijkstra, Arlo Griffiths, Alexey Kirichenko, Adam Łajtar, Polly Lohmann, Sven Ouzman and Charlotte Roueché.

The preparation of the workshop as well as this publication was funded by the Deutsche Forschungsgemeinschaft (DFG; German Research Foundation) under Germany's Excellence Strategy – EXC 2176 'Understanding Written Artefacts: Material, Interaction and Transmission in Manuscript Cultures', project no. 390893796. The research was conducted within the scope of the Centre for the Study of Manuscript Cultures (CSMC) at the Universität Hamburg.

We would also like to record our gratitude to Alessandro Bausi and Michael Friedrich for their initial encouragement and enduring support of this endeavour; to the members of the CSMC working groups Theory and Terminology (TnT) and Situating Graffiti for their constructive comments and suggestions on previous instantiations of this introduction; to Caroline Macé for her selfless help on numerous occasions during the inception of this volume and masterful management of the editorial process; to Eva Locher at De Gruyter for her enthusiastic support of this book; to Kristen de Joseph and Philip Saunders for punctilious copyediting and Imre Galambos for careful typesetting of the volume; and to Javier Abarca for his kind invitation to present and promote this book at the Unlock Book Fair and the Tag Conference: Name Writing in Public Space 2023.

References

As'ad, Khaled and Jean-Baptiste Yon (2001), *Inscriptions de Palmyre: Promenades épigraphiques dans la ville antique de Palmyre* (Guides archéologiques, 3), Beirut, Damascus and Amman: Presses de l'Institut français du Proche-Orient.

Avramidis, Konstantinos and Myrto Tsilimpounidi (eds) (2017), *Graffiti and Street Art: Reading, Writing and Representing the City*, Abingdon: Routledge.

Bachmann-Medick, Doris (2012), 'Culture as Text. Reading and Interpreting Cultures', in Birgit Neumann and Ansgar Nünning (eds), *Travelling Concepts for the Study of Culture* (Concepts for the Study of Culture, 2), Berlin: De Gruyter, 99–118.

Baird, Jennifer A. and Claire Taylor (2011), *Ancient Graffiti in Context*, New York: Routledge.

Baird, Jennifer A. (2015), 'Private Graffiti? Scratching the Walls of Houses at Dura-Europos', in Rebecca Benefiel and Peter Keegan (eds), *Inscriptions in the Private Sphere in the Greco-Roman World* (Brill Studies in Greek and Roman Epigraphy, 7), Leiden: Brill, 11–31.

Baird, Jennifer A. and Claire Taylor (2016), 'Ancient Graffiti', in Ross 2016, 17–26.

Bakker, Lothar and Brigitte Galsterer-Kröll (1975), *Graffiti auf römischer Keramik im Rheinischen Landesmuseum Bonn* (Epigraphische Studien, 10), Cologne: Rheinland-Verlag.

Balzani, Marcello, Marco Calliei, Matteo Fabbri, Andrea Fasano, Claudio Montani, Paolo Pingi, Nicola Santopuoli, Roberto Scopigno, Frederico Uccelli and Alberto Varone (2004), 'Digital

Representation and Multimodal Presentation of Archeological Graffiti at Pompei', in Kevin Cain, Yiorgos Chrysanthou, Franco Niccolucci and Neil Silberman (eds), *VAST 2004: The 5th International Symposium on Virtual Reality, Archaeology and Cultural Heritage*, Goslar: Eurographics Association, <doi:10.2312/VAST/VAST04/093-103> (accessed on 19 May 2023).

Bateman, John, Janina Wildfeuer and Tuomo Hiippala (2017), *Multimodality: Foundations, Research and Analysis: A Problem-Oriented Introduction* (Mouton Textbook), Berlin: De Gruyter.

Bausi, Alessandro, Michael Friedrich and Marilena Maniaci (eds) (2020), *The Emergence of Multiple-Text Manuscripts* (Studies in Manuscript Cultures, 17), Berlin: De Gruyter.

Benefiel, Rebecca R. (2010), 'Dialogues of Ancient Graffiti in the House of Maius Castricius in Pompeii', *American Journal of Archaeology*, 114/1: 59–101.

Benefiel, Rebecca R. (2014), 'Ancient Graffiti in Pompeian Domestic Spaces', in Werner Eck and Peter Funke (eds), *Öffentlichkeit – Monument – Text: XIV Congressus Internationalis Epigraphiae Graecae et Latinae 27.–31. Augusti MMXII. Akten*, Berlin: de Gruyter, 494–496.

Benefiel, Rebecca, Sara Sprenkle, Holly M. Sypniewski and Jamie White (2017), 'The Ancient Graffiti Project: Geo-Spatial Visualization and Search Tools for Ancient Handwritten Inscriptions', *DATeCH2017: Proceedings of the 2nd International Conference on Digital Access to Textual Cultural Heritage*, 2: 163–168, <doi:10.1145/3078081.3078104> (accessed on 26 May 2023).

Bîrzescu, Iulian (2006), 'Some Ceramic Inscriptions from Istrian Sanctuaries: The Naukratis Approach', in Alexandra Villing and Udo Schlotzhauer (eds), *Naukratis: Greek Diversity in Egypt. Studies on East Greek Pottery and Exchange in the Eastern Mediterranean*, Oxford: Oxbow Books, 169–174.

Bloch, Stefano and Susan A. Phillips (2021), 'Graffiti, Crime, and Street Culture', in Jeffrey Ian Ross (ed.), *Routledge Handbook of Street Culture*, Abingdon: Routledge, 77–89.

Burghardt, Manuel, Franziska Hertlein, Bastian Hinterleitner, Constantin Lehenmeier and Thomas Spröd (2015), 'A Crowdsourced Approach for the Documentation and Transcription of Graffiti in Public Restrooms', in Franjo Pehar, Christian Schlögl, Christian Wolff (eds), *Re:inventing Information Science in the Networked Society. Proceedings of the 14th International Symposium on Information Science (ISI 2015), Zadar, Croatia, 19th–21st May 2015*, Glückstadt: Verlag Werner Hülsbusch, 160–164, <urn:nbn:de:bvb:355-epub-357069> (accessed on 26 May 2023).

Carè, Barbara (2022), 'Pavement Design and Game Boards from Public Spaces of Ancient Athens: A Review Across the Board', *Board Game Studies Journal*, 16/1: 225–249.

Carletti, Carlo (2021), 'At the Origins of European Pilgrimage: The Devotional Graffiti of the Anglo-Saxons in Rome (Seventh–Ninth Centuries)', in Felle and Ward-Perkins 2021b, 77–89.

Castillo Gómez, Antonio (2020), 'Words on Walls: An Approach to Exposed Writing in Early Modern Europe', *Journal of Early Modern Studies*, 9: 57–82.

Champion, Matthew (2012), 'The Medium Is the Message: Votive Devotional Imagery and Gift Giving amongst the Commonality in the Late Medieval Parish', *Peregrinations: Journal of Medieval Art and Architecture*, 3/4: 103–123, <https://digital.kenyon.edu/perejournal/vol3/iss4/3> (accessed on 19 May 2023).

Champion, Matthew (2015), *Medieval Graffiti: The Lost Voices of England's Churches*, London: Ebury Press.

Champion, Matthew (2021), 'Accepted and Acceptable? Attitudes to Historical Graffiti Inscriptions in the Medieval Church', unpublished paper read at the workshop 'Scratched,

Scrawled, Sprayed: Towards a Cross-Cultural Research on Graffiti', Centre for the Study of Manuscript Cultures, University of Hamburg, 5 March 2021.

Chaniotis, Angelos (2011), 'Graffiti in Aphrodisias: Images – Texts – Contexts', in Baird and Taylor 2011, 191–207.

Chaniotis, Angelos, Thomas Corsten, Ronald S. Stroud and Rolf A. Tybout, (eds) (2007), *Supplementum Epigraphicum Graecum*, 53, Leiden: Brill.

Cole, Caroline M. (1991), 'Oh Wise Woman of the Stalls', *Discourse & Society*, 2/4: 401–411.

Cosentino, Antonino, Samantha Stout and Carmelo Scandurra (2015), 'Innovative Imaging Techniques for Examination and Documentation of Mural Paintings and Historical Graffiti in the Catacombs of San Giovanni, Syracuse', *International Journal of Conservation Science*, 6/1: 23–34.

Crist, Walter, Anne-Elizabeth Dunn-Vaturi and Alex de Voogt (2016), *Ancient Egyptians at Play: Board Games across Borders*, London: Bloomsbury.

Daryaee, Touraj (2017), 'Middle Persian Graffiti on Sasanian and Arab-Sasanian Coins at the American Numismatic Society', in Marek Jan Olbrycht (ed.), *Collectanea Iranica et Asiatica: Iran and Western Asia in Antiquity. New Perspectives* (Anabasis, 8), Rzeszów: Uniwersytetu Rzeszowskiego, 265–274.

Davis, Stephen J. (2020), 'Anastasia, Thecla, and Friends: Archaeological and Epigraphic Evidence from the Shenoutean Women's Monastery of Atripe', *Le Muséon*, 133/3–4: 259–287.

Dawdy, Shannon Lee (2016), *Patina: A Profane Archaeology*, Chicago: University of Chicago Press.

de Voogt, Alex (ed.) (1995), *New Approaches to Board Games Research: Asian Origins and Future Perspectives*, Leiden: International Institute for Asian Studies.

de Voogt, Alex (2012), 'Mancala Players at Palmyra', *Antiquity*, 84: 1055–1066.

de Voogt, Alex, Anne-Elizabeth Dunn-Vaturi and Jelmer W. Eerkens (2013), 'Cultural Transmission in the Ancient Near East: Twenty Squares and Fifty-eight Holes', *Journal of Archaeological Science*, 40: 1715–1730.

de Voogt, Alex, Maria Nilsson and John Ward (2020), 'The Role of Graffiti Game Boards in the Understanding of an Archaeological Site: The Gebel el-Silsila Quarries', *Journal of Egyptian Archaeology*, 106/1–2: 123–132.

Di Segni, Leah (2021), 'Jewish Devotional Graffiti and *Dipinti* in the Holy Land', in Felle and Ward-Perkins 2021b, 31–46.

Dirven, Lucinda and Maartje van Gelder (2018), 'Inleiding: Graffiti van de oudheid tot heden', *Tijdschrift voor Geschiedenis*, 131/1: 1–15.

Dundes, Alan (1966), 'Here I Sit: A Study of American Latrinalia', *The Kroeber Anthropological Society Papers*, 34: 91–105.

Eisewicht, Paul and Laura-Maria Lintzen (2022a), 'Einleitung – Zur Vielfalt der Graffiti-Forschung', in Eisewicht and Lintzen 2022b, 1–4.

Eisewicht, Paul and Laura-Maria Lintzen (eds) (2022b), *Dirty Hands: Interdisziplinäre Perspektiven auf die Graffiti-Szene*, Wiesbaden: Springer.

Elliott, Tom, Gabriel Bodard, Hugh Cayless et al. (2006-2022), *EpiDoc: Epigraphic Documents in TEI XML*, <https://epidoc.stoa.org/> (accessed on 25 August 2023).

Emberling, Geoff and Suzanne Davis (eds) (2019), *Graffiti as Devotion: Along the Nile and Beyond*, Ann Arbor: Kelsey Museum of Archaeology, University of Michigan.

Felle, Antonio (2021), 'Inscriptions, Graffiti, Graffiti *devotionis causa*: Some Concluding Notes and Reflections', in Felle and Ward-Perkins 2021b, 177–180.

Felle, Antonio E. and Bryan Ward-Perkins (2021a), 'Introduction', in Felle and Ward-Perkins 2021b, xvii–xx.

Felle, Antonio E. and Bryan Ward-Perkins (eds) (2021b), *Cultic Graffiti in the Late Antique Mediterranean and Beyond*, Turnhout: Brepols.

Ferem, Mark (2006), *Bathroom Graffiti*, New York: Mark Batty Publisher.

Finkel, Irving L. (ed.) (2007), *Ancient Board Games in Perspective: Papers from the 1990 British Museum Colloquium, with Additional Contributions*, London: British Museum Press.

Fleming, Juliet (2001), *Graffiti and the Writing Arts of Early Modern England*, London: Reaktion Books.

Fraenkel, Béatrice (2010), 'Writing Acts: When Writing Is Doing', in David Barton and Uta Papen (eds), *The Anthropology of Writing: Understanding Textually Mediated Worlds*, London: Continuum, 33–43.

Frederick, Ursula K. (2009), 'Revolution is the New Black: Graffiti/Art and Mark-making Practices', *Archaeologies. Journal of the World Archaeological Congress*, 5: 210–237, <doi.10.1007/s11759-009-9107-y> (accessed on 30 March 2023).

Frederick, Ursula K. (2014), 'Shake Well Midden: An Archaeology of Contemporary Graffiti Production in Perth, Western Australia', *Australian Archaeology*, 78: 93–99, <https://doi.org/10.1080/03122417.2014.11682004> (accessed on 30 March 2023).

Friedrich, Michael and Cosima Schwarke (eds) (2016), *One-Volume Libraries: Composite and Multiple-Text Manuscripts* (Studies in Manuscript Cultures, 9), Berlin: De Gruyter.

Gabel, Jenny, Christof Berns, Sebastian Bosch, Jost Eickmeyer, Kaja Harter-Uibopuu, Natalie Martin, Ann Lauren Osthof, Johann Anselm Steiger and Frank Steinicke (2022), 'Immersive Inscribed Spaces: Bringing Virtuality to Written Artefacts for Humanities', *i-com: Journal of Interactive Media*, 21/1: 7–18.

Graf, Ann M. (2018), 'Facets of Graffiti Art and Street Art Documentation Online: A Domain and Content Analysis, <https://dc.uwm.edu/etd/1809> (accessed on 15 March 2023).

Graf, Ann M. (2019), 'Warrant Revealed and an Institutional Response: The AAT and Graffiti Art', *Nasko*, 7: 183–189.

Graf, Ann M. (2020), 'Domain Analysis of Graffiti Art Documentation: A Methodological Approach', in Marianne Lykke, Tanja Svarre, Mette Skov and Daniel Martínez-Ávila (eds), *Knowledge Organization at the Interface: Proceedings of the Sixteenth International ISKO Conference 2020*, Aalborg: Ergon, 161–170, <doi.org/10.5771/9783956507762> (accessed on 15 March 2023).

Griffiths, Arlo (2021), 'A Very First Exploration of Graffiti as an Epigraphic Category in South East Asia up to ca. 1500 CE', unpublished paper read at the workshop 'Scratched, Scrawled, Sprayed: Towards a Cross-Cultural Research on Graffiti', Centre for the Study of Manuscript Cultures, University of Hamburg, 5 March 2021.

Hall, Mark A. (2019), 'Whose Game is it Anyway? Board and Dice Games as an Example of Cultural Transfer and Hybridity', *Archimède: archéologie et histoire ancienne*, 6: 199–212.

Hamburger, Jeffrey F. (2011), 'The Iconicity of Script', *Word & Image*, 27/3: 249–261.

Harmanşah, Ömür (2018), 'Graffiti or Monument? Inscription of Place at Anatolian Rock Reliefs', in Ragazzoli et al. 2018, 49–64.

Hawkins, John D. (1998), 'Tarkasnawa king of Mira, "Tarkondemos", Boğazköy Sealings and Karabel', *Anatolian Studies*, 48: 1–31.

Hentschel, Elke (1987), 'Women's Graffiti', Multilingua: Journal of Cross-Cultural and Interlanguage Communication, 6/3: 287–308.

Historic England (2021), *Graffiti on Historic Buildings: Removal and Prevention*, Swindon: Historic England.

Holler, Robin (2014), 'GraffDok – A Graffiti Documentation Application', in Anna-Lena Lamprecht and Tiziana Margaria (eds), *Process Design for Natural Scientist: An Agile Model-Driven Approach*, Heidelberg: Springer, 239–252, <https://doi.org/10.1007/978-3-662-45006-2_19> (accessed on 30 March 2023).

Htun Khaing (2016), 'Defacing Bagan', *Frontier Myanmar*, 4/13, <https://www.frontiermyanmar.net/en/defacing-bagan/> (accessed on 26 May 2023).

Ishizawa, Yoshiaki (2015), 'The World's Oldest Plan of Angkor Vat: The Japanese So-called Jetavana, an Illustrated Plan of the Seventeenth Century', *Journal of Khmer Studies*, 13: 47–61.

Jacquet-Gordon, Helen (2003), *The Graffiti of the Khonsu Temple Roof at Karnak: A Manifestation of Personal Piety* (Oriental Institute Publications, 123), Chicago: Oriental Institute Chicago Press.

JEPSY (2022), 'The Real Deal', in Eisewicht and Lintzen 2022b, 5–12.

Karkoon, Rashi (2023), 'Erasing Heritage through Love Tagging', unpublished paper read at the conference 'Tag: Name Writing in Public Space', Hamburg, 1 July 2023.

Keegan, Peter (2014), 'Graffiti and Dipinti as *monumenta* and *verba*: Marking Territories, Creating Discourse in Roman Pompeii', in Werner Eck, Peter Funke, Marcus Dohnicht, and Klaus Hallof (eds), *XIV Congressus Internationalis Epigraphiae Graecae et Latinae 27. – 31. Augusti MMXII*, Berlin: De Gruyter, 497–498.

Keegan, Peter (2015), *Graffiti in Antiquity*, Abingdon: Routledge.

Kienitz, Sabine (2022), 'Schreiben, um gehört zu werden: Zur Materialität religiöser Kommunikation im Medium des Anliegenbuchs', *Rheinisch-Westfälische Zeitschrift für Volkskunde*, 67: 178–196.

Kirichenko, Alexey (2021), 'Beyond the Programmed? Multigraphic Content in Buddhist Monuments of Upper Burma', unpublished paper read at the workshop 'Scratched, Scrawled, Sprayed ... and Drawn: Multigraphic Graffiti across Times and Cultures', Centre for the Study of Manuscript Cultures, University of Hamburg, 2 July 2021.

Kobiałka, Dawid (2019), 'Living Monuments of the Second World War: Terrestrial Laser Scanning and Trees with Carvings', *International Journal of Historical Archaeology*, 23/1: 129–152.

Kruschwitz, Peter and Virginia L. Campbell (2009), 'What the Pompeians Saw: Representations of Document Types in Pompeian Drawings and Paintings (and Their Value for Linguistic Research)', *Arctos*, 43: 57–84.

Kruschwitz, Peter (2010), 'Writing on Trees: Restoring a Lost Facet of the Graeco-Roman Epigraphic Habit', *Zeitschrift für Papyrologie und Epigraphik*, 173: 45–62.

Kütter, Jochen (2008), *Graffiti auf römischer Gefäßkeramik aus Neuss Berichte aus der Geschichtswissenschaft*, Aachen: Shaker Verlag.

Łajtar, Adam (2018), 'The Constantinopolitan Creed in an Inscription from the Monastery Church on Kom H in Dongola', in Włodzimierz Godlewski, Dorota Dzierzbicka and Adam Łajtar (eds), *Dongola 2015–2016: Fieldwork, Conservation and Site Management* (Polish Centre of Mediterranean Archaeology: Excavation Series, 5), Warsaw: University of Warsaw Press, 37–46.

Łajtar, Adam (2020), *A Late Christian Pilgrimage Centre in Nubia: The Evidence of Wall Inscriptions in the Upper Church at Banganarti* (*Journal of Juristic Papyrology* Supplements, 39), Leuven: Peeters.

Łajtar, Adam (2021), 'Cultic Graffiti in Christian Nubia (Sixth to Fifteenth Centuries)', in Felle and Ward-Perkins 2021b, 159–176.

Łajtar, Adam and Jacques van der Vliet (2009), 'Wall Inscriptions in a Burial Vault under the Northwest Annex of the Monastery of on Kom H (Dongola 2009)', *Polish Archaeology in the Mediterranean*, 21: 330–337.
Lea, Daniel (2006), 'Intertextuality', in Peter Childs and Roger Fowler (eds), *The Routledge Dictionary of Literary Terms*, Abingdon: Routledge, 121–123.
Lohmann, Polly (2018a), 'Fünf Graffiti auf römischen Gefäßen aus Speyer', in Ulrich Himmelmann, Bettina Hünerfauth and Jutta Winkelmann (eds), *Fundsache Speyer: vom Stadtrand bis zum Domplatz* (Archäologische Denkmäler in der Pfalz, 6), Mainz: Generaldirektion Kulturelles Erbe – Rheinland-Pfalz, 51–52.
Lohmann, Polly (2018b), *Graffiti als Interaktionsform: Geritzte Inschriften in den Wohnhäusern Pompejis*, Berlin: De Gruyter.
Lohmann, Polly (ed.) (2018c), *Historische Graffiti als Quellen: Methoden und Perspektiven eines jungen Forschungsbereichs*, Stuttgart: Franz Steiner.
Lohmann, Polly (2020), 'Historical Graffiti: The State of the Art', *Journal of Early Modern Studies*, 9: 37–57.
Lovata, Troy (2015), 'Marked Trees: Exploring the Contexts of Southern Rocky Mountain Arboglyphs', in Lovata and Olton 2015, 91–104.
Lovata, Troy and Elizabeth Olton (eds) (2015), *Understanding Graffiti: Multidisciplinary Studies from Prehistory to the Present*, Walnut Creek: Left Coast Press.
Ludwig, Johannes Baptista aka JBL (2022), 'I Spot with My Little Eye: Malen und Fame betrachtet aus einer Komplementärperspektive', in Eisewicht and Lintzen 2022b, 121–134.
MacMullan, Ramsay (1982), 'The Epigraphic Habit in the Roman Empire', *The American Journal of Philology*, 103/3: 233–246.
Mailer, Norman (1966), *Cannibals and Christians*, New York: Dial Press.
Mallea-Olaetxe, Joxe (2000), *Speaking through the Aspens: Basque Tree Carvings in California and Nevada*, Reno: University of Nevada Press.
Manzo, Andrea (2020), 'The Great Aksumite Decorated Stelae: Architectural Characteristics, Functions, and Meanings', *Aethiopica*, 23: 7–31.
Marciniak, Marek (1981), 'Une inscription commémorative de Deir el-Bahari', *Mitteilungen des Deutschen Archäologischen Instituts, Abteilung Kairo*, 37: 299–303.
Marraccini, Manuele (2020), 'Urbino's Graffiti: From the Wall to the Exhibition', *Journal of Early Modern Studies*, 9: 195–202.
Masilamani, Rachel (2008), 'Documenting Illegal Art: Collaborative Software, Online Environments and New York City's 1970s and 1980s Graffiti Art Movement', *Art Documentation. Journal of the Art Libraries Society of North America*, 27/2: 4–14.
Matsui, Dai and Arakawa Shintaro (eds) (2017), *Tonkō sekkutsu ta-gengo shiryō shūsei* 敦煌石窟多言語資料集成, Tokyo: Tōkyō Gaikokugo Daigaku Ajia Afurika gengo bunka kenkyūjo.
Matsumoto, Mallory E. (2022), 'Archaeology and Epigraphy in the Digital Era', *Journal of Archaeological Research*, 30: 285–320.
Meade, Melissa (2015), 'Latrinalia in a Room of One's Own: Language, Gender, Place', in Lovata and Olton 2015, 33–46.
Mulvin, Linda and Steven E. Sidebotham (2003), 'Roman Game Boards from Abu Sha'ar (Red Sea Coast, Egypt)', *Antiquity*, 78/301: 602–617.
Murphy, Dan (2013), 'Egypt's Antiquities Face Bigger Problems than Chinese Graffiti: How a Young Chinese Boy Defaced an Ancient Egyptian Temple, and Unwittingly Joined a Long Tradition in the Process', *The Christian Science Monitor*, 28 May 2013,

<https://www.csmonitor.com/World/Security-Watch/Backchannels/2013/0528/Egypt-s-antiquities-face-bigger-problems-than-Chinese-graffiti> (accessed on 18 January 2023).

Naveh, Joseph (1979), 'Graffiti and Dedications', *Bulletin of the American Schools of Oriental Research*, 235: 27–30.

Niemann, Sven (2022), 'INGRID – Das Informationssystem Graffiti in Deutschland', in Wilke, Thomas and Michael Rappe (eds), *HipHop im 21. Jahrhundert. Medialität, Tradierung, Gesellschaftskritik und Bildungsaspekte einer (Jugend-)Kultur*, Wiesbaden: Springer VS, 267–288.

Nikitin, Alexander B. (1993), 'Middle Persian and Some Other Graffiti on Sasanian Coins from the Moscow Collection', *Iran*, 31: 99–101.

Nilsson, Maria (2015), 'Gebel el Silsila: Field Report from the Main Quarry', *Journal of Intercultural and Interdisciplinary Archaeology*, 2: 147–191.

Norfolk Medieval Graffiti Survey (2017), *Medieval Graffiti Survey: Volunteer Handbook. Revised Oct. 2017*, <http://www.medieval-graffiti.co.uk/Volunteer%20Handbook%20NMGS.pdf> (accessed on 19 June 2023).

Nowakowski, Pawel (2021), 'Pilgrims and Seafarers: A Survey of Travellers' Graffiti from the Aegean Islands', in Felle and Ward-Perkins 2021b, 111–135.

O'Donald, Megan (2018), 'The ROTAS "Wheel": Form and Content in a Pompeian Graffito', *Zeitschrift für Papyrologie und Epigraphik*, 205: 77–91.

Ouzman, Sven (2021), 'Prose Has Its Cons: An Archaeological Understanding of Graffiti as Material Culture – Lessons from the Global South', unpublished paper read at the workshop 'Scratched, Scrawled, Sprayed ... and Drawn: Multigraphic Graffiti across Times and Cultures', Centre for the Study of Manuscript Cultures, University of Hamburg, 2 July 2021.

Patrois, Julie (2013), 'Río Bec Graffiti: A Private Form of Art', *Ancient Mesoamerica*, 24/2: 433–447.

Perrottet, Tony (2016), 'Tourists Gone Wild', *The New York Times*, 9 December 2016, <https://www.nytimes.com/2016/12/09/opinion/sunday/tourists-gone-wild.html> (accessed on 18 January 2023).

Pyke, Gillian (2019a), 'The Ceramic Material from Athribis: The 2007/8–2010/11 Excavation Seasons,' in Marcus Müller, Mohamed El-Bialy and Mansour Boraik (eds), *Athribis V: Archäologie im Repit-Tempel zu Athribis 2012–2016*, Cairo: Institut français d'archéologie orientale, 221–294.

Pyke, Gillian (2019b), 'The Ceramic Material from Athribis: The 2012/13–2014/15 Excavation Seasons,' in Marcus Müller, Mohamed El-Bialy and Mansour Boraik (eds), *Athribis V: Archäologie im Repit-Tempel zu Athribis 2012–2016*, Cairo: Institut français d'archéologie orientale, 295–362.

Pope, Jeremy (2019), 'Figural Graffiti from the Meroitic Era on Philae Island', in Emberling and Davis 2019, 71–86.

Porció Tibor (2014), 'Some Peculiarities of the Uygur Buddhist Pilgrim Inscriptions', in Christoph Cueppers and Max Deeg (eds), *Searching for the Dharma, Finding Salvation: Buddhist Pilgrimage in Time and Space*, Lumbini: Lumbini International Research Institute, 157–178.

Powers, Stephen (1999), *The Art of Getting Over: Graffiti at the Millennium*, New York: St. Martin's Press.

Purcell, Nicholas (1995), 'Literate Games: Roman Urban Society and the Game of Alea', *Past and Present*, 147: 3–37.

Rachiele, Valentina (2020), 'Multimedia and Interaction Design in the "Stone with a Story" Project', *Journal of Early Modern Studies*, 9: 203–212.

Ragazzoli, Chloé (2017), *La grotte des scribes à Deir el-Bahari: La tombe MMA 504 et ses graffiti* (Mémoires de l'Institut Français d'Archéologie Orientale, 135), Cairo: Institut français d'archéologie orientale.

Ragazzoli, Chloé (2018), 'The Scribes' Cave: Graffiti and the Production of Social Space in Ancient Egypt circa 1500 BC', in Ragazzoli et al. 2018, 23–36.

Ragazzoli, Chloé, Ömür Harmanşah and Chiara Salvador (2018) 'Introduction', in Ragazzoli et al. 2018, 1–15.

Ragazzoli, Chloé, Ömur Harmanşah, Chiara Salvador and Elizabeth Frood (eds) (2018), *Scribbling through History: Graffiti, Places and People from Antiquity to Modernity*, London: Bloomsbury Academic.

Reisner, Robert (1971), *Graffiti: Two Thousand Years of Wall Writing*, Chicago: Henry Regnery.

Relph, Edward (1976), *Place and Placelessness*, London: Pion.

Rippl, Gabriele (2015), 'Introduction', in Gabriele Rippl (ed.), *Handbook of Intermediality: Literature – Image – Sound – Music* (Handbooks of English and American Studies, 1), Berlin: De Gruyter, 1–32.

Ritsema van Eck, Marianne (2018), 'Graffiti in Medieval and Early Modern Religious Spaces: Illicit or Accepted Practice? The Case of the Sacro Monte at Varallo', *Tijdschrift voor Geschiedenis*, 131/1: 51–72.

Robert, Jörg (2014), *Einführung in die Intermedialität* (Einführungen Germanistik), Darmstadt: Wissenschaftliche Buchgesellschaft.

Rodriguez, Amardo (2015), 'On the Origins of Anonymous Texts That Appear on Walls', in Lovata and Olton 2015, 21–31.

Rogers, Janine (2018), 'Graffiti and the Medieval Margin', in Ragazzoli et al. 2018, 175–188.

Ross, Jeffrey Ian (ed.) (2016), *Routledge Handbook of Graffiti and Street Art*, Abingdon: Routledge.

Roueché, Charlotte (2014), 'Using Civic Space: Identifying the Evidence', in Werner Eck and Peter Funke (eds), *Öffentlichkeit – Monument – Text: XIV Congressus Internationalis Epigraphiae Graecae et Latinae 27.–31. Augusti MMXII*, Berlin: De Gruyter, 135–158.

Sarti, Raffaella (2020), 'Editorial', *Journal of Early Modern Studies*, 9: 7–26.

Schädler, Ulrich (1994), 'Latrunculi: Ein verlorenes strategisches Brettspiel der Römer', in Günther G. Bauer (ed.), *Homo Ludens. Der Spielende Mensch 4*, Munich: Verlag Emil Katzenbichler, 47–67.

Schädler, Ulrich (1998), 'Mancala in Roman Asia Minor', *Board Games Studies*, 1: 10–25.

Schädler, Ulrich (2009), '*Pente grammai*: The Ancient Greek Board Game *Five Lines*', in Jorge Nuno Silva (ed.), *Board Games Studies Colloquium XI, Proceedings*, Lisbon: Associaçâo Ludus, 173–196.

Shimizu Junzō 清水潤三 (1965), 'Ankōru watto sekichū ni nokoru Nihonjin bokusho no chōsa アンコール・ワット石柱にのこる日本人墨書の調査', in Matsumoto Nobuhiro 松本信広 (ed.), *Indoshina kenkyū: Tōnan'ajia inasaku minzoku bunka sōgō chōsa hōkoku* インドシナ研究：東南アジア稲作民族文化綜合調査報告, vol. 1, Yokohama: Yūrindō Shuppan, 221–265.

Stern, Karen B. (2018a), *Writing on the Wall: Graffiti and the Forgotten Jews of Antiquity*, Princeton: Princeton University Press.

Stern, Karen B. (2018b), 'Carving Lines and Shaping Monuments: Mortuary Graffiti and Jews in the Ancient Mediterranean', in Ragazzoli et al. 2018, 145–156.

Strehle, Samuel (2008), 'Fortsetzung des Aufstands mit anderen Mitteln? Eine kultursoziologische und medientheoretische Analyse des Graffiti-Writings', in Samuel Strehle and

Sacha Szabo (eds), *Unterhaltungswissenschaft: Populärkultur im Diskurs der Cultural Studies*, Marburg: Tectum, 11–36.

Stumpf, Christiane (2013), *Toilettengraffiti: Unterschiedliche Kommunikationsverhalten von Männern und Frauen*, Frankfurt: Peter Lang.

Subías Pascual, Eva (2003), *La Corona Immarcescible: Pintures de l'Antiguitat Tardana de la Necròpolis Alta d'Oxirinc (Mínia, Egipte)* (Sèrie Documenta, 1), Tarragona: Institut Català d'Arqueologia Clàssica.

Summerfield, Chantel (2012), 'Trees as a Living Museum: Arborglyphs and Conflict on Salisbury Plain', in Nicholas J. Saunders (ed.), *Beyond the Dead Horizon: Studies in Modern Conflict Archaeology*, Oxford: Oxbow Books, 159–171.

Sur les murs: histoire(s) de graffitis (2018), Paris: Éditions du patrimoine, Centre des monuments nationaux.

Talloen, Peter (2018), 'Rolling the Dice: Public Game Boards from Sagalassos', *Herom: Journal of Hellenistic and Roman Material Culture*, 7/1–2: 97–132.

Thomov, Thomas (2014), 'Four Scandinavian Ship Graffiti from Hagia Sophia,' *Byzantine and Modern Greek Studies*, 38/2: 168–184.

Tianshui Maijishan shiku yishu yanjiusuo 天水麥積山石窟藝術研究所 (1998): *Tianshui Maijishan* 天水麥積山 (Zhongguo shiku 中國石窟), Beijing: Wenwu chubanshe.

Trahan, Adam (2016), 'Research and Theory on Latrinalia', in Ross 2016, 92–102.

Tsakos, Alexandros (2019), 'Materiality and Physicality of Medieval Manuscripts from Christian Nubia', *Cahiers d'études africaines*, 59: 967–992.

Tuan Yi-Fu (1974), *Topophilia: A Study of Environmental Perceptions, Attitudes, and Values*, Englewood Cliffs, NJ: Prentice-Hall.

Tuan Yi-Fu (1977), *Space and Place: The Perspective of Experience*, Minneapolis: University of Minnesota Press.

Ünal, Ahmet (1989), 'Drawings, Graffiti and Squiggles on the Hittite Tablets: Art in Scribal Circles', in Kutlu Emre, Barthel Hrouda, Machteld Mellink and Nimet Özgüç (eds), *Anatolia and the Ancient Near East: Studies in Honor of Tahsin Özgüç*, Ankara: Türk Tarih Kurumu Basimevi, 505–513.

Valente, Riccardo and Daniela Orenia (2017), 'Survey and Drawings for the Study and Enhancement of Ancient Wall Graffiti: The Case of the Baptistery of Castiglione Olona', *DISEGNARECON*, 10/19: 1–10, <https://disegnarecon.univaq.it/ojs/index.php/disegnarecon/article/view/277> (accessed on 15 March 2023).

Valente, Riccardo and Luigi Barazzetti (2020), 'Methods for Ancient Wall Graffiti Documentation: Overview and Applications', *Journal of Archaeological Science. Reports*, 34: 1–13, <https://doi.org/10.1016/j.jasrep.2020.102616> (accessed on 15 March 2023).

Valente, Riccardo, Luigi Barazzetti, Mattia Previtali and Fabio Roncoroni (2019), 'Considerations on the Use of Digital Tools for Documenting Ancient Wall Graffiti', in Alesso Cardaci, Francesco Fassi and Fabio Remondino (eds), *The International Archives of the Photogrammetry, Remote Sensing and Spatial Information Sciences, Volume XLII-2/W9, 2019, 8th Intl. Workshop 3D-ARCH "3D Virtual Reconstruction and Visualization of Complex Architectures", 6–8 February 2019, Bergamo, Italy*, Göttingen: Copernicus, 731–737, <doi.org/10.5194/isprs-archives-XLII-2-W9-731-2019> (accessed on 15 March 2023).

van Belle, Jean-Louis and Anne-Sophie Brun (2020), *Le graffiti-signature: reflet d'histoire*, Brussels: Éditions Safran.

Verhoeven, Geert, Benjamin Wild, Jona Schlegel, Martin Wieser, Norbert Pfeifer, Stefan Wogrin, Lothar Eysn, Massimiliano Carloni, Bernhard Koschiček-Krombholz, Adolfo Molada Tebar,

Johannes Otepka-Schremmer, Camillo Ressl, Martina Trognitz and Alexander Watzinger (2022), 'Project Indigo – Document, Disseminate & Analyse a Graffiti-Scape', *The International Archives of the Photogrammetry, Remote Sensing and Spatial Information Sciences, 9th Intl. Workshop 3D-ARCH "3D Virtual Reconstruction and Visualization of Complex Architectures", 2–4 March 2022, Mantua, Italy,* 46/2/W1 Göttingen: Copernicus, 513–520, <https://doi.org/10.5194/isprs-archives-XLVI-2-W1-2022-513-2022> (accessed on 30 March 2023).

Weiss-König, Stephan (2010), *Graffiti auf römischer Gefäßkeramik aus dem Bereich der Colonia Ulpia Traiana / Xanten* (Xantener Berichte, 17), Mainz: Philipp von Zabern.

Widura, Anne (2015), *Spielräume: Kulturhistorische Studien zum Brettspiel in archäologischen Kontexten*, Leidorf: Rahden.

Wilcken, Ulrich (1932), 'Das Leydener Klammersystem', *Archiv für Papyrusforschung*, 10/3–4, 211–212.

Wild, Benjamin, Geert J. Verhoeven, Martin Wieser, Camillo Resi, Jona Schlegel, Stefan Wogrin, Johannes Otepka-Schremmer and Norbert Pfeifer (2022), 'AUTOGRAF – AUTomated Orthorectification of GRAFfiti Photos', *Heritage*, 5: 2987–3009, <https://doi.org/10.3390/heritage5040155> (accessed on 30 March 2023).

Wimmer, Hanna, Dmitry Bondarev, Janina Karolewski and Vito Lorusso (2015), 'A Heuristic Tool for the Comparative Study of Manuscripts from Different Manuscript Cultures', *Centre for the Study of Manuscript Cultures Occasional Papers*, 3, <doi.org/10.25592/uhhfdm.9800> (accessed on 26 May 2023).

Wu Cheng'en (2012), *The Journey to the West*, tr. and ed. Anthony C. Yu, revised edn, Chicago: The University of Chicago Press.

Youkhana, Eva and Larissa Förster (eds) (2015), *Grafficity: Visual Practices and Contestations in Urban Space*, Paderborn: Wilhelm Fink.

Young, Alison (2014), *Street Art, Public City: Law, Crime and the Urban Imagination*, Abingdon: Routledge.

Africa

Ursula Verhoeven

Writing Wherever Possible and Meaningful: Graffiti Culture in Ancient Egypt

Context, Terminology, Documentation

Abstract: After an introduction about scribes, writing culture, scripts and literacy in Ancient Egypt, the close relationship between text and image in many domains, including graffiti, is addressed. Several text genres are found in graffiti, as well as on mobile artefacts, because such texts belonged to the didactic curriculum and cultural knowledge. The various evidence of graffiti-like inscriptions on landscape formations, tombs, and temples over more than three millennia can be characterized only briefly and selectively. The use and definitions of the term 'graffiti' and similar labels in Egyptology are presented and discussed with reference to various criteria. In the end, the evolution of the documentation techniques is sketched, and the author reflects on her own experiences with inked graffiti (*dipinti*) inside a rock tomb in Asyut.

1 Introduction

In Ancient Egypt, at least in the higher strata of society, writing and images were media that played a central role in almost all aspects of life: in the civilization's extensive administration and trade, the maintenance of their culture of knowledge, the representation of the king's ideology, and the differentiated funerary and religious ideas and arrangements. Becoming a 'scribe' in this society not only meant being relieved of menial, physical labour (Fig. 1), but education and extensive knowledge promised status, a good income, and maybe a high office, even up to the royal court.

Moreover, it opened up the possibility of being able to create one's own, permanent tomb, with a rich burial equipment and high-quality decoration that should be effective beyond death: offering formulae inscribed in the name of the tomb owner, on the one hand, and depictions of the tomb owner in the contexts of fishing, fowling, agriculture, cattle herding, marshland activities, and festive family scenes with relatives, on the other, intended to guarantee that the needs of this worldly life would be continuously satisfied in the netherworld.

https://doi.org/10.1515/9783111326306-002

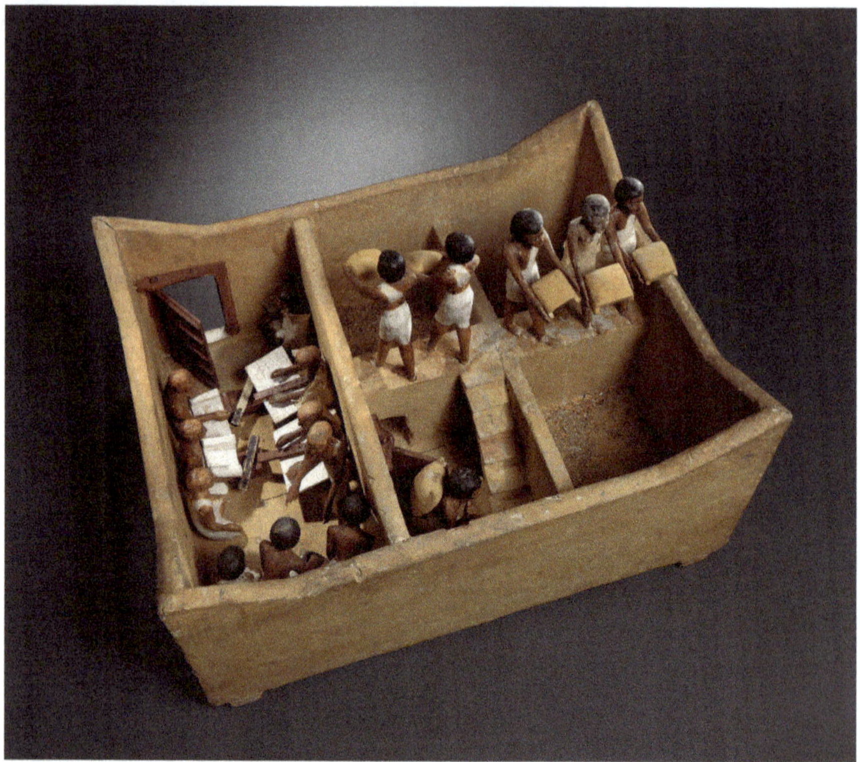

Fig. 1: Wooden model showing the work of scribes; scribes with papyrus rolls and wooden writing tablets (left) noting what workers carry into the granary (right); from Theban Tomb TT 280, *c.* 1981–1975 BCE; The Metropolitan Museum of Art, New York, 20.3.11; public domain.

Incidentally, tools for writing – rushes, palettes, pigments, and wooden boards or papyri – are also represented among grave goods. However, scribes were also bearers of social communication beyond orality, and acted as agents of the transmission and preservation of cultural wisdom and memory.[1] The status of a scribe can be recognized in an inscription of the nomarch Khety II in his monumental rock tomb at Asyut, dating to the twenty-first century BCE. He states: 'Every scribe and every scholar who is skilful in his work, apt in writing, apt in wisdom ... he

1 Cf. e.g. the recent works by Allon and Navrátilová 2017; Cancik-Kirschbaum and Kahl 2018, 70–72, 86–87; Pinarello 2015; Ragazzoli 2010; Ragazzoli 2019.

should become an elder of his city, praised in his nome, and I will vouch for him as his advocate in the necropolis'.[2]

Of course, at most, only one per cent of the people of the country were educated,[3] being involved in administrative sectors or the broad culture of knowledge and therefore able to produce textual graffiti. The vast majority of society was not at all able to read or write; they worked, for example, as craftsmen, peasants, hunters, fishermen, quarrymen, washers, cooks and soldiers, not to mention women of all social contexts, with different tasks and professions.

In addition to the hieroglyphic inscriptions and pictorial scenes present everywhere in temples and tombs and on statues, stelae, obelisks, and other monuments – always according to Ancient Egyptian decorum – graffiti texts and/or images are also found throughout the country, painted or carved in places of both natural and artificial origin; these, however, are less elaborate than the official inscriptions. On the issue of delimiting and valuing such categories of images and texts as 'graffiti' in a contemporary sense, the emic view should first be considered: affixing texts or pictures to or inside buildings of an official, religious or funerary character, or on rocks and the like, was obviously not forbidden or illegal in Ancient Egypt, and there is generally no evidence of intentional erasure, reckless overpainting or any anti-graffiti techniques.

The so-called graffiti, *dipinti* or rock inscriptions (for the terminology, cf. Section 5 below) were therefore part of Ancient Egyptian written culture, mostly executed by educated scribes and regarded as self-representation, testimony of personal piety, or interest in older monuments. Further, we sometimes find short name graffiti that do not seem to come from a practised hand. That some of the figural graffiti, carved lines or symbols were made by illiterate persons may be assumed,[4] but the purpose of an image or magical symbol may be more important than a text, and 'while texts could be conceived only by a minority, figures could be perceived by all'.[5]

It is revealing that the authors of graffiti did not conceal their names; it was generally important to mention one's name (and sometimes also title, genealogy and the date) when the scribe wanted to demonstrate that he had visited a special place or asked for the help of gods in his daily life or on a journey to a foreign place. On the other hand, we also find anonymous texts and images, where it was seemingly unnecessary to leave a signature.

---

2 Cf. Cancik-Kirschbaum and Kahl 2018, 53 (tomb Siut IV, 66–71). English translation by the author.

3 Baines and Eyre 2007, 67–70.

4 Staring 2011, 148.

5 Staring 2018, 96.

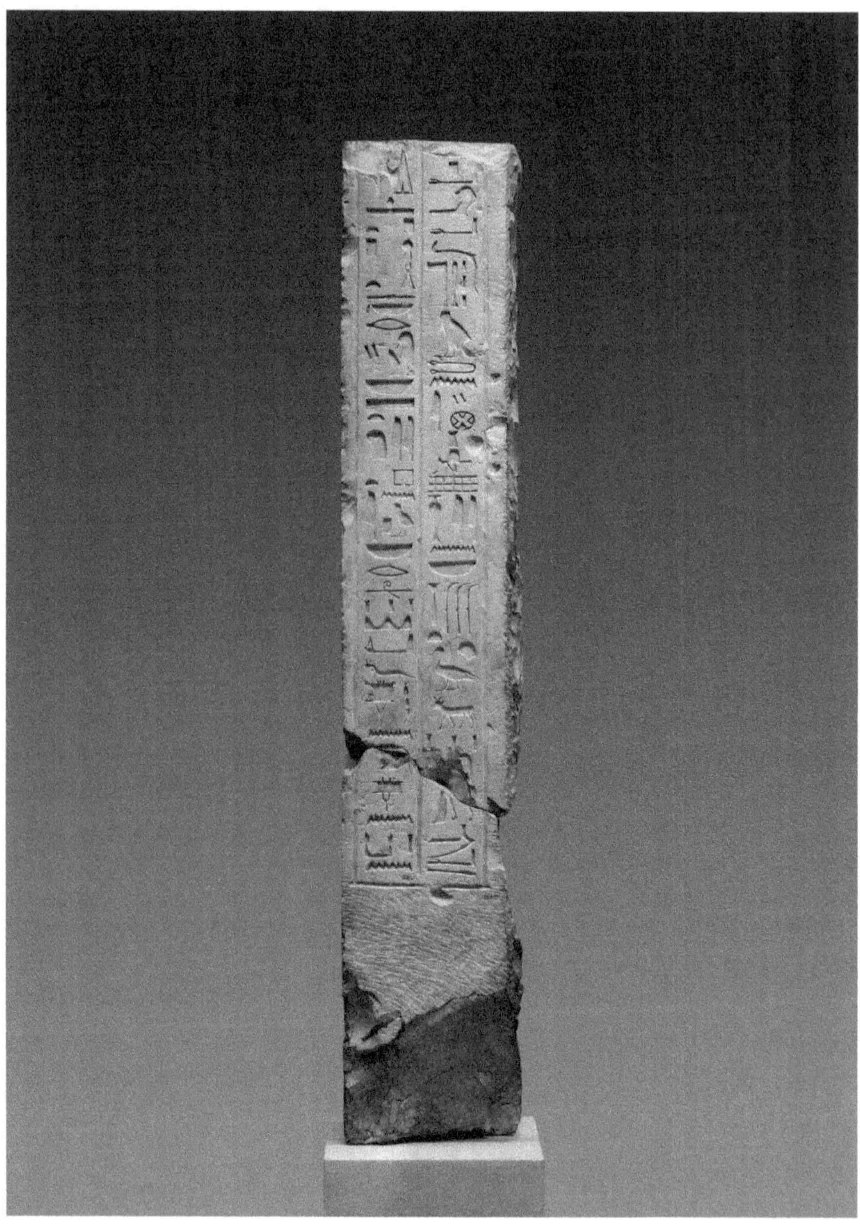

Fig. 2: Hieroglyphic inscription; door jamb of the tomb of Sitepihi from Abydos, *c.* 1479–1458 BCE; The Metropolitan Museum of Art, New York, 00.460; public domain.

Following this emic view, it is interesting to ask if the Ancient Egyptian language itself differed between normal texts/inscriptions and graffiti. There was no difference in the labelling of a text based on its support, the circumstances or the writer; the language distinguishes only the type of script: execution in the form of detailed hieroglyphs is called *mdww nṯr* (or *sẖꜣ n mdww nṯr*) '(script of) the words of god'. It may be raised or engraved in relief, painted in colour or monochrome, and made of any material, even gold and precious stones, but also inked on diverse surfaces. The writing direction may be from left to right or right to left, in columns or lines (Fig. 2).

Cursive handwriting, on the other hand, is referred to simply as *sẖꜣ* 'script' in the case of hieratic script, and later as *sẖꜣ šꜥ.t* 'epistolary' for the more abbreviated demotic script (cf. below). These scripts are always written from right to left, sometimes in columns (earlier and also later on), but mainly in lines (cf. Fig. 3, purposely selected from the same time span as the object in Fig. 2).

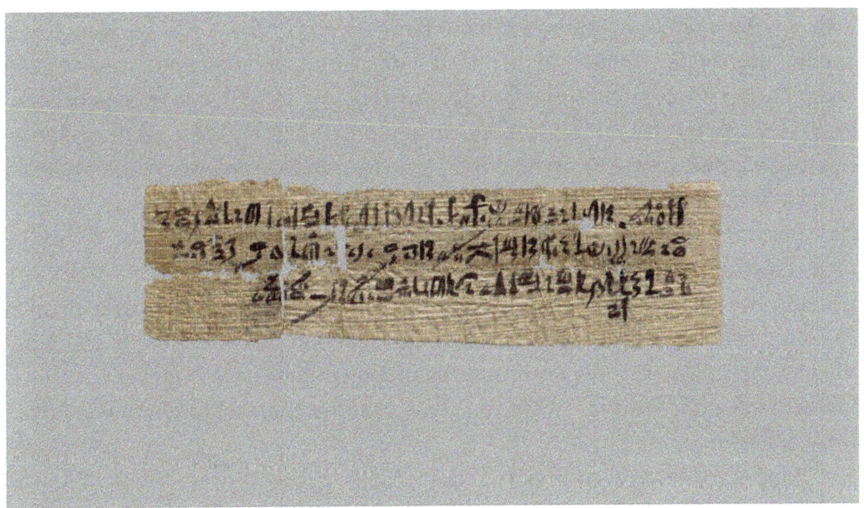

Fig. 3: Letter written in hieratic script on papyrus; from Deir el-Bahari, *c.* 1479–1458 BCE; The Metropolitan Museum of Art, New York, 27.3.560; public domain.

The hieroglyph for the general terms 'script', 'scribe', and 'written document' is the sign that shows the tools of handwriting: a rush container, a bag for pigments, and a palette. The cursive scripts were usually written in ink on papyrus, leather, linen, stuccoed wooden writing tablets, clay or limestone sherds, but were sometimes also applied to stuccoed walls, wooden coffins, stone objects or rock surfaces, in which cases the characters may have been painted or engraved.

While hieroglyphic and hieratic graffiti were in use for more than three millennia, demotic graffiti spanned one millennium, being found mainly in temples, from the time of Darius I (522–486 BCE) until the fifth century CE. Further, Egyptian monuments also bear Phoenician, Carian, Greek, Latin, Aramaic, Coptic and of course Arabic graffiti,[6] along with the names and dates of many travellers over the last three centuries.

2 The multigraphic aspect of graffiti

In Ancient Egypt, the visual character of the figurative hieroglyphs led to a connection between text and image that was obvious and never severed. This can be observed in the elaborate decorative programmes of tombs and temples, where hieroglyphs nearly always accompany large pictures. The script itself is also a combination of phonemes and pictorial characters: the writing system is a refined combination of phonetic signs (e.g. 𓅓 for /*m*/, 𓆑 for /*f*/), ideograms or logograms (e.g. 𓁷 for 'face', 𓃒 for 'bull'), and determinatives or classifiers denoting the semantic category of the word (𓀀 after words for men and their names, 𓁐 for women, 𓉐 for buildings etc.). This close connection also extends to large wall decorations: a life-sized and detailed depiction of one tomb owner can be read, for example, as a monumental personal classifier of his name, which appears in the accompanying inscription but lacks the 𓀀 sign after his name. On the other hand, representations of men, gods, actions etc. were often accompanied by captions to identify and contextualize an otherwise anonymous or meaningless image, for example, 'Offering wine' next to a representation of two jars in front of a god.

Many of the rock inscriptions on desert roads, in the Cataract region of Aswan and in the quarry of Hatnub are supplemented by pictures of the named author (Fig. 4), which evoke the combination of text and image on Ancient Egyptian stelae or decorative scenes in tombs.

6 For references to the Late Period, cf. Darnell 2020, 1122. Cf. also Ragazzoli et al. 2018.

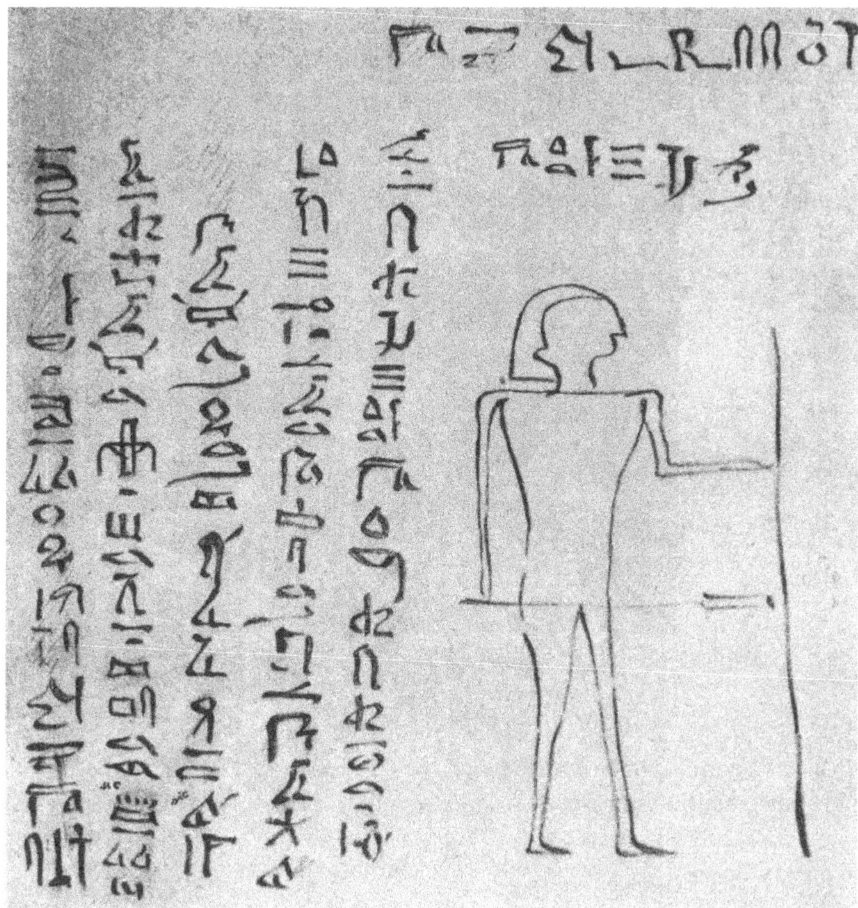

Fig. 4: Hieratic graffito; Quarry of Hatnub, *c.* 2000 BCE; after Anthes 1928, Plate 13.

The text of this graffito says 'Year 20 of the nomarch Aha-nakht, his son Khnum-iqer' (above the figure). 'What was said by the scribe Khnum-iqer: I am a scribe according to his [i. e. a superior's] heart's desire, with a cool body, who displaces heat, praised by all whom he meets, and free from blasphemy. I have come here to Hatnub to fetch calcite alabaster for making monuments to (the goddess) Unut, the Lady of Unu, for the health of Aha-nakht; may he live [and] be prosperous and healthy'.[7]

7 Translation by the author.

Sometimes, graffiti images actually illustrate what the visitors did during their stay in the desert region. One carved graffito in Wadi el-Hol, after a date in regnal year 17 of an unnamed ruler from the Middle Kingdom (c. 2137–1781 BCE), reads '... Spending the day by the scribe NN beneath this mountain, on holiday together with the people who are with him';[8] nearby sketches of singers and the goddess Hathor as a cow point to a ritual festival context.[9]

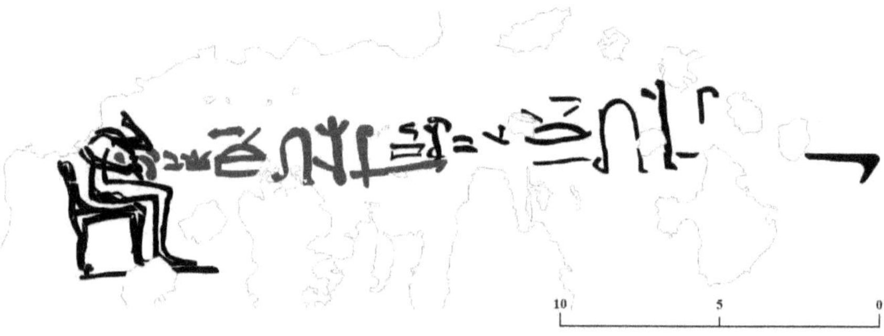

Fig. 5: Hieratic *dipinto* TS6 of 'The Royal Scribe Kha-em-waset'; Tomb N13.1 at Asyut, *c.* 1350 BCE; facsimile courtesy of Svenja A. Gülden and Ursula Verhoeven (Cf. Verhoeven 2020b, Plate 267).

Inside the corpus of inked visitors' graffiti (*dipinti*) in rock tomb N13.1 at Asyut, text statements are sometimes complemented by a picture, mainly for self-representation (Fig. 5) or piety to gods.[10] This custom has also been noticed in Theban tomb graffiti.[11]

3 Interaction between graffiti and texts on mobile artefacts

The texts of the typical visitors' graffiti of the Eighteenth Dynasty, which refer to the special monuments on which they were placed, may have the following

8 Darnell 2002, 129.

9 Darnell 2020, 1123–1124 with Fig. 57.3; cf. also the connection with Hathor in the Asyut *dipinti*: Gervers 2020, 394–395; Verhoeven 2020b, 265–266, 284–286.

10 Gervers 2020, 394–396; Verhoeven 2020b, 312, Plates 195, 267.

11 Den Doncker 2012.

structure: 'The scribe NN came to see the beautiful temple of (god) NN, and he found it more beautiful in his heart than any other temple. Then he said: may the heaven rain with fresh myrrh and drip incense onto the roof of the temple of (god) NN. Made by the scribe NN.'[12] Interestingly, this type of text was obviously practised by pupil scribes,[13] who wrote this formula on mobile artefacts, namely ostraca coming from Western Thebes.[14] Conversely, exercises in painting animals were normally sketched on ostraca, but practising animal sketches as *dipinti* on a tomb wall is also found.[15]

The school curriculum of the New Kingdom (*c.* 1500–1100 BCE) contained several didactic texts, namely teachings allegedly by former kings or high officials from the Old and Early Middle Kingdoms (between *c.* 2600–1900 BCE). These deal with administration management ('The Teaching of Ptahhotep') or conspiracies and assassination at the royal court ('The Teaching of King Amenemhat'); share experiences and thoughts about loyalty ('The Teaching of Kairsu') or life and death ('The Teaching of Hardjedef', 'The Teaching for Merikare'); or describe the scribe's profession as the best compared to all strenuous trades ('The Teaching of Khety').[16] As suggested by archaeological finds, mainly from the village of Deir el-Medina, these teachings were often reproduced in copies of various lengths, sometimes as short as a single paragraph, written on papyrus or ostraca. In one exceptional case, visiting scribes from local priestly families copied many paragraphs from seven different works of this didactic literature corpus as *dipinti* on the walls of rock tomb N13.1 at Asyut which must have been a destination for school trips from time to time.[17] In one very long copy, the scribe even arranged his lines in two columns, as he would have done on papyrus.[18] The visiting scribes looked for suitable places where they could place their long hieratic *dipinti* texts amid the tomb decoration: their focus was the large pictures of the tomb owner, which may have reminded them of the famous officials who were the alleged authors of the teachings. The kilts in the images of the tomb owner provided the perfect background for writing *dipinti*, not only because of their size and bright colour, but also because the kilt was the place for writing in the typical cross-legged position of scribes, who stretched a papyrus roll over the kilt around their thighs. Sometimes, only the typical header 'Beginning of the teaching made by ...' was

12 Translation by the author; cf. Verhoeven 2020b, 220–226.
13 Fischer-Elfert 2003, 132; cf. Gervers 2020, 392.
14 Hassan 2013; Hassan 2017; Ragazzoli 2016; Ragazzoli 2017, 83–85.
15 Gervers 2020, 391–393.
16 Cf. Burkard and Thissen 2015, 89–122, 183–200.
17 Verhoeven 2020b; overview on pp. 240–242.
18 Verhoeven 2020b, 150–153 (TS25).

written, which is also found as *dipinti* in the Ramesside temples of Abydos and Medinet Habu.[19]

Another widespread work is the so-called 'schoolbook' *Kemyt*, a compilation of texts in the form of a letter used for training scribes in an archaic writing style and letter phraseology. Parts of it are preserved in inked script on several hundreds of objects, like wooden tablets, limestone ostraca, potsherds, and papyrus.[20] Some words or sentences of it, however, were also copied as *dipinti*, maybe during school excursions to different places.[21]

Other text genres widely used in Egyptian funerary or other religious contexts are offering formulas and appeals to the living who will pass by. These texts are traditionally inscribed in monumental hieroglyphs on behalf of a tomb owner or on a dedicatory stela erected in a temple area. Two visitors of the old Asyutian tomb N13.1 placed such texts as *dipinti* on the walls and hoped that it would work in the same way for their own memory. The scribe Men wrote: 'Oh you scribe, lecture priest, purification priest, singer at the harp who tells stories to his lord at the right time, you should recite: 'An offering ... for the soul of the scribe Men, son of the purification priest Upuauty, born of the lady of the house Nut'.[22]

4 Significance of graffiti for Egyptological research

Despite the first recording of a graffiti text in 1799 and the use of the term 'graffito' by Mariette since 1850, early Egyptologists were mostly interested in such inscriptions because of the dates and names they recorded.[23] The larger graffiti, which were also called rock inscriptions, were studied intensively, since they yielded important data on history, chronology, prosopography and economy.

19 Cf. the mentions in Verhoeven 2020b, 17–18.

20 Motte 2022.

21 Demarée 2009; Verhoeven 2020b.

22 Translation by the author; cf. Verhoeven 2020b, 160–161, 234–237.

23 Salvador 2020, 435–436.

4.1 Desert graffiti

More than a hundred years ago, documentation of the countless graffiti in the mountain area of Western Thebes began.[24] During the Nineteenth and Twentieth Dynasties (1292–*c.* 1075 BCE), thousands of graffiti were left by members of the workmen's village Deir el-Medina. The recent study of this material has yielded various new insights into the organization of the 'gang' that worked in the royal tombs of the Valley of the Kings. The graffiti on their daily route over the mountain to work were easily executed with a flintstone, and mentioned their name, title, and sometimes family members. They seemed to have served as a medium for commemorating the mentioned persons within the community and a guarantee of future immortalization.[25] In the following Twenty-First Dynasty (until 945 BCE), graffiti are found in a wider environment, and the content has changed; in this period, the Theban necropolis scribes came to 'check the mountain', looking for old tombs or safe places for new burials for high-priests, and *cachettes* for mummies from robbed graves.[26]

Only recently have graffiti by members of caravan trails and travellers to the oases of the Libyan Desert been examined professionally by the first Theban Desert Road Survey. The graffiti are from all periods, starting *c.* 3200 BCE until the Middle Ages. Some are historically very important, for example for the reconstruction of the northern expansion of the Theban rulers around 2100 BCE.[27]

4.2 Temple graffiti

Graffiti in Egyptian temples have increasingly been studied over the last decades, in many places and by various scholars.[28] In the Khonsu Temple at Karnak, built between *c.* 1200 and 1000 BCE, 334 graffiti were left on the roof of the colonnade around the large open court. They date from all periods of the first millennium BCE until the Christian era. Two-thirds are hieroglyphic, hieratic or demotic texts, with or without footprints; the rest depict creatures or objects. The names and titles show that the footprints did not belong to travellers, but to members of the clergy attached to the temple itself. These graffiti were interpreted as substitutes

24 Spiegelberg 1921.
25 Rzepka 2014, cf. conclusions 275–276.
26 Rzepka 2014, 274.
27 Darnell 2002. For further places and material, cf. also Darnell 2013; Ragazzoli et al. 2023, Part I.
28 Thissen 1989; Marciniak 1974; Jacquet-Gordon 2003; Cruz-Uribe 2008; Frood 2010; Dijkstra 2012; Frood 2013; Sabek 2016; Ragazzoli et al. 2023, Part III.

for a temple statue or stela, which could be erected in the forecourt of the temple only by high officials in the government or religious hierarchy, but not by simple priests of the temple. Since the latter had access to the temple and its roof, they used this kind of simple manifestation to establish their presence at temple festivals forever, like a statue, and to be protected by the gods of the temple for as long as possible. The text of the rightmost column of the inscription in Fig. 6 entreats the god Khonsu, 'Let my name endure in your temple forever and ever'.[29]

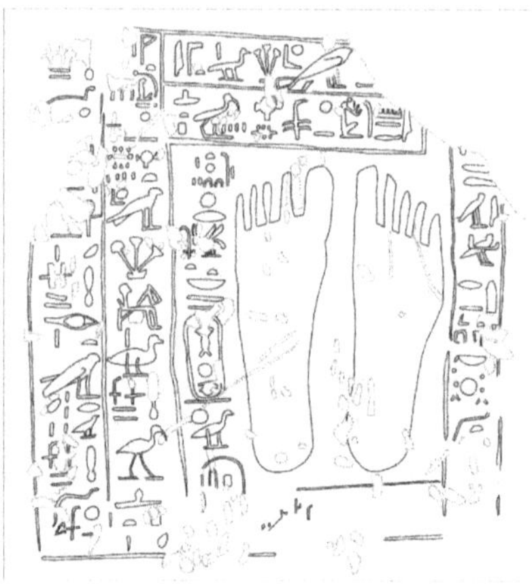

Fig. 6: Incised footprint with hieroglyphic inscription; roof of the temple of Khonsu at Karnak, 576 BCE; courtesy of the Oriental Institute of the University of Chicago (CC-BY 4.0); cf. Jacquet-Gordon 2003, Plate 106, no. 275; van Pelt and Staring 2019, 4, Fig. 3.

On the contrary, the Roman-era graffiti in the open forecourt of the temple of Khnum, on Elephantine Island, show that visitors came on at least some occasions throughout the year, and merchants left their names on booths for selling wares at festivals.[30]

4.3 Tomb graffiti

In the current century, efforts to document and study the (mainly inked) visitors' graffiti of ancient tombs have intensified. Hana Navrátilová began her research

29 Jacquet-Gordon 2003, 3–5.
30 Dijkstra 2020; cf. also Krapf 2020.

on visitors' graffiti of the New Kingdom in the Memphite necropolis (Giza, Saqqara, Dahshur, Meidum, also Abusir)[31] around the same time that the present author did in the newly discovered tomb N13.1 of the rock necropolis of Asyut/ Middle Egypt.[32] Somewhat later, Chloé Ragazzoli began studying a large number of graffiti in the so-called 'grotte des scribes' in the mountain of Deir el-Bahari in Western Thebes,[33] as well as in several private Theban tombs.[34] The authors of

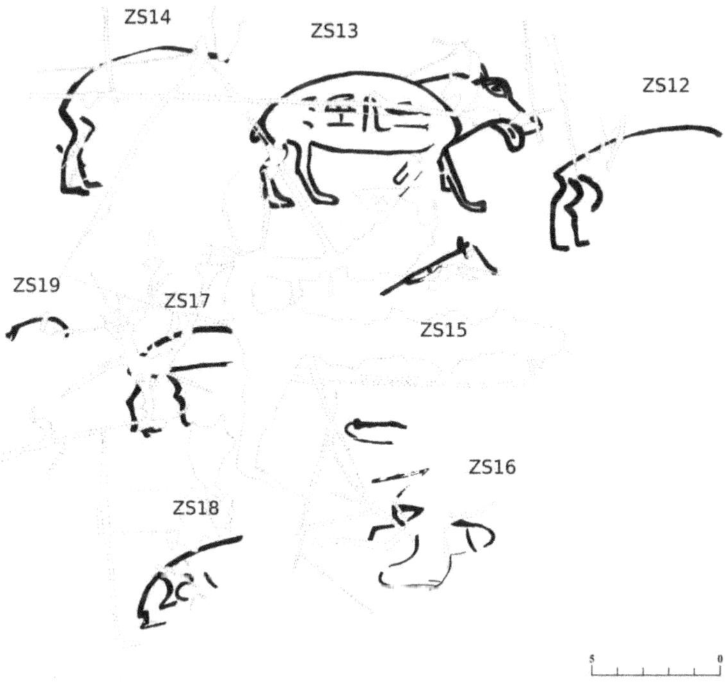

Fig. 7: *Dipinto* of a hippopotamus with the signature 'made by scribe Men' (ZS13+TS9), accompanied by several exercise drawings; Tomb N13.1 at Asyut, *c.* 1350 BCE; facsimile courtesy of Eva Gervers (cf. Gervers 2020, Plate 368).

31 Navrátilová 2007; Navrátilová 2015.

32 Verhoeven 2020b.

33 Ragazzoli 2017.

34 Ragazzoli 2011; Ragazzoli 2013; Ragazzoli 2018; and Ragazzoli forthcoming. Cf. also the contributions on tomb graffiti at various places in Part II of Ragazzoli et al. 2023.

these graffiti of the New Kingdom were mostly priests and scribes of different stages, and the text genres are quite similar in all of them: signatures, names and titles, dates, visitor formulae, and votive and piety texts, but also satiric and erotic allusions in text and/or image.[35] Some scholars concentrated on figural graffiti and *dipinti* left in tombs: Den Doncker has found that the re-composition, adaptation or refashioning of the original tomb decoration took place in these sketches,[36] while Staring concluded that the application of graffiti 'effectively replenishes the value of the monument'.[37] Gervers described how teachers used graffiti to demonstrate how to sketch a figure, and pupils followed them in exercises found nearby (Fig. 7).[38]

The documentation of secondary additions like graffiti is fortunately no longer neglected, as its study has yielded important insights. One research question of Egyptology is why these visitors' graffiti started in the time of the New Kingdom. After the troubled times period of foreign domination, the state consolidation at the beginning of the Eighteenth Dynasty coincided with a heightened interest in the past. In this temporal and socio-cultural environment, more or less educated men visited ancient monuments of the Old and Middle Kingdoms, like temples and royal or private tombs, and left graffiti or *dipinti* with the typical, above-mentioned types of short and longer texts and/or pictures. They wanted to memorialize themselves for the future within the context of ancient funerary or religious architecture, and sometimes asked for the support from the ancestors or gods through the promised offering. Moreover, they used their visits to study, copy, and sometimes reinterpret special motifs in the original, ancient decoration.

It is not possible, in this connection, to address all the primary sources and the topics that are currently being treated in the field of Ancient Egyptian graffiti internationally. Peden's 2001 monograph[39] delivers a good chronological overview of most of the rock inscription material and all other kinds of graffiti. In 2020, the author herself published a chapter on the terminology and distribution of ancient visitors' graffiti and *dipinti*,[40] and in the same year, two articles in Oxford Handbooks presented the relevant issues in synoptic form.[41] For further areas

35 For the last group, cf. Ragazzoli 2017, 109–117; Verhoeven 2009; Verhoeven 2020b, 232–233.
36 Den Doncker 2012, 31.
37 Staring 2011, 154.
38 Gervers 2020, 346–350.
39 Peden 2001.
40 Verhoeven 2020b, 15–19.
41 Darnell 2020; Salvador 2020.

of research, one may also look to the numerous topics of recent Egyptological conferences, papers and anthologies on graffiti.[42]

5 Labels and definitions

Amid the rich and varied textual and pictorial evidence of Ancient Egypt, arriving at a definition of 'graffiti' is not an easy task. So far, researchers have developed several definitions, based on various categories and criteria,[43] to differentiate 'graffiti' from the larger field of 'inscriptions', but not without problems and overlaps. The following paragraphs aim to present and discuss the main criteria:

a) Artificial vs. natural surface
If the surface on which something is applied is of artificial origin, like the walls of tombs or temples or even stelae,[44] the term 'graffiti' or 'graffiti proper' is often used, in contrast to a natural surface like a rock, where an applied text or picture is called a 'rock inscription' or 'rock drawing', 'rock art' as the case may be. In parallel, the term 'rock graffiti' was and still is used as well.[45]

b) Surface designed vs. not designed
A recent definition summarizes that the term 'graffiti' could indicate 'all those texts, signs, marks, and drawings that have been deliberately marked on a surface that was not designed to receive them'.[46] Under this definition, inscriptions and drawings on natural surfaces, like granite rocks in the Cataract region or the rock formations in the wadis and deserts, which

---

42 Conferences such as 'Clamour from the Past: Graffiti, Rock Inscriptions and Secondary Epigraphy from Ancient Egypt', June 2019, Cairo (cf. Ragazzoli et al. [eds] 2023); 'Making and Experiencing Graffiti in Ancient and Late Antique Egypt and Sudan', December 2021, Leiden, <https://www.nino-leiden.nl/event/making-and-experiencing-graffiti-in-ancient-and-late-antique-egypt-and-sudan> (accessed on 11 August 2022). For papers, the University of Münster's *Aegyptiaca* bibliographic database <https://aegyptiaca.uni-muenster.de/> currently contains 275 entries for the keyword 'graffiti', half of which date from 2005 onwards (accessed on 15 March 2022). A relevant anthology is Ragazzoli et al. 2018.

43 Cruz-Uribe (2008, 197–225) has listed and annotated sixteen criteria or facets that graffiti may have had in Egypt. Some keywords are: unofficial, flat surface, individually motivated, intended to be permanent, not intended to desecrate earlier inscriptions, different purpose than the surface originally had, outside the realm of control, textual, representational or combined, using whatever convenient technology is available, excised from or added to the surface, intended to be recognizable to those of the same culture, visibility, convenient height, contextual significance, written in a shaded area, not in a still-functioning sacred area, found in a dynamic location.

44 Staring 2017.

45 References and discussion in Darnell 2020, 1110.

46 Salvador 2020, 435 with references.

were not designed by humans for writing, would belong to the category of graffiti, contrary to the criteria in a).

c) Primary vs. secondary inscription

This differentiation is based on whether the text or image is part of the original decoration (of a tomb, temple or even stela) or if it is a secondary addition, reflection, comment etc.[47] In this respect, the primary rock inscriptions are not graffiti. Yet we can observe that the first rock inscriptions (as well as visitors' graffiti and *dipinti*) often attracted other, later inscriptions, sometimes forming large clusters over a very long time span. In the desert region of the Upper Egyptian city Elkab, there is a prominent rock on which hundreds of carvings and inscriptions were made from prehistoric times onwards.[48] We thus find secondary activities alongside primary ones of the same character. The prehistoric motifs are on a surface that was not designed (Fig. 8), while the surface of the later ones was designed (Fig. 9).

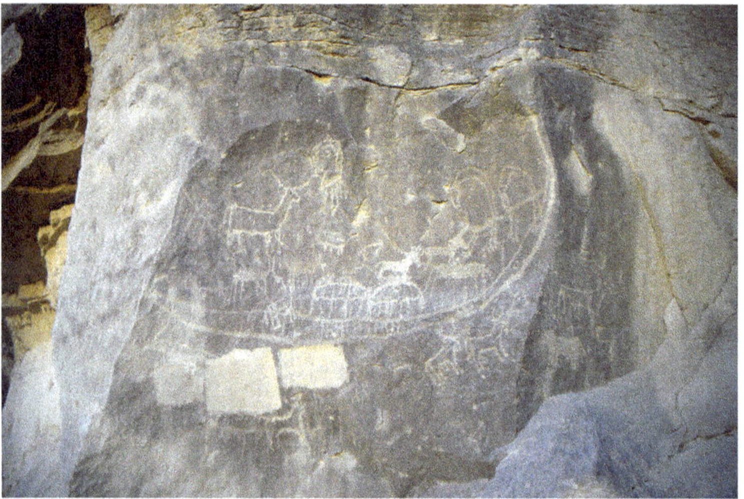

Fig. 8: Rock art; Vulture Rock at Elkab; prehistoric; photograph courtesy of Ursula Verhoeven (The Asyut Project).

Ragazzoli introduced the term 'secondary epigraphy' for graffiti-like additions that are 'personelle, non sanctionnée par l'autorité, informelle', while traditional epigraphy should be 'impersonelle, officielle, formelle'.[49] For Ancient Egypt, it is difficult to determine what was official or non-official in its content; the textual parts of 'graffiti' may well be formal or formulaic; others possibly informal, personal or even coarse; and there are also literary works, hymns and songs executed in calligraphy, but in a secondary graffiti-like context. Visitors'

47 See already Helck 1952 ('Sekundärinschriften'); Ragazzoli 2017, 4–5; Ragazzoli forthcoming.
48 Vandekerckhove and Müller-Wollermann 2001.
49 Ragazzoli 2017, 4–5.

texts in particular use formulaic phrases, and it is questionable whether their prohibition, permission or sanctioning by an authority played an important role, as already indicated above. On the contrary, Staring states that the additions in tombs are part of the primary function of that place as 'an integral part of the so-called visitors' cult'.[50]

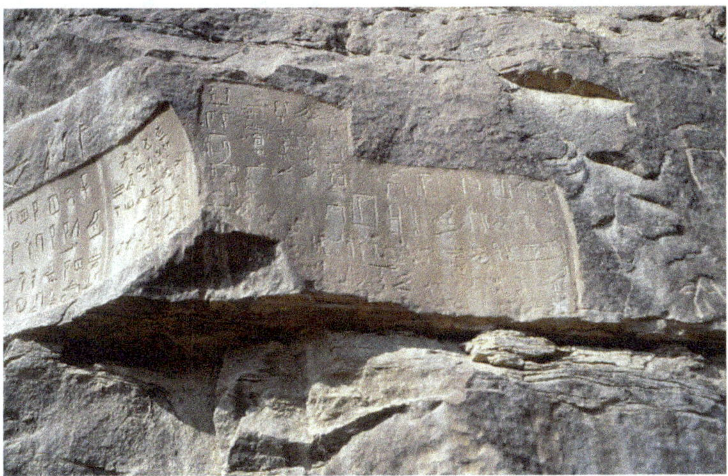

Fig. 9: Rock inscriptions; Vulture Rock at Elkab, *c.* 2250 BCE; photograph courtesy of Ursula Verhoeven (The Asyut Project).

d) Planned vs. spontaneous intent

Our modern sensitivities often harbour another notion of what is meant by graffiti: the term comes to mind in connection with single letters or signs, words, texts or pictures that were applied in a way that was seemingly accidental, unplanned, momentary, cursory, carelessly, and quickly done etc. The term '*en-passant*-Inschriften' has been introduced with respect to these features.[51] Vandekerckhove and Müller-Wollermann based their work on the definition of classic epigraphy (cited in n. 10 of RAC XII, Sp. 641), and their own conclusion came after discussion of four criteria: 'Graffiti sind das Resultat einer direkten Äußerung des Affektes des Menschen' ('Graffiti are the result of a direct expression of the affect of the person'), especially because they constitute a subjective, spontaneous expression and were not previously edited by educated specialists, as would be the case for rock inscriptions.[52] However, recent research has pointed out that graffiti in Ancient Egypt were not always spontaneously created, but were normally the outcome of a routine exercise, a part

50 Staring 2018, 81.

51 Wildung 1975.

52 Vandekerckhove and Müller-Wollermann 2001, 9–11. Quote on p. 11.

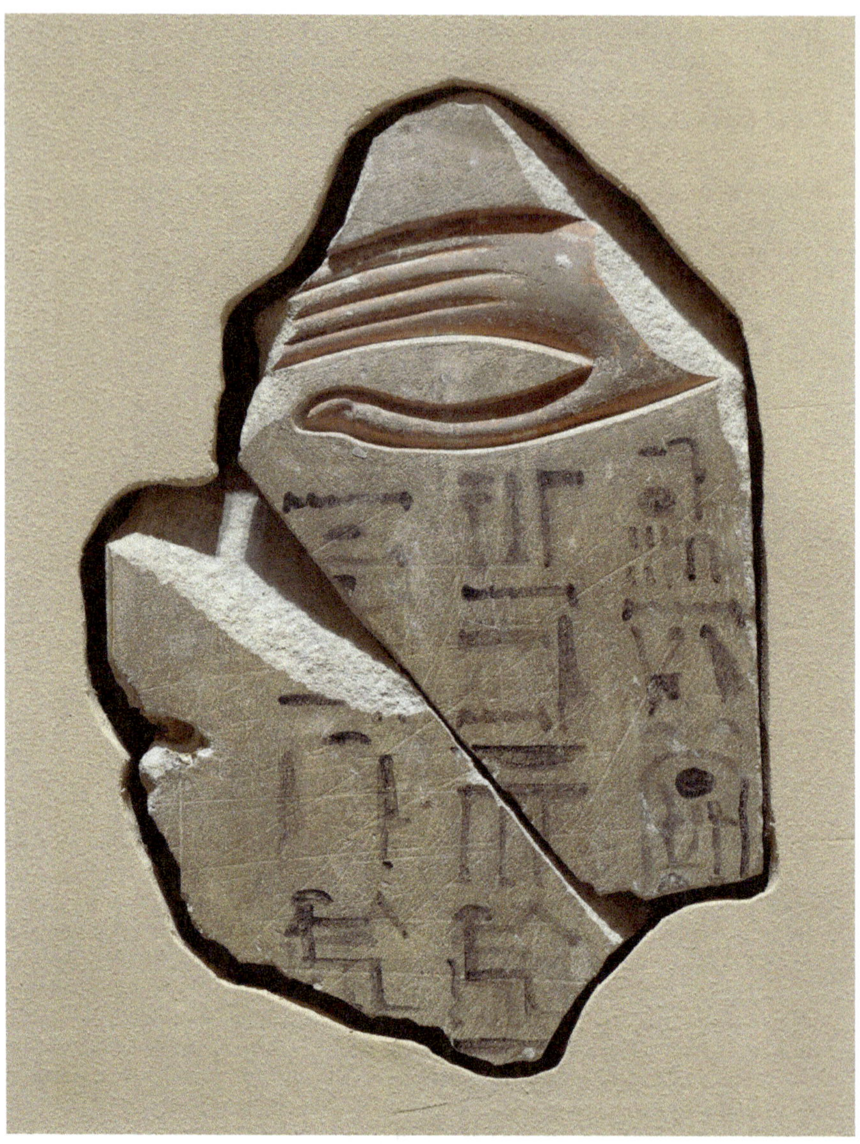

Fig. 10: Limestone block with hieroglyphic *dipinto*; from Deir el-Bahari, *c.* 2051–2000 BCE and 1287 BCE; The Metropolitan Museum of Art, New York, 23.3.26; public domain.

of rational communication, dependent on their time and context, and could entail reciprocity with the entities addressed.[53]

e) Monumental vs. cursive script
Another terminological tradition combines the surface with the writing style. Hieroglyphic 'rock inscriptions' are distinguished from 'rock graffiti' executed in carved hieratic characters.[54] In between these categories, the travertine quarries of Hatnub offer two main types – red-inked texts in hieratic, called 'graffiti', and carved hieroglyphs, known as 'inscriptions' (as defined by Anthes) – but recent surveys have also discovered hybrid formats: red-pigment hieroglyphic texts, as well as carved hieratic (or hieraticizing) texts (and images).[55] This distinction is also not helpful for a definition of graffiti, because there are hieroglyphic ink graffiti made by visitors to ancient tombs in Asyut[56] as well as in Thebes, e.g. the block from the Tomb of Khety (TT 311) in Fig. 10, whose inked hieroglyphs were made by the High Priest of Amun Nebnetjeru more than 700 years after the relief decoration.

f) Subgroups of graffiti by kind of making (scratched vs. inked)
A special distinction was initially used in the field of classical archaeology with reference to the procedure for making the secondary elements, regardless of the surface: *graffiti* is thus the regular term for carved or scratched items, and *dipinti* for painted or inked texts and figures (mainly in Pompeii), mirroring the use of the Italian terms. These categories and definitions are spreading in Egyptology now,[57] but 'graffiti' as a generic term for both kinds of making is also used.

g) Subgroups of graffiti by text genre, location and function
The content, text genre, place, and context, as well as the motives of graffiti makers, have been crucial to the elaboration of certain graffiti subgroups, by which Egyptologists categorize 'exploration and desert graffiti, temple graffiti, piety graffiti, visitors' graffiti'.[58] The last group is also called 'tourist graffiti',[59] as well as 'Besucherinschriften' as opposed to 'Votivinschriften'.[60]

These labels and descriptions demonstrate how formulating a general definition of graffiti, with the aim of drawing connections with other kinds of Ancient Egyptian inscriptions, is a difficult task due to the complexity of the relevant features and their overlap. The best solution seems to be that one should always define their personal use of the term with respect to the corpus examined. For instance, Staring formulated a very convincing definition concerning New Kingdom graffiti

53 Staring 2018, 80–81.
54 Rzepka 2014.
55 Enmarch and Gourdon 2020, 6.
56 Verhoeven 2020b, 116, Plates 97b, 249 (TW26).
57 Cf. Verhoeven 2020b, 15–16; Salvador 2020, 434.
58 Ragazzoli 2018, 24ff.
59 Negm 1998.
60 Wildung 1975.

in Saqqara tombs as including ‘writings and drawings that are incised, scratched or painted onto extant architectural features and non-portable objects’.[61]

6 Methods of documentation

Recently, Salvador has characterized the documentation of graffiti in detail in terms of four steps: ‘(1) a preliminary survey, (2) recording, (3) collation, and (4) a post-recording process’.[62] The following aspects may explain and supplement her remarks.

After one has located a site containing graffiti during a survey, the on-site documentation should take many factors into account, namely the kind, formation and light circumstances of the location within the landscape or architecture, the original decoration of the monument (tomb wall paintings or temple reliefs) and the presence of other graffiti. The Ancient Egyptian graffiti scribes chose their writing spaces with respect to accessibility, visibility and significance of the context. Further, the availability of writing or scratching tools and the time they could spend in a suitable place were important conditions for making graffiti.

In Egypt, the recording of graffiti, mainly inside ancient buildings, can often start only after restoration activities, which concern not only the quality of the stone walls, but also the stucco or plaster on which the graffiti were placed. Sometimes, the question may arise whether a drawing, graffito or another element from later millennia should be removed to present the relics of Pharaonic times in a clear manner. Such destruction of the history of a monument should be avoided because the whole range of activities in a special place or context is connected and important to different disciplines (Coptology, Classics, Islamic history,[63] anthropology, sociology etc.) and their research questions.

Starting in the nineteenth century and until the 1970s, squeezes (‘Papierabdrücke’, ‘Abklatsche’)[64] were used for the documentation of incised inscriptions and sometimes also for graffiti, though graffiti was long considered to have low value as a research topic. The advantage was that these squeezes were very detailed and accurate and could be stored for a long time.[65] The disadvantage, of

61 Staring 2018, 82.

62 Salvador 2020, 436–444.

63 E.g. Ahmed-Mohamed 2020.

64 Cf. Salvador 2020.

65 E.g. the squeezes from the years 1834 to 1910 in the archive of the ‘Altägyptisches Wörterbuch’: <https://aaew.bbaw.de/archive/abklatsch-archiv> (accessed on 15 March 2022).

course, was the fact that small parts of the surface and even traces of colour could be inadvertently removed.

Until 2017, Egyptian epigraphy relied on the tradition of fixing large transparencies onto walls and tracing the lines with different-coloured felt-tip pens. These facsimiles were therefore drawn by hand and on a 1:1 scale, copying the primary and secondary elements in their context and in relation to each other, complemented by the marking of destroyed areas and lost colours, as well as further comments. This method had the advantage of requiring no electricity in the field, and the transparencies could be taken home or scanned and printed at reduced sizes at local Egyptian copy shops as a basis for further research both on site and at home. Since 2018, the Egyptian Ministry for Antiquities has forbidden this method, due to its danger to surfaces and the increasing development of modern digital methods like high-resolution digital photography, photogrammetry, infra-red photographs,[66] 3D documentation, and videos etc.

Even so, photography has been an additional means of documentation for over a hundred years, but remains very dependent on light conditions. The sunlight can often be mirrored to light up the inner rooms of a tomb or temple, while movable artificial lights (and torches) can illuminate an area from various directions, which helps to detect shadows of scratched lines or faded ink traces. Despite this, photographs often cannot reproduce all the details of a damaged surface and graffiti traces, even those that are visible to the naked eye when standing directly before the wall. If the surface is a kind of stucco, it could also happen that the ink is completely faded, but the very thin engraved lines produced by the rush are still visible.

Besides, professional photography is very time-consuming, not only due to exposure problems, but also depending on the location and the position of the object: for example, when a graffito is found several metres high, under the ceiling of a temple building that was full of debris when the visitor wrote it, but is empty today.

While researchers in the past used to produce the final facsimiles of the graffiti by hand and from the original, the modern method is to use high-resolution photographs and graphic design software like Adobe Illustrator to draw the facsimile digitally. The photograph must first be checked with respect to scale and distortion and can then be edited in terms of contrast and brightness; further, the program D-Stretch allows for better recognition of red-coloured texts or images. For background elements, ink, damage, line numbering, comments, date,

66 Navrátilová 2015.

and producer, one should always reserve different layers in the digital facsimile document.

Where inked graffiti is concerned, Egyptologists have different habits in reproducing the ink consistency: some try to colour the signs, according to their current condition, in different shades of grey with a lead pencil;[67] others prefer a purely blackish shade within the outlines, as was originally intended by the scribe.[68] The moment of dipping, namely when the ancient scribes took fresh ink, is interesting for the writing process, and if it is visible, one should mark this in the facsimile.[69] Another detail to be documented is the sequence of strokes: if this is recognizable, it should also be recorded for later palaeographical studies, which can help to identify a personal handwriting style (Fig. 11).[70]

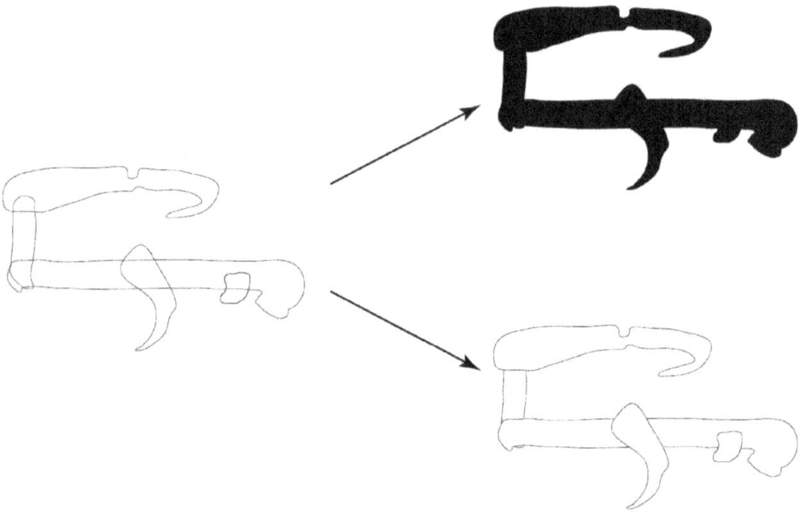

Fig. 11: Facsimiles of a hieratic form of the hieroglyph 𓈖 *mn*; after Gülden 2018, Fig. 9.

Of course, all possible measurements should also be documented, not only by a scale on the photograph. Necessary data include the maximal height and width of the whole text or single letters, and the minimal distance from the floor and

67 Dorn 2011.
68 Verhoeven 2020b.
69 Verhoeven 2020b, 304.
70 Cf. Gülden 2018.

potentially also to the ceiling, as well as to the right and left corners of a wall. The visibility axis may also be of interest with respect to the lighting and perception by passers-by at different times of day.

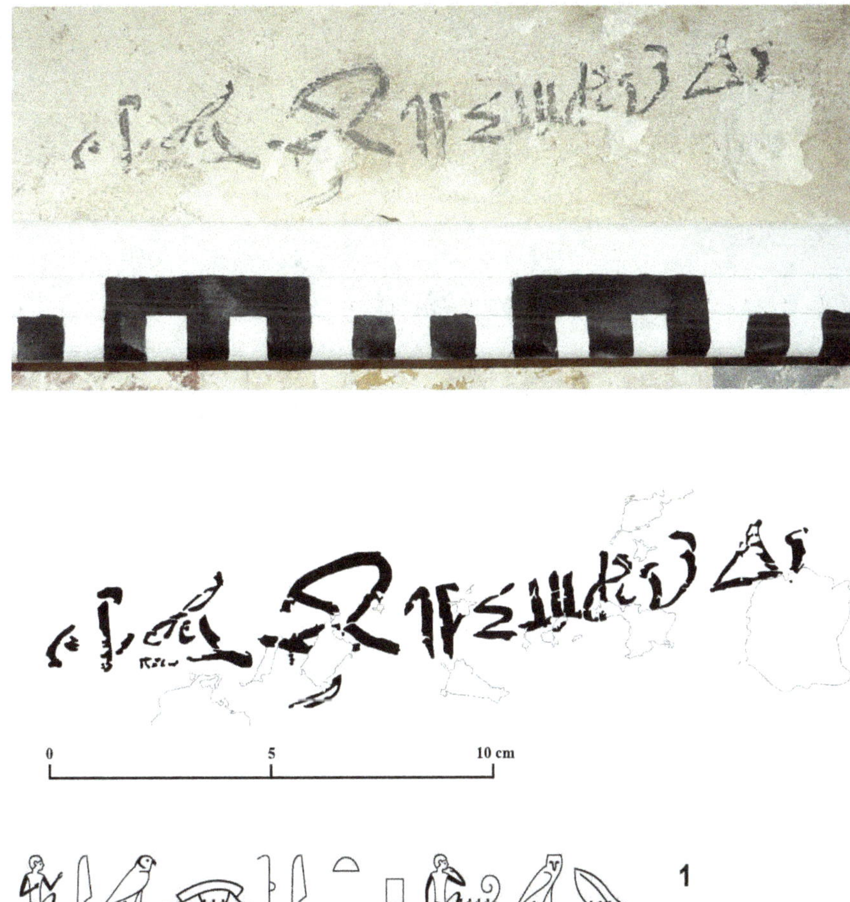

sḏm ptr Ḥrj
'Hear and behold Hori!'

Fig. 12: Votive *dipinto* TS29; Tomb N13.1 at Asyut, *c.* 1200 BCE; photograph courtesy of Jochem Kahl (The Asyut Project); facsimile courtesy of Svenja A. Gülden and Ursula Verhoeven; hieroglyphic transliteration, transcription and translation by Ursula Verhoeven.

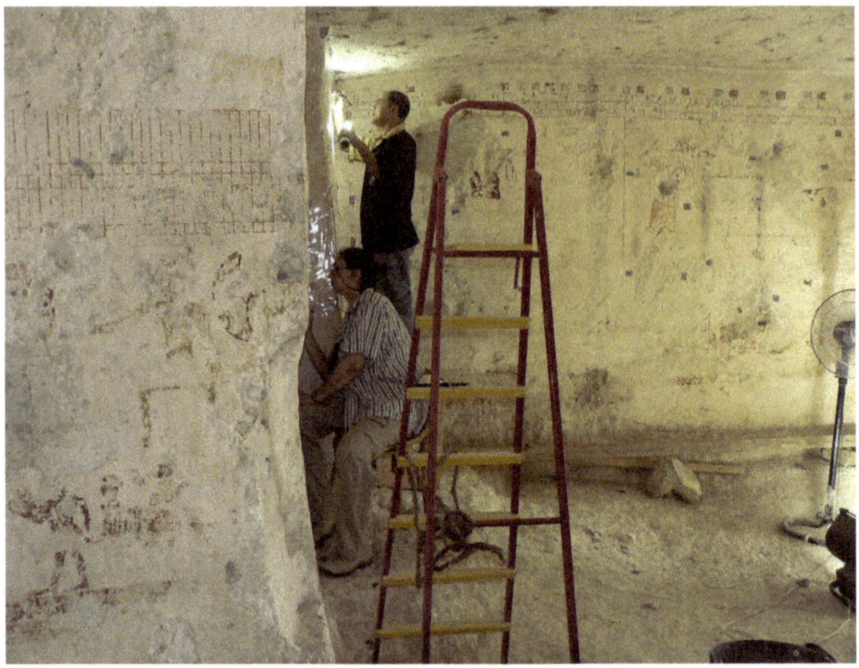

Fig. 13: Epigraphic work; Tomb N13.1 at Asyut, 2006; photograph courtesy of Jochem Kahl (The Asyut Project).

As mentioned above, the next step is collating the facsimile and other documentation details in front of the original wall, and is absolutely necessary after or in between phases of research. A second person with an independent view should be involved for control if possible. Presenting the material to colleagues and students can also help to detect unconscious misinterpretations.

At the same time, the hieroglyphic or (cursive) hieratic characters of the graffito or *dipinto* text are transliterated into standard hieroglyphs. This is necessary to make the outcome of the decipherment both clear and legible to all colleagues not specialized in the respective forms of cursive signs. This transliteration into hieroglyphs can be realized in two different ways: by a trained researcher's hand on paper, or with a digital program like JSesh[71] or VisualGlyph[72]. The orientation and layout of the original graffito or *dipinto* should be maintained (Fig. 12). The

71 <https://jsesh.qenherkhopeshef.org> (accessed on 14 August 2022).

72 <https://visualglyph.software.informer.com> (accessed on 14 August 2022).

transliteration is accompanied by the Egyptological transcription of the signs into a modern transcription font, and by a translation with commentary.

In the next step, not only should the content of graffiti be compared with similar sources in the corpus and from other places and regions, but the signs themselves can also be studied palaeographically. Inked characters can reveal the handwriting of a specific person[73] and an exact time span for the dating of the graffito. A comparison between inked and scratched graffiti by the same person is difficult, but possible.[74] On the other hand, one should be mindful that writing in different body postures and on a vertical, smooth and absorbent surface like a stuccoed wall produces different writing habits and forms of signs than on a horizontally placed papyrus sheet or ostracon.[75] In any case, palaeography analysis – traditionally in tables on paper, or digitally, with different methods of reproduction and ample metadata and photographs of the entire document at hand improves the research possibilities.[76]

In my own research on visitors' *dipinti* inside rock tomb N13.1 at Asyut, the documentation was influenced by the circumstance that we were never sure if we could return to the site the next year or if the tomb would remain untouched. The first step, after discovering the tomb in 2005, was to take non-professional photographs of the original state of the decoration and the already visible graffiti. Then, after completely cleaning the tomb of debris, several restorers, the draftsman of the original decoration and I had to work step by step and side by side to copy the inked graffiti (Fig. 13).

During the 2006 season, I copied all the related graffiti I could find using felt-tip pens on transparencies that were copied onto long rolls of paper. In subsequent seasons, my colleague Svenja Gülden accompanied the project team and helped in collating, taking measurements and photographing details, alongside a professional photographer who could work only from time to time, as other findings and excavations also had to be documented in the necropolis mountain. In the following years, Svenja Gülden produced all the digital facsimiles in close collaboration with the author.

The final edition[77] was published in two volumes; the first contained the documentation, translation and analysis of the historical, local and religious

73 Verhoeven 2020b, 261–264, 270–272.
74 Dorn 2015. Cf. also Rzepka 2014, 43.
75 Gülden 2022.
76 Gülden, Krause and Verhoeven 2020. Cf. the online palaeographic database of the Mainz Academy project 'Altägyptische Kursivschriften', <https://aku-pal.uni-mainz.de> (accessed on 14 August 2022).
77 Verhoeven 2020b.

context, text genres, agents and motives behind this very special find. One of the chapters also looked for reasons and criteria to choose a place for a *dipinto* depending on brightness, height, free space and its relation to motifs of the original decoration and already existing visitors' inscriptions. Another chapter treated the different methods of writing (carving, ink colours, dippings of the rush, corrections by the scribes themselves, categories of mistakes they made), writing types (hieroglyphs or hieratic) and layouts (formats, number of lines or columns, spatia and combinations of text, and image). The second is a folio volume of the plans, photographs, facsimiles and hieroglyphic transliterations. However, while the high-resolution photographic material could be enlarged on the screen during research, for the reader of the printed version, it may be difficult to comprehend the readings. After the publisher releases the rights in five years from the date of publication, an online version will also be available, in which the photos can easily be enlarged.

7 Conclusion

The legacy of graffiti in various places in Ancient Egypt, from around at least 3200 BCE, must be viewed against the background of the special importance of writing and imagery. Being able to read and write was a privilege of the elite, and conferred not only good career opportunities, but also access to knowledge of real and supernatural matters. The immortalization of one's own name or the protection of deities, for example, during desert expeditions, could be realized in graffiti or rock inscriptions in a very personal way.

Graffiti were scratched or inked (*dipinti*) in hieroglyphs, hieratic, demotic or Coptic script in places of natural or artificial origin, and there were no official restrictions against such activities. The combination of names or texts with figurative images is omnipresent, based in part on the already pictorial nature of the hieroglyphic writing system.

With the beginning of the New Kingdom (*c.* 1500 BCE), the special genre of visitors' graffiti emerged, testifying to visits by scribes to ancient temples and tombs. People also left offering formulae or calls to the living who would later read these texts. Formulaic graffiti texts were obviously practised in school lessons and, conversely, famous literary texts that have survived mainly on papyri and ostraca were sometimes practised as *dipinti*. The definitions of graffiti and *dipinti* versus other types of inscriptions (and pictures) are not without problem, and may be based on different parameters.

The method of documentation has changed considerably since the nineteenth century, from squeezes, free-hand copies and facsimiles to photographs of increasing quality that now allow for digital tracing. However, due to the graffiti's state of preservation, extensive surveys and several collations are still necessary on site. Yet the study of graffiti and *dipinti* has grown substantially in the last twenty years, revealing the scientific value of these mostly spontaneous, personal and unofficial legacies.

References

Ahmed-Mohamed, Youssef (2020), 'Texte und Zeichnungen aus islamischer Zeit', in Verhoeven 2020a, 407–444, Plates 170–179.

Allon, Niv and Hana Navrátilová (2017), *Ancient Egyptian Scribes: A Cultural Exploration*, London: Bloomsbury Egyptology.

Anthes, Rudolf (1928), *Die Felsinschriften von Hatnub nach den Aufnahmen Georg Möllers* (Untersuchungen zur Geschichte und Altertumskunde Ägyptens, 9), Leipzig: Hinrichs [repr. Hildesheim: Olms, 1964].

Baines, John and Christopher Eyre (2007), 'Four Notes on Literacy', in John Baines (ed.), *Visual and Written Culture in Ancient Egypt*, Oxford: Oxford University Press, 63–94.

Burkard, Günter and Heinz J. Thissen (2015), *Einführung in die altägyptische Literaturgeschichte I: Altes und Mittleres Reich* (Einführungen und Quellentexte zur Ägyptologie, 1), 5th edn, Berlin: LitVerlag.

Cancik-Kirschbaum, Eva and Jochem Kahl (2018), *Erste Philologien: Archäologie einer Disziplin vom Tigris bis zum Nil*, Tübingen: Mohr Siebeck.

Cruz-Uribe, Eugene (2008), *Hibis Temple Project 3: The Graffiti from the Temple Precinct*, San Antonio, TX: Van Siclen Books & Tambopata Partners.

Darnell, John Coleman (2002), *Theban Desert Road Survey in the Egyptian Western Desert I: Gebel Tjauti Inscriptions 1–45 and Wadi el Hôl Inscriptions 1–45* (Oriental Institute Publications, 119), Chicago: Oriental Institute of the University of Chicago.

Darnell, John Coleman (2013), *Theban Desert Road Survey II: The Rock Shrine of Paḥu, Gebel Akhenaton, and Other Rock Inscriptions from the Western Hinterland of Qamûla* (Yale Egyptological Publications, 1), New Haven, CT: Yale Egyptological Seminar.

Darnell, John Coleman (2020), 'Rock Art, Rock Inscriptions, and Graffiti', in Ian Shaw and Elizabeth Bloxam (eds), *The Oxford Handbook of Egyptology*, Oxford: University Press, 1111–1137.

Demarée, Rob (2009), 'A Hieratic Graffito in the Tomb of Ptahemwia', *Saqqara Newsletter*, 7: 11–12.

Den Doncker, Alexis (2012), 'Theban Tomb Graffiti during the New Kingdom: Research on the Reception of Ancient Egyptian Images by Ancient Egyptians', in Katalin Anna Kóthay (ed.), *Art and Society: Ancient and Modern Contexts of Egyptian Art. Proceedings of the International Conference Held at the Museum of Fine Arts, Budapest, 13–15 May 2010*, Budapest: Museum of Fine Arts, 23–34.

Dijkstra, Jitse H. F. (2012), *Syene I: The Figural and Textual Graffiti from the Temple of Isis at Aswan* (Beiträge zur ägyptischen Bauforschung und Altertumskunde, 18), Darmstadt: Philipp von Zabern.

Dijkstra, Jitse H. F. (2020), 'Of Fish and Vendors: The Khnum Temple Graffiti Project', in Svenja C. Dierksen and Lena S. Krastel (eds), *Epigraphy through Five Millennia: Texts and Images in Context* (DAI Karo Sonderschrift, 43), Wiesbaden: Harrassowitz, 61–71.

Dorn, Andreas (2011), *Arbeiterhütten im Tal der Könige* (Aegyptiaca Helvetica, 23), Basel: Schwabe.

Dorn, Andreas (2015), 'Diachrone Veränderungen der Handschrift des Nekropolenschreibers Amunnacht, Sohn des Ipui', in Ursula Verhoeven (ed.), *Ägyptologische „Binsen"–Weisheiten I-II: Neue Forschungen und Methoden der Hieratistik* (Abhandlungen der Akademie der Wissenschaften und der Literatur Mainz, Geistes- und sozialwissenschaftliche Klasse, Einzelveröffentlichung, 14), Stuttgart: Steiner Verlag, 175–218.

Enmarch, Roland and Yannis Gourdon (2020), *Quarry Epigraphy at Hatnub* <https://livrepository.liverpool.ac.uk/3093960/1/Hatnub%20Graffiti%20article.pdf> (accessed on 15 March 2022).

Fischer-Elfert, Hans-Werner (2003), 'Representations of the Past in the New Kingdom Literature', in John Tait (ed.), *'Never Had the Like Occurred': Egypt's View of the Past*, London: Routledge, 119–137.

Frood, Elisabeth (2010), 'Horkhebi's Decree and the Development of Priestly Inscriptional Practices in Karnak', in Ladislav Bareš, Filip Coppens and Květa Smoláriková (eds), *Egypt in Transition: Social and Religious Development of Egypt in the First Millennium BCE*, Prague: Charles University, Faculty of Arts, 103–128.

Frood, Elisabeth (2013), 'Egyptian Temple Graffiti and the Gods: Appropriation and Ritualization in Karnak and Luxor', in Deena Ragavan (ed.), *Heaven on Earth: Temples, Ritual and Cosmic Symbolism in the Ancient World*, Chicago: The Oriental Institute, 285–318.

Gervers, Eva (2020), 'Zeichnungen von Besuchern des Neuen Reiches', in Verhoeven 2020a, 325–405, Plates 344–368.

Gülden, Svenja A. (2018), 'Paläographien und Hieratogramme – digitale Herausforderungen', in Svenja A. Gülden, Kyra van der Moezel and Ursula Verhoeven (eds), *Ägyptologische „Binsen"–Weisheiten III: Formen und Funktionen von Zeichenlisten und Paläographie* (Abhandlungen der Akademie der Wissenschaften und der Literatur Mainz, Geistes- und sozialwissenschaftliche Klasse, Einzelveröffentlichungen, 15), Stuttgart: Steiner Verlag, 83–109.

Gülden, Svenja A. (2022), 'Materialität, Textsorten, Schreiberhände – eine experimentelle digitale Analyse zu Schriftzeichen der 18. Dynastie', in Svenja A. Gülden, Tobias Konrad and Ursula Verhoeven (eds), *Ägyptologische „Binsen"–Weisheiten IV: Hieratisch des Neuen Reiches. Akteure, Formen und Funktionen* (Abhandlungen der Akademie der Wissenschaften und der Literatur Mainz, Geistes- und sozialwissenschaftliche Klasse, Einzelveröffentlichungen, 17), Stuttgart: Steiner Verlag, 221–277.

Gülden, Svenja A., Celia Krause and Ursula Verhoeven (2020), 'Digital Palaeography of Hieratic', in Vanessa Davies and Dimitri Laboury (eds), *The Oxford Handbook of Egyptian Epigraphy and Palaeography*, Oxford: Oxford University Press, 634–646.

Hassan, Khaled (2013), 'A Visitor's Hieratic Ostracon Concerning the Temple of Deir el-Bahari', *Bulletin de l'institut français d'archéologie orientale*, 113: 183–192.

Hassan, Khaled (2017), 'The Longest Visitor's Ostracon Concerning the Tempel of Deir el-Bahri', *Bulletin de l'institut français d'archéologie orientale*, 117: 281–292.

Helck, Wolfgang (1952), 'Die Bedeutung der ägyptischen Besucherinschriften', *Zeitschrift der Deutschen Morgenländischen Gesellschaft*, 102 (NF, 27): 39–46.

Jacquet-Gordon, Helen (2003), *The Graffiti on the Khonsu Temple Roof at Karnak: A Manifestation of Personal Piety* (Oriental Institute Publications, 123), Chicago: The Oriental Institute.

Krapf, Tobias (2020), 'Vom Hofpflaster zur dritten Dimension: Der Kontext der Graffiti des Chumtempelvorhofs von Elephantine', in Svenja C. Dierksen and Lena S. Krastel (eds), *Epigraphy through Five Millennia: Texts and Images in Context* (DAI Karo Sonderschrift, 43), Wiesbaden: Harrassowitz, 157–167.

Marciniak, Marek (1974), *Les inscriptions hiératique du Temple de Thoutmosis III* (Deir el-Bahari, 1), Warsaw: PWN.

Motte, Aurore (2022), 'Kemit, Writing-Boards, and Palaeographic Studies', in Svenja A. Gülden, Tobias Konrad and Ursula Verhoeven (eds), *Ägyptologische „Binsen" –Weisheiten IV: Hieratisch des Neuen Reiches. Akteure, Formen und Funktionen* (Abhandlungen der Akademie der Wissenschaften und der Literatur Mainz, Geistes– und sozialwissenschaftliche Klasse, Einzelveröffentlichungen, 17), Stuttgart: Steiner Verlag, 341–383.

Navrátilová, Hana (2007), *The Visitors' Graffiti of Dynasties XVIII and XIX in Abusir and Northern Saqqara* (The Visitors' Graffiti, 1), Prague: Czech Institute of Egyptology.

Navrátilová, Hana (2015), *Visitors' Graffiti of Dynasties 18 and 19 in Abusir and Northern Saqqara: With a Survey of the Graffiti at Giza, Southern Saqqara, Dahshur and Maidum*, 2nd rev. edn, Wallasey: Abercromby Press.

Negm, Maged (1998), 'Tourist Graffiti from the Ramesside Period', *Discussions in Egyptology*, 40: 115–123.

Peden, Alexander J. (2001), *The Graffiti of Pharaonic Egypt: Scope and Roles of Informal Writings (c. 3100–332 BC)* (Probleme der Ägyptologie, 17), Leiden: Brill.

Pinarello, Massimiliano Samuele (2015), *An Archaeological Discussion of Writing Practice: Deconstruction of the Ancient Egyptian Scribe* (GHP Egyptology, 23), London: Golden House.

Ragazzoli, Chloé (2010), 'Weak Hands and Soft Mouths: Elements of a Scribal Identity in the New Kingdom', *Zeitschrift für Ägyptische Sprache und Altertumskunde*, 137: 157–170.

Ragazzoli, Chloé (2011), 'Lire, inscrire et survivre en Égypte ancienne: les inscriptions de visiteurs du Nouvel Empire', in Christian Jacob (ed.), *Lieux de savoir 2: Les mains de l'intellect*, Paris: Albin Michel, 290–311.

Ragazzoli, Chloé (2013), 'The Social Creation of a Scribal Place: The Visitors' Inscriptions in the Tomb Attributed to Antefiqer (TT 60) (With Newly Recorded Graffiti)', *Studien zur Altägyptischen Kultur*, 42: 269–323, Plates 26–27.

Ragazzoli, Chloé (2016), 'Genres textuels et supports matériels: une inscription de visiteur comme exercice sur ostracon (Ostracon University College 31918)', *Nehet*, 4: 65–173.

Ragazzoli, Chloé (2017), *La grotte des scribes à Deir el-Bahari: la tombe MMA 504 et ses graffiti* (Mémoires de l'institut français d'archéologie orientale, 135), Cairo: Institut français d'archéologie orientale.

Ragazzoli, Chloé (2018), 'The Scribes' Cave: Graffiti and the Production of Social Space in Ancient Egypt Circa 1500 BC', in Ragazzoli et al. 2018, 23–36.

Ragazzoli, Chloé (2019), *Scribes: les artisans du texte en Égypte ancienne*, Paris: Les Belles Lettres.

Ragazzoli, Chloé (forthcoming), *L'épigraphie secondaire dans les tombes thébaines*, 2 vols, [rpt. habilitation thesis, University of Paris, 2016].

Ragazzoli, Chloé, Ömür Harmanşah, Chiara Salvador and Elizabeth Frood (eds) (2018), *Scribbling through History: Graffiti, Places and People from Antiquity to Modernity*, London: Bloomsbury Academics.

Ragazzoli, Chloé, Khaled Hassan and Chiara Salvador (eds) (2023), *Graffiti and Rock Inscriptions from Ancient Egypt: A Companion to Secondary Epigraphy* (Bibliothèque d'Etude 182), Cairo: Institut français d'archéologie orientale.

Rzepka, Slawomir (2014), *Who, Where and Why: The Rock Graffiti of Members of the Deir el-Medina Community*, Warsaw: University of Warsaw, Institute of Archaeology, Department of Archaeology of Egypt & Nubia.

Sabek, Yasser (2016), *Die hieratischen Besucher-Graffiti, ḏsr-ꜣḫ.t in Deir el-Bahari* (Internet Beiträge zur Ägyptologie und Sudanarchäologie, 18), London: Golden House Publications.

Salvador, Chiara (2020), 'Graffiti', in Vanessa Davies and Dimitri Laboury (eds), *The Oxford Handbook of Egyptian Epigraphy and Palaeography*, Oxford: Oxford University Press, 434–447.

Spiegelberg, Wilhelm (1921), *Ägyptische und andere Graffiti (Inschriften und Zeichnungen) aus der thebanischen Nekropolis*, 2 vols, Heidelberg: Winter.

Staring, Nico T. B. (2011), 'Interpreting Figural Graffiti: Case Studies from a Funerary Context', in Maarten Horn, Joost Kramer, Daniel Soliman, Nico Staring, Carina van den Hoven and Lara Weiss (eds), *Current Research in Egyptology 2010: Proceedings of the Eleventh Annual Symposium, Leiden University 2010*, Oxford: Oxbow Books, 145–156.

Staring, Nico T. B. (2017), 'Graffiti on a Thirteenth Dynasty Stela from Abydos (Louvre C8)', in Camilla Di Biase-Dyson and L. Donovan (eds), *The Cultural Manifestations of Religious Experience: Studies in Honour of Boyo G. Ockinga* (Ägypten und Altes Testament, 85), Münster: Ugarit–Verlag, 251–262.

Staring, Nico T. B. (2018), 'Products of the Physical Engagement with Sacred Space: The New Kingdom Non-Textual Tomb-Graffiti at Saqqara', in Ben J. J. Haring, Kyra V. J. van der Moezel and Daniel M. Soliman (eds), *Decoding Signs of Identity: Egyptian Workmen's Marks in Archaeological, Historical, Comparative and Theoretical Perspective* (Egyptologische Uitgaven, 32), Leiden and Leuven: Nederlands Instituut voor het Nabije Oosten and Peeters, 79–112.

Thissen, Heinz Josef (1989), *Die demotischen Graffiti von Medinet Habu: Zeugnisse zu Tempel und Kult im ptolemäischen Ägypten* (Demotische Studien, 10), Sommerhausen: Gisela Zauzich–Verlag.

Vandekerckhove, Hans and Renate Müller-Wollermann (2001), *Die Felsinschriften des Wadi Hilâl* (Elkab, 6), 2 vols, Turnhout: Brepols.

van Pelt, W. Paul and Nico Staring (2019), 'Interpreting Graffiti in the Saqqara New Kingdom Necropolic as Expressions of Popular Customs and Beliefs', *Rivista del Museo Egizio*, 3 <http://doi.org/10.29353/rime.2019.2577>.

Verhoeven, Ursula (2009), 'Die wie Kraniche balzen: Männerphantasien zur Zeit Amenhoteps III. in Assiut', in Dieter Kessler, Regine Schulz, Martina Ullmann, Alexandra Verbovsek and Stefan Wimmer (eds), *Texte – Theben – Tonfragmente: Festschrift für Günter Burkard* (Ägypten und Altes Testament, 76), Wiesbaden: Harrassowitz, 434–441.

Verhoeven, Ursula (ed.) (2020a), *Dipinti von Besuchern des Grabes N13.1 in Assiut* (The Asyut Project, 15), Wiesbaden: Harrassowitz.

Verhoeven, Ursula (2020b) [with the collaboration of Svenja A. Gülden], 'Besuchertexte, Lehren und Lieder des Neuen Reiches', in Verhoeven 2020a, 1–323, Plates 1–343.

Wildung, Dietrich (1975), 'Besucherinschriften', in Wolfgang Helck and Eberhard Otto (eds), *Lexikon der Ägyptologie I*, Wiesbaden: Harrassowitz, 766–767.

Seth M. Markle

'Spray It Loud': Hip Hop Graffiti Culture and Politics in Dar es Salaam, 2003–2018

Abstract: This essay is a critical examination of the origins and evolution of hip hop-influenced graffiti in Dar es Salaam, Tanzania (East Africa). It sets out to explore questions of identity, criminality, visual aesthetics, independent entrepreneurship, social group dynamics, mentorship, and grassroots community organizing. Informed largely by multi-sited ethnographic research conducted between 2003 and 2018, 'Spray It Loud' seeks to show how the embrace and practice of graffiti writing among urban Tanzanians in a hip hop cultural context can shed significant light on processes of transnational identity formation and community building in Africa's neoliberal era. While hip hop has given Tanzanian graffiti writers a sense of purpose and belonging, economic motivations and the lack of competition and rivalry among and between the low number of hip hop graffiti artists and crews have stagnated the movement's growth and expansion in Tanzania's most populated city.

1 'I write because no one listens': An introduction

A crucial component of hip hop graffiti's appeal stems from its ability to respond to the social realities of the world with the right combination of words, symbols, and colors. For the Tanzanian graffiti writers quoted above, their aspirations stretch beyond the confines of the movement's traditionally rooted core values and codes of conduct, suggesting that, whether produced legally or illegally, hip hop graffiti is in a constant state of redefinition, being reimagined in relation to the changing times and a graffiti writer's lived reality.[1] This essay deals with the rarely studied hip hop art form of graffiti in Africa. It sheds light on the multi-layered ways in which a group of Tanzania graffiti artists from Dar es Salaam, Tanzania, known as the Wachata Crew (WCT) [pronounced wa-chaw-ta], have engaged in illegal and legal cultural making acts, using graffiti as a tool for individual and collective self-fashioning in a neo-liberalized urban society. I argue that sanctioned graffiti in urban Tanzania constitutes a practice of hip hop

1 Rose 1994, 41–47; Chang 2005, 73–76.

https://doi.org/10.1515/9783111326306-003

agency, a way for marginalized youth and young adults to forge individual and community identity, and voice socio-political perspectives. The graffiti writers the reader will encounter in this essay – Mejah, Local Fanatics, Kalasinga, and Medy[2] – not only define themselves as hip hop artists, but also as educators, mentors, cultural organizers, and independent entrepreneurs. I set out to analyze Wachata Crew and its role in the making of a relatively new urban subculture of hip hop graffiti writing, first by addressing hip hop and graffiti's transnational origins in the country, then by assessing the aesthetics and message of WCT's graffiti art productions and its grassroots community building practices, and finally, by examining the crew as a micro-business enterprise.

Hip hop is a cultural movement founded by African American and Afro-Caribbean youth in the South Bronx, New York City in the early 1970s. Through its four main mediums of expression – rapping, breakdancing, deejaying, and graffiti – hip hop is used to 'articulate the pleasures and problems' of urban life.[3] For this essay, I employ the phrase 'hip hop graffiti' to connote a specific type of public surface writing associated with the hip hop movement from 1973 onwards.[4] Practiced by urban youth disenfranchised because of their race and class, graffiti is defined by its leading founders as one of the core artistic elements of hip hop. Also referred to as 'writers', graffiti artists primarily use aerosol spray-paint cans to communicate messages and attain recognition (i.e., fame).[5] It is a form of contemporary public art comprised of abstract and interlocking lettering styles, vibrant colors, and characters that can be both legally and illegally produced primarily on public and private property surfaces. To examine the nature and meaning of Wachata Crew's 'affinitive investment in hip-hop'[6] is to uncover the strategic ways graffiti writers interact with and through a hip hop frame of reference, how they theorize and practice graffiti writing, how hip hop shapes their ideological positionalities and perceptions of self and social organization, and how their strategies of community building speak to everyday desires of belonging and economic survival. This case study is not to claim Tanzania graffiti writing's exceptionality. Rather, it is to provide ethnographic insight into how graffiti art culture and ideologies are localized and contingent, profoundly shaped by social, political, and economic lived realities.

---

2 Mejah is pronounced May-Jah; Kalasinga is pronounced Kah-la-sing-ga; Medy is pronounced Med-ee.

3 Rose 1994, 2.

4 One more point on terminology here: In Hip Hop Studies, hip hop graffiti is simply called graffiti. Because this edited volume explores various types of graffiti, specificity was necessary.

5 For example, see Fricke and Ahearn 2002; Cooper 2004; Forman and Neal 2012.

6 Holt 2019, 9.

1.1 Literature review

This essay is informed by two bodies of ever-expanding, interdisciplinary scholarship. One of them analyzes contemporary graffiti while the other focuses on Tanzanian youth culture. One of the strengths of the former lies in its varied unpacking of the intersection between art and criminality. Urban geographers, sociologists, anthropologists, and linguistics have framed graffiti as a form of street-oriented communication of the disempowered that contests power and authority through the counterhegemonic occupation of public and private spaces in cities.[7] This essay enters this conversation about the relationship between hip hop graffiti writing and institutional policing with the question: What are the implications when graffiti artists reject illegal forms of writing as an expressive tactic of spatial resistance to urban inequalities? While scholars' singular focus on breaking the law has elicited insights into how visual artists exercise political agency, it also points to the need for interpreting graffiti movements more holistically and outside major global North cities.[8]

The scholarship on postcolonial Tanzanian urban youth culture has also opened opportunities for the study of graffiti in a hip hop context. Scholars have shown how the government's abandonment of socialism in favor of neoliberal capitalism, which was characterized by uneven and unequal urbanization processes, led to the disenfranchisement and criminalization of youth living in cities. In identifying correlations between neoliberal globalization and the social repression of youth, a handful of scholars have examined how Tanzanians have adopted and refined African Diaspora cultural ideas and practices such as Rastafarianism and hip hop to forge resistive group and individual identities in response to their alienation.[9] Critical inquiries of aesthetics, linguistics, commercialization, political discourse, and gender dynamics have enhanced the study of Tanzanian hip hop but there is yet to be a full-length study on the graffiti art in the country despite it being in existence for over twenty years.[10] 'Spray It Loud' seeks to fill in the gaps (no pun intended) in both literatures, entangling rather than disentangling graffiti with hip hop cultural and knowledge production and

7 Some examples include Abdelmagid 2013; Benavides-Vanegas 2005; Campos 2015; Creswell 1996; Docuyanan 2000; Gross, Walkosz and Gross 1997; Heinsohn 2015; Jaffe, Rhiney and Francis 2012; Moreau and Alderman 2011; Schacter 2019.

8 Jaffe, Rhiney and Francis 2012, 1–2.

9 See Englert 2008; Gesthuizen and Haas 2000; Moyer 2005; Remes 1999; Stroeken 2005; Fast and Moyer 2018; Casco 2006.

10 See Clark 2014, 144–148; Clark 2018; Perullo 2011, 84–90.

paying more focused attention on the careerist and community-building aspirations of graffiti writers.

1.2 Methodology

As someone who strongly identifies with hip hop culture, I was guided by a deep interest in how hip hop is lived and anchors urban Tanzanians' daily lives. To unpack Tanzanian hip hoppers' social imaginaries and cultural practices, I had to embark on the path of the hip hop ethnographer and oral historian.[11] The research for this essay is therefore drawn from prolonged multi-sited ethnographic fieldwork I conducted in Dar es Salaam between 2003-2018, where I made seven visits for periods of time ranging from three months to thirteen months, carrying out twenty-three recorded oral history and qualitative interviews, mostly in English, with ten practitioners of Tanzania hip hop graffiti writing (Tanzanian and non-Tanzanian), including multiple structured interviews with the four core members of Wachata Crew who are the focus of this study. The application of oral history and long-term ethnography was informed by an awareness of hip hop graffiti's status in the country as a sub-culture-in-becoming with few practitioners, and not extensively documented by the state and news media. In allowing my interlocutors to define what hip hop means to them on their own terms, the employment of this mixed method approach helped open a window onto how a diasporic culture is localized. Direct interpersonal modes of interaction with graffiti writers in intimate spaces over extended periods of time further allowed me to gain insights into questions about intragroup social dynamics and processes of creative production hidden from public view.

The centrality of visual storytelling to hip hop graffiti production necessitated that I supplement my research by incorporating visual methods while also taking into consideration hip hop graffiti's short temporal life span in the material world due to factors such as deterioration or replacement. I, therefore, used photographic data collection as a tool for historical preservation, but also to track shifts and changes in the crew's politics and aesthetic development over time.[12] This essay contains photographs taken in the field at different points in time, most of which are no longer in physical existence, to provide context for readers

11 Important ethnographic scholarship on hip hop and hip hop graffiti informed this essay; see Brown 1999; Gauthier 2001; Kramer 2010; Lachmann 1988; Lee 2009.

12 In documenting the graffiti scene in Tanzania, specifically, I collected over 300 digital photographs capturing a range of settings.

unfamiliar with hip hop graffiti and contemporary urban Tanzania, more generally, to chart the crew's artistic growth, and to deepen my analysis on artist/art intention from a visual perspective.

2 Towards a transnational history of hip hop graffiti in Dar es Salaam

Hip hop's emergence in urban Tanzania is a story of entanglement. The commercialization and global spread of hip hop functioned in symbiosis and conflict with the neo-liberalization of Tanzania's economy and society.[13] The country birthed its first generation of practitioners and enthusiasts in the mid-1980s during the country's shift from one-party state-led socialism called 'Ujamaa na Kujitegemea' [Kiswahili for African Socialism and Self Reliance] to a mode of capitalism based on private ownership and a multi-party democratic system. The harsh economic realities that came with this shift – extreme underemployment, forced urban migration, drastic cuts in social services that led to a sharp rise in education costs – were acutely felt by Dar es Salaam's growing youth population. Finding themselves in dire situations, they gravitated to hip hop, identifying with African American urban lived experience of marginalization and disenfranchisement.[14]

Deejays and club promoters played key generative roles in carving out social spaces for youth in the city to express themselves primarily through breakdancing and rapping. By the mid-1990s, a Kiswahili rap industry was fueled by privately owned radio stations and advances in and greater access to hip hop commodities from abroad and recording technologies, becoming the most dominant element of hip hop practiced in the country by youth and young adults. Although hip hop graffiti was pretty much non-existent throughout the early years of hip hop in Tanzania during the 1980s and 1990s, WCT graffiti writers see themselves as part of a non-hip hop graffiti writing tradition rooted in Tanzania's socialist era. One could find names of people on public walls written in charcoal, an indigenous style of graffiti that dates back to the socialist era:

> [G]raffiti has been around since the late 1970s during the time of Ujamaa (African Socialism) when most Tanzanians had no access to the Western Hemisphere nor Europe, the internet and [*sic*] the computer technology in general. The youth along the coastal towns of Dar es

---

13 Perullo 2011, 84–142.

14 Zavara Mponjika interview with author, July 2011; KBC interview with author, June 2018; Mejah Mbuya interview with author, June 2012.

> Salaam, Tanga, Mtwara and Zanzibar started to 'storeaway' in ships that came in and left the country, and some, riskly [*sic*] made it to Europe and the West. Through photographs and letters sent back home to relatives and friends who still held the dream of becoming seamen or just storing away for the sake of making it to Europe, escaping the hardships in the late 1970s to early 1980s when the Tanzanian economy was in bad shape right after the Tanzania-Uganda war that sent dictator Idi Amin Dada into exile, youth started tagging their real names and nicknames on city walls using charcoal which was available in any homestead and was easy to use in 'leaving a mark'.[15]

Predating hip hop graffiti was also an urban public art culture featuring iconographic portraits of African American hip hop artists, namely rappers, such as 2Pac, Biggie, Jay Z, and 50 Cent painted in acrylic on the walls of general stores and barbershops and hair salons. Hip hop graffiti pieces done with spray paint cans and containing salient stylistic features like abstract lettering, etc., did not appear in Dar es Salaam for public viewing until about early 2000's when Zaki, a graffiti writer from South Africa, produced 'CURE', a mural alluding to the HIV/Aids epidemic that was ravaging the continent in the 1990s. From here, the hip hop graffiti's origin story becomes one about international alliance building, mentorship, and patronage from foreign embassies, NGOs, and corporations.

Sela-One is considered the first non-Tanzanian graffiti artist who contributed to the art form's gradual spread in the city. Kiswahili for Gangsta One, Sela was a German student studying away for a year at the University of Dar es Salaam in the early 2000s. Sela-One was a prolific writer. His tags, throw ups, and pieces were located all over the city, which inspired some Tanzanians to take up the art. While Sela-One was covering Dar's public and private walls in 2005 and 2006, Mejah was illegally tagging anti-economic globalization messages at strategic locations like bus stops, major bus stations, and the bathroom walls of restaurants and nightclubs. He was aware of Sela-One's work and purposefully sought him out. When they connected, Sela-One taught Mejah, who back then went by the aliases Ghost and Souljah of Fortune, more techniques of the trade to improve the aesthetics of his tags without compromising speed. At this point in the nascent movement, the first era of hip hop graffiti was connected to illegality and anonymity yet without eliciting an urgent need for institutional policing.

'Hip hop saved my life. That is all I can say when it comes to what hip-hop has done for me!' wrote Mejah in a short essay that appeared in a book about hip

15 Wachata Crew, 'The History of Graffiti Art in Tanzania', <http://wachatacrew.blogspot.com/2012/07/the-history-of-graffiti-art-in-tanzania.html>, posted on 26 July 2012 (accessed on 7 December 2022).

hop in Africa in 2015.[16] In a 2011 interview with Mejah for a global hip hop blog, he shared with me how and why he became a graffiti artist:

> Being a graffiti artist never crossed my mind at the time when I discovered hip-hop back in 1988. Although I could draw, I was more caught up in the MCing and DJing art forms. Bboying, though, was big at that time too, but during my school days I was trying to be a rapper. I even attempted to perform Nas' 'Ain't Hard To Tell' in 1995 at a high school talent show. It was an ugly performance! On that day I learned that MCing was not my thing. In 2001, after I graduated from university, I moved to Cape Town (South Africa) where the graffiti scene was huge, and I knew that graffiti was my piece of the hip-hop equation [...]. It was then and there that I decided to use graffiti to deliver social justice messages. In terms of how graffiti appealed to me, I think that goes back to when I started to read *The Source* magazine in the early 1990s. I discovered that hip hop was about struggle, so whenever my eyes came across *The Source* I would first read about hip hop, then I'd flip to the social and political sections and read about the Black Panthers, the transatlantic slave trade, U.S. Civil Rights movement, the Nation of Islam and the Prison Industrial Complex, etc. And in doing so, I had more of an understanding of MCs like Rakim compared to most of my peers in terms of the topics they were rapping about. When I became a graffiti artist, I fulfilled my dream to be a part of the hip-hop community and, secondly, to deliver social justice messages.[17]

Mejah not only wanted to belong to a global community and make a social impact but also add a missing hip hop element to Tanzania's scene. When he re-settled in Dar es Salaam in 2002, he started illegally tagging anti-capitalist globalization slogans mainly on public surfaces in and around dala dala (bus) stops spread throughout the city. In addition to 'Mkapanization', named after then Tanzanian president Benjamin Mkapa, he tagged 'Coco-Colonization'. Both tags were clever pejoratives in reference to forces of neo-liberalization complicit in the marginalization of urban youth in the country. Once he gained more confidence and improved his technique to two-dimensional bubble letters, he started writing upon the request of neighborhood hip hop crews looking to add a hip hop graffiti aesthetic to their respective neighborhoods and social gathering spots.

Mejah's encounter with skilled graffiti writers was not limited to Sela-One. His maturation as a more technically skilled and professional-oriented graffiti writer, which would lead him to form Wachata Crew, owed a great deal to the mentorship of Charles Hargrove, also known as Kool Koor, an African American hip hop graffiti pioneer. Born in 1963 to parents who were painters, Hargrove grew up in the birthplace of hip hop, the South Bronx, and got into graffiti when he saw his peers doing it. As a teenager, Hargrove attended the Art and Design

16 Mbuya 2014, 174.
17 Mejah Mbuya interview with author, June 2012.

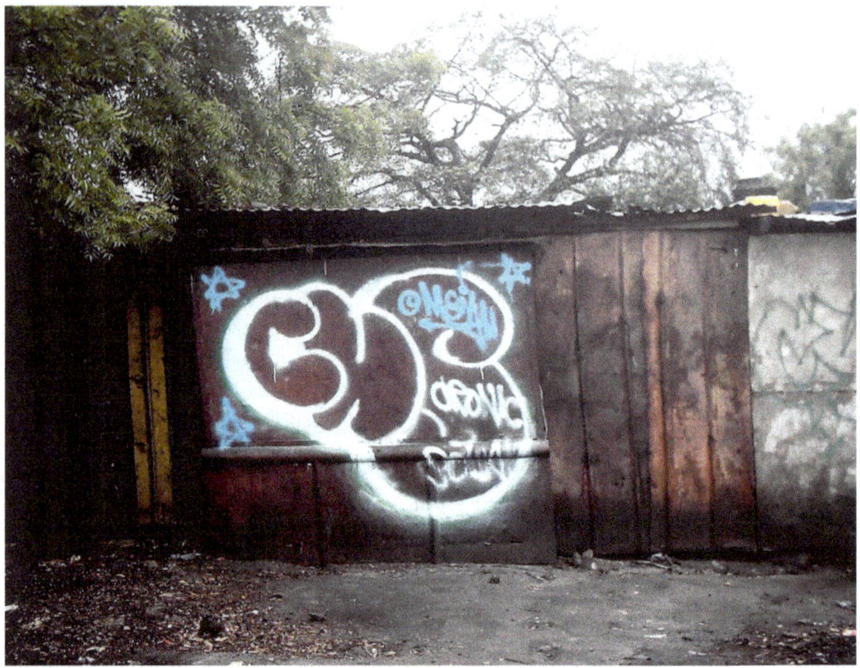

Fig. 1: A Throw Up of CNS (Chronic Souljahs) by Mejah, Dar es Salaam, 2006; photograph © Seth M. Markle.

school in Manhattan where he studied architecture and illustration. His formative arts education, however, came from outside of school during his daily commute from the South Bronx to midtown, which further introduced him to a city in the throes of a graffiti revolution.[18] Going by the name Kool Koor, he soon joined the pioneering graffiti crew Tag Master Killers. Although he never painted top-to-bottom pieces on the exterior of subway trains, he gained fame as an interior subway tagger of the 2, 3, and 4 lines. In 1982, at the age of sixteen, he exhibited his graffiti-on-canvas at the famous Fashion Moda, an Avant Garde gallery in the Bronx and one of the first to open its doors to showcasing graffiti artists. Two years later, in 1984, his expressionistic use of spray paint that produced 'space-aged' and 'futuristic' inspired work earned him an exhibition in Brussels, along with fellow American artists Keith Haring, Jean-Michel Basquiat, and Futura 2000. He returned and

18 See Rose 1994, 41–47.

settled in Brussels in 1989, becoming a driving force in the city's street art scene as an artist, mentor, educator, and advocate to the present day.[19]

In 2007, Koor traveled to Dar and facilitated a series of graffiti workshops at WaPi. Founded in the same year, WaPi, short for 'Words and Pictures', was a hip hop cultural showcase hosted and sponsored by the British Council. 'I met him there', Mejah revealed to me in 2011. 'He was being sponsored by Montana-Cans, so he decided to do a graffiti workshop and I happened to be there. From that time, Koor shared with us techniques and the basics of graffiti, which we did not know. From there everything came into place'.[20] WaPi marked the first organized event that introduced graffiti art to urban youth and the public. Held every Saturday of the month, the British Council opened its space for hip hop practice and performance, which included allowing its ivory-white painted walls to be covered in graffiti. Over fifty youth participated in the workshop, and Mejah used the turnout and positive reception to identify and recruit the most skilled artists into what became Tanzania's first hip hop graffiti crew called Wachata Crew, Kiswahili slang for 'graffiti', or 'to put your signature'. Joining Mejah were Local Fanatics, Kalasinga, and Medy – all younger novices born and raised in Dar who showed advanced talent and commitment to the practice when they attended WaPi events.[21]

Kool Koor's return to Dar es Salaam in 2009 to facilitate another series of graffiti workshops resulted in further hands-on mentorship of the Wachata Crew.

> Kool Koor's effect was physically seen after attending his graffiti workshop in 2009 in Dar es Salaam. He's the first one to introduce us to Montana spray cans, which were completely different from what we were using at that time and what was available in our shopping stores. He taught us different techniques on how to handle spray cans, making straight lines and how to blend colors. Although some of us were self-taught artists, Kool Koor was the first person who we physically witnessed doing graffiti.[22]

---

19 AB-Ancienne Belgique, 'HipHop: The First Element with... Chuck "Kool Koor" Hargrove' [Video], <https://youtu.be/k-htZCJR_-U>, posted on 10 November 2014 (accessed on 15 June 2016); Snoekx 2021; also see Munsell and Tate 2020.

20 Mejah Mbuya interview with author, June 2012.

21 Kalasinga interview with author, August 2011; Kalasinga interview with author, April 2016; Medy interview with author, August 2011; Medy interview with author, April 2016; Mizani interview with author, June 2011; Local Fanatics interview with author, May 2018. There were other founding members such as Edo T, Mizani, D-Man, and Biggie, but they have either left the crew or loosely affiliated.

22 Mejah Mbuya interview with author, June 2012.

Koor's mentorship ushered in mechanical and stylistic instruction, insight into how to sketch an outline, how to hold and manipulate a spray paint can, how to fade, how to give dimension, and, most important, how to conserve paint.

Between 2007 and 2009, WCT crew devoted its energies to technical skills development, setting up chapters in Moshi and Mwanza, training novices, designing a fashion line, asset mapping and building a network of contacts and connections. This period also marked a turning away from unsanctioned graffiti-ing writing.

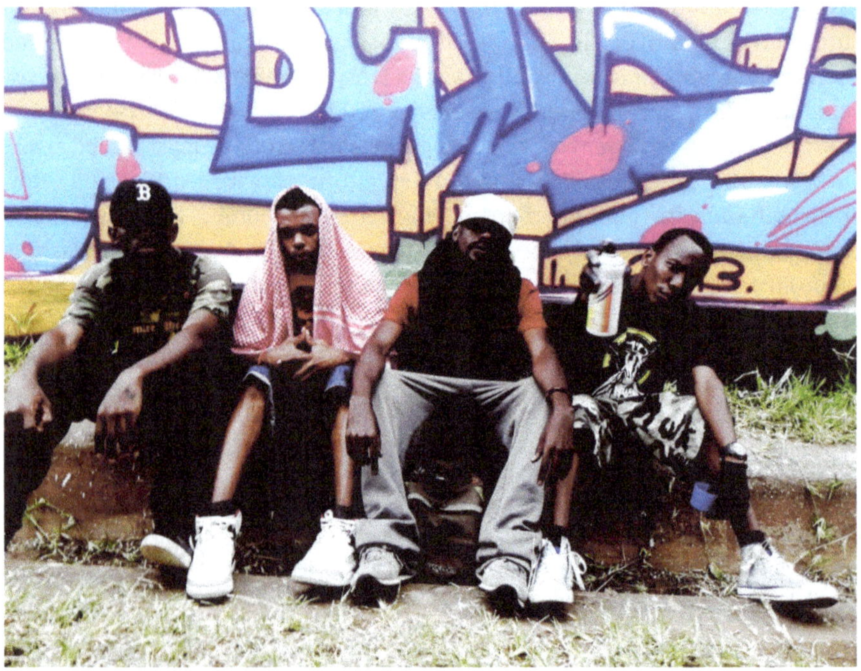

Fig. 2: Wachata Crew (l-r: Local Fanatics, Kalasinga, Mejah, and Medy), Dar es Salaam, 2014; photograph © Seth M. Markle.

3 'There's always time for art': Hip hop graffiti aesthetics and messaging

As committed practitioners, Wachata Crew members are chiefly concerned with doing graffiti and presenting it as art for the public. By focusing on the production of sanctioned murals or 'pieces' (graffiti slang term for masterpiece) over illicit tagging, they find joy and excitement in utilizing the physical urban landscape as their canvas. While WCT has presented its art on fishing boats, vehicles, sneakers, t-shirts, bodies, bedsheets, and even the shell of turtles, it prefers the exterior concrete walls that surround and demarcate public and private property ownership mainly because it is the most accessible for public consumption and engagement given their ubiquity throughout the city.[23]

The crew produces graffiti murals with four objectives in mind: 1) to showcase their artistic talents in hip hop performance style, 2) to beautify the city making it more aesthetically pleasing, 3) to educate and incite critical thought and debate by conveying messages of cultural and political importance to Tanzanians, and 4) to introduce hip hop graffiti as art, not vandalism.[24] The location of a piece is determined by a few factors. WCT seeks out permission first. Most importantly, if not doing a mural at a cultural event on interior walls of NGO compounds, it also seeks out sites with the most potential for visibility by the public such as main roads, bus stations, and popular restaurants and bars. After identifying the location for a piece, the crew discuss and think about a theme or message, and then sketch in pencil and/or markers a basic outline on paper, usually in a black bounded notebook, known to graffiti writers as blackbooks. This process of selecting and confirming a location and outlining a piece can range in time, from weeks to months. It is not uncommon for one crew member to think of a thematic-driven piece with the intention of having all members involved in its completion.

WCT primarily uses aerosol or spray-paint cans of varying quality, preferring, like most writers, elite products like Montana cans over the local ones imported from the United Arab Emirates. Their murals incorporate a combination of abstract lettering styles, characters (i.e., people and animals), objects like books, microphones, speakers, turntables, city skylines, palm trees, and hats, and the blending, fading, and shading of multiple colors. Producing the mural is an exercise in teamwork. Each member is assigned a task. Local Fanatics, who is considered among the crew as the most technically skilled, is responsible for constructing the outline. Once completed, the other members do fill-ins, blending, shading – giving dimensionality to the image(s). The time it takes to complete a mural varies on the size and pace of the writers. On several occasions, I have observed WCT work at a leisurely pace, listening to rap music on a wireless speaker

---

23 Jaffe, Rhiney and Francis 2012, 2–3.

24 I have come to these conclusions from attending a number of crew meetings, informal conversations, and formal interviews with crew members over a fifteen-year period.

and using the opportunity to socialize with each other, document the process for social media, and most importantly, to directly engage with onlookers who typically stand or sit transfixed by the creation process.

Most of WCT murals are constructed around a theme or message; sometimes straightforward and easy to understand, other times requiring some effort in deciphering. The crew sees its artwork as dialogic, offering commentary and critique grounded in ongoing social issues that percolate in Tanzania society. In multiple pieces produced at different points in time, WCT's art has tackled the issue of education in Tanzania from various vantage points, from addressing the systemic exclusion of Muslim girls to promoting the empowering effect of basic literacy. It also engages in acts of memorialization by honoring Tanzania's socialist past with a portrait of Julius Nyerere, the nation's first president and major theorist of African socialism. In other pieces, messages of pan-African solidarity are articulated in a portrait of President Barack Obama, the first African American elected president in US history, which was produced in 2008 at an event celebrating his election. It created a stencil of Walter Rodney, the Afro-Guyanese historian and pan-Africanist who taught at the University of Dar es Salaam in the 1960s, raising his fist in the air. The crew also calls on its audience to be proactive citizens with murals that are meant to raise awareness about climate change, animal poaching in the nature reserve parks, cycling to reduce traffic congestion, HIV and AIDS prevention, and contamination of and access to clean water. In most instances, WCT purposefully tries to speak to women by designing women characters and/or messaging about women-specific issues. 'Womens [*sic*], they have a power in the community', Medy said to me. 'Most of my work, I like to paint on womens [*sic*]. I believe that women are the line to the community. So, when you use women to deliver the message to the community, it will be easier for people to catch it than like youth like men or boys to deliver the message'.[25]

Some pieces are more minimalistic in their design but equally provocative, such as a peace sign painted in the colors of the Tanzanian national flag, flanked by the words 'Amani' (Kiswahili for 'peace') on the left side and 'Tanzania' on the right side. This was a call for safe elections amid ongoing political violence between the ruling party, Chama Cha Mapinduzi (CCM) and its main opposition, Chama cha Demokrasi na Maendeleo (CHADEMA).

25 Medy interview with author, May 2018.

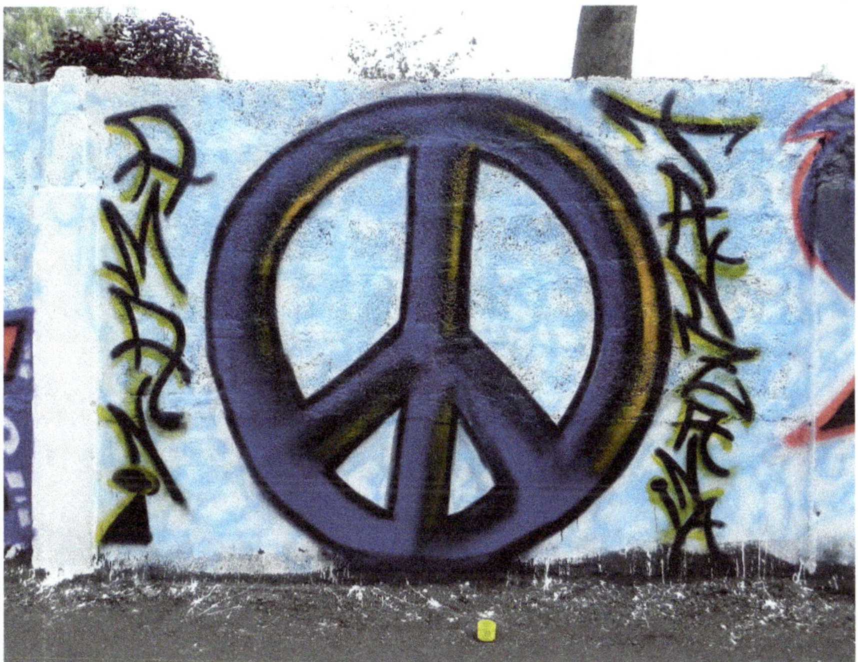

Fig. 3: Wachata Crew graffiti piece 'Amani Tanzania', Arusha, 2013; photograph © Seth M. Markle.

Other pieces are more abstract, making the message harder to decode. Take for example a 2014 piece titled 'Panya Rodi' [Kiswahili for 'Rat Road'] that I observed being produced on the wall of a semi-constructed house in Kigamboni, a section of the city located on a peninsula where I was living at the time. That same year, a disorganized protest march led by unemployed youth who referred to themselves as rats unfolded in response to the municipal government's banning of informal sector jobs dominated by youth in and around the commercial center. When these youth took to the streets, brandishing machetes to voice their grievances over the lack of employment opportunities, they were violently repressed by the Tanzania police force. WCT produced a mural that took direct aim at the state, trying to explain to the people the root cause of the issue.[26]

26 Daniel Dieng, 'T1AP Mejah_TOAP002' [Video], <https://vimeo.com/118317406>, posted 30 January 2015 (accessed on 8 July 2021), 00:00:00–00:02:21.

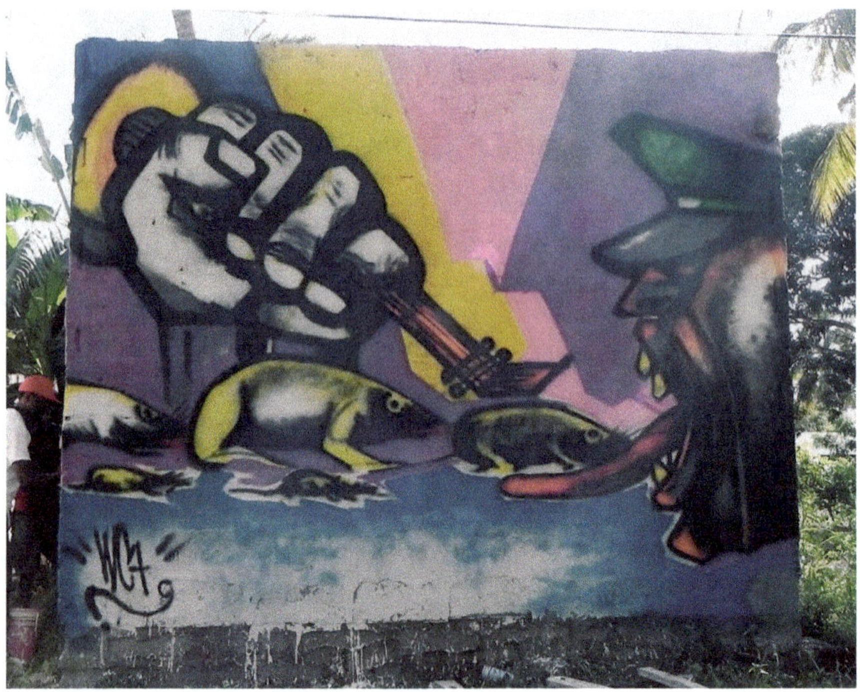

Fig. 4: Wachata Crew graffiti piece 'Panya Rodi', Dar es Salaam, 2014; photograph © Seth M. Markle.

On the upper left-hand corner is the image of the police officer's muscular hand crushing an acoustic guitar. On the right is a profile of police officer's head, wearing a standard policeman's hat. The police officer's mouth is agape, exposing sharpened, yellow-tinted teeth and a red elongated tongue extending outward and draping over the bottom teeth and lip onto the ground like a ramp. Located at the bottom of the wall, sandwiched in between the hand and face of the policeman, are three rats in a line, one already positioned on the policeman's tongue while the others are moving in the direction of the policeman's mouth. The use of monotone and dark colors of the main objects in the piece evokes a somber tone indicative of the three actions taking place while the vibrant background colors of blue, pink, purple, and yellow give the piece its trademark WCT identity.

The guitar symbolizes a tool of employment, a coping mechanism, and an object of survival in the city. In portraying the youth as rats, WCT was portraying them from the perspective of the state. Youth are to be viewed as an annoyance and nuisance. The size of the head and hand of the policeman in comparison to the smaller-sized youth, passive and disempowered in the way they capitulate, positions them as victims when confronted with state power and authority. It is a mural about the government eating its youth by restricting their opportunities for self-employment with policy and violence. 'In graffiti', Mejah said in interview for a short documentary film documenting the making of the mural, 'I feel the pleasure of seeing somebody who didn't know, now they know something'.[27] By far this piece is the crew's most radical production, one that is more explicit in its criticism of the CCM-led government.

Over the five hours it took to produce the mural, I watched from afar as Mejah would converse with people passing by, most of them youth. Then and there, I came to understand the strategic importance of the piece's location. It was in plain view on an off-road leading from a main road to a primary school. Every day, youth dressed in the standard school uniforms, a light blue-collar shirt under a blue wool V-neck sweater, tan shorts for boys and navy-blue skirts with pleats for girls, walked this road with their book bags in tow. On this day, they would stop and watch, and I would follow Mejah as he approached them to explain the meaning of the mural. 'They will tell others', he told me afterwards.

Over time, WCT has developed an aesthetic style tied to its use of vibrant colors, a mix of Kiswahili and English words, and characters to convey messages with socio-political and cultural meaning. While they remain deeply invested in abstract lettering and multi-dimensional imagery, the crew has become more concerned with execution, making sure their message is of high technical quality and easy to understand. I have noticed that since John Magufuli was elected president in 2015, political messaging that explicitly critiques the state is lacking. Nicknamed the 'Bulldozer', Magufuli, unlike his predecessor, was intolerant of criticism and proved so by gaining an infamous reputation for silencing journalists, musicians, cartoonists, and activists up until his mysterious death in 2021.[28] I asked Local Fanatics if he was reluctant in doing political hip hop graffiti with Magufuli in power:

> The previous president had no problem with graffiti and that's why many of the cartoon artists in magazines and newspapers used drawing [*sic*] without any problems. He would laugh and smile and call you names, and he was comfortable with it. But the president we have right now? No. It's a little bit crazy and it's not safe. It's not safe.[29]

---

27 Daniel Dieng, 'T1AP Mejah_TOAP002' [Video], <https://vimeo.com/118317406>, posted 30 January 2015 (accessed on 8 July 2021), 00:02:22–00:02:29.

28 Human Rights Watch 2020, 552–558.

29 Local Fanatics interview with author, May 2018.

4 'Kuyonesha Upendo wa Kweli Hip Hop': Community building and belonging

WCT's hip hop identity is not singularly located in the adoption of a core hip hop artistic element. Visual and aural markers of committed belonging to a national hip hop community within a global hip hop nation are also evidenced in the crew members' embrace of hip hop representational acts of speaking and dressing.[30] Moreover, rap music has been the soundtrack of their youth and adult lives with each member having his own memories of how lyrics influenced the ways they see themselves and the world. More importantly, Wachata Crew hold a very clear ideological stance on what hip hop is and how the culture should be perceived and practiced in the city. This is encapsulated in the phrase the crew employs on its Facebook account: 'Kuyonesha Upendo wa Kweli Hip Hop'. In English, the phrase means 'to show love for true hip hop'. By adopting a group-based approach to hip hop community building, WCT performs a form of active citizenship focused on contributing to the growth and development of Tanzanian hip hop culture as a unified movement. This ideological commitment to preserving and growing 'true hip hop', and promoting its positive values and principles, explains the crew's ongoing participation in and creation of cultural events/showcases as well as arts-education initiatives targeting youth, novices, and young women.

From what I have observed from WCT activities over the years is that to live or to represent 'true' hip hop is to devote oneself to a life of cultural responsibility, engaging in event planning work, oftentimes in collaboration with NGOs, foreign embassies, radio stations and television broadcasting companies, and indigenous and foreign hip hop artists and collectives. At these events, hip hop is presented, first and foremost, as an inclusive arts-based movement that is comprised of four artistic elements and can be used as a tool to foster creative expression, nonviolent competition, and community.

Two oppositional stances are implied in the crew's identification with this principle of showing one's love for true hip hop. Firstly, there is a desire to challenge popular and corporate media's reduction of hip hop to rap, occluding from the view the other three foundational elements that make up the culture, including graffiti writing. Secondly, WCT's form of civic engagement aims to neutralize or counter hip hop voices that glorify misogyny, homophobia, materialism, violence, crime, and drug abuse. This community-building role also seeks to elevate the status of graffiti writing, presenting it as a distinctive hip hop performance

---

30 See H. Samy Alim et al., 2011.

style and mode of cultural and political expression. Cultural events allow for WCT to reach a wide audience, especially youth, inviting them into curated spaces that present a wholistic and positive image of hip hop culture while nurturing technical skills development in hip hop art forms.

Unlike commissioned work for multinational companies, which I will discuss in the next section of this essay, hip hop events, especially ones organized by WCT itself, serve as platforms that cultivate cultural and professional legitimacy. It provides the group a greater freedom in its self-expression than paid work where they are beholden to content requirements of their paid customers. According to Local Fanatics: 'When someone gives you commissioned work, he controls everything. Me, being an artist, I'm not free to design my own thing. From him, from the company, you just have orders: "Do this. Put this. Put this."'[31] At WCT's annual anniversary showcase held at Nafasi Art Space, a nonprofit organization dedicated to the arts, WCT members do live exhibitions without having to follow any stipulations or guidelines other than to showcase their technical skills and points of view.[32]

Because of WCT's ideological opposition to illegal graffiti writing, cultural events are the most viable means for promoting and growing hip hop graffiti. They provide safe spaces for artists of varying skill levels and, in the process, position graffiti as a legitimate form of visual art. In 2018, during my most recent visit to Dar es Salaam before the outbreak of COVID pandemic, I was struck by the stagnant growth of graffiti art. After eleven years of existence, there is only a small number of practitioners. I was determined to talk to WCT members, curious about whether they saw this stagnancy as an unintended outcome of its efforts to delegitimize illegal graffiti writing. Medy, who came to graffiti through practicing on interior walls of one of his friends' compounds, explained his reasons to me for being against illicit writing:

> I don't prefer illegal graffiti. If you want to speak something, just speak your mind. If you want to speak your mind, you have to be calm. So, when you go to the wall and start doing illegal, you won't be comfortable to express what you want to say. So, I don't, and I won't do illegal graffiti in my life. Yeah.[33]

31 Local Fanatics interview with author, May 2018.

32 While cultural events can result in payment for their services, normally WCT uses its own resources (money and supplies) to participate in and/or organize events. This is another example of how it shows their 'love for true hip hop'.

33 Medy interview with author, May 2018.

I pressed him by asking whether he thought being a true graffiti writer is to be a criminal, to do it without permission because that was the essence of the art form – Medy was unconvinced and steadfast in his opposition. 'No', he politely retorted. 'I don't agree with that because graffiti is not about crime, you know, graffiti is an artist's expression. So, if you want to express something, you have to be, you have to think, you have to look at what you are going to address to the people. So, if you are going to go fast and you don't set down what you're going...it would be like you are wasting your time. And mostly, at least nowadays, graffiti artists in the world are trying to express their feeling compared to the other generation. I'm not saying bad for them, but they show us the way, but we have to take from there to the other level. So, for this world, we don't have to do illegal graffiti'.[34]

My interviews with Kalasinga and Local Fanatics yielded very similar arguments about their understanding of hip hop graffiti as art. Time and patience were valuable weapons in the production process given the mechanical challenges that come with working with spray paint cans. Both had engaged in illegal graffiti writing before joining WCT in 2007, and relayed humorous yet cautionary tales about rushing their work and being chased and caught by police, security guards, and property owners. But once WCT was formed, the crew became more resolute in denouncing illicit graffiti practices. For Kalasinga, there were other risks at stake, namely the potential for criminalization of the crew itself without actually doing unsanctioned work:

As Wachata Crew we don't do illegal graffiti because we are the only crew who do graffiti in Tanzania. You see? So, it's easy for us to be recognized when we'd do that thing. Yeah. They could say that this is Wachata Crew [...]. So, for us, we can't do that because we are the only crew who do this. And sometimes they could say it's Wachata but maybe it's our students because we have taught so many young graffiti artists to do it.[35]

WCT involvement in the production of cultural events also allows for the forging and strengthening of hip hop networks of solidarity on local, national, regional, and international spheres. It has collaborated with a host of Tanzanian hip hoppers in Dar es Salaam as well as in other Tanzanian cities and towns, such as Arusha, Bagamoyo, and Mwanza. Its regional and translocal networks and connections have led to WCT's attendance at hip hop festivals and participation in collaborative art projects in the United States and multiple countries in Africa and Europe. Moreover, through its connection to Kool Koor, the crew's

34 Medy interview with author, May 2018.
35 Kalasinga interview author, May 2018.

mentor, WCT is a member of his global coalition of graffiti writers called 'Spray It Loud'.[36]

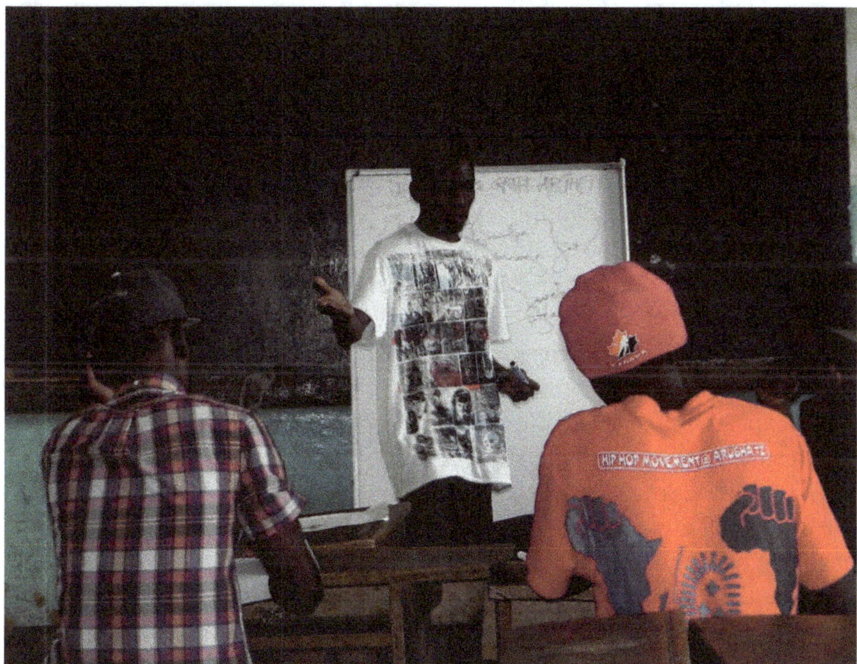

Fig. 5: Wachata Crew graffiti workshop, Arusha, 2013; photograph © Seth M. Markle.

WCT take seriously what is referred to in the global hip hop community as the 'Fifth Element of Hip Hop'. It is an element that promotes both the dissemination and consumption of knowledge for self and community improvement.[37] Thus, WCT artists feel responsible for training and educating the next generation of hip hop graffiti writers. As a result, WCT has designed and implemented a workshop-based curriculum oriented toward hip hop cultural knowledge and graffiti skills technical training. To be a graffiti writer is to not only master mechanics and techniques, but also to learn about hip hop cultural history, values, and codes

36 Msia K. Clark, 'HHAP Episode 31: Wachata Crew on Graffiti and Hip Hop Culture in Tanzania', <https://hiphopafrican.com/wachatacrew/>, posted on 10 December 2018 (accessed on 29 December 2018).
37 Gosa 2015, 56–70.

of conduct. Students are first introduced to the history of graffiti in Philadelphia and New York City, where they are exposed to tagging and subway graffiti art as well as to various lettering styles. The workshop also comprises a lecture on how it spread to Tanzania. Here, WCT explain the difference between illegal and legal graffiti writing, and how the former is not applicable to Tanzania's situation. After addressing the salient features of the history and culture, students practice writing on sheets of paper with pens, markers, and pencils and then later take what they've learned to an actual wall using spray paint cans. Through these workshops, WCT's curriculum is crafted in quite deliberate ways that explicitly encourage legal hip hop graffiti practice.

Women Xpress is the most cutting edge of WCT's arts education initiative in that it strategically aims to introduce and train young women in hip hop graffiti. The project was first conceptualized in 2013 after WCT members spoke to an African American woman hip hop researcher who asked the crew why there weren't any Tanzanian women graffiti artists. Four years later, after visiting Nairobi and being exposed to women graffiti artists there, WCT went into action. 'But last year I remember when we went to Nairobi [Kenya], we found some female graffiti writers and when we came back here', Medy recalled. 'I told our fellow crew member we had to do our idea right now because when we used to train girls but most of them are not from [here, they] were foreigners. So, and, uh, we, as a people, we embrace the culture here. Why don't you go take people from the street and teach them how to be a graffiti writer? So, from there we find a place to start, and it was almost like one month workshop with the girls. And we worked with almost like twelve girls. From there, we taught them how to use can, how to sketch'.[38] In working with an expatriate woman living in Dar who also was a graffiti writer, WCT secured the funds to support implement the project.[39]

Medy further explained why recruiting and training women in graffiti art was so important, revealing to me that 'if you empower women, you create generation to be better'.[40] WCT also links the absence of women practitioners to traditional gender roles. In one Facebook post WCT proclaimed:

> ...If you are an African, grew up here...remember when you came from school as a boy and after meal you will run to play soccer with your friends? While your sister younger than you will be sent to fetch water or collect firewoods [*sic*]? Or how many African women has been deprived [of] education just because they happened to be girls? Cammon [*sic*] man...be

38 Medy interview with author, May 2018.

39 Kalasinga interview with author, May 2018.

40 Ibid.

> honest to your self..Boys in African [*sic*] have more access to MORDEN [*sic*] KNOWLEDGE THAN WOMEN...period![41]

In 2016, a graffiti exhibition was held at a popular bus station, featuring artists of Women Xpress. BBC TV covered the event, which was later posted on the crew's YouTube channel. In this short feature, BBC notes how, in Tanzania, graffiti has gone from 'uchafuzi wa mazingira na uhuni' (pollution and hooliganism) to an artform that has 'imeleta tija kubwa kiuchumi' (i.e., brought greater economic productivity).[42] Women Xpress illustrates the crew's continued commitment to women's empowerment and graffiti professionalization. In adopting a gendered approach to recruitment and training, WCT has sought to provide an avenue through which to challenge women's marginal role in Tanzanian hip hop movement.[43] Moreover, its attempt at increasing women's participation in hip hop graffiti, which is evident in its thematic-oriented pieces combined with its education-based training work, has helped to challenge their own assumptions – not to mention the hip hop community's – concerning gender roles in Tanzanian urban society. What WCT learned over three years doing Women Xpress is that women are excellent students. In contrast to the children and male novice writers in their teens and twenties, young women students have exhibited greater patience in the development and maturation of their technical skills in the graffiti writing.[44]

5 Hip hop graffiti and urban entrepreneurialism

One of the early murals that WCT produced was called 'Hali Mbaya', Kiswahili for 'Hard Times', a wild style piece that sums up what many urban dwellers think about life in the city being a constant struggle. The Dar of the 2000s, the city I have been exposed to, is a city of contrasts. On the one hand, I have seen an explosion of foreign capital investment evidenced in high-rise building constructions, movie theaters, shopping centers and malls, and cosmopolitan restaurants catering to elites, expatriates, tourists, and an emergent middle class. On the other, one can't ignore air pollution, extreme traffic congestion, slums, heroin

41 Wachata Crew Facebook profile, <https://www.facebook.com/wctcrew>, posted on 19 December 2012 (accessed on 7 December 2022).
42 Wachata Crew, 'WomenXpress 2016 (Tanzania)' [Video], <https://youtu.be/p4W4T2-sK7M>, posted on 4 July 2019 (accessed on 7 December 2022).
43 Clark 2014, 144–167.
44 Local Fanatics interview with author, May 2018; Kalasinga interview with author, May 2018.

addiction, chronic unemployment, youth idleness, and rising political violence. I have come to understand the crew's anti-illegal graffiti position and how a potential public, corporate and government backlash would close already limited economic opportunities for commissioned work for graffiti writers.

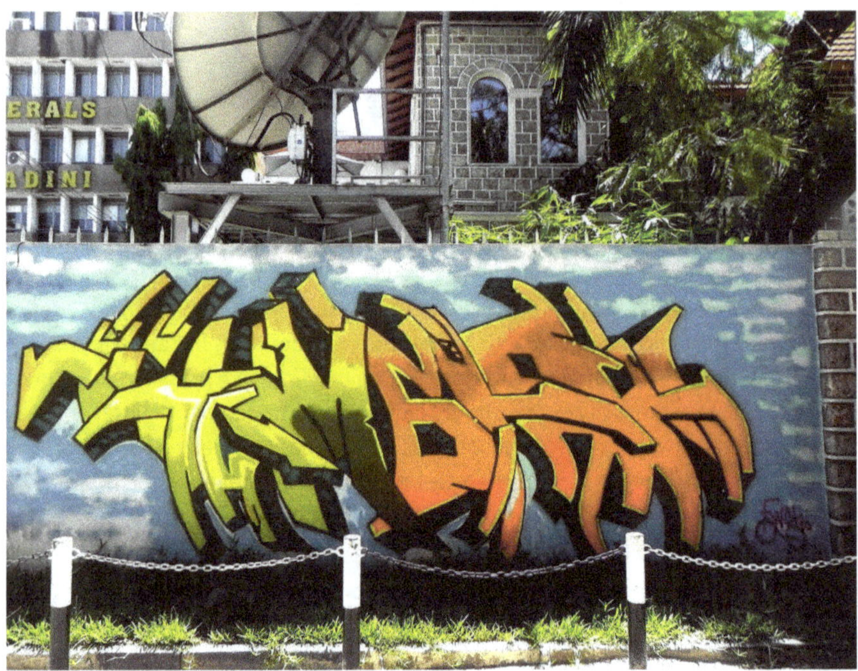

Fig. 6: Wachata Crew graffiti piece 'Hali Mbaya', Dar es Salaam, 2016; photograph © Seth M. Markle.

As the CCM-led government continues to push a neo-liberal discourse of development, WCT artists have taken great strides in professionalizing their work with dreams of making a living from their art. They do this by promoting legal graffiti writing as a profession, over time adopting an approach that revolves around seven core revenue streams. In addition to making money on producing commissioned pieces, they also design, print, and sell their own t-shirts and redesign and sell used sneakers; redesign the interior décor of spaces using acrylic paint, consult for hip hop-themed events, teach graffiti classes, produce graffiti for Tanzanian rap music videos, and produce and sell art on traditional canvas.[45] This is not to say that they don't need to supplement their incomes with other sources of employment outside graffiti. Mejah concentrates a lot of his energy and time on his eco-tourism business. Local Fanatics became a very successful tattoo artist until he got married and felt uncomfortable serving his majority women clientele. Medy, for the past couple of years, is becoming a very talented puppeteer, appearing on local television shows geared towards children. Apart from Mejah, the other three crew members are heavily reliant on their graffiti art skills for their economic well-being.[46]

Mejah is the intellectual force behind transforming WCT into a micro-business enterprise. Using his own capital for the crew's startup funds, he helped the crew become an official Limited Liability Company (LLC) as well as set up a bank account. He currently holds the position of head of marketing while the roles of 'distribution officer', 'head of procurement', and 'senior designer' are occupied by Kalansinga, Medy, and Local Fanatics, respectively.[47] When I asked Local Fanatics what they do with the money made from commissioned work, he stated:

> We have a bank account where we put all the money in there. We also have our merchandise: we sell our own products like t-shirts and sneakers. The money is put into the bank account, but if you do graffiti for Wachata Crew at least you have to get paid. So, some percentage of the money has to go to us and then the rest in the bank...That's how it works.[48]

In 2014, I accompanied WCT to Taweza (Kiswahili for 'we are capable'), a nonprofit organization dedicated to public service advocacy. The crew was paid to redecorate its library. While there, I sat down with a Taweza staff member, an Indo-Tanzanian in his early-to-mid-twenties who went by the name Elamin. He told me that Taweza contracted WCT to 'spice up our work environment' and to 'make us feel like the kinds of things we do in the office and for our visitors who come to the office – to make all of us feel as if there is hope in doing what it is we do'. He went on to talk about how WCT's artwork creates a 'vibe' with its images

---

45 Carol Anande, 'Wachata Crew and Their Debut on Canvas at NafasiArtspace', <http://carolanande.blogspot.com/2014/10/wachata-crew-and-their-debut-on-canvas.html>, posted on 10 October 2014 (accessed on 11 January 2016); Valerie Amani, 'STREET ART: Engaging the Youth in Tanzania's Metropolis', <https://emergentartspace.org/forum/71007/>, posted on 29 July 2019 (accessed on 1 June 2022).

46 For other examples of scholarship on the professionalization of graffiti, see Bowan 1999; Kramer 2010; Lachmann 1988.

47 Nafasi Art Space, 'Wachata Crew', <https://www.nafasiartspace.org/portfolio/wachata-crew/> (accessed 8 July 2020).

48 Local Fanatics interview with author, May 2018.

of faceless characters playing, jumping, and generally having fun. 'So, I think the colors, the images, the scenery, the faceless characters describe that that kind of vibe is not restrictive to any one person, to any one region or any one kind of vision for Tanzania, but it's really about what people want for themselves. And so, I'm very happy that Wachata Crew is doing this'.[49] As an organization made up of young adults in the twenties and thirties, staff members like Elamin grasped the art form's ability to generate excitement and cultivate community.

In turn, WCT is fully aware how hip hop graffiti is so strongly associated with youth and coolness, so much so that the crew has used this stereotypic association to its advantage, resulting in paid contracts from some of the country's biggest and most influential corporations. Currently, due to WCT's efforts, graffiti in Dar is seen as a modern, urban, and stylish form of public art, which has provided the crew with a consistent source of income throughout its short history.

Despite booking multiple paid murals per year, WCT still faces challenges in its efforts to professionalize hip hop graffiti and make an honest living. One challenge is avoiding economic dependency on NGOs, foreign governments, and multinational corporations, the core financiers of hip hop graffiti in the country. Another challenge has to do with perception and exploitation. 'They like graffiti, but they don't want to pay for it', Medy told me toward the end of one interview. For every commissioned work, there are two that don't work out due to disagreements over pay. WCT has held firm to its rates, allowing for, and often initiating, the cancelation of contracts rather than accepting less for its labor. This is not a problem for graffiti artists per se but indicative of how visual artists in general have historically been co-opted and exploited in the country.[50] Every request is one of negotiation, and WCT hopes that advocating for pay equity will influence other graffiti writers in refusing low wage offers for commissioned work.[51]

By being the progenitors of Tanzanian hip hop graffiti, WCT has also become the progenitors of a model of hip hop entrepreneurialism for graffiti writers. However, in being the first and most skilled hip hop graffiti artists, WCT finds itself in a paradoxical situation as a result of having monopolized the industry. This raises concerns, at least for me, about graffiti culture's growth and its role as a source of income for other aspirating writers. Do More Together and East Side Boys are two hip hop graffiti crews that have emerged in the past 5 years only to disband due to a lack of economic opportunities doing graffiti.[52] WCT has recognized this

49 Elamin interview with author, Summer 2013.
50 Makukula 2019, 201–202.
51 Mejah Mbuya interview with author, June 2018.
52 Andrew Munuwa interview with author, June 2018.

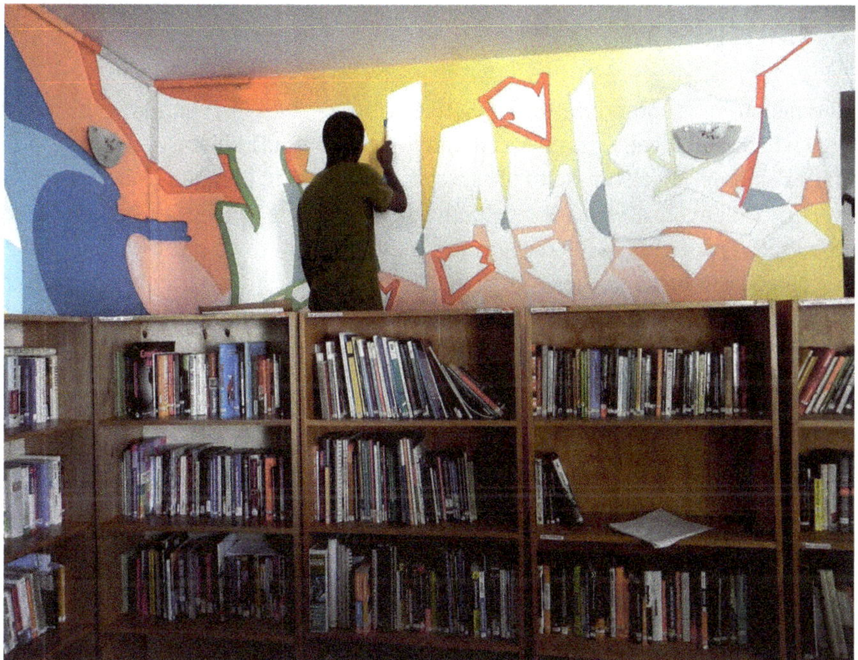

Fig. 7: Wachata Crew commissioned work at Taweza, Dar es Salaam, 2014; photograph © Seth M. Markle.

problem to an extent, but it believes it is the lack of discipline and commitment to honing one's craft that is preventing them from getting paid for their art.[53] Would the crew be as open to training the next generation if a competitor of equal talent and organization started to secure grants and corporate contracts? WCT's attempts at professionalization have yet to show how one can make money from this form of art outside the crew itself. Thus far, it operates at a sub-cultural level that has not expanded the opportunity, having not gone mainstream to the extent that WCT cannot fulfill the demand for commissioned work.

53 Local Fanatics interview with author, May 2018.

6 Conclusion

The debate over intention, over whether 'true' or 'real' hip hop graffiti is that which is done illegally, has informed my study on graffiti history and culture in Dar es Salaam. What I came to observe as I traversed in and out of the scene between 2003 and 2018 was an attempt by artists to create a localized version of hip hop graffiti, one that gives recognition to its criminal roots but by no means is beholden to it. From its inception to its current manifestation, hip hop graffiti in Dar has undergone an urban-based localization process through which it has become a legitimate pursuit of economic employment, of creative expression, of pleasure, and of socio-political discourse.

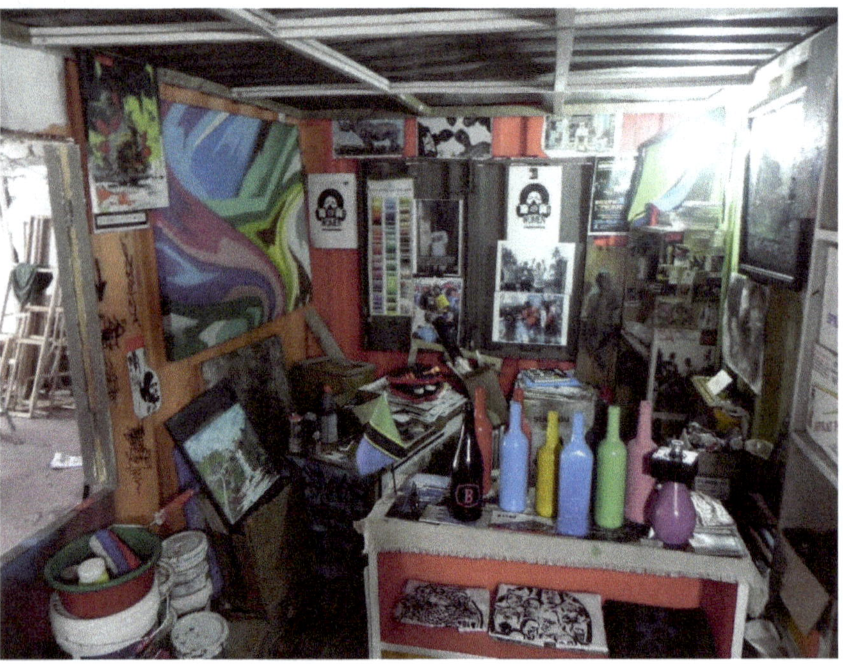

Fig. 8: Wachata Crew Studio, Nafasi Art Space, Dar es Salaam, 2018; photograph © Seth M. Markle.

As the first crew of its kind in the city, WCT embraces its role as hip hop pioneers and gatekeepers. The respect it has accrued has positioned the crew as an authority in defining what constitutes hip hop and hip hop graffiti in the country. To ensure its positive reception as well as one's economic needs being met, WCT partners with NGOs and uses arts education to prevent or contain the proliferation of illegal writing to the extent that hip hop graffiti in the city is publicly acceptable. Its decision to move away from illicit graffiti writing stems from an acute understanding of their own socio-economic realities. WCT has crafted a hip hop identity cultivated through a commitment to professionalizing and legitimizing hip hop graffiti and building a unified hip hop movement in the process. It has trained, and continues to train, the next generation of writers, particularly young women, while also pursuing self-employment opportunities. These activities are indicative of a hip hop ethics of cultural responsibility that seeks to preserve and promote hip hop as a positive and empowering culture.

In this essay, I have tried to put forth a complex portrait of the benefits and dilemmas of creating a localized graffiti art movement and of the meanings and experiences of hip hop for a crew of Tanzanian graffiti practitioners in Dar es Salaam. I have observed WCT evolve as a collective that uses graffiti to narrate stories, teach 'the people', and make a living. Its hardened oppositional stance to illegal graffiti in Tanzania signifies an engagement in a type of hip hop theorizing that refuses to conform to a purist definition of the practice but rather seeks to legitimize a careerist-oriented approach.

Acknowledgements

Asanteni sana [Thank you very much] to Mejah, Medy, Kalasinga and Local Fanatics of Wachata Crew, for bringing me into their lives and sharing with me their stories. A special thanks must also go to Cody Maldonado and Mikey Bankston (R.I.P.), two undergraduate students who assisted me in aspects of this research.

References

Interviews with author

Elamin (Taweza), Summer 2013.
Kalasinga, August 2011.
Kalasinga, April 2016.
Kalasinga, May 2018.
KBC interview, June 2018.
Local Fanatics, May 2018.
Mbuya, Mejah, June 2012.
Mbuya, Mejah, June 2018.

Medy, August 2011.
Medy, April 2016.
Medy, May 2018.
Mizani, June 2011.
Mponjika, Zavara, July 2011.
Munuwa, Andrew, June 2018.

Secondary sources

Abdelmagid, Yakein (2013), 'The Emergence of the Mona Lisa Battalions: Graffiti Art Networks in Post-2011 Egypt', *Review of Middle East Studies*, 47/2: 172–182.

Alim, H. Samy, John Baugh and Mary Bucholtz (2011), 'Global Ill-Literacies: Hip Hop Cultures, Youth Identities, and the Politics of Literacy', *Review of Research in Education*, 35: 120–146.

Benavides-Vanegas, Farid Samir (2005), 'From Santander to Camillo and Che: Graffiti Resistance in Contemporary Colombia', *Social Justice*, 32/1: 53–61.

Campos, Ricardo (2015), 'Youth, Graffiti, and the Aestheticization of Transgression', *Social Analysis: The International Journal of Anthropology*, 59/3: 17–40.

Casco, Jose Arturo Saavedra (2006), 'The Language of the Young People: Rap, Urban Culture and Protest in Tanzania', *Journal of Asian and African Studies*, 41/3: 229–248.

Chang, Jeff (2005), *Can't Stop Won't Stop: A History of the Hip Hop Generation*, New York: Picador.

Clark, Msia Kibona and Mickie Mwanzia Koster (eds), *Hip Hop and Social Change in Africa: Ni Wakati*, Lanham: Lexington Books.

Clark, Msia Kibona (2014), 'Gender Representations among Tanzanian Female Emcees', in Clark and Koster 2014, 144–167.

Clark, Msia Kibona (2018), *Hip-Hip in Africa: Prophets of the City and Dustyfoot Philosophers*, Athens: Ohio University Press.

Docuyanan, Faye (2000), 'Governing Graffiti in Contested Urban Spaces', *Political and Legal Anthropology Review*, 23/1: 103–121.

Englert, Birgit (2008), 'Ambiguous Relationships: Youth, Popular Music and Politics in Contemporary Tanzania', *Wiener Zeitschrift für kritische Afrikastudien*, 8: 71–96.

Fast, Danya and Eileen Moyer (2018), 'Becoming and Coming Undone on the Streets of Dar es Salaam', *Africa Today*, 64/3: 3–26.

Gauthier, Louise (2001), 'Confessions of an Ethnographer: Reflections on Fieldwork with Graffiti Writers in Montreal', *Anthropologica*, 43/2: 273–276.

Gesthuizen, Thomas and Peter-Jan Haas (2000), 'Ndani ya Bongo: Kiswahili Rap Keeping it Real', in Frank Gunderson and Gregory Barz (eds), *Mashindano! Competitive Music Performance in East Africa*, Dar es Salaam: Mkuki na Nyota, 279–294.

Gosa, Travis L. (2015), 'The Fifth Element: Knowledge', in Justin A. Williams (ed.), *The Cambridge Companion to Hip-Hop*, Cambridge: Cambridge University Press, 56–70.

Gross, Daniel D., Barbara Walkosz and Timothy D. Gross (1997), 'Language Boundaries and Discourse Stability: "Tagging" as a Form of Graffiti Spanning International Borders', *ETC: A Review of General Semantics*, 54/3: 275–285.

Heinsohn, Bastian (2015), 'Critical Voices from the Underground: Street Art and Urban Transformation in Berlin', in Jill E. Twark and Axel Hildebrandt (eds), *Envisioning Social Justice in Contemporary German Culture*, Woodbridge: Boydell and Brewer, 119–141.

Holt, Kevin C. (2019), 'Emcee Ethnographies: A Brief Sketch of U.S. Hip-Hop Ethnography', *Current Musicology*, 105: 6–20 <https://doi.org/10.7916/cm.v0i105.5400>.

Human Rights Watch (2020), *World Report 2020: Events of 2019*, New York: Seven Stories Press.

Jaffe, Rivke, Kevon Rhiney and Cavell Francis (2012), '"Throw Word": Graffiti, Space and Power in Kingston, Jamaica', *Caribbean Quarterly*, 58/1: 1–20.

Kramer, Ronald (2010), 'Painting with Permission: Legal Graffiti in New York City', *Ethnography*, 11/2: 235–253.

Lachmann, Richard (1988), 'Graffiti as Career and Ideology', *American Journal of Sociology*, 94/1: 229–250.

Lee, Jooyoung (2009), 'Open Mic: Professionalizing the Rap Career', *Ethnography*, 10/4: 475–495.

Makukula, Dominicus Z. (2019), *The Development of Visual Arts in Tanzania from 1961 to 2015: A Focus on the National Cultural Policy and Institutions' Influences*, PhD thesis, Freie Universität Berlin.

Mbuya, Mejah (2014), 'Tanzanian MCs vs. Social Discourse', in Clark and Koster 2014, 174–177.

Moreau, Terri and Derek H. Alderman (2011), 'Graffiti Hurts and the Eradication of Alternative Landscape Expression', *Geographical Review*, 101/1: 106–124.

Moyer, Eileen (2005), 'Street-Corner Justice in the Name of Jah: Imperatives of Peace among Dar es Salaam Street Youth', *Africa Today*, 51/3: 31–58.

Munsell, Liz and Greg Tate (eds) (2020), *Writing the Future: Basquiat and the Hip-Hop Generation*, Boston: Museum of Fine Arts.

Perullo, Alex (2011), *Live from Dar es Salaam: Popular Music and Tanzania's Music Economy*, Bloomington: Indiana University.

Remes, Pieter (1999), 'Global Popular Music and Changing Awareness of Urban Tanzanian Youth', *Yearbook for Traditional Music*, 31: 1–26.

Rose, Tricia (1994), *Black Noise: Rap Music and Black Culture in Contemporary America*, Hanover: University Press of New England.

Schacter, Rafael (2019), 'From Pollution to Purity: The Transformation of Graffiti and Street Art in London (2005–17)', in Christopher Tilley (ed.), *London's Urban Landscape: Another Way of Telling*, London: UCL Press, 403–425.

Snoekx, Kurt, (2021), 'Graffiti Legend Kool Koor Turns the Tables on History', *Bruzz*, posted on 24 May 2021, <https://www.bruzz.be/en/culture/art-books/graffiti-legend-kool-koor-turns-tables-history-2021-02-24> (accessed on 7 December 2022).

Stroeken, Koen (2005), 'Immunizing Strategies: Hip-Hop and Critique in Tanzania', *Africa: Journal of the International African Institute*, 75/4: 488–509.

America

Jarosław Źrałka

Incised Images among the Palaces and Temples: The Content and Meaning of Pre-Columbian Maya Graffiti

Abstract: The pre-Columbian Maya civilisation flourished in the jungles of Central America, where many monumental centres developed with examples of sophisticated architectural complexes, such as pyramids, temples, palaces and ball courts. The interiors of some of these buildings were inscribed or painted with depictions that escape the canons of classic Maya art and are usually described as 'graffiti'. Maya graffiti constitute one of the most fascinating but still poorly studied aspects of pre-Columbian art. This chapter deals with several different aspects of pre-Columbian Maya graffiti, such as their architectural and archaeological contexts, dating and meaning. We will also elaborate on the subject of an exact definition of graffiti in the scientific discourse of Maya and Mesoamerican studies. As we will demonstrate, the style and content of graffiti are highly complex and may reflect different authors and diverse motivations behind their creation. This contribution will also deal with the iconographic diversity of the ancient Maya graffiti corpus, pointing out differences and similarities to graffiti from other pre-industrial societies.

1 Introduction

The pre-Columbian Maya civilisation flourished in an area now covered by southeastern Mexico, Guatemala, Belize, western Honduras and El Salvador, which encompasses about 324,000 km². The pre-Hispanic history of the Maya is divided into three major periods: Preclassic (2000 BCE–250 CE), Classic (250–950 CE) and Postclassic (950–1521 CE). The apogee of the Maya civilisation is the Classic period, when many cities flourished in this area, ruled by kings holding the prestigious title of *k'uhul ajaw* or 'divine lord'. The most powerful Maya kingdoms of the Classic period were Tikal (in present-day Guatemala) and *Kaanul* or the Snake kingdom, with capitals first in Dzibanche and then in Calakmul (in present-day

https://doi.org/10.1515/9783111326306-004

Mexico).[1] It is the Classic period when the most outstanding examples of Maya architecture and art were created. Most of the Maya graffiti documented so far can also be attributed to the Classic period and they prevail in a region denominated the Maya Lowlands.

Graffiti in the Maya area encompass all representations (incised, painted or prepared with other techniques) that appear on buildings, specifically on their plaster surfaces, but are not part of the original design or architectural context of these structures. Incising was the main technique for creating graffiti, however, they could also be made with other techniques, such as painting, gouging, printing or sketching with charcoal. These representations are further characterized by poor artistic quality when compared to official Maya art known from courtly or royal contexts.[2] As such, graffiti are secondary additions that were not part of the original programme or original artistic and architectural vision at the time of the construction of the buildings where they are documented.[3] Thus, I adopt a broad definition of graffiti that is formed mainly on a qualitative and technological basis, in a manner similar to other Mediterranean researchers who argue that graffiti should encompass both images and texts rendered in places or on portable objects which were not intended to carry such depictions[4] (also see the discussion below).

In this chapter, I would like to discuss various topics related to the theme of Maya graffiti, such as the techniques of their rendition, iconography, dating, stylistic variability and authorship. Before delving into that, however, I will focus on a short presentation of the history of research on Maya graffiti, to show how views about this type of *unofficial* art have evolved and the current state of research. I will also try to present the most up-to-date interpretations of the function and meaning of Maya graffiti and show both the common features and differences between Maya graffiti and graffiti of other ancient cultures.

2 History of investigations into Maya graffiti

The subject of graffiti has been marginalised and ignored in Maya studies for many decades. If we look at the opinions of the first scholars studying pre-Columbian Maya ruins, we will see that graffiti were, in most cases, interpreted as the

1 Martin and Grube 2008; Martin 2020.

2 See, e.g., Coe and Kerr 1997; Miller and Martin 2004.

3 Źrałka 2014b, 50–51.

4 See, e.g., Langner 2001; Baird 2011, 50–52; Chaniotis 2011, 196.

work of young pre-Columbian vandals, pre-Columbian or colonial visitors who were not contemporaneous with the occupation of the city, 'bored or inattentive novices', squatters or even childish scribbles or doodles.[5] Nevertheless, there were also those among the early researchers who associated graffiti with the original inhabitants of pre-Columbian buildings.[6]

A new epoch in studying Maya graffiti starts with the investigations of the Tikal Project carried out in one of the most majestic and monumental pre-Hispanic Maya cities of Central America, located in today's northern Guatemala. This project was conducted between 1956 and 1970 by the University of Pennsylvania Museum. During this research, the first systematic documentation of all graffiti was undertaken and the first (and, as yet, the only) monograph fully devoted to the subject of Maya graffiti for a single Maya site was published.[7] This was largely due to Helen Trik (née Webster) and Michael Kampen, the two researchers who were in charge of documenting hundreds of Tikal graffiti located in the monumental core of this ruined city. However, what is interesting and merits attention is that Webster and Kampen had different views on interpreting Tikal graffiti. For Webster, graffiti were contemporaneous to the growth of the city and had been made by the original inhabitants of Tikal.[8] She distinguished some descriptive drawings among the Tikal graffiti which were related to the lives of the elites, and depictions that were supposed to be offered to deities in the expectation of healing from diseases and other favours in return. Kampen, on the other hand, saw in graffiti acts of desecration of abandoned structures.[9] In 1995, William Haviland and Anita de Laguna Haviland, who were also members of the UPENN Museum Tikal Project, came up with a very different and controversial model according to which most graffiti from Tikal had been made during altered states of consciousness.[10] Their work was influenced by studies by David Lewis-Williams and Thomas Dowson relating most Palaeolithic cave paintings to shamanistic rituals and visions.[11]

In 1999 George Andrews – who studied pre-Columbian Maya architecture for several decades – proposed in his important and influential work entitled *Architectural Graffiti and the Maya Elite* that Maya graffiti can be interpreted as a kind

5 Thompson 1898; Tozzer 1913, 160; Gann 1918, 95; Gann 1924, 247; Thompson 1954; and Thompson 1966, 10–11.
6 Maler 1911, 56–61; also see Ruppert and Denison 1943, 36.
7 Trik and Kampen 1983.
8 Webster 1963.
9 Kampen 1978.
10 Haviland and Haviland 1995.
11 Lewis-Williams and Dowson 1988.

of popular art which was created by members of Maya elites occupying structures within which these images were documented. Andrews proposed that graffiti document important places, objects, people and events in the life of local elites.[12] This view was further developed and supported by investigations at Nakum in Guatemala, where many examples of graffiti were recorded between 1999 and 2001 by Bernard Hermes, Justyna Olko and myself.[13] We found that simple models relating Maya graffiti with one specific period or one-directional interpretation do not reflect the complex chronological, thematic and architectural diversity of graffiti. Our research showed that most Nakum graffiti can be associated with Classic period people living in (or visiting) structures where these works are found. Hence, most graffiti are contemporaneous with the occupation and development of this and most other Maya centres where they were documented. However, there are also depictions that can be situated in a post-abandonment period based on their style and stratigraphic or architectural context.[14]

The beginning of the twenty-first century saw a growing interest in Maya graffiti as more and more examples of this kind of art were being discovered at different Maya sites. A group of scholars from Valencia organised an important conference (*I Workshop Internacional de grafitos prehispánicos: los grafitos mayas*) in 2008 which was fully devoted to this topic. Consequently, a whole volume on Maya graffiti was published presenting examples from many different sites and leading the study of this subject along a new path.[15] One of the outcomes of this scientific event was also a creation of the so-called Maya Graffiti International Database, accessible online at http://grafitos.artemaya.es/. This database contains graffiti recorded at many Maya sites and, as such, constitutes a very useful resource for both scholars and laypersons.

Recent years have witnessed a further interest in this subject, which resulted in the publication of both short articles or reports on newly discovered and previously known graffiti,[16] a book wholly devoted to this topic and written by the author of this chapter,[17] and a doctoral dissertation defended by Núria Feliu at the University of Valencia.[18] This vast group of publications includes an

12 Andrews 1999.

13 Hermes, Olko and Źrałka 2001 and 2002.

14 Hermes, Olko and Źrałka 2001 and 2002; Źrałka and Hermes 2009.

15 Vidal Lorenzo and Muñoz Cosme, 2009.

16 Patrois 2013; Kováč 2014; Mayer 2014; Źrałka 2014b; Navarro-Castillo, Sheseña and Pincemin 2017; McCurdy, Brown and Dixon 2018; Olton 2018; Watkins et al. 2020; also see Callaghan et al. 2017; Tokovinine and Fialko 2019.

17 Źrałka 2014a.

18 Feliu 2019.

interesting article by Leah McCurdy, Kathryn Brown and Neil Dixon,[19] who studied a collection of graffiti from a palace room in the El Castillo complex at Xunantunich (Belize). They proposed that these graffiti might have been the result of training and teaching novice scribes. However, as demonstrated by Rosamund Fitzmaurice, Tia Watkins and Jamie Awe,[20] it is hard to believe that the scribes would practice on stucco plaster instead of the materials Maya scribes usually worked on, such as bark paper, stone, ceramics (painting) or others (e.g. bone, shell). These are media that were popularly employed by Maya and other Mesoamerican artists during pre-Hispanic times.[21] In addition, there are sites (Rio Bec or Nakum) which feature many examples of graffiti but very few or no official art, such as carved monuments.

Finally, a seminar on ancient, medieval and modern graffiti was organised by Rosamund Fitzmaurice, Tia Watkins and Ioannis Nakas at the Institute of Archaeology, University College London, in March 2019. The papers from the conference were then published in the UCL 'Papers from the Institute of Archaeology' (2021). This volume contains two chapters on pre-Columbian Maya graffiti[22] and presents important new data concerning the subject.

3 Techniques and locations

The definition of Maya graffiti is based largely on their archaeological and architectural context and the technology of their rendition. Hence, it is worth devoting some space at this point to the subject of techniques used to produce this type of art.

Incising is a predominant technique of execution of Maya graffiti (Fig. 1a). More than 90 % of all graffiti were created via this technique. Some tests of experimental archaeology[23] indicate that incised graffiti must have been rendered mostly with sharp stone tools, such as a chert, or obsidian implements with which graffitists would make incisions into the stucco surface of masonry structures. Other techniques of rendering graffiti include gouging, which involved removing large parts of stucco from walls in order to create contours of the representations desired (Fig. 1b). The next category are the so-called punctate graffiti

19 McCurdy, Brown and Dixon 2018.
20 Fitzmaurice, Watkins and Awe 2021, 68.
21 Coe and Kerr 1997.
22 Fitzmaurice, Watkins and Awe 2021; Helmke and Źrałka 2021.
23 Carrascosa, Pérez and Mora 2009.

formed by round, shallow holes perforated into the surface of walls by drilling and/or chipping stucco (Fig. 1c–d). They almost always form geometric designs. Some of these representations may be related to counting or calendrical and astronomical notations.

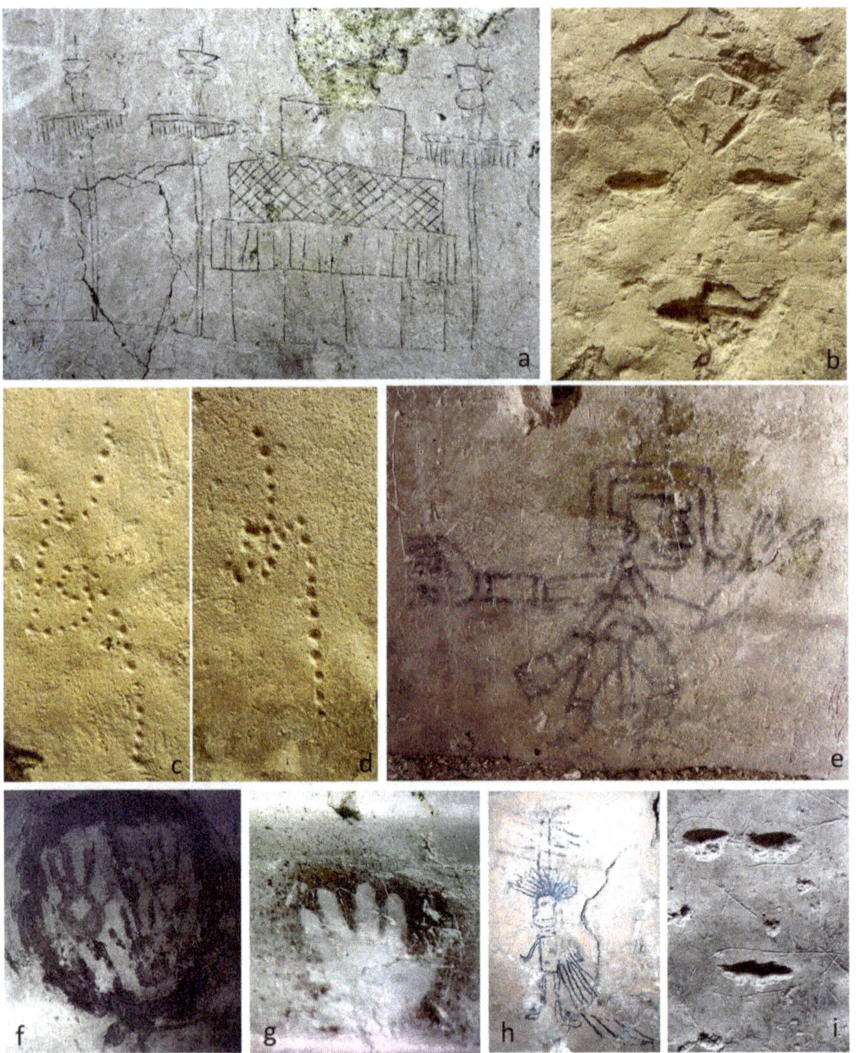

Fig. 1: Photographs representing different techniques of making Maya graffiti: a) incision; b) gouging; c-d) punctate graffiti; e) painting; f) printing (positive); g) printing (negative); h) graffiti made with charcoal, and i) composite technique (gouging and incision).

Another group is painted graffiti (Fig. 1e). Most of these were created with black paint, but there are also examples painted with green, red and even representations made with the use of several colours (polychrome graffiti). The latter have been recently documented in La Blanca and El Chilonche by a team of Spanish scholars.[24] It should be stressed that some researchers[25] did not categorise such depictions as graffiti but classified them as 'painted designs'. In my opinion, however, painting should be considered as one of the techniques of graffiti (as is the case in other ancient cultures[26]). It is the architectural context that should be treated as the main factor determining whether a given representation should be classified as graffiti or not. Thus, graffiti should include representations made in various techniques (including incising, painting and gouging) that do not belong to the original decoration and context of a given building but are secondary additions. A similar discussion concerns representations that were imprinted (they were usually made with utilising paint impressed on the surface of walls with human palms) since some Mayanists do not consider such depictions as graffiti. Nevertheless, the context of these depictions prompts us to consider them as graffiti too. Imprinted graffiti can be further divided into two subcategories: positive and negative prints. Positive prints were produced by the application of paint to the palm and imprinting them on a plaster surface (Fig. 1f). Negative prints, on the other hand, are human hands outlined by paint on a stucco surface (Fig. 1g).

We should also mention that some Maya graffiti were made with charcoal (these are known from at least four Maya sites) (Fig. 1h). Finally, we can also distinguish composite graffiti[27] made via more than one technique (usually incision and gouging) (Fig. 1i).

Summing up, we can argue that the main elements that define Maya graffiti are their architectural context (graffiti are defined as secondary additions to various architectural features) and the technique of execution (graffiti in the Maya area are mainly depictions incised on walls but could also be made with other techniques described above). Moreover, as I have already mentioned, graffiti are also characterized by a low-quality style of rendition when compared to examples of official art known from the Maya civilization.

As far as the spatial and architectural context of Maya graffiti is concerned, most of them were recorded in palaces or residential structures inhabited by members of elite families. Palace buildings are usually multiroom constructions

24 Feliu 2019.

25 See, e.g., Orrego and Larios 1983, 93–94; Mayer, 1998 and 2009.

26 See Peden 2001; Baird 2011; Baird and Taylor 2011a, 3; Źrałka 2014b.

27 See Kampen 1978; Źrałka 2014a, 93–94.

which bear masonry benches used by the original inhabitants as places to sleep and sit within their interiors. Nevertheless, a third of the graffiti also figure inside temple buildings, which are most often located on pyramidal platforms. Graffiti usually appear on stucco coatings covering interior walls of structures, between 0.5 and 1.60/1.70 metres above the floor, i.e. at the height most appropriate for people creating this type of art who worked in a sitting or standing position. Graffiti were also rendered on doorway jambs, benches (on both their sides and tops) and floors. Bench tops and floors usually have representations of boards representing a very famous Mesoamerican game of chance called *patolli* (see below) since these were very suitable places for playing this game.[28] Areas situated close to benches at Nakum and many other Maya sites usually have the largest concentration of graffiti because benches were places where people spent a lot of time.

4 Thematic content

The study of the Maya graffiti iconography is a very important issue since it can help us to determine the authorship and motivations behind their creation. The iconographic content of Maya graffiti is very rich. Apart from many individual representations, it also includes more complex scenes that can be described as narrative and usually involve a group of people who could be shown close to architectural buildings and/or participating in complex activities. These narrative scenes capture the most important events of a socio-political and social character, such as ceremonies, parades, human sacrifices and martial scenes.

All known Maya graffiti can generally be ascribed to at least 14 categories (see Fig. 2), the most popular of which are representations of people, animals, geometric designs, handprints, representations of architectural buildings, followed by depictions of deities, sexual symbols and other unidentified elements.[29]

Representations of people constitute the largest group of the graffiti corpus. Apart from simple silhouettes, this group also contains depictions of richly attired members of Maya elites, including presumed depictions of kings or elites who carry important emblems of power or are shown sitting on thrones or being carried on elaborate palanquins (Figs 3, 10 and 12m). There are also depictions of

28 Źrałka 2014a, 179–184.
29 See Źrałka 2014a.

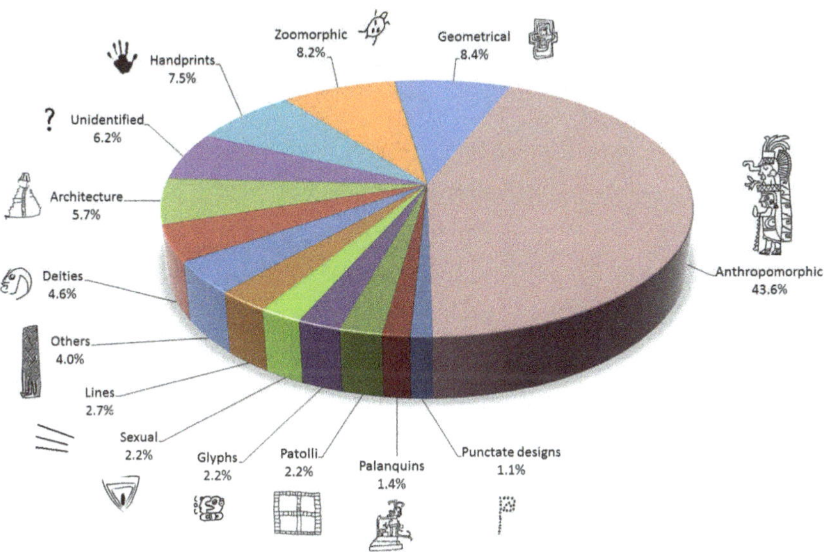

Fig. 2: Percentual content of different categories of Maya graffiti.

warriors equipped with typical Maya weaponry (spears and shields) and musicians playing different instruments, mostly trumpets or rattles (Fig. 3i-t). There are also depictions of captives, some of which form complex scenes in which the prisoners are shown in scenes of torture or sacrifice. An interesting collection of graffiti representing individual captives or as part of more complex scenes come from one set of buildings in Tikal: Group G (Structures 5E-58 and 5E-55). Here we can see a group of captives sitting one after the other, with their hands tied and lips pierced (?) (Fig. 4a). The same constructions also bear depictions of a person tied to a pole and butchered (Fig. 4b) as well as an individual stretched over a sacrificial stone with his chest opened after a heart removal[30] (Fig. 4d). The authors of some of these graffiti might have witnessed these terrifying scenes as they were able to reproduce many details of sacrifices including the terrible pain visible on the faces of the prisoners and torture victims. It can be assumed that these scenes could have taken place in close proximity to the building complex described in Tikal. The presence of such scenes among graffiti may indicate that their creators wanted to commemorate moments and events that were particularly memorable to them and the local community.

30 Orrego and Larios 1983; Źrałka 2014a, Plate 9.

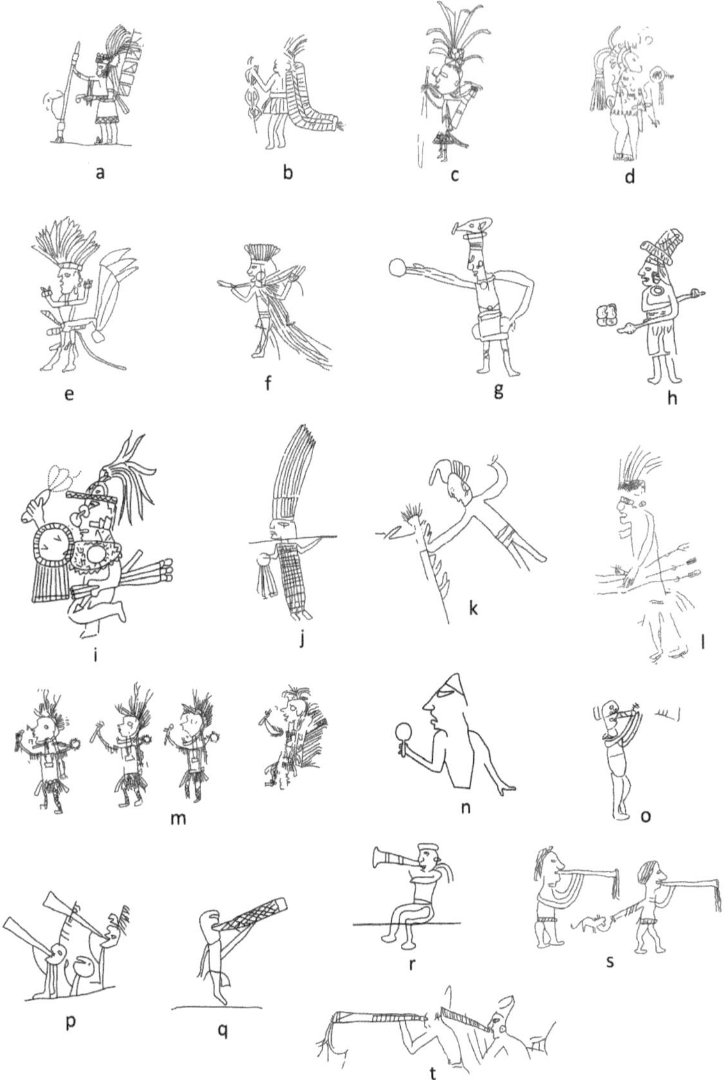

Fig. 3: Anthropomorphic graffiti from different Maya sites; note the depictions of richly attired individuals (a-f), a ballplayer (g), warriors (i-l) and musicians playing trumpets and rattles (m-t); a) Tikal, Structure 5D-43; b) Tikal, Temple VI; c) Tikal, Structure 5D-43; d) Tikal, Structure 3D-40; e) Tikal, Temple II; f) Tikal, Temple VI; g) Tikal, Maler's Palace; h) Tikal, Maler's Palace; i) Santa Rosa Xtampak, Palace; j) Chichen Itza, Palacio de los Falos; k) Nakum, Structure Y; l) La Sufricaya, Structure 1; m) Kakab, Structure 1; n) Tz'ibatnah, Casa de las Pinturas; o) Dzibanche, Small Acropolis, Building I; p) Río Bec V, Structure IV; q) Río Bec A, Structure 5N2; r) Río Bec B, Structure 6N1; s) Tikal, Structure 5D-52-1; and t) Nakum, Structure A.

Many of the representations of human beings from the graffiti corpus are very similar in composition to depictions known from 'official' art, especially from polychrome Maya ceramics that frequently feature court scenes involving elites receiving visitors and drinking prestigious beverages; Maya ceramics also depict dignitaries participating in processions or parades involving captives or focused on ritual activities. Thus, we may surmise that the authors of many of the narratives described above participated in scenes immortalized in the form of graffiti, especially if we consider that these depictions were rendered inside palaces or sacred buildings located in the central part of many Maya centres which staged the most important events involving many religious and socio-political activities, including the exposure, torture and sacrifice of captives.

Representations of animals are also very popular among Maya graffiti. However, the exact identification of animal species is difficult in many cases due to the simplicity of their representation. Nevertheless, we can see that the most popular groups of animals depicted are birds, snakes and felines – in other words – powerful animals that are also frequently seen in official art or which played an important role in the daily and religious life of the Maya people. Some depictions classified as animals may also represent deities. This is especially the case with representations of at least some snakes that are shown floating and bearing feathers (in the latter case, they may represent a very famous Mesoamerican deity: a feathered serpent) (Fig. 5). One beautiful scene from Nakum merits special attention: it features a group of birds catching fish (see Fig. 6).

Representations of architecture form another important category of Maya graffiti. In fact, most representations of architectural buildings in Maya art come from the corpus of graffiti since official Maya art is almost devoid of scenes of buildings. Architectural constructions that we find among graffiti include both large multi-terraced pyramids (which are especially well-known from the largest Maya centres where true examples of such architectural constructions exist [Tikal, Yaxha, Nakum, Chicanna, Chichen Itza]), as well as simple buildings, many of which depict structures made of perishable materials with very high, pointed roofs covered by leaves (Fig. 7). Consequently, the graffiti corpus permits us to see what perishable architecture looked like or the decorations of some buildings. We can also find an interesting graffiti at Tikal featuring a ball court consisting of two parallel structures with sloping walls. The scene depicts the actual game taking place in the middle of the court with several players involved (Fig. 7k).[31] Palanquins constitute the next important group that can be distinguished in the graffiti corpus. Apart from simple palanquins that are depicted empty or with dignitaries

31 Trik and Kampen 1983, Fig. 46.

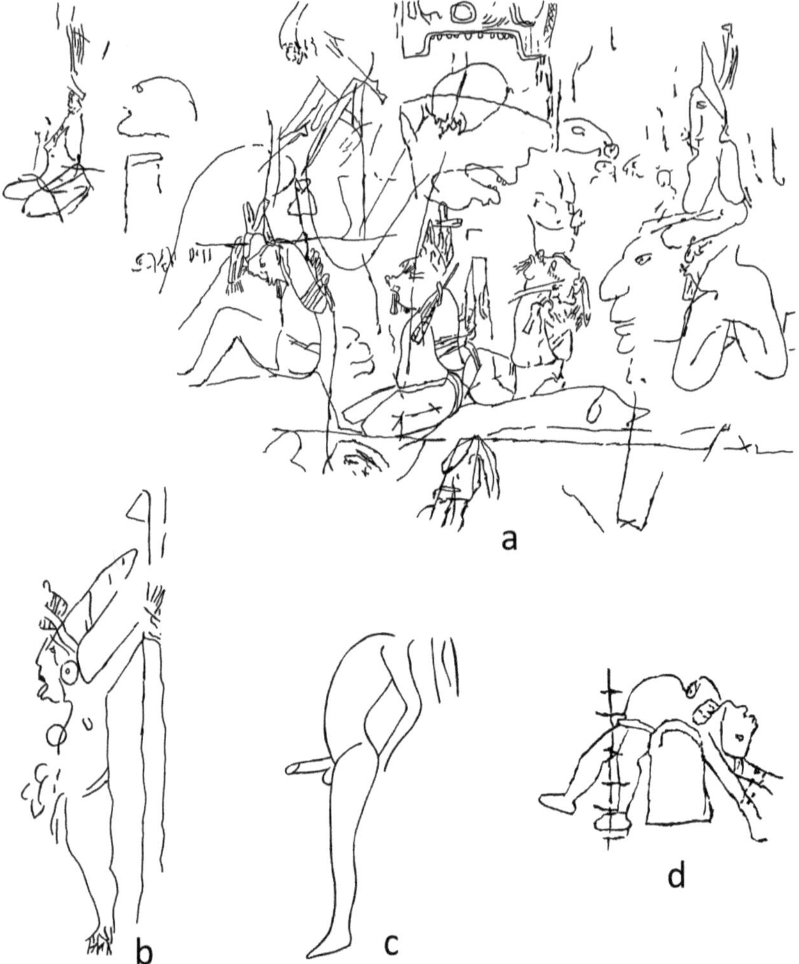

Fig. 4: Representations of tortured or sacrificed captives from Tikal, a) Structure 5E-58; b) Structure 5E-55-2; c) Structure 5E-58; and d) Structure 5E-58; all graffiti are incised.

sitting inside, there are also elaborate palanquins with effigies of patron deities (Fig. 8a-b).[32] Such objects are shown to have been carried by the Maya to battle fields and constituted desirable trophies during the conflicts. Kings might have been taken to the battlefields riding such palanquins.[33] Since these objects have

32 Źrałka 2014a, 127–128; Olton 2018.
33 Martin 2020, 168.

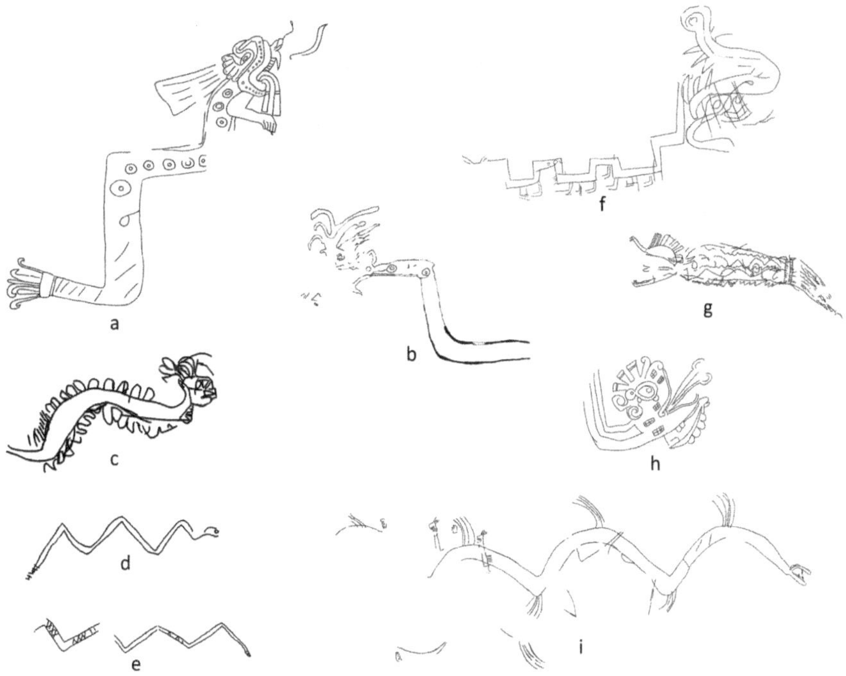

Fig. 5: Representations of snakes, feathered serpents and reptile-like creatures, a-b) Nakum Structure E; c) Tikal Structure 3D-40; d-e) Tikal, Structure 5D-52-1; f) Nakum Structure W; g) Nakum Structure 61-1; h) Chichen Itza Structure 2D1; and i) Nakum Structure W.

not survived, it can be assumed that they were made of perishable materials, such as wood, paper and textiles. The seizure of palanquins with images of gods by the enemy party meant great success for the victor and humiliation for the loser, whose patron deities were symbolically captured.[34] The largest collection of such palanquins rendered in the form of graffiti is known from Tikal, where similar objects were also represented in official art as trophies taken after the conflict with three enemy centres with which Tikal waged wars: Calakmul, El Peru and Naranjo. The trophy palanquins were shown on wooden lintels installed in the giant Temples I and IV of Tikal.[35]

34 Martin 1996; Martin and Grube 2008, 44–45; Źrałka 2014a, 127–128, Plates 38 and 3.
35 Jones 1987; Martin 2020, 166–172.

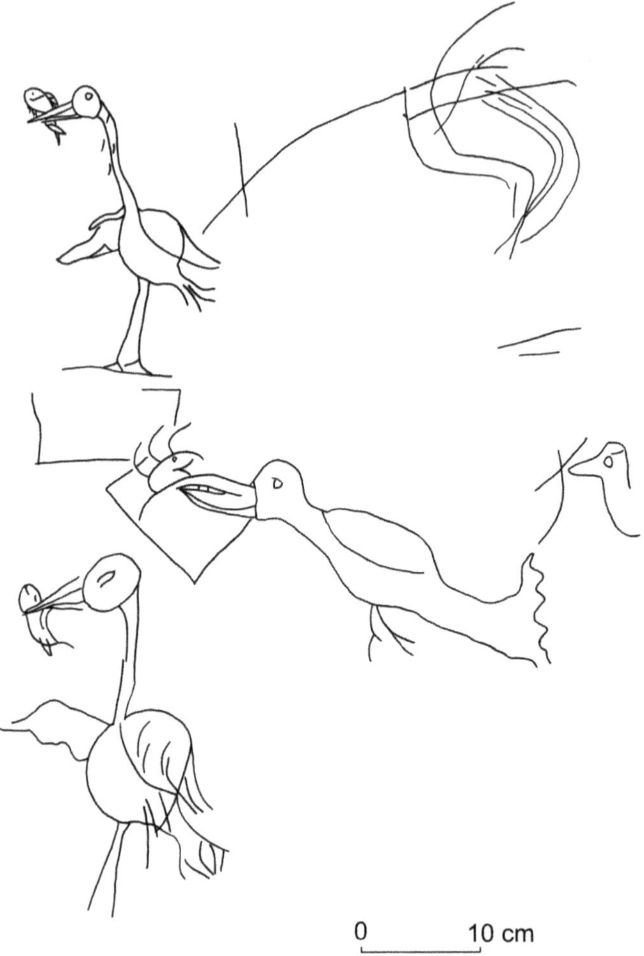

Fig. 6: Graffiti featuring birds catching fish from Nakum Structure D.

Representations of deities constitute about 4.6 % of the whole graffiti corpus and usually feature the most important supernatural beings of the Maya pantheon, such as the sun deity, Chahk (the god of rain) or the maize god (Fig. 8c-j). The latter deity is typically rendered as a young male shown in a dancing position (see Fig. 8i-j). There is also a group of representations that depict human beings with fantastic features that can be classified as supernatural beings. Their exact identification is difficult in many cases due to the simplicity of representation or state of preservation.

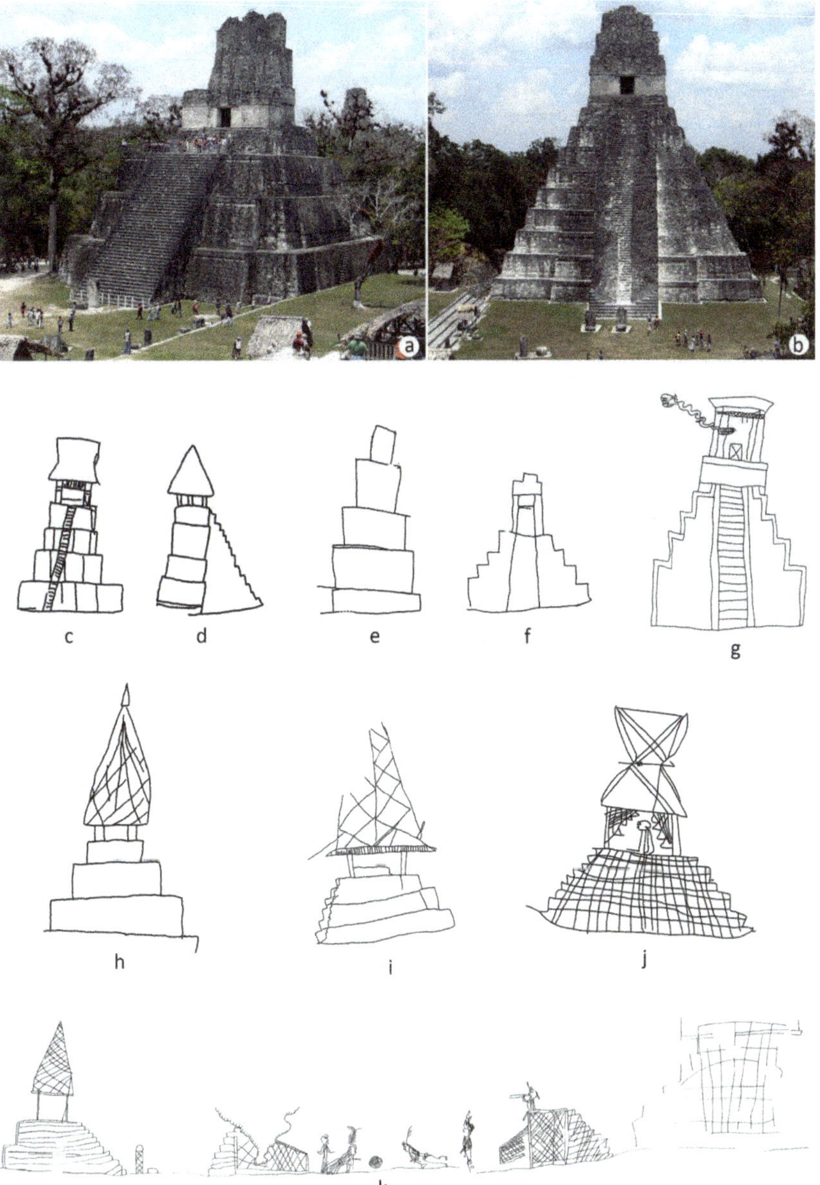

Fig. 7: Representations of various architectural buildings in the corpus of Maya graffiti, a-b) large pyramidal temples from Tikal (Temples II and I); c-g) graffiti featuring pyramidal temples documented at Tikal (c-f come from Temple II); h-j) platforms topped by buildings with roofs made of perishable materials (h – Tikal, Temple II; i – Nakum Structure G; j – Rio Bec V, Structure IV); and k) ball court scene from Tikal Structure 5D-43.

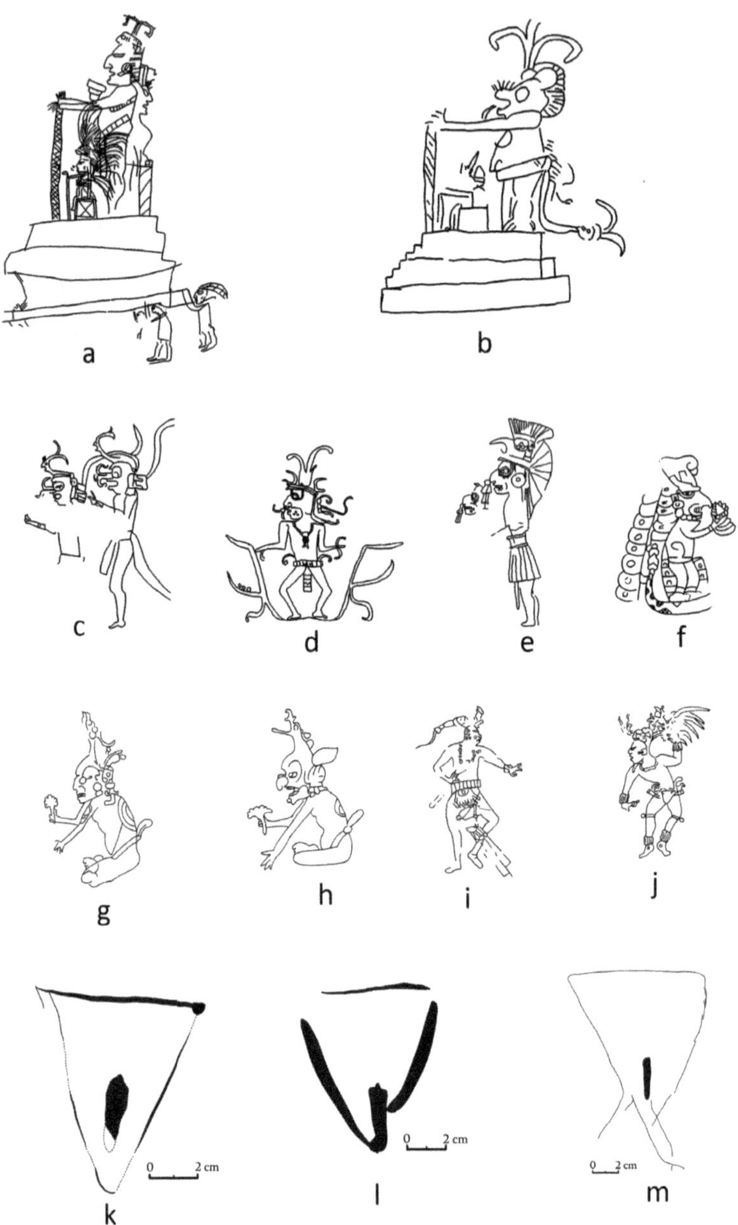

Fig. 8: Palanquins with patron deities (a-b), representations of deities (c-j) and vulva symbols (k-m); a-b) Tikal, Maler's Palace; c) Tikal, Temple I; d) Tikal, Temple II; e) Tikal, Maler's Palace; f) Pasion del Cristo, Structure 1; g-h) Tikal, Structure 5D-33-2; i) Copan, Oropendola Structure; j) Tikal, Maler's Palace; and k-m) Nakum, Structures 61-1, D and E.

Sexual symbols constitute the next category. So far, 71 have been documented at 10 sites. Most are vulvas (Fig. 8k-m), and only three cases are representations of phalluses. The dating of many vulva symbols is debatable; their style and location (on upper parts of the walls, above a level of collapse stones of masonry structures) indicate that they might have been created during the Postclassic period, i.e. after most Classic Maya centres in the Lowlands had been abandoned.[36]

Inscriptions, which constitute the vast majority of the graffiti documented in ancient cultures of the Mediterranean Basin, form a very small group among Maya graffiti (about 2 %). They have been documented at 16 sites so far, and the total number of glyphic graffiti exceeds 60 examples, most of which are known from Tikal.[37] They usually include separate glyphs, such as dates or numbers. In a few cases, some longer inscriptions have also been documented at Tikal and Cahal Pech.[38] Most of the glyphic graffiti record names, dates or simple numbers as well as astronomical notations (Fig. 9).[39] Calendar Round dates are especially popular in this group. A Calendar Round was a Mesoamerican cycle of 52 years that was formed by a combination of a 260-day count (*tzolkin*) and a 365-day solar year (*haab*). Thus, each Calendar Round date gives the position of a day in both *tzoklin* and *haab* counts (Fig. 9). However, when the number of Maya glyphic graffiti is compared with the quantity of texts from other ancient cultures, a drastic difference may be observed. Most documented graffiti in ancient Egypt, Greece and Rome are textual.[40] This brings us to an interesting topic concerning the level of literacy among the ancient Maya. Some scholars have already postulated[41] that reading and writing might have been a very limited skill among the pre-Hispanic Maya, and was most probably restricted to the upper echelons of Maya society. This statement can be largely supported by the extremely low proportion of hieroglyphic texts in the Maya graffiti corpus.

The next category is particularly interesting as it is related to a pre-Columbian game of chance known in Mesoamerica as *patolli*. Players of this game used portable boards made on a mat that could be easily rolled up. *Patolli* boards could also be scratched onto stucco floors or benches of masonry Maya buildings,

36 Patrois and Nondédéo 2009, 53; Źrałka 2014a, 140–141.

37 Trik and Kampen 1983; Źrałka 2014a, Table 1; Helmke and Źrałka 2021.

38 Trik and Kampen 1983; Helmke and Awe 2012, Fig. 14; Helmke and Źrałka 2021.

39 Saturno et al. 2012; Callaghan et al. 2017, Figs 8 and 10g; Helmke and Źrałka 2021.

40 Tanzer 1939; Lang 1974, 1976; Peden 2001; Varone 2002; Navrátilová 2007; Benefiel 2010; Benefiel 2011; Benefiel 2018, 101–103.

41 Houston 1994, 39; Źrałka 2014a, 139.

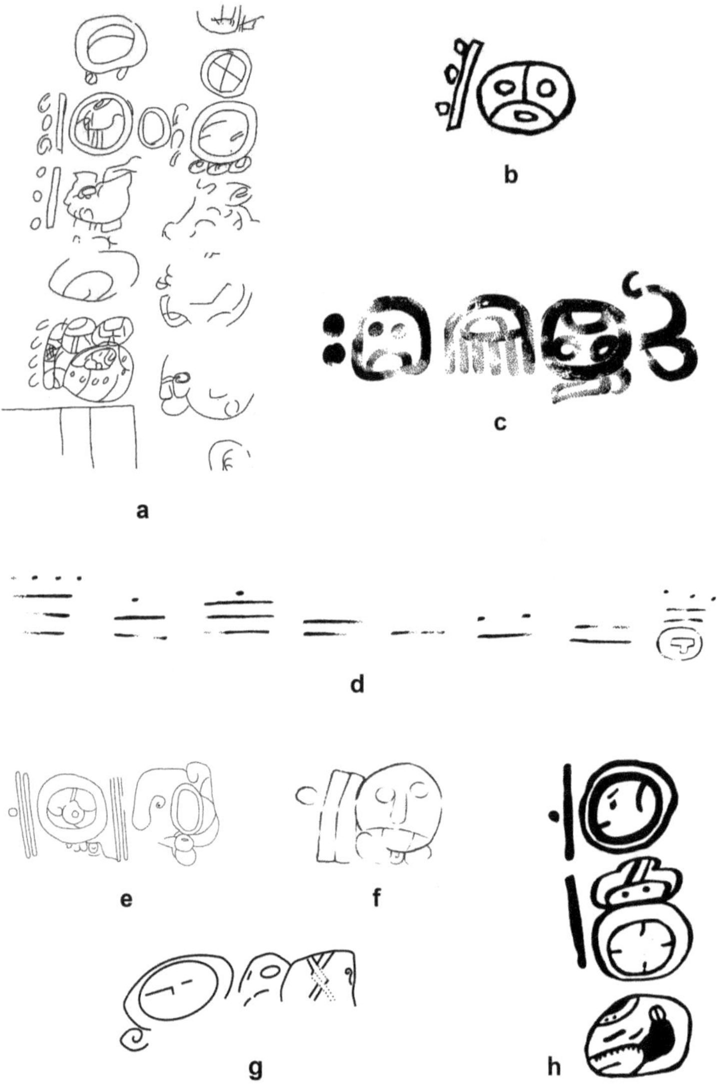

Fig. 9: Hieroglyphic graffiti represented by calendrical notations documented at various Maya sites, after Helmke and Źrałka 2021: Fig. 6; a) longer text headed by the Calendar Round date 6 K'an 7 Pax, Tikal, Str. 5C-49, Room 1; b) tzolkin date 8 Ajaw, Tikal, Temple II, roofcomb, Chamber 2; c) painted text featuring the tzolkin date 2 Ajaw, Tikal, Str. 5E-55-2nd; d) numeric array closed by the tzolkin date 13 Ik' from Tikal Str. 5E-55-2nd; e) Calendar Round date 11 Manik 10 Xul, Nakum, Str. E, Chamber 1; f) tzolkin date 11 Ajaw, Xunantunich, Str. A-13, Room 7; g) Calendar Round date from Tzibatnah, Casa de las Pinturas; and h) painted Calendar Round date 6 Men 5 Yaxk'in from Dzibilchaltun, Str. 1-sub.

which is where they are usually found.[42] There was not one universal and common board for a *patolli* game but several, which sometimes differed in shape and the number of internal spaces or registers (Fig. 10).[43] As far as the rules are concerned, players moved counters (which were usually coloured stones) along all the spaces of the *patolli* board. The players moved their counters according to the throw of a die (dices were usually beans with numbers inscribed on them). The winner was the first to advance through all the spaces of the board. By 2014, I was able to count 72 examples of *patolli* boards in the whole Maya area (2.2 % of the whole corpus). However, new examples have recently been documented, especially at the Maya site of Xunantunich in Belize where 12 new *patolli* boards etched on bench surfaces or on floors have been recorded.[44] An interesting set of *patolli* boards incised on the floor of a ball court at Copan (Honduras) has also been published recently by William and Barbara Fash.[45] The latter find may indicate that there might have been some association between a ball court game and a *patolli* game. In fact, some ethnohistoric documents from the colonial period confirm connections between the games and their association with gambling.[46]

As previously mentioned, some of the graffiti categories (e.g. anthropomorphic, zoomorphic or architectural) can create more complex scenes that can be described as 'narrative'. The latter usually involve several individuals who are shown in the context of dynamic activity; such scenes often take place next to buildings. This group includes processions, sacrifices, sexual intercourse, enema scenes and hunting. There is also one representation of a ball court scene with ball players playing on the court. Processions merit special attention and have been documented at many Maya sites. They are usually located close to architectural buildings and involve people of high status who are being carried on palanquins or shown in a walking position but accompanied by servants: people carrying umbrellas, banners or musicians (see Fig. 11). There are also several processions involving warriors. Some of these scenes may mirror the local topography and architecture of the sites where they were documented. This is a case of some graffiti from Yaxha in Guatemala that feature processions shown close to

42 Swezey and Bittman 1983; Gallegos Gómora 1994; Fitzmaurice, Watkins and Awe 2021.
43 Źrałka 2014a, Table 2.
44 Watkins et al. 2020; Fitzmaurice, Watkins and Awe 2021.
45 Fash and Fash 2015, Fig. 5.
46 See Durán 1971, 318–319; Fitzmaurice, Watkins and Awe 2021, 65.

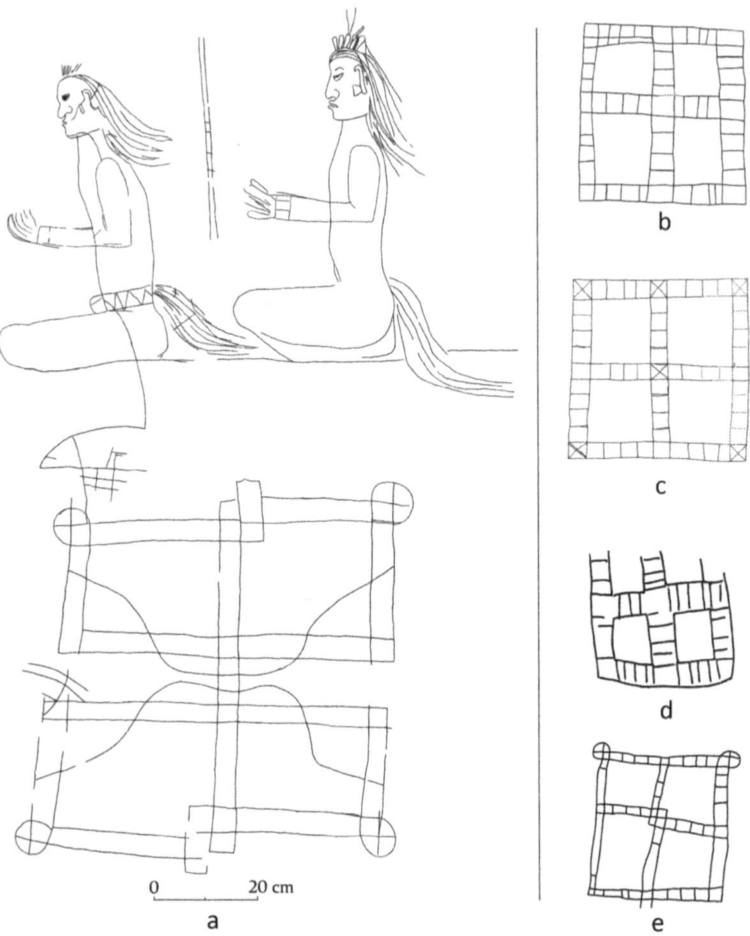

Fig. 10: Representations of patolli boards used during a famous Mesoamerican game of chance; a) scene from Nakum Structure Y incised on a stucco covering of a masonry bench, it may feature two individuals playing patolli; b-e) patolli boards from different Maya sites (b – Calakmul Structure VII, c – Tikal, Structure 5G-4, d – Tz'ibatnah, Casa de las Pinturas, e – Rio Bec B, Structure 6N1).

large pyramids.[47] One complex scene from Yaxha shows terrain that rises upwards (to the left of the viewer) with a group of people holding umbrellas close to whom tall banners are visible. Further to the right, we can see a figure (of a ruler?)

47 Źrałka and Hermes 2009.

carried on a litter, in front of which one individual – who seems to be conducting the procession – is walking (Fig. 11c). A building in the form of a pyramid is shown next to the banners. The whole scene could commemorate an event that took place in the southern part of Yaxha, where the topography of the terrain is similar to that which is depicted in the graffiti. This scene was incised into the wall of the palace building located in the southern part of Yaxha (South Acropolis), from where the viewer could observe the event commemorated in the form of the graffiti described.

Other interesting complex scenes that merit some attention depict sacrifices, especially one type that is usually referred to as a 'scaffold sacrifice'.[48] Interestingly, this type of sacrifice is barely seen in official art but has been documented at several Maya centres in the graffiti corpus. Scaffold sacrifice involved tying the victim to a scaffold-like construction or two vertical poles. The victim was subsequently killed by celebrants who threw arrows or spears at his body (Fig. 12 and possibly also Fig. 4c). This sacrifice had a very complex agricultural symbolism among the Aztecs. The throwing of the arrows was associated with the insertion of the planting stick into the soil, which was symbolically represented by the body of the prisoner. The blood droplets that fell onto the soil evoked the rain that would guarantee a good harvest. This ritual might have also been practiced among the Maya in the context of the ascension of a new ruler.[49]

5 Style and agents of Maya graffiti

Although incised graffiti form a rather coherent group, their style betrays various authors with different artistic skills. Some are very crude representations which, in many cases, are difficult to identify due to their highly simplified style. Their authors had no artistic preparation, though their content is also often related to the Classic Maya elites and elite culture. In this group, we can also find representations that, based on their style and method of depiction, might have been created by children. Katherine Huntley[50] demonstrated that the figurative graffiti from Campanian sites in Italy include many examples most probably made by children. This assumption can be backed by psychological studies concerning the

48 Taube 1988.
49 Taube 1988; van Akkeren 1999; Źrałka 2014a, 168–171.
50 Huntley 2011.

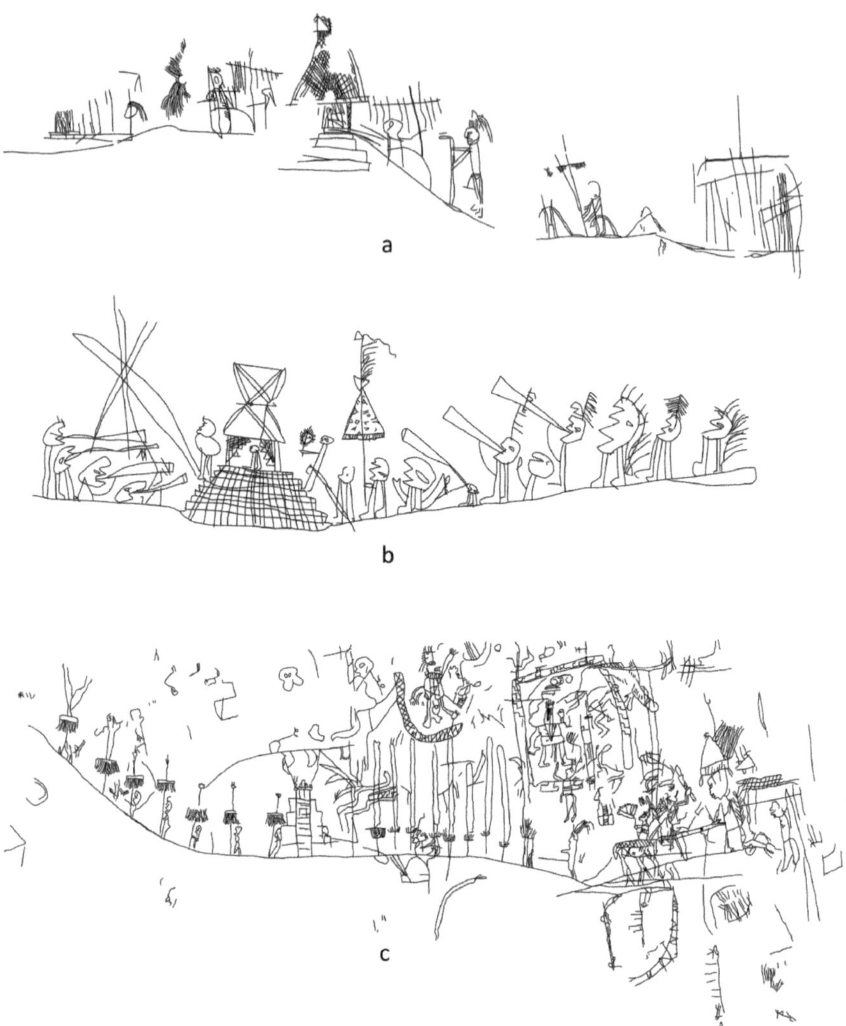

Fig. 11: Graffiti featuring complex narrative scenes (processions) from several Maya sites a) Rio Bec, Group A, Structure 5N2; b) Rio Bec, Group V, Structure IV; and c) Yaxha, Structure 375.

biological growth of children and how they depict things, since they usually illustrate what they know rather than what they see about a specific subject or person.[51] By applying this approach to a corpus of Maya graffiti, I was able to find a group of representations which fit the same category and that were most probably

51 For further characterization of this model, see Huntley 2011.

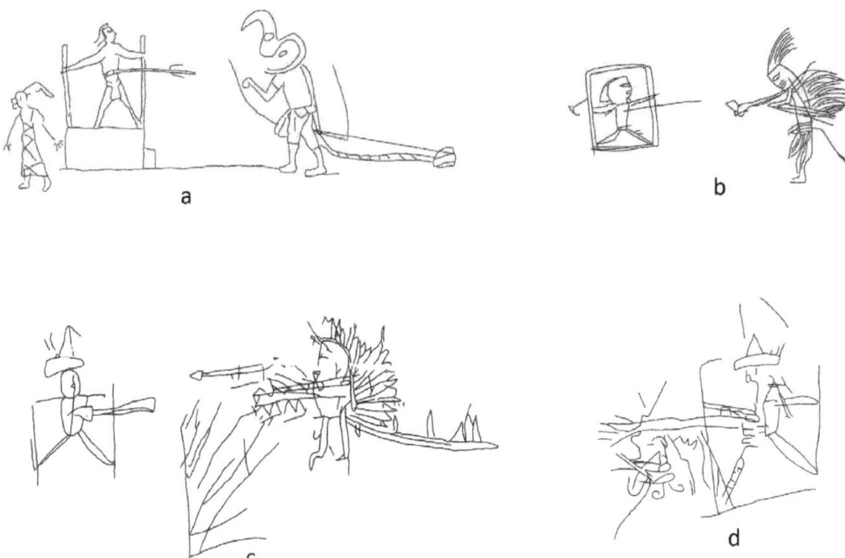

Fig. 12: 'Scaffold sacrifice' scenes documented at Tikal Temple II (a), Rio Bec D, Structure 7N1 (b) and Nakum Structure G (c-d).

rendered by children (Fig. 13a-h). These are usually crude figurative representations of people and animals.[52] Other Mayanists, such as Scott Hutson[53] as well as Julie Patrois and Philippe Nondédéo,[54] have also suggested that some Maya graffiti were created by children. Hutson argued that creating graffiti can be viewed as an important element of a child's growth and socialisation as well as an act of recreating the world that encircles them – 'in a miniaturized form that they can control'.[55]

We can also discern images of a fine style among the Maya graffiti characterized by the use of very thin, flexible and exact incisions (Fig. 13i-m). This group shows many affinities with official art of the Late Classic period (600–800 CE), and especially with the paintings from polychrome ceramics. It includes representations of people, animals, architecture, deities, glyphic texts and other symbols. These graffiti must have been executed by experienced artists, some of whom

52 Źrałka 2014a, 208–211.

53 Hutson 2011.

54 Patrois and Nondédéo 2009, 44.

55 Hutson 2011, 421.

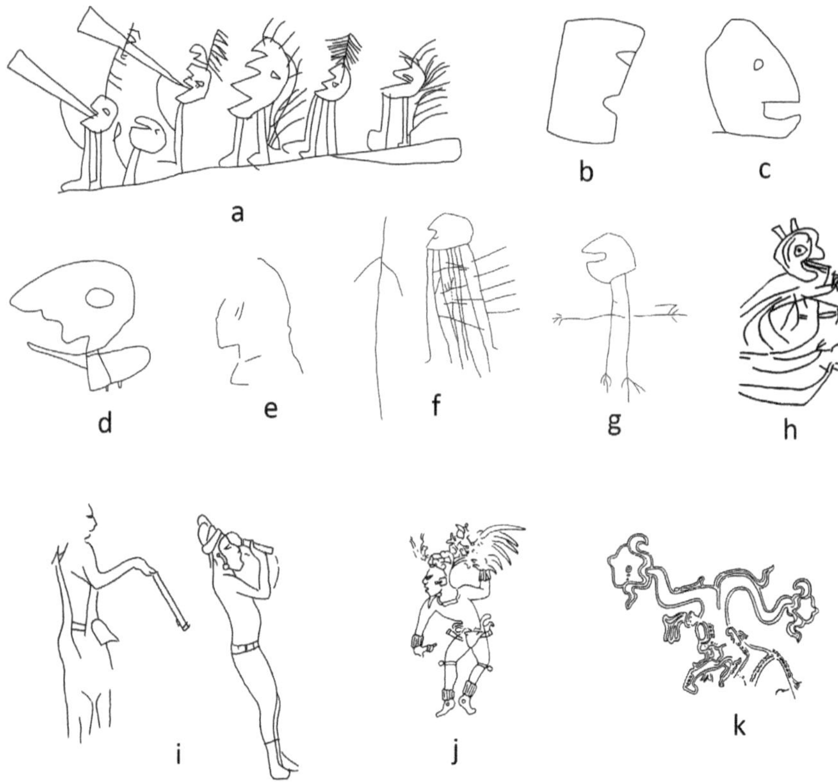

Fig. 13a–k: Stylistic diversity of Maya graffiti: a-h) crude graffiti that, based on their form, might have been rendered by children; a) Río Bec V, Structure IV; b) Río Bec A, Structure 5N-2; c) Río Bec V, Structure IV; d) Tz'ibatnah, Casa de las Pinturas; e) Tz'ibatnah, Casa de las Pinturas; f) Tikal, Structure 5D-50; g) Tikal, Structure 3D-40; h) Tikal, Structure 3D-40; i) Nakum, Structure Y; j) Tikal, Structure 5D-65 (Maler's Palace); k) Palenque, Temple of the Inscriptions.

were probably responsible for creating the best examples of Maya art, such as polychrome ceramics painted with intricate scenes and other examples of elite art (sculptures, reliefs or examples of portable art).

The rich corpus of Maya graffiti also contains images which differ from the canons of the Classic Maya art. In this group, we can find images that are sometimes described as 'Mexicanized' or of 'foreign' origin. Some of them show influences of the pan-Mesoamerican Mixteca-Puebla style characteristic of the Postclassic period (Fig. 13n-p). However, they cannot be attributed to 'Postclassic squatters' since their execution is skilful and manifests knowledge of official elite art canons of this period. These Postclassic graffiti can be related to the

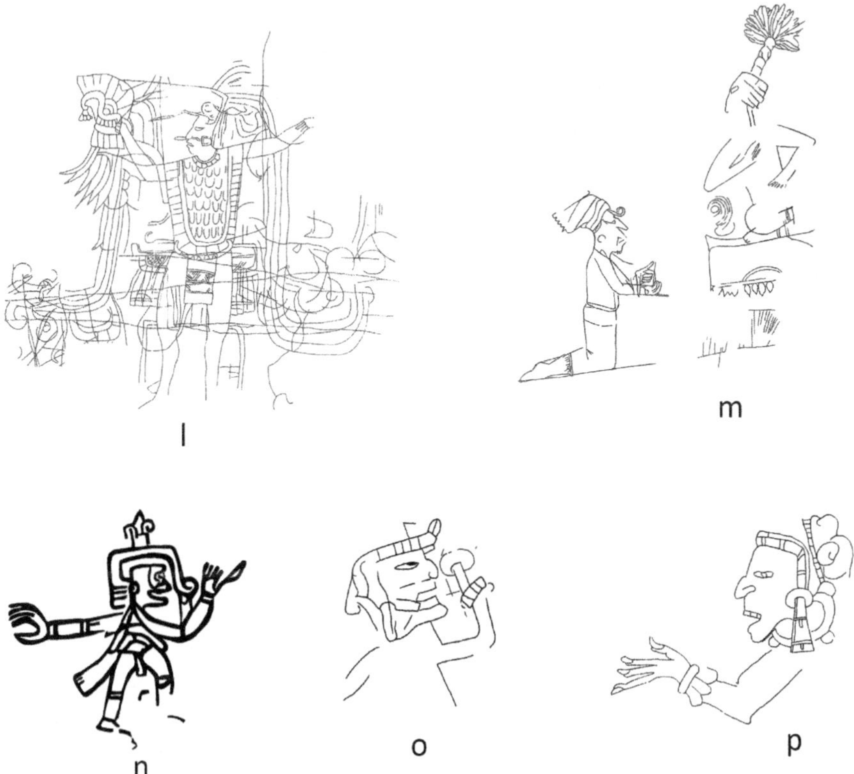

Fig. 13l–p: Stylistic diversity of Maya graffiti: i-m) fine style graffiti similar to the best examples of official Maya art; n-p) graffiti that can be ascribed to the Mixteca-Puebla style dated to the Postclassic period; l) Tikal, Structure 6F-27 (Temple VI); m) La Blanca, Structure 6J1; n) Nakum, Structure E; o) Nakum, Structure 61-1; and p) Tikal, Structure 5C-13 (Bat Palace).

Postclassic occupation documented archaeologically at various Maya sites (including Tikal, Nakum and Yaxha), which might have been temporarily visited for different purposes by people who were aware of the canons prevailing in contemporary art.

6 Conclusions

If we look at the Maya graffiti in a broad sense or perspective, we may be tempted to present a few characteristics or conclusions. Graffiti from most Maya centres depict people, places, objects and scenes (e.g. rituals) which are strictly related to the Classic Maya elites and the 'elite culture'. In other words, they are inspired by courtly life since they indicate knowledge about existing canons in art and activities strictly related to courtly life: elite members, musicians, warriors, specific gestures, paraphernalia, costumes, rituals and other upper-class activities.[56] There are hieroglyphic texts present which also fit the same category of courtly activity. As such, most graffiti cannot be associated with simple peasants or squatters who reoccupied previously abandoned structures, as some scholars proposed in the past. There are no scenes which could be tied to the life of common people (e.g. agricultural work, pottery making, food production). Moreover, some graffiti from Nakum, Naranjo, Holmul, Tikal, Palenque, Xunantunich and La Blanca[57] rival the best examples of official art known from carved monuments and paintings. We should also stress that most Maya graffiti come from residential, palace buildings and their authors were most probably the original inhabitants of these constructions.

Based on the corpus of Maya graffiti available, we can conclude that they constituted a form of individual expression of elite members, most of whom wanted to record the events, people and places which played an important role in their lives. Some events reflected in narrative scenes (sacrifices, procession scenes) must have made a great impression on the local people who decided to commemorate them in the form of graffiti. Thus memorialisation and commemoration might have been major motivations for creating graffiti at many, if not most, Maya sites. As such, we may describe and envision graffiti as pictures designed to evoke important events, places or objects for those who viewed them.

Another interesting conclusion that can be drawn is the prevailing presence of representations of deities and supernatural beings in sacred places such as temples or shrines. This tendency can be observed at several Maya sites, including Tikal, Cival or Holmul.[58] These images might have been created as an act of prayer, spiritual experience and devotion, in a way similar to some graffiti known from medieval and early modern European churches, which contain prayer formulas or motifs related to the Christian religion.[59] As such, an act of etching or painting deities or supernatural figures documented in many Maya buildings might have served to communicate and interact with these entities and to make pleas and prayers to them. We should also remember that, according to the Maya,

56 Cf. Webster 1963; Andrews 1999; Źrałka 2014b, 51; Olton 2018.
57 See Vidal Lorenzo and Muñoz Cosme 2009a; Źrałka 2014a; Tokovinine 2021.
58 Cf. Estrada-Belli 2011, 106–108; Tokovinine 2021.
59 See Pritchard 1967; Plesch 2002 and 2007.

the world around them was alive, and this applied not only to nature, but also to architectural buildings and portable objects. They were all animated and had souls. Temples or pyramidal structures were perceived as sacred mountains which were abodes of gods and ancestors as well as paradisiac loci. Entrances conducting to these structures symbolically led to the underworld.[60] As such, creating of at least some graffiti in their interiors or exteriors might have had an exceptional ritual significance; it was an act of prayer, reverence and communication with supernatural beings that these structures embodied or contained.

Of course, some graffiti had more practical meanings since – as we have already discussed – there is a large collection of *patolli* boards which must have been used for this famous Mesoamerican game of chance. However, at some sites (e.g. Nakum), we can also find 'smaller versions' of *patolli* boards etched on walls, in other words, in places not suitable for conducting games. In these cases, authors were most probably trying to evoke the game (game remembrance) and topics associated with it.

Most Maya graffiti from the Classic period structures must have come from the last moments of occupation of these buildings since the interiors of Maya buildings were replastered, therefore, what we usually document are depictions covering the last layer of plaster on the walls. Hence, we might argue that a large part of Maya graffiti from Classic buildings can be dated temporarily to the eighth century CE, which was the apogee of Maya civilisation. However, we should also remember that there are structures and graffiti that can be dated to earlier and later periods (Preclassic and Postclassic, respectively).

The corpus of Maya graffiti contains scenes that can be dated to post-abandonment contexts based both on their style and architectural-archaeological context.[61] This group includes both simple graffiti that might have been rendered by 'common people' who temporarily reoccupied abandoned structures or complexes in various Lowland Maya sites. However, as has been mentioned previously, we can also assign to this group some representations that may be linked with the elite culture of Postclassic times and betray connections with the Mixteca-Puebla international style associated with elite courts. There are also graffiti which were most probably created just before the abandonment[62] or which were rendered on Postclassic buildings.[63]

60 See Taube 2004; Stone and Zender 2011, 132–133.
61 Patrois and Nondédéo 2009, 53; Patrois 2013; Źrałka 2014a, 190.
62 See Fitzmaurice, Watkins and Awe 2021, 69.
63 Źrałka 2014a, 190.

There are also graffiti dating back to the Preclassic period, preceding the apogee of the Maya civilisation. Although there are few such examples and they come mainly from buildings covered and sealed by later architecture, their themes also refer to the elite culture. Among the Preclassic graffiti, we have anthropomorphic images, representations of deities, mat designs (the mat was an important symbol of power in Mesoamerica) as well as zoomorphic depictions and glyphic texts.[64]

Thus, it is clear that although most of the graffiti from the Maya area can be associated with the Classic period and the greatest development of Maya culture, we also find representations that are dated both to the Preclassic period and Postclassic and later periods. Some of them can also be associated with post-abandonment contexts.

All in all, graffiti are an extremely valuable source of information about the pre-Hispanic Maya culture. They represent a kind of private record of unknown authors, residents or visitors of the buildings in which we discover this type of art. They often depict scenes unknown from official art. Thus, they can fill gaps in our knowledge concerning many aspects of the ritual and daily life of the pre-Columbian Maya.

Figure Credits

Figure 1: Photographs © Jarosław Źrałka (a-e, h) and courtesy of Karl Herbert Mayer (f-g).

Figure 2: After Źrałka 2014a, 105.

Figure 3: Illustration credits: a-h) processed by Jakub Źrałka after Trik and Kampen 1983; i) redrawn by Katarzyna Radnicka after Andrews 1999, Fig. 71; j) redrawn by Katarzyna Radnicka after Martín and Smith 2009, Fig. 20; k) redrawn by Izabela Jurkiewicz after Calderón et al. 2004, Fig. 108; l) redrawn by Piotr Kołodziejczyk after Estrada-Belli et al. 2009, Fig. 6a; m) drawing by Guido Krempel, courtesy of Guido Krempel and Karl H. Mayer; n) drawing by Milan Kováč, courtesy of SAHI Project and Milan Kováč; o) courtesy of Proyecto Arqueológico Dzibanche; p-q) redrawn by Katarzyna Radnicka after Patrois and Nondédéo 2009, Fig. 15k-l; r) redrawn by Katarzyna Radnicka after Patrois and Nondédéo 2009, Fig. 15j; s) redrawn by Piotr Kołodziejczyk after Webster 1963, Fig. 38; t) drawing by Justyna Olko.

Figure 4: Redrawn by Izabela Jurkiewicz after Orrego and Larios 1983, Plates 17, 8B, 23A, 19A respectively.

Figure 5: Illustration credits: a), f-g) and i) drawing by Jarosław Źrałka; b) redrawn by Izabela Jurkiewicz after Calderón et al. 2004, Fig. 10; c-e) processed by Jakub Źrałka after Trik and Kampen 1983; h) redrawn by Izabela Jurkiewicz after Tozzer 1957, Fig. 246.

64 Źrałka 2014a, 187–188.

Figure 6: Drawing by Katarzyna Leboch.

Figure 7: Illustration credits: a-b) photographs by Jarosław Źrałka; c-h) processed by Jakub Źrałka after Trik and Kampen 1983, Figs 34, 36b, 8b and 38b; i-j) redrawn by Katarzyna Radnicka after Calderón et al. 2004, Fig. 47 and Patrois and Nondédéo 2009, Fig. 20e; k) after Trik and Kampen 1983, Fig. 46.

Figure 8: Illustration credits: a-e) and g) processed by Jakub Źrałka after Trik and Kampen 1983; f) redrawn by Izabela Jurkiewicz after Mayer 1997, Fig. 1; h) and j) processed by Jakub Źrałka after Webster 1963, Figs 21 and 7; i) drawing by Joanne Baron, courtesy of Ricardo Agurcia Fasquelle and Oropondola Project; k-m) drawing by Piotr Kołodziejczyk.

Figure 9: Illustration credits: a) after Trik and Kampen 1983, Fig. 29c; b) after Trik and Kampen 1983, Fig. 40c; c) drawing by Christophe Helmke; d) drawing by Christophe Helmke; e) drawing by Justyna Olko; f) drawing by Christophe Helmke; g) drawing by Milan Kováč; h) drawing by Izabela Jurkiewicz after Andrews and Andrews 1980, Fig. 112.

Figure 10: Illustration credits: a) drawing by Katarzyna Radnicka; b) redrawn by Izabela Jurkiewicz after Gallegos Gómora 2001, Fig. 51; c) after Trik and Kampen 1983, Fig. 92; d) drawing by Milan Kováč; courtesy of SAHI Project and Milan Kováč; e) redrawn by Piotr Kołodziejczyk after Patrois and Nondédéo 2009, Fig. 19.

Figure 11: Illustration credits: a-b) redrawn by Katarzyna Radnicka after after Patrois and Nondédéo 2009, Figs 20d-e; c) drawing by Jarosław Źrałka, Katarzyna Radnicka and PDS Project, courtesy of Bernard Hermes.

Figure 12: Illustration credits: a) redrawn by Piotr Kołodziejczyk after Webster 1963, Fig. 23; b) redrawn by Piotr Kołodziejczyk after Patrois and Nondédéo 2009, Fig. 20a; c-d) redrawn by Katarzyna Radnicka after Calderón et al. 2004, Figs 33 and 53.

Figure 13: Illustration credits: a-c) redrawn by Katarzyna Radnicka after Patrois and Nondédéo 2009, Figs 20d and 15u-v respectively; d-e) redrawn by Piotr Kołodziejczyk after Kováč 2010, Figs III-66 and III-83; f-g) redrawn by Piotr Kołodziejczyk after Trik and Kampen 1983, Figs 53e and 4 respectively; h) processed by Jakub Źrałka after Trik and Kampen 1983, Fig. 1; i) drawing by Katarzyna Radnicka; j) processed by Jakub Źrałka after Webster 1963, Fig. 7; k) redrawn by Izabela Jurkiewicz after Ruz Lhuillier 1992, Fig. 118; l) processed by the author after Trik and Kampen 1983, Fig. 96c; m) drawing by La Blanca Archaeological Project, courtesy of Cristina Vidal Lorenzo and La Blanca Archaeological Project; n) drawing by the author and Justyna Olko; o) drawing by the author; and p) processed by Jakub Źrałka from Trik and Kampen 1983, Fig. 16.

References

Andrews, George (1999), 'Architectural Graffiti and the Maya Elite', in George Andrews (ed.), *Pyramids and Palaces, Monsters and Masks: The Golden Age of Maya Architecture* (3 vols), vol. III: Architecture of the Rio Bec Region and Miscellaneous Subjects, Lancaster (CA): Labyrinthos, 221–261.

Andrews IV, Wyllys and Wyllys Andrews V (1980), *Excavations at Dzibilchaltun, Yucatan, Mexico* (Publication 48), New Orleans: Middle American Research Institute, Tulane University.

Baird, Jennifer A. (2011), 'The Graffiti of Dura-Europos: A Contextual Approach', in Baird and Taylor 2011b, 49–68.

Baird, Jennifer A. and Claire Taylor (2011a), 'Ancient Graffiti in Context: Introduction', in Baird and Taylor 2011b, 1–19.

Baird, Jennifer A. and Claire Taylor (eds) (2011b), *Ancient Graffiti in Context*, New York: Routledge.

Benefiel, Rebecca R. (2010), 'Dialogues of Ancient Graffiti in the House of Maius Castricius in Pompeii', *American Journal of Archaeology*, 114: 59–101.

Benefiel, Rebecca R. (2011), 'Dialogues of Graffiti in the House of the Four Styles at Pompeii (*Casa dei Quattro Stili*, I.8.17, 11)', in Baird and Taylor 2011b, 20–48.

Benefiel, Rebecca R. (2018), 'Gladiators, Greetings and Poetry: Graffiti in First Century Pompeii', in Chloé Ragazzoli, Ömür Harmanşah, Chiara Salvador and Elizabeth Frood (eds), *Scribbling through History: Graffiti, Places and People from Antiquity to Modernity*, London: Bloomsbury, 101–116.

Calderón, Zoila, Varinia Matute, Jarosław Źrałka, Sławek Konik and Wiesiek Koszkul (2004), *Memoria anual de actividades: unidad de arqueologia local, año 2004*, unpublished report, Guatemala City: Instituto de Antropología e Historia de Guatemala.

Callaghan, Michael G., Brigitte Kovacevich, Karla J. Cardona Caravantes, Melvin Rodrigo Guzmán Piedrasanta, Dawn Crawford and Mary Clarke (2017), 'La comunidad preclásica en Holtun, Guatemala: vista del Grupo F', in Barbara Arroyo, Luis Méndez Salinas and Gloria Ajú Álvarez (eds), *XXX Simposio de Investigaciones Arqueológicas en Guatemala, 2016*, Guatemala City: Museo Nacional de Arqueología y Etnología, 93–106.

Carrascosa Moliner, Begoña, Montserrat Lastras Pérez and Francisca Lorenzo Mora (2009), 'La conservación de los grafitos de La Blanca: investigaciones sobre materiales, procesos y técnicas', in Vidal Lorenzo and Muñoz Cosme 2009b, 119–132.

Chaniotis, Angelos (2011), 'Graffiti in Aphrodisias: Images–Texts–Contexts', in Baird and Taylor 2011b, 191–207.

Coe, Michael and Justin Kerr (1997), *The Art of the Maya Scribe*, New York: Thames and Hudson.

Durán, Diego (1971), *Book of the Gods and Rites and the Ancient Calendar*, translated and edited by Fernando Horcasitas and Doris Heyden, Norman: University of Oklahoma Press.

Estrada-Belli, Francisco (2011), *The First Maya Civilization: Ritual and Power before the Classic Period*, New York: Routledge.

Estrada-Belli, Francisco, Aleksandre Tokovinine, Jennifer M. Foley, Heather Hurst, Gene A. Ware, David Stuart and Nikolai Grube (2009), 'A Maya Palace at Holmul, Peten, Guatemala and the Teotihuacan "Entrada": Evidence from Murals 7 and 9', *Latin American Antiquity*, 20/1: 228–259.

Fash, William and Barbara Fash (2015), 'Apuesta, guerra ritual e identidad en el juego de pelota de Mesoamérica', in María Teresa Uriarte (ed.), *El juego de pelota mesoamericano: temas eternos, nuevas aproximaciones*, Mexico City: Universidad Nacional Autónoma de México, 37–66.

Feliu Beltrán, Núria (2019), *Los grafitos mayas: clasificación tipológica y aproximación a su significado*, unpublished doctoral dissertation, Universitat de Valénica.

Fitzmaurice, Rosamund, Tia Watkins and Jaime Awe (2021), 'Play and Purpose: The Relationship between Patolli and Graffiti at Xunantunich, Belize', *Papers from the Institute of Archaeology*, 31/1: 60–92 <https://doi.org/10.14324/111.444.2041-9015.1286>.

Gallegos Gómora, Miriam Judith (1994), 'Un patolli prehispánico en Calakmul, Campeche', *Revista Española de Antropología Americana*, 24: 9–24.

Gallegos Gómora, Miriam Judith (2001), *Costumbres funerarias y organización social en Calakmul: excavaciones en la estructura VII. Una interpretación*, Campeche: Universidad Autónoma de Campeche, Centro INAH Tabasco.

Gann, Thomas (1918), *The Maya Indians of Southern Yucatan and Northern British Honduras* (Bureau of American Ethnology Bulletin, 64), Washington, D.C.: Smithsonian Institution.

Gann, Thomas (1924), *In an Unknown Land*, New York: Charles Scribner's Sons.

Haviland, William and Anita de Laguna Haviland (1995), 'Glimpses of the Supernatural: Altered States of Consciousness and the Graffiti of Tikal, Guatemala', *Latin American Antiquity*, 6/4: 295–309.

Helmke, Christophe and Jaime Awe (2012), 'Ancient Maya Territorial Organisation of Central Belize: Confluence of Archaeological and Epigraphic Data', *Contributions in New World Archaeology*, 4: 59–90.

Helmke, Christophe and Jarosław Źrałka (2021), 'Writing amidst the Scribbles: The Role and Place of Writing in Ancient Maya Graffiti', *Papers from the Institute of Archaeology*, 31/1: 93–120 <https://doi.org/10.14324/111.444.2041-9015.1287>.

Hermes, Bernard, Justyna Olko and Jarosław Źrałka (2001), 'En los confines del arte: los graffiti de Nakum, (Petén, Guatemala) y su contexto arquitectónico, arqueológico e iconográfico', *Anales del Instituto de Investigaciones Estéticas*, 23/79: 29–69.

Hermes, Bernard, Justyna Olko and Jarosław Źrałka (2002), 'Entre el arte elitista y el arte popular: los graffiti de Nakum, Petén, Guatemala', *Mexicon*, 24/6: 123–132.

Houston, Stephen (1994), 'Literacy among the Pre-Columbian Maya: A Comparative Perspective', in Elizabeth Hill Boone and Walter D. Mignolo (eds), *Writing without Words: Alternative Literacies in Mesoamerica and the Andes*, Durham and London: Duke University Press, 27–49.

Huntley, Katherine (2011), 'Identifying Children's Graffiti in Roman Campania: A Developmental Psychological Approach', in Baird and Taylor 2011b, 69–89.

Hutson, Scott (2011), 'The Art of Becoming: The Graffiti of Tikal, Guatemala', *Latin American Antiquity*, 22/4: 403–426.

Jones, Christopher (1987), 'The Life and Times of Ah Cacau, Ruler of Tikal', in *Primer Simposio Mundial sobre Epigrafía Maya*, Guatemala City: Asociación Tikal, 107–120.

Kampen, Michael (1978), 'The Graffiti of Tikal, Guatemala', *Estudios de Cultura Maya*, 6: 155–180.

Kováč, Milan (2010), 'Excavaciones en "La Casa de Las Pinturas". Operación 3', in Milan Kováč and Ernesto Arredondo Leiva (eds), *Excavaciones en el Peten Noreste: Tz'ibatnah I. Temporada 2010*, Bratislava: Instituto Eslovaco de Arqueología e Historia, 34–83.

Kováč, Milan (2014), 'El arte privado de una casa maya: los grafitos de Tz'ibatnah, Guatemala', in Cristina Vidal Lorenzo and Gaspar Muñoz (eds), *Artistic Expressions in Maya Architecture: Analysis and Documentation Techniques* (BAR International Series, 2693), Oxford: Archaeopress, 31–42.

Lang, Mabel (1974), *Graffiti in the Athenian Agora*, Princeton: American School of Classical Studies at Athens.

Lang, Mabel (1976), *The Athenian Agora XXI: Graffiti and Dipinti*, Princeton: The American School of Classical Studies at Athens.

Langner, Martin (2001), *Antike Graffitizeichnungen: Motive, Gestaltung und Bedeutung*, Wiesbaden: Ludwig Reichert.

Lewis-Williams, David and Thomas Dowson (1988), 'The Signs of All Times: Entoptic Phenomena in Upper Palaeolithic Art', *Current Anthropology*, 29/2: 201–245.
Maler, Teobert (1911), *Explorations in the Department of Peten, Guatemala: Tikal* (Memoirs of the Peabody Museum of Archaeology and Ethnology, 5/1), Cambridge, MA: Harvard University.
Martin, Simon (1996), 'Tikal "Star War" against Naranjo', in Martha J. Macri and Jan McHargue (eds), *Eighth Palenque Round Table, 1993,* electronic version downloaded from <www.mesoweb.org>.
Martin, Simon (2020), *Ancient Maya Politics: A Political Anthropology of the Classic Period 150–900 CE*, Cambridge: Cambridge University Press.
Martin, Simon and Nikolai Grube (2008), *Chronicles of the Maya Kings and Queens: Deciphering the Dynasties of the Ancient Maya*, 2nd edn, London: Thames and Hudson.
Mayer, Karl Herbert (1997), 'Maya Drawings and Graffiti at Pasion del Cristo II, Campeche', *Mexicon*, 19/2: 23–25.
Mayer, Karl Herbert (1998), 'La terminología de la decoración mural maya', *La pintura mural prehispánica en México*, 8–9: 7–10.
Mayer, Karl Herbert (2009), 'Ancient Maya Architectural Graffiti', in Vidal Lorenzo and Muñoz Cosme 2009b, 14–27.
Mayer, Karl Herbert (2014), 'Ancient Graffiti at Kakab, Yucatan, Mexico', in Cristina Vidal Lorenzo and Gaspar Muñoz (eds), *Artistic Expressions in Maya Architecture: Analysis and Documentation Techniques* (BAR International Series, 2693), Oxford: Archaeopress, 19–30.
McCurdy, Leah, Kathryn Brown and Neil Dixon (2018), 'Tagged Walls: The Discovery of Ancient Maya Graffiti at El Castillo, Xunantunich', *Research Reports in Belizean Archaeology*, 15: 181–193.
Miller, Mary and Simon Martin (2004), *Courtly Art of the Ancient Maya,* New York: Thames and Hudson.
Navarro-Castillo, Marx, Alejandro Sheseña and Sophia Pincemin (2017), 'The Maya Graffiti of Plan de Ayutla, Chiapas', *Latin American Antiquity*, 29/2: 386–393.
Navrátilová, Hana (2007), *The Visitors' Graffiti of Dynasties XVIII and XIX in Abusir and Northern Saqqara* (The Visitors' Graffiti, 1), Prague: Czech Institute of Egyptology.
Olton, Elizabeth (2018), 'A New Look at Maya Graffiti from Tikal', in Chloé Ragazzoli, Ömür Harmanşah, Chiara Salvador and Elizabeth Frood (eds), *Scribbling through History: Graffiti, Places and People from Antiquity to Modernity*, London: Bloomsbury, 117–130.
Orrego, Miguel and Rudy Larios (1983), *Reporte de las investigaciones arqueológicas en el Grupo 5E-11, Tikal*, Guatemala City: Instituto de Antropología e Historia.
Patrois, Julie (2013), 'Río Bec Graffiti: A Private Form of Art', *Ancient Mesoamerica*, 24/2: 433–447.
Patrois, Julie and Philippe Nondédéo (2009), 'Los grafitos mayas prehispánicos en la microregión de Río Bec (Campeche, México)', in Vidal Lorenzo and Muñoz Cosme 2009b, 29–59.
Peden, Alexander (2001), *The Graffiti of Pharaonic Egypt: Scope and Roles of Informal Writings (c. 3100–332 B.C.)*, Leiden-Boston-Köln: Brill.
Plesch, Véronique (2002), 'Memory on the Wall: Graffiti on Religious Wall Paintings', *Journal of Medieval and Early Modern Studies*, 32/1: 167–197.
Plesch, Véronique (2007), 'Using or Abusing? On the Significance of Graffiti on Religious Mural Paintings', in Luís Urbano Afonso and Vítor Serrão (eds), *Out of the Stream: Studies in Medieval and Renaissance Mural Painting*, Newcastle: Cambridge Scholars Publishing, 42–68.
Pritchard, Violet (1967), *English Medieval Graffiti*, Cambridge: Cambridge University Press.

Ruppert, Karl and John H. Denison Jr. (1943), *Archaeological Reconnaissance in Campeche, Quintana Roo, and Peten*, (Publication, 543), Washington D.C.: Carnegie Institution of Washington.

Ruz Lhuillier, Alberto (1992), *El Templo de las Inscripciones, Palenque*, 2nd edition, Mexico City: Fondo de Cultura Económica.

Saturno, William, David Stuart, Anthony Aveni and Franco Rossi (2012), 'Ancient Maya Astronomical Tables from Xultun, Guatemala', *Science*, 336/6082: 714–717.

Stone, Andrea and Marc Zender (2011), *Reading Maya Art: A Hieroglyphic Guide to Ancient Maya Painting and Sculpture*, London: Thames and Hudson.

Swezey, William and Bente Bittman (1983), 'El rectángulo de cintas y el patolli: nueva evidencia de la antigüidad, distribución, variedad y formas de practicar este juego pre-colombino', *Mesoamerica*, 6: 373–410.

Tanzer, Helen (1939), *The Common People of Pompeii: A Study of the Graffiti*, Baltimore: The Johns Hopkins Press.

Taube, Karl (1988), 'A Study of Classic Maya Scaffold Sacrifice', in Elizabeth Benson and G. Griffin (eds), *Maya Iconography*, Princeton: Princeton University Press, 331–351.

Taube, Karl (2004), 'Flower Mountain: Concepts of Life, Beauty, and Paradise among the Classic Maya', *RES: Anthropology and Aesthetics*, 45: 69–98.

Thompson, Eduard Herbert (1898), 'Ruins of Xkichmook, Yucatan', *Publications of the Field Columbian Museum, Anthropological Series*, 2/3, 209–230.

Thompson, Eric S. (1954), *The Rise and Fall of Maya Civilization*, 1st edn, Norman: University of Oklahoma Press.

Thompson, Eric S. (1966), *The Rise and Fall of Maya Civilization*, 2nd edn, Norman: University of Oklahoma Press.

Tokovinine, Alexandre (2021), 'Lecture 26: Ancient Maya Graffiti and Dipinti' <https://www.youtube.com/watch?v=gc6VB1CAYQc&t=163s> (accessed on 11 February 2022).

Tokovinine, Aleksandre and Vilma Fialko (2019), 'En el cerro de los colibríes: el patrón divino y el paisaje sagrado de la ciudad de Naranjo', in Barbara Arroyo, Luis Méndez and Gloria Ajú (eds), *XXXII Simposio de Investigaciones Arqueológicas en Guatemala, 2019*, Guatemala City: Museo Nacional de Arqueología y Etnología, 825–838.

Tozzer, Alfred (1913), *A Preliminary Study of the Prehistoric Ruins of Nakum, Guatemala* (Memoirs of the Peabody Museum of American Archaeology and Ethnology, 5/3), Cambridge (MA): Harvard University.

Tozzer, Alfred (1957), *Chichén Itzá and Its Cenote of Sacrifice: A Comparative Study of Contemporaneous Maya and Toltec* (Memoirs of the Peabody Museum of Archaeology and Ethnology, 11–12), Cambridge (MA): The Peabody Museum.

Trik, Helen and Michael Kampen (1983), *The Graffiti of Tikal* (Tikal Report, 31), Philadelphia: The University Museum, University of Pennsylvania.

van Akkeren, Ruud (1999), 'Sacrifice at the Maize Tree: Rab'inal Achi in Its Historical and Symbolic Context', *Ancient Mesoamerica*, 10/2: 281–295.

Varone, Antonio (2002), *Erotica Pompeiana: Love Inscriptions on the Walls of Pompeii* (Studia Archaeologica, 116), Rome: L'Erma di Bretschneider.

Vidal Lorenzo, Cristina and Gaspar Muñoz Cosme (2009a), 'Los grafitos de La Blanca: metodología para su estudio y análisis iconográfica', in Vidal Lorenzo and Muñoz Cosme 2009b, 99–118.

Vidal Lorenzo, Cristina and Gaspar Muñoz Cosme (eds) (2009b), *Los grafitos mayas* (Cuadernos de arquitectura y arqueología maya, 2), Valencia: Ediciones UPV.

Watkins, Tia, Claire Ebert, Gabriela Saldaña, Jorge Can and Jaime Awe (2020), 'Continued Investigations of Graffiti at Plaza A-III: The 2019 Excavations at Structure A13', in Claire Ebert, John Walden, Julie Hoggarth and Jaime Awe (eds), *The Belize Valley Archaeological Reconnaissance Project: A Report of the 2019 Field Season*, Flagstaff: Department of Anthropology, Northern Arizona University, 125–136.

Webster, Helen (1963), 'Tikal Graffiti', *Expedition Magazine*, 6/1: 37–47.

Źrałka, Jarosław (2014a), *Pre-Columbian Maya Graffiti: Context, Dating and Function*, Kraków: Alter.

Źrałka, Jarosław (2014b), 'Maya Graffiti in a Wider Cultural and Geographic Context', in Cristina Vidal Lorenzo and Gaspar Muñoz (eds), *Artistic Expressions in Maya Architecture: Analysis and Documentation Techniques* (BAR International Series, 2693), Oxford: Archaeopress, 43–56.

Źrałka, Jarosław and Bernard Hermes (2009), 'Los grafitos prehispánicos de los sitios Nakun y Yaxhá (Petén, Guatemala): su contexto arqueológico, iconográfico y cronológico', in Vidal Lorenzo and Muñoz Cosme 2009b, 133–158.

Alexander Araya López

Graffiti and the Media: Between Politics, Art and Vandalism

Abstract: In this chapter, the diversity of contemporary graffiti practices is studied by exploring the main media narratives that shape the public debate on 'graffiti'. Firstly, a typology of graffiti practices is proposed based on the motivation and circumstances of their production. Both the communicative and non-communicative aspects of these practices are examined, while addressing the role of spatial politics, power and the public sphere in the sociological analysis of these cultural products. Secondly, five media discourses apropos of graffiti practices are discussed, namely the medical-epidemiological, legal, criminogenic, social value and artistic value narratives. Unauthorized forms of graffiti – which include political graffiti, tagging and pichação/pixação – are perceived as damaging to the social body, as compared to more 'aesthetic' forms of graffiti, such as street art and hip-hop graffiti.

1 Introduction

Graffiti is a complex and diverse series of social practices that have continuously captured media attention. In 1971, *The New York Times* published a short story about Taki 183, 'a Manhattan teenager who writes his name and his street number everywhere he goes'.[1] In the article, the reader learns about this 'subculture' of young people, who enjoy being recognized by their peers. Two important details in this story relate to our understanding of contemporary graffiti practices: first, the unidentified journalist describes the negative impact of 'tagging' in New York City, explaining that 'to remove such words, plus the obscenities and other graffiti in subway stations, it cost 80,000 manhours, or about $300,000, in the last year, the Transit Authority estimates'. In the following pages, strategies to eliminate and regulate graffiti practices will be discussed, including references to emblematic cases of police abuse. The second important detail is a verbatim quotation of Demetrius (a.k.a. Taki 183) in which he allegedly trivializes the costs of graffiti removal while pointing to the unfairness of public aesthetics and spatial

1 '"Taki 183" Spawns Pen Pals' 1971.

https://doi.org/10.1515/9783111326306-005

politics: 'Why do they go after the little guy? Why not the campaign organizations that put stickers all over the subways at election time?'[2]

In this chapter, graffiti practices will be explored by tracking the main media narratives about graffiti works and their producers in contemporary urban scenarios. The chapter is divided into four sections. The first section explores the notion of the public sphere, power and spatial politics in relation to graffiti, including a typology of these practices. Although graffiti practices share some similarities wherever the phenomenon is found, there are important differences that must be considered in terms of cultural understanding, societal value, legislation, policing and media coverage. After a short description of the methods, this theoretical analysis of graffiti practices will focus on a typology of media narratives in the second section, highlighting how these discourses shape both the practices and their producers. The third section of this empirically based study addresses the anti-graffiti strategies employed by both local authorities and private individuals or businesses. The discussion in both the second and third section centres around various graffiti practices in Brazil. The final section presents the main conclusions and identifies several paths for future research on graffiti practices, its media narratives and its policing.

2 Understanding graffiti practices: Spatial politics, power and the public space

There is a vast debate regarding spatial politics and the ways in which 'we' – the inhabitants of a given space – are expected to behave or not behave. In the past, spatial arrangements of the 'public space' were significantly less regulated, and as Sennett has pointed out, there has been a complex historical process by which the publicness of our acts has been defined.[3] While some behaviours have been deemed acceptable in public, other behaviours and cultural practices have been displaced to the private realm, and each society has also defined the method and degree of punishment for any transgressive behaviour. The concept of 'we' in this context is often a neutralized, all-encompassing idea of a given collectivity, and tends to hide or segregate those who do not necessarily fit the archetype of membership. In this sense, while some individuals move through urban spaces and the cities with relative freedom, enjoying 'full membership' because of their

2 '"Taki 183" Spawns Pen Pals' 1971.
3 Sennett 1977; Sennett 1990.

social status or 'privilege', other individuals are excluded from these 'same' spaces, navigating them while experiencing stigma and feelings of not belonging. As Goffman has explained in his seminal book on stigma, these disenfranchised individuals frequently devise strategies to minimize their stigma.[4]

Lefebvre and Harvey have observed that the production of contemporary urban spaces cannot be disconnected from the reproduction of society under capitalism.[5] Urban spaces are designed to supply the needs of the system, a spatial rationality that favours the transport of commodities, raw resources, people, information and other materials that facilitate capital accumulation.[6] These spaces are symbolically violent, and according to Lefebvre, in their monumentality they 'mask the will to power and the arbitrariness of power beneath signs and surfaces which claim to express collective will and collective thought'.[7] For this analysis, the notion of monumentality has been expanded to look beyond 'monuments', which are often the target of political graffiti,[8] to include other infrastructure that could be considered 'monumental', such as skyscrapers, transport systems (i.e., rail transport, airports etc.), headquarters of businesses and corporations and governmental buildings. Although these spaces have dominant or preferred uses, alternative uses are not necessarily precluded, and countless forms of spatial appropriation may emerge. In her sociological analysis of space, Löw explains how several 'spaces' can coexist within the same physical space, while pointing out that 'we' experience the city differently depending on multiple factors, such as age, sex/gender, social class and race/ethnicity.[9]

The idea of the 'right to the city' has been extensively discussed as part of the resistance against spatial exclusion. According to Lefebvre, this right implies access to the centre, a privileged space of power.[10] In his interpretation of this right, Harvey states that this notion not only includes the right to access the common resources available in the city (in which respect public aesthetics should be considered a shared good), but also the right to participate in the (democratic) processes of shaping the city itself.[11] The practices of occupying spaces, resistance and 'wars of words' that challenge dominant narratives may be considered part of a

4 Goffman 1963.
5 Lefebvre 1991; Harvey 2001.
6 Harvey 2001, 81.
7 Lefebvre 1991, 143.
8 Siwi 2016.
9 Löw 2001; Löw 2010.
10 Lefebvre 1996.
11 Harvey 2012.

functioning democratic system,[12] because they aim at correcting deficits within democratic institutions and improving the political participation of marginalized/disenfranchised subsets of the population.

Proposing a '*criminological verstehen*'[13] of these unauthorized and transgressive social practices, Ferrell et al. observe that this analysis should not be detached from idealized notions of decency and community.[14] Indeed, considering the dichotomy of 'crime as culture' and 'culture as crime', Ferrell proposes to understand criminal behaviour as subcultural behaviour, 'collectively organized around networks of symbol, ritual, and shared meaning', while also observing 'the reconstruction of cultural enterprise as criminal endeavor'.[15] As mentioned above, the practice of inscribing on a wall is not necessarily illegal or controversial when it is practised in the private realm, but the same behaviour is considered a 'crime' or 'vandalism' when it takes place in unauthorized public spaces.

Following Habermas and Ferrell, the discussion of public matters – including both the idea of the city and public spaces and the definition of 'crime' – is perceived as key in democratic societies.[16] It is through such public debate that consent is reached or attempted, which would theoretically offer disenfranchised groups the possibility of expressing their political views on a given subject. However, the political power of these counterpublics,[17] diasporic publics,[18] or subaltern publics[19] is limited, and the emergence of participatory deficits within democratic institutions has also been acknowledged.[20] As Parkinson has pointed out, there are reasons 'to be concerned about the ongoing availability of spaces for the performance of democratic roles, including limits to the ability of some sections of the public to access collective arenas and resources'.[21]

Because these diverse collectives experience various levels of disenfranchisement and vulnerability, their relationship with power structures changes according to context. Indeed, while the 'normalized' idea of political contestation might

---

12 Routledge 2017.

13 '*Criminological verstehen*' is an adaptation on Weber's formulation of *verstehen*, which includes processes of 'interpretive understanding' and 'sympathetic participation' that would allow the researcher to develop a 'methodology of attentiveness' (Ferrell 1999, 400).

14 Ferrell, Hayward and Young, 2008.

15 Ferrell 1999, 403–404.

16 Habermas 1990; Ferrell 1999.

17 Warner 2002.

18 Avritzer and Costa 2004.

19 Fraser 1990.

20 Markovits 2005.

21 Parkinson 2012, 88.

take the form of the written/oral word in terms of signature collection, lobbying and petitions, these subaltern publics might prefer 'alternative' forms of political participation, including both embodied politics (for example, performance or dance)[22] as well as audio-visual strategies (ranging from holograms to political graffiti).

The multifaceted nature of graffiti phenomena can be summarized in an introductory typology based on the intended motivation of the producers and the circumstances of their production. This typology includes several practices that are usually labelled as 'graffiti' in media stories or specialized literature, but there is extensive debate about the specific boundaries of each category. For example, the emergence of zones of tolerance and the recognition of spaces traditionally appropriated by graffiti producers have contributed to 'legalizing' some of these works, even if other 'graffiti' producers – or even scholars in the field – might not consider these 'authentic' graffiti. In this sense, although there are some contradictions in the definition of what graffiti is, the typology allows us to theoretically differentiate some of these productions, even if a certain piece or written statement fits in more than one 'type':

a) **political graffiti**, in the sense of any legal or illegal *street propaganda or political campaigning*, which includes both hegemonic and 'countercultural' or counter-hegemonic discourses;
b) **sponsored or branded graffiti** as a 'new' form of *outdoor advertising* in order to promote certain goods or services associated with local or global businesses and corporations;
c) **commissioned or 'official' graffiti** to designate works realized *under the supervision* or *with the explicit approval* of institutions (local governments, NGOs and churches) as a way to promote social values, health campaigns, environmental awareness etc. This category includes forms of *muralism* that are (mis)labelled as graffiti;
d) **street art (and hip-hop graffiti)**, in the sense of any authorized (negotiated) or illegal transformation of the *public aesthetics* (counter-aesthetics could be also included) in order to improve or challenge the appearance of a given urban or rural landscape. Street art is *freely* created by individuals or groups, without the support of any local institution or business. This category refers to graffiti practices that are not co-opted;
e) **territorial graffiti** to refer to the use of inscriptions, signs and other varieties of symbols created to delimit the *geographical-symbolic presence* of an individual or collective, which includes the 'individual' practice of *tagging* (*pixação*) and any territorial demarcation of space by urban or rural gangs, independent of any links of these groups to organized crime, drug dealing or any other potential risky behaviour (as in the case of soccer/football gangs).

It is important to emphasize that these 'types' of graffiti are often hard to separate, and that the combination of two or more such types is common. Indeed, in

22 Avritzer and Costa 2004.

recent studies on graffiti, the evolution and intertwinement of these practices can be observed. Franco has tracked the emergence of graffiti art in Brazil, linking its origins to political graffiti during the dictatorship.[23] Similarly, Austin has explored the wide complexity of graffiti practices in New York City.[24] Furtado and Zanella have further pointed out that during the sixties, Brazilian graffiti became a way to oppose the official spaces of public debate and artistic expression, constituting a sort of countercultural movement aimed at creating new civil liberties.[25] Some specialized publications on graffiti have also observed the mixture of these graffiti practices; for example, street art in Oaxaca has been used as part of the political activism of local schoolteachers campaigning for better working conditions (constituting a mixture of political graffiti and street art).[26]

3 Methods

This theoretical analysis is based on my previous systematic revision of news articles, op-eds and editorials that discuss graffiti practices in two Latin American newspapers, namely *Folha de São Paulo* in Brazil and *La Nación* in Costa Rica, in the period between 2001 and 2010.[27] A total of 682 articles from the Brazilian newspaper were collected and coded, while 246 articles were considered for the Costa Rican case. These media texts were collected with a series of keywords that included terms such as 'graffiti', 'street art' and *pichação/pixação*.[28] For the

---

23 Franco 2009.

24 Austin 2001.

25 Furtado and Zanella 2009, 1283.

26 Nevaer and Sendyk 2009.

27 Araya López 2015. *Folha de São Paulo* (www.folha.uol.com.br) is part of the Grupo Folha media group, established in 1921. It was the most widely read Brazilian newspaper between 2002 and 2009 (but the second most in 2010). *La Nación* (www.nacion.com), founded in 1946, is the main newspaper of the media corporation Grupo Nación S.A., which also includes the newspapers *El Financiero* and *La Teja*. Both *La Nación* and *Folha de São Paulo* contribute to shaping the political debate in their respective countries, and could be labelled as conservative and business-oriented, although their journalistic work allows for some pluralism.

28 In the Brazilian data, searching for the word *grafite* also yielded results related to the *Grafite* column by cartoonist Paulo Caruso; the soccer player Edinaldo Batista Libânio (a.k.a. Grafite); the term *grafite* as a form of the chemical element carbon; *grafite* as a color in fashion, cars and computer design; and finally, *grafite* as an artistic technique and pencil material, as in the context of requirements for school or university tests. All these results were excluded from the sample. *Pichado* and *pichada* were also excluded. For the Costa Rican data, the word *graffiti* was the main search term, with *grafitero* and *grafitera* included as well. Given the common misspelling

present chapter, more recent news articles from Brazil as well as media stories from other countries have been included with the explicit purpose of updating the main findings of the previous study.

In the Brazilian case, the term *pichação*, a noun derived from the verb *pichar*, refers to messages written on public and private surfaces that do not satisfy the aesthetic criteria for artwork, generally being political or economic protests or even forms of interpersonal communication. *Pixação*, or *pixo*, in a distinction made by its own producers, describes a practice of Brazilian youth – some of them marginal or belonging to the periphery, though not exclusively – that may be characterized as an autochthonous form of writing (calligraphy) typically found in large metropolises such as São Paulo, Rio de Janeiro or Belo Horizonte. The *pixação* is usually inscribed in black ink (in Portuguese, *tinta*), and is further characterized by its non-communicative nature and aggressive counter-aesthetic. Both *pichação* and *pixação* have been included in the analysis because they are frequently discussed in the media stories alongside other graffiti practices.

The qualitative analysis is based in three main tasks, as proposed by Tonkiss:[29] a) identifying key themes and arguments; b) looking for variations in the text; and c) paying attention to silences. The present study has not considered quantitative content analysis methodology for three main reasons: first, the definitions of coding categories used in quantitative analysis are often underpinned by qualitative judgements. Second, the counting of words reproduces dominant themes and narratives, reinforcing the power of these categories. Third, quantitative/content analysis presupposes a shared world of meaning that lies in the content of the articles. One example in relation to graffiti production may be the alleged criminogenic nature of the practice: even when this type of discourse appears a few times in the media articles analysed, it is impossible to know the impact of such statements, especially when pronounced by an important source, such as a local authority or 'academic' expert. For this specific chapter, other empirical information has been selected from social media and specialized graffiti publications, as well as from documentaries and movies produced with the participation of graffiti writers, artists and *pixadores* (practitioners of *pixação*).

---

of the word, an additional search was done for *grafitti*. The term *pintada* was not included in this research, though it is sometimes used colloquially to refer to this social practice.

29 Tonkiss 2004.

4 Typology of media narratives: Graffiti practices and their producers

A large quantity of graffiti is produced in the streets and on public surfaces without capturing the attention of global or local media outlets. Given this, before describing the five media discourses related to graffiti practices, it is worth revisiting some essential criteria for determining *newsworthiness*. According to Martini,[30] these criteria include: (a) novelty, such as new and up-to-date information, with the event as a turning point; (b) originality, impressibility and unpublished character, as criteria that could reinforce the idea of novelty and foster curiosity about the event; (c) the future evolution of the event, considering the development of the event itself and the possibilities for relating it with other news events; (d) importance and severity, the impact the event could have on society as a whole, the possible transformations both in the present and in the future, and the element of shock; (e) geographical proximity of the event to a given society (a local event is more likely to be selected as newsworthy); (f) magnitude, as in the number of people or places involved and the quantity of individuals, groups or spaces affected by the event; (g) hierarchy of the involved figures, their popularity and public sympathy towards them; and finally, (h) the inclusion of displacements, as in the case of massive migrations, public rallies and demonstrations, travels of any important public figure and similar changes of location or spaces.

Based on this, graffiti practices are often reported in the media because they effectively satisfy several newsworthiness criteria. In the case of established 'street art' or 'graffiti' artists such as Banksy or the Brazilian twin brothers OSGEMEOS (Otavio Pandolfo and Gustavo Pandolfo), their works are immediately relevant for media outlets, as they are recognized artists both in the streets and within high-status art institutions (Fig. 1). An example of this is the collaboration of said artists in New York City in 2013.[31] Similarly, the 2008 'attack' on the São Paulo Biennial organized by several *pixadores* – which led to the arrest and imprisonment of *pixadora* Caroline Pivetta da Mota – became a news story due to its unprecedented nature, while offering 'shocking' images and a potential evolution of the original event.[32]

30 Martini 2000.
31 Zeveloff 2013.
32 Araya López 2020.

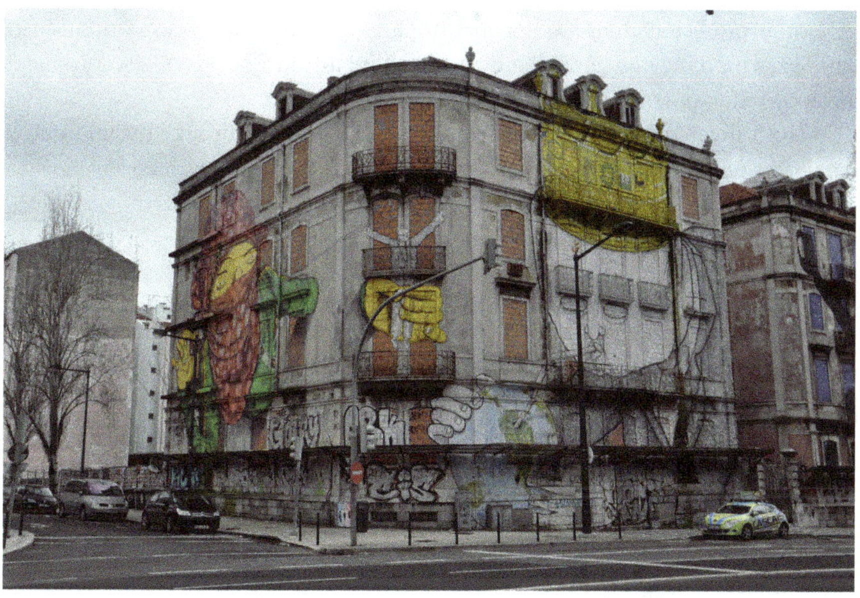

Fig. 1: An artwork by OSGEMEOS (Brazil) and Blu (Italy) in Lisbon, which is a more communicative form of graffiti, with bright colours and enjoyable aesthetics; photograph © Alexander Araya López, 2013.

In both the *Folha de São Paulo* and *La Nación*, there was a perceived evolution of media narratives on 'graffiti'. In the first years under analysis (approximately 2001 to 2004), graffiti practices were mostly described as criminal activity or vandalism. However, these narratives subtly changed to incorporate more palatable forms of street art and hip-hop graffiti: these practices are portrayed in a positive light throughout the period under review, which may be a direct result of the celebrated position that some elite graffiti producers have achieved both among the 'public' and in art institutions in Brazil and abroad. Their works are appreciated due to their aesthetic and economic value. Some arguments against graffiti (and street art) refer to its attributed US-American origin and to the lower-class or ghettoized aspect of the practice. However, graffiti seems to have conquered the upper class, at least through consumption and appreciation, if not directly through production. The legal and commissioned types of the practice have been openly recognized and fostered by local authorities. *Pichação/pixação* is presented mostly in negative terms at the beginning of the period under research (approximately 2001 to 2006), but is perceived more positively at the end (2007 to 2010). This may be a direct result of the actions of *pixadores* themselves, who have fought for recognition both in the media and in art institutions. Since 2008, *pixadores* have not only protested their exclusion through (violent) acts of appropriation of spaces (which may be considered as forced inclusion), but have also produced their own documentary movies, books and scholarship.

The following five types of discourses were identified through the qualitative analysis mentioned above:[33]

4.1 The medical-epidemiological discourse

In this first narrative, graffiti is perceived as a contagious social practice that is damaging to the social body. This contagiousness seems to work on two levels: it is conceived as a social practice that originates in the periphery and moves towards the centre, while at the same time moving from the 'lower classes' to the 'upper classes'. This narrative was particularly visible in relation to writing practices such as tagging and *pichação/pixação*.[34] The producers are perceived as 'less than human' or 'non-human', and often compared to animals and organisms that spread disease (e.g., rats, pigs, insects and germs). In this discourse, the producers are illiterate and unable to understand basic notions of decency and community, which coincides with the analysis of Ferrell as described above.[35] The main risk of this medical-epidemiological discourse of graffiti practices is that the solution proposed for dealing with them, and especially with the producers, is based on eradication. Having constructed them as a danger to society, local authorities and the police may decide to physically remove them from the city (either through forceful exclusion or via state-sanctioned murder) – as these 'young people' were allegedly less than human in the first place. In short, this medical-epidemiological discourse facilitates the suspension of basic human rights. Although this narrative was limited to a few media stories and declined in frequency in the last years under study, recent cases of excessive police brutality against graffiti producers in Colombia, Brazil and the United States could represent the factual 'eradication' of individuals that have been constructed as a 'societal threat'. This discourse was reproduced by some journalists and by authors of weekly columns or op-eds.

In the documentary *Pixo*, which was created by *pixadores* in Brazil to promote their own narratives of the practice, several images show these young male producers effortlessly climbing the façades of buildings while systematically

33 Araya López 2015.

34 Araya López 2020, 177.

35 Ferrell 1999.

placing their inscriptions on the walls.[36] This same documentary includes a short scene in which one of the *pixadores* confesses his inability to read basic Portuguese,[37] while excelling at reading *pixo* (which is characterized as a different code). Through these images, the documentary describes the territoriality of the practice, which could explain why those who oppose the practice exploit its comparison with animality. Moreover, graffiti writers, taggers and *pixadores* are not the only subset of the marginalized population that has been targeted by such medical-epidemiological discourse; some media texts also mentioned homeless people or drug users as part of this campaign in 'defence of civility'.

4.2 The legal discourse

The second media narrative of graffiti practices focuses on a broader discussion of the law. In this discourse, the issue with graffiti is not necessarily its 'contaminating' nature, but its unauthorized transgression and what this implies in terms of a society of law-abiding citizens. Again, this narrative was particularly prominent in the case of graffiti writing, tagging, *pichação/pixação* and political graffiti (Fig. 2). In this sense, the producers are recognized as human and not necessarily uneducated or ignorant, but are nonetheless individuals characterized by a lack of something, be it respect for common heritage or for the legal system. These media texts understood the motivation behind these graffiti practices (for example, physical exclusion or political disenfranchisement), but the tactics employed by these 'dissenters' were considered 'inappropriate'. This discourse relates to the aforementioned political participation of subaltern/diasporic and counterpublics, which would be 'more appropriate' if they utilized the official channels designated by democratic institutions (from the perspective of those in power). Although some graffiti practices may be read as a form of civil, democratic or aesthetic disobedience under this narrative,[38] the discourse mainly focused on promoting respect for the legal order.

Considering graffiti practices as a 'clear' violation of the law, the solutions for dealing with the producers have included fines, community service and other forms of societal retribution or 'punishment'. In the documentary *Pixo*, several *pixadores* report extrajudicial punishment in their interactions with local police.[39]

36 Wainer and Oliveira 2009.

37 De Barros e Silva 2010.

38 Celikates 2016; Markovits 2005; Neufeld 2015.

39 Wainer and Oliveira 2009.

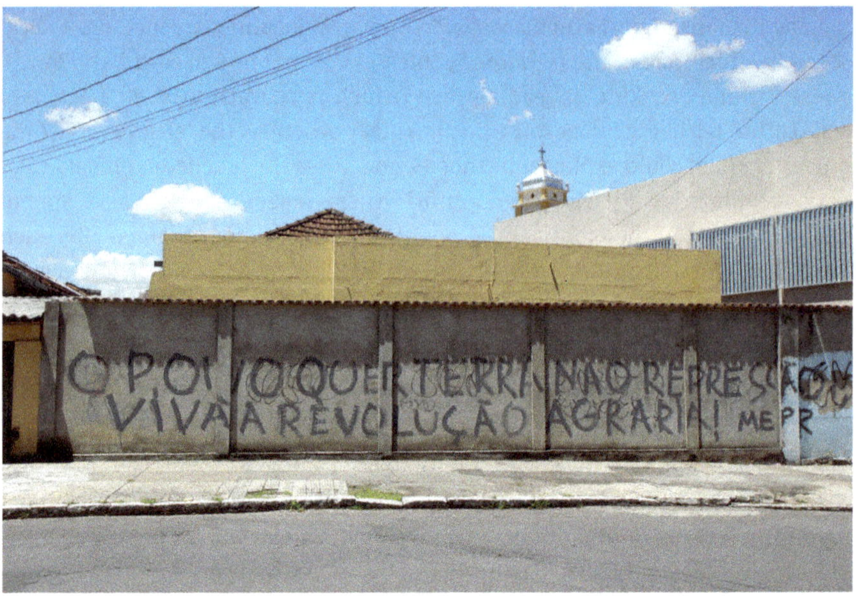

Fig. 2: A political inscription by the Movimento Estudantil Popular Revolucionário (MEPR, 'Popular Revolutionary Student Movement') campaigning for an agrarian revolution in Brazil; photograph © Alexander Araya López, 2010.

It could be argued that in the case of political graffiti, if a citizen engages in 'illegal' graffiti practices to promote a given cause or denounce a harm, and if she is already 'punished' by the democratic system through exclusion or limited political participation, is additional punishment a solution for her transgressions? In relation to the 'attack' at the São Paulo Biennial in 2008, the arrested *pixadora* experienced such an escalated punishment, as her lack of a legal address allegedly became the main justification for her imprisonment, in contrast to the other *pixador*, who was arrested at the event and later released.[40] In this discourse, both the 'law' and 'democracy' are constructed as ideals that offer every citizen the same degree of protection or participation, with the nuances of both law and democracy *in practice* remaining unacknowledged.

40 Araya López 2020.

4.3 The criminogenic discourse

The third narrative identified in the media texts presented graffiti practices as a gateway to more serious and violent forms of crime. In short, graffiti practices are considered a first violation of the law, and if the 'transgressors' are not punished for their acts, they develop a sense of confidence that can potentially lead them to other criminal pursuits, ranging from drug dealing to rape or murder. This narrative was not so frequent in the media texts, but it was discernible. In Brazil, some regions of São Paulo – such as Cracolândia (Crackland), in which drug trafficking and consumption are relatively common – are characterized by the prevalence of tagging, political graffiti and *pichação/pixação*. It could be argued that derelict places are spaces in which 'criminal activity' accumulates, with graffiti practices being just another manifestation of disorder and societal decay, instead of being the direct cause of the criminal behaviour.

However, it is evident that unauthorized graffiti practices include some level of 'criminal activity', which might include trespassing, destruction of private property (for example, a padlock) or even minor theft (i.e., of spray cans, paint, brushes etc.). Given the territorial nature of some graffiti practices, the potential for rivalry between competing groups also cannot be excluded, which could turn violent or 'criminal' in nature. The main risk associated with this narrative, as with the medical-epidemiological discourse, is that it ignores the structural forces that play a role in the reproduction of chaotic, 'criminal' spaces, while scapegoating the individuals as the main actors in these processes. The popularity of this criminogenic approach may be traced back to the 'Broken Windows theory',[41] an approach that has been widely contested for its inherent unfairness towards racial minorities and other vulnerable populations.[42]

Media outlets frequently exploit these unverified relationships to add shock value to their stories. In the case of *pixadores* in Brazil, TV shows such as *Conexão Repórter*, presented by journalist Roberto Cabrini, have portrayed the practice among other episodes treating controversial societal issues, including sexual child abuse within the Catholic church, high-end prostitution or even cannibalism. Unlike other media publications, in which the *pixação* may be presented as exclusively masculine, this show also featured the voices of some female *pixadoras*, despite some degree of stereotypical and oversexualized representation of the women in this movement, which could be damaging.[43] Female participants in

41 Kelling and Wilson 1982.

42 Ferrell, Hayward and Young, 2008; Thompson 2015; Jay and Conklin 2017.

43 Araya López 2020, 188.

pixação were perceived as 'rare' or 'secondary players', and even in the case of Caroline Pivetta da Mota – who became a central figure in the public debate about *pixação* due to her role in the 2008 'attack' on the São Paulo Biennial and her later imprisonment – media stories frequently highlighted her 'womanhood' and her 'novice' role in the practice. The dominant discourse is to present the practice as exclusively masculine and aggressive.

4.4 The social value discourse

In contrast to the media narratives discussed above, the social value discourse centres on the positive aspect of graffiti practices, ranging from the improvement of urban aesthetics to the potential entrepreneurialism of the producers. This discourse was used in relation to graffiti practices that characterize themselves as being authorized and having a 'pleasant' aesthetic. Graffiti practices are considered a form of public art, and could potentially contribute to educating the population in the form of specific 'awareness campaigns', ranging from public health to environmental preservation. Indeed, in several news stories, graffiti practices were considered a way out of the 'destructive' *pichação/pixação* lifestyle and practices, and workshops for rehabilitating *pixadores* and transforming them into graffiti artists were promoted in the media. In terms of aesthetics, these workshops would prescribe more enjoyable, colourful and 'creative' (art)works, therefore taming the transgressive and non-communicative aspects of the *pixação*.

These graffiti practices are frequently sponsored by local or international businesses, NGOs or governmental authorities, and although they are referred to as 'graffiti', these sanctioned artworks could more accurately be categorized as muralism.[44] Instead of damaging the social body, graffiti practices in this narrative contribute to fostering a sense of belonging within a community or the city, and they are in harmony with ideas of heritage and civility. The main characteristic of these graffiti practices is their communicative purpose, contrary to other works, which may be encrypted and refuse to address society as a whole, as may be the case for *pichação/pixação* or tagging.

In the Brazilian scenario, the social value of graffiti as a practice – mostly in impoverished communities – is related to its capacity to foster self-esteem, offering at-risk young people the opportunity to get involved in something creative

44 In the Costa Rican case, one awareness campaign, aimed at discouraging illegal street racing, featured an artwork presenting two scenarios – 'life' versus 'death' – at different speeds (80 km/h vs 180 km/h). The news article in *La Nación* referred to this work as both graffiti and mural.

and productive, rescuing them from their potential involvement in criminal activities. Graffiti is offered among other courses and classes conceived as prevention strategies aimed at transforming life in these communities and mitigating a series of social issues (from drug dealing and addiction to health and education). Some of these projects were linked to local youth organizations, such as Cidade Escola Aprendiz or Quixote Spray Arte. The at-risk youth who participate in these workshops and learn to create (authorized) graffiti works could allegedly profit from this knowledge by inserting themselves in the art market, predominantly through entrepreneurism.

4.5 The artistic value discourse

The final narrative in the media texts highlights the artistic nature of graffiti practices, independently of whether they are found in the streets or within art institutions. Graffiti, mostly associated with the global hip-hop movement, is perceived as an art, a way to beautify the city and improve the physical landscape (Fig. 3). The street art located on public and private surfaces, the creation of zones of tolerance for graffiti production, and the inclusion of the practice in the realm of galleries and museums are included in this representation. As a result, the products may be used for the decoration of houses or businesses as well as in advertising. This discourse generally applies to the category of street art and forms of hip-hop graffiti.

In relation to the producers, these individuals are characterized as artistic and creative youth who may have succeeded in the formal art market. Some creators are elevated to the category of celebrities, with their own fandom. Some examples in the Brazilian scenario include OSGEMEOS and their collaborators Nina (Nina Pandolfo) and Nunca (Francisco Rodrigues da Silva). These graffiti artists have acquired international recognition, and often they are active participants in global graffiti culture.[45] In this sense, their works are not only welcomed and celebrated, but officially promoted (though this does not mean that their works are not threatened). Indeed, it could be argued that both the creation and the removal of the works of these graffiti artists is frequently tracked by local and global media.[46]

---

45 Araya López 2017.

46 Some graffiti producers move between the legality and 'illegality' of the practices, oftentimes creating their (art)works in authorized spaces or in collaboration with local authorities, while also creating unauthorized (art)works, political graffiti or even *pixação*.

FOLHA DE S.PAULO COTIDIANO domingo, 28 de março de 2004 C3

O PROCESSO Os Gêmeos, dupla de grafiteiros mais conhecida no Brasil e no exterior, durante pintura sob viaduto na baixada do Glicério, no centro de São Paulo

Belezura subversiva

GRAFITE TOMA DE ASSALTO A PAISAGEM DE SP, GANHA STATUS DE ARTE E SEDUZ JOVENS

FERNANDA MENA

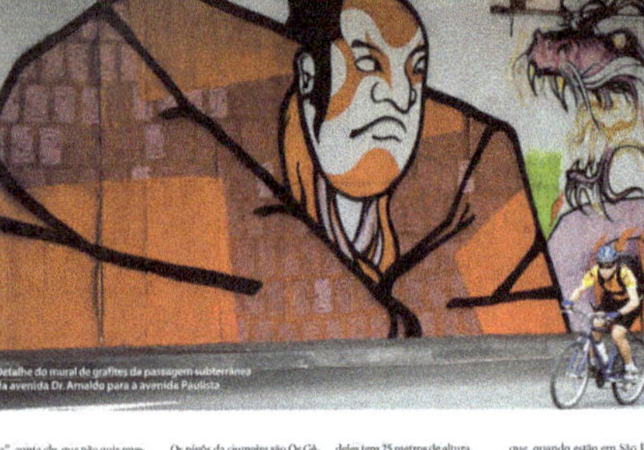

Detalhe do mural de grafites da passagem subterrânea da avenida Dr. Arnaldo para a avenida Paulista

Grafite de SP é vanguarda mundial

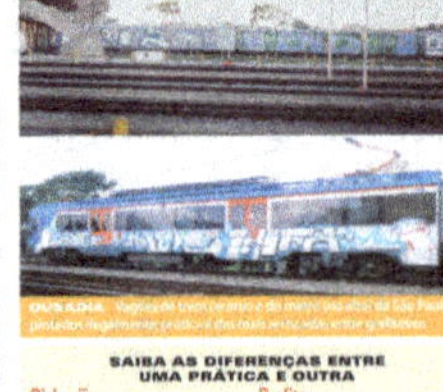

SAIBA AS DIFERENÇAS ENTRE UMA PRÁTICA E OUTRA

Pichação / Grafite

Grafiteiro critica falta de espaço

Fig. 3: The *Folha de São Paulo* article 'Belezura subversiva' ('Subversive Beauty', 28 March 2004, C3) reports on how graffiti transformed São Paulo, coexisting between the categories of 'vandalism' and 'art'; © Folha de S.Paulo/Folhapress; reproduced with permission.

Although there is evidence that the producers of unauthorized forms of tagging and *pichação/pixação* have campaigned against the commodification of graffiti practices, and have 'attacked' graffiti exhibitions hosted at established art institutions (e.g., the 'attacks' on the Choque Cultural gallery and at the São Paulo Biennial in 2008), these producers have also engaged in the commercialization of their own cultural products, creating artworks and documentaries either for the consumption of their peers or to prevent the appropriation of their aesthetics/art by other actors in the formal and informal art markets.[47]

5 Anti-graffiti and anti-*pichação/pixação* strategies and policing

Although graffiti practices have achieved some recognition in many cities and countries, the 'fight' against unauthorized or 'unaesthetic' forms of graffiti is commonplace. Local authorities in São Paulo have implemented several official strategies to tackle such forms of graffiti and *pichação/pixação*; these plans were covered extensively in the *Folha de São Paulo*. The first such project was Operação Belezura (Operation Beauty), under the administration of Mayor Marta Suplicy (Partido dos Trabalhadores). Secondly, in 2005, several articles referred to anti-*pichação* strategies adopted by Mayor José Serra (Partido da Social Democracia Brasileira). The third campaign was the Cidade Limpa (Clean City) law, signed by Mayor Gilberto Kassab (Democratas) (Fig. 4). News stories reported on the scope of these campaigns, referring to the economic costs of both graffiti and *pichação/pixação* as well as statements from those affected by the phenomenon or the expectations of the local inhabitants regarding these campaigns.

The main strategy has been the physical removal of graffiti or *pichação/pixação* by clean-up campaigns. These operations may include volunteer groups that take part in graffiti removal efforts, or private businesses that specialize in such services and are therefore compensated by local authorities. Although clean-up campaigns are theoretically an effective way to reduce the visual impact of graffiti practices, this eradication strategy requires consistency, given that the newly cleared spaces become an invitation for graffiti producers to re-appropriate them. A recent controversial case in Brazil involved the Mayor of São Paulo, João Doria (Partido da Social Democracia Brasileira), who continued the long tradition

47 Siwi 2016.

FOLHA DE S.PAULO SEGUNDA-FEIRA, 14 DE SETEMBRO DE 2009 cotidiano C3

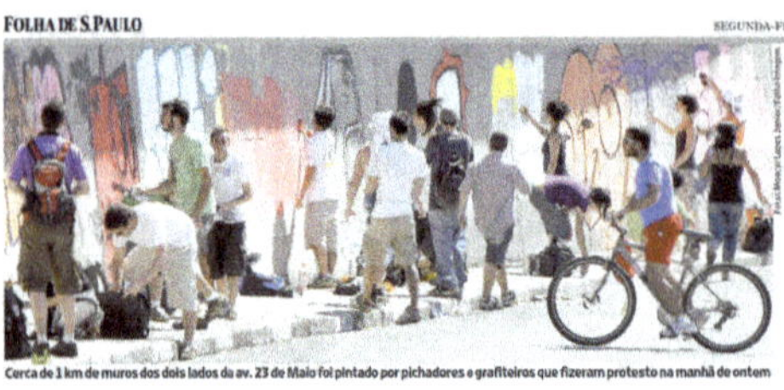

Cerca de 1 km de muros dos dois lados da av. 23 de Maio foi pintado por pichadores e grafiteiros que fizeram protesto na manhã de ontem

150 pichadores atacam a av. 23 de Maio em protesto

Nove jovens chegaram a ser detidos pela PM; ato foi organizado contra o "cinza de Kassab"

Frases como "Fora Kassab", "Fora Sarney", "Fiquem pelados" e "Seja feliz, mate um político" foram pichadas na avenida

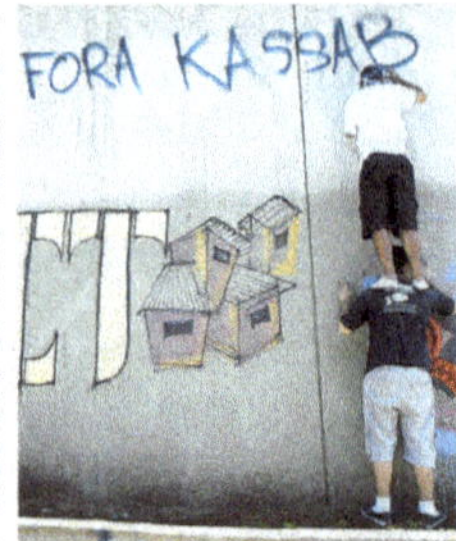

'Fora Kassab' e 'Fora Sarney' estavam entre frases pichadas

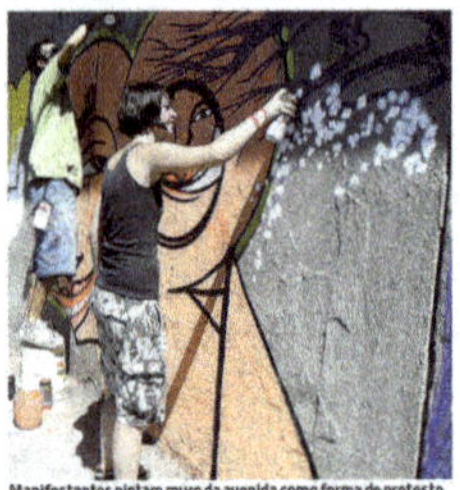

Manifestantes pintam muro da avenida como forma de protesto

TRANSPORTE

Detran abre três novos postos de atendimento na capital

VIOLÊNCIA

Chacina deixa três mortos em favela de Santo André

JOGO

Pela 2ª vez, PM fecha bingo clandestino em Higienópolis

MORTES

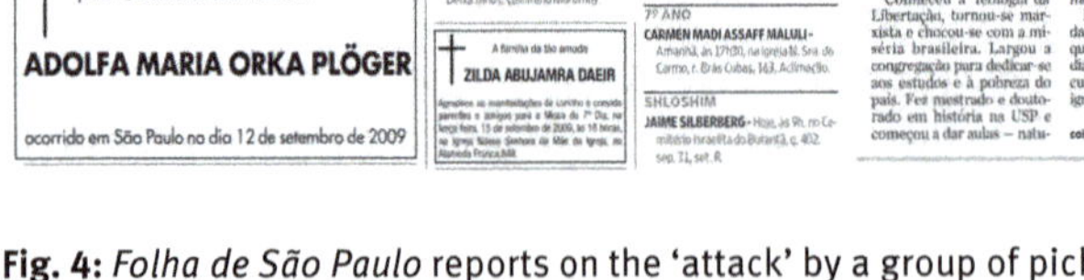

Melhoramentos Florestal S.A. comunica com pesar o falecimento da senhora

ADOLFA MARIA ORKA PLÖGER

ocorrido em São Paulo no dia 12 de setembro de 2009

VICTOR VINCENT VALLA (1937-2009)

Dedicou-se a estudar a pobreza brasileira

Fig. 4: *Folha de São Paulo* reports on the 'attack' by a group of pichadores on May 23 Avenue, which was a response to the clean-up campaign authorized by Mayor Gilberto Kassab (14 September 2009, C3); © Folha de S.Paulo/Folhapress; reproduced with permission.

of (failed) projects to beautify the city.[48] As part of his campaign against *pichação/pixação*, one of the biggest avenues in the city, Avenida 23 de Maio (May 23 Avenue) – internationally known for its outstanding graffiti art – was painted grey.[49] The following declaration by graffiti artist Mauro Sergio Neri da Silva (a.k.a. Veracidade) addresses the issue of spatial politics and the impossibility of finding a common aesthetic that satisfies us all:

> 'The new administration chose to get rid of this graffiti in a sensationalist way. Though they said the project was against vandalism and tagging, they also painted over graffiti at the same time.' The day after finding his wall covered in grey, Da Silva began gently sponge-washing the paint off, revealing the bright colours beneath but police officers stopped him and hauled him to the police station, where he was charged with committing an 'environmental crime'. Soon, journalists gathered at the police station as well and by the time he was released a few hours later, his plight had evolved into a symbolic case in the simmering fight over graffiti's place in São Paulo – between competing definitions of what makes a beautiful city.[50]

Other artists, including the renowned OSGEMEOS, questioned the mayor's tactics. A court decision was needed to prevent the removal of additional graffiti works, which subsequently required approval from local authorities on the matter of cultural heritage.[51]

A second strategy to eliminate or significantly reduce the quantity of unauthorized graffiti is based on the (ab)use of legislation. In this sense, laws and other local policies could be enacted to target those who engage in unauthorized graffiti production, with punishment ranging from community service to fines to incarceration. In Brazil, some legislation has targeted the possession of materials for graffiti production with heavy fines, technically making the sale of spray cans to underage youth 'illegal'. The spray cans also include a disclaimer stating that *pichação* is a crime; here the term may refer to both political graffiti and to *pixo/pixação* (as referred to by its own producers).[52]

Abuses of the law have also been reported by graffiti producers, a problem that has been mentioned in some media texts: for example, news articles on the female *pixadora* arrested during the 'attack' on the São Paulo Biennial. These abuses include the application of laws that were created for other purposes (e.g. to fight organized crime or against criminal incitement) against graffiti

48 Araya López 2015, 141–142.
49 Sims 2017.
50 Sims 2017.
51 Paulo 2019.
52 Araya López 2020.

producers.[53] In the documentary *Pixo* (Fig. 5), *pixadores* describe various forms of extrajudicial punishment exerted by the police, including forcing them to drink paint or to chew a paint roller.[54] In informal conversations with graffiti producers, they have also reported that police authorities have tied them to outdoor public infrastructure in cold weather – but that often it is possible to 'escape' punishment by bribing the police officers or arguing that their work is 'graffiti', alluding to its aesthetic value as opposed to the non-communicative and transgressive *pixo*. In Belo Horizonte, a group of *pixadores* known locally as 'Pixadores de Elite' were the target of a 2016 police operation; their punishment included wearing ankle bracelets to prevent them from going out at night.[55]

The physical eradication of graffiti producers is a more complex issue. In recent years, several 'scandals' involving the police and graffiti writers, taggers and *pixadores* have been widely discussed in Colombia, the United States and Brazil. In Colombia, the 2011 death of Diego Felipe Becerra, a.k.a. Tripido, a 16-year-old student, led to an investigation into police corruption, considering that police officers had planted evidence and manipulated the crime scene to make it look like a confrontation with an armed robber.[56] The case caused additional outrage when Canadian singer Justin Bieber was allegedly provided a police escort while creating graffiti in central Bogotá.[57] In South Florida, Israel 'Reefa' Hernandez-Llach, an 18-year-old graffiti artist, died after he was shocked in the chest with a stun gun in 2013. The police officer involved in this case, Jorge Mercado, was not prosecuted as his actions were considered 'legally justified'.[58] Both the family and the wider graffiti community have advocated for justice, and his life and death have inspired a movie.[59] A year later, Delbert 'Demz' Rodriguez Gutierrez, aged 21, was spotted by police officers in Miami while tagging a building and fled the scene. He later died due to severe brain injury after being struck by an unmarked police car.[60] According to local media, 'Rodriguez was struck at the height of Art Basel week, as thousands of visitors descend on Miami Beach and Miami for one of the biggest art fairs in the world. Wynwood, which has gained international renown in large part because of its street art, has become central to the festival'.[61]

---

53 Aguiar 2016.
54 Wainer and Oliveira 2009.
55 Aguiar 2016.
56 Acosta Villada 2021.
57 Brodzinsky 2013; 'Críticas a Policía' 2013.
58 Madigan 2015.
59 Kavana Dornbusch 2021.
60 Rabin 2014.
61 Rabin 2014.

E4 ilustrada DOMINGO, 15 DE JUNHO DE 2008 FOLHA DE S.PAULO

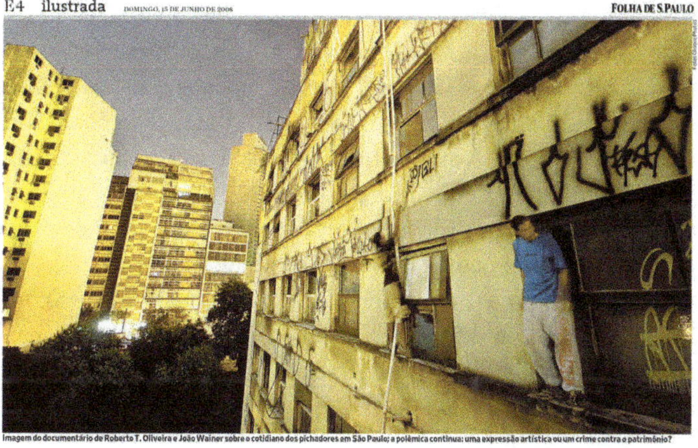

Imagem do documentário de Roberto T. Oliveira e João Wainer sobre o cotidiano dos pichadores em São Paulo; a polêmica continua: uma expressão artística ou um crime contra o patrimônio?

Documentário mostra ação de pichadores em SP

Filme registra jovens escalando edifícios e desvenda seus códigos de conduta

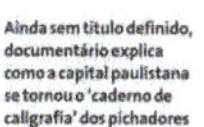

Ainda sem título definido, documentário explica como a capital paulistana se tornou o 'caderno de caligrafia' dos pichadores

THIAGO NEY
DA REPORTAGEM LOCAL

A pichação é uma expressão artística ou um crime contra o patrimônio? A polêmica questão voltou a ser notícia na última quarta, 11 de junho, quando Rafael Augustaitiz, 24, aluno de artes visuais da Belas Artes, foi detido ao pichar, com amigos, muros e paredes da faculdade paulistana. Para Augustaitiz, o ato foi seu trabalho de conclusão de curso. Para a faculdade, foi vandalismo.

Discutir se a pichação é uma expressão artística ou um crime contra o patrimônio é o que faz um documentário que acaba de ser filmado em São Paulo.

Os diretores do filme (ainda sem título), os irmãos Roberto T. Oliveira e João Wainer —este último, fotógrafo da **Folha**—, negociam com distribuidoras o lançamento nos cinemas.

O documentário não apenas registra diversas ações de pichadores (ou "pixadores", como eles grafam), mas desvenda alguns dos códigos de conduta.

Inscrições e desenhos, que para muitos não passam de rabiscos sem sentido, possuem significado próprio entre as turmas de pichadores.

Por exemplo, há várias categorias (ou modalidades) de pichação. "Agenda" é aquela feita em muros baixos; na "janela", pintam-se os espaços entre as janelas de um edifício; a "escalada" é a mais "nobre" (e a mais perigosa): transportando latas de spray em mochilas, os pichadores escalam edifícios para carimbar o topo dos prédios.

Caderno de caligrafia

"São Paulo é como um caderno de caligrafia, e os muros e paredes da cidade são os espaços em branco que vão ser preenchidos pelos pichadores", explica um dos entrevistados no filme. "Meu 'picho' está na pele de São Paulo", diz outro.

Ex-pichador, Djan, 24, é o fio condutor do documentário. Ele começou a pichar aos 12 anos. Hoje está parado; ganha a vida filmando ações de pichadores e vendendo DVDs em lojas do centro de São Paulo.

"Não basta rabiscar um muro para ser aceito entre os pichadores; é preciso conhecer quem é do meio, as turmas, fazer amizades", conta. Pichadores ignoram propositalmente as convenções de linguagem. "Criam regras próprias", diz Djan.

O que motiva um jovem a escalar um edifício para pintar seu nome e o de sua turma?

"A adrenalina, a superação", responde à **Folha** Diego, 22, que picha desde 2003. "Não temos o apoio de ninguém, nem da nossa família. É apenas pela adrenalina."

No filme, Gilberto Dimenstein, colunista da **Folha**, observa: "São pessoas invisíveis à sociedade. Não querem que a existência deles seja nula".

Estilo paulistano

Diferentemente do grafite, que tem uma preocupação estética, a pichação é feita com traços rudes, brutos, crus. É uma comunicação "fechada", que não tem a intenção de dialogar com a cidade.

A pichação praticada em São Paulo, com linhas elásticas, retas, formou um estilo próprio, que chama a atenção de especialistas de vários países.

"Em São Paulo, o estilo das letras é formalizado, quase como um alfabeto. Há uma conexão entre a pichação e os desenhos feitos em Nova York no final dos anos 1960", afirma a fotógrafa e escritora norte-americana Martha Cooper, que tem o grafite e as artes urbanas como focos de trabalho.

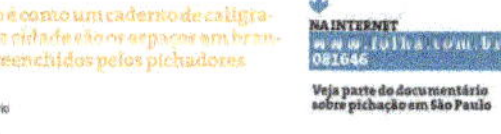

"São Paulo é como um caderno de caligrafia, e os muros da cidade são os espaços em branco que vão ser preenchidos pelos pichadores"

PICHADOR
em entrevista no documentário

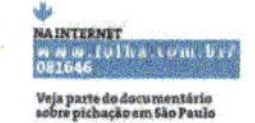

NA INTERNET
www.folha.com.br/081646

Veja parte do documentário sobre pichação em São Paulo

O QUE DIZEM E O QUE FAZEM

As gírias e os tipos de pichação

CATEGORIAS

Agenda	Muro baixo, mais fácil de pichar; cada turma de pichadores costuma ter várias "agendas"
Janela	Subir pelo lado de fora do edifício e pichar entre as janelas
Invasão	Invadir um edifício, subir pelo elevador e pichar o topo do prédio
Escalada	Subir um edifício alto pelo lado de fora

GLOSSÁRIO

Avenida de escândalos	Rua ou avenida de grande movimentação, cujos muros são muito procurados pelos pichadores
Pico de estouro	Topo de casa ou de edifício com bastante visibilidade
Point	Bares e festas que servem de ponto de encontro dos pichadores
Jeguerê	O que dois ou mais pichadores fazem, um em cima do outro, para alcançar um ponto alto de um muro
Soscar	Deixar a letra bem grossa, usando lata de spray
Grife	Nomes das uniões de gangues de pichadores
Molhou	Chegou a polícia
Bruxo	Policial

Fernando Donasci/Folha Imagem

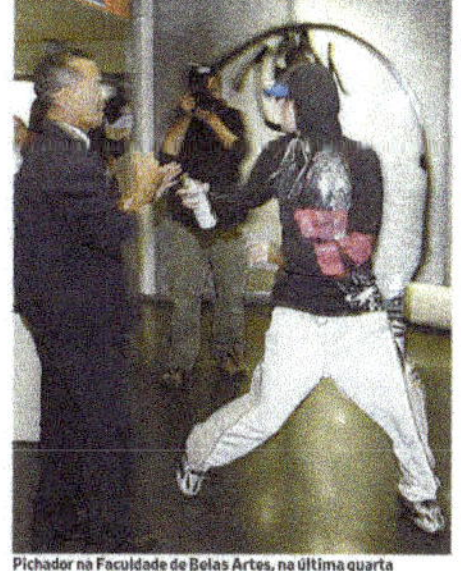

Pichador na Faculdade de Belas Artes, na última quarta

'É um crime, mas é arte também', diz especialista

DA REPORTAGEM LOCAL

É crime. Mas é arte. A opinião é da fotógrafa e escritora norte-americana Martha Cooper, especialista em arte urbana. "Como arte, pode ser comparada com caligrafia. Demanda conhecimento e prática para ser feita bem. Mas quando essa escrita é feita sem permissão, numa superfície que tem proprietário, então é ilegal."

Em comunicado, a Polícia Militar afirma que é necessário "um esforço conjunto, envolvendo todas as esferas de governo, a polícia e a própria comunidade, a fim de dar um basta a essa prática causadora de poluição visual, que além de danificar os imóveis esteticamente, causando prejuízos financeiros, traz conseqüências também à estética, ao paisagismo urbano e ao próprio ambiente".

De acordo com o artigo 65 da Lei 9.605/98, a pichação é crime ambiental passível de detenção de três meses a um ano, além de multa.

No documentário dirigido por João Wainer e Roberto T. Oliveira, vários pichadores afirmam que preferem ser "zoados" pela polícia (ter corpo e rosto pintados com spray, por exemplo) a sofrer processos judiciais.

Monumentos públicos

Rafaela Bernardes, do Departamento do Patrimônio Histórico da Prefeitura de São Paulo, diz que a pichação em monumentos públicos "é um problema sério", mas cujas ocorrências vêm diminuindo.

Ela calcula que 5% dos monumentos históricos de São Paulo (a cidade possui cerca de 400 no total) estejam pichados. "São pichações que não conseguimos remover. É necessário fazer uma restauração."
(TN)

Fig. 5: The documentary *Pixo*, here reported by *Folha de São Paulo* (15 June 2008, E4), explored the practice of *pixação* from the perspective of the producers, describing their political views, their interactions with the police and their lives in São Paulo; © Folha de S.Paulo/Folhapress; reproduced with permission.

In 2014, the *pixadores* Alex Dalla Vecchia Costa and Ailton dos Santos, 32 and 33 years old respectively, were also killed in a controversial encounter with police officers in São Paulo. Though their relatives argue that they went into the building where they were killed with the explicit purpose of practising *pixo*,[62] local police authorities have contested this story, stating that the young men were 'robbers' caught in the act. In 2017, a local judge ruled that the police acted in legitimate defence and absolved the officers involved in the incident, a decision that was later confirmed in another court trial in 2018.[63] Though these cases may be considered relatively 'infrequent', and each of these 'killings' involves complex issues such as race, migration status, age, gender and social class, the legal decision to protect police officers could be read as a 'concealed' deterrence strategy targeting 'graffiti' producers and *pixadores* (Fig. 6).

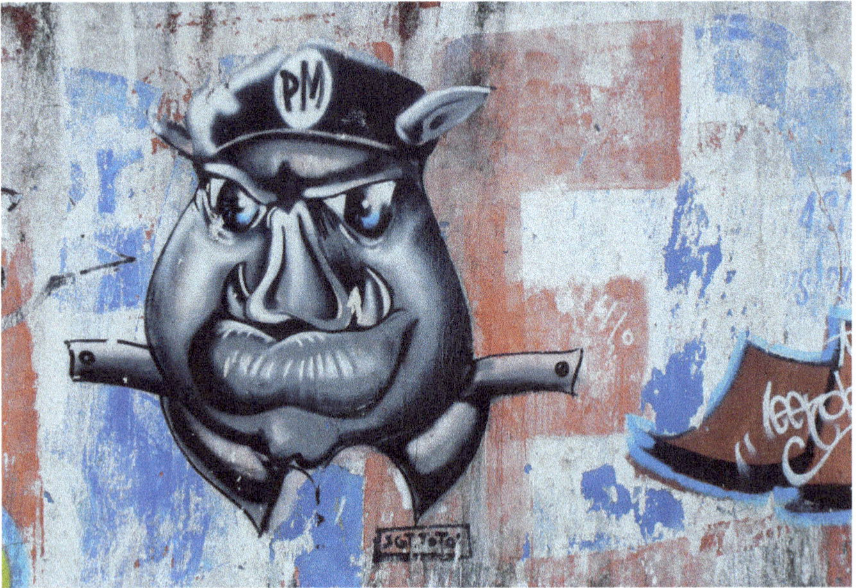

Fig. 6: A graffiti in Belo Horizonte depicts a military police officer as a wild pig; photograph © Alexander Araya López, 2010.

62 Phillips 2018.
63 Tomaz 2018.

6 Conclusions

This chapter has explained how contemporary graffiti practices are a complex urban phenomenon that requires an analysis based on spatial politics, power and the notion of the public sphere. The term 'graffiti' seems to be used freely in several media outlets, and at least five different types of graffiti practices have been identified: political graffiti, sponsored or branded graffiti, commissioned or 'official' graffiti, territorial graffiti and street art. In relation to media narratives on this diversity of graffiti practices, there are five main discourses. The medical-epidemiological discourse portrays graffiti as contagious, with the producers being reduced to a less-than-human or non-human status. The legal discourse emphasizes the alleged vandalism of the practice, while considering the producers to be uneducated individuals lacking respect for society and common heritage. The criminogenic discourse perceives graffiti practices as the gateway to a criminal career, with its producers engaging in more serious forms of crime because of a perceived 'immunity' to social punishment. The final two discourses are highly intertwined, and include the social value discourse, which centres on the positive effects that graffiti practices produce in a given society, ranging from a sense of belonging to education through various awareness campaigns. This narrative refers particularly to forms of authorized graffiti, which are often promoted as a way out of illegal forms of graffiti production such as tagging, political graffiti and *pichação/pixação*. Finally, the artistic value discourse further perceives graffiti practices as 'art', including their potential commercialization in established art institutions and the private market. This chapter also points out how these diverse narratives are linked to anti-graffiti strategies, including the erad ication of graffiti works and of their producers and forms of legal and extrajudicial punishment.

To conclude, several recommendations for future research are proposed: while there is an extensive literature on graffiti production, the popularity of graffiti practices from the perspective of consumers has been overlooked, as has research on the self-proclaimed 'victims' of graffiti practices. In terms of consumption, social media accounts that promote graffiti on Twitter or Instagram could be tracked and analysed to understand how graffiti is consumed by global audiences. It could be argued that the popularity of graffiti on the internet and in other cultural products (e.g. books, movies, clothing) has contributed to the positive shift in media narratives of graffiti practices. In relation to the 'victims' of graffiti practices, ethnography of buildings/spaces frequently targeted by graffiti producers combined with in-depth interviews of those affected by these forms of writing could be useful in exploring the 'real impact' that graffiti productions have on local inhabitants and private business, which may go beyond the economic damages frequently highlighted in the media to include affective, psychological or emotive dimensions. Although this chapter briefly explores anti-graffiti strategies and the role of the police in specific cases, there is a lack of research on how police officers understand graffiti practices, their perceptions of the legality or appropriateness of extrajudicial punishment, and their consumption of palatable forms of authorized graffiti (street art).

Regarding the artistic value discourse, the inclusion of street art in established art institutions has yielded a series of other cultural products that monetize graffiti practices, including documentaries/movies, books, clothing, souvenirs, graffiti tours etc. More research is needed to explore how profitable these 'commodities' are and whether the graffiti artists are compensated in any way. Finally, regarding *pichação/pixação*, tagging and political forms of graffiti, the effectiveness of these graffiti practices as a form of radical politics, civil/democratic or aesthetic disobedience should be studied, particularly considering that some of these practices aim at correcting inherent deficits within democratic institutions, and that political graffiti has been used to protest a wide variety of social issues, from mass tourism to the climate crisis to societal restrictions during the COVID-19 pandemic.

Acknowledgements

The author wishes to thank the *Folha de São Paulo*/Folhapress for the kind permission to reproduce original pages from their news articles in this chapter.

References

Acosta Villada, Camilo (2021), 'Diego Becerra: condenan a abogado y cinco policías por alterar escena del crimen', *El Espectador*, 20 October 2021 <https://www.elespectador.com/bogota/diego-becerra-condenan-a-abogado-y-cinco-policias-por-alterar-escena-del-crimen/> (accessed on 10 January 2023).

Aguiar, Leandro (2016), 'Arte coletiva ou formação de quadrilha? Por que pichadores de BH têm de usar tornozeleiras eletrônicas', *BBC News Brasil*, 18 November 2016 <https://www.bbc.com/portuguese/brasil-38007787> (accessed on 10 January 2023).

Araya López, Alexander (2015), *Public Spaces, Stigmatization and Media Discourses of Graffiti Practices in the Latin American Press: Dynamics of Symbolic Exclusion and Inclusion of Urban Youth*, PhD thesis, Freie Universität Berlin.

Araya López, Alexander (2017), 'Conflicted Celebrity in Media: Graffiti Artists and Pixadores in the Brazilian Press', in Jackie Raphael and Celia Lam (eds), *Becoming Brands: Celebrity, Activism and Politics*, Toronto: WaterHill Publishing, 56–69.

Araya López, Alexander (2020), 'The Pichadora Girl: Politics of Art Institutions, Legal and Extrajudicial Punishment and the "Pixo" as Transgressive Social Practice', in Lucy Finchett-Maddock and Eleftheria Lekakis (eds), *Art, Law, Power: Perspectives on Legality and Resistance in Contemporary Aesthetics*, Oxford: Counterpress, 176–197.

Austin, Joe (2001), *Taking the Train: How Graffiti Art Became an Urban Crisis in New York City*, New York: Columbia University Press.

Avritzer, Leonardo and Sérgio Costa (2004), 'Teoria crítica, democracia e esfera pública: Concepções e usos na America Latina', *Dados*, 47/4: 703–728.

Brodzinsky, Sibylla (2013), 'Artist's Shooting Sparks Graffiti Revolution in Colombia', *The Guardian*, 30 December 2013 <https://www.theguardian.com/world/2013/dec/30/bogota-graffiti-artists-mayor-colombia-justin-bieber> (accessed on 10 January 2023).

Celikates, Robin (2016), 'Democratizing Civil Disobedience', *Philosophy and Social Criticism*, 42/10: 982–994.

'Críticas a Policía por acompañar a Justin Bieber a pintar grafitis' (2013), *El Espectador*, 31 October 2013 <https://www.elespectador.com/bogota/criticas-a-policia-por-acompanar-a-justin-bieber-a-pintar-grafitis-article-455751/> (accessed on 10 January 2023).

De Barros e Silva, Fernando (2010), '"zfkolprajwlitdaniurdx"', *Folha de S. Paulo*, 6 June 2010 <https://www1.folha.uol.com.br/fsp/opiniao/fz0607201003.htm> (accessed on 10 January 2023).

Ferrell, Jeff (1999), 'Cultural Criminology', *Annual Review of Sociology*, 25: 395–418.

Ferrell, Jeff, Keith Hayward and Jock Young (2008), *Cultural Criminology*, London: SAGE Publications.

Franco, Sérgio Miguel (2009), *Iconografias da Metrópole: Grafiteiros e Pixadores representando o Contemporâneo*, MA thesis, University of São Paulo.

Fraser, Nancy (1990), 'Rethinking the Public Sphere: A Contribution to the Critique of Actually Existing Democracy', *Social Text*, 25–26: 56–80.

Furtado, Janaina Rocha and Andréa Vieria Zanella (2009), 'Graffiti e cidade: sentidos da intervenção urbana e o proceso de constituição dos sujeitos', *Revista Mal-Estar e Subjetividade, Universidade de Fortaleza*, 9/4: 1279–1302.

Goffman, Erving (1963), *Stigma: Notes on the Management of Spoiled Identity*, New York: Touchstone.

Jay, Mark and Philip Conklin (2017), 'Detroit and the Political Origins of "Broken Windows" Policing', *Race & Class*, 59/2: 26–48.

Habermas, Jürgen (1990), *Strukturwandel der Öffentlichkeit: Untersuchungen zu einer Kategorie der bürgerlichen Gesellschaft*, Frankfurt am Main: Suhrkamp.

Harvey, David (2001), *Spaces of Capital: Towards a Critical Geography*, Edinburgh: Edinburgh University Press.

Harvey, David (2012), *Rebel Cities: From the Right to the City to the Urban Revolution*, London: Verso.

Kavana Dornbusch, Jessica (2021), 'Miami Graffiti Artist Reefa, Who Died by Police Taser, Didn't Want to Be Invisible', *The Miami Herald*, 9 May 2021 <https://www.miamiherald.com/opinion/op-ed/article251270674.html> (accessed on 10 January 2023).

Kelling, George L. and James Q. Wilson (1982), 'Broken Windows: The Police and Neighborhood Safety', *The Atlantic*, March 1982 <https://www.theatlantic.com/magazine/archive/1982/03/broken-windows/304465/> (accessed on 10 January 2023).

Lefebvre, Henri (1991), *The Production of Space*, tr. Donald Nicholson-Smith, Oxford: Basil Blackwell.

Lefebvre, Henri (1996), *Writings on Cities*, tr. and ed. Eleonore Kofman and Elizabeth Lebas, Oxford: Blackwell Publishers.

Löw, Martina (2001), *Raumsoziologie*, Frankfurt am Main: Suhrkamp.

Löw, Martina (2010), *Soziologie der Städte*, Frankfurt am Main: Suhrkamp.

Madigan, Nick (2015), 'No Charges for Officer in Miami Taser Death', *The New York Times*, 23 July 2015 <https://www.nytimes.com/2015/07/24/us/no-charges-for-officer-in-miami-taser-death.html> (accessed on 10 January 2023).

Markovits, Daniel (2005), 'Democratic Disobedience', *The Yale Law Journal*, 114/8: 1897–1952.

Martini, Stella (2000), *Periodismo, noticia y noticiabilidad*, Bogotá: Grupo Editorial Norma.

Neufeld, Jonathan A. (2015), 'Aesthetic Disobedience', *The Journal of Aesthetics and Art Criticism*, 73/2: 115–125.

Nevaer, Louis E.V. and Elaine Sendyk (2009), *Protest Graffiti Mexico: Oaxaca*, New York: Mark Batty Publisher.

Parkinson, John R. (2012), *Democracy and Public Space: The Physical Sites of Democratic Performance*, Oxford: Oxford University Press.

Paulo, Paula Paiva (2019), 'Justiça de SP condena Doria e a Prefeitura por remoção de grafites na 23 de Maio', *O Globo*, 26 February 2019 <https://g1.globo.com/sp/sao-paulo/noticia/2019/02/26/justica-de-sp-condena-doria-e-a-prefeitura-por-remocao-de-grafites-na-23-de-maio.ghtml> (accessed on 10 January 2023).

Phillips, Dom (2018), 'São Paulo: Taggers Killed for Their Art Show Dangers of City's Graffiti Culture', *The Guardian*, 1 August 2018 <https://www.theguardian.com/cities/2018/aug/01/brazil-graffiti-artist-sao-paulo> (accessed on 10 January 2023).

Rabin, Charles (2014), 'Graffiti "Tagger" Dies after Being Hit by Miami Police Car', *The Miami Herald*, 10 December 2014 <https://www.miamiherald.com/news/local/crime/article4296547.html> (accessed on 10 January 2023).

Routledge, Paul (2017), *Space Invaders: Radical Geographies of Protest*, London: Pluto Press.

Sennett, Richard (1977), *The Fall of the Public Man,* London: Penguin Books.

Sennett, Richard (1990), *The Conscience of the Eye: The Design and Social Life of Cities*, New York: Alfred A. Knopf.

Sims, Shannon (2017), 'Paint It Grey: The Controversial Plan to "Beautify" São Paulo', *The Guardian*, 23 February 2017 <https://www.theguardian.com/cities/2017/feb/23/sao-paulo-street-art-paint-over-joao-doria-brazil-graffiti> (accessed on 10 January 2023).

Siwi, Marcio (2016), 'Pixação: The Story behind São Paulo's "Angry" Alternative to Graffiti', *The Guardian,* 6 January 2016 <https://www.theguardian.com/cities/2016/jan/06/pixacao-the-story-behind-sao-paulos-angry-alternative-to-graffiti> (accessed on 10 January 2023).

'"Taki 183" Spawns Pen Pals' (1971), *The New York Times*, 21 July 1971 <https://www.nytimes.com/1971/07/21/archives/taki-183-spawns-pen-pals.html> (accessed on 10 January 2023).

Thompson, J. Phillip (2015), 'Broken Windows: The Origins of the "Broken Windows" Policy', *New Labour Forum*, 24/2: 42–47.

Tomaz, Kleber (2018), 'TJ mantém absolvição de PMs que mataram pichadores; "marginais", diz desembargador sobre vítimas', *O Globo*, 29 September 2018 <https://g1.globo.com/sp/sao-paulo/noticia/2018/09/29/tj-mantem-absolvicao-de-pms-que-mataram-pichadores-marginais-diz-desembargador-sobre-vitimas.ghtml> (accessed on 10 January 2023).

Tonkiss, Fran (2004), 'Analysing Text and Speech: Content and Discourse Analysis', in Clive Seale (ed.), *Researching Society and Culture*, London: Sage, 367–382.

Wainer, João and Roberto T. Oliveira (2009), 'Pixo' [Documentary], <https://vimeo.com/29691112> (accessed on 10 January 2023).

Warner, Michael (2002), *Publics and Counterpublics*, New York: Zone Books.

Zeveloff, Julie (2013), 'Banksy Collaborated with Brazilian Graffiti Artists For Today's NYC Installation', *Business Insider India*, 18 October 2013 <https://www.businessinsider.com/banksy-os-gemeos-collaboration-2013-10> (accessed on 10 January 2023).

Central and East Asia

Matsui Dai

Old Uyghur Graffiti Inscriptions from Central Asia

Abstract: This paper introduces the results of recent research on Old Uyghur-Turkic graffiti inscriptions from Central Asia. Most of these, written on the walls of Buddhist sanctuary cave temples (in Turfan, Xinjiang, and in Dunhuang, Gansu), consist of the memorial writings of pilgrims and visitors. These graffiti inscriptions demonstrate the diversity of Old Uyghur literary culture and Buddhist cults, as well as various aspects of their daily lives that are undetectable from the enormous Buddhist religious canons; examples of religious practices conducted by visitors and pilgrims at cave temples; and the nodes and terminals of their geographical network.

1 Introduction

The Old Uyghurs[1] were Turkic nomads who built an empire on the Mongolian Plateau in the mid-eighth century CE. With their powerful cavalry force, they flourished amid the Silk Road trade between Tang China and western Eurasia. As the Uyghur nomadic empire collapsed in the mid-ninth century, a considerable part of the Uyghur population migrated to and occupied eastern Central Asia or the eastern part of the Tianshan Mountains (in present-day Xinjiang, People's Republic of China), where they established the West Uyghur kingdom. During the late ninth and tenth centuries, the Turkic Uyghurs linguistically Turkicized the native inhabitants of Chinese or Indo-Iranian origin in the oasis cities of the region, which came to be regarded as *turkistān*, 'the land of the Turks', in Iranian sources. In turn, the religions and sedentary culture of the native inhabitants gradually influenced the Uyghur nomads: though the Uyghurs had adopted Manichaeism in the late eighth century, most of them converted to Buddhism after the westward migration, influenced by the sedentary Tocharians and Chinese, whose Buddhist culture had been established in the Tarim Basin since the earliest centuries of the Christian era. Some of the Uyghur nomads adopted a mercantile

1 The Old Turkic ethnonym Uyghur is also Romanized as Uigur, Uighur, or Uygur, all of which derive from the form *'WYXWR* = *Uyγur* in Uyghur script.

https://doi.org/10.1515/9783111326306-006

lifestyle and became more active in interregional trade throughout the Silk Road. From the earliest stages, they enjoyed close contact with Dunhuang 敦煌, a neighbouring oasis state at the westernmost edge of the Gansu Corridor. At the beginning of the thirteenth century, the Uyghurs placed themselves under the jurisdiction of the emerging Mongol empire, and a considerable number of Uyghurs participated in the Mongol administration as bureaucrats or commercial agents, extending their sphere of activity to Eurasia – from China in the east to Anatolia in the west – through the late fourteenth century. Consequently, these Buddhist Uyghurs were mostly absorbed into the local societies.[2]

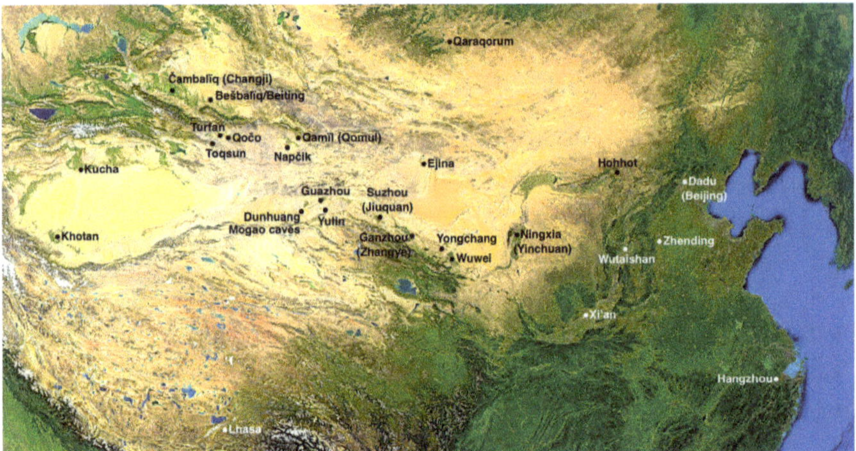

Fig. 1: Map with geographical names related to the present paper.

At the turn of the twentieth century, Europe and Japan dispatched expeditions to ruined oases and archaeological sites in Xinjiang and Gansu, respectively. In particular, expeditions to ruins around Gaochang 高昌 (→ Uyg. *Qočo*) – the ancient winter capital of the Uyghur kingdom, in the Turfan (= Tulufan 吐魯番) basin of Xinjiang – and the Mogao 莫高 cave temples of Dunhuang were the most successful in yielding a great number of paper fragments of textual materials in various

2 Successive waves of Islamization had forced the Buddhist Uyghurs of East Turkestan to migrate to the Gansu region by the early sixteenth century. Eventually, the identity of the ethnic 'Uyghurs' of East Turkestan, which had been closely linked with Buddhist culture, was replaced by 'Muslim' or 'Turk'. The term 'Uyghur' as a generic political appellation for the Turkic Muslim people of modern Xinjiang was not adopted until the early twentieth century, and has scarce continuity with the Old Uyghurs as a historical entity.

languages and scripts belonging to the millennium from the third to fourteenth centuries CE. Among these paper materials are Old Uyghur texts written in the Old Uyghur-Turkic language in the Uyghur script and generally dated between the ninth and fourteenth centuries. The majority of the Old Uyghur texts concern the Buddhist canons, while a smaller number are related to Manichaeism or the Christian Church of the East (the so-called 'Nestorian Christians'). These religious texts are significant sources for the religious and cultural history of the Old Uyghurs and their Eurasia-wide activities. Secular documents also serve to reconstruct the daily socio-economic aspects of Uyghur history. For more than a century after the excavation, studies on the history of the Old Uyghurs in Turfan and Dunhuang were based mainly on the philological decipherment and textual editing of these unearthed paper materials.[3]

However, another type of Old Uyghur religious text – the inscriptions and graffiti written on the walls of the Buddhist cave temples of Xinjiang and Gansu – have piqued the interest of scholars in this field. This paper presents information on these Old Uyghur wall inscriptions and graffiti and their significance, mainly as the textual sources for the reconstruction of the history of the Old Uyghurs in Central Asia.[4]

2 Definition of Old Uyghur graffiti inscriptions and brief research history

Texts in various languages including Chinese, Sanskrit, Tibetan, Tocharian, Tangut, Mongolian as well as Old Uyghur that were written or inscribed on the walls of the Buddhist cave temples in Xinjiang and Gansu can be collectively designated in Chinese as *tiji* 題記 'memorial writing', which is generally classified into two categories.[5]

3 For a survey of Old Uyghur studies up to 2009, see Matsui 2009.

4 There are also non-textual graffiti by Old Uyghurs on wall paintings or paper; see, for example, Zieme 1977, 271 and Tafel XIII.1 = Zieme 2015a, 122; Raschmann 2009, 188, 189, 222; Zieme 2013a, 182–183, 192; Zieme 2013b, 55, 193; Zieme 2013c, 15, 37 (pict. 19); Raschmann and Sertkaya 2016, 91, 279; Yakup and Li Xiao 2019, 417. Thus far, the known number thereof is too low to enable considerable collective analysis.

5 For examples of the Chinese inscriptions at the Buddhist cave temples, see Dunhuang yanjiuyuan 1986.

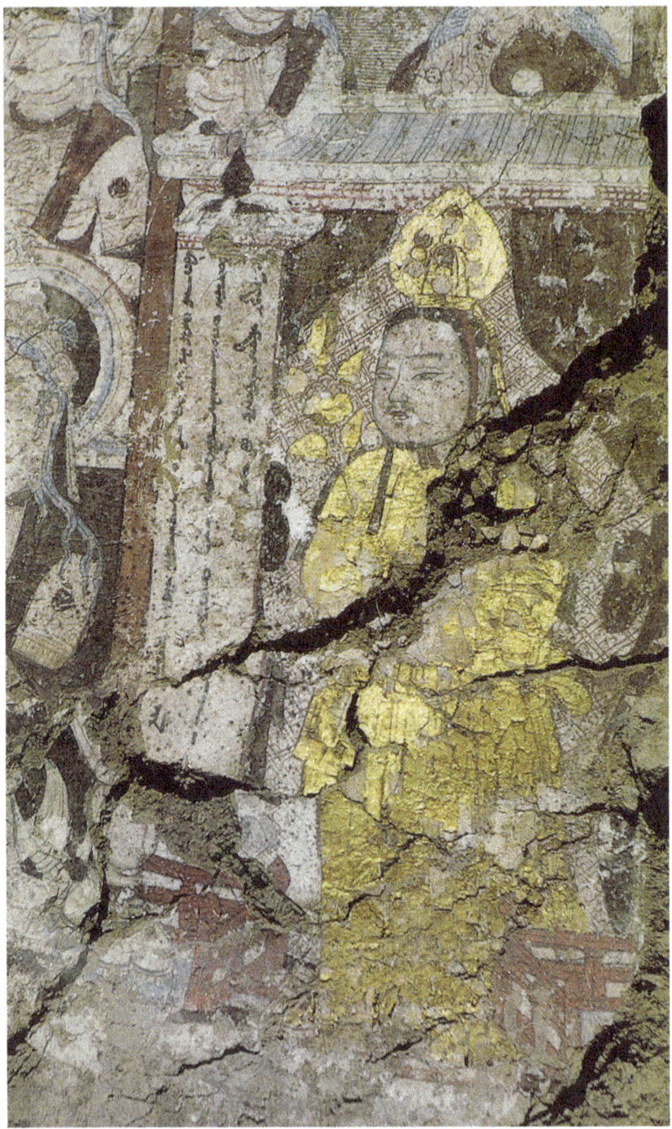

Fig. 2: Portrait of the West Uyghur King as a donor and his 'identity inscription'; the Buddhist temple ruins of Bešbalïq (Beiting 北庭), Jimsar, Xinjiang, *c.* tenth to eleventh century CE; based on Zhongguo shehui kexueyuan kaogu yanjiusuo 1991, Colour Plate X. The text reads: ₁*kün ay tngri-lär-tä qut bulmïš [buya]n ornanmïš alpïn ärdämin el* ₂*tutmïš üčünč arslan bilgä xan* 'Arslan-Bilgä Khan III, who was given divine charisma by the sun and moon gods and was provided with meritorious virtue, and [who] ruled the realm with his bravery and manliness'; cf. Umemura 1996, 364.

The first category is called *bangti* 榜題 or *timing* 題銘 in Chinese, which can be interpreted as 'title inscriptions', 'identity inscriptions', or 'explanatory inscriptions'. They usually appear on commissioned wall paintings, either in a space specifically assigned for this in the main painting or in a rectangular cartouche (*ti'e* 題額) beside the accompanying portraits of the wall paintings' donors (*gongyangren* 供養人). Inscriptions of this category were generally written or inscribed based on the wishes of the donors, the majority of whom were political rulers or local leaders and their families, offering material support to the religious communities.[6] Even shorter inscriptions, simply declaring the identity, name, and title of each donor, can offer a more concrete image of the people who supported these religions (Fig. 2). Some of the longer ones include praise of their meritorious deeds—such as construction and renovation of monastic facilities, or donations to religious communities—or expressions of their religious wishes and desires, and therefore deserve the special designation of 'donor inscriptions' (Fig. 3), which may be parallel to the Chinese technical term *gongdeji* 功德記 'record of meritorious deeds'. Most of the identity or donor inscriptions in Old Uyghur date from the tenth to eleventh centuries, a period for which information on the Uyghurs is quite scarce in the narrative historical record. Therefore, these inscriptions can be valuable sources for grasping the structures of political power or social community that supported Uyghur Buddhism in Central Asia.[7]

Another category is broadly designated as *youren manti* 游人漫題 in Chinese, 'visitors' graffiti' in English; these graffiti do not necessarily relate to the content of the Buddhist wall paintings nor to the donor portraits featured there (Fig. 4), but were written by visitors to Buddhist cave temples or other religious sites. Their contents are generally commemorative (Uyg. *ödig*) of their visits or religious pilgrimages to the sanctuary cave temples. Quite a few of them have only a couple of words—the visitor's name, their actions, and sometimes the deities worshipped[8]—though longer ones may include the date, the visitor's place of birth or departure,

---

6 See Zieme 2013b and Zieme 2013c for an overview of Old Uyghur donor portraits on various materials and their corresponding texts. We have many Chinese inscriptions with textual explanations of the Buddhist connotations of the scenes or deities depicted in the wall paintings, while Old Uyghur ones of this kind are not as many. See e.g. von Le Coq 1913, 38; Russel-Smith 2005, 91–96; Mirkamal and Yang Fuxue 2012; Zieme 2013c, 8; Li Gang and Kadir 2020, *passim*; Chen Aifeng, Chen Yuzhen and Matsui 2020, *passim*; Zieme 2021b.

7 Especially those left in the Dunhuang grottoes are of historical significance as evidence for the close relationship between the West Uyghur kingdom and the Dunhuang region. See e.g. Moriyasu 2008; Matsui 2014; Matsui 2017, 4–5.

8 See, e.g. Matsui 2017, no. 49, *buyan qy-a* (a personal name only), no. 5, *arqaži bitidim* 'I, Arqaži, wrote (this)', no. 81, *adityazen yükünürmän* 'I, Adityazen, venerate', no. 64, *tngri maitri bodistv*

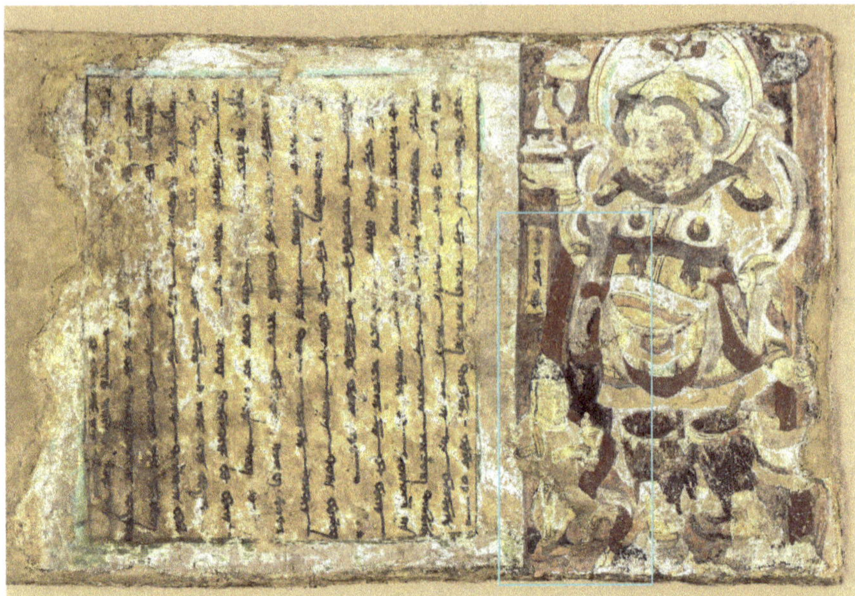

Fig. 3: Donor inscriptions on a Buddhist wall painting of the West Uyghur period; Bezeklik Cave 46, Turfan, Xinjiang, *c.* tenth to eleventh century CE; VD 831, the State Hermitage Museum, St Petersburg (formerly IB 8622a, the Berlin Turfan collection); based on Zieme 2022, 433, Fig. 4, with modifications. Encircled is the portrait of a male donor with a cartouche displaying his name, Boruγčï. In the longer Uyghur inscription on the left, the donor Boruγčï declares his wish to transfer the merit he earned from constructing the cave temple (*v(ï)rxar*) – perhaps '(after) destroying the Manichaean(?) monastery ($_2$*[manis]dan? buzturup*)' – to his family; cf. Zieme 2022, 433–434.

and the duration of their stay at the cave temple, offering detailed information about the reality of Old Uyghur Buddhist religious practice at the cave temples.[9] Some scribes even declare the motive of their visit and their wish to obtain enlightenment and to transfer the merit of their pilgrimage to their family, as also commonly expressed in donor inscriptions, reflecting their religious sentiment, enthusiasm, and piety as Buddhists. Furthermore, in many cases, the scribes expected their graffiti to remain long afterwards and be witnessed by future visitors.[10] In view of their content, it would not be reasonable to define such writings

'Holy Bodhisattva Maitreya!', no. 94, *bo mančuširi bodistv* 'This Bodhisattva Mañjuśrī!'; Li Gang and Zhang Hailong 2021b, *passim*.

9 See Section 4 of the present paper.

10 See the examples cited below.

as 'ephemeral graffiti' and to strictly distinguish them from '(identity or donor) inscriptions': the previous scholarly works have used not only simply 'graffiti' or 'scribbles', but also such terms as 'visitors' graffiti', 'pilgrim inscriptions', 'memorial inscriptions', and 'postscripts to pilgrimage', according to the content of the writings. The most appropriate umbrella term—to comprehensively indicate their nature, written occasionally and carelessly but piously, as a memorial—may be 'graffiti inscriptions'.[11]

The majority of the Old Uyghur texts on the cave walls can be classified as graffiti inscriptions with mainly Buddhist content, though they have not received as much scholarly attention as the paper manuscripts from these sites. One reason for this may be that they were regarded as rather worthless due to their lacking any direct connection with the images in the wall paintings.[12] Moreover, compared to the quantity of easily transportable paper manuscripts, the number of wall fragments that the European and Japanese expeditions cut down from the caves and brought to various holding institutes and offered to academic circles was much smaller. Although the explorers did not neglect to photograph the graffiti inscriptions at the ruins or cave temples, deciphering the Uyghur inscriptions based solely on photographs might lead to misinterpreting stains or shadows on the wall surface as strokes of the Uyghur script.[13] The direct investigation of the originals still extant in the cave temples of Xinjiang and Dunhuang was indispensable to preparing a reliable philological edition of the Old Uyghur graffiti inscriptions.

Since the 1980s, specialists in Old Uyghur studies have conducted fieldwork in Xinjiang and Dunhuang and produced editions of Old Uyghur graffiti inscriptions as significant sources for the history of the Old Uyghurs and Central Asian Buddhism. As a result of his fieldwork, Moriyasu Takao published several Manichaean graffiti inscriptions on wall paintings in the Buddhist cave temples of Bezeklik (= Baizikelike 柏孜克里克) in the Turfan basin, displaying the historical interaction between Manichaeism and Buddhism around the tenth to eleventh centuries.[14] Through direct investigation of the originals, the present author revised the previous facsimile-based edition of the graffiti inscriptions of the Yulin 榆林 caves

---

11 See also Zieme 2013c, 7; Porció 2014, 162–163, n. 37.

12 Porció 2014, 158–159.

13 We may note that Paul Pelliot prepared eye copies of many Old Uyghur graffiti inscriptions during his investigations of the Dunhuang caves in 1908, though they could not help being inaccurate. See Matsui 2008b, 29; Matsui 2017, nos 3, 16, 34, 35, 44, 53, 65.

14 Moriyasu 1991, 18–30; Moriyasu 2004a, 17–32.

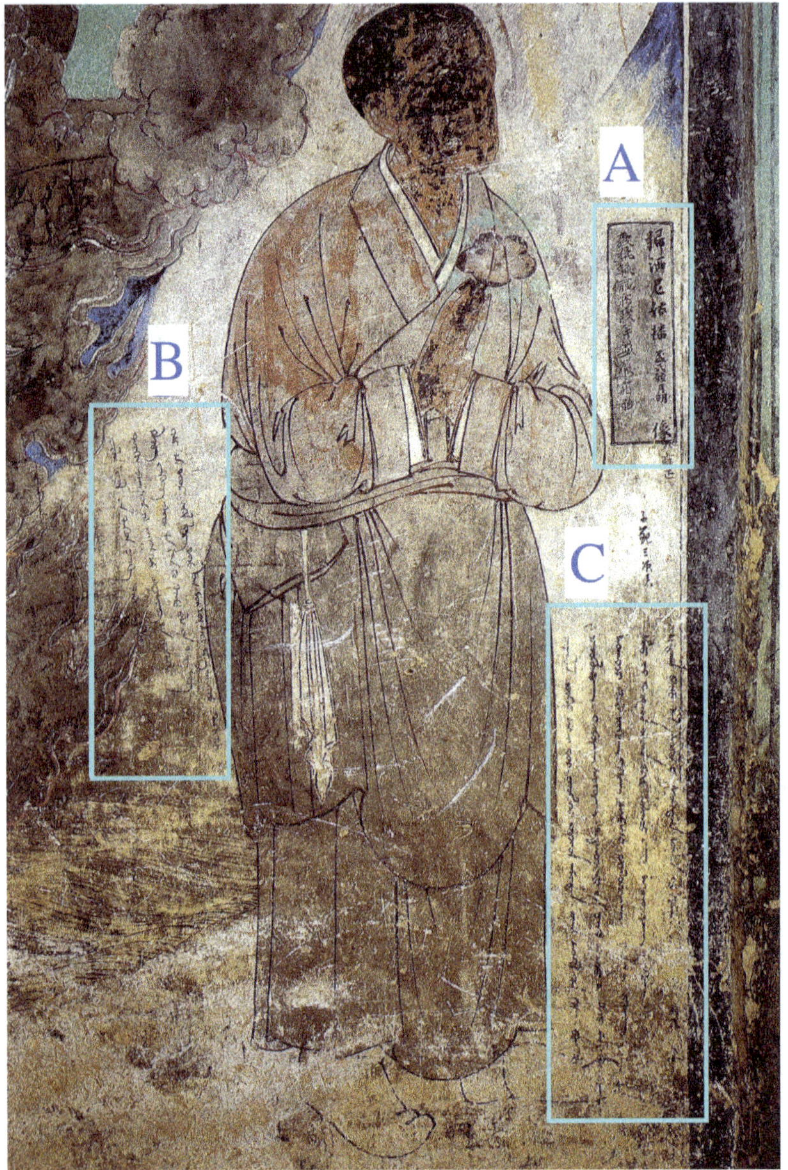

Fig. 4: A nun portrait of the Xixia period; Mogao Cave 61, Dunhuang, Gansu, *c.* eleventh to twelfth century CE; based on Duan Wenjie (ed.) 1996, 144 (Fig. 183), with modifications. A: Tangut-Chinese bilingual identity inscription attached to the nun portrait; Sato 2017, 343. B: Uyghur graffiti of the thirteenth to fourteenth century by a visitor from Ningxia; Matsui 2017, no. 13. C: Mongolian graffiti in alliterative verse of the thirteenth to fourteenth century; Matsui 2017, no. 12.

of Guazhou 瓜州, in the environs of Dunhuang, and highlighted their significance as sources for Old Uyghur history from the tenth to fourteenth centuries.[15]

Around the same time, Porció Tibor conducted a pioneering qualitative analysis of graffiti inscriptions through a comparison with various types of Old Uyghur Buddhist literature, including colophons and alliterative verse texts in paper manuscripts or on temple banners. As a result, he detected many common features in their formulas and wording, and established the significance of Old Uyghur graffiti inscriptions not as 'simple old touristic "scribbles" with silly content', but as textual sources exhibiting a Uyghur Buddhist literary culture.[16] Notably, in his analysis, Porció took account of Old Uyghur memorial writings and scribbles on the margins or back sides of Buddhist scrolls that were also left at the cave temples by Uyghur visitors or pilgrims, and consequently have quite a similar character as the graffiti inscriptions on the walls.[17]

Only thirty-three graffiti inscriptions were treated in Porció's paper, though; many more have since been made available to researchers. Peter Zieme edited twelve inscriptions attached to a Brāhmaṇa painting from the Bezeklik caves,[18] and offered a brief but informative overview of the graffiti inscriptions.[19] The present author continued his field research in Dunhuang and Xinjiang to produce a series of articles.[20] A Buddhist pagoda established in Hohhot (~ Kökeqota = Huhehaote 呼和浩特), Inner Mongolia, in the eleventh century also preserves twenty Old Uyghur graffiti of the Mongol Yuan era comparable with those from Xinjiang and Dunhuang.[21] In 2017, the present author provided a comprehensive edition of some 260 Old Uyghur graffiti inscriptions as a result of fieldwork on around 150 caves in the Dunhuang area,[22] including ones predating the Mongol period.[23] This edition was followed by investigations of a considerable number of

15 Matsui 2008b. Cf. Hamilton and Niu Ruji 1998.

16 Porció 2014. This work is helpful as a brief survey of research on Old Uyghur graffiti inscriptions, though it lacks reference to those published by Umemura and Min 1995.

17 See Porció 2014, 161, 164–167, 172, 173, where he labels them as 'manuscript inscriptions'. On Uyghur visitors to Buddhist cave temples who left memorial writings on cave walls and the backs of Buddhist scrolls, see Matsui 2021, 38–41, and Figs 11 and 12 in the present paper.

18 Zieme 2013a.

19 Zieme 2013c, 7–10.

20 Matsui 2013; Matsui 2014; Matsui 2015; Matsui 2016a.

21 Bai Yudong and Matsui 2016.

22 Matsui 2017. For a Chinese and an English paper based on this edition, see Matsui 2018; Matsui 2019.

23 Matsui 2017, 6.

Old Uyghur inscriptions at the newly excavated temple ruins of the Toyoq (~ Tuyuq = Tuyugou 吐峪溝) caves near Turfan,[24] as well as the more fragmentary materials yielded by earlier expeditions.[25]

Such developments in the textual and archival situation enable further progress in the study of Uyghur graffiti inscriptions in various respects.[26]

3 A variety of scripts, languages, ethnicities and religions

First, we must consider the variety of scripts that the Old Uyghurs used. Most of their graffiti inscriptions were written in the so-called Old Uyghur script, and a smaller number in the Brāhmī, Tibetan, 'Phags-pa, and Syriac scripts.[27]

Graffiti inscriptions in the Brāhmī script, of Indic origin, were retrieved by the German Turfan expeditions and assembled by Dieter Maue;[28] Kitsudō Kōichi detected many more such instances in the Dunhuang caves.[29] More recently, the archaeological investigations of the Toyoq caves, Turfan, yielded further new materials.[30]

The number of Brāhmī graffiti inscriptions in the Old Uyghur language is smaller than those in Indic (Sanskrit) or Tocharian languages, which were also sometimes written by ethnic Uyghurs. For example, in the Dunhuang caves, the monk Adityazen left twenty-nine graffiti in Brāhmī,[31] seven of which were paired with his Old Uyghur graffiti (Fig. 5),[32] while in five other graffiti he used solely the

---

24 Yakup and Li Xiao 2019; Fu Ma and Xia Lidong 2021; Li Gang and Zhang Hailong 2021a; Li Gang and Zhang Hailong 2021b.

25 Raschmann 2020, 215–229; Chen Aifeng, Chen Yuzhen and Matsui 2020; Zieme 2021b; Zieme 2022; Matsui 2022.

26 See also Raschmann 2020, 204–215, for an overview of recent research trends in Old Uyghur graffiti epigraphy.

27 For the variety of the scripts used by the Old Uyghurs, see von Gabain 9–41; Ölmez 2017, 189–209. See also Moriyasu 2004b, 228–232, on the chronological classification of the Uyghur script.

28 Maue 1996; Porció 2014, 162–163.

29 Kitsudō 2017a.

30 Li Gang and Zhang Hailong 2021b, nos 13, 39, 40(?), 52(?), 82, 83.

31 Kitsudō 2017a, nos 1–4, 6–8, 11, 13, 14, 16–18, 20–23, 25, 28, 30–32, 35, 36, 39–43.

32 Kitsudō 2017a, no. 24 and Matsui 2017, no. 175; Kitsudō 2017a, no. 28 and Matsui 2017, no. 184; Kitsudō 2017a, no. 28 and Matsui 2017, no. 193; Kitsudō 2017a, no. 34 and Matsui 2017, no. 210; Kitsudō 2017a, no. 36 and Matsui 2017, no. 222; Kitsudō 2017a, no. 39 and Matsui 2017, no. 231;

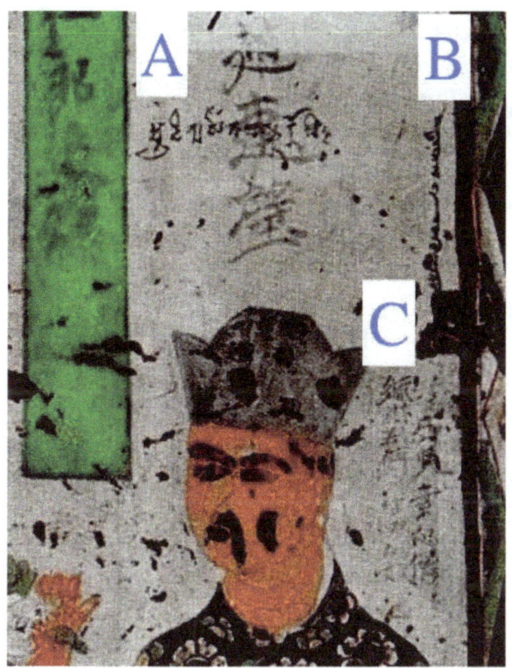

Fig. 5: Graffiti inscriptions by Adityazen; Yulin Cave 19, Guazhou, Gansu, *c.* tenth to twelfth century CE; based on Dunhuang yanjiuyuan (ed.) 2014, 84 (Fig. 51), with modifications. A: Brāhmī Sanskrit graffiti by Adityazen; Kitsudō 2017a, no. 34. B: Uyghur graffiti by Adityazen; Matsui 2017, no. 210. C: Bilingual graffiti of Tangut ^{1}*hu* ^{2}*leu* ^{1}*kyin* (← Chin. Fu Liujin 傅六斤) and Chin. *Fu Liujin nan Anu* 傅六斤男阿奴 'Fu Liujin and his son Anu', but not referring to the male donor portrait; Arakawa 2017, 298.

Uyghur language and script:[33] he was apparently multilingual in Sanskrit, Tocharian and Uyghur, as suggested by his name, Adityazen, deriving from Sanskrit *Ādityasena* via the Tocharian intermediate form *Ādityaseṃ*.[34] According to the information in his graffiti, Adityazen came to Dunhuang from Bešbalïq (the ruined city of Beiting 北庭 in Jimsar = Jimusaer 吉木薩爾 county, Xinjiang), seemingly during the West Uyghur period. Focusing on his graffiti, Kitsudō demonstrated

Kitsudō 2017a, no. 41 and Matsui 2017, no. 260. Kitsudō 2017a, no. 40 and Matsui 2017, no. 249 may also be paired.

33 Matsui 2017, nos 16, 44, 81, 190, 224.

34 We find further evidence of Indic-Uyghur bilinguals in the Dunhuang graffiti inscriptions: Matsui 2017, no. 158 and Kitsudō 2017a, no. 24; Matsui 2017, no. 88 and Kitsudō 2017a, no. 32; Matsui 2017, no. 173 and Kitsudō 2017a, no. 33.

the close cultural ties between the Tocharian-Uyghur Buddhists in East Turkestan and Chinese Buddhists around Dunhuang.[35]

Buddhist Uyghurs were heavily influenced by Chinese Buddhism throughout the tenth to fourteenth centuries; therefore, unsurprisingly, they inserted Chinese characters in their memorial writings and scribbles on paper materials as well as in graffiti inscriptions on cave walls.[36] Paul Pelliot reported a Uyghur-Chinese bilingual graffiti in Dunhuang, written by a Uyghur scribe named Ayïš-Qaya, but this had been lost until recently.[37] Another Uyghur graffiti from Hohhot ends in two Chinese characters, which seem to be a translation of a common Uyghur phrase and were probably read in the Uyghur language (Fig. 6).[38]

The Tibetan elements of Uyghur Buddhism have mainly been detected in Old Uyghur Tantric texts of the Mongol period and are generally considered reflections of the prestige that the Mongol imperial family of the Yuan dynasty afforded to Tibetan Buddhism in the thirteenth and fourteenth centuries.[39] Such a situation may likewise be evinced by the Old Uyghur graffiti inscriptions of the Mongol period, which newly attest many Tibetan names of Uyghur pilgrims and visitors.[40] Recently a Uyghur-Tibetan bilingual graffiti of the Mongol period was discovered in a cave near Turfan.[41]

Among the Old Uyghur texts related to Tibetan culture, one unique instance is the Old Uyghur Buddhist catechism written in Tibetan script, which was retrieved from the so-called Cangjingdong 藏經洞 'Library Cave' of Dunhuang (Mogao Cave 17) and then dated to before the eleventh century. The text reflects the Sarvāstivādin tradition prevalent in the Tocharian Buddhism of East Turkestan, which led the Uyghurs to convert to Buddhism.[42] Through our fieldwork in Dunhuang, we have newly discovered Tibeto-Uyghur graffiti from an older period (Fig. 7C): the scribe, with a name of Tocharo-Uyghur origin (Tib. *Sang ga seng* ← Uyg. *Sangazen* ← TochA. **Saṅghaseṃ* ← Skt. *Saṅghasena*), used the Tibetan script

35 Kitsudō 2017b.

36 Matsui 2010, 707; Porció 2014, 163; Matsui 2017, no. 269; Matsui 2021, Text D.

37 Matsui 2017, no. 23.

38 On the Chinese characters inserted into Uyghur texts, some of which were read in the Uyghur language, see, e.g. Shōgaito 2004, 322; Shōgaito 2014, 14–27.

39 See, e.g. Zieme 1992, 40–42; Elverskog 1997, 13; Zieme 2015b, 877–878.

40 E.g. Uyg. *čospal* < Tib. *chos dpal* ; *dorčïpal* < *rdo rje dpal* ; *luqpal* < *lugs dpal?*; *sangpo* < *bzang po* ; *šakyapal* ~ *šakyapa* < *sha kya dpal*. See Matsui 2017, 7.

41 Tulufanxue yanjiuyuan 2020, 103, and Plate 2, Fig. 7.

42 Moriyasu 1985; cf. Maue and Röhrborn 1985. See also Maue 1996, 210–222, on the Uyghur fragments in Tibetan script in the Berlin Turfan collection, which cannot definitively be dated to the pre-Mongol period.

to leave graffiti in the Uyghur language, and was even accompanied by a Tibetan colleague with the title *sha 'pi* 'novice' (← Uyg. *šabi* ← Chin. *shami* 沙彌).[43] This instance merits attention from the viewpoint of Buddhist cultural interaction between the Uyghurs and Tocharians in the region covering East Turkestan

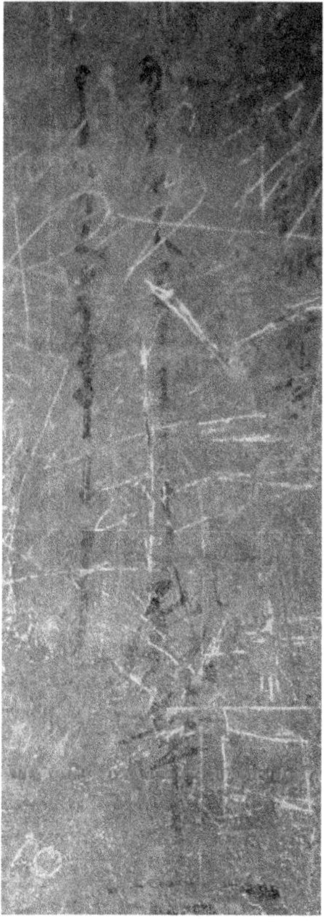

Fig. 6: Uyghur graffiti with Chinese characters; The White Pagoda, Hohhot, Inner Mongolia, *c.* thirteenth to fourteenth century CE; based on Bai Yudong and Matsui 2016, 73. The text reads: $_{1}$*taqïγu yïl törtünč ay-nïng* $_{2}$*beš yangï-qa tonga ạrs[la]n ša* 戲筆 '$_{1\text{-}2}$On the fifth day of the fourth month (of) the Rooster year. $_{2}$I, Tonga-Arslan-Ša, wrote (this) for fun'. The Chinese *xibi* 戲筆 'wrote for fun' might correspond to Uyg. *erikip bitidim* 'I wrote in boredom'; see Bai Yudong and Matsui 2016, Text P.

43 Iwao 2017, no. 59. The scribe Sang ga seng is likely identical to the scribe of two Brāhmī Sanskrit graffiti, Saṅghasene (← Skt. *Saṅghasena*). See Kitsudō 2017a, nos 26, 27.

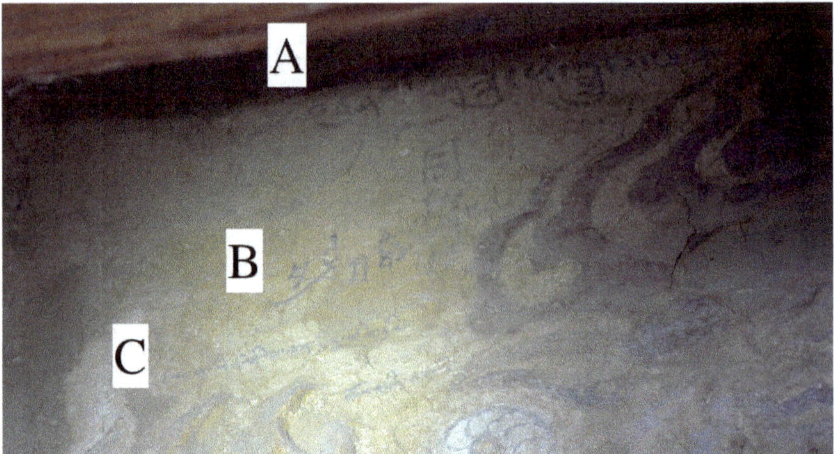

Fig. 7: Graffiti inscriptions in Tibetan and Brāhmī scripts; The 'Stupa of Maitreya' (Cishita 慈氏塔), Dunhuang, Gansu, *c.* tenth to twelfth century CE; after Matsui and Arakawa 2017, Fig. 2, with modifications. A: Tibetan graffiti; Iwao 2017, no. 58. B: Brāhmī graffiti by the Tocharian-Uyghur pilgrim Adityazen; Kitsudō 2017a, no. 22. C: Uyghur graffiti in Tibetan script by Sangazen, followed by another line in Tibetan: $_1$*sang ga seng shi la ['an di di] gyin drim* (← Uyg. *sanggazen šila[vandi tä]gindim*) 'I, Sangazen-*šilavanti*, arrived here'; $_2$*chos sprin sha 'pi* 'Chos sprin, the novice'; Matsui *apud* Iwao 2017, no. 59.

and Gansu, where the Tibetan script was in popular use in the ninth to twelfth centuries.[44] The novice Tsunpa (Uyg. *yangï tsunpa* = Tib. *btsun pa sar pa*), a Uyghur pilgrim from Qamïl (present-day Qomul = Hami 哈密, Xinjiang), who left bilingual Uyghur-Tibetan graffiti inscriptions in the Yulin caves, should also belong to a similar historical context.[45]

The 'Phags-pa script was invented in 1269 CE by the Imperial Preceptor (*dishi* 帝師) of the Mongol Yuan court, and can therefore be used as a dating marker for graffiti inscriptions of the following period.[46] Only one Old Uyghur graffiti in the 'Phags-pa script was available to Porció,[47] although our fieldwork retrieved a

44 For the use of the Tibetan script in the East Turkestan and Gansu in the ninth to twelfth centuries, see e.g. Takeuchi 2012.

45 His graffiti had been regarded as dating to the Mongol period, though Kitsudō has suggested an earlier date. Cf. Porció 2014, 162; Matsui 2017, nos 185, 202, 211, 220, 226, 251, 258; Iwao 2017, nos 61, 65, 67, 69, 72, 76, 79, 80, 81, Kitsudō 2017a, 167.

46 See Zieme 1998 on the Uyghur or Turkic materials in 'Phags-pa script that were known to researchers at the time.

47 Cf. Matsui 2017, no. 51 (= Matsui 2019, Text B), line 6.

further twenty-one instances of the script, a considerable number of which were written in Old Uyghur (Fig. 8C).[48] These instances allow us to speculate that the Uyghurs of the Mongol period were susceptible to the cultural trends of the Mongol Yuan Imperial court.

In contrast, the literary culture of the Uyghurs strongly influenced the Mongols in various respects, as has been detected through research on contract documents and Buddhist scriptures in both languages.[49] This is corroborated by the Mongol graffiti inscriptions from Dunhuang, the formulas and wording of which are almost parallel to those of the Uyghurs.[50] Below, I present typical examples of Uyghur and Mongolian graffiti inscriptions, whose content is mostly parallel, sharing such elements as: [1] the date; [2] the name(s) of the visitor or pilgrim; [3] their activities (arrival/visit, veneration, departure/return, offerings, writing, etc.); [4] the name of the scribe (frequently substituted by [2]); and [5] the closing, which often includes [5a] the scribe's wish to transfer the merit of their pilgrimage, that the inscription be seen by posterity, etc.

Uyghur:

$_1$*qutluγ qoyn yïl altïnč ay yägrmi [....]* ....[1]
$_2$*biz qur? buq-a [....]K taγ buq-a elig?*
$_3$*tüz tämür bašlap kim? kun ''LD(...)-ta y(...)* ....[2]
$_4$*bo taγ süm-lär-kä kälip barïr-ta* ....[3]
$_5$*män taγ buq-a* ....[4]
kenki-kä körgü bolzun tep ....[5a]
$_6$*bir iki käzig bitidim* ....[5]

[1] $_1$The fortunate Sheep year, the sixth month, on the [....] day.
[2] $_2$We, Qur?-Buqa, [....]K, Taγ-Buqa, Elig?, $_3$Tüz-Tämür, and [the people?] in Kim?-Kun-[....],
[3] $_4$came to these mountain temples, and on departure,
[4] $_5$I, Taγ-Buqa, [5a] saying 'May (this writing) be seen by posterity!',
[5] $_6$wrote a couple of lines.

(Matsui 2017, no. 63)

48 Matsui 2017, nos 31, 122, 131, 144, 191, 195, 199, 213, 263. Furthermore, the language of nos 10 and 124 is indiscernible, though they are written alongside graffiti in the Uyghur language. Nos 104 and 112 are in Mongolian; no. 123, in Chinese; we have not yet deciphered the texts of nos 9, 11, 107, 117, 127, 188 and 245, enough to discern their languages.
49 E.g., Cleaves 1955; Matsui 2016b; Shōgaito 1991.
50 See, e.g. Matsui 2017, nos 13, 63, 147, 169, 228, 230.

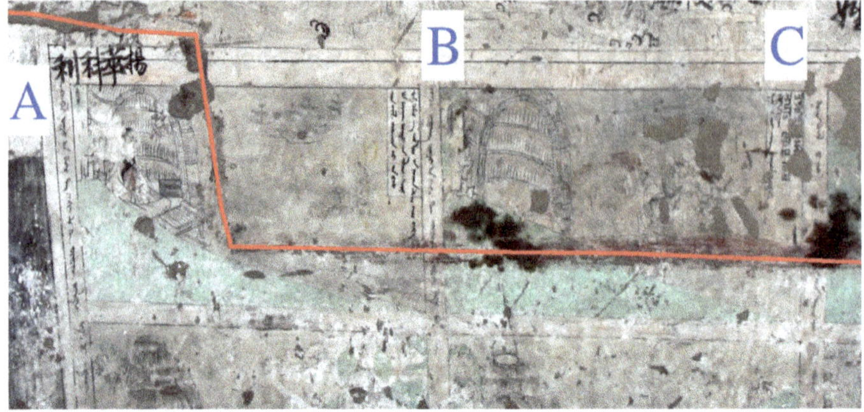

Fig. 8: Graffiti inscriptions in Uyghur and 'Phags-pa scripts; Yulin Cave 3, Guazhou, Gansu, *c.* thirteenth to fourteenth century CE; based on the online colour version of Liu Yongzeng 2014, Fig. 7 <https://news.artron.net/20161111/n883482.html> (accessed on 5 March 2022), with modifications. A: Uyghur, with two Mongolian words at the end: *šakyapal uday-qa barïr-ta kenki-lär-kä ödig qïldïm qutuytu boltuyai* 'I, Šakyapal, in leaving for Uday (= Wutaishan), made (this) record for posterity. [Mongolian] May it be fortunate!'; Matsui 2017, no. 128. B: *täväči tutung uday-qa barïr-ta kenki-lär-kä ödig qïldïm sadu bolzun* 'I, Täväči-*tutung*, in leaving for Uday (= Wutaishan), made (this) record for posterity. May it be good!'; Matsui 2017, no. 130. C: Lines 2–4 are in 'Phags-pa script, but in the Uyghur language: $_{2}$*män* $_{3}$*män luqpal* $_{4}$*yükü[n]dü[m]* 'I, Luqpal, venerated (here)'; Matsui 2017, no. 131.

Uyghur:

$_{1}$*quḍluy taqïyu yïl bešinč ay on beš-tä* .... [1]
$_{2}$*män luqpal šakyapal ṭorčïpal üčägü* .... [2=4]
kälip bo ïduq buqar-$_{3}$*qa yụkünüp bardïmïz* .... [3, 5]
bo buyan-ï alqu quḍrulmaq ol
$_{4}$*yana tapmaq-lar-ï bolzun tep tedi* .... [5a]

[1] $_{1}$The fortunate Hare year, the fifth month, on the fifteenth day.
[2=4] $_{2}$We, Luqpal, Šakyapal, and Dorčïpal, three of us,
[3, 5] came (here), $_{2\text{-}3}$venerated this sacred (cave) temple, and departed.
[5a] This meritorious deed is to exempt all (living beings). And they shall find (this writing)! Thus (I) said.

(Matsui 2017, no. 147)

Uyghur:

$_{1}$*qut-luγ yunt yïl törtünč ay-nïng* $_{2}$*ygrmi säkiz-kä* .... [1]
qaču-nïng taγ süm-kä $_{3}$*yüküngäli kälip*
yükünüp yanar-ta .... [3]
män $_{4}$*darm-a širi bitiyü tägindim* .... [2=4, 5]

[1] $_{1}$The fortunate Horse year, the fourth month, $_{2}$on the twenty-eighth day.
[3] Coming to and venerating the mountain temple of Qaču (← Guazhou 瓜州), and on return,
[2=4,5] $_{5}$I, Darmaširi, humbly wrote (this).

(Matsui 2017, no. 198)

Mongolian:

$_{1}$*morin ǰil doluγan sara-yin γurban sinede* ....[1]
$_{2}$*yung čang vuu-ača iregsed* ....[3]
bi dorǰi en-e $_{3}$*süm-e-ṯür mörgüǰü* ....[2=4, 3]
šaču-yin süm-e-$_{4}$*ṯür odbai* ....[3, 5]
qoyin-a üǰeküi boltuγai ....[5a]

[1] $_{1}$The Horse year, the seventh month, on the third day.
[2=4] $_{2}$I, Dorǰi, [3] who came from the Yung-čang (← Yongchang 永昌) Circuit, $_{3}$venerated this sacred (cave) temple and [5] $_{4}$departed for the temple of Šaču (← Shazhou 沙州 = Dunhuang). [5a] May (this writing) be seen in the future!

(Matsui 2017, no. 169)

Mongolian:

$_{1}$*bečin ǰil doluγan sara-yin* $_{2}$*dörben sinede* ....[1]
bi [....] dorǰi ....[2=4]
$_{3}$*süm-e-ṯür mörgüǰü γarba* ....[3, 5]

[1] $_{1}$The Monkey year, the seventh month, on the fourth day.
[2=4] $_{2}$I, Dorǰi, [3, 5] $_{3}$venerated (this cave) temple and $_{4}$departed.

(Matsui 2017, no. 177)

In the tenth to fourteenth centuries, a small population of Turkic peoples, including Uyghurs, were believers in the Christian Church of the East. Besides the Uyghur script, they also used the Syriac script, mainly for ecclesiastic texts.[51] Some

51 See Zieme 2015a for the Christian Uyghur texts.

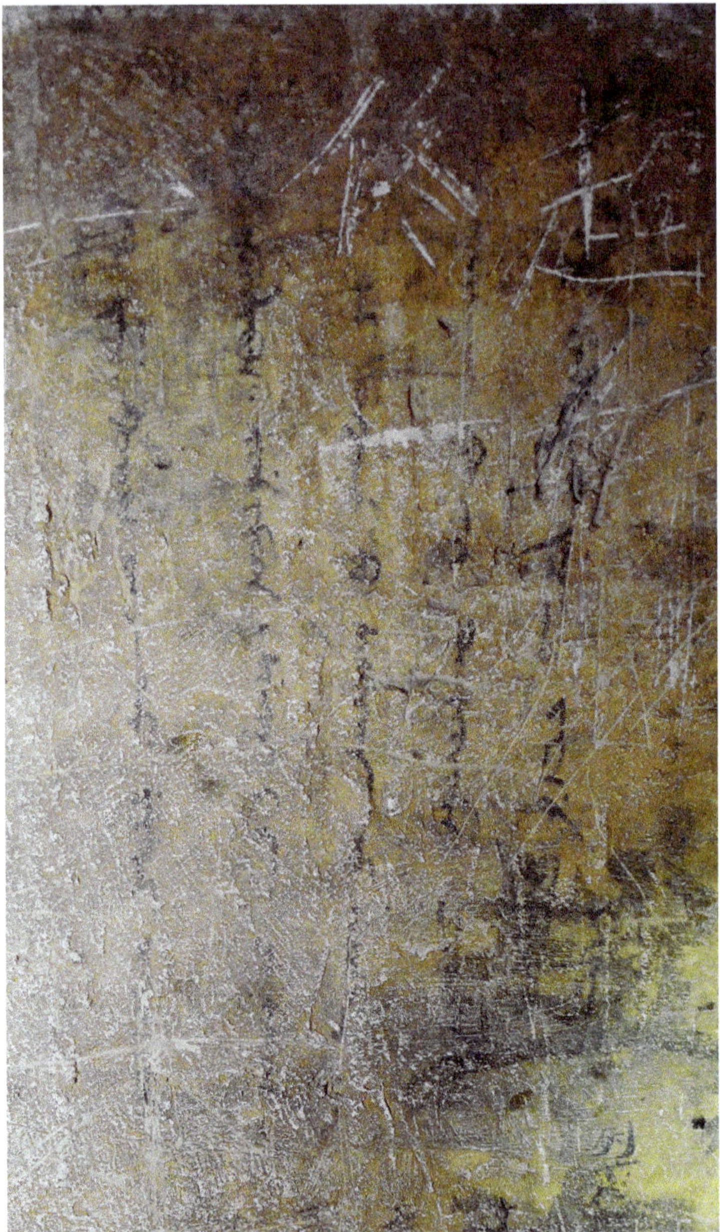

Fig. 9: Uyghur graffiti inscription, with a Christian prayer in Syriac in the fifth line; White Pagoda, Hohhot, Inner Mongolia, *c.* thirteenth to fourteenth century CE; based on Bai Yudong and Matsui 2016, 74.

of these Christians occasionally visited Buddhist sanctuaries to leave their graffiti inscriptions in the Uyghur and Syriac languages in Uyghur and Syriac scripts.

During the Mongol period, the Buddhist 'White Pagoda' of Hohhot, Inner Mongolia, was supported financially by the Christian princes of the Turkic Önggüd tribe (hereditary sons-in-law of the Mongol Emperors), and attracted not only Buddhist but also Christian visitors who left their memorials on the inner wall. Alongside twelve Syro-Turkic graffiti inscriptions,[52] we have detected two Uyghur-Turkic ones related to the Christian Church of the East.[53] One of them, cited below, mentions two visitors with Christian names (*Pilipoz* ← Syriac *pylypws* 'Philip', and *Yušimut* ← Sogdian *ywšmbd* 'Sunday', deriving from Middle Iranian), and puts a Christian prayer in Syriac in its fifth line, clearly displaying affiliation with the Church of the East:

> $_{1}$*küskü yïl t[o]quzunč ay yeti otuz-qa* $_{2}$*[bi]z pilipoz yuş̤imut qïrqïz? y-a-čï bačay?* $_{3}$*[mon]gol?-day munčayu bo suburyan-nï körgäli* $_{4}$*kälü? täginip bitiyü tägintimiz čïn'ol* $_{5}$*('m)yn w(ḥyl) lš(...) 'bdk pyl(ypws)*

> $_{1}$Monkey year, the ninth month, on the twenty-seventh day.
> $_{2}$We, Pilipoz, Yušimut, Qïrqïz?, Y-a-čï, Bačay?, $_{3}$Mongolday? – these people humbly came to watch this pagoda, $_{4}$and wrote (this). This is true.
> $_{5}$[Syriac] Amen! May Pilipoz, Your slave, be encouraged ....
>
> (Bai Yudong and Matsui 2016, Text Q. See Fig. 9).

According to the text ($_{3}$*bo suburyan-nï körgäli* 'to watch this pagoda'), this group of Uyghurs, including at least two Christians, apparently visited the White Pagoda of Hohhot on purpose. However, it is more likely that the Christian Uyghurs regarded the Buddhist pagoda as a tourist site than a target of religious worship.[54]

On the other hand, a Syro-Uyghur graffiti inscription we have recently retrieved from the Yulin caves apparently shares the same formula as the Buddhist graffiti inscriptions cited earlier, and suggests contact between their epistolary cultures:

52 Borbone 2013.

53 Bai Yudong and Matsui 2016, Texts C, Q; Takahashi 2019, 638.

54 Cf. Borbone 2013, 61. See also Zieme 2011, 179–180, who refrains from interpreting the Buddhistic phrase in a Syro-Uyghur Christian booklet as a kind of syncretism between Buddhism and Christianity.

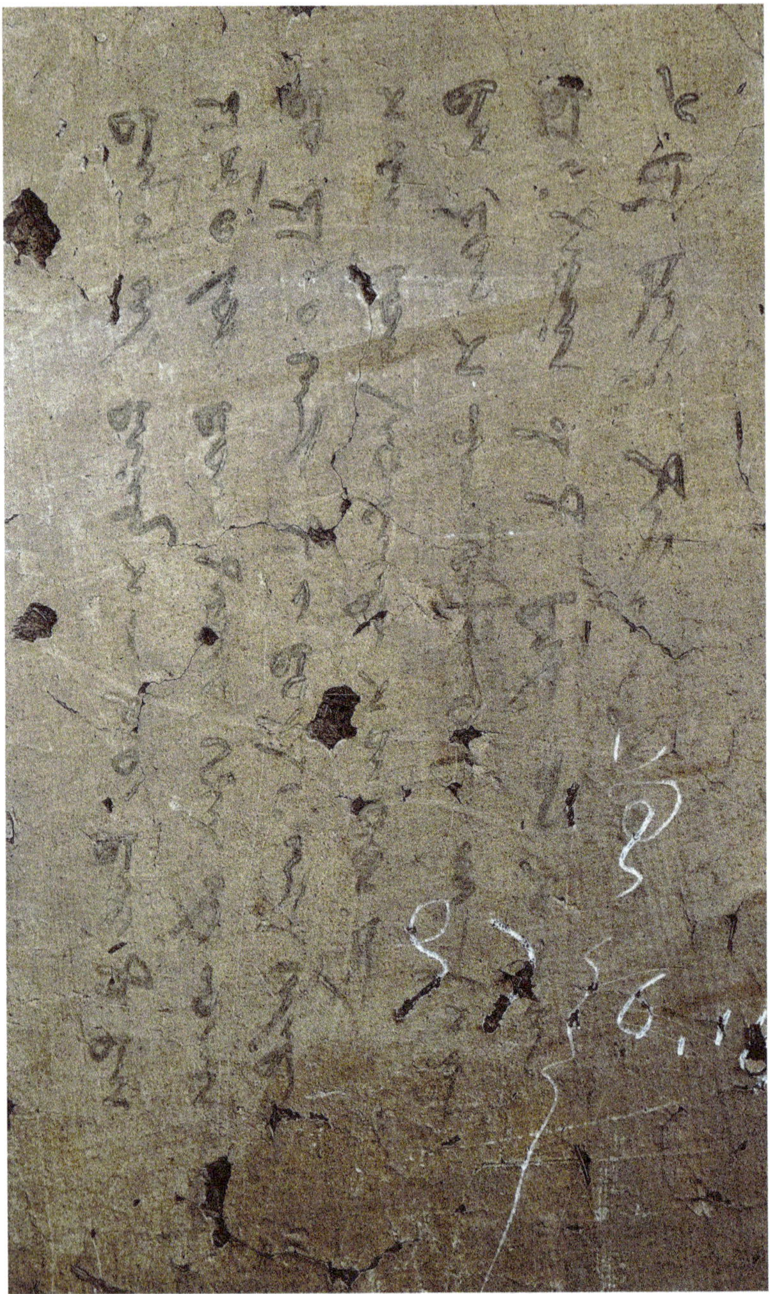

Fig. 10: Syro-Uyghur graffiti inscription; Yulin Cave 16, Guazhou, Gansu, *c*. thirteenth to fourteenth century CE; based on Matsui and Arakawa 2017, Fig. 5.

$_1$*bečin yïl bešinč ay on beš-tä*	........................[1]
biz $_2$*xaču-luy buyan temür*	
natanayel yōḥannān	........................[2=4]
$_3$*bo xaču-nïng tay buxar-ïnga kälip*	
$_4$*iki kün tezginip üč sorma* $_5$*bir xoyn*	
ašïn sökünüp yenä ya[n]ïp $_6$*bartïmïz*	........................[3, 5]
yad bolzun amin $_7$*abamuya tegi amin*	........................[5a]

[1] $_1$Monkey year, the fifth month, on the fifteenth day.
[2=4] $_2$(We) Buyan-Temür, Natanayel, and Yōḥannān of Guazhou, [3] $_3$came to this mountain temple of Guazhou, $_4$visited (the caves) for two days, $_{4-5}$venerated with (the offering of) a meal (*aš*) of three (bottles? of) wheat beer (*sorma*) and one sheep, and then [5] $_{5-6}$started on our way back.
[5a] $_{6-7}$May (this) be memorialized! Amen! For ever! Amen!

(Matsui 2017, no. 197. See Fig. 10).

As revisited in Section 4 below, this Syro-Uyghur graffiti inscription also implies that these Christian Uyghurs participated in Buddhist feasts conducted at the Yulin caves and even offered a donation to the Buddhist monastery. The cultural and religious contact between Buddhist and Christian Uyghurs deserves further scholarly attention and investigation.

Though few in number, some Old Uyghur graffiti inscriptions attest scribes or authors with Muslim names of Arabo-Persian origin: for example, Uyg. *Sul(a)yman* ← Sulaymān; *Uḍman* ← Uṯmān; *Axmat* ← Aḥmad; *Ïqbal-Sang* ← Iqbāl Sang.[55] These names do not directly witness their religious affiliation with Islam: perhaps they were children of mixed Buddhist and Muslim parentage.[56] Even in the case that they were Muslims, they likely visited the Buddhist sanctuaries simply as attractions, similarly to some of the Christian Uyghurs.[57]

55 Bai Yudong and Matsui 2016, Texts A, D; Matsui 2017, nos 61, 105.

56 According to Marco Polo, the Turkic Önggüd tribe, who adopted the Christianity of the Church of the East, ruled the city of Tiande 天德 (→ *Tenduc*, present-day Hohhot), which was also inhabited by a people called the *argon* (← Turkic *aryun*), 'born of the two races, of the lineage of those Tenduc who worship idols [= Buddhists] and those who worship by the law of Mahomet [= Muslims]'. See Moule and Pelliot 1938, 182; Pelliot 1959, 48–51.

57 Bai Yudong and Matsui 2016, 51–53; Matsui 2017, 8.

4 Old Uyghur graffiti inscriptions as Buddhist literature

As mentioned above, one of Porció's most significant contributions was identifying common elements between graffiti inscriptions and Old Uyghur Buddhist colophons.[58] His analysis is supported by many newly available materials. The Uyghur authors of graffiti inscriptions frequently expressed their wishes to achieve Buddhahood (Uyg. *burxan qutï* = Chin. *foguo* 佛果),[59] be reborn in the Pure Land (*sukavadi uluš*),[60] become a buddha (*burxan bol-* = Chin. *chengfo* 成佛),[61] and transfer their meritorious deeds to the living and deceased (Chin. *huixiang* 迴向).[62] One instance from Dunhuang wishes to encounter Maitreya or the future Buddha, and its text is almost parallel to one of the colophon texts from Turfan:

> $_{1}$*br(a)xmazen qaytso gunazen* $_{2}$*yüküngäli käldimz*
> *bo buyan* $_{3}$*küčintä maitri tngri burxan* $_{4}$*birlä oqadmatïn odγuraq* $_{5}$*tuš bolmaqï bolzun*
>
> $_{1\text{-}2}$We, Braxmazen, Qaytso, and Gunazen, came (here) to venerate.
> $_{2\text{-}3}$Through this merit, $_{3\text{-}5}$may (we) surely encounter Holy Buddha Maitreya without delay!
>
> (Matsui 2017, no. 88)

> $_{1}$*ärdinig bošγunγalï tutγalï-ï* $_{2}$*oqïγalï oqïtγalï bititgäli-i* $_{3}$*bitigäli ögrätig qïlmïš kärgäk*
> $_{4}$*bo avant tïltaγ üzä kenki* $_{5}$*burxan-larïγ oqadmatın* $_{6}$*odγuraq tuš* $_{7}$*bolγay-sizlär*
>
> In order to learn and retain the (*dharma*) jewel; in order to recite (it), and to have (others) recite and copy (it); and in order to write (it), one must do exercises. $_{4}$Through these causes, $_{5\text{-}7}$you will surely encounter the future Buddhas without delay!
>
> (Kasai 2008, 84–85, lines 153[1]–159[7])

---

58 Porció 2014, 166–174.
59 Matsui 2017, nos 79, 219, 231.
60 Matsui 2017, no. 176.
61 Bai Yudong and Matsui 2016, Text R; Li Gang and Zhang Hailong 2021b, nos 29, 37.
62 Beside Matsui 2017, no. 147 cited above, also see nos 173, 182, 252.

Porció also noticed examples of stanzaic alliterative poems among the graffiti inscriptions from Turfan.[63] Similar stanzaic alliterative graffiti inscriptions have been retrieved not only from Turfan but also from Dunhuang.[64] A long graffiti inscription of fifteen stanzas from Yulin Cave 34,[65] seemingly written by the above-mentioned pilgrim Adityazen, is noteworthy from the viewpoint of Uyghur Buddhist culture and literature. Its first seven stanzas are allotted to the life story of Buddha Śakyamuni and the spread of his doctrine by *arhat*s (→ Uyg. *arxant*). The latter eight stanzas are praise of the 'Mountain Hermitage' (*tay aryadan*), that is, the Yulin cave temples. This alliterative poem reveals that Buddhist Uyghurs worshipped the sanctuary cave temples that were generally established in the mountain gorge.[66] Another graffiti inscription in memory of a pilgrimage to Hohhot contains alliterative praise of Mañjuśrī Bodhisattva, the text of which substantially parallels a small stanzaic poem on a fragment discovered at Singgim, near Turfan:[67]

$_5$*alqu? biraman?-lar-nïng körgülüki?*
$_6$*adroq? adroq? dintar-lar-nïng yüküngülüki?*
$_7$*arïy? maxa[ya]n? nom-lar-nïng soq-a? öztözi?*
$_8$*ary-a mančuširi-qa yükünürmän*

$_5$(He is) to be seen by all Brahmans(?);
$_6$(He is) is to be venerated by various(?) monks;
$_7$ (He is) exactly(?) the essential nature(?) of the pure *dharma*s of Mahāyāna(?);
$_8$I venerate the Noble Mañjuśrī!

(Bai Yudong and Matsui 2016, 45, Text T)

63 Porció 2014, 166–167, citing only Zieme 1985, Text 60b, from Turfan.
64 Hamilton and Niu Ruji 1998, Inscription G = Matsui 2017, no. 172; Zieme 2013a, 188–189; Matsui 2017, nos 93, 137; Fu Ma and Xia Lidong 2021, I-2 = Li Gang and Zhang Hailong 2021a, K10-B-Z4; Fu Ma and Xia Lidong 2021, II-7 = Li Gang and Zhang Hailong 2021a, K10-B-Z2; Fu Ma and Xia Lidong 2021, III-2 = Li Gang and Zhang Hailong 2021a, K10-B-Y1; Li Gang and Zhang Hailong 2021b, no. 67.
65 Matsui 2017, no. 249.
66 The Uyghur phrases for the Dunhuang cave temples, 'Mountain Hermitage' or 'Mountain Temple' (*tay vrxar ~ tay buqar ~ tay süme*), parallel the Chinese *shansi* 山寺 'Mountain Temple' and Tangut (Xixia) ^{1}*shyan* ^{2}*miq'* ^{2}*'yen*; the Mongolian phrase for the Dunhuang caves, *ayula-yin süme* 'Mountain Temple', should be a translation of the Uyghur. See Matsui 2017, 19.
67 Bai Yudong and Matsui 2016, 45–46.

₁*kertgünč-lüg tïnly-lar-nïng yükünggülüki*
₂*kinayan maxayan nom-lar soq-a öz tözi*
₃*kirsiz arïy mančuširi-qa yükünürbiz*

₁(He is) to be venerated by living beings having the faith, ₂and (He is) exactly the essential nature (of) the *dharma*s of Hīnayāna and Mahāyāna.
₃We venerate the Pure Mañjuśrī!

(Zieme 1985, 146, no. 32)

Their textual similarity over a geographically broad range may reflect the Uyghurs' knowledge of popular texts or formulaic phrases of the Mañjuśrī cult.

5 Daily Buddhist practices of the Uyghurs

The huge number of manuscripts and fragments of Old Uyghur Buddhist canons unearthed in Central Asia demonstrate the variety of Buddhist works and cults (e.g. Maitreya, Avalokieśvara, Amitāyus/Amitābha, Mañjuśrī) spreading among the Uyghurs.[68] However, these materials offer limited information on the daily lives of the Buddhist Uyghurs who produced them. Notably, the majority of Old Uyghur Buddhist works were discovered in the Buddhist cave temples at Turfan and Dunhuang. Consequently, they should be closely related to the religious practices of the Uyghur monks dwelling at the cave temples, as well as those of visitors and pilgrims. The details provided by the Uyghur graffiti inscriptions—the number of people for each delegation and pilgrimage, their duration of stay, the religious practices they conducted at the caves, etc.—are indispensable to grasping the historical background of Uyghur Buddhism.

Regarding the duration of visits, one graffiti inscription recounts that the scribe, named Buyan-Qaya, left his hometown Suzhou 肅州 (→ Uyg. *Sügčü*, present-day Jiuquan 酒泉) in Gansu three years prior and stayed at the Dunhuang Mogao caves for seven months.[69] The circumstances that enabled him to undergo such a long-term pilgrimage deserve historical investigation.

In addition, the graffiti inscriptions refer to various religious practices. The first one mentioned is the Old Uyghur term *pakčan (~ bakčan)* 'summer retreat',

68 For a brief overview of Old Uyghur Buddhist literature, see e.g. Elverskog 1997; Zieme 2015b.
69 Matsui 2019, Text A. On his route from Suzhou to Mogao, Buyan-Qaya passed by the Yulin caves, leaving memorial inscriptions there. See Matsui 2019, Texts D–H.

which refers to the three months of the rainy season, during which the Buddhist monks conducted intensive religious training.[70] The Uyghurs paraphrased the term *pakčan*, of Tocharian origin, as *üč ay* 'three months (of summer retreat)' in their own tongue (Fig. 11).[71]

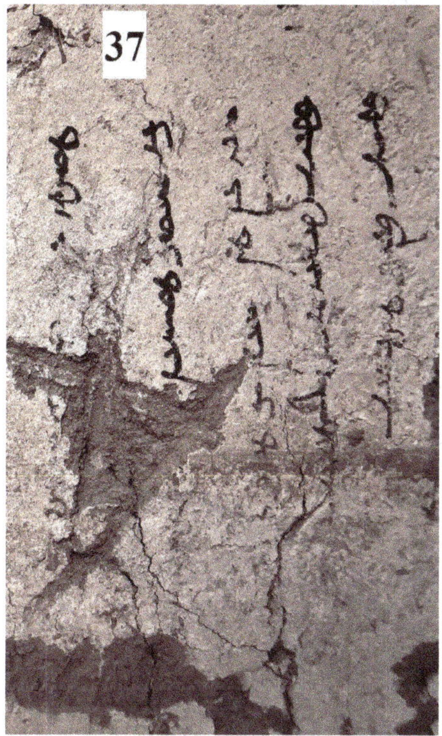

Fig. 11: Uyghur graffiti in memory of a stay of *üč ay* 'three months', a figurative term for Buddhist summer retreat; Cave 26 of the West Zone of the Toyoq grottoes, Turfan, Xinjiang, *c.* thirteenth to fourteenth century CE; based on Li Gang and Zhang Hailong 2021b, no. 37 (Fig. 13). The text reads: $_{1}$*tonguz yïl ye[tin]č? (ay) säki[z ....]* $_{2}$*män qïtay toɣrïl [....] bo? tïyoq?* $_{3}$*qïsïl-ta üč ay tur(u)? (tägintim? bo?)* $_{4}$*buyan küčintä käd toyïn (.......)* $_{5}$*burxan bolu täginäyin* '$_{1}$The Boar year, the seventh? month, on the [.... day]. $_{2}$I, Qïtay-Toɣrïl, $_{3}$humbly? stayed? in the gorge of Toyoq? (*tïyoq*) for (the summer retreat of) three months. Through (this?) $_{4}$meritorious deed, Käd-Toyïn, [....] $_{5}$we shall become Buddha!'; after Matsui 2021, Text B, with modifications.

70 Matsui 2017, no. 231; Niu Ruji and Zieme 1996, 46, 49, 52; Wilkens 2021, 98.

71 Fu Ma and Xia Lidong 2021, 186; Matsui 2021, 40 = Li Gang and Zhang Hailong 2021b, no. 37.

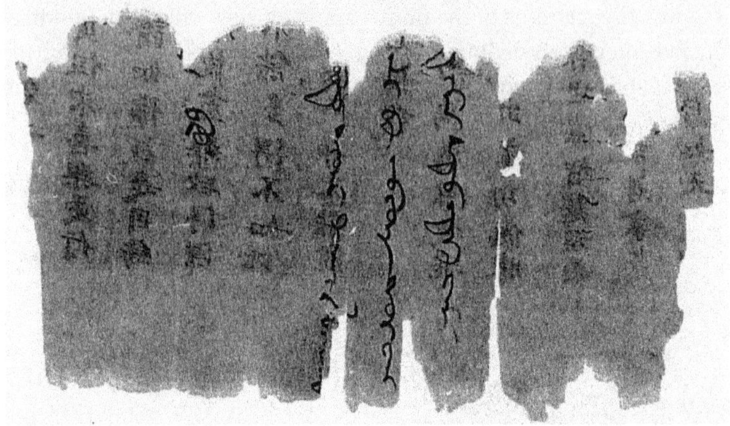

Fig. 12: A Uyghur scribble written on the back of a Chinese Buddhist scroll; seemingly from the Toyoq caves, Turfan, Xinjiang, *c.* thirteenth to fourteenth century CE; Dx 9569, Institute of Oriental Manuscripts, Russian Academy of Sciences, St Petersburg; based on Matsui 2021, 41; text: Matsui 2021, Text C. The scribe, $_1$Qïtay-Toɣrïl, is probably the same one who produced the graffiti in Fig. 11.

These graffiti suggest that the Turfan and Dunhuang cave temples in the gorge, remote from cities and villages, were used for training during the summer retreat. One of the manuscripts of the Old Uyghur version of the Buddhist work *Maitrisimit* ('Encounter with Maitreya') was copied by a Uyghur monk as part of his practice during the summer retreat.[72] Though we do not find many mentions of the summer retreat (*pakčan*) or its paraphrase *üč ay* 'three months (of summer retreat)' in graffiti inscriptions on cave walls or in manuscript colophons, Buddhist Uyghurs would have considered copying or reading Buddhist texts at cave temples an important part of their religious training during the summer retreat (Fig. 12).

Other religious practices conducted by Uyghur Buddhist pilgrims and visitors were meditation (Skt. *dhyāna* → Uyg. *dyan* ~ Chin. *chan-ding* 禪定) and learning (Uyg. *bošyut* ; *nom tut-* 'to keep the *dharma* ; to learn'). Sometimes meditation and learning are mentioned alongside their duration[73] to suggest that the Buddhist

72 Kasai 2008, 192–193.

73 Matsui 2017, nos 37 (15 days), 146 (3 days), 165 (10 days), 197 (2 days), 231 (3 months); Fu Ma and Xia Lidong, 2021, I-15 (20 days?). Another instance, on a fragment of a cave wall from Turfan (TU 406 in the State Hermitage, St Petersburg), attests to *bir ay-lïq bošyut* 'learning for one month'. Li Gang and Zhang Hailong 2021b, no. 49, also suggests a one-month stay at the cave temple. Cf. Matsui 2010, 708–709; Porció 2014, 113.

monasteries at the cave temples prepared training programmes for low-ranked monks and laymen. One stanza of an alliterative poetic graffiti emphasizes that 'the living place of the Bodhisattvas is the *dharma*', and recommends that future readers learn (*bošyut*) *dharma*.[74]

Besides the summer retreat, Buddhist religious feasts were conducted on various occasions. The fifteenth day of the fifth month of the lunar calendar was one of the most important feast days for Dunhuang Buddhist monasteries. In the ninth to eleventh centuries, it was customary for the local Chinese government of Dunhuang to conduct the *guanzhai* 官齋 'official Buddhist feast' on that day. This custom was seemingly inherited by the Tanguts in the eleventh and twelfth centuries, and later by Uyghurs under the Mongols, as suggested by many Old Uyghur and Mongolian graffiti inscriptions dated to this occasion in the Dunhuang caves.[75] The aforementioned Syro-Uyghur Christian graffiti of Yulin Cave 16 also has the same date, and its authors, the Christian Uyghurs, stayed there for more than two days.[76] Apparently, they participated in and enjoyed the Buddhist feast on that day, leaving offerings for the monastery and a memorial graffiti.

Mainstream Buddhism had six *poṣadha* (→ Uyg. *posat* ~ Chin. *busa* 布薩) days, namely the eighth, fourteenth, fifteenth, twenty-third, twenty-ninth, and thirtieth of every month of the lunar calendar. On these days the monks conducted a repentance ceremony and preached to laypeople. The Buddhist Uyghurs likewise followed this code, as suggested by memorial graffiti written on 'the day of the *poṣadha* commandment' (*posat bačay kün*).[77] A newly introduced Uyghur graffiti inscription from the Toyoq cave refers to the fourteenth day of the fourth month as *suv yayïš kün* 'the day of flowing water', likely a type of feast day.[78] There are many more instances of Uyghur memorial graffiti on the back sides of Chinese Buddhist manuscripts brought from the Toyoq caves to the St Petersburg collection, and their dates are worthy of further comparative analysis.[79]

---

74 Zieme 2013a, 188–189.

75 Matsui 2017, nos 56, 97, 110, 111, 119, 121, 129, 138, 141, 142, 145, 146, 147, 275.

76 Matsui 2017, no. 197; Matsui 2018, 38–39. See also the text cited in Section 2 above.

77 Matsui 2017, nos 167, 168, 201. For similar instances of Uyghur Buddhist colophons, see Kasai 2008, 56, 132, 133, 209, 240.

78 Li Gang and Zhang Hailong 2021b, 26, relate 'the day of flowing water' to the Buddhist ceremony of *yufojie* 浴佛節 'Buddha Bathing Festival', though this ceremony should have been held on the Buddha's birthday, that is, the 8th of the 2nd/4th month.

79 Matsui 2004, 61. One of the texts (4b Kr/12, now renumbered as SI 4029 at the Institute of Oriental Manuscripts of the Russian Academy of Sciences, St Petersburg) is dated to the eighth day of the second month, that is, Śākyamuni Buddha's birthday.

Some caves depicted the Buddha or principal deities on their central pillar or set their statues on a main, central seat. In such caves, the ritual of *weirao* 圍遶 'to circle the Buddha three times with one's right shoulder facing in' would have been conducted. In the Hohhot Buddhist pagoda, climbing up the internal spiral staircase and circumambulating the corridor would correspond to the *weirao* ritual, which was apparently referred to as *tägzinmäk* 'to revolve, rotate' (← v. *tägzin-* ~ *täzgin-*) in Old Uyghur.[80] This Uyghur phrase was also used in graffiti in Dunhuang and Turfan, seemingly in its original sense 'to travel around; to visit many grottoes'.[81] Newly published instances from the Toyoq caves attest to the practice of 'pulling the pearl/jewel' (*mončuq tart-*), the reality of which is not well understood, though it apparently entails the Buddhist rosary (Chin. *shuzhu* 數珠).[82]

Sometimes the pilgrims mentioned their offerings (*čodpa*, *yaγïš*) to the monastery, such as fruit (*yemiš*), sheep (*qoyn*), and beer (*sorma*).[83] We may cite an instance written by a local Uyghur governor in memory of his visit to a cave of Dong-Qianfodong 東千佛洞 'the Eastern Thousand-Buddha Caves', some 150 km east of the Dunhuang Mogao caves. The term *daruγačï* 'governor general', a loanword from Mongolian, clearly dates this inscription to the Mongol period.

> $_{1}$*qoyn yïl* aram *ay on üč-tä* $_{2}$*qaču-nïng čopan-ï-nïng oγlï* $_{3}$*äsän quḍluγ atlïγ q(aču)-ta* $_{4}$*daruγačï bolup taγ-qa barïp kali* $_{5}$*tungur-täki on beš kiši birlä kali tungur-*$_{6}$*ta taγ sümä qonïp bo bitig-ni* $_{7}$*bitip bardïmïz ärti bo bitig-ni* $_{8}$*biz-tin sangïk qalγan? yemiš-lär* $_{9}$*uluγ kenki-lär körüp qaqïmïš bolmazun* $_{10}$*män tämür äsän qutluγ bitiγ[ü]* $_{11}$*qodtïm qut[luγ bolzun]* $_{12}$*ädgü-lüg kälzün* $_{13}$*nišanim č[ïztïm]*
>
> $_{1}$The Sheep year, the first month, on the thirteenth day.
> $_{2}$[I,] the son of the mayor of Guazhou, $_{3-4}$named Äsän-Qutluγ, have been (assigned to) the governor general (*daruγačï*) of Guazhou, visited (caves in) the mountain, $_{5-6}$stayed at the mountain temple of the Kali caves (Uyg. *tungur* ← Chin. *dongku* 洞窟 'cave, grotto') together with fifteen people (resident) in the Kali caves, $_{7}$wrote this writing, and we have departed. $_{8-9}$Even seeing the (small quantity of) fruit left for the monastery by us, $_{9}$may the noble posterity not be angry! $_{10}$I, Tämür and Äsän-Qutluγ, wrote and $_{11}$left (this). May it be auspicious! $_{12}$May prosperity come! $_{13}$I drew my mark (here).
>
> (Matsui 2017, no. 281. See Figs 13 and 14)

---

80 Bai Yudong and Matsui 2016, Texts J, R, T.
81 Matsui 2017, no. 197; Li Gang and Zhang Hailong 2021b, no. 47.
82 Fu Ma and Xia Lidong 2021, 187–188, explain this practice as counting the 108 beads on the Buddhist rosary, while Li Gang and Zhang Hailong 2021a, 161, interpret it simply as 'meditation'.
83 Matsui 2017, nos 37, 146, 159, 183, 281; Li Gang and Zhang Hailong 2021b, no. 66.

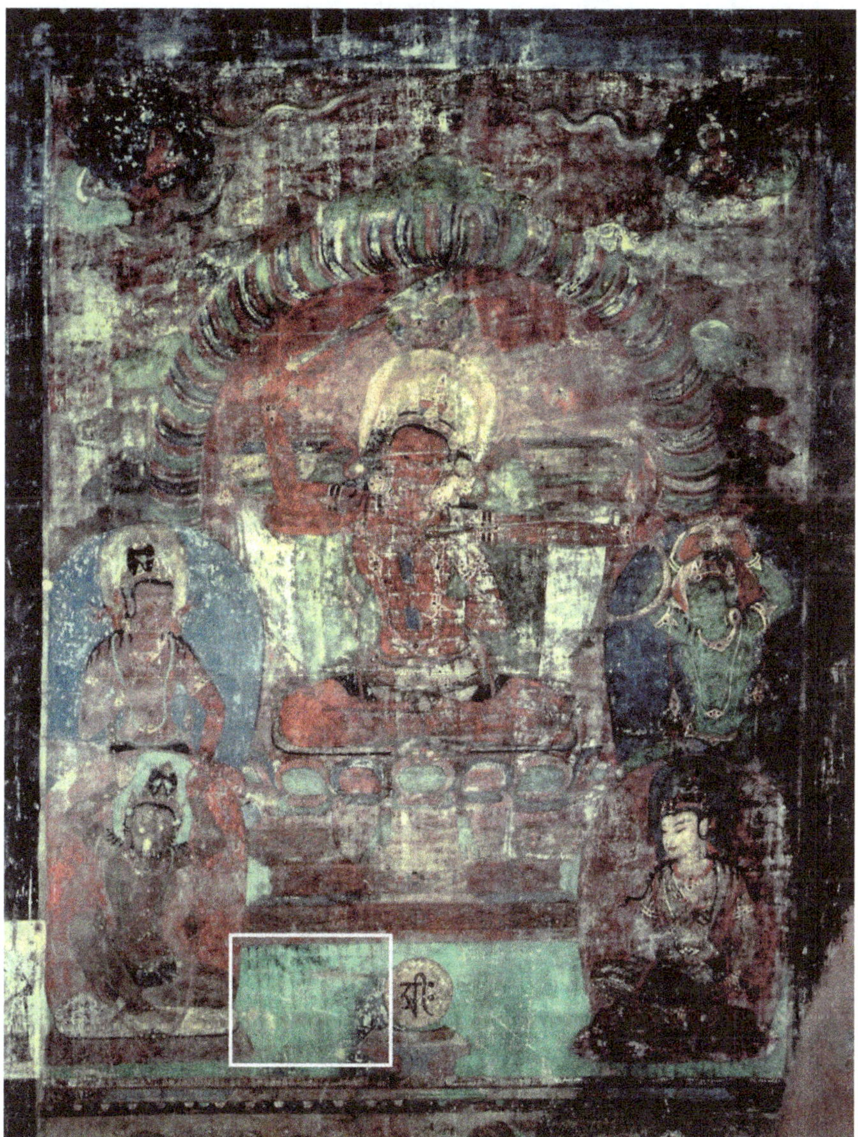

Fig. 13: The wall painting of Four-armed Mañjuśrī Bodhisattva of the Xixia period; Dong-Qianfodong Cave 2, Guazhou, Gansu, *c.* eleventh to twelfth century CE; based on Zhang Baoxi 2012, 103 (Plate 5), with modifications.

Fig. 14: Uyghur graffiti inscription in the encircled space in Fig. 13; Dong-Qianfodong Cave 2, Guazhou, Gansu, *c.* thirteenth to fourteenth century CE; based on Zhang Baoxi 2012, 66 (Fig. 49); text: Matsui 2017, no. 281.

This graffiti inscription may suggest that the visitor and author, Äsän-Qutluγ, conducted his pilgrimage in token of his assignment to the governor general of Guazhou. In contemporaneous Yuan China, local governors generally paid great honour to Buddhist, Taoist, and Confucian monasteries in the regions under their control, and it was their important duty to maintain those monastic facilities: fulfilling this duty earned them the great admiration of local society, and even homages in memory of this deed were prepared by Chinese literati and realized as stele inscriptions.

Äsän-Qutluγ, however, may have chosen the immediate reward of self-praise instead of future kudos from others. The phrase 'even seeing the (small quantity of) fruit left for the monastery by us, may the noble posterity not be angry!' should not be understood literally, but interpreted as a modest expression for his sizeable donation to the monastery. Local governor chiefs (as seen in other graffiti inscriptions), as well as envoys (*elči*) from the Mongol royal families, also

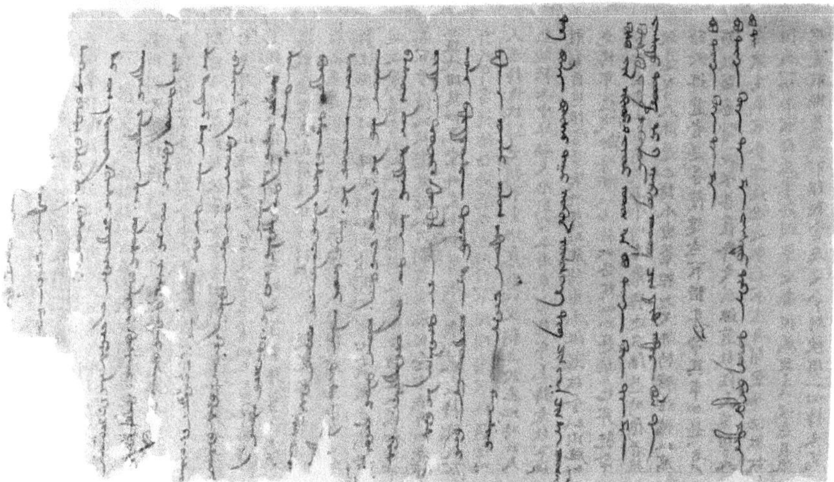

Fig. 15: Uyghur memorial writings (lines 18–24 from left) on the back side of a Chinese Buddhist scroll; seemingly from the Toyoq caves, Turfan, Xinjiang, *c.* thirteenth century CE; SI 4033 (4b Kr/16a); Institute of Oriental Manuscripts, Russian Academy of Sciences, St Petersburg; based on Institute of Oriental Manuscripts, Russian Academy of Sciences and the Toyo Bunko 2021, 378 (Plate 22). The text reads: $_{19}$*küskü yïl ikinti ay yeti otuz-qa bo tavγač küen-tä män* $_{21}$*yaqšidu tutung qy-a erikip o[l]urup čïzdïm ödig bolzun* '$_{19}$The Rat year, the second month, on the twenty-seventh day. On this Chinese scroll, I, $_{21}$Yaqšidu-*tutung*, staying (here) in boredom, depicted (this). May it be memorialized!'; cf. Matsui 2010, 700; Institute of Oriental Manuscripts, Russian Academy of Sciences and the Toyo Bunko 2021, 251, no. 553.

supported the Buddhist monasteries with such material donations.[84] It is also highly likely that lay visitors were required to make donations to be allowed to leave memorial inscriptions on the walls of the sanctuary caves.

While Mahayana Buddhism generally prohibits eating meat, the aforementioned Syro-Uyghur Christian graffiti from the Yulin cave openly mentions sheep (*xoyn* ~ *qoyn*) as food (*aš*), that is, to be slaughtered.[85] Both a twelfth-century Chinese source and Marco Polo in the Mongol era further report that Buddhist Uyghurs practised the ritual slaughtering of sheep, which could be referred to in Uyghur as *čodpa*, derived from the Tibetan *mchod pa* 'offering; sacrifice'.[86]

84 Matsui 2017, nos 15, 37, 145, 167, 215.

85 Matsui 2017, no. 197; Matsui 2018, 38–39. Also see Section 2 above in the present paper.

86 As Uyghur words for 'offering, donation', *lab* (← Skt. *labhā*) and *bušï* (← Chin. *bushi* 布施) had taken root not only among the Buddhist Uyghurs, but also among the Manichaens and Christians. See Matsui 2008b, 24–25; Matsui 2017, 83. Cf. Porció 2014, 173.

Interestingly, some pilgrims and visitors expressed their honest feelings about religious activities in the graffiti inscriptions on the cave walls: for them, a stay at the cave temples and the associated religious practices were boring (*erikip* ← v. *erik-* 'to be bored').[87] One pilgrim even complains that the training (*iš küč*) at the summer retreat (*üč ay*) is distressing (*sïqïš*).[88] Many other Uyghur Buddhist pilgrims also recorded such feelings in their memorial scribbles in the margins or on the back sides of Chinese Buddhist scrolls, from which they learned Buddhism during their stay at the cave temples (Fig. 15).[89]

6 Geographical sphere of Old Uyghur pilgrimages and travels

As mentioned above, the Uyghurs placed themselves under the jurisdiction of the Mongol Empire in the early thirteenth century. Many Uyghurs were appointed high officials and bureaucrats of the Mongol courts, and under the Mongols, they vastly extended their sphere of activity across the eastern half of Eurasia, as attested by Chinese narrative and biographical sources of the Mongol Yuan era.[90] The Old Uyghur Buddhist texts retrieved from Turfan and Dunhuang include a large number of block-print fragments published by technologically advanced printing offices in Yuan China, suggesting the Uyghurs' close Buddhist cultural ties across the eastern half of Eurasia.[91] Such circulation of Buddhist works and merchandise from China is also attested by some secular Uyghur documents.[92]

87 Fu Ma and Xia Lidong 2021, I-10; Li Gang and Zhang Hailong 2021a, 163; Li Gang and Zhang Hailong 2021b, nos 10, 56, 76.

88 For *sïqïš* 'distress, heavy burden', I modify the previous readings and interpretations by Fu Ma and Xia Lidong 2021, 184–186 (*saqïš* 'number') and Li Gang and Zhang Hailong 2021a, 158–159 ('finished').

89 Matsui 2004, 51; Matsui 2010, 703; Porció 2014, 165.

90 For examples of Uyghur families of noble bureaucrats who migrated to China proper and culturally assimilated into China, see Brose 2005.

91 See Zieme and Kudara 1985, 29–35 on the Old Uyghur Buddhist canons printed in the Yuan capital of Dadu 大都, present-day Beijing, and in Hangzhou 杭州, the former capital of the Southern Song dynasty.

92 See Moriyasu 1982 for Old Uyghur letter correspondence, excavated from Dunhuang, on the transaction of Uyghur Buddhist canons being translated by Uyghur high priests of the Yuan court; see Moriyasu 1988 on the circulation of *qïngsay tavar* 'damask of Hangzhou' (Uyg. *qïngsay* ← Chin. Xingzai 行在, an alias of Hangzhou) as a luxury item among Buddhist Uyghurs.

Declaring the homeland or starting point of the scribes, Old Uyghur visitors' graffiti and pilgrim inscriptions can provide evidence for the reality of the geographically extensive mobility of the Uyghurs. In particular, the graffiti inscriptions of the Dunhuang grottoes may reveal a sphere of activity extending from their homeland in East Turkestan (Fig. 1). Of the Uyghur (and Mongol) visitors and pilgrims to Dunhuang in the Mongol era, the majority of those from the west were inhabitants of *Qamïl* (present-day Qomul = Hami 哈密),[93] while those from the east came mainly from *Sügčü* = Suzhou (present-day Jiuquan).[94] Both Qomul and Suzhou were neighbouring cities of Dunhuang, and, during the Mongol period, the Uyghur inhabitants of the latter were mostly immigrants from East Turkestan. Also attested are *Bešbalïq*, *Qočo*, *Turpan* (= Turfan = Tulufan 吐魯番), *Čambalïq* (present-day Changji 昌吉, west of Urumchi = Wulumuqi 烏魯木齊), and *Napčik* (present-day Lapchuq = Lafuqueke 拉甫卻克, *c.* 65 km west of Qomul) as the main cities of the Uyghur kingdom,[95] as well as *Qamču* (← Ganzhou 甘州, present-day Zhangye 張掖), *Yung-čang* (← Yongchang 永昌, between Zhangye and Wuwei 武威), and *Isinai* (→ Yijinai 亦集乃 of Yuan, the ruined city of Khara-khoto or Heishuicheng 黑水城 in present-day Ejina 額濟納, Inner Mongolia) along the Gansu Corridor.[96]

In addition to the main cities of Uyghur habitation, pilgrims also came from more distant places. Two Dunhuang graffiti were written by a visitor from *Tangut-čölgä* 'the Circuit of the Tanguts', which corresponds to Yuan-era name Xixia-lu 西夏路 (= Ningxia-lu 寧夏路), that is, present-day Yinchuan 銀川 in the Ningxia Hui Autonomous Region, north-west China.[97] Two groups of visitors arrived at the Yulin caves from further east, *Aqbalïq* ~ *Aq-Balïq* 'the White City', the Turkic toponym for the city of Zhending 眞定, present-day Zhengding 正定 in the Hebei Province of China proper (Fig. 16).[98] We also see that pilgrims left the Yulin caves for *Uday*, a partial transcription of Chinese Wutaishan 五臺山 or Mt Wutai, the

93 Matsui 2017, nos 39, 53, 161, 220, 226, 251.

94 Matsui 2017, nos 20, 32, 50, 78, 137, 149, 163, 165, 167, 180, 230, 246, 250, 261.

95 Matsui 2017, nos 13, 31, 37, 162, 248, 231.

96 Matsui 2017, nos 169, 176, 227, 255.

97 Matsui 2013, 43–44; Matsui 2017, nos 13, 14. Cf. Fig. 4 (B) above.

98 Matsui 2016a, 285; Matsui 2017, nos 160, 208. The Uyghur-Turkic *Aqbalïq* ~ *Aq-Balïq* is referred to as *achbaluch* by Marco Polo, and corresponds to the Mongolian *Čayan-Balyasun* 'the White City', which is transcribed as *Čaġān Balġasūn* in the Persian source of the Ilkhanid Iran. See Moule and Pelliot 1938, 257; Pelliot 1959, 8–9; Sugiyama 1990, 15–16.

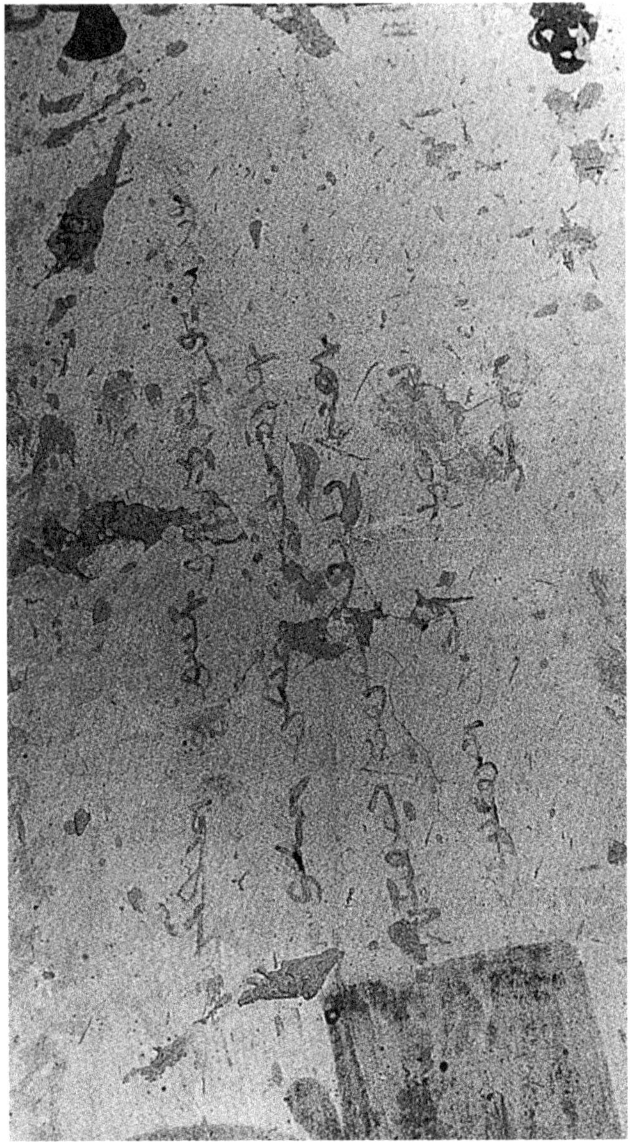

Fig. 16: Uyghur graffiti inscription by visitors from Aqbalïq (present-day Zhengding); Yulin Cave 12, Guazhou, Gansu, *c.* thirteenth to fourteenth century CE; after Hamilton and Niu Ruji 1998, 168. The text reads: $_1$*biz aqbalïq-ta liu sinpo lu ödigä* $_2$*sigu (..)D(...)W üčägü qaču* $_3$*süm kälip* 'We three, Liu Sinpo, Lu Ödigä, and Sigü (..)D(...)W of Aqbalïq, came (to) the temple of Guazhou, and ....' (Matsui 2017, no. 160, lines 1–3). The first two visitors have apparently Chinese surnames (*Liu* and *Lu*), while the name of the third, *Sigu*, seems to be a transcription of a Tangut surname ^{2}*si:* ^{2}*gyu* (→ Chin. *Jiwu* 即兀).

renowned sanctuary of Manjuśri Bodhisattva, located in Shanxi Province, North China (Fig. 5 A, B).[99]

Notably, these minor nodes and terminals of the Buddhist Uyghur pilgrimage network overlap with the locations of the one hundred Buddhist temples to which Yïymïš (→ Chin. Yiheimishi 亦黑迷失), a distinguished Uyghur official of the Yuan court, made donations.[100] The White Pagoda of Hohhot also received pilgrims from cities in the Uyghurs homeland of East Turkestan, such as *Qamïl*, *Čambalïq*, and *Toqsïn* (present-day Toqsun = Tuokesun 托克遜, ca. 80 km to the west of Turfan).[101] The extent of the Buddhist Uyghur spheres of mobility and pilgrimage was likely closely related to the commercial activities of Uyghur merchants on the Silk Road.[102] Furthermore, the Buddhist networks extending to Jiangsu, Zhejiang and Fujian were likely shared with Christian Uyghurs.[103]

7 Conclusion

This paper has described the Old Uyghur texts written on walls of Central Asian Buddhist cave temples by Uyghur visitors and pilgrims as 'graffiti inscriptions', and outlined their contents and peculiarities from the viewpoint of Old Uyghur history of the tenth to fourteenth century.

The variety of scripts and languages used in the graffiti inscriptions clearly reflects the multilingual and multi-religious culture established among the Old Uyghurs, and their interaction with other cultural entities such as Indo-Tocharian, Tibetan, Chinese, and Mongolian.

As Porció has previously pointed out, the Old Uyghur graffiti inscriptions of the Buddhist cave temples are of course to be related to Buddhist culture, and find a position within Uyghur Buddhist literature, sharing various elements with paper manuscripts and block prints. Considering how casually and carelessly these

---

99 Matsui 2014, 38; Matsui 2017, nos 128, 130; Kasai 2020, 27; Raschmann 2020, 206–207; Zieme 2021c, 231–232.

100 See Chen Dezhi 2008; Matsui 2016a, 286–287; Bai Yudong and Matsui 2016, 47–53; and Fu Ma 2022, for the inscription in honor of Yïymïš preserved at the Quanzhou Maritime Museum (Quanzhou 泉州, Fujian). Among the destinations of his donations, we find Zhendìng 眞定 (= Uyg. *Aq-Balïq*), Ningxia 寧夏 (= Uyg. *Tangut*), and Xiliang 西涼 (present-day Wuwei).

101 Bai Yudong and Matsui 2016, Texts E, J, K, L, T.

102 Noteworthy in this respect is a Uyghur contract document of an agreement to drive a Buddhist master (*baxšï*) and his loads from Heishuicheng to Suzhou. See Umemura and Matsui 2008, 185–186. Furthermore, see Matsui 2008a, 170–171.

103 Matsui 2016a, 287–290; cf. Bai Yudong and Matsui 2016, 47, 49–51, 53.

graffiti inscriptions were written, the Buddhist literary elements they contain may reflect what kinds of clichés and stock phrases were extracted from the canonical texts and used daily among Buddhist Uyghurs.

The graffiti inscriptions also display various aspects of the daily activities of Uyghur pilgrims and visitors to the cave temples. They devoted themselves to Buddhist practices and disciplines, during which they produced the manuscripts of Old Uyghur Buddhist works that have come down to us. Alongside such piety (as also discerned in Buddhist manuscript colophons), however, some of the graffiti inscriptions disclose their true feelings that Buddhist practices and discipline were not always joyful for them.

The geographical sphere of Uyghur travel and pilgrimage can be detected from information in the graffiti inscriptions. It has been revealed by both the Old Uyghur texts unearthed in Central Asia and Chinese narrative sources that Buddhist and Christian Uyghurs extended their range of activity across the eastern half of Eurasia, especially in the thirteenth and fourteenth centuries. The information from graffiti inscriptions likewise suggests such a situation, in addition to offering more details on the increase of Uyghur mobility in the Mongol period; moreover, it allows for evaluating the religious significance of each cave temple site as a Buddhist sanctuary.

The arguments I have presented above, however, may still be regarded as tentative, as they are based on the corpus of Old Uyghur graffiti inscriptions, which is far from complete. I have conducted fieldwork on Dunhuang Uyghur graffiti at only some 150 of the 800-odd caves of the Dunhuang grottoes; smaller Buddhist cave sanctuaries scattered throughout East Turkestan and the Gansu Corridor also reportedly preserve Old Uyghur graffiti inscriptions that have not yet been made available to researchers.[104] While we may also expect new archaeological findings from present-day Xinjiang, especially the Turfan region, the materials previously excavated or retrieved, as well as those offered in my edition, deserve further analysis and revision.

It may be noted that Uyghur graffiti inscriptions have thus far mainly been transcribed with the naked eye or photographed with rather simple equipment. However, the graffiti inscriptions on the walls of the Central Asian cave temples are fading, becoming fainter and being more difficult to decipher and photograph. Moreover, they could be accidentally damaged or broken amid preservation work on the cave wall, if adequate precautions are not taken. We expect that further developments in optical scientific methods will aid in detecting and deciphering

104 For yet unedited Old Uyghur graffiti, see, e.g. Zhongguo shehui kexueyuan kaogu yanjiusuo 1991, *passim*; Raschmann 2020.

the faded graffiti inscriptions, and that exhaustive investigations will rigorously collate data from graffiti inscriptions at various archaeological sites.

Summing up, the historical reality of the Old Uyghurs – as seen from their graffiti inscriptions – will always need future revisions and amendments in the light of new textual information. It is also a future task to elucidate the connection between Buddhist Uyghur religious trends and their preference in pilgrimage caves, comparing the textual information from graffiti inscriptions with Buddhist mural paintings. For a holistic investigation of Old Uyghur graffiti inscriptions, it is necessary to constantly search for new methodologies.

Acknowledgement

This work was supported by JSPS KAKENHI Grant Number JP20H013240.

Abbreviations

Chin. = Chinese
Skt. = Sanskrit
Tib. = Old Tibetan
Uyg. = Old Uyghur
v. = verbal stem

References

Arakawa, Shintarō 荒川慎太郎 (2017), 'Tonkō sekkutsu Seika-bun daiki meibun shūsei' 敦煌石窟西夏文題記銘文集成, in Matsui and Arakawa 2017, 241–333.

Borbone, Pier Giorgio (2013), 'More on the Priest Särgis in the White Pagoda', in Li Tang and Dietmar W. Winkler (eds), *From the Oxus River to the Chinese Shores*, Berlin: Lit, 51–65.

Brose, Michael C. (2005), *Subjects and Masters: Uyghurs in the Mongol Empire*, Western Washington: Western Washington University.

Chen Aifeng 陳愛峰, Chen Yuzhen 陳玉珍 and Matsui Dai 松井太 (2020), 'Da-Taoergou di-9 ku bashisi dachengjiuzhe tuxiang bukao' 大桃兒溝第 9 窟八十四大成就者圖像補考, *Dunhuang yanjiu* 敦煌研究, 5: 63–76.

Chen Dezhi 陳得芝 (2008), 'Cong Yiheimishi shenfen kan Make Boluo' 從亦黑迷失身份看馬可波羅, *Yanjing xuebao* 燕京學報, 26: 39–57.

Cleaves, Francis Woodman (1955), 'An Early Mongolian Loan Contract from Qara Qoto', *Harvard Journal of Asiatic Studies*, 18: 1–49.

Duan Wenjie 段文傑 (ed.) (1996), *Zhongguo Dunhuang bihua quanji 10: Dunhuang, Xixia, Yuan* 中國敦煌壁畫全集 10: 敦煌西夏元, Tianjin: Tianjin renmin meishu chubanshe.

Dunhuang yanjiuyuan 敦煌研究院 (ed.) (1986), *Dunhuang Mogaoku gongyangren tiji* 敦煌莫高窟供養人題記, Beijing: Wenwu chubanshe.

Dunhuang yanjiuyuan 敦煌研究院 (ed.) (2014), *Yulinku* 榆林窟, Nanjing: Jiangsu meishu chubanshe.

Durkin-Meisterernst, Desmond, Simone-Christiane Raschmann, Jens Wilkens, Marianne Yaldiz and Peter Zieme (eds) (2004), *Turfan Revisited: The First Century of Research into the Arts and Cultures of the Silk Road*, Berlin: Dietrich Reimer.

Elverskog, Johan (1997), *Uygur Buddhist Literature*, Turnhout: Brepols.

Fu Ma 付馬 (2022), 'Hanghaijia Yiheimishi de muyu shiyan' 航海家亦黑迷失的母語誓言, *Haijiaoshi yanjiu* 海交史研究, 3: 61–70.

Fu Ma 付馬 and Xia Lidong 夏立棟 (2021), 'Comprehensive Study on Old Uighur and Chinese Wall Inscriptions in Room B of Newly Excavated Cave 26 in Tuyuq Grottoes, Turfan', *Acta Orientalia Academiae Scientiarum Hungaricae*, 74/2: 181–206.

Gabain, Annemarie von (1974), *Alttürkische Grammatik*, 3rd edn, Wiesbaden: Otto Harrassowitz.

Geng Shimin 耿世民 and Zhang Baoxi 張寶璽 (1986), 'Yuan Huigu-wen "Zhongxiu Wenshusi-bei" chushi' 元回鶻文《重修文殊寺碑》初釋, *Kaogu xuebao* 考古學報, 2: 253–264 and Plates 19–20.

Hamilton, James and Niu Ruji 牛汝極 (1998), 'Inscriptions ouïgoures des grottes bouddhiques de Yulin', *Journal Asiatique*, 286: 127–210.

Institute of Oriental Manuscripts, Russian Academy of Sciences and the Toyo Bunko (eds) (2021), *Catalogue of the Old Uyghur Manuscripts and Blockprints in the Serindia Collection of the Institute of Oriental Manuscripts, RAS*, Vol. 1, Tokyo: The Toyo Bunko.

Iwao, Kazushi 岩尾一史 (2017), 'Tonkō sekkutsu Chibetto-go meibun shūsei' 敦煌石窟チベット語銘文集成, in Matsui and Arakawa 2017, 199–239.

Kasai, Yukiyo (2008), *Die uigurischen buddhistischen Kolophone* (Berliner Turfantexte, 26), Turnhout: Brepols.

Kasai, Yukiyo (2020), 'The Bodhisattva Mañjuśrī, Mt. Wutai, and Uyghur Pilgrims', *BuddhistRoad Paper*, 5/4: 3–39.

Kitsudō, Kōichi 橘堂晃一 (2017a), 'Tonkō sekkutsu Burāfumī moji daiki meibun shūsei' 敦煌石窟ブラーフミー文字題記銘文集成, in Matsui and Arakawa 2017, 163–198 and Figs 1, 2, 8.

Kitsudō, Koichi 橘堂晃一 (2017b), 'Bezekuriku sekkutsu kuyō biku-zu saikō' ベゼクリク石窟供養比丘圖再考, in Miyaji Akira 宮治昭 (ed.), *Ajia bukkyō bijutsu ronshū, Chūō Ajia 1, Gandāra – Tōzai Torukisutan* アジア佛教美術論集：中央アジア 1：ガンダーラ～東西トルキスタン, Tokyo: Chūō kōron bijutsu shuppan, 523–550.

Li Gang 李剛 and Umar Kadir 吾買爾・卡得爾 (2020), 'Tulufan baixiha shiku cancun Huigu-wen tiji shaokao' 吐魯番伯西哈石窟殘存回鶻文題記少考, *Studies on the Inner Asian Languages*, 35: 25–37.

Li Gang 李剛 and Zhang Hailong 張海龍 (2021a), 'Tulufan Tuyugou 10-hao ku xinfaxian zhi Huigu-wen tiji kaoshi' 吐魯番吐峪溝 10 號窟新發現之回鶻文題記考釋, *Xiyu yanjiu* 西域研究, 1: 152–164.

Li Gang 李剛 and Zhang Hailong 張海龍 (2021b), 'Uyghur Wall Inscriptions Newly Discovered in the Cave 26 of the Tuyuq Grottoes of Turfan (II)', *Studies on the Inner Asian Languages*, 36: 23–59.

Liu Yongzeng 劉永增 (2014), 'Guazhou Yulinku di-3 ku de niandai wenti' 瓜州榆林窟第 3 窟的年代問題, *Yishu sheji yanjiu* 藝術設計研究, 4: 16–23.

Matsui, Dai 松井太 (2004), 'Shivushidu Yakushidu kankei monjo to Toyoku sekkutsu no Bukkyō kyōdan' シヴシドゥ・ヤクシドゥ關係文書とトヨク石窟の佛教教團, in Moriyasu

Takao 森安孝夫 (ed.), *Chūō Ajia shutsudo bunbutsu ronsō* 中央アジア出土文物論叢, Kyoto: Hoyu shoten, 41–70.

Matsui, Dai (2008a), 'A Mongolian Decree from the Chaghataid Khanate Discovered at Dunhuang', in Peter Zieme (ed.), *Aspects of Research into Central Asian Buddhism: In Memoriam Kōgi Kudara*, Turnhout: Brepols, 159–178.

Matsui, Dai (2008b), 'Revising the Uigur Inscriptions of the Yulin Caves', *Studies on the Inner Asian Languages*, 23: 17–32.

Matsui, Dai (2009), 'Recent Situation and Research Trends of Old Uigur Studies', *Asian Research Trends: New Series*, 4: 37–59.

Matsui, Dai (2010), 'Uigur Manuscripts Related to the Monks Sivšidu and Yaqšidu at "Abita-Cave Temple" of Toyoq', in Xinjiang Tulufanxue yanjiuyuan 新疆吐魯番學研究院 (ed.), *Tulufanxue yanjiu: di-san jie Tulufanxue ji Ou-Ya youmu minzu de qiyuan yu qianxi guoji xueshu yantaohui lunwenji* 吐魯番學研究：第三屆吐魯番學暨歐亞游牧民族的起源與遷徙國際學術研討會論文集, Shanghai: Shanghai guji chubanshe, 697–714.

Matsui, Dai 松井太 (2013), 'Tonkō sho sekkutsu no Uiguru-go daiki meibun ni kansuru sakki (I)' 敦煌諸石窟のウイグル語題記銘文に關する劄記（一）, *Jinbun shakai ronsō* 人文社會論叢, 30: 29–50.

Matsui, Dai 松井太 (2014), 'Tonkō sho sekkutsu no Uiguru-go daiki meibun ni kansuru sakki (II)' 敦煌諸石窟のウイグル語題記銘文に關する劄記（二）, *Jinbun shakai ronsō* 人文社會論叢, 32: 27–44.

Matsui, Dai 松井太 (2015), 'Dunhuang Mogaoku Anxi Yulinku de Huigu-yu tiji' 敦煌莫高窟・安西榆林窟的回鶻語題記, in Abdurishid Yakup 阿不都熱西提·亞庫甫 (ed.), *Xiyu: Zhongya yuwen-xue yanjiu* 西域——中亞語文學研究, Shanghai: Shanghai guji chubanshe, 210–225.

Matsui, Dai (2016a), 'Mengyuan shidai Huigu Fojiaotu he Jingjiaotu de wangluo' 蒙元時代回鶻佛教徒和景教徒的網絡, in Xu Zhongwen 徐忠文 and Rong Xinjiang 榮新江 (eds), *Make Boluo, Yangzhou, Sichouzhilu* 馬可·波羅，揚州，絲綢之路, Beijing: Beijing daxue chubanshe, 283–293.

Matsui, Dai (2016b), 'Uigur-Turkic Influence as Seen in the Qara-Qota Mongolian Documents', in Nikolaj N. Telicin and J. N. Šen (eds), *Aktual'nye voprosy tjurkologičeskix issledovanij: K 180-letiju kafedry tjurkskoj filologii Sankt-Peterburgskogo gosudarstvennogo universiteta* (*Актуальные вопросы тюркологических исследований: К 180-летию кафедры тюркской филологии Санкт-Петербургского государственного университета*), Sankt-Peterburg: Kafedra tjurkskoj filologii SPbGU, 559–564.

Matsui, Dai 松井 太 (2017), 'Tonkō sekkutsu Uiguru-go Mongoru-go daiki meibun shūsei' 敦煌石窟ウイグル語・モンゴル語題記銘文集成, in Matsui and Arakawa 2017, 1–160 and Figs 1, 3–7, 11.

Matsui, Dai 松井 太 (2018), 'Yulinku di-16 ku Xuliya-zi Huigu-wen Jingjiaotu tiji' 榆林窟第 16 窟叙利亞字回鶻文景教徒題記, *Dunhuang yanjiu* 敦煌研究, 2: 34–39.

Matsui, Dai (2019), 'Remarks on Buyan-Qaya, a Uighur Buddhist Pilgrim to Dunhuang', in Zekine Özertural and Gökhan Şilfeler (eds), *Unter dem Bodhi-Baum: Festschrift für Klaus Röhrborn anlässlich des 80. Geburtstags überreicht von Kollegen, Freunden und Schülern*, Göttingen: Vandenhoeck & Ruprecht, 209–224.

Matsui, Dai (2021), 'Two Remarks on the Toyoq Caves and Abita Qur "Abita Cave"', *Pis'mennye Pamiatniki Vostoka (Письменные памятники Востока)*, 18/3: 37–50.

Matsui, Dai (2022), 'Bir Eski Uygur duvar metnine göre Koço Uygur krallığında Budist manastırların himayesi', in Osman Fikri Sertkaya, Günay Karaağaç and Mesut Şen (eds), *Prof. Ceval Kaya armağanı*, Ankara: Akçağ, 335–345.

Matsui, Dai 松井太 and Arakawa Shintarō 荒川慎太郎 (eds) (2017), *Tonkō sekkutsu tagengo shiryō shūsei* 敦煌石窟多言語資料集成, Fuchu (Tokyo): Research Institute for Languages and Cultures of Asian and Africa, Tokyo University of Foreign Studies.
Maue, Dieter (1996), *Alttürkische Handschriften, Teil 1: Dokumente in Brāhmī und tibetischer Schrift*, Stuttgart: Franz Steiner.
Maue, Dieter and Klaus Röhrborn (1984), 'Ein "buddhistischer Katechismus" in alttürkischer Sprache und tibetischer Schrift (Teil 1)', *Zeitschrift der Deutschen Morgenländischen Gesellschaft*, 134: 286–313.
Maue, Dieter and Klaus Röhrborn (1985), 'Ein "buddhistischer Katechismus" in alttürkischer Sprache und tibetischer Schrift (Teil 2)', *Zeitschrift der Deutschen Morgenländischen Gesellschaft*, 135: 68–91.
Mirkamal, Aydar 阿衣達爾・米爾卡馬力 and Yang Fuxue 楊富學 (2012), 'Dunhuang Mogaoku 464-ku Huigu-wen bangti yanjiu' 敦煌莫高窟 464 窟回鶻文榜題研究, *Minzu yuwen* 民族語文, 3: 78–81.
Moriyasu, Takao (1982), 'An Uigur Buddhist's Letter of the Yüan Dynasty from Tun-huang', *Memoirs of the Research Department of the Tōyō Bunko*, 40: 1–18.
Moriyasu, Takao 森安孝夫 (1985), 'Chibetto moji de kakareta Uiguru-bun Bukkyō kyōri mondō (P. t. 1292) no kenkyū' チベット文字で書かれたウイグル文佛教教理問答（P. t. 1292）の研究, *Osaka Daigaku Bungakubu kiyō* 大阪大學文學部紀要, 25: 1–85 and 1 plate.
Moriyasu, Takao 森安孝夫 (1988), 'Tonkō shutsudo Gen-dai Uiguru monjo chū no Kinsai donsu' 敦煌出土元代ウイグル文書中のキンサイ緞子, in *Enoki Hakushi shōju kinen tōyōshi ronsō* 榎博士頌壽記念東洋史論叢, Tokyo: Kyūko shoin, 417–441.
Moriyasu, Takao 森安孝夫 (1991), *Uiguru-Manikyō-shi no kenkyū* ウイグル=マニ教史の研究 = *Osaka Daigaku Bungakubu kiyō* 大阪大學文學部紀要, 31–32.
Moriyasu, Takao (2004a), *Die Geschichte des uigurischen Manichäismus an der Seidenstraße*, Wiesbaden: Harrassowitz.
Moriyasu, Takao (2004b), 'From Silk, Cotton and Copper Coin to Silver: Transition of the Currency Used by the Uighurs during the Period from the 8th to the 14th Centuries', in Durkin-Meisterernst et al. 2004, 228–239.
Moriyasu, Takao (2008) 'Chronology of West Uighur Buddhism', in Peter Zieme (ed.), *Aspects of Research into Central Asian Buddhism: In Memoriam Kōgi Kudara,* Turnhout: Brepols, 191–227.
Moule, Arthur Christopher and Paul Pelliot (1938), *Marco Polo: The Description of the World*, Vol. 1, London: George Routledge & Sons.
Niu Ruji 牛汝極 and Peter Zieme (1996), 'The Buddhist Refuge Formula: An Uigur Manuscript from Dunhuang', *Türk Dilleri Araştırmaları*, 6: 41–56.
Ölmez, Mehmet (2017), *Köktürkçe ve Eski Uygurca dersleri*, İstanbul: Kesit.
Pelliot, Paul (1959), *Notes on Marco Polo*, vol. 1, Paris: Imprimerie nationale.
Porció Tibor (2014), 'Some Peculiarities of the Uygur Buddhist Pilgrim Inscriptions', in Christoph Cueppers and Max Deeg (eds), *Searching for the Dharma, Finding Salvation: Buddhist Pilgrimage in Time and Space*, Lumbini: Lumbini International Research Institute, 157–178.
Raschmann, Simone-Christiane (2009), *Alttürkische Handschriften, Teil 14: Dokumente, Teil 2*, Stuttgart: Franz Steiner.
Raschmann, Simone-Christiane (2020), 'Pilgrims in Old Uyghur Inscriptions: A Glimpse behind Their Records', in Carmen Meinert and Henrik Sørensen (eds), *Buddhism in Central Asia I: Patronage, Legitimation, Sacred Space, and Pilgrimage*, Leiden: Brill, 204–229.

Raschmann, Simone-Christiane and Osman Fikri Sertkaya (2016), *Alttürkische Handschriften, Teil 20: Alttürkische Texte aus der Berliner Turfansammlung im Nachlass Reşid Rahmeti Arat*, Stuttgart: Franz Steiner.

Russell-Smith, Lilla (2005), *Uygur Patronage in Dunhuang*, Leiden: Brill.

Satō, Takayasu 佐藤貴保 (2017), 'Tonkō sekkutsu Seika-ki Kanbun bokusho kokubun shūsei' 敦煌石窟西夏期漢文墨書・刻文集成, in Matsui and Arakawa 2017, 335–362.

Shōgaito, Masahiro (1991), 'On Uighur Elements in Buddhist Mongolian Texts', *Memoirs of the Research Department of the Toyo Bunko*, 49: 27–49.

Shōgaito, Masahiro (2004), 'How Were Chinese Characters Read in Uighur?', in Durkin-Meisterernst et al. 2004, 321–324.

Shōgaito, Masahiro (2014), *The Uighur Abhidharmakośabhāṣya Preserved at the Museum of Ethnography in Stockholm*, Wiesbaden: Harrassowitz.

Sugiyama, Masa'aki 杉山正明 (1990), 'Gen-dai Mou-kan gappeki meireibun no kenkyū (I)' 元代蒙漢合壁命令文の研究(一), *Studies on the Inner Asian Languages*, 5: 1–31 and 2 plates.

Takahashi, Hidemi (2019), 'Syriac Christianity in China', in Daniel King (ed.), *The Syriac World*, London: Routledge, 625–652.

Takeuchi, Tsuguhito (2012), 'Old Tibetan Buddhist Texts from the Post-Tibetan Imperial Period (Mid-9th C. to Late 10th C.)', in Cristina Scherrer-Schaub (ed.), *Old Tibetan Studies: Proceedings of the 10th Seminar of the International Association for Tibetan Studies*, Leiden: Brill, 205–215.

Tulufanxue yanjiuyuan 吐魯番學研究院 (2020), 'Tulufan Baixiha shiku fajue jianbao' 吐魯番伯西哈石窟發掘簡報, *Tulufanxue yanjiu* 吐魯番學研究, 1: 92–106 and Plates 1–2.

Umemura, Hiroshi (1996), 'A Qočo Uyghur King Painted in the Buddhist Temple of Beshbalïq', in Ronald E. Emmerick (ed.), *Turfan, Khotan und Dunhuang*, Berlin: Akademie Verlag, 361–378.

Umemura, Hiroshi 梅村坦 and Matsui Dai 松井太 (2008), 'Uiguru-moji Thuruku-go monjo' ウイグル文字テュルク語文書, in Yoshida Jun'ichi 吉田順一 and Chimeddorji チメドドルジ (eds), *Harahoto shutsudo Mongoru monjo no kenkyū* ハラホト出土モンゴル文書の研究, Tokyo: Yuzankaku, 183–199.

Umemura, Hiroshi 梅村坦 and Min Byung-hoon 閔丙勳 (1995), 'Gug-lib Jung-ang Bag-mul-gwan jang Be-je-keu-lig byeog-hwa Wi-gu-leu myeong-mun si-seog' 國立中央博物館藏베제크릭壁畫 위구르銘文試釋, *Mi-sul cha-ryo* 美術資料, 55: 119–155.

von Le Coq, Albert (1913), *Chotscho*, Berlin: Dietrich Reimer.

Wilkens, Jens (2021), *Handwörterbuch des Altuigurischen*, Göttingen: Universitätsverlag Göttingen.

Xie Zhiliu 謝稚柳 (1955), *Dunhuang yishu xulu* 敦煌藝術叙錄, Shanghai: Shanghai chuban gongsi.

Yakup, Abdurishid and Li Xiao (2019), 'A Philological Investigation of the Old Uighur Pilgrim Inscriptions Recently Discovered in the Cave NK 10 in the Tuyoq Grottoes of Turfan', *Acta Orientalia Academiae Scientiarum Hungaricae*, 72/4: 399–417.

Zhang Baoxi 張寶璽 (2012), *Guazhou Dong-Qianfodong Xixia shiku yishu* 瓜州東千佛洞西夏石窟藝術, Beijing: Xueyuan chubanshe.

Zhongguo shehui kexueyuan kaogu yanjiusuo 中國社會科學院考古研究所 (1991), *Beiting Gaochang Huigu fosi yizhi* 北庭高昌回鶻佛寺遺址, Shenyang: Liaoning meishu chubanshe.

Zieme, Peter (1977), 'Zwei Ergänzungen zu der christlichen Handschrift T II B 1', *Altorientalische Forschungen*, 5: 271–272 and Plates XIII–XIV.

Zieme, Peter (1985), *Buddhistische Stabreimdichtungen der Uiguren* (Berliner Turfantexte, 13), Berlin: Akademie-Verlag.
Zieme, Peter (1992), *Religion und Gesellschaft im Uigurischen Konigreich von Qočo*, Opladen: Westdeutscher Verlag.
Zieme, Peter (1998), 'Turkic Fragments in 'Phags-pa Script', *Studies on the Inner Asian Languages*, 13: 63–69 and Plates XVI–XVII.
Zieme, Peter (2011), 'Notes on the Religions in the Mongol Empire', in Anna Akasoy, Charles Burnett and Ronit Yoeli-Tlalim (eds), *Islam and Tibet*, Farnham: Ashgate, 177–187.
Zieme, Peter (2013a), 'A Brāhmaṇa Painting from Bäzäklik in the Hermitage of St. Petersburg and Its Inscriptions', in Tatiana Pang, Simone-Christiane Raschmann and Gerd Winkelhane (eds), *Unknown Treasures of the Altaic World in Libraries, Archives and Museums*, Berlin: Klaus Schwartz, 181–195.
Zieme, Peter (2013b), 'Stifter und Texte von der Seidenstraße nach Zeugnissen des altuigurischen Buddhismus', in Barbara Schuler (ed.), *Stifter und Mäzene und ihre Rolle in der Religion*, Wiesbaden: Harrassowitz, 43–55 and 190–193.
Zieme, Peter (2013c), 'Some Notes on Old Uighur Art and Texts', in Ryūkoku Daigaku Ajia bukkyō bunka kenkyū sentā 龍谷大学アジア仏教文化研究センター (ed.), *Torufan no bukkyō to bijutsu: Uiguru bukkyō wo chūshin ni* トルファンの仏教と美術：ウイグル仏教を中心に / *Buddhism and Art in Turfan: From the Perspective of Uyghur Buddhism*, Kyoto: Ryūkoku Daigaku Ajia bukkyō bunka kenkyū sentā, 5–42.
Zieme, Peter (2015a), *Altuigurische Texte der Kirche des Ostens aus Zentralasien*, Piscataway: Gorgias Press.
Zieme, Peter (2015b), 'Local Literatures: Uighur', in Jonathan A. Silk, Oskar von Hinüber and Vincent Eltschinger (eds), *Brill's Encyclopedia of Buddhism, vol. 1: Literature and Languages*, Leiden: Brill, 871–882.
Zieme, Peter (2020), 'Notes on the Interpretation of the Toyok Inscription of the West Uyghur Kingdom', *Studies on the Inner Asian Languages*, 35: 1–24.
Zieme, Peter (2021a), 'Merit Transfer and Vow According to an Old Uyghur Buddhist Text from Qočo/Gaochang', *Annual Report of the International Research Institute for Advanced Buddhology at Soka University*, 24: 217–229.
Zieme, Peter (2021b), 'Scenes from the Lotus Sūtra: An Old Uygur Temple Banner with Cartouche Inscriptions', *Manuscripta Orientalia*, 27/1: 3–19.
Zieme, Peter (2021c), 'Mount Wutai and Mañjuśrī in Old Uigur Buddhism', in Susan Andrews, Jinhua Chen and Guang Kuan (eds), *The Transnational Cult of Mount Wutai*, Leiden: Brill, 223–237.
Zieme, Peter (2022), 'Avalokiteśvara mit altuigurischen Inschriften aus der Bäzäklik-Grotte 46', in Ines Konczak-Nagel, Satomi Hiyama and Astrid Klein (eds), *Connecting the Art, Literature, and Religion of South and Central Asia: Studies in Honour of Monika Zin*, New Delhi: Dev, 431–436.
Zieme, Peter and Kudara Kōgi 百濟康義 (1985), *Uiguru-go no Kanmuryōjukyō* ウイグル語の觀無量壽經, Kyoto: Nagata Bunshōdō.

Nadine Bregler

Chinese Graffiti in Dunhuang?

Abstract: This contribution looks at materials from Dunhuang that are relevant to the study of graffiti. As can be observed from statements in poems preserved on the verso of one Dunhuang scroll, the practice of scratching names into cave walls was not always welcomed, regardless of the skills of the writer. An analysis of the textual structure of nine inscriptions from Mogao Cave 108 reveals telling differences between the inscriptions, which were likely done by persons of different social standings. Among them, one inscription is also found as one of several mnemonic lines on as many as ten Dunhuang manuscripts. This suggests similar functions for the blank spaces on walls and manuscripts. Since the mnemonic lines on the manuscripts indicate an educational context, it is very likely that students also scratched these lines onto the walls.

1 Introduction

On cliffs and building walls all over China, a great wealth of famous inscriptions is preserved, ranging from ancient to modern times. These inscriptions show the impressive degree to which people interacted with the spaces surrounding them.[1] Over the centuries, inscriptions were appreciated for both their textual and calligraphic qualities. They were collected, preserved and circulated in the form of rubbings, further copied and emulated by calligraphers, and finally, studied by historians. However, as elsewhere, no great interest was taken in collecting inscriptions that were deemed ephemeral and not prestigious or serious enough – the only exception being poems written on walls, especially if authored by renowned figures.[2] Such inscriptions oftentimes appear in places where they

1 Harrist 2008 uses four case studies to show how the functions fulfilled by distinct types of inscriptions differ, depending on location, time, and historical circumstances. Xue Lei 2019 demonstrates how inscriptions that arose in originally distinct spheres constantly became embedded in new socio-political contexts. For the Song era, Zhang Cong 2005 shows the different functions of inscriptions at inns, made by travelling official-scholars and their female relatives.

2 An introduction to the culture of inscribing poems on walls is provided by Liu Lingdi 2011. For poems inscribed during the Tang era, see Yan Jihua 2008. Dudbridge 2018, 165–166 considers factors such as the randomness, coincidences and selective processes that led verses on walls to

https://doi.org/10.1515/9783111326306-007

were not originally intended to appear, and likely without the consent of the respective owners or authorities. The surfaces were therefore usually neither designed nor prepared to carry such inscriptions, commonly referred to in scholarship as 'graffiti'.[3]

Among the places where pre-modern Chinese examples of such inscriptions are preserved *in situ* is the Buddhist temple complex known as the Mogao Caves, one of the many religious sites of the Dunhuang region at the western margin of the medieval Chinese Empire. On occasions such as the Lantern Festival on the fifteenth day of the first lunar month, the caves were lit up with oil lamps, offering the contemporary viewer a particular visual experience.[4] In addition, contemporaries often donated temple caves in honour of their deceased relatives, who were portrayed as worshippers on the cave walls.[5] Thus, people donated money to produce lavish wall paintings, while others would scribble on them.

The cave walls preserve a great number of inscriptions in a variety of languages; these have been less studied in terms of who left them behind and why. Matsui Dai categorizes such inscriptions in the Old Uyghur language under the umbrella term 'graffiti inscriptions' and shows that they may appear to be written rather carelessly on certain occasions, but generally point to visits and religious pilgrimages. He convincingly shows that these inscriptions are situated within the daily life experiences of the Old Uyghurs and are evidence of interactions with other cultures, such as Tibetan and Chinese.[6] Chinese inscriptions, including graffiti, are likewise documented in the various photographic reproductions of the murals.[7] Among other inscriptions, Li Zhengyu collected those that were engraved or painted on walls by students.[8] A more recent study of Chinese visitor inscriptions in the Mogao Caves has been conducted by Wang Liping.[9]

---

be jotted down in the notebooks of passers-by or travellers. Such verses would then gradually be included in authorized collections under the names of authors.

3 See the introduction to this volume.

4 Wu 2002. For a study on the spatial experience of the caves, see Wu 2023.

5 On the construction of the grottoes and their relation to the donors, see Sheng and Xia 2022, 58–67.

6 Matsui, this volume. On the state of art of epigraphy in the Dunhuang region, the inscriptions' appearance on walls and their terminology, see ibid.

7 See for instance the early photographs in Pelliot 1920–1924, and the recent publication of the photographs of the Lo Archive in Ching 2021. Nowadays, pictures of the murals can also be conveniently accessed online, for instance via artstor.org.

8 Li Zhengyu 1987.

9 Wang Liping 2014.

The material presented here is too scarce to draw decisive conclusions. Instead, these preliminary observations show the potential for the study of ancient graffiti practices. First, two poems written on a Dunhuang manuscript will be analysed in some detail, since their content suggests that the practice of inscribing names into the niches was not welcomed by everyone.[10] Secondly, nine inscriptions from Mogao Cave 108 will be introduced and compared. Since neither photographs nor line drawings of these inscriptions are available, the main approach here consists of an analysis of structure and content of these inscriptions as preserved in textual editions. The differences in their structure and content give reason to assume different kinds of inscriptions, which were written by people of various identities and social standing. Lastly, a line found in one of the inscriptions from the Mogao Cave is also paralleled in as many as ten Dunhuang manuscripts. This link will be considered to illustrate the similar function of blank spaces on walls and in manuscripts.

2 Two poems on the verso of Dunhuang scroll P.2641

Nearly ever since wall inscriptions first appear in Chinese historical sources, there have been complaints about the practice of scribbling on walls.[11] Of the four poems on the verso of Dunhuang scroll P.2641, the second and third warn pilgrims about the sufferings of hell should they intend to engrave their names on the cave walls:[12]

厶人述	**Told by someone**
1 白壁從來好丹青	[I] always appreciated the coloured paintings on the white walls,
2 無知箇箇亂題名	[But] ignorant people inscribed [their] names in a disorderly fashion.

10 The library cave with the Dunhuang manuscripts is estimated to have been sealed in the early eleventh century CE. For a comprehensive introduction to the library cave and the early dispersal of the manuscripts, see Rong Xinjiang 2013, 79–108. The manuscripts will be referred to here by their abbreviated signatures. For instance, the signature 'Pelliot chinois' followed by a number, used for manuscripts in the Bibliothèque nationale de France (BnF), are referred to using the letter 'P' and the respective numbers. Likewise, the press mark 'Or.8210/S.(*number*)' for manuscripts kept at the British Library is given as 'S.(*number*)'.

11 See for instance the complaints discussed by Wu 1995, 194 and by Harrist 2008, 44.

12 The scroll measures 29.4 to 30.4 cm × 165 cm. There are 4 sheets in total. The first sheet is 37.7 cm long; the other three are 42.3 to 42.6 cm long. The manuscript is published in the online catalogue accessible via the BnF website <gallica.bnf.fr>.

3 三塗地獄交誰忍	Who can bear the three paths of hell?
4 十八湔銅灌一瓶	With one jar poured of the scalding copper of the eighteen [hells] [down one's throat].[13]
5 鐫龕必定添福利	Carving the niches certainly increases merit,
6 鑿壁多層[14]證無生	[But] chiselling the wall on multiple levels[15] is a testimony of birthlessness.
7 為[16]報往來遊翫者	For the sake of those travelling for pleasure,
8 輒莫於此騁書題	Better not to impetuously inscribe here.

依韻	**With the same rhyme**
1 白壁雖然好丹青	Even though [I] appreciated the coloured paintings on the white walls,
2 無間[17]迷愚難悟醒	The restless deluded [ones] are difficult to awaken.[18]
3 縱有百般僧氏巧	Even if there are all sorts of skills in the monk family,[19]
4 也有文徒書號名	[And] also literate fellows writing their names,
5 空留佳妙不題宣	It is [still] best to leave empty space and not inscribe public announcements,
6 却入五趣陷塵境	Otherwise one enters into the five realms of being and falls into the world of dust.
7 為[20]報往來遊觀者	For the sake of those sightseeing,
8 起聽前詞□□□	Better start listening to the preceding song [...]

In these poems, various terms are used for the act of inscribing. The Chinese terms often reflect slightly different acts based on the content or material that is being inscribed. Various lines reveal more about the aims of the inscribing and what was inscribed. For instance, in the second line of the first poem, the writer complains that everyone has 'inscribed [their] names in a disorderly fashion' (*luan ti ming* 亂題名), and the fourth line of the second poem ends with 'writing [their] names' (*shu haoming* 書號名).[21] In addition, the fifth line of the second poem urges the reader (or listener) to leave the walls blank and not to 'write public announcements' on them (*ti xuan* 題宣).

---

13 This is one of the eighteen hells, which are variously described. For an introduction, see Eberhard 1967, 24–59.

14 The manuscript has *ceng* 層, which literally means 'layers'. Xu Jun 2000, 116 proposes to read *ceng* 曾 ('once').

15 This possibly refers to inscribing stupas in different spots.

16 The manuscript has *wei* 唯; the reading here follows Xu Jun 2000, 116.

17 The manuscript has *jian* 簡; the reading here follows Xu Jun 2000, 116.

18 This likely refers to those who ignorantly inscribe walls.

19 Most likely, this relates to writing skills of the monks.

20 The manuscript has *wei* 唯; the reading here follows Xu Jun 2000, 116.

21 *Shu* means 'to write down' or 'record'. Used as noun, it refers to writing and script, more specifically to a certain style of writing or calligraphy.

What can be seen from both poems on the verso is that someone objected to individuals inscribing their names on walls. This is clearly not even tolerated when done by skilled writers, such as 'monks' (*seng shi* 僧氏) or 'literate fellows' (*wen tu* 文徒), which are terms that are most likely used satirically here.[22] Since the Dunhuang manuscripts contain only these two poems in which such matters are addressed, is difficult to ascertain how widespread such criticism was and whether there were regulations or even punitive measures against inscribing on walls.

The circumstances under which these two poems were written on the verso of the Dunhuang scroll along with two other poems are likewise difficult to assess.[23] On the scroll, a prose text without a title precedes the four poems and concerns the restoration of one of the Mogao Caves (Fig. 1).[24] This prose text and the four poems are written on the verso of the scroll, meaning that they are later additions, not the original incentives for the production of this paper manuscript.[25] The texts are neatly structured overall, and three of the four poems have titles. The lack of extensive revisions and corrections suggests at least that the prose text was copied *from* a wall, contrary to being a draft text that was later to be inscribed *on* a wall.[26] However, it remains unclear whether the four poems were also originally inscribed on a wall following the prose text; if they were collected from different sources, such as other walls or further manuscripts; or if they were only composed upon having copied the prose text in the manuscript. As for what kinds of inscriptions may have bothered the composers of these poems, one can turn to the cave walls themselves.

22 See the fourth and fifth lines of the second poem.

23 For instance, there is no colophon providing further information on when and by whom these poems were written. There are additional texts after the blank space in the second half of the manuscript: among others, a 'record of meritorious deeds' (*gongde ji* 功德記), in which the restoration of another cave is mentioned. See Xu Jun 2000, 117–118.

24 Sørensen 2020, 10 indicates that the cave in question is Mogao Cave 130.

25 The scroll is made of four sheets, each of which contains one report on the recto. The reports concern expenditures made on the occasion of festivals and for guests such as messengers from Khotan, with mentions of quantities of food such as flour and oil. See the BnF's online catalogue. The dates provided after each report indicate the period when Cao Yuanzhong 曹元忠 (r. 939–974 CE) was the local ruler (Ma De 1994, 43).

26 For a study of the epigraphic material that has survived in Dunhuang manuscripts, see Galambos 2009.

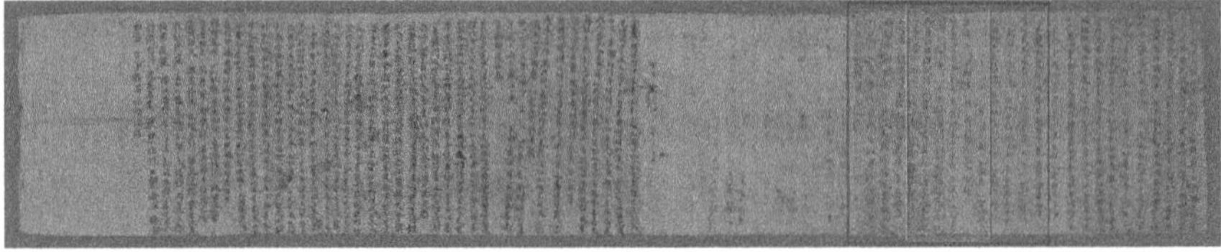

Fig. 1: The verso of the scroll Pelliot chinois 2641; paper, 29.4–30.4 × 165 cm; Bibliothèque nationale de France (BnF); the first half of the scroll contains the prose text on the restoration of a cave followed by the four poems; the red square shows the location of the four poems; the blue square indicates the two poems containing criticism of the practice of inscribing names on the murals; courtesy of the BnF.

3 The nine inscriptions from Mogao Cave 108

Inscriptions from the Mogao Caves have been published in Chinese collections such as *Dunhuang Mogao ku gongyangren tiji* 敦煌莫高窟供養人題記 from 1986 and the more recent *Dunhuang Mogao ku tiji huibian* 敦煌莫高窟題記彙編 from 2014.[27] The material collected in these two editions mainly concerns inscriptions by 'donors' (*gongyangren* 供養人) who provided financial support to the temple, but there are also names and dates inscribed by pilgrims, as well as a few poems. The editions unfortunately record only the texts and do not offer visual reproductions. Nothing is therefore known about the spatiality of the nine inscriptions of Mogao Cave 108 to be analysed in the following, for example how they were placed and how they interrelated with each other.[28] In both editions, the nine inscriptions are sorted under 'visitors' graffiti' (*youren manti* 游人漫題).[29]

The nine inscriptions were not placed directly on the cave walls. Instead, they were written on the brim of the southern rockface outside the cave.[30] Moreover, as early as 1987, only one year after the publication of the first edition, the inscriptions are reported as 'having already come off' (*jin yi boli* 今已剝離).[31] While it is unclear exactly which architectural structure is meant and how and why the inscriptions came off, this remark is a reminder that the caves as they

27 Dunhuang yanjiuyuan 1986 and Xu Ziqiang, Zhang Yongqiang and Chen Jing 2014.

28 Unfortunately, only a few photographic reproductions of Mogao Cave 108 could be found. There is for instance only one blurred picture in Pelliot 1920–1924 and two photographs in Ching 2021, vol. VII, 156, showing the donor figures of Cao Yuande and Cao Yijin.

29 The translation for the term has been adopted from Matsui, this volume.

30 See Dunhuang yanjiuyuan 1986, 53 and Xu Ziqiang, Zhang Yongqiang and Chen Jing 2014, 124.

31 Li Zhengyu 1987, 36.

appear today are often incomplete, for example missing the wooden porches at the entrances.[32]

Most of the nine inscriptions are very short and incomplete, likely due to their illegibility on the wall. For some, only a few legible characters are preserved. Therefore, it is difficult to make statements about their exact content. Nevertheless, it becomes clear that the inscriptions featured different kinds of content. As far as the content is still legible, several inscriptions revolve around topics such as visiting the caves for pilgrimage.[33] Among them, some inscriptions consist merely of dates.[34] While frustrating for the modern scholar, this is fairly typical of this kind of incidental text elsewhere as well.[35]

In the following, I will introduce the inscriptions according to their sequence in the source publications. The first inscription consists of a long prose text, a poem and a concluding colophon. The latter indicates that the inscription was done by a certain Zhang Yingrun 張盈潤, who explains in much detail that he came to the Mogao Caves while on a military campaign.[36] Zhang Yingrun mentions he was reminded of the greatness of the ten thousand Buddhas while wandering through the grottoes. After being motivated to devote himself to Buddhism again, he states that he 'thus inscribed shallow verses [onto the wall]' (*zhe ti qian ju* 輒題淺句).[37] The subsequent poem can be understood as an abbreviated and poetic version of this long explanation. The colophon afterwards states that Zhang Yingrun inscribed the poem in the year 949 CE, which is the period when Cao Yuanzhong 曹元忠 (r. 944–974 CE) was the local ruler.[38] Zhang is referred to as the 'Clerk to the Governor' (*jiedu yaya* 節度押衙); thus, he was a man of considerable social standing. Zhang Yingrun is also known from further Dunhuang

32 For a study on the architecture of the exterior structures of the caves, see Zhou Zhenru 2022. The appendix includes pictures of the timber-structured façades and drawings on the structures of the caves.

33 The records often consist of only a few characters, of which most are set in brackets to further highlight the uncertainty of their readings.

34 For instance, the two lines recorded as the fourth inscription. For the Chinese dating systems, see Galambos 2020, 95–96.

35 Ragazzoli et al. 2018.

36 Contrary to the editions that understand the inscription as 'visitor graffiti' (*youren manti* 游人漫題), this inscription has also been described as 'Poem inscribed on a wall; with preface; one piece' (*tibishi bing xu yi shou* 題壁詩並序一首) (Li Zhengyu 1987, 36).

37 Dunhuang yanjiuyuan 1986, 54 and Xu Ziqiang, Zhang Yongqiang and Chen Jing 2014, 125.

38 On Cao Yuanzhong, see Rong Xinjiang 2013, 46.

manuscripts;[39] for example, his name is mentioned in a text in which the completion of a stupa in the following year, 950 CE, is celebrated. Here, Zhang is mentioned as a sponsor of paintings.[40]

This long votive inscription has very serious content. It stands to reason that the expression about inscribing 'shallow verses' falls into the category of modest speech and should not be taken entirely at face value. It is unclear whether Zhang had permission to inscribe it. It is possible that he felt entitled to do so, for instance because he served in an official position. He may also have sponsored more than just the paintings from the following year. Pending further evidence, it therefore remains an open question whether this inscription may be classified as a graffiti inscription.

In comparison, the following eight shorter inscriptions show notable structural differences. Since the seventh inscription is still comparatively long and legible, I will present it here in more detail; additional evidence from the remaining shorter inscriptions will be cited where applicable.[41] The seventh inscription mentions the monk Daozhen 道真 (*c.* 915–*c.* 987 CE) and his associates, who are said to have set up a ritual site below the slope of Shengwang 聖王 Temple at Mt. Sanwei 三危.[42] This is followed by a date that most likely corresponds to the year 950 CE;[43] the whole inscription ends with a four-line poem.

Both the first and the seventh inscriptions begin with a prose text. However, compared to the first inscription, the sequence of the poem and colophon or date is inverted in this seventh inscription: the date comes first, and the poem only afterwards. In addition, names are not provided in the same place. In the first inscription, a colophon provides the date and the name Zhang Yingrun. Compared to this, in the seventh inscription, the name Daozhen appears directly in the descriptive first line and *not* in the next line with the date. This suggests that Daozhen did not inscribe the text himself, but is merely mentioned in it.

39 In a note on a Dunhuang manuscript, which is merely a torn slip of paper, Zhang is mentioned as a student of Lingtu Monastery. The year mentioned here corresponds to the year 927 CE. This note is on manuscript P.5011 (Li Zhengyu 1987, 35, n. 91).

40 Dunhuang manuscript P.3390 (Li Zhengyu 1987, 36, n. 94). The text also mentions that Zhang Yingrun was a former student of Lingtu Monastery, where he studied together with a certain *śramaṇa* Derong 德榮 (Li Zhengyu 1987, 36).

41 This is not to say that all of the other inscriptions have all the elements found in the seventh inscription.

42 The same monk is also mentioned on the first text in P.2641, concerning the restoration of a Mogao Cave in the years 948 to 949 CE. On Daozhen, see Sørensen 2020. For a tentative translation of the seventh inscription up until the date, see Sørensen 2020, 9.

43 Sørensen 2020, 9, n. 16.

The reasons for such structural differences are difficult to ascertain without knowing how the inscriptions originally looked, especially since we cannot assess the quality of the handwriting. However, experience shows that colophons usually indicate the end of a text. It is therefore plausible that either some or all three elements of the seventh graffiti inscription were done by different persons and under distinct circumstances. The seventh inscription and several others may have looked quite different from the first inscription by Zhang Yingrun.

A second difference concerns the dating. The colophon by Zhang Yingrun provides the regnal year as the second year of the Qianyou 乾祐 period (949 CE), which allows us to accurately determine the corresponding date in the Gregorian calendar. The colophon reads:[44]

> 乾祐二年六月三日節度押衙張盈潤題
> The third day of the sixth month of the second year of the Qianyou period, inscribed (*ti* 題) by the Clerk to the Governor Zhang Yingrun.

The seventh inscription continues the year count from the previous era, Tianfu 天福, up to the fifteenth year (950 CE), although officially it had ended in 947 CE.[45] Likewise, the date of the third inscription mentions the fourteenth year of the Tianfu era (949 CE).[46] While it is not uncommon for the former era name to remain in use for some time, it is a notable difference compared to the first inscription by Zhang Yingrun.[47]

A third difference is that in the colophon by Zhang Yingrun, the name is followed by the word 'inscribed' (*ti* 題). In the seventh inscription, there is no name mentioned after the date, but only the statement 'travelled and noted this; that's it' (*you ji zhi er* 遊記之耳). Similar wording appears in as many as three more of the nine inscriptions. The third line of the second inscription reads '(in his own)

---

44 Dunhuang yanjiuyuan 1986, 54 and Xu Ziqiang, Zhang Yongqiang and Chen Jing 2014, 125.
45 The Tianfu 天福 era was used by the two emperors of the later Jin 後晉 era (936–947 CE) for another eight years, from 936 to 944 CE. The reign title was changed to Kaiyun 開運 for the final three years. The first emperor of the next dynasty, the Later Han 後漢 (947–950 CE), continued to use the reign title Tianfu for another year (947 CE). He also seamlessly continued the year count, subsuming three years of the Kaiyun era under the twelfth year of the Tianfu reign. The subsequent Qianyou 乾佑 era was used from 948 to 950 CE (Wan Guoding 1978, 101).
46 Dunhuang yanjiuyuan 1986, 54 and Xu Ziqiang, Zhang Yongqiang and Chen Jing 2014, 125.
47 This is not unusual, especially in times when the dynasties or emperors frequently changed. As shown by Qu Jian 2022, the continuation or abolition of older era dates is also often closely linked to changes in socio-political identities. For instance, people also used the Xuantong 宣统 era date (1909–1911 CE) well into the beginning of the Republican period (1912–1949 CE).

hand, Kong Yi noted [this] down' (*ji shou Kong Yi ji* 洎手孔壹記).[48] In the second line of the eighth inscription, directly after mentioning that someone paid respect to the Buddha, we find the statement 'written and noted down by [my] own hand' (*zi shou shu ji* 自手書記). Lastly, in the first line of the two dates in the ninth inscription, the last two characters are 'noted down; that's it' (*ji er* 記耳). These formulas closely resemble the statement 'I was here', a common phrase in graffiti of all times and places. Moreover, the phrase 'written and noted down by [my] own hand' (*zi shou shu ji* 自手書記) offers intriguing parallels with the formulas used in colophons or dates on Dunhuang manuscripts, especially on manuscripts belonging to an educational context.[49] Such graffiti inscriptions appear much more likely to be the target of criticism than the first inscription by Zhang Yingrun.

4 The third line of the fifth graffiti inscription found in Dunhuang manuscripts

It is very likely that there were also students among the individuals inscribing on walls, even though they did not always mention their name and status. An exemplary case of this is an inscription on the southern wall of Mogao Cave 199 corresponding to the year 917 CE.[50] Here, a 'student' (*xueshilang* 學使郎) of Longxing 龍興 Monastery is mentioned, without a name being provided afterwards.[51]

In addition, one line from the fifth inscription of Mogao Cave 108 is preserved in as many as ten Dunhuang manuscripts, many of which can be situated in an educational context. This suggests that the appearance of this line on the wall was the result of a similarly off-the-cuff action as its appearance in the manuscripts. Because of their similar function, scribbles on manuscripts have previously been

48 The character *ji* 洎 is provided in brackets in the two editions, therefore indicating a suggestion for a rather illegible character. Given the context, it is understood here as *zi* 自 ('own').

49 For actions indicated in colophons, see for example Galambos 2020, 98. Additional aspects will be examined in my dissertation on Dunhuang manuscripts containing collections of literary texts. For instance, it is not always clear whether and how a colophon and a line with a date differ from each other. In addition, there are several possibilities for translating the character *ji* 記 – 'to note', 'to record' or 'to remember' – and the frequently occurring term 'note(d) this down; that's it' (*ji zhi er* 記之耳), especially in relation to other actions mentioned above, such as 'to write' (*shu* 書) or 'to copy' (*xie* 寫).

50 Li Zhengyu 1987, 35, entry 82 describes the inscription as an 'inscription by a traveller' (*youren tiji* 游人題記).

51 For terms for 'students', see Galambos 2020, 97.

compared to 'graffiti'.[52] In the following, I will look at the line as it is preserved in Dunhuang manuscripts and how it reflects a phenomenon similar to the usage of blank space on walls.

Not much can be revealed about this line from the content as recorded in the two editions, except for the information provided in the latter half of the third line, which states, '[...] Second, don't become familiar with the wine shop' ([...] *Di er mo gong jiu jia qin* 第二莫共酒家親). In the Dunhuang manuscripts, this line is often part of a longer list of maxims.[53] The precise wording in the manuscripts exhibits slight variations, especially in the fourth line. One of the more complete versions reads:[54]

第壹郎君須立身	First, you must establish yourself
第貳莫共酒家親	Second, don't become familiar with the wine shop
第三君不見生生鳥[55]	Third, don't you see the double-headed bird[56]
第四為酒送其身[57]	Fourth, [don't] dedicate your life to wine

These lines are clearly not a self-contained poem. For instance, it is unlikely that the lines of a poem would begin with such words as 'First' (*di yi* 第一), 'Second' (*di er* 第貳) and 'Third (*di san* 第三). It is also striking that the third line has one

52 Scott-Warren 2018 demonstrates that much can be gained from situating books in their changing social and historical environments to understand the manifold situations and aims that led to the additional writings, which range from notations of ownership and marks of having visited a place or seen a book to openly shaming or praising books or individuals. Rogers 2018 argues that medieval manuscripts are by definition products that usually involve many contributors, and furthermore points out that it was a common practice to write on architectural spaces as well as in circulating manuscripts. For considerations concerning the usage of blank margins in manuscripts, see also the introduction of Ragazzoli et al. 2018, 159–162.

53 The manuscripts have been collated by Xu Jun (2000, 880) and supplemented in Xu Jun 2002, 70–71. The signatures are P.2604, P.3666, P.4052, P.5557, S.707, S.3724, S.4295, S.5711 and BD07220. One additional scroll is kept in the Fu Ssu-Nien Library at the Academia Sinica, Taiwan. For photographs, see Fang Guangchang 2013, 120–147. For a description of this scroll and its content, see ibid., 10–13.

54 Scroll S.4295. Apart from the line recorded from Mogao Cave 108, the counting at the start of each line is only preserved in one of the ten manuscripts.

55 On the scroll, there is only one character *sheng*. The other manuscripts have two *sheng*, with the second *sheng* written as a reduplication mark. Therefore, the addition of the second *sheng* follows Xu Jun 2002, 71.

56 This bird, called the *jīvajīvaka* (Skrt.), has one body in the form of a bird and two heads with human faces, which depend on each other in life and death (Ci Yi 1989, 4287).

57 This character is written as *xin* 新 ('new') in the manuscript, but as *shen* 身 ('body') on all further manuscripts. The reading as *shen* here therefore follows Xu Jun 2002, 71.

more syllable than the other lines.[58] In addition, the last characters of the first and fourth lines are identical. This suggests that instead of being a proper poem, these lines are something else. Each line probably refers to a popular saying, originally longer, that is only cited here by its opening words.[59] The counting at the beginning may have served as a mnemonic device.[60]

Several indications suggest that these mnemonic lines were familiar to and learned by students. For example, the term 'establishing oneself' (*li shen* 立身) likely alludes to the section on establishing oneself in another text learned by students, the 'Classic of Filial Piety' (*Xiaojing* 孝經).[61] Indeed, the beginning of this line also appears on the verso of a manuscript with the 'Classic of Filial Piety' as the main or 'core' content.[62] In addition, the second to fourth lines are also included in a passage of a long humorous text known often to have been copied by students, entitled 'Discussion between Tea and Wine' (*Cha jiu lun* 茶酒論).[63]

The ten manuscripts on which the mnemonic lines are written have different book forms. Seven of them are scrolls, one is a booklet and one is a paper fragment; lastly, one manuscript is a paper patch formerly attached to a scroll.[64]

Notably, the mnemonic lines never constitute the core content of their manuscripts. Instead, just like the so-called 'student poems', the lines appear in blank spaces throughout the ten manuscripts, for instance on the cover of the booklet (Fig. 2).[65] In addition, the lines appear in the blank space after the core content on the recto (Fig. 3) or throughout the verso of the scrolls (Fig. 4).[66] On the versos, the lines co-occur with other, remarkably diverse texts, mainly written by different

---

58 The second character *sheng* 生 is written with reduplication marks. Therefore, in the manuscripts, the third line is as long as the others. However, when vocalized, the line is longer.

59 Xiang Chu 2006, 580, n. 1, for example, refers to the second line as a 'contemporary popular saying' (*dangshi suyu* 當時俗語).

60 See Wang Mingqin 2004, who describes texts abbreviated to their initial lines and written in four directions as a mnemonic tool for Qin officials.

61 See Galambos 2020, 129, n. 301, who also provides the exact passage.

62 Scroll S.707, described by Galambos 2020, 129. For the definitions of core and paracontent, see Ciotti et al. 2018.

63 Xu Jun 2002, 70–71. These are the original titles as they appear in the manuscript. The 'Discussion between Tea and Wine', for example, is preserved in P.2718. For this text, see Xiang Chu 2006, 566–585. For a translation of the text, see for example Mair and Erling 2009. The text is also discussed in Benn 2015.

64 For the paper patch, see Giles 1957, 235. For scroll S.2607, from which several more paper patches like the present one were removed, see Giles 1957, 239.

65 For 'student poems', see Galambos 2020, 104–112.

66 Such scattered writings attest to specific patterns, according to which further manuscripts presumably belong to an educational context can be identified. See Galambos 2016.

hands with comparable skills, for example poems as well as texts relating to Buddhism and divination. In some cases, the mnemonic lines are repeated more than once; in other cases, the text is not written in its entirety and only the first characters of the line appear.

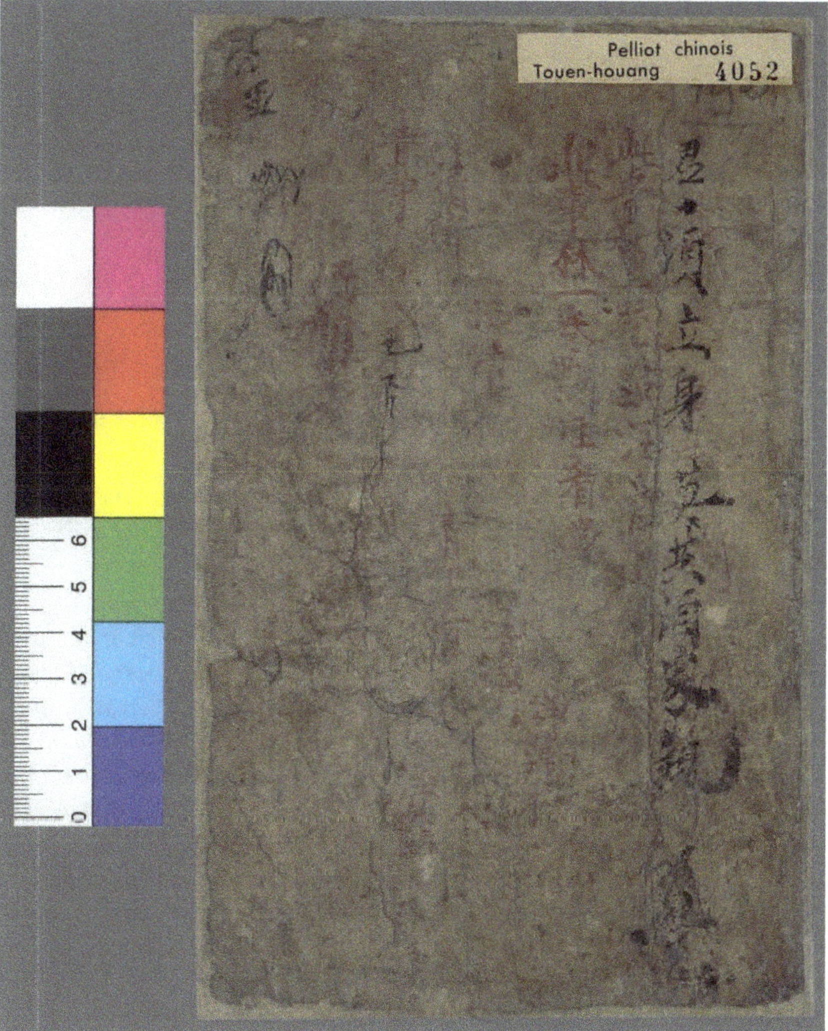

Fig. 2: Cover of the booklet Pelliot chinois 4052; paper, 21.5 × 13.5 cm; Bibliothèque nationale de France (BnF); the incomplete mnemonic line is written in black ink at the far right; courtesy of the BnF.

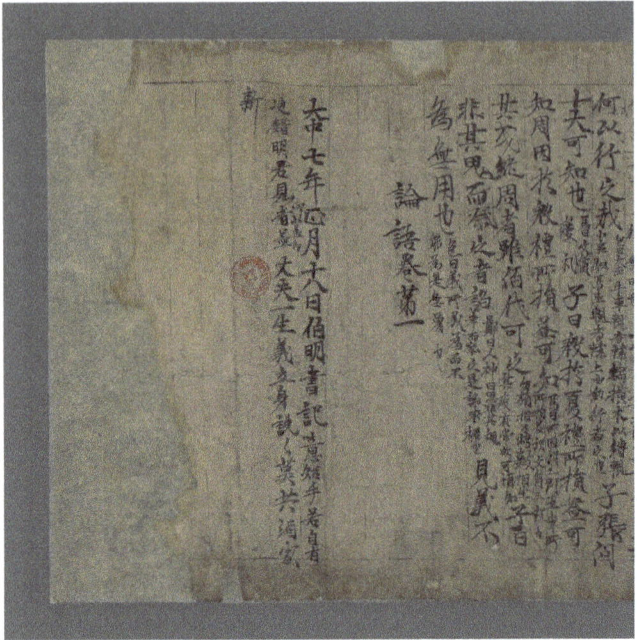

Fig. 3: Recto of Pelliot chinois 2604 (section view); paper, 28.8–29.6 × 104.2 cm; Bibliothèque nationale de France (BnF); the mnemonic line begins after another poem beneath the colophon; courtesy of the BnF.

The manuscripts have different core content. Three manuscripts contain texts known to have been copied by students, such as the 'Rhapsody on the Swallow, One *Juan*' (*Yanzi fu yi juan* 燕子賦一卷), the 'Classic of Filial Piety, One *Juan*' (*Xiaojing yi juan* 孝經一卷) and the 'Thousand Character Classic, One *Juan*' (*Qianziwen yi juan* 千字文一卷).[67] In the other manuscripts, the core content is often written in considerably better hands. There are various texts, such as Buddhist texts and a collection of *dhāraṇīs*.[68] This suggests that in addition to making their own manuscripts, students could, to a certain degree, access manuscripts that were produced by others, and leave their additions on them.

67 For these texts, see scroll P.3666, scroll S.707 and patch S.5711, respectively. For texts copied by students, see Galambos 2020, 100–104.

68 For Buddhist texts, see S.3724 and the scroll kept in the Fu Ssu-nien Library at Academia Sinica, Taiwan. The collection of *dhāraṇīs* is contained in S.4295.

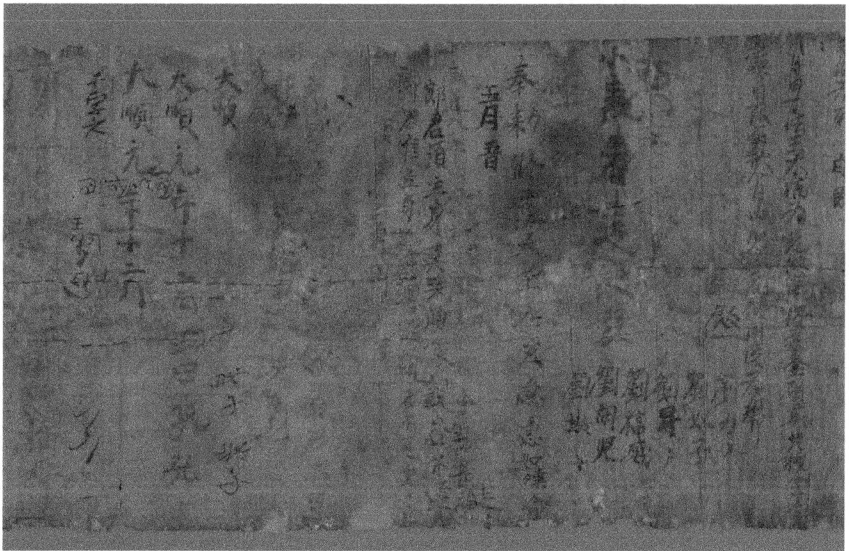

Fig. 4: Section of the verso of scroll Pelliot chionois 3666; paper, dimensions unknown; Bibliothèque nationale de France (BnF); containing the beginnings of the mnemonic lines and various other content, such as dates; courtesy of the BnF.

5 Conclusion

The Mogao Caves played an important role in the religious life of Dunhuang. Therefore, it is very likely that far more inscriptions were left by visitors, of which only a limited number have been recorded in modern publications.

In two poems on the verso of Dunhuang scroll P.2641, the practice of inscribing one's name onto painted walls is clearly condemned. Since the two poems on the verso of Dunhuang scroll P.2641 are the only testament to this attitude in the Dunhuang manuscripts, it is difficult to estimate how far-reaching was the criticism against such practices of inscribing, what kinds of inscriptions were generally perceived as unwanted, and whether inscriptions other than those discussed here were included. Both poems specifically mention the disorderly incising of names, without referring to any further textual forms.

The analysis of the structure and content of the inscriptions recorded for Mogao Cave 108 suggests that different kinds of inscriptions existed, likely done by a great variety of people with different identities and social standings. The first record is an inscription by the official Zhang Yingrun; the inscription is datable to the year 949 CE. This inscription is not a clear-cut case, since it remains uncertain whether he was entitled to inscribe it or whether he assumed the authority to do so on his own. Although it is unclear whether this inscription generally gave much reason for complaint, it is less likely due to the serious content of the inscription and the status of the inscriber.

The following eight shorter inscriptions consist of dates, names and formulas mentioning visits, and therefore partially match the subjects of complaint in the two poems. It is more likely that, at least for the author of the two poems, such inscriptions were considered transgressive. They therefore fall within the narrow definition of graffiti. Here we face the problem that our source publication has transcribed the texts without providing an image of their original format; thus, crucial information is unavailable to us. A great variety of graffiti inscriptions must have existed on other walls, too, yet have since been washed off or faded away.

Connections between the content of inscriptions on the Mogao Cave wall and the Dunhuang manuscripts attest to the fact that there are similarities in function between graffiti inscriptions on walls and scribbles in the blank spaces of manuscripts. Three of the wall inscriptions contain formulas indicating that someone travelled to a place or wrote something down. Similar formulas appear frequently in colophons in student manuscripts or in short notes on the verso of scrolls, which also suggests that this was a common practice. In addition, the fifth wall inscription contains one line that appears in as many as ten Dunhuang manuscripts. Since the mnemonic lines on these manuscripts belong to an educational context, it is very likely that the fifth inscription on the wall was also written by a student and, like several of the graffiti inscriptions, may not have looked very neat. It becomes apparent that the whole age group of adolescents is underrepresented in the records from Dunhuang; only a few traces remain in the form of student names or terms to designate students. There may have been assemblies or schooling that took place in or near the caves. Just as students commonly wrote notes in manuscripts, they also used the space on cave and temple walls for writing and drawing when they were bored.

It is difficult to ascertain in retrospect whether inscriptions by renowned individuals in the region, such as the one by Zhang Yingrun, gave much reason for complaint. In addition, there are indications that some texts originating as graffiti inscriptions may very well have been perceived as valuable already in contemporary times, not least when a famous name is mentioned: for instance, the seventh inscription, which is likely a graffiti inscription based on the structure of the content, may have been created by more than one person. Since the prose text of this inscription mentions the monk Daozhen, who was renowned in the Dunhuang region, the status and later historical value of this inscription are likely to have shifted often over time.

References

Benn, James A. (2015), *Tea in China*, Honolulu: University of Hawai'i Press.

Ching, Dora C.Y. (ed.) (2021), *Visualizing Dunhuang: The Lo Archive Photographs of the Mogao and Yulin Caves*, 9 vols, Princeton: Princeton University Press.

Ci Yi 慈怡 (ed.) (1989), *Foguang da cidian* 佛光大辭典, Beijing: Shumu wenxian chubanshe.

Ciotti, Giovanni, Michael Kohs, Eva Wilden, Hanna Wimmer and the TNT Working Group (2018), 'Definition of Paracontent' (*CSMC – Occasional Paper* no. 6) <http://doi.org/10.25592/uhhfdm.9814> (accessed on 26 January 2023).

Dudbridge, Glen (2018), 'Verses on Walls in Medieval China', in Ragazzoli et al. 2018, 163–174.

Dunhuang yanjiuyuan 敦煌研究院 (ed.) (1986), *Dunhuang Mogaoku gongyangren tiji* 敦煌莫高窟供養人題記, Beijing: Wenwu chubanshe.

Eberhard, Wolfram (1967), *Guilt and Sin in Traditional China*, Berkeley: University of California Press.

Fang Guangchang 方廣錩 (ed.) (2013), *Zhongyang yanjiuyuan lishi yuyan yanjiusuo Fu Sinian tushuguan cang Dunhuang yishu* 中央研究院歷史語言研究所傅斯年圖書館藏敦煌遺書, Taipei: Zhongyang yanjiuyuan lishi yuyan yanjiusuo.

Galambos, Imre (2009), 'Manuscript Copies of Stone Inscriptions in the Dunhuang Corpus: Issues of Dating and Provenance', *Asiatische Studien/Etudes asiatiques*, 63/4: 809–826.

Galambos, Imre (2016), 'Scribbles on the Verso of Manuscripts Written by Lay Students in Dunhuang', *Tonkō shahon kenykū nenpō* 敦煌寫本研究年報, 10: 497–522.

Galambos, Imre (2020), *Dunhuang Manuscript Culture: End of the First Millennium*, Berlin: De Gruyter.

Giles, Lionel (1957), *Descriptive Catalogue of the Chinese Manuscripts from Tunhuang in the British Museum*, London: British Museum.

Harrist, Robert E. (2008), *The Landscape of Words: Stone Inscriptions from Early and Medieval China*, Seattle: University of Washington Press.

Li Zhengyu 李正宇 (1987), 'Dunhuang xuelang tiji jizhu' 敦煌學郎題記輯注, *Dunhuangxue jikan* 敦煌學輯刊, 1: 26–40.

Liu Lingdi 劉玲娣 (2011), 'Tibi: shi ci zai gudai de "wangluo" chuanbo' 題壁：詩詞在古代的"網絡"傳播, *Baoding xueyuan xuebao* 保定學院學報, 24/6: 79–83.

Ma De 馬德 (1994), '"Mogao ku zai xiu gongde ji" kao shu' "莫高窟再修功德記"考述, *Sheke zongheng* 社科縱橫, 4/40: 43–44.

Mair, Victor H. and Hoh Erling (2009), *The True History of Tea*, London: Thames & Hudson.

Pelliot, Paul (1920–1924), *Les grottes de Touen-Houang: peintures et sculptures bouddhiques des époques des Wei, des T'ang et des Song*, Paris: Geuthner.

Qu, Jian 瞿見 (2022), 'From "Xuantong" to "Republic": The Change in the Year Notation in the Contract Documents from the Qingshui River Basin Area' 從"宣統"到"民國"：清末民初清水江潔約文書中的紀念更替, paper presented at the conference 'Standardisation of Written Artefacts in East Asia', Centre for the Study of Manuscript Cultures, Universität Hamburg, 17–19 August 2022 <https://www.csmc.uni-hamburg.de/register-workshop27/programme.pdf> (accessed on 29 January 2023).

Ragazzoli, Chloé, Ömür Harmanşah, Chiara Salvador and Elizabeth Frood (eds) (2018), *Scribbling through History: Graffiti, Places and People from Antiquity to Modernity*, London: Bloomsbury.

Rogers, Janine (2018), 'Graffiti and the Medieval Margin', in Ragazzoli et al. 2018, 175–195.

Rong Xinjiang 榮新江 (2001), *Dunhuangxue shiba jiang* 敦煌十八講, Beijing: Beijing daxue chubanshe.

Rong, Xinjiang 榮新江 (2013), *Eighteen Lectures on Dunhuang*, tr. Imre Galambos (Brill's Humanities in China Library, 5), Leiden: Brill [translation of Rong Xinjiang 2001].

Scott-Warren, Jason (2010), 'Reading Graffiti in the Early Modern Book', *Huntington Library Quarterly*, 3: 363–381.

Sheng, Yanhai and Xia Shengping (2022), 'An Exploration on Stature Creation and Grotto Construction of Donors in Ancient Dunhuang', *International Journal of Engineering and Advanced Technology Studies*, 10/3: 58–67.

Sørensen, Henrik H. (2020), 'The Life and Times of Daozhen: A Saṃgha Leader and Monk Official in Dunhuang during the 10th Century', *BuddhistRoad Paper*, 5.3 <doi.org/10.13154/rub.br.144.121>.

Wan Guoding 萬國鼎 (1978) (ed.), *Zhongguo lishi jinianbiao* 中國曆史紀年表, Beijing: Zhonghua shuju.

Wang Liping 王立平 (2014), 'Mogaoku Hanwen youren tiji shiliao jiazhi tanxi' 莫高窟漢文遊人題記史料價值探析, *Dunhuangxue jikan* 敦煌學輯刊, 3: 43–59.

Wang Mingqin 王明欽 (2004), 'Wangjiatai Qin mu zhujian gaishu' 王家台秦墓竹簡概述, in Ai Lan 艾蘭 and Xing Wen 邢文(eds), *Xinchu jianbo yanjiu* 新出簡帛研究, Beijing: Wenwu chubanshe.

Wu, Hung (1995), *Monumentality in Early Chinese Art and Architecture*, Stanford: Stanford University Press.

Wu, Hung (2002), 'What is Dunhuang Art?', in Annette Juliano and Judith Lerner (eds), *Nomads, Traders and Holy Men Along China's Silk Road*, Turnhout: Brepols, 7–10.

Wu, Hung (2023), *Spatial Dunhuang: Experiencing the Mogao Caves*, Seattle: University of Washington Press.

Xiang Chu 項楚 (2006), *Dunhuang bianwen xuan zhu (zeng ding ben)* 敦煌變文選注 (增訂本), Beijing: Zhonghua shuju.

Xu Jun 徐俊 (2000), *Dunhuang shiji canjuan jikao* 敦煌詩集殘卷輯考, Beijing: Zhonghua shuju.

Xu Jun 徐俊 (2002), 'Dunhuang xieben shige xu kao' 敦煌寫本續考, *Dunhuang yanjiu* 敦煌研究, 5: 65–72.

Xu Ziqiang 徐自強, Zhang Yongqiang 張永強 and Chen Jing 陳晶 (2014) (eds), *Dunhuang Mogaoku tiji huibian* 敦煌莫高窟題記彙編, Beijing: Wenwu chubanshe.

Xue, Lei (2019), *Eulogy for Burying a Crane and the Art of Chinese Calligraphy*, Seattle: University of Washington Press.

Yan Jihua 嚴紀華 (2008), *Tangren tibishi zhi yanjiu* 唐人題壁詩之研究, Taipei: Hua Mulan wenhua chubanshe.

Zhang, Cong (2005), 'Communication, Collaboration, and Community: Inn-Wall Writing During the Song (960–1279)', *Journal of Song-Yuan Studies,* 35: 1–27.

Zhou, Zhenru (2022), 'From Earth to Heaven: An Architectural Spectacle of the Dunhuang Mogao Caves', *Athanor*, 39: 171–192 <doi.org/10.33009/FSU_athanor131171>.

Minna Valjakka

Transcribed Flows and Arrhythmias: 'Graffiti' in Relation to Epigraphic and Artistic Trajectories in Today's Mainland China

Abstract: Chinese culture is characterized by an affluence of practices, well-elaborated methods and refined aesthetics in the domain of writing – independently of and in relation to the visual arts, religion and socio-political objectives. Given the prominence of such intricate forms of agency, aims and appreciation criteria, denoting anything written, inscribed, brushed or sprayed in public spaces as 'graffiti' confuses more than it clarifies. Based on long-term research in and beyond the major cities of mainland China, the aim of this paper is to shed light on the main characteristics of the varied and even contradictory notions of 'graffiti', and the challenges this concept highlights for understanding the intersections of writing, art, social status, public space, politics and policy. Through diachronic and synchronic, locally embedded and cross-cultural analysis, I propose a more flexible framing based on investigating the resonances, discrepancies and confluences of 'graffiti' and its related practices. This approach illuminates the continuously changing interrelations and undercurrents of 'graffiti' by a continuous un- and remapping of the constellation of concepts, their significations and the manner in which they are defined by cultural policies and socio-political norms. It can also enable the investigation of forthcoming manifestations and their interactions through local, regional and international settings.

1 The importance of un- and remapping conceptual constellations

The past decades have brought forward novel perceptions, practices and policies regarding 'graffiti' and its enduring presence across cultural contexts and historical periods. Until the twenty-first century, graffiti had mainly been studied through the lenses of epigraphy, history, social sciences, political studies and cultural studies. During the past two decades it has also become a key topic of study in art history. Given the broad disciplinary fascination with 'graffiti', the

https://doi.org/10.1515/9783111326306-008

presence of partially overlapping, contradictory and parallel definitions and evaluation criteria is unavoidable. This is particularly true of studies that aim for diachronic or synchronic investigations in and between varied geographical locations, methods and agency of 'graffiti'. Providing clear classifications is even more challenging if the research aims not only to reflect on, but also define 'graffiti' differently from the closely interrelated concepts of 'inscriptions', 'epigraphs', 'tags', 'street art', and 'murals/muralism', among others. Scholars are increasingly recognizing the need for in-depth contextualization, the acknowledgement of intention, techniques and content, and more refined conceptual categories with potentially clarifying attributes, such as ancient graffiti, hobo graffiti, latrinalia and graffiti art.[1] At the same time, the interpretations of 'graffiti' as a criminal, subcultural or political manifestation of resistance, identity formation and vandalism have greatly broadened and changed to include artistic self-expression and even officially commissioned projects by local and national governments.[2]

When these concepts and practices are considered beyond the Euro-American contexts in which they are presumed to originate, they are inevitably mediated, transformed and redefined for local cultural purposes and socio-political conditions. Formulating meaningful cross-cultural approaches is challenging and requires a renewed acknowledgement of local epistemological, ontological and conceptual trajectories and their possible intersections with regional and international exchanges in related fields of knowledge. Instead of seeking one predefinition of 'graffiti' or 'graffiti in China', I propose, it is far more beneficial to acknowledge the existence of a constellation of local concepts, their connotations and evaluation criteria as an essential starting point for any cross-cultural or transhistorical research. By mapping some of the most prominent practices of writing in public spaces, this paper aims to offer an analytical model as a point of departure for further studies. This approach, I believe, will also facilitate research on similar phenomena in other cultural contexts.

Scholars addressing forms of writing in China have often recognized these terminological discrepancies, but without further problematizing the issues.

1 For an insightful introduction to these phenomena and their interpretations, see Baird and Taylor 2011; Ross 2016.

2 For an example of these changes in China, see Pan 2014, and in Singapore, Chang 2019. An intriguing examination of the interrelations of 'graffiti' and 'street art' with modern art is provided by Feral Diagram 2.0; see e.g. Graffuturism, 'Daniel Feral Releases Feral Diagram 2.0 at Futurism 2.0 "Symmetry across Centuries"', <http://graffuturism.com/2012/09/24/daniel-feral-releases-feral-diagram-2-0-at-futurism-2-0-symmetry-across-centuries/>, posted on 24 September 2012 (accessed on 23 March 2022). However, what is missing from the diagram is murals/muralism, for instance, Chicano/a murals.

Some of them have aimed to solve such conceptual challenges with different approaches. The difficulties in building a comprehensive transhistorical analysis are self-evident, as the Chinese language is rich with words of subtle but essential differences in meaning. The major challenge is that 'graffiti' is a foreign term with no clearly equivalent concept in Chinese. The obstacles to translating the notion of 'graffiti' to the Chinese cultural context are highlighted by its various translations. The most frequently used terms that come closest to its original connotations in Euro-American scholarship are *tuya* 塗鴉 ('doodling'), *tuya yishu* 塗鴉藝術 ('graffiti art') and *pen* 噴 ('to spray'), all with slightly different emphases of intention, method and appreciation.

This conceptual richness is further complicated by the different connotations of the sister concepts *jietou yishu* 街頭藝術 ('street art') and *bihua* 壁畫 ('mural', 'wall painting', 'fresco'). The former is more commonly understood in China today as performing arts enacted on the streets (e.g. singing), while the latter has deep-rooted historical origins as religious paintings in temples, cave temples and tombs. In the twentieth and twenty-first century, new forms of painting on walls, such as political peasant paintings (*nongminhua* 農民畫) and graffiti commissioned to celebrate the 2008 Olympic Games, have further added to the complexity of categorizing these different forms of writing and painting.[3] As some of the previous studies emphasize, it is essential to take local traditions, variations and signification processes into account instead of simply using a framing based on non-Chinese traditions.[4] Such exploration entails accepting the *continuous fluidity* of these concepts and even their *contradictory local usages*. As one Chinese graffiti writer summarized, 'If you bring together five of us and ask us define "graffiti", we will not be able to agree'.[5]

Amid the growing variations in 'graffiti' practices and their definitions, I propose that a more comprehensive investigation of the intricate multidimensional dynamics of 'graffiti' and its related transhistorical and contemporary phenomena (e.g. calligraphy, street art and murals) can contribute to a more nuanced understanding of how 'graffiti' is perceived and valued. Instead of aiming for any one definition of 'graffiti' or its forms, or framing it through another

3 For more details on a graffiti wall created for the Beijing Olympics, see Valjakka 2016. *Nongminhua* is a broad stylistic category of arts including a variety of medium and created mainly by peasant-artists varying from amateurs to (semi-)professionals. Even today, some contemporary and collaborative paintings on walls are called as *nongminhua*; see Valjakka 2018, 308–309.

4 Valjakka 2011; Valjakka 2018; Zhang 2017.

5 Personal communication, 9 October 2012; recorded in the author's field notes of an informal discussion with a Chinese graffiti writer who prefers to remain anonymous. Translations from Chinese to English by the author unless otherwise noted.

umbrella concept, this approach aims to illuminate its continuously changing significations.

Developing this kind of flexible framing is challenging. It will require a continuous un- and remapping of the relevant constellation of concepts, their connotations and agency, and the manner in which they are defined by cultural policies and socio-political norms. Yet through such a fluid and malleable framing, it will also be possible to investigate new and still forthcoming manifestations and their flows through local, regional and international settings. Especially in cross-cultural studies, we can better understand the long-lasting allure of 'graffiti' by paying attention to changing conditions, aims and forms. By this, I do *not* mean that everything scribbled, inscribed or brushed on any surface should be considered 'graffiti', because that would imply the blunt application of the concept from the European context to other localities, but quite the contrary: instead of positioning any one concept as the key signifier, the aim here is to encourage an approach based on multiple concepts (in various languages) and their flexible interrelatedness. By examining the forms, concepts and manifestations of and related to 'graffiti' in mainland China, and how they are transformed when exceeding national borders, I aim to shed light on more than just the challenges, contingencies and discrepancies of studying 'graffiti' as a cross-cultural historical and aesthetic phenomenon.

My interest in graffiti and street art in their various guises began in contemporary art areas in Beijing and Shanghai in 2005 and 2006. Since then, my growing interest in artistic and creative practices in urban public spaces has expanded geographically and thematically. My ongoing, locally embedded research has taken me to eighteen cities in East and Southeast Asia, some of which I have lived in for years, others that I visit on a regular basis. Through this long-term multisite study, I have traced the intricate and dynamic variations of 'graffiti' across these regions, observing how it is prone to fluctuations in terms of policy and regulation: its forms, roles and possibilities vary greatly from one city to another and even between neighbourhoods. What is tolerated can even depend on the ownership of a specific wall and the time of the year. Hence, examining these changing situations and nuances will benefit our understanding of these interdependences also in the future.

Chinese culture is characterized by an affluence of practices, well-elaborated methods and refined aesthetics in the domain of writing – independently and in relation to the visual arts, religion and socio-political objectives. Given their specific site and materiality (e.g. a name sign of a pavilion in a garden), indexical subjects (e.g. a reference to a poem) and forms of agency (e.g. the status of the author), these varied manifestations are viewed through intricate evaluation criteria that often require versatile knowledge of Chinese culture, history and socio-political ideologies. Consequently, a detailed historical analysis or a generalized theorization of multiple epigraphic manifestations and their value structures is neither a feasible nor meaningful approach here. Rather, by focusing on the current situation through both diachronic and synchronic analysis, taking into account both local and translocal cultural flows, I investigate the multiple notions of 'graffiti' in mainland China and the major challenges of this conceptual approach. The aim of this paper is to shed light on the main characteristics of the varied and even contradictory notions of 'graffiti' and the challenges this concept highlights for understanding the intersections of writing, art, social status, public space, politics and policy. To do so, the first part of this essay addresses the forms and values of writing from a historical perspective, as well as their importance to contemporary discourses and terminology. The second part examines the new forms of 'graffiti' that emerged since the 1990s and that (to some extent) draw inspiration from – but also clearly redefine – 'graffiti' as it was conceived from the late 1960s onwards in the US and Europe.

2 Historical trajectories of calligraphy in and for the public

> Like ritual and dance, calligraphy as 'doing' and 'using' through practice, is at once a physical and social act. It involves not only conscious and unconscious knowledge, but expresses a state of mind and body that reflects personal feelings, social values and cultural beliefs.[6]

The long-standing trajectories of calligraphy (*shufa* 書法) as an indicator of the socio-political and cultural status of the object, site, author, commissioner or person commemorated (e.g. inscriptions in a tomb) has lent itself to manifold traditions, discourses and conceptual approaches of writing in China. Since the earliest existing examples of writing – originating from the late Shang period (*c.* 1600–*c.* 1046 BCE) as inscriptions on animal bones, turtle shells and bronze vessels used in divination and sacrificial rituals[7] – epigraphic manifestations have embodied various permutations of religious, socio-political and aesthetic values and connotations. Many factors, such as the production of paper in the late Han

6 Wen 1999, 32.

7 Known as 'oracle bone script' (*jiaguwen* 甲骨文). For more information and recent research, see Li 2017.

dynasty (206 BCE–220 CE), facilitated the evolvement of calligraphy written with brush and ink. The development of calligraphic styles added to the appreciation of the aesthetic qualities of writing. This paved the way for the perceptions of writing as a form of self-cultivation besides being an essential medium for documenting practices, events, beliefs and guidelines. During the Six Dynasties (222–589 CE), the foundations of the discourse on calligraphy were set, and it became recognized as an independent form of aesthetic self-expression among the scholarly elite.[8] As a result, calligraphy became a highly valued practice, known together with poetry and painting as one of the 'three perfections' (*san jue* 三絕) and reaching its maturity in the Tang dynasty (618–907).[9] Throughout the centuries, the significance of calligraphy has not diminished, but rather diversified by extending to new cultural and societal realms with innovative forms and further refined aesthetic criteria. For instance, to the distinguished reformer, political activist and art/calligraphy theorist, Kang Youwei (1858–1927), 'painting and calligraphy were not only central components of a civilisation, they symbolized its highest achievements'.[10]

Guided by the multitude of socio-cultural and political transformations in China, the transhistorical mediations of calligraphy, poetry and writing have had various manifestations across both public and private spheres. To respond to the main inquiries posed in the introduction of this book, it is most informative to briefly focus on historical forms of writing in (semi)public spheres, some of which are known as 'public calligraphy' (*tizi* 題字). How do these expressions resonate or recede with notions of 'graffiti', most often understood as an unsolicited and relatively impermanent informal inscription by an unknown individual? What would we gain or lose if this conceptual approach were extended to include a commissioned, carefully engraved and gilded poem written by an honoured historical figure, maintained and copied for hundreds of years out of aesthetic appreciation?

Besides their engravings on temples, tombs, monuments and steles,[11] esteemed flows of brush were reproduced on rocks, wooden plates and mountain-sides to

8 Harrist 1999, 7; Barrass 2002, 17.

9 For the inherent interrelations of these forms of expression, see e.g. Fong 2014; Murck and Fong 1991; Sullivan 1999. For detailed studies on styles and forms of traditional calligraphy, see Harrist and Fong 1999; Ouyang and Fong 2008.

10 Wong 2016, 8.

11 Pietro De Laurentis' (2021, 1–28) recent study examines the historic and artistic value of the famous Buddhist stone inscription *Ji Wang shengjiao xu*, engraved on a stele erected in 673 CE at Hongfu Si Monastery. The stele is now kept as a national treasure (*guobao* 國寶) in a museum dedicated to tablets in Xi'an. Based on the semi-cursive style of Wang Xizhi (303–361 CE), known

bring added value to scenic spots, gardens and other significant sites. As Yueh-ping Yen asserts, 'Chinese landscape is never complete without some calligraphic inscription'.[12] The 'stone inscriptions' (*moya* 摩崖 or *moya shike* 摩崖石刻) embedded in the landscape and carved on the surface of the earth create an embodied reading experience for viewers who will travel and climb to read them. In so doing, these poems, prayers, sutras, names of Buddhist deities, imperial words, historical records and anecdotes create, among other things, multidimensional aesthetic and semiotic resonances with the surrounding sceneries. At the same time, being written for peers, future travellers, gods, spirits and ancestors, they elucidate the significant historical, religious and political layers that the sites have accumulated throughout the centuries.[13] To some degree, a person may have expected 'to gain literary immortality' through engravings at popular sites.[14] Mount Tai, one of the five sacred mountains and the site of an imperial pilgrimage, is one of the most illuminating examples of the significant cultural, historical, artistic and aesthetic aura of calligraphy in relation to religion, politics, landscape, rock formations and cultural identity (see Fig. 1). In 1987, Mount Tai was designated as a World Heritage site, which enhanced the international recognition of inscribed landscapes as heritage.[15]

The original texts of these inscriptions were often written on paper with brush and ink by noted dignitaries, and then copied, engraved and sometimes further inlaid, gilded or painted (in red) by craftsmen on the physical item (a sign board) or at the site (a mountain).[16] Through such transmission processes, both the permanence and appreciation of these inscriptions were clearly enhanced as the materiality of the writing transformed from rather ephemeral paper into stones, cliffs or other more durable surfaces. What added to the value of these writings was not only the aesthetic quality of the brushstrokes and the semiotic resonances of the written words, but also the social status of the person who

---

as 'the undisputed epitome of calligraphic art' and 'the aesthetic ideal for the rest of Chinese art history', De Laurentis proposes that this stele can be perceived as a work of calligraphic art and further as 'Buddhist calligraphy', a distinct form of Buddhist art. As such, it is an instructive example of the current research on changing perceptions and notions at the interface of calligraphy and art.

12 Yen 2004, 1.

13 A valuable in-depth study of stone inscriptions is found in Harrist 2008.

14 Strassberg 1994, 5. Some of these inscriptions are closely related to travel writing as a form of literary culture. For more on landscape not as a visual but as a written form, see also McDowall 2009.

15 Harrist 2008, 289.

16 See e.g. Harrist 2008.

wrote them. The enduring appreciation of these writings were further mediated to the broader public through rubbings, copies and prints to be studied for prac-

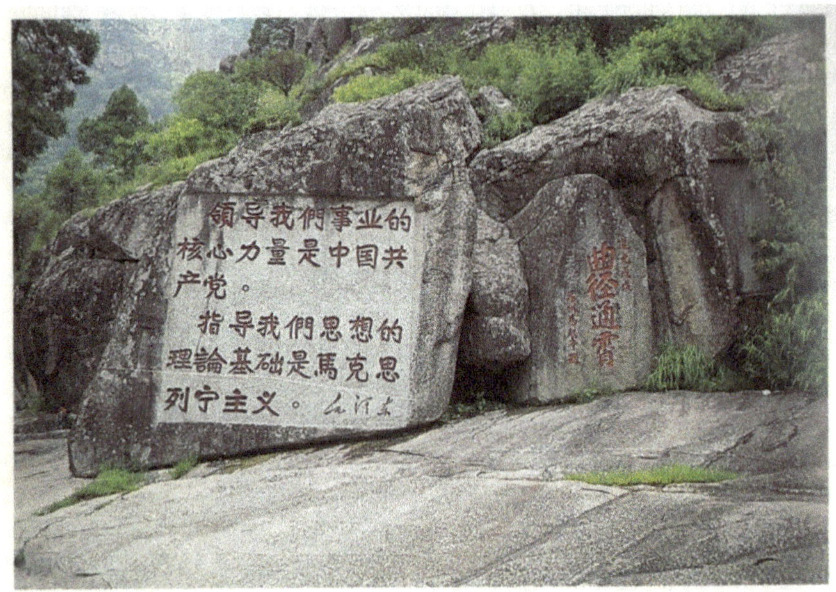

Fig. 1: Stone inscriptions in Mount Tai, 1979; on the left, a quotation from Mao Zedong; on the right, classical poetry; photograph © Pertti Seppälä.

tising calligraphy. Such recirculation processes and intermediality across multiple materials, together with the aim of self-cultivation as a civilized citizen, could be perceived as one of the salient characteristics distinguishing public calligraphy in China from historical 'graffiti' in the European context. Indeed, calligraphy is an invaluable and inseparable part of cultural heritage in China, and its connoisseurship is deeply rooted in historical and cultural specificities that, in turn, require some knowledge of these local trajectories of writing. I suggest that labelling these aesthetically appreciated inscriptions in a landscape as 'graffiti' would not only devalue their cultural importance, but also pave the way for misreading their inherent and intricate signification processes. For instance, it is common to find a great variety of short historical inscriptions at scenic sites, such as 'inscribed names' (*timing* 題名). But as Robert Harrist reminds us, the cultural and social conditions of their production often set them clearly apart from the usual notion of 'graffiti' in the Western context. As an example, in the Song dynasty (960–1125 CE), government officials would proudly confirm their presence with carved inscriptions.[17]

As the discussions above already indicate, a multitude of writing practices and forms of circulation existed in imperial China. Some sporadic records indicate how unsolicited and occasionally antagonistic writings on walls, rocks and caves have existed since the second century.[18] However, a better-documented form of public writing is the ephemeral poems that the mobile elite brushed on the walls of guesthouses and other sites. Such 'writing *in* place' (*tibishi* 題壁詩, literally 'verses on walls'), also known as 'inscriptions left behind' (*liuti* 留題), emerged in the Six Dynasties Period (220–589 CE), and while it did not become prominent until the Tang dynasty (618–906 CE), it 'remained a standard part of poetic practice during subsequent dynasties'.[19] According to Glen Dudbridge, copying the verses and responding to them on paper made them more tangible than their original versions on ephemeral whitewashed mud walls, although the processes of transmission were governed by chance. This transmitted literature not only reveals the personal feelings of both men and women in specific settings and circumstances, but also the reflections and contemplations of those who reacted to these writings in their notebooks and collections. As a result, it is perceived by literary scholars 'as a distinct branch of China's poetic heritage'.[20] The significance of ephemeral poetry written with brushes on walls is characterized also by Judith Zeitlin as a

> legitimate cultural practice in which individuals left inscriptions on the walls of public buildings (mainly temples, inns, taverns, courier stations, and government offices) – written mementos, which sometimes could not only enhance the cultural value of a spot but even put it on the map.[21]

Even though these 'verses on walls' are an inherent part of appreciated Chinese literary tradition, Dudbridge intriguingly refers to these poems as 'graffiti'. He concludes his study by asserting how, despite the ephemerality and randomness of its later mediation, 'Writing graffiti is not merely a fleeting, contingent act by perishable human beings. It is also a feature of human cultures that can, in the right circumstances, transcend and outlive those cultures themselves'.[22]

---

17 Harrist 2008, 273–275.
18 Harrist 2008, 44. See also Ledderose 1979, 31.
19 Zeitlin 2003, 74.
20 Dudbridge 2016.
21 Zeitlin 2003, 74.
22 Dudbridge 2016, 20.

Compared to the more official and esteemed tonalities of 'stone inscriptions', it seems that, for Dudbridge, the informal and personal intentions behind the writing and the casual nature of the act of writing itself (written by the person him/herself) are some of the characteristics that may render writing on a wall to be perceived as 'graffiti'.

Zeitlin, however, provides a more analytical take on how 'graffiti' and *tibishi* might relate or differ. To her, a clear difference is that of intention, because 'graffiti are generally understood to be a form of defacement, to compromise the integrity and value of the public surfaces on which they appear'.[23] Similar connotations of 'graffiti' as defacement can be found in Harrist's study, when he differentiates between the 'early records of public writing sanctioned by religious or political authority' and 'unofficial, transgressive inscriptions that have been termed graffiti by modern scholars'.[24] Intriguingly, though, Zeitlin also points out how graffiti and *tibishi* share the aim of leaving a mark behind to indicate one's presence at a location. Yet the main difference 'between contemporary urban graffiti and *tibishi*' is that, while the former 'tend to evoke a sense of immediacy, the present, forced confrontation, *tibishi* tend to elicit a melancholy response of pastness and loss'.[25] Even if this interpretation of partially different intentions is valid to some extent, it nevertheless is based on a relatively limited perception of 'urban graffiti', which in the twenty-first century has evolved into a rich cultural phenomenon in terms of forms, media, goals and content (to be addressed in the latter part of this chapter).

Here it suffices to summarize that, as these examples and discourses demonstrate, practices of writing in China are informed by intricate assessment and definition criteria which resonate differently with the prevailing understandings of 'graffiti'. Even though calligraphy is generally recognized to present a unity of aesthetic sensitivities and the erudition of the author, not all historical writings are equally perceived as works of art today. Style, content, intention, form, size and agency are firmly correlated and form the basis of any analysis and evaluation of a manifestation. While the aesthetics of brush strokes are unquestionably important, calligraphy is not to be taken only as a form of art, but rather as 'a social and political institution'.[26] Power relations and (political/religious) ideologies accordingly have an impact on the canonization processes of calligraphy. This, in turn, directly informs perceptions of some forms of calligraphy as cultural heritage.

---

23 Zeitlin 2003, 74.
24 Harrist 2008, 44.
25 Zeitlin 2003, 77–79.
26 Kraus 1991, x.

3 Modern transformations of writing in public

Similarly, for a nuanced understanding of calligraphy in the modern period, more holistic contextualizations and conceptualizations are essential. Writing in and for the public has taken on new semiotic meanings, forms of visibility and intentions – while also carrying forward existing ones. Besides continuing to exist in (semi-)natural settings, public writing has gained greater prominence at the nexus of the tangible built environment, infused with new societal activities and political ideologies. Amid growing urbanization, writing in cities has been used to inform, regulate, educate, allure, entice and aestheticize. From shop signs to political slogans and from handwritten notices to advertisement banners, the modern urban space has been filled with inscriptions written in varied calligraphic styles, chosen to resonate with the intention and the site. These novel works of calligraphy have not necessarily been appreciated as art objects, but their reception has depended on their possible ephemerality, the quality of their materials, their forms of production (e.g. printing) and their commerciality.

The growing prominence of calligraphy has inspired Yen to explore the importance of 'social calligraphy'. For him, this implies 'situations when the significance of calligraphy has escaped the confines of literati's studies, aestheticians' theoretical rumination and art historians' stylistic analysis, when calligraphy becomes part of everyday life and carries with it the power and influence that affects people's social life'.[27] One category of social calligraphy is 'public calligraphy' (*tizi*), some instances of which have been used for political purposes.[28]

After the establishment of the People's Republic of China (PRC) in 1949, the presence of political calligraphy in public space gained unprecedented significance. The brushwork of political figures became a permanent feature of public life. In particular, Mao Zedong's words and calligraphy penetrated all layers of ordinary people's lives 'on a scale unmatched by anyone in Chinese history'.[29] However, writing political calligraphy was not reserved for leaders only, but was practised by politically active institutions and individuals as well. Among the various forms of political calligraphy in public, one of the most well-known is the so-called 'big-character posters' (*dazibao* 大字報), handwritten in ink on paper. *Dazibaos* had already been used in twentieth-century political movements, but they gained new importance during the first decades of the PRC, and especially

27 Yen 2004, 3–4.
28 Yen 2004, 15–24.
29 Yen 2004, 2; see also Kraus 1991.

amid the mass mobilization of the Cultural Revolution (1966–1976), when political calligraphy was perceived as a kind of cultural performance.[30] This originally accepted and encouraged form of public writing, allowing anyone to take part in political discussion, had its momentum during the Democracy Wall movement in 1978 and 1979, before hanging such posters began to be denounced in 1980.[31]

Inevitably, as Yen further asserts, 'Calligraphy woven in the social fabric of everyday life can no longer be seen simply as an artistic pursuit or aesthetic consideration'.[32] Thus the socio-political processes and objectives that sparked writing in public space are integral not only for the permanent forms of public and political calligraphy by esteemed political leaders but also for the passing manifestations by individual citizens. Hence, though it is not unusual that big-character posters are perceived as an early form of 'graffiti' in China by people keen to promote the universality of 'graffiti' in (social) media, the socio-political and cultural conditions in which people wrote *dazibao*, or were required to do so – necessarily following specific norms – clearly sets the phenomenon apart from the general notions of 'graffiti' in the existing Euro-American scholarship.

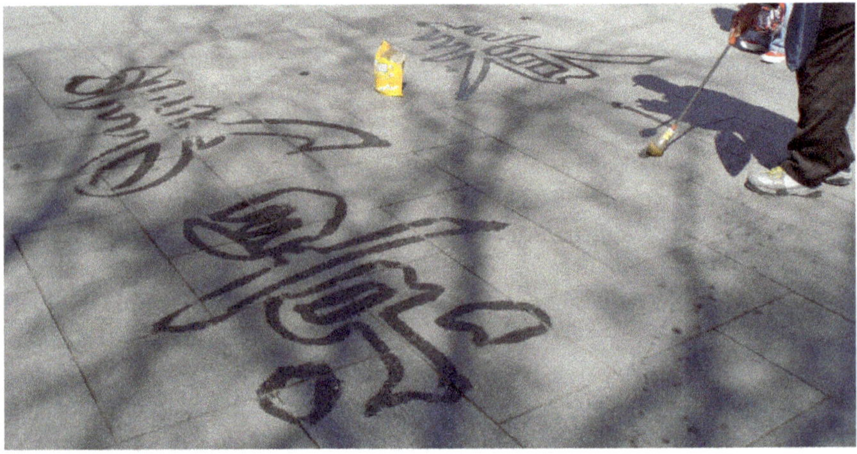

Fig. 2: 'Water calligraphy' (*dishu*) in Beihai, Beijing, 2007; photograph © Minna Valjakka.

30 Yen 2004, 61–63; see also Kraus 1991.

31 Kraus 1991.

32 Yen 2004, 4.

Along with some major changes in arts and culture in general, both calligraphy and other public writing reached new frontiers at the end of twentieth century, mainly due to technological and ideological developments. One major form of public calligraphy, revived after the political turmoil, is practised by elderly residents in parks, squares, walking districts, avenues and leisure areas (see Fig. 2). 'Evanescent calligraphy', as Yen calls it,[33] is less a political expression than a leisure activity, mainly for men. By simply tipping a large brush or a brush-shaped sponge into water and writing out the evaporating characters, or their mere outlines, poems and anecdotes are composed directly on the ground. Often also called 'water calligraphy' or 'street calligraphy' – although a more direct translation would be 'earth' or 'ground calligraphy' (*dishu* 地書) – this form of engagement with the tangible public space adds another dimension to current discussions on the performativity of writing (by whom, to whom and for what purposes).

As a form of urban social activity that has continued to be practised in the twenty-first century, this type of calligraphy allows for simultaneously performing 'a sense of self and public space'.[34] For Angela Zito, it is also an example of 'recurring sociality' through the formation of temporary assemblies and 'communities of personal significance under the stressful pressures of rapid change' amid the demolition and redevelopment of the post-Maoist, post-Socialist urban infrastructure.[35] Though *dishu* is primarily a social activity, and the content of the inscriptions also matters, their aesthetic quality is of the utmost importance. At the same time, the (im)materiality of this practice highlights yet another dimension of enhanced appreciation through ephemerality rather than permanence. Regardless of these aesthetic aspects, *dishu* is not usually considered art because of the social status of the people practising it (non-artists); however, it is not vandalism either, and referring to it as graffiti would blur or even erase some of the original aesthetic values and intentions of this practice of self-cultivation.

33 Yen 2004, 112.

34 Zito 2014, 11, 13. See also the documentary *Writing in Water* (2012) directed and written by Angela Zito.

35 Zito 2014, 13. For an eye-opening visual documentation, see also Chastanet 2013.

4 New modalities of writing in public in the twenty-first century

While many of the previously discussed forms of social and public calligraphy are still prevalent in the contemporary environment, the twenty-first century has further reshaped and added to the intricate dynamics of agency, intention and forms of writing in public spaces. For instance, writing poems in (semi-)public sites is not an unknown practice today either; instead of the elite, however, the poetry anonymously written by pen and brush on the walls of abandoned buildings is more likely to be left by a migrant worker. This extension of agency to new social classes is even more apparent in the great variety of advertisements for services and certificates, from plumbing to fake diplomas (see Fig. 3). These notices are usually stencilled, brushed or written on walls, and include only a mobile phone number alongside an indication of the type of service offered. Intriguingly, Elizabeth Parke suggests that these *handwritten* advertisements for falsified documentation (*banzheng* 辦證) by and for migrant workers represent a contemporary form of public calligraphy. By mirroring these two acts of writing in public – one sophisticated, authorized and signed, the other illegal, anonymous and hastily made, yet both entailing individual physical movement – she proposes that

> Thinking of public calligraphy is illuminating when conceptualizing how power is communicated and immortalized through the gestural act of calligraphy. In contrast to the writing of phone numbers that is regarded as a public nuisance and disease, calligraphy by those in power is both welcomed and expected. This agonistic relationship between those in power and those with little power, both of whom write in public, is indicative of the current urban condition in China.[36]

As Parke further elaborates, this 'numerological graffiti' exposes the public secrets behind urbanization, namely the inherent exploitation of migrant workers.[37] Therefore it offers a public presence of invisible individuals from the margins and breaks through the official rhetoric dominating the public domain in cities. Given the growing surveillance of public spaces and emphasis on the cleanliness of urban infrastructure, such handwritten advertisements are relatively rare in the important areas of the main cities, such as luxury shopping areas, business

36 Parke 2018, 276.
37 Parke 2018, 277.

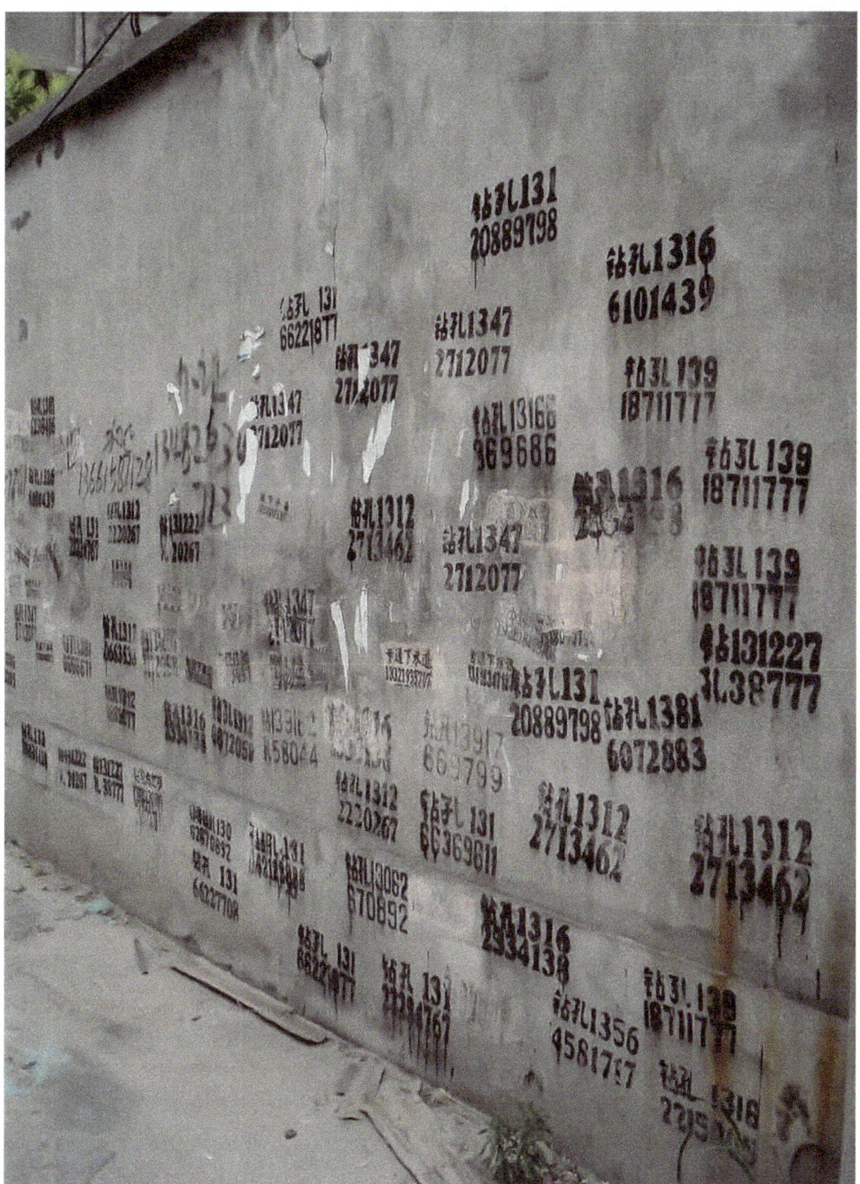

Fig. 3: Stencilled advertisements of services, drilling holes (*zuankong*); Shanghai, 2006; photograph © Minna Valjakka.

centres and politically important quarters. In general, however, in recent years, advertisement stickers have become more common than handwritten advertisements, because the act of pasting one can pass unnoticed.

Besides these anonymously written brief inscriptions, poems and ads, a great variety of inscriptions are found in public spaces today. As at heritage sites and other scenic places across the globe, epigraphs, signatures and initials scribbled by tourists are a common problem in mainland China too. Bilingual signs urging against 'graffiti' are not uncommon, for instance at the Great Wall of China. In these occasions, the most common term used is *kehua* 刻畫 ('to scrawl').[38] Despite great efforts to discourage people from writing, autographs are still left by both Chinese and foreign tourists, causing heated debates over how and to what extent heritage must be protected. Though traditional practices of leaving brief notes or poetry at precious sites are studied and appreciated, as mentioned above, these kinds of unsolicited inscriptions of names with no aesthetic intention are nowadays regarded as vandalism, destroying highly valued monuments and places. The clear element of defacement apparently renders them more easily denoted as 'graffiti' in English, whereas in Chinese, the words used for these markings imply scrawling, scribbling and engraving.

Other anonymous epigraphic practices also co-exist in the fringes of the urban fabric, but apparently, since they are not appreciated as a social phenomenon, they have only recently begun to attract scholarly attention. One such example is 'bathroom graffiti', whose semi-public setting provides enough privacy and safety to reveal one's intimate thoughts on sex and love in a society where 'graffiti in public places is an unwelcomed and prohibited behaviour'.[39] According to Dan Wang and colleagues, what may appear as immoral or uncivilized behaviour from the perspective of traditional Chinese culture can be interpreted as having 'the symbolic appearance or resistance or rebelliousness'.[40] As a result, 'bathroom graffiti' can be a valuable source for examining the social and psychological lives of students, aspects of femininity and masculinity, gender differences and the willingness to address issues that are prohibited from being discussed elsewhere.[41]

Notions of resistance through 'graffiti' can occasionally be found on the streets, regardless of the growing surveillance and censorship across major cities. In Ciqikou, a historical district of Chongqing, residents began writing on the walls

---

38 See e.g. Hu 2017.
39 Wang et al. 2020, 945–946.
40 Wang et al. 2020, 946.
41 Wang et al. 2020.

as a strategy of resistance against redevelopment projects.[42] This ‘spatial poetics’, as Nick Smith calls it, was informed by four spatial dimensions, namely territory, place, scale and network. It was actively used to manipulate (un)coded space and to create rhetorical effects. Residents employed collective anonymity together with tactics of visual and textual appropriation of colours, words, slogans, and paints from official language displayed in public space to formulate the multidimensional de- and recoding of their neighbourhood. To a degree, the residents’ graffiti can be claimed to represent their rightful resistance, as Smith elaborates. They insightfully adopted the existing discourse for their own purposes. Even if the graffiti was ordered to be painted over, the shared affect of the graffiti allowed the residents to voice and defend their own values in this temporarily formed and claimed discursive space. Whereas this kind of graffiti can be ‘poetically de-naturalizing the party-state’s monopolistic claim to urban territory’ it would require further studies to examine if it can truly fulfil Smith’s proposition to offer possibilities for alternative urban futures.[43]

Nonetheless, Smith’s results resonate to some extent with Hong Zhang and Brian Chan’s findings on how protest graffiti in Macao ‘is meaningful as a form of political participation which challenges the conventional order’.[44] Yet, Macao’s socio-political conditions and cultural traditions render it a distinctive location to engage with and examine graffiti in ways that are not necessarily possible in mainland Chinese cities.[45] Furthermore, the past decade in Hong Kong has underlined the need for a detailed and localized historical contextualization, which is not possible in this short contribution. It suffices here to point out that the Umbrella Movement in 2014 was an unprecedented display of civil disobedience and social activism that inspired innumerable artistic and creative methods, including some protest graffiti.[46] Similar manifestations continued to emerge openly until the national security law was passed in June 2020, criminalizing any verbal or oral subversion.[47]

42 Smith 2020.

43 Smith 2020, 596–597.

44 Zhang and Chan 2020, 515.

45 For an in-depth study on Macao, see also Zhang 2017.

46 Valjakka 2020.

47 Hong Kong Government, ‘The Law of the People’s Republic of China on Safeguarding National Security in the Hong Kong Special Administrative Region’, <https://www.elegislation.gov.hk/fwddoc/hk/a406/eng_translation_(a406)_en.pdf>, published 2020, (accessed on 3 March 2022).

If we accept the claim that 'graffiti have a definitive and even existential link to margins',[48] then most of the historical public or social calligraphy in China could not be further from this notion of 'graffiti'. However, they may still bear more personal, even critical tones as a social practice, as, for instance, writing a poem with critical undercurrents is not an unknown practice. Yet, as discussed above, some of the practices of writing in twenty-first-century public spaces are indeed connected with the margins – not only in tangible space, but also through the social status and invisibility of the people involved. Regardless of the highly sophisticated surveillance of public spaces in mainland Chinese cities, some subversive and socio-politically critical public writing may still exist. Not all areas are fully covered by CCTV, and some citizens simply wish to make their stances known to the public, for instance when defending their neighbourhoods, temples or other emotionally significant sites. Whereas the documentation and study of these practices has become increasingly difficult – almost impossible – new methods and forms of voicing concern are actively being developed (e.g. online). However, for our discussion, it is more relevant to address new forms of contemporary graffiti in mainland China that are both based on and exceed 'writing', and often bear more artistic and aesthetic intentions in urban public spaces.

5 Artistic resonances in relation to calligraphy, graffiti and public space

In the last decades of the twentieth century, new performative and abstract dimensions of calligraphy were explored by both calligraphers and contemporary artists. Extending from conceptual art to performance and new media art, Chinese calligraphy is attracting unprecedented international interest in art galleries, museums and biennales in the twenty-first century. Some of these artists have also experimented with public spaces or used their own bodies as a 'canvas' for writing. One of the most well-known examples of the latter is Zhang Huan's *Family Tree* (2000), created after he moved to New York (see Fig. 4).[49] Infused with the discourses of traditional and contemporary arts, cultural heritage, identity and their interdependences, these artistic endeavours are nevertheless

48 Ragazzoli, Harmanşah and Salvador 2018, 10.
49 For an informative introduction to modern and contemporary takes on calligraphy, see Barrass 2002 and Hearn 2013.

beyond the scope of this chapter. Instead, the focus will be maintained on transformative examples in the public space of mainland China.

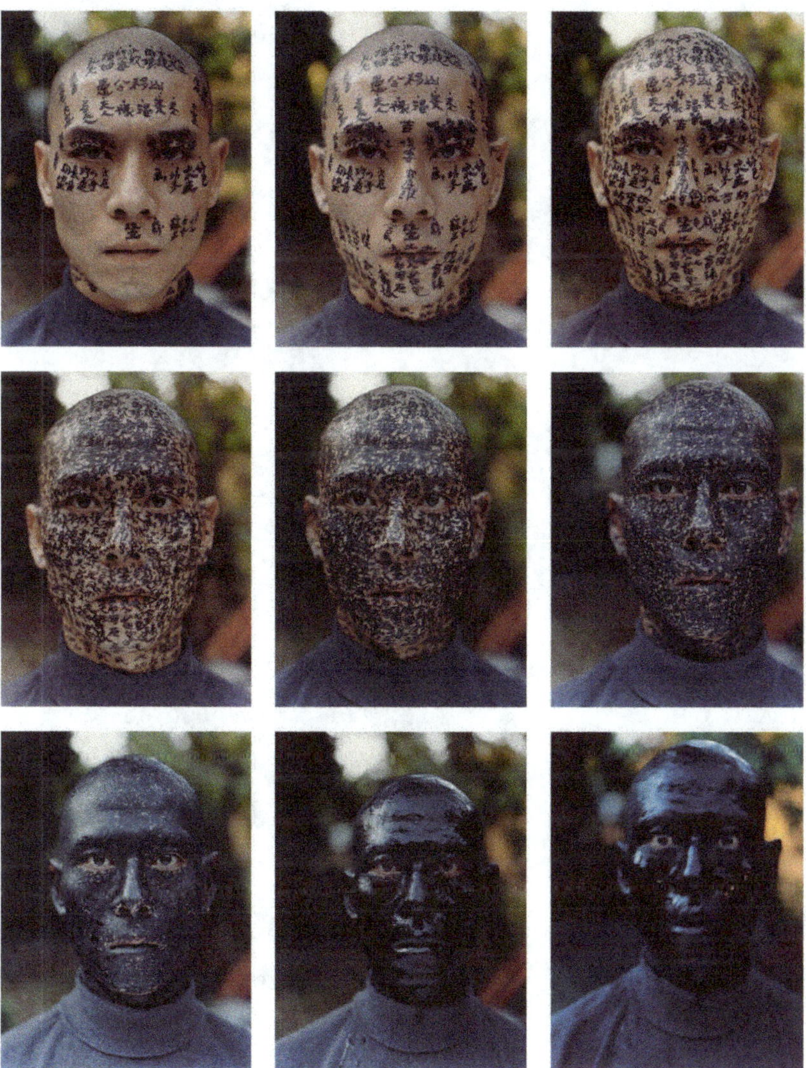

Fig. 4: Zhang Huan's *Family Tree*. 2000; courtesy of the Museum of Fine Arts, Houston; Museum purchase funded by the Caroline Wiess Law Accessions Endowment Fund; 2008.538. A-.I © Zhang Huan; photograph © The Museum of Fine Arts, Houston; Thomas R. DuBrock.

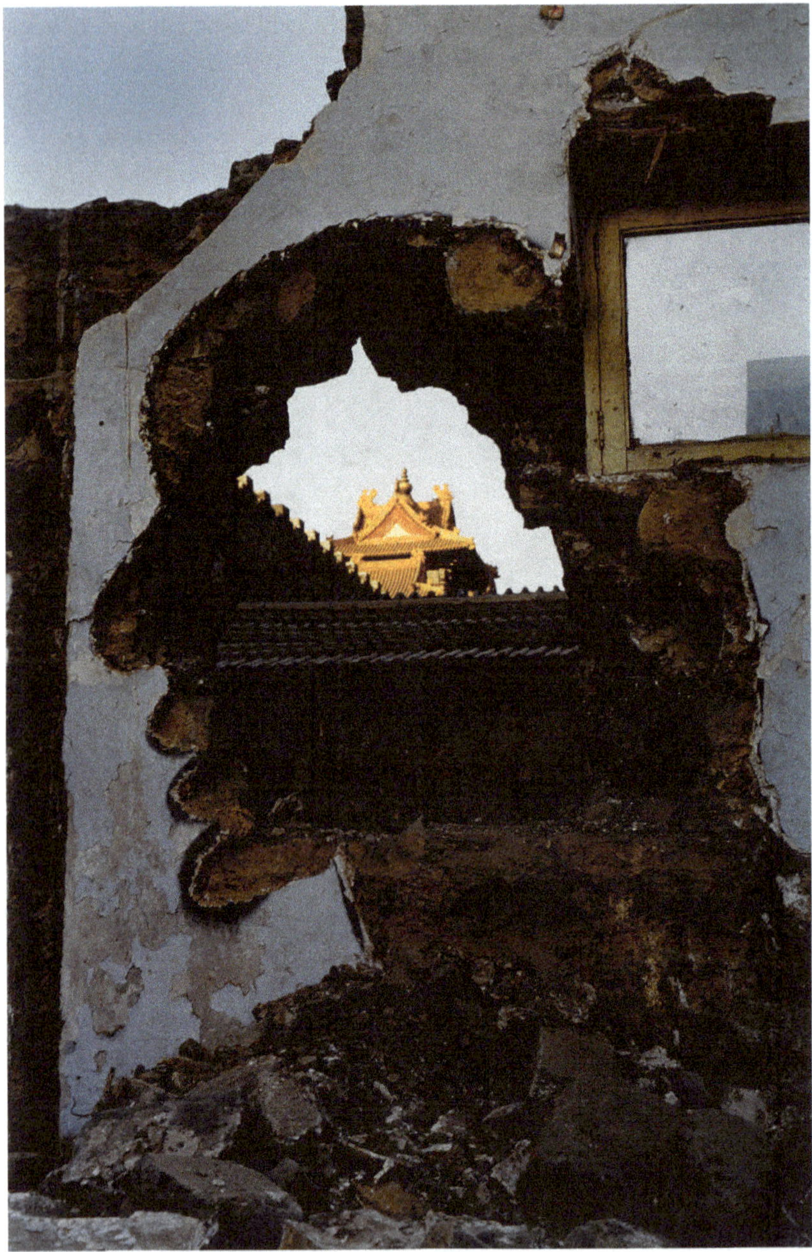

Fig. 5: Zhang Dali; *Demolition: Forbidden City*, Beijing, 1998; courtesy of the Museum of Fine Arts, Houston; gift of Anne Wilkes Tucker in memory of Robert Holland Chaney; 2008.541; photograph © The Museum of Fine Arts, Houston; Thomas R. DuBrock.

Zhang Dali's (b. 1963) *Dialogue* (*Duihua* 對話) series consists of dozens of spray-painted or chiselled silhouettes of his own profile on the walls of Beijing from 1995 to 2005 (see Fig. 5). He has also created similar images on canvas with paint and neon lights.[50] Intriguingly, Zhang's works on the streets gained prominence as the starting point of 'graffiti' in China. Yet for Zhang, as he explains in an interview, it is primarily a contemporary art project, and despite tagging and spraying on the streets, he does not consider himself a 'graffiti writer' (*penzi* 噴子) or 'graffiti artist' (*tuya yishujia* 塗鴉藝術家). Furthermore, Zhang has not been collaborating with the contemporary graffiti scene or any of the graffiti crews in Beijing.[51] Though the project caught the interest of the art world, nevertheless, as Wu Hung asserts, it seemingly failed in its attempt to instigate dialogue in the urban environment.[52] However, Zhang Dali's oeuvre demonstrates how essential it is to acknowledge the complex mediation processes not only across national borders in the 1990s, but also between different genres of art and graffiti: his practices were inspired by his encounters with graffiti while living in Bologna, before moving back to Beijing.[53]

Such translocal mediation processes were not only stimulated by visits outside of China, but were also enhanced by European, North American and Australian graffiti writers and street artists travelling to or living in mainland Chinese cities. Some specific sites, such as Moganshan Road in Shanghai, were known as (semi-)legal sites to paint.[54] Furthermore, films, media, magazines and the internet helped to promote exchange at the beginning of the twenty-first century.

Due to such exchange and the keen interest in developing new forms of self-expression, a small but relatively lively 'graffiti scene' developed, especially in the major cities of mainland China. Since the early days, the emphasis has been on artistic practices and aesthetics. The clear majority of people involved are art students or young professionals from creative industries (e.g. designers). Although the participants do not (and will not) fully agree on what constitutes 'graffiti', and whether it should or should not be based on mastering the alphabetic writing system, many of them are inspired, to a degree, by the letter-based 'hip hop graffiti' or 'modern graffiti' originating in the United States and Europe. Some 'old-school' Chinese graffiti writers still aim to 'keep it real', but local conditions and

50 Valjakka 2016; Valjakka 2018.

51 Valjakka 2016; Valjakka 2018. Cf., for instance, Marinelli 2004, Pan 2014 and Wu 2000.

52 Wu 2000.

53 Valjakka 2018, 295–296.

54 For an illuminating documentation of Moganshan Road, see Dezio 2010.

aspirations are inevitably transforming the phenomenon to respond to the local needs, and it is not common, for instance, to illegally paint (i.e. 'to bomb') trains.

Table 1: Contemporary graffiti events; © Minna Valjakka.

Year	Event	City / Country
2008	Wall Lords Asia	Beijing (CN), Shanghai (CN), Taipei (TW), Hong Kong, Shenzhen (CN, finals)
2009	Wall Lords Asia	Incheon (KR), Taipei (TW), Wuhan (CN), Shanghai (CN, finals)
2010	Wall Lords Asia	Makati, Manila (PH), Kuala Lumpur (MY), Singapore (SG), Taipei (TW), Bangkok (TH), Bandung (ID), Shanghai (CN, finals)
2010	Meeting of Styles (Asia)	Kuala Lumpur (MY)
2011	Wall Lords Asia	Chengdu (CN), Singapore (SG), Kuala Lumpur (MY), Marikina, Manila (PH), Bangkok (TH), Seoul (KR), Bandung (ID), Taipei (TW, finals)
2011	Meeting of Styles (Asia)	Changsha (CN)
2012	Wall Lords Asia	Bangkok (TH), Makati, Manila (PH), Shanghai (CN), Taipei (TW), Seoul (KR), Taipei (TW, finals)
2012	Meeting of Styles (Asia)	Guangzhou (CN)
2013	Meeting of Styles (Asia)	Shenzhen (CN)
2014	Meeting of Styles (Asia)	Manila (PH), Shenzhen (CN), Bangkok (TH), Singapore
2015	Meeting of Styles (Asia)	Wuhan (CN), Chiang Mai (TH), Iloilo City, Cebu City, Davao City, Manila (PH)
2016	Meeting of Styles (Asia)	Manila (PH); Zhuzhou (CN); Kuala Lumpur (MY); Pattaya (TH)
2017	Meeting of Styles (Asia)	Manila (PH), Wuhan (CN), Bangkok (TH), Saigon (VN)
2018	Meeting of Styles (Asia)	Bangkok (TH), Kuala Lumpur (MY), Wuhan (CN), Manila (PH), Hue (VN)
2019	Meeting of Styles (Asia)	Kuala Lumpur (MY), Bangkok (TH), Manila (PH)
2019	Wall Lords Asia	Kunming (CN), Surabaya (ID), Yilan (TW)
2022	Meeting of Styles (Asia)	New Taipei City (TW), Manila (PH), Karanganyar (ID)
2023	Meeting of Styles (Asia)	Karanganyar (ID)

Additional support for developing the scene and individual skills in an urban environment with a high level of surveillance and limited access to walls is provided by specific graffiti events and exhibitions. Among others, Wall Lords Asia and Meeting of Styles (Asia) have toured in and outside of mainland China since 2008 and 2010, respectively (see Table 1), and have been vital platforms for graffiti writers and artists to spray together. These events have brought together mainly

Chinese, Asian and European enthusiasts to display their highest skills. Whereas Meeting of Styles (Asia) is open to different forms of graffiti and hosts a great variety of works, Wall Lords Asia is defined by the organizers as a 'letter-based

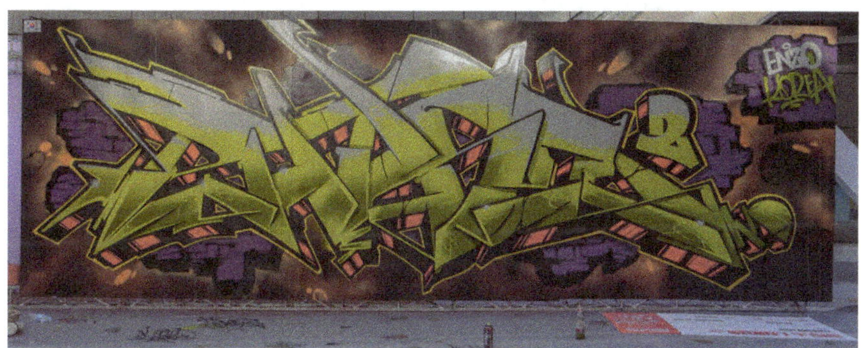

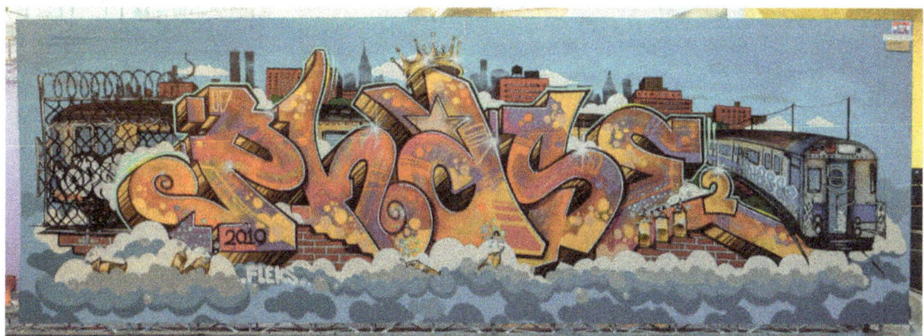

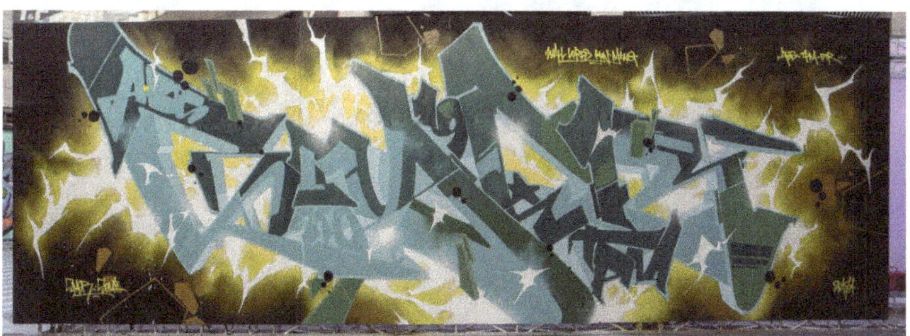

Fig. 6: Wall Lords Asia in Kunming, 2019; top: the award-winning work by ENZO; middle: the work by the second-place winner FLEKS; bottom: a work by one of the judges, SMER; photographs © Zemok.

graffiti battle'. These contests often attract the most dedicated practitioners from Asia, and the quality is generally high. Understandably, since 2019, when Kunming hosted Wall Lords Asia (see Fig. 6), there has been a pause in organizing these kind of events in mainland China.

Fig. 7: Anonymously painted work during the Meeting of Styles, Wuhan, 2015; photograph © Minna Valjakka.

Whereas contemporary graffiti in Euro-American contexts is often openly informed by social and political criticism, this is not the case in mainland China. Some critical perceptions may be implied, but they are seldom directly antagonistic. The anonymously and swiftly sprayed figure in a closed factory in Wuhan during the 2015 Meeting of Styles is unusually straightforward in its message (see Fig. 7). The intertextual notions of lack of freedom it illustrates derive directly from Li Hua's (1907–1994) woodcut *Roar!*, created in 1935 and circulated widely in Chinese newspapers. The bound male figure is a mirror image of the original work, depicted with only one hand and foot visible, and with a spray can instead of a dagger.

Graffiti events and walls are known to be organized and sponsored by city officials and local institutions for various political and social purposes. For instance, a graffiti wall was commissioned by officials to support the 2008 Beijing Olympics.[55] More recently, rural villages have become the newest locations for various 'graffiti' festivals, programmes and events as part of their revitalization aims. More often than not, these events concern murals focusing on portraits, nature, animals and scenery, not writing. In addition, these murals are more commonly painted with other techniques (e.g. with brush and acrylic paint) than with spray-paint. It is therefore also possible to perceive them as public art, as Meiqin Wang elaborates.[56]

Because some of the major characteristics of these myriad practices, usually known as graffiti art (*tuya yishu*) or spraying (*pen*), are quite the opposite of the original elements of hip hop graffiti (e.g. the emphasis on illegality and focus on trains), it may be more feasible to use the conceptual approach of 'contemporary graffiti' to denote this new phenomenon that has emerged in mainland Chinese cities since the 1990s.[57] As Gehao Zhang points out, this is not fully unproblematic either, because it is challenging to clearly differentiate what constitutes 'traditional' or 'contemporary'.[58] While (trans)historical analysis may help somewhat in this respect, what is even more conceptually challenging is defining how contemporary graffiti might differ from street art or murals. One option is indeed to use clarifying attributes such as 'letter-based graffiti'.

What is perhaps more important, however, is to emphasize how the practices in mainland China today are *not* to be perceived as mere imitations of their foreign predecessors, but quite the contrary. Whereas the questions of 'Chinese'

---

55 Valjakka 2011, 84.

56 Wang 2022.

57 Valjakka 2011; see also Valjakka 2018.

58 Zhang 2017, 921–922.

versus 'Western' or 'American' styles are unavoidable, some graffiti writers and artists in China are keen to explore and develop their own novel takes at the intersection of Chinese calligraphy, hip hop graffiti and art. One such case, as Adriana Iezzi analyses in detail, is the Kwanyin Clan crew, with their versatile oeuvre at the intersection of calligraphy, landscape painting, graffiti, poetry and art. These tendencies resonate with the traditional aesthetic values and notions of the cultivated literati.[59]

For Tin, a member of the Kwanyin Clan crew, calligraphy and graffiti represent two different eras and forms of art from two cultures. What they share in common is the creation process, based more on perception and sensibility (*ganxing* 感性) than on sight (*shijue* 視覺), but their aesthetic practices and interests differ greatly. The use of calligraphy and Chinese characters in the early years of the Kwanyin Clan originated from the aspiration to trace back and to endorse their identity and ethnicity: a kind of an 'adoration of symbols' (*fuhao chongbai* 符號崇拜). However, capturing the traditional aesthetics does not imply the application of calligraphic rules. Instead, they were more keen to explore how graffiti could portray notions of traditional aesthetics and their fragmentation. Because the comprehension of aesthetic has changed due to modernization, 'calligraphy' offers a different perspective from the predominant 'progressive view of modernity'. Exploring the changes and tensions between old and new, and their own reflections on them, is an inherent part of the Kwanyin Clan's creative work.[60]

6 Spatio-aesthetic dynamics of 'graffiti' in the twenty-first century

Guided by a transhistorical approach, I have chosen examples from various eras and forms to demonstrate how the categories of 'traditional', 'modern' and 'contemporary', in relation to writing, art and aesthetics, are fluid and co-exist in public space today. While the current manifestations of writing and their evaluation criteria are obviously rooted in the long-standing Chinese traditions of calligraphy, social interrelation and politics, they are also informed by modern understanding of 'art' and translocal interactions today.

---

59 Iezzi 2019; Iezzi 2020.
60 Tin, personal communication with the author, 2 February 2023.

Writing in public in China by an individual citizen was (and still is) *not* necessarily antagonistic nor related to socio-political issues. Because it is likely that many examples have vanished unrecorded throughout the centuries, it is obviously impossible to assess their forms and modalities in detail. Yet based on the existing information and inscriptions, and taking into account that the ability to read and write was also defined to some extent by one's social status, writing in public during the imperial era was most likely practised by the people of a relatively high social background for a great variety of purposes. Since the late nineteenth century, but even more so in the twentieth century, premised upon cultural and socio-political turmoil, calligraphy became more closely related to political reform and discourse in public space. Gradually, citizens from various walks of life began to take part in public discussions through writing in public. For a relatively brief time, in the mid-twentieth century, writing in public was mainly political. Today, political slogans and texts are still dominant in public spaces as discursive tools, but the forms of agency and writing together with accepted vocabulary are more restricted.

Perhaps because the concept of 'graffiti' was first conceived by a nineteenth-century classical archaeologist working in Pompeii to denote an ephemeral material practice, it bears the connotations of a 'fragile, poetic voice from the deep past'.[61] However, for much of its history and still today, the word 'graffiti' has often evoked notions of criminality, vandalism, social ills and political antagonism. Given the rich variety of practices, values and connotations of writing in China, and its interdependencies with other artistic practices throughout the centuries, this foreign concept has rather limited relevance to the socio-political and cultural context of China. At the same time, mediality and materiality are essential factors in understanding writing in public in China and how it interrelates with practices of calligraphy and art.

Calligraphy – whether it is practised in public or private, with spray-paint, marker pen, water or ink – can be seen as one transhistorical trajectory of Chinese cultural practices. The continuous presence of the culturally revered examples has shaped perceptions of what kind of writing, where and by whom is still accepted. For instance, it could be argued that because traditional forms of inscriptions were mainly reserved for eminent male figures, these gendered socio-historical modalities even have repercussions for the possibilities and acceptance of female agency in public space today. Clearly, fewer women than men are taking part in 'water calligraphy' or spray-painted 'letter-based graffiti'.

61 Ragazzoli, Harmanşah and Salvador 2018, 1.

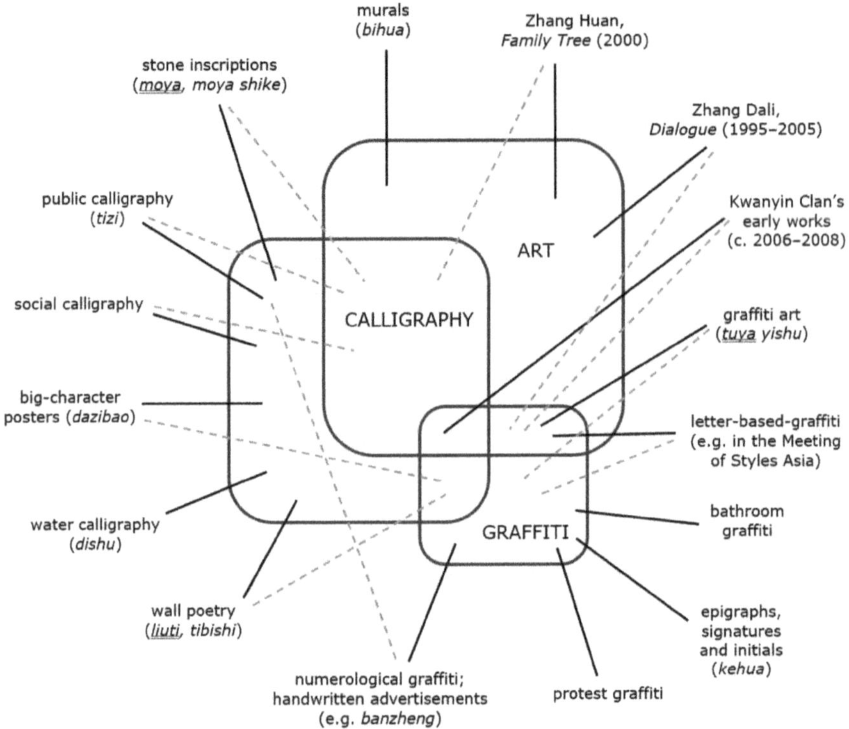

Fig. 8: Constellation of concepts; © Minna Valjakka.

Premised upon a study of resonances, discrepancies and confluences of 'graffiti' and its related practices, I propose some analytical methods for more nuanced contextualization. The diagram above aims to elucidate the intricate interrelations between three major categories of calligraphy, art and graffiti, and some of the major forms of writing practices discussed in this paper (see Fig. 8). The second objective of the diagram is to demonstrate that, regardless of new perceptions of these three concepts today, none of them fully encompasses the other two. The black solid line between the example and the conceptual realm points out the most common primary connotation today and its position in the conceptual constellation, whereas the grey dashed line indicates the secondary implication. The connotations are not always equally strong regardless of the similar lines used for the sake of clarity. Obviously, this diagram is only able to offer a preliminary take on these shifting perceptions and can – and hopefully will – be further problematized by future research by adding, for instance, cultural heritage as the fourth conceptual realm into the discussion.

It is impossible to take into account all the relevant criteria for understanding the interrelatedness of processes, forms, intentions and evaluations in a two-dimensional illustration. As discussed above, some of the primary criteria that have a direct impact on the perceptions of these forms include, but are not limited to: (1) the socio-political status of the author; (2) the aesthetic qualities of the writing (including also its materiality and permanence/ephemerality); (3) the role of the manifestation (unsolicited or commissioned; and, if commissioned, by whom); (4) the intention of the manifestation (social, political, commercial, artistic); (5) the form of agency (individual, collaborative, shared). As has been emphasized, these criteria should not be taken as clear dichotomies or opposing positions, but rather, as fluid and continuously changing qualities in a multidimensional web.

This diagram, nevertheless, serves to move the analysis and perceptions of 'graffiti' beyond any simplified linear, dichotomic or directly comparative approach aiming to prioritize one specific definition, concept or evaluation criteria above the other. As such, it aims to encourage further studies on these evolving practices across national borders.

References

Baird, J.A. and Claire Taylor (eds) (2011), *Ancient Graffiti in Context*, New York: Routledge.

Barrass, Gordon S. (2002), *The Art of Calligraphy in Modern China*, Berkeley: University of California Press.

Chang, T. C. (2019), 'Writing on the Wall: Street Art in Graffiti-free Singapore', *International Journal of Urban and Regional Research*, 43/6: 1046–1063.

Chastanet, François (2013), *Dishu: Ground Calligraphy in China*, Stockholm: Document Press.

Clunas, Craig (2007), *Empire of Great Brightness: Visual and Material Cultures of Ming China, 1368–1644*, Honolulu: University of Hawai'i Press.

De Laurentis, Pietro (2021), *Protecting the Dharma through Calligraphy in Tang China: A Study of the Ji Wang Shengjiao Xu*, Abingdon: Routledge.

Dezio (2015), *No Scribble*, Shanghai: *s.n.*

Dudbridge, Glen (2016), 'How Verses on Walls Found a Universal Voice in Notebook Literature', *East Asian Publishing and Society*, 6/1: 5–21.

Fong, Wen C. (1999), 'Chinese Calligraphy: Theory and History', in Harrist and Fong 1999, 29–84.

Fong, Wen C. (2014), *Art as History: Calligraphy and Painting as One*, Princeton: Princeton University Press.

Harrist, Robert, E. (1999), 'Reading Chinese Calligraphy', in Harrist and Fong 1999, 3–27.

Harrist, Robert E. (2008), *The Landscape of Words: Stone Inscriptions from Early and Medieval China*, Seattle: University of Washington Press.

Harrist, Robert E. and Wen C. Fong (eds) (1999), *The Embodied Image: Chinese Calligraphy from the John B. Elliott Collection*, Princeton: Art Museum, Princeton University in association with Harry N. Abrams.

Hearn, Maxwell K. (2013), *Ink Art: Past as Present in Contemporary China*, New York: Metropolitan Museum of Art.

Hu, Ximeng (2017), 'Calls for Protection of Great Wall as Multilingual Graffiti on Bricks Shock the Public', *People's Daily Online*, 18 August 2017, <http://en.people.cn/n3/2017/0818/c90000-9257316.html> (accessed on 9 March 2023).

Iezzi, Adriana (2019), 'The Kwanyin Clan: Modern Literati Graffiti Writers: An Aesthetic and Text Analysis of Their Main Artworks', *Annali di Ca' Foscari. Serie Orientale*, 55: 395–448.

Iezzi, Adriana (2020), '"Sinization" Against "Westernization" in Beijing Contemporary Graffiti? A Comparison between the Kwan-Yin Clan and the ABS Crew', in Chiara Piccinini and Elisa Maria Giunipero (eds), *Italian Association for Chinese Studies: Selected Papers, 3, 2020*, Venice: Cafoscarina, 92–106.

Kraus, Richard Curt (1991), *Brushes with Power: Modern Politics and the Chinese Art of Calligraphy*, Berkeley: University of California Press.

Li, Zong-kun (ed.) (2017), *A Legacy of Elegance: Oracle Bones Collection from The Chinese University of Hong Kong*, Hong Kong: The Chinese University of Hong Kong Press.

Liu, Yuan Sheng and Tom Dartnell (2020), *Beijing Graffiti*, Atglen: Schiffer.

Marinelli, Maurizio (2004), 'Walls of Dialogue in the Chinese Space', *China Information*, 18: 429–462.

McDowall, Stephen (2009), *Qian Qianyi's Reflections on Yellow Mountain: Traces of a Late-Ming Hatchet and Chisel*, Hong Kong: Hong Kong University Press.

Murck, Alfreda and Wen C. Fong (1991), *Words and Images: Chinese Poetry, Calligraphy, and Painting*, New York: Metropolitan Museum of Art.

Ouyang, Zhongshi and Wen C. Fong (eds) (2008), *Chinese Calligraphy*, New Haven: Yale University Press.

Pan, Lu (2014), 'Who Is Occupying Wall and Street: Graffiti and Urban Spatial Politics in Contemporary China', *Continuum*, 28/1: 136–153.

Pan, Lu (2015), *Aestheticizing Public Space: Street Visual Politics in East Asian Cities*, Bristol: Intellect.

Parke, Elizabeth (2018), 'Out of Service: Migrant Workers and Public Space in Beijing', in Minna Valjakka and Meiqin Wang (eds), *Visual Arts, Representations and Interventions in Contemporary China: Urbanized Interface*, Amsterdam: Amsterdam University Press, 261–284.

Ragazzoli, Chloé, Ömür Harmanşah and Chiara Salvador (2018), 'Introduction', in Chloé Ragazzoli, Ömür Harmanşah, Chiara Salvador and Elizabeth Frood (eds), *Scribbling through History: Graffiti, Places and People from Antiquity to Modernity*, London: Bloomsbury, 1–16.

Ross, Jeffrey I. (ed.) (2016), *Routledge Handbook of Graffiti and Street Art*, Abingdon: Routledge.

Smith, Nick R. (2020), 'Spatial Poetics Under Authoritarianism: Graffiti and the Contestation of Urban Redevelopment in Contemporary China', *Antipode*, 52/2: 581–601.

Strassberg, Richard E. (1994), *Inscribed Landscapes: Travel Writing from Imperial China*, Berkeley: University of California Press.

Sullivan, Michael (1999), *The Three Perfections: Chinese Painting, Poetry, and Calligraphy*, New York: George Braziller [1st edn 1980].

Valjakka, Minna (2011), 'Graffiti with Chinese Characteristics', *The Copenhagen Journal of Asian Studies*, 29/1: 31–61.

Valjakka, Minna (2015), 'Negotiating Spatial Politics: Site-Responsiveness in Chinese Urban Art Images', *China Information*, 29/2: 253–281.

Valjakka, Minna (2016), 'Claiming Spaces for Urban Art Images in Beijing and Shanghai', in Ross 2016, 357–362.

Valjakka, Minna (2018), 'Translocal Site-Responsiveness of Urban Creativity in Mainland China', in Valjakka and Wang 2018, 285–315.

Valjakka, Minna (2020), 'Co-authoring the Space: The Initial Lennon Wall Hong Kong in 2014 as Socially Engaged Creativity', *Cultural Studies*, 34/6: 979–1006.

Wang, Dan, Adam John Privitera, Yueyuan Jiang and Ziyan Zai (2020), 'What Does Bathroom Graffiti Reveal about Young Adults in China?', *Journal of Youth Studies*, 23/7: 945–958.

Wang, Meiqin (2022), 'Public Art in Rural China: The Case of Dongtou Village Graffiti Festival', in Meiqin Wang (ed.), *Socially Engaged Public Art in East Asia: Space, Place, and Community in Action*, Wilmington: Vernon Press, 85–118.

Wei, Lia and Michael Long (2021), 'Entexted Heritage: Calligraphy and the (Re)making of a Tradition in Contemporary China', *China Perspectives*, 3: 41–51.

Wong, Aida Yuen (2016), *The Other Kang Youwei: Calligrapher, Art Activist, and Aesthetic Reformer in Modern China*, Leiden: Brill.

Wu, Hung (2000), 'Zhang Dali's Dialogue: Conversation with a City', *Public Culture*, 12/3: 749–768.

Yen, Yuehping (2004), *Calligraphy and Power in Contemporary Chinese Society*, London: Routledge.

Zeitlin, Judith T. (2003), 'Disappearing Verses: Writing on Walls and Anxieties of Loss', in Judith T. Zeitlin and Lydia H. Liu (eds), *Writing and Materiality in China: Essays in Honor of Patrick Hanan*, Boston: Harvard University Asia Center, 73–132.

Zhang, Gehao (2017), 'Fengshui Your Graffiti: Embodied Spatial Practices in the "City of Gambling"', *Cultural Studies*, 31/6: 918–940.

Zhang, Hong and Brian Hok-Shing Chan (2021), 'Protest Graffiti, Social Movements and Changing Participation Frameworks', *Journal of Language and Politics*, 20/4: 515–538.

Zhang, Hong and Brian Hok-Shing Chan (2022), 'Differentiating Graffiti in Macao: Activity Types, Multimodality and Institutional Appropriation', *Visual Communication*, 21/4: 560–580.

Zito, Angela (2014), 'Writing in Water, or, Evanescence, Enchantment and Ethnography in a Chinese Urban Park', *Visual Anthropology Review*, 30/1: 11–22.

Intermezzo

Sanja Ewald in conversation with Mirko Reisser

The Spray Can as an Attitude to Life between Illegal Action and Commercial Art: A Conversation on the Emergence of a Modern Graffiti Form with the Artist Mirko Reisser alias DAIM

Mirko Reisser belongs to the Hamburg graffiti generation of the 1980s and is considered one of the best-known graffiti artists worldwide. His style is characterised by the modern graffiti form of 'style writing', in which the self-selected pseudonym takes centre stage as lettering. In addition to his artistic activities, he has built and maintained a graffiti collection for over thirty-five years, which was initially biographically motivated by his own artistic activities. Thus, to this day, he has kept every sketch he has ever made and every photograph of every graffiti he has sprayed himself. In addition, there are photographs by other graffiti artists, publications, newspaper articles, magazines in which graffiti was mentioned, as well as materials from within the scene, such as sketchbooks or correspondence from artists. The collection focuses on the Hamburg area of the eighties and nineties.

Sanja Ewald works on Reisser's archive from a cultural studies perspective. In this interview, which was conducted exclusively for this volume, she shows how closely the archive and knowledge are interwoven with the person Mirko Reisser.

They talk about Reisser's own artist biography and the development of a lively Hamburg graffiti scene in the eighties and nineties, which produced numerous illegal and legal graffiti. They also discuss the understanding of the different conceptualisations of graffiti, the phenomenon of transience, and possibilities of preserving and storing graffiti.

First of all, I would be interested to know what exactly the modern graffiti form of writing entails. What elements can be included? What constitutes writing for you personally?

The so-called graffiti writing came to Europe in the early eighties through the hip-hop context of the subway-inspired graffiti from New York, and simply means that

https://doi.org/10.1515/9783111326306-009

one writes and does not work figuratively. In this graffiti form, characters are always just the decorative accessory; the essence of graffiti writing is always the writing; if this is missing, it is an unfinished picture for a graffiti writer. We also had character sprayers within the scene in the eighties and nineties, but they were only a very small part of the graffiti sprayers.

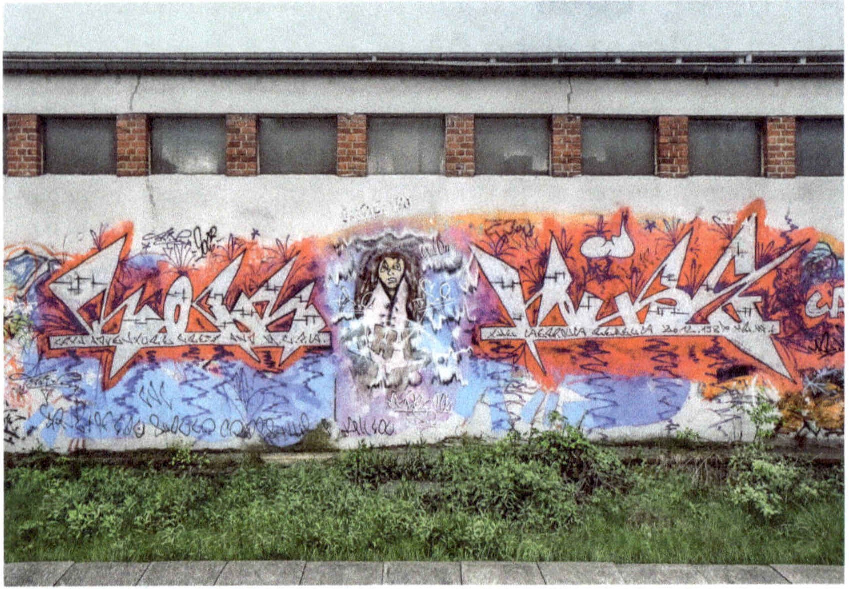

Fig. 1: Graffiti writing 'Rock da House' by MR. W, Stellingen, Hamburg, 1989; photograph © MRpro and VG Bild-Kunst, Bonn 2023. Creative Commons license terms for re-use do not apply to this image. Further permission may be required from the rights holder.

A character can be anything?

Anything figurative. It can also be a landscape in the background or a forest, a mountain range or even houses. But, as a rule, they tend to be comic figures or photorealistic images.

Have different styles and contents developed within writing?

At the end of the sixties and beginning of the seventies, in the USA, there were first tags, the quickly written signatures. Since sprayers wanted to stand out more and more from the countless tags that eventually appeared on the walls, these became increasingly complex but also larger through additional elements, such as curves, strokes, arrows or clouds, for example, by making the individual lines of the letters thicker and giving them an outline. This is how the large-format pieces slowly developed. And at some point, the so-called style writing developed. That was also what we did a lot of in the Hamburg scene in the eighties and nineties.

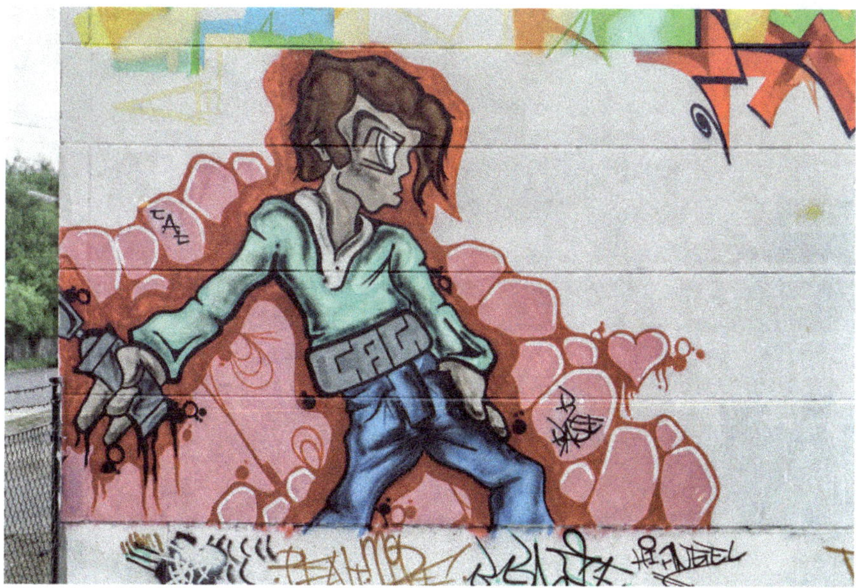

Fig. 2: Character 'CAC' by B-BASE, Hamburg, 1990; photograph © MRpro and VG Bild-Kunst, Bonn 2023. Creative Commons license terms for re-use do not apply to this image. Further permission may be required from the rights holder.

What is the exact difference between graffiti writing and style writing?

While 'graffiti writing' simply means writing, the term 'style' refers to writing as a complex structure of letters. And, at the same time, 'style' is also the individual style. For me, the philosophy behind style writing has always been the idea that the name still forms the basis, but the letters of a style have to dance, that is, you want to get movement into the letters. This can be achieved in different ways. For example, the so-called wild styles appeared, really crass, wild font styles that are full of jags and lines and can look super aggressive. And, of course, there is also,

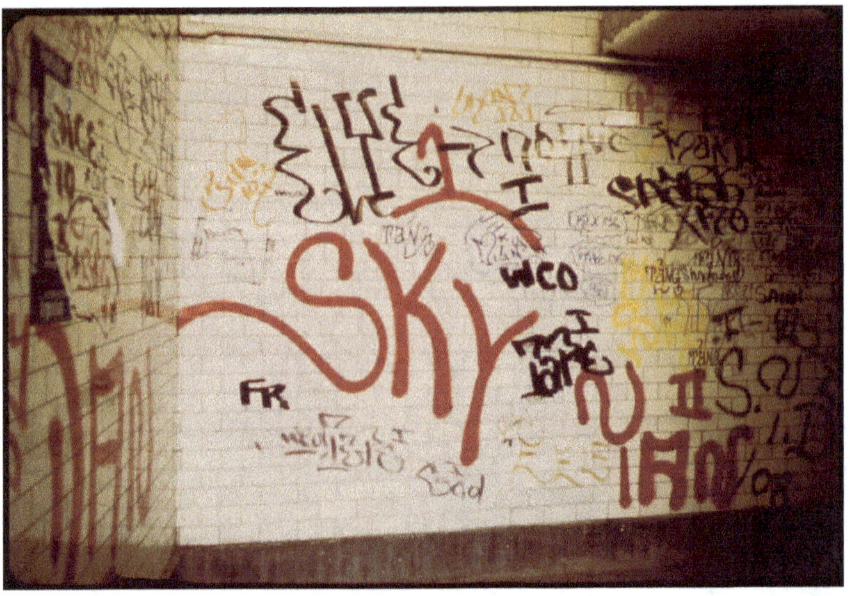

Fig. 3: Heavily tagged New York City Subway station, May 1973; U.S. National Archives photo no. 412-DA-5784; original caption: 'Vandals Have Spray-Painted Messages on Walls of This Subway Station (116th Street)'; photograph by Erik Calonius, courtesy of the National Archives.

for example, the very curved bubble style, which is very clear and, thus, appears rather sweet, friendly and cheerful.

Do I understand correctly that style writing is no longer about readability and is much more about recognition and individualisation?

Exactly. Through this form of writing, the name suddenly becomes much more of an image than simply a written word. The requirement for me, and certainly for many others, was to spray one's own style, which is one's own name in a style that should be unmistakable, in order to gain recognition among one's own community in turn. Thus, legibility was no longer a priority at all, especially not for outsiders.

So, writing and image merge into a pictoriality and are perceived as a whole?

That is exactly what style writing is!

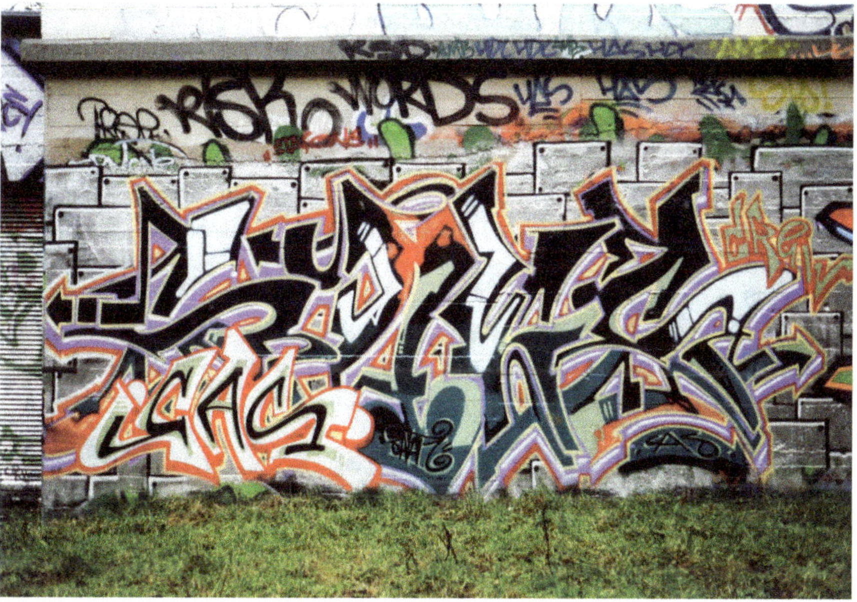

Fig. 4: Wild style by SATAN, Sternschanzenbunker, Hamburg, 1998; photograph © MRpro and VG Bild-Kunst, Bonn 2023. Creative Commons license terms for re-use do not apply to this image. Further permission may be required from the rights holder.

Are the letterings made up of real letters or can they also be fictitious?

The Latin alphabet usually forms the basis and the regularities of the letters also have to be observed. But it is possible to build up a letter in such a complex way or to layer it and interweave it with other additional elements in such a way that the letter dissolves and is no longer recognisable.

But the letter still follows rules?

Yes, there are certain rules. Even if I as a sprayer, for example, totally blow up an A and make it complex by overlaying the letter and shooting a thousand arrows through it, an A can never look like an O, then the A wouldn't be an A anymore. To understand: I and other sprayers started out very simply with normal letters and became increasingly complex and abstract by layering a lot of elements on top of them. If you were to take all these elements away again, you would be able to recognise very clear letters again.

Is a name also chosen with the consideration of which letters appear?

My first name was CAZA, like the French comic artist. The name was rather difficult for me at the time, because it was made up of letters that I didn't like at all. For a while I actually drew different letters and thought about which individual letters I liked and which letters work well in combination and together make sense or a readable word. That's how the name DAIM developed.

Must a spray name always have a mixture of consonants and vowels so that it makes a readable name? Or can a pseudonym also be unpronounceable because it consists only of vowels, for example?

Of course, that also exists. But that's more typical for crews as an abbreviated name. And I also wanted to have a real name, because within the scene, we often address each other by our writer names. There are people in the scene who don't even know what my real name is.

Did you call each other by your sprayer names to protect yourselves? To maintain anonymity and prevent the real name from slipping out to someone?

Exactly, or to distinguish oneself or because the real name was uncool. I'm a bit ambivalent about it, because I never internalised my sprayer name DAIM so much that I really had the feeling that it was my own name. Today, I also call myself Mirko Reisser as an artist. But there were also writers who adopted their sprayer name in everyday life, even with their family.

How did you finally come up with your sprayer name DAIM?

I like the combination of letters, the shape that these letters form together. Especially in the variation with the i-dot, which always gives the lettering a bit of a pyramid shape. I write a lowercase 'i', although I write a capital D and A and M. The 'i' seems perfectly protected between the stable A and the stable M, which have a supporting function within the name. The D, on the other hand, threatens to roll forward, but is caught by the A and, at the same time, has enough room for its fat belly. And this combination of letters also has enough bearing surface to place it on the ground. With flying letters, this lettering does not work as well.

That's important to think about, because the style extremely changes whether it sits or flies. The different possibilities play a big role, especially in illegal spraying: do I want to make the graffiti big and monstrous and fill a lot of surface with my letters and have as little background as possible? Or do I, instead, want to have flying letters, which leaves a lot more possibilities for the background?

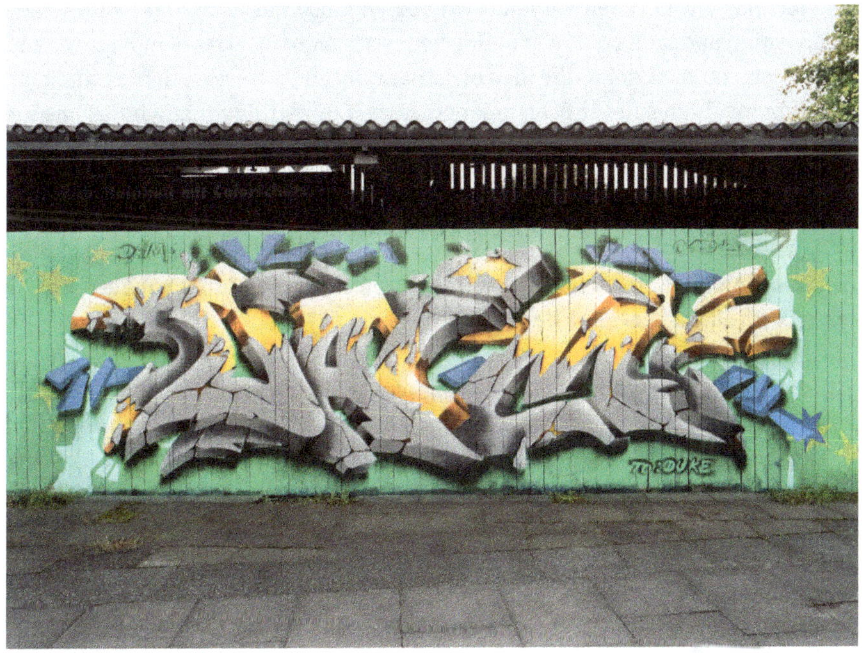

Fig. 5: Mirko Reisser's (DAIM) early graffiti 'The Departure', Hamburg, 1993; photograph © MRpro and VG Bild-Kunst, Bonn 2023. Creative Commons license terms for re-use do not apply to this image. Further permission may be required from the rights holder.

Is this also a reason why people sometimes had several pseudonyms? To find themselves and first try out what works for them?

As a rule, most sprayers have several names. There were even the so-called ABC stylists, sprayers who could style through the entire ABC. They had their own style for each letter and could put it all together and just write a different name. That's totally cool! I've never styled through the whole ABC before.

Really? Not even for fun?

No. Maybe that's also untypical for the scene. But for me personally, it was always much more a self-portrait, these four letters, this style: DAIM - That's me. For other sprayers, this idea of a portrait perhaps was not so much in the foreground, they simply had a different motivation to style letters or develop their own style. My stuff has always been very constructed and also has a lot to do with image composition and tension. If you define your style more in terms of movement and form, then you're closer to the idea of calligraphy and also close to breakdancing and dancing. I have never been a dancer myself, but I think that when someone comes out of this dance tradition and then also discovers graffiti for themselves, you are physically involved in a completely different way.

Is it a technique that inscribes itself in the whole body and that you have to learn first? Like a sport or a dance?

The main difficulty with illegal spraying was that, as a sprayer, you worked directly on a wall, without any aids, so you could only spray for an arm's length at a time. So I had to practise that if I went out of my own field of vision, my arm would still always stay in the same position and I would carefully go along a little bit so that the line would stay straight. Only those who were really well practised could still walk while spraying. In addition, while spraying, you had to step back repeatedly and see if the proportions and the individual lines were right, which was especially difficult to see at night in the semi-darkness. This whole dynamic is also a certain kind of dance.

I would like to talk about the terminology of the term 'graffiti': What constitutes graffiti for you, where do you situate yourself conceptually and where do you demarcate yourself from other concepts?

Even though we in the first German sprayer scene did not question the term 'graffiti', but accepted it as a fixed term coming from the USA, I would still say that the terminology basically has to develop first and sometimes also has to be discussed controversially. For example, there were always sprayers, especially from the early beginnings in the USA, who rejected the term graffiti. There was a time when it was called 'aerosol art' or just 'writing' or 'style writing', not 'graffiti writing'. Later, in Germany, there was mainly the discussion between the different styles. On the one hand, whether ‘graffiti writing’, or pure writing, is something different from figurative work. On the other hand, there is the distinction between graffiti and street art, which existed before American graffiti came over here, but which was taken up by many people outside the scene as ‘good graffiti’ or ‘beautiful graffiti’. Suddenly, we were all supposed to be street artists within the writing scene and that’s when we distanced ourselves as classic graffiti writers or as graffiti sprayers, and made it clear that street art has little connection with what we do. Nowadays, there is also the generic term urban art, which includes many different forms.

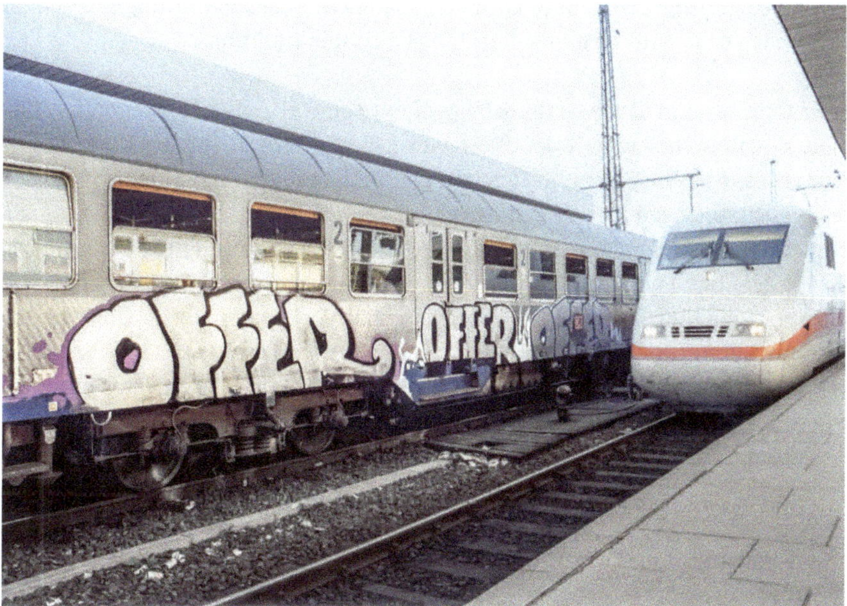

Fig. 6: Illegally sprayed trains by OFFER in Hamburg, *c.* 1994–1995; photograph © MRpro and VG Bild-Kunst, Bonn 2023.

Have you realised that in the external perception, graffiti is actually a rather old term?

Yes, I have. What is striking here is that the attributions of the different terms for different styles or categories always came from the outside. Within the scene, we didn’t feel the need to distinguish ourselves, because we didn’t feel before that cave paintings or even classical graffiti in ancient Rome had anything to do with our art. Nevertheless, in the scene, we suddenly had to partly distance ourselves from newspaper articles and attributions, for example, when journalists wrote about our graffiti and targeted the Italian word *sgraffito* as the original word for graffito. For us internally, it was always graffiti in the singular and graffiti in the plural. If someone said graffito, they already outed themselves as someone from the outside.

Is there no direct consensus for you to say here: 'I see that the term graffiti writing can be applied to both antiquity and my art, because writing is a similar act in each case and the name graffiti has a certain tradition'?

From today's point of view, I think that when a political graffiti sprayer puts a complete slogan in the city or wants to convey a clear message, there are many more references to the historical, the ancient graffiti than to graffiti writing, which was really just about the idea of getting one's name out into the city. I think it's important to understand that I started to get interested in graffiti in adolescence, in the late eighties. I wanted to distance myself from everything at that time. I wanted to have something of my own, something special, to explicitly separate myself from my parents or from adults. Of course, within the scene, we were also aware of the books that were published in Germany from the nineties onwards by adults who researched graffiti, and we also realised that there was a connection to historical concepts. But we didn't see ourselves in this tradition at all back then.

Would you also draw the conceptual distinction via age, via generations?

Yes, I would, and additionally via illegality, because the scene is still sustained by illegality today. Let's say illegal graffiti was no longer there, then there would be a few artists out there painting colourful pictures in the urban space. But it wouldn't be the same.

Nevertheless, the external perception has also shifted over the decades and graffiti has also gained recognition in the general public, hasn't it?

Spraying developed quickly in Hamburg in the late eighties/early nineties, which is exactly when I started. Outsiders started to recognise graffiti and sometimes commissioned work. That would not have been possible one or two years before. That led to a new development; suddenly you didn't just want to please your friends with your graffiti, but also outsiders, maybe to get a commission or simply to develop the perspective of seeing graffiti writing as art and as a profession.

Is it mainly the artistic perspective that has developed?

Yes, no one started spraying graffiti in the eighties and nineties because they saw themselves as artists; in the beginning there was no motivation to make art.

And do you feel that legality and illegality can be translated as financing and not financing artworks? Could both run parallel or did you also move a bit out of the scene as soon as you sprayed commercially?

If you first gained respect within the scene illegally and then sprayed legally and earned money with it, then you were still respected. But if you started as a legal commission painter and never worked illegally, then you had no respect in the scene. And personally, I've always thought you don't really understand graffiti if you haven't also sprayed illegally. A spray can alone doesn't make you a graffiti sprayer. The nice thing for me was always that everything went in parallel. I always really enjoyed the fact that I could spray illegally or legally, huge but also extremely small, during the day and at night. I could draw in my black books or on paper or spray on walls and other surfaces.

What do you think motivates people to write graffiti then and now? What motivated you back then?

I still find this question fascinating today. I think it's about the basic need to step out of the anonymity of a big city and become visible. But also about doing something completely unknown, something very special and new. That's why I personally can't understand how people can still get involved with graffiti today.
In my case, I started listening to hip-hop music in the mid-eighties, which was very closely related to graffiti. And that's also how I made my first pencil sketch, which I then transferred to cardboard with sharpies and in paint. But it was also clear to me that these were only preliminary stages that weren't worth much and that only the sprayed graffiti was the finished work. And then, in the summer of

1989, when I was sitting in my room with two friends, we spontaneously decided to grab some spray cans from my parents' basement and just spray some graffiti outside on the nearest electricity box. In the middle of the day. It was a whole new world for me and since that moment I have never taken the spray can out of my hand again.

To stay with this concept of value, which I find really beautiful: what is the value of graffiti in urban space? How does graffiti change the space itself? Does it have some kind of aesthetic strategy for you?

Looking back, I think it's a pity that my own horizon as a young person was very limited. From the graffiti photos from the eighties and nineties, you can see today that within the scene, we didn't see graffiti in a larger context at all. We were only ever concerned with spraying our own image and photographing that, without considering the context of the place.

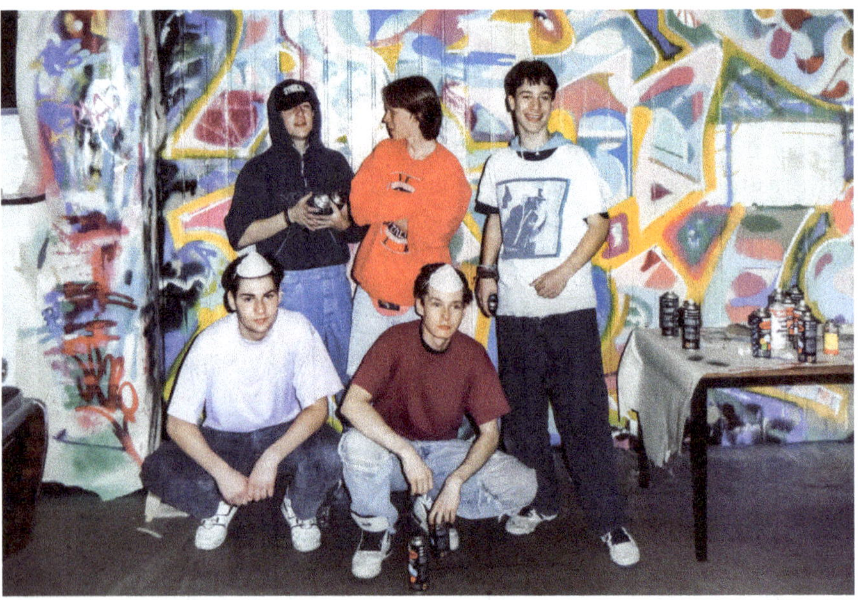

Fig. 7: Mirko Reisser (below, right side) with sprayer friends, Kewen, Cedric (Björn Warns), Mac and EloOne (Ole Warns), Hamburg, 1990; courtesy of Andreas Müller © VG Bild-Kunst, Bonn 2023. Creative Commons license terms for re-use do not apply to this image. Further permission may be required from the rights holder.

Does this mean you didn't notice the surroundings and the space itself?

It was a bit of an absolute ego act. That also fits in with the fact that the scene was so dominated by boys. Graffiti was a great way to show what you can do, to fight and compete. I always experienced it as a very positive way of measuring myself, even if I was always competing with friends.

Did you see any interaction directly in the space through graffiti? Did graffiti writings have a direct relation to each other, a kind of communication?

From the mid-nineties onwards, concept walls appeared, on which several sprayers painted a picture together and not just styles that were added next to each other. But there was also stress within the scene and graffiti was crossed out (German: 'gecrossed'), that is, overwritten by someone else, and then there was a reaction and someone crossed out in return. This led to direct interactions on the wall, superimposed layers, some of which can still be found today.

It seems like it was also about conquering space or the wall. Were there territorial boundaries or did you feel free to write wherever you wanted?

It was always a conquest of space! It wasn't about painting a beautiful picture, but about leaving your name and occupying spaces... That's how, as a teenager, I got to know my city in an incredibly intense way. Especially because I constantly travelled and walked along all the railway lines in this city, not only to leave my name, but also to be the first to see and photograph the latest graffiti. I couldn't look that up on any map. And, of course, I also looked to see where there were cool or brand-new spots. Sometimes I didn't know how to get to the area that I saw from the train and had to find out how to get to it illegally via the railway grounds in order to quickly take a photo before the next suburban train came and someone called security. That means I had to spend a lot of time and energy to get to this area first.

The procedure you are now describing requires local knowledge. Did you also travel to other cities?

Yes, I travelled a lot to Munich, Frankfurt or Switzerland, for example, and had my contacts there. Especially the graffiti sprayers from the eighties built a big national network. There are crazy stories about how sprayers recognised each other mainly by their appearance: many who listened to hip-hop wore wide laces in thick trainers and a hoodie. Nobody else wore that. And so people could talk to each other and ask, 'Yo, do you spray too?' That's how friendships were formed that still exist today.

Are there places where different graffiti writers immortalize themselves across national borders? Some kind of place of pilgrimage.

In the early years, there were certain places: for example, Stalingrad in Paris or the flea market halls in Munich, which then became really important halls of fame, that also got around in the scene. You had to go there. Nowadays, there are many such spaces all over the world. For example, Venice Beach in Los Angeles in the middle of the beach, with palm trees and the sea behind it. That's a spot where sprayers line up. But you spray a picture there, take a photo and five minutes later the next sprayer is standing on the wall and sprays over your picture again. So, it's just about being there and having a photo of your painting on that wall.

Another question would be about urban space versus interior space. Would you say that modern graffiti or style writing can also work indoors?

For me personally, it has always been about conquering space and discovering new spaces through graffiti. The moment I make something on site, I enter that space and that space doesn't have to be an outdoor space or an urban space. It can also be a museum space, which for me is also a public space that needs to be conquered. That was absolutely part of it for me as an artist. But I also started spraying canvases at an early age and had my first gallery exhibition in 1991, and I was also part of a large museum exhibition at the Altona Museum in 1991. That's how I've always transported my graffiti into interior spaces.

What is the difference for you between working on a canvas and working in a room?

The format of the canvas is, of course, very limited and can be transported at will without having any real reference to the room in which it hangs. But when I spray directly onto walls, I exploit the dimensionality of the space, because then I'm not just designing the wall, but the whole room. Of course, a wall work is temporary and, therefore, unique, because the graffiti disappears irretrievably after the exhibition period. Nevertheless, such a work always remains closely connected to the space for me, since it was explicitly planned and realised for this one space and cannot exist for any other space.

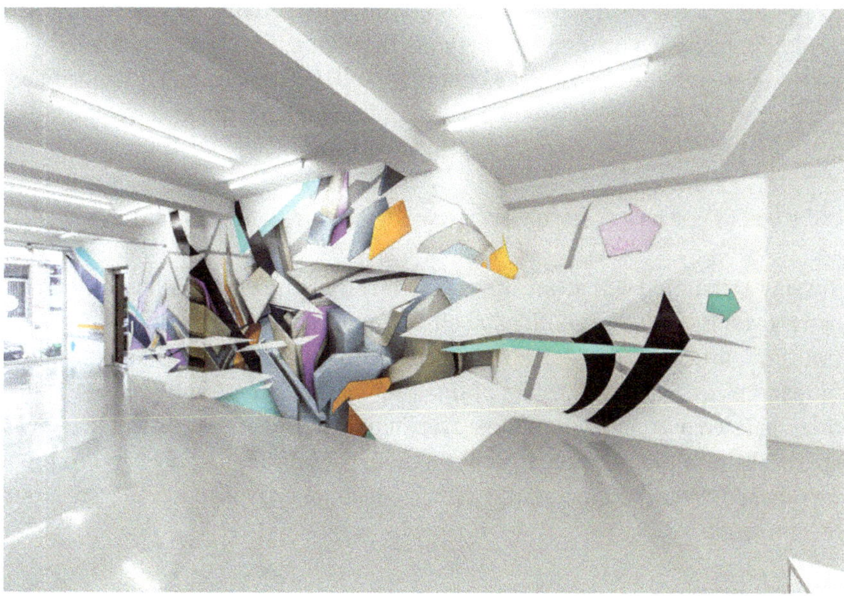

Fig. 8: An example of a space completely designed by DAIM: a view of the work 'Coming out of Hopfenburg' from the exhibition *Taking Over* at Borchardt Gallery, Hamburg, 2021; photograph courtesy of Galerie Borchardt © VG Bild-Kunst, Bonn 2023. Creative Commons license terms for re-use do not apply to this image. Further permission may be required from the rights holder.

The theme of non-repeatability and the irretrievable is really an important and interesting point.

Yes, and although I only ever write my name and have a very strong repetition in my subject matter, it is still different from a musician or dancer who repeats a certain song or dance over and over again. But I paint each picture uniquely only for this one room.

This brings us to the last topic and the outlook on the storage and transience of graffiti. What meaning does the knowledge of past graffiti have for you? How do you store your own work?

I don't even want to imagine where the graffiti scene would be today without the two New York photographers Martha Cooper and Henry Chalfant. Then graffiti probably wouldn't even have developed around the globe. Photos are important to preserve graffiti, but also to make graffiti transportable and bring it to the world. Since I grew up with photography through my grandpa and my father, I have always felt the need to take photos as well. On the one hand, to document my own work, but also as a source of inspiration for what others have done.

Were you or you as a scene always aware of the transience of graffiti?

Yes, my generation was aware of the ephemeral nature of graffiti, because in my early years in 1989/90, graffiti was already persecuted so harshly that sprayed trains in particular were quickly cleaned up. But we also had a few legal spots, for example, on the gymnasium of the Altona grammar school; there we sometimes painted over our own pictures every month because there wasn't that much space. We also took photographs of these legal graffiti for storage and as proof for other sprayers, because graffiti like that meant hard work and you were proud of your work.

Was the storage always through photography and you kept that for yourself?

Yes, I always photographed everything of mine and my crew mates, but also everything else I saw in the urban space that I liked, even in other cities.

As a last question, I would like to have a prediction, also in view of the digital age, for storage.

Personally, I tend to focus my collection on the initial period of the 1980s and 1990s, which is the analogue era. It's important to sift through materials and archive them because quite a lot has already gone. It's a lot of work, but it's important. I have negatives that are fourty years old and they look like they did on the first day, even though they haven't been taken care of much. But, of course, over the course of thirty-five years, I've also had different data that I've had to store and different steps of digitisation. I always have to keep up with technology: in the very beginning, storage was on 3.5" floppy disks with 1.44 MB of space, then came ZIP disks with 100 MB of space, then the CD-ROM, DVD-ROM and Blue Ray. Today, I have everything on hard drives, backed up several times in different locations and protected against burglary and fire. And at some point, I also added digital photography, which now has a relatively good quality even with mobile phones. With the surplus of data, the biggest challenge nowadays is to contain the mass and ask: what should be archived – and what can be forgotten?

South and West Asia

Ingo Strauch

Graffiti in Ancient India: Towards the Definition of a Genre of Indian Epigraphy

Abstract: The paper examines the use of the term graffiti in Indian epigraphy. In discussing the different categories of objects commonly associated with this term, it argues for a more differentiated approach that takes into account the function of these texts in their material and cultural context. Based on this approach, pottery inscriptions should preferably be excluded from the category of graffiti. Instead, most of the inscriptions that are often referred to as 'pilgrims' and travelers' records' do seem to fall into this category. The paper aims at a more precise characterisation of the varieties of graffiti in an Indian cultural environment using four exemplary cases from different geographical and historical contexts. Since most of the corpora of graffiti have not yet been researched even fundamentally, a future study will primarily have a comprehensive documentation of the existing sites as its task.

1 Introduction

The category of graffiti as a distinct genre has not yet been firmly established in Indian[1] epigraphy. Instead, the term is used with different meanings based on either the technical features of an inscribed text (= 'short, scratched inscription'), the character of the signs ('non-alphabetic ideographic inscription'), or the function and character of the text ('informal, non-official inscription'). This terminological confusion is not completely baseless, as the inscriptions described as graffiti according to these different usages share a number of features. They are often short, inscribed on objects on which they are not primarily intended to be inscribed and not written on behalf of official agents, such as religious or non-religious authorities. A similar vague usage – combining technical and functional

1 I use the terms 'Indian' and 'India' here and throughout the article with reference to 'Indian culture'. Consequently, the article also deals with material from modern Pakistan, Sri Lanka, Uzbekistan and even Yemen.

https://doi.org/10.1515/9783111326306-010

features – can be observed in other fields of epigraphy, where graffiti are defined in the broadest sense as:

> any kind of text or drawing scratched, scrawled, painted, or marked in any manner *on material not primarily designed for writing* (such as wax tablets) with a sharp object – although sometimes chalk, coal, or paint were used (*dipinti*, *tituli picti*; their inclusion is sometimes questioned, but practical and analytical reasons would suggest their use). Graffiti may range from simple scratch marks to elaborate wall paintings. [...] They were common in the Greek and Roman worlds, often carved not only on walls and monuments, but also objects, in particular pottery. Although epigraphists, historians, and paleographers find it difficult to define the category, graffiti, both in Greek and Latin epigraphy, form a special group among inscriptions. Graffiti are regularly characterized by *accidental, personal, spontaneous, arbitrary, or immediate production*, and mostly executed in various forms of *cursive script*. They include figure drawings, often added as illustrations.[2]

The study of graffiti as important witnesses of ancient cultures has considerably increased our sensitivity towards these objects over the past few decades.[3] At the same time, this new research put the utility of this broad definition into question and calls for a more differentiated approach that considers the functions, formats and material contexts of graffiti. Starting with a brief overview of the use of this term in Indian epigraphy, this paper attempts to propose a refined typology of inscriptions hitherto referred to as graffiti based on their formal features and material contexts. Since many of these inscriptions have not yet been published and studied, a brief outlook on the prospects for the study of Indian graffiti is given in conclusion.

2 How does Indian epigraphy use the term graffiti?

Richard Salomon uses the term graffiti in various contexts in his work *Indian Epigraphy – A Guide to the Study of the Inscriptions in Sanskrit, Prakrit, and the Other Indo-Aryan Languages* (1998), the most comprehensive and reliable survey of Indian inscriptions to date. He applies this term to the probably non-alphabetic signs that are incised into numerous potsherds, mostly from South and Western India. He calls short Brāhmī inscriptions on potsherds from Anuradhapura graffiti, and, finally, the term is also used for the inscriptions found along the Karakorum

2 Hahn 2013, emphasis mine.
3 See e.g. Baird and Taylor 2011; Keegan 2014; Lohmann 2018; Ragazzoli et al. 2018.

Highway in the Upper Indus River Valley, which Salomon alternatively labels as 'pilgrims' and travelers' records'.[4] In none of these places is the specific meaning of the term explained. What do all these graffiti have in common, and does this similarity justify the use of this term?

2.1 Non-alphabetic (?) signs on potsherds as graffiti

Indian archaeologists usually refer to potsherds with signs that are undeciphered and probably do not represent alphabetic characters as graffiti potsherds. Potsherds with an inscription, on the other hand, are usually not referred to by this term in these publications.

The most comprehensive study of these non-alphabetic signs is K. Rajan's *Early Writing System: A Journey from Graffiti to Brāhmī* (2015). According to Rajan, it is possible to distinguish three categories among the pottery signs found in a burial context: 1. potter's marks, 2. owner's marks and 3. clan marks.[5]

Based on this usage, the first definition of graffiti contrasts them with legible, alphabetic texts: all we can read, is an inscription; all we cannot read, is a graffito. The definition that can be derived from this would be: 'a (short) sequence of scratched illegible signs on pottery'.

2.2 Short inscriptions on potsherds as graffiti

The term graffiti is also occasionally used for short inscriptions on pottery, in most cases the names of the vessel's owners.[6] Harry Falk uses the term for the Brāhmī inscriptions on these potsherds in his study of pottery inscriptions from the Sri Lankan Buddhist site Tissamaharama.[7] He does not give an explanation

---

4 Regarding non-alphabetic signs on South and West Indian pottery: 'graffiti found on megalithic and chalcolithic pottery from southern and western India', see Salomon 1998, 10; regarding the Brāhmī inscriptions on potsherds from Anuradhapura, see Salomon 1998, 12; regarding inscriptions in the Indus river Valley: 'Most of these inscriptions are brief graffiti or travelers' records but are nonetheless of considerable historical, cultural, and linguistic importance', see Salomon 1998, 143, and 'graffiti in Kharoṣṭhī', see Salomon 1998, 44; and regarding the inscriptions from Sigiriya: 'literary graffiti from Sīgiri', see Salomon 1998, 151.

5 Rajan 2015, 62.

6 As Salomon (1998, 12) did concerning the Brāhmī inscriptions on potsherds from Anuradhapura. As Hahn's definition shows, this usage is also found in other fields of epigraphy, especially regarding inscribed pottery from the Greek and Roman world.

7 Falk 2014.

for this usage, but it can be suggested that it was mainly the technical aspect that favoured the use of the term graffiti: the inscriptions from Tissamaharama were scratched on the potsherds after firing. Nearly all the Tissamaharama inscriptions are indications of ownership, mainly quite short and giving just the name of the owner, sometimes accompanied by his/her title or function or the name of the object owned. Both this character and the technique of scratching relates them, of course, to the graffiti potsherds from South India. Based on this alternative use of the term, we would have to suggest a second, more inclusive definition of graffiti: 'a (short) sequence of scratched (legible or illegible) signs on pottery'.

2.3 'Pilgrims' and travelers' records' as graffiti

Salomon introduced in his *Indian Epigraphy* for the first time – as far as I am aware – the category of 'pilgrims' and travelers' records', which he defined as 'brief inscriptions recording the visits of pilgrims [...] often found at various sites, especially on the walls or pathways of temples and other sacred sites of Buddhist, Brahmanical, and Jaina affiliation'.[8] Salomon highlights the following features:

- 'most commonly' pilgrim's name in the nominative or stem form, or in the genitive case.
- possible extension through additional information (title, verbal formulation *praṇamati* 'bows', *likhitam* 'written', *ihāgata-*, *iha prāpta-* 'came here'), and
- occurrence in clusters.

Although most of these inscriptions are very short, Salomon also refers to longer texts (e.g. in Jāgeśvar). Salomon highlights inscriptions in ornate scripts, such as the 'Ornate Brāhmī' and the so-called 'shell-script', as a special category among the 'pilgrims' and travelers' records'.

Interestingly, he avoids the term 'graffiti' in his chapter on 'pilgrims' and travelers' records', which he, however, repeatedly used for short inscriptions left by travelers, pilgrims or other visitors (see above n. 4). Again, the terminological choice is not completely obvious and we cannot be sure that Salomon's 'graffiti *or* travelers' records'[9] really aims at an identification of both terms and their possible synonymous use. In this case, the informal, unofficial character of the inscriptions would seem to have informed the use of the term graffiti. At the same time, their brevity also seems to have played a certain role.

8 Salomon 1998, 121–122.
9 Salomon 1998, 143, emphasis mine.

Brevity, however, is not a characteristic of one of the perhaps most impressive collections of graffiti from ancient South Asia: the hundreds of poems left by visitors at the impressive site of Sigiriya (Sri Lanka). Their first editor, the eminent Sri Lankan epigraphist Senarath Paranavitana, labelled them 'Sigiri Graffiti' in his monumental edition,[10] a designation that was also adapted by Salomon, who calls them 'literary graffiti'.[11] As Paranavitana's introduction makes clear, the choice of this term was mainly due to their non-official character. They were left on a highly polished wall ('mirror wall') along the way to a rock surface that was (and still is) equipped with paintings of semi-nude women that has attracted visitors from far away.[12]

Taking all this evidence together, a possible definition of this type of graffiti would be: 'non-official, often short inscriptions left on a public space that was originally not intended to be inscribed'. The technical character of these graffiti is of secondary importance. They can be scratched into plaster (as in Sigiriya), chiselled in stone (as in most Indian sites) or 'bruised' on rock surfaces (as along the Karakorum Highway).

3 The formal features and material contexts of Indian graffiti – steps towards a typology

The use of the term 'graffiti' has, so far, been rather arbitrary, as this brief survey makes clear. Even if a clear single definition of this term might be impossible, we should try to distinguish between different types of graffiti, based on the identification of primary and secondary features that would allow the use of the term. According to the survey above, the primary features of a graffito would be its accidental and personal character and its execution on a material or surface not assigned for writing. The technique and script are certainly secondary features that are finally not decisive when it comes to the application of the term. However, even this distinction will not avoid certain 'grey' areas where a mixture of only some of these (primary and secondary) features is found. I will test this approach in the following discussion by looking more closely at the different categories of inscriptions referred to as graffiti in the secondary literature.

10 Paranavitana 1956.

11 Salomon 1998, 151.

12 Paranavitana 1956, vol. 1, vii–xii.

3.1 Inscribed pottery

Pots or potsherds with inscriptions are attested from archaeological sites all over India. Most of them belong to Buddhist monasteries; only the inscribed potsherds from Tamil Nadu were apparently found in a non-Buddhist context. The documentation of these objects is still quite rudimentary and, in many cases, short references in archaeological reports without further details are our only sources, hardly allowing for a systematic study.[13] Fortunately, recent archaeological work has paid more attention to this type of material and allows a first step towards its systematic description. I suggested the following typology for pottery inscriptions in a recent paper on pottery inscriptions from Buddhist sites in Āndhradeśa:[14]

A. Individual possession inscriptions

This type of inscription is found on pottery (but also on other utilitarian objects, such as lamps) at numerous archaeological sites on the subcontinent and beyond, the most important among them being Kara Tepa (in modern Uzbekistan), Salihundam and Vaḍḍamānu (both in Āndhradeśa). The inscriptions are inscribed (either scratched or painted) on the outside of the object and designate a person's individual ownership of the object inscribed. The short texts generally consist of the person's name (and title) in the genitive case, often supplemented by the designation of the object (such as *pāti* 'dining plate') and sometimes a further specification that characterises the object as individual property (Sanskrit *paudgalika* 'personal, individual', Middle Indic *pogalika*). Thus, the general structure could be defined as follows:

> [Name] [title] (gen.) [*pāti etc.*] [[*pogalika*-]]
> [[Personal]] [dining plate] of [title] [Name].

An interesting variety that is typical of the Northwest adds a formula that prohibits the theft of the object: Sanskrit *na kenacid hartavyam* 'not to be taken away by anyone'.[15]

13 For a survey on references to inscribed potsherds in archaeological records, see Ray 1987.

14 Strauch forthcoming.

15 Cf. for this formula and its use on different types of objects, Falk 2000. For a stone box with this formula, see Falk 2020–2021, 127–129. It is remarkable that the formula is used here in connection with a donation inscription. Falk suspects that the box may have served as a container for birch bark manuscripts.

Based on the uncertain meaning of the so-called non-alphabetic graffiti on potsherds from South and Western India, it is difficult to determine their function. Since these signs occur in Tamil Nadu in the same context and at the same time as the inscription written in the Tamil Brāhmī script[16] it seems possible to assume a similar function for both types of inscriptions. Accordingly, these 'graffiti' most probably designate the ownership of the objects inscribed.

B. Collective possession inscriptions

These inscriptions are more or less identical with the individual possession inscriptions in terms of their formula and use on the objects. Unlike the previous category, they are meant to denote the collective ownership by a monastery (*vihāra*) or a community (*saṃgha*). Consequently, they do not use the term *paudgalika* 'personal'. Instead, they sometimes refer to other terms, such as *paribhoga* 'object of use', in Tissamaharama *prasādaparibhoga*, translated by Falk as 'object of use on the platform'.[17]

C. Donative inscriptions

This category comprises the largest variety of formulae that largely depend on the epigraphical practice of the region to which they belong. In their shortest variant, they simply contain the donor's name in the genitive case, followed by the nouns *dāna* 'gift' or *deyadharma* 'pious gift', sometimes supplemented by the designation of the object and the recipient.

This formula can be largely extended, parallel to donative texts on other types of objects, such as sculptures or architectural elements, especially in the northwest. In many cases, these donative texts contain a formula that explicitly indicates the recipient of the gift, 'typically with the phrase "to the universal community, in the possession of the masters of the X school" (*saghe caturdiśe acaryaṇa X-aṇa parigrahe*)'.[18] This had led some scholars to assume a possessive character of these texts which would primarily denote the rightful owner of that object

16 According to Rajan 2015, 269–270, 'one may presume that nearly 99 % of them are personal names. The remaining 1 % also carry personal names along with attributes prefixed or suffixed to the main personal names [...]. The occurrences of exclusive non-personal names like *nikama* are very rare and constitute a negligible percentage'.

17 Falk 2014, 78–80.

18 Salomon 2002, 354.

rather than the act of donation.[19] In rare cases, the formula above can even be replaced or extended by a reference to an individual recipient.[20] In view of their hybrid character, I have proposed calling this subtype of donative inscriptions 'donative-cum-possession inscriptions'.

Inscriptions on pottery usually follow a clearly established formula, often related to formulae of other types of epigraphs. Thus, the donative inscriptions clearly reproduce the formulae found on sculptures, reliefs or other objects. Possession inscriptions are also not limited to ceramics, but can also be found on other objects. Most inscriptions on pottery do not generally seem to be the result of spontaneous and individual production, but have to be perceived as part of an administrative tradition of the community to which they belong.

Based on this character and on the functional diversity of pottery inscriptions and their formal differences (in terms of formulae, techniques and length), I propose avoiding the term graffiti for inscriptions on pottery, whether they are scratched or not, legible or not, long or short. It seems more appropriate to refer to these inscriptions according to their function, for example, as possession or donative inscriptions.[21] If anything, they show only secondary features of a graffito; none of the primary features seem to apply here.

3.2 'Pilgrims' and travellers' records'

This group certainly comes closest to what is commonly referred to as graffiti. As has been mentioned above, Salomon subsumes a large variety of inscriptions here reaching from scratched names on the walls of caves and temples to the thousands of diverse texts along the Karakorum Highway. As in the case of the pottery inscriptions, the documentation of many of the sites is far from satisfactory – with some important exceptions discussed below. A systematic comparative study of the material has never been carried out. We have, at least, access to some of the texts for a few sites, such as Bhuilī (Mirzapur district, Uttar Pradesh),[22]

19 Exemplarily, Salomon 2002, 354–355; Fussman 2011, 41; Falk 2014, 47.

20 See Strauch forthcoming.

21 There are other less frequent types of pottery inscriptions that are not covered in the survey above, e.g. abecedary inscriptions (Cf. Strauch forthcoming).

22 Pilgrim records of the seventh/eighth century CE, 'engraved on different parts of the rocky hillock in the village' (ARIE 1961–1962, 9), near a Hanuman temple. Published in ARIE 1961–1962, 136–139, nos B.909–966).

Devaprayāg (Garhwal district, Uttar Pradesh),[23] Jāgeśvar (Almora district, Uttarakhand)[24] and Muṇḍeśvarī (Kaimur district, Bihar),[25] all mentioned by Salomon.[26] However, the information is rather limited due to the general absence of illustrative material or detailed descriptions. Moreover, many more sites could be added to those briefly mentioned by Salomon, most of them undocumented and unstudied.[27]

A special category of these texts is represented by the so-called shell-script (or *śaṅkhalipi*) inscriptions,[28] executed in a highly ornate fashion that makes reading so far impossible (cf. below Fig. 11). They are often found side by side with other graffiti. According to Richard Salomon, these inscriptions 'are particularly common in Bihar and central India' and can roughly be dated between the fourth/fifth and eighth/ninth centuries CE. In most cases, they seem to represent personal names.[29] Salomon documented altogether 640 inscriptions of this type from 67 different sites from nearly all parts of the subcontinent, with the 'apparent exception of the northwest and the far south'.[30]

The present discussion can only provide a preliminary assessment of all the material and offer guidance for further studies. I will present four paradigmatic cases in the following from various periods and different cultural and geographical contexts, which may allow some preliminary conclusions about the character of 'pilgrims' and travellers' records', their formal features and their contexts.

23 About 40 'inscriptions in characters of different type: Brāhmī, Ornamental Brāhmī, and Devanāgarī' (Chhabra 1953–1954, 133), from *c.* the fourth up to the seventeenth century CE. The Brāhmī inscriptions – exclusively Sanskrit proper names – are published by Chhabra (1953–1954). The texts are inscribed on a rock behind a Raghunātha temple.

24 Pilgrim records of the eighth to tenth century CE on the walls and pillars of the Mṛtyuñjaya temple and adjacent shrines. Published by D. Ch. Sircar (1961–1962, 250–254).

25 Pilgrim records in Brāhmī and 'shell-script', partially published by Salomon 1976 and 1983. For this remarkable place, see also Neuss 2003.

26 Salomon 1998, 122.

27 See below, part 3.

28 For a comprehensive survey of these inscriptions, see Salomon 1980, supplemented by Salomon 1986.

29 Salomon 1986, 111–112.

30 Salomon 1986, 143.

3.2.1 Case 1: The inscriptions and drawings from the Hoq cave at Socotra

I will begin this brief survey with the texts and drawings from the Hoq cave on the island of Socotra.[31] Although far from the Indian subcontinent, the majority of the inscriptions and drawings were left by Indian seafarers – so it might be permissible to include this site in the present survey.

Belgian speleologists discovered hundreds of inscriptions and drawings here in 2000 which had been left in a huge natural cave by visitors in the first centuries of the Common Era. The texts and drawings were left on the surfaces of stalactites and stalagmites, on walls and rocks (see Fig. 1).

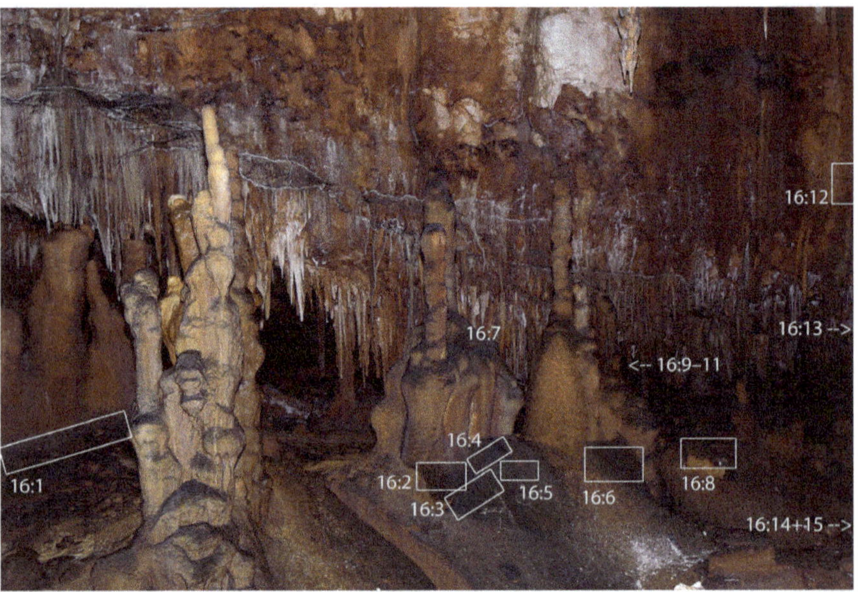

Fig. 1: Site 16 at the Hoq cave, with graffiti indicated; after Strauch 2012, 196.

They are executed in different techniques: they could be made by hand with the chalk or mud found inside the cave. Occasionally, they were simply written or drawn on the surface of the soft sand that covers portions of the cave floor. Alternatively, they were written with pieces of charcoal from the lamps that were used to illuminate the cave's interior, or scratched into the surface of the rock with a

31 References and citations of inscriptions follow the catalogue of inscriptions and drawings in Strauch 2012.

piece of a broken stalagmite or stalactite. All these techniques witness the *ad hoc* character of the inscriptions and drawings. The visitors simply used the material found in the cave, probably without the previous intention of doing so, but possibly inspired by the texts and drawings they found when they came to this place. Nearly all inscriptions are executed in a rather cursive type of script. Hence, all these features would certainly qualify the Hoq corpus as graffiti *par excellence*, combining all primary and secondary features of the broad definition: they are apparently the result of an 'accidental, personal, spontaneous, arbitrary, or immediate production, and mostly executed in various forms of cursive script'.[32]

Further research could identify the inscriptions as belonging to different scripts and languages: the majority (nearly 200) were left by Indian visitors, and fewer inscriptions are written in South Arabian, Aksumite, Greek and Bactrian.[33]

As the Indian and Greek inscriptions make clear, the visitors were sailors who had landed on the island and evidently used their time there to visit the cave.[34] It is not completely clear what motivated their visit, but there is some inscriptional evidence that the cave was perceived as a sacred space. The extraordinary natural beauty might, of course, have contributed to the attraction of the place.

I have distinguished the following two main categories of inscriptions in my study of the Indic material:

A. Personal inscriptions

Most of the inscriptions (*c.* 90 %) report the presence of a person at the site. As the cave is rather long (about 2 km), the visitors had to walk past several (already inscribed) spots. Consequently, some names are attested more than once on the way through the cave. Inscriptions of this type contain only the person's name, either in the nominative (or stem) form, but more often in the genitive case. The personal name can be supplemented by the father's name, a reference to a provenance, profession or title, and a verbal form, most frequently *prāpta* 'has come'. As a typical example of this more developed type of personal inscriptions, I cite:

> (11:22): *śivaghoṣaputro rudranaṃndi prāptaḥ* 'Rudranandin, son of Śivaghoṣa, has come (here)'.

32 Hahn 2013.

33 For the identification of an inscription in the hitherto undeciphered 'Kushan script', see Bonman et al. 2023, 322-323.

34 The Indians refer to themselves repeatedly as *navika* 'sailor', one of the Greek epigraphs (11:26) refers to a ναύκληρο[ς], translated by Bukharin as ship owner (Strauch 2012, 142).

B. Religious devotional texts

Probably due to the character of the visitors, this category is much less represented and consists only of two clearly identifiable texts left by a person named Rahavasu. They refer to the historical Buddha Śākyamuni in different expressions in the genitive case, without any indication of the donative or venerating character of the inscription. As an example, I cite:

> (14:28): *bhagavato gotamasa na[bha]katasa. rahavasu*. 'For the Lord Gautama, the lion (?). Rahavasu (= personal name)'.

It is not clear what exactly the intention of these inscriptions was, but their religious character is underpinned by numerous drawings of an apparently religious nature. While such symbols as the trident (*triśūla*) or *pūrṇaghaṭa* ('auspicious vase with lotus emerging') must be taken as rather generic auspicious symbols without any clear affiliation to one of the Indian religious communities, two surviving drawings of *stūpa*s clearly point to a Buddhist background of the 'artist'.

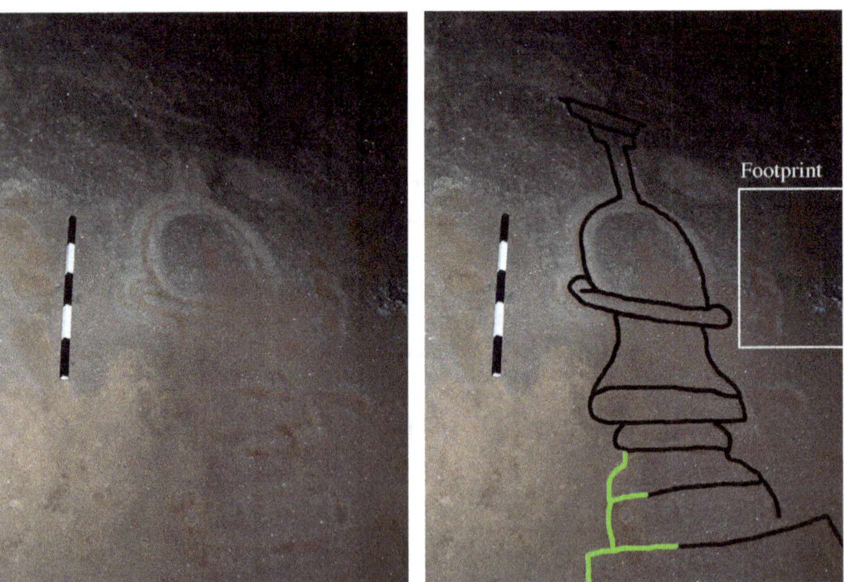

Figs 2–3: The *stūpa* drawing at site 13, with a footprint on the upper right; after Strauch 2012, 167.

These drawings are also remarkable in terms of their technique: they were apparently drawn by hand in the soft sand of the cave where they remained for more than 1500 years until the Belgian visitors documented them (Figs 2–3).

At the time of this documentation, the *stūpa* drawings were accompanied by the still visible footprints of the artist and his name, which is legible as *iśaradasa* (Sanskrit Īśvaradāsa) (= 13:5). The same person has left his name three times on the central 'wall'.

This 'wall' is of special importance for the architecture of the cave. It is actually a curtain of columns with only two very narrow passages, dividing the cave into two large parts. Visitors had to use one of the two passages to reach the rear part of the cave – as the distribution of names shows, not everyone knew of the existence of this rear part. The 'wall' can easily be mistaken for the end of the cave, unless a trained guide shows the visitors the passages. In any case, this spot was apparently very attractive to the visitors. Nearly 50 identifiable texts are found here; some of the visitors even left their names more than once (Figs 4–5).

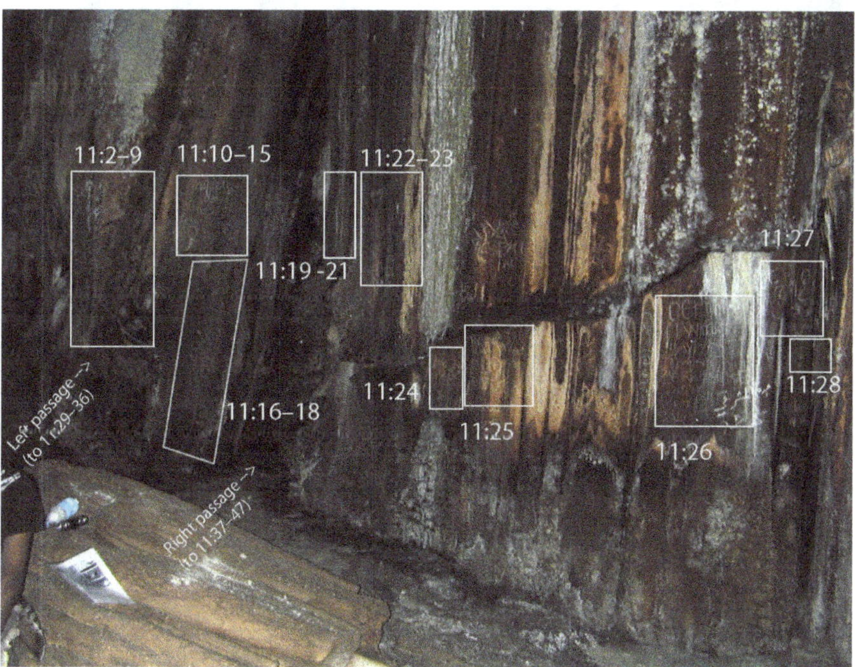

Fig. 4: General view of the 'wall' with graffiti 11:2–11:28 indicated; after Strauch 2012, 123.

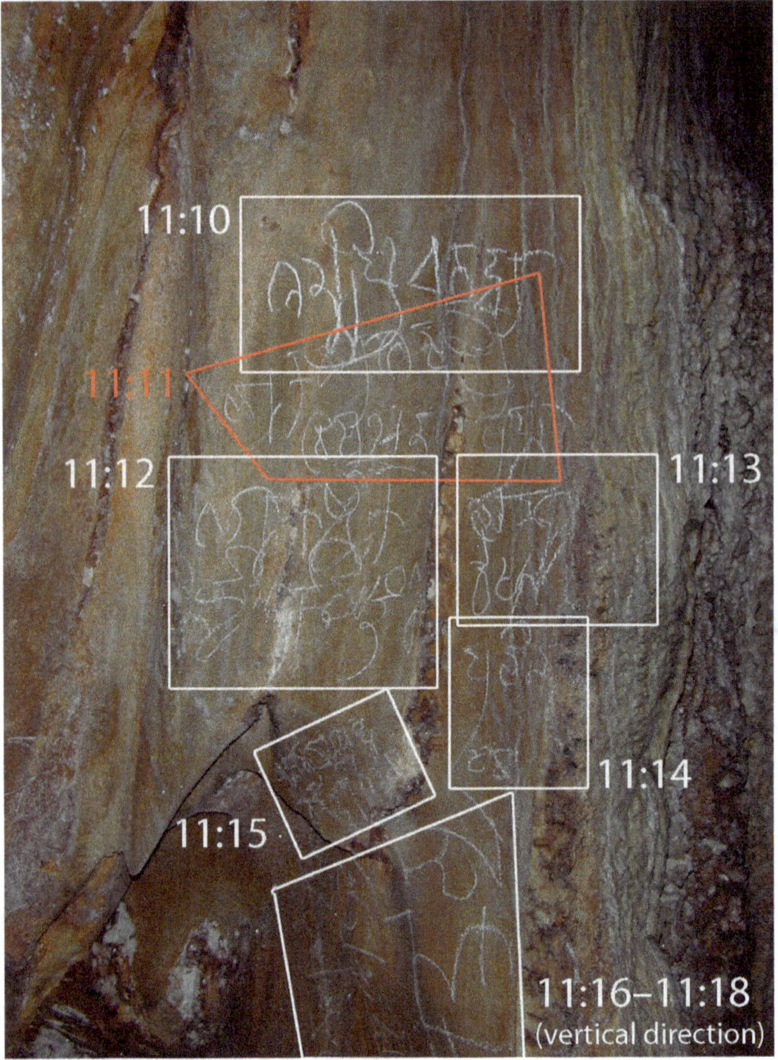

Fig. 5: Close-up view of the graffiti 11:10–11:18; after Strauch 2012, 124.

This attraction is perhaps also partly due to the soft surface of the 'wall', which makes it easy to scratch. Modern visitors (after 2000) have also chosen to write their names here (cf. Fig. 4, Arabic names above 11:25).

3.2.2 Case 2: The inscriptions and drawings from the Upper Indus Valley

As I had already noticed in 2012 (cf. also Strauch 2019), the corpus of Hoq graffiti – as we may call them by now – shares many features with the inscriptions and drawings found in the Upper Indus River valley in Northern Pakistan. The overwhelming majority of these objects have now been published thanks to the impressive work of the Heidelberg Academy Project *Felsbilder und Inschriften am Karakorum-Highway.*[35] Despite the nearly complete publication, a comprehensive study of this material is still a *desideratum.*[36]

The sites documented are located along the ancient route connecting Gandhara with the region of Xinjiang. The inscriptions testify to a variety of ethnic groups who used this route from probably the first up to the fourteenth century CE, among them Indians (in Kharoṣṭhī and Brāhmī scripts), Sogdians,[37] Bactrians, Tibetans and Chinese. Both inscriptions and drawings are usually found together, 'bruised' into the surface of free-standing rocks or rock formations that had been covered by a patina ('desert varnish'), with the help of a pointed stone or metal instrument.[38] While most of the drawings represent 'folk beliefs' and local traditions (they include depictions of animals and various symbols), there are a huge number of Buddhist drawings of a mostly remarkable artistic quality (Fig. 6).

This distinguishes the Karakorum corpus clearly from the Hoq evidence. As the inscriptions show, the people who frequented the ancient Karakorum route were also Buddhist 'professionals', i.e. monks or artists. These Buddhist drawings were not *ad hoc* creations of occasional visitors, but – as the accompanying inscriptions show – were commissioned by influential locals, most probably in order to create places for worship at these spots for the travelling caravans. The religious graffiti of Northern Pakistan redefined the existing landscape. Apparently, an ancient technique attested by thousands of petroglyphs on rock surfaces along the Karakorum Highway was adapted by local Buddhists to create

35 For the editions, photographs and studies of the Karakorum material, see the series *Antiquities of Northern Pakistan* and *Materialien zur Archäologie der Nordgebiete Pakistans*. The following sites have so far been covered by these publications: Oshibat (Bemmann and König 1994), Shatial (Fussman and König 1997), Hodar (Bandini-König 1999), Shing Nala and Gichi Nala (Bandini-König and von Hinüber 2001), Dadam Das (Bemmann 2005) and Thalpan (Bandini-König 2003, 2005, 2007, 2009, 2011, 2013).

36 For a good summary on the sites and the importance of these findings for the history of Buddhist transmission, see Neelis 2011, 268–287.

37 For Sogdian graffiti from the Upper Indus River valley, see the contribution by Carlo G. Cereti in this volume.

38 Neelis 2011, 268.

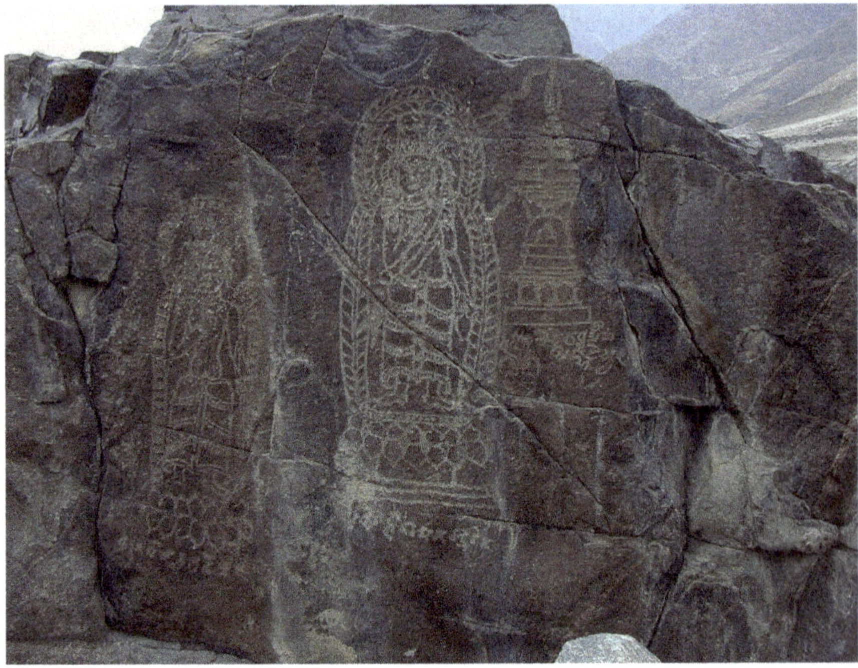

Fig. 6: Bodhisattva and stūpa drawings at Chilas I donated by Siṅhoṭa; photograph © Ingo Strauch; for the inscriptions, cf. von Hinüber 1989b, 86, nos 83–85.

new spaces for religious activities. Buddhist drawings include numerous depictions of *stūpa*s, Buddhas, Bodhisattvas, and even narratives, in particular scenes from Buddha's previous lives as described in various *Jātaka*s (cf. e.g. the *Śibi-Jātaka* at Shatial). In a few cases, several Buddha and Bodhisattva drawings can be attributed to a single donor. Although it is mostly impossible to determine a sequence of epigraphs and drawings at one particular site, it seems logical to regard these consecrating drawings and inscriptions as the initial phase of these sites. They probably motivated subsequent visitors to memorialise their presence at the site.

Roughly speaking,[39] the inscriptions can be divided into two groups: personal inscriptions reporting the presence of people at the site and inscriptions of a religious character.

39 A detailed study of the entire corpus is beyond the scope this article. There are other types of inscriptions, such as label inscriptions that accompany drawings (for the Hindu deities Vāsudeva-

The first group shares many features with the personal inscriptions from Hoq. The editor of the Brāhmī inscriptions, Oskar von Hinüber (1989a), identified the following types:

Type 1: 'contains only names either in the nominative or endingless, or less often in the genitive case';
Type 2: combines the names 'with verbs meaning "has come, has arrived"';
Type 3: additional information is indicated, such as
a) professions,
b) castes and tribes,
c) religious status
d) official titles.

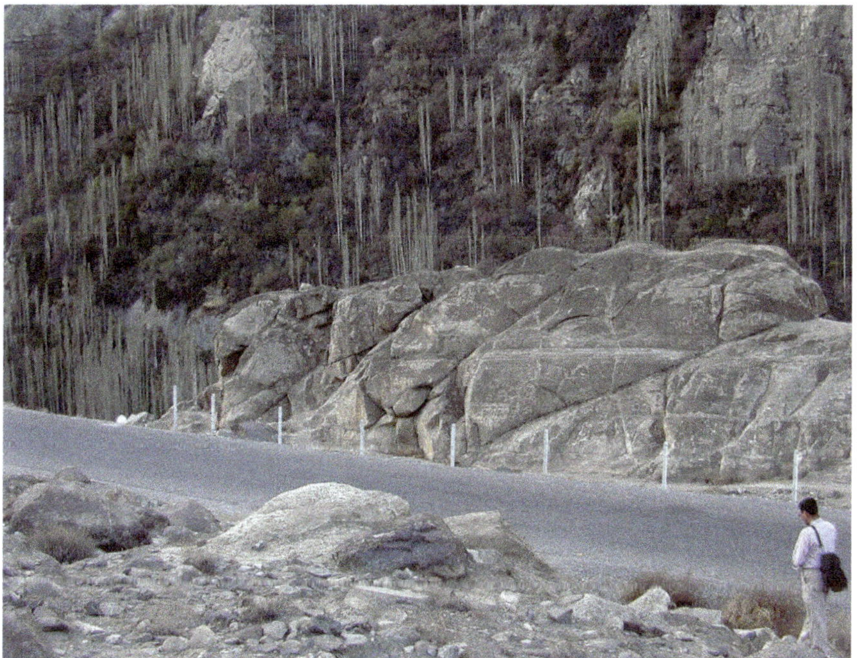

Fig. 7: The rock of Haldeikish covered with graffiti; photograph © Ingo Strauch.

Kṛṣṇa and Baladeva-Balarāma at Chilas II) or even official inscriptions by local kings in eulogical *praśasti* style (cf. von Hinüber 1989a, 57–60).

Inscriptions of this type can cover huge surfaces, partly overlapping each other, such as in Haldeikish (see Fig. 7).

As typical example for this type I cite: *ādītyo iha gata* 'Ādītya (Sanskrit Āditya) came here' (Shatial-West).[40]

The group of religious inscriptions is much more developed than in the Hoq corpus and comprises different types of texts. Texts of a religious character generally accompany a religious drawing. Depictions of *stūpa*s or Buddhas and Bodhisattvas are frequently designated as a religious donation (*deyadharma*).[41] Their formula corresponds to that of Buddhist donative inscriptions (see above), such as: *devadharmo yaṃ priyanandaputra dharmasihe* 'Pious gift (of) Dharmasiha, son of Priyananda' (Thalpan Ziyarat).[42]

Another type of religious text is represented by veneration formulae that are also often combined with images of Buddhas and Bodhisattvas, or *stūpa*s.[43] The names of Tathāgatas and Bodhisattvas mentioned in these inscriptions suggest a relationship to Buddhist protective texts (*dhāraṇī*). These inscribed texts also possibly fulfilled a protective function.[44] They are not always clearly associated with the accompanying drawings, but often seem to function as labels for these drawings, as, for example, the figure of a Tathāgata that is accompanied by the legend *namo āryā vipaśis tathāgatāya. sārdhaṃ siṅ(h)oṭena* 'Veneration to the Tathāgata, the noble Vipaśyin. Together with Siṅhoṭa' (Chilas I).[45]

These labels also occur in the stem form (or nom. case?), for example, in Thalpan, where a *stūpa* drawing is labelled as *śākyamuni tathāgata* and one of the two accompanying drawings of Bodhisattvas is identified as *maṃjuśrī bodhisatva*.[46]

The multitude of inscriptions and drawings along the Karakorum Highway represent a variety of texts and images. In the case of the personal inscriptions, a spontaneous and unofficial character of their production can be assumed—their designation as graffiti seems, therefore, justified. The religious inscriptions and the drawings that are related to them are more difficult to evaluate. The donative formulae and their careful execution do not speak in favour of a spontaneous creative act. It seems more as if these objects were intentionally placed at strategically important sites along the trade routes in order to create places for religious worship. Contrary to the personal graffiti that are often carelessly distributed on

40 von Hinüber 1989a, 44, no. 16.
41 von Hinüber 1989b, 77–86.
42 von Hinüber 1989b, 75, no. 69.
43 von Hinüber 1989b, 86, 91–99.
44 von Hinüber 1989b, 99.
45 von Hinüber 1989b, 84, no. 79.
46 von Hinüber 1989b, 88, nos 86, 87.

any surfaces available, most of the religious drawings and texts seem to be carefully arranged. They are carried out by the same techniques and often on the same surfaces as the personal graffiti but seem to fulfil a completely different function and follow different formal patterns. It is hard to believe that they are the result of an 'accidental, personal, spontaneous, arbitrary, or immediate'[47] production. If we decide to call these objects graffiti, we have to be aware of this distinctively different character.

3.2.3 Case 3: The Sigiriya graffiti

A completely different type of inscriptions is represented by the unique corpus of graffiti on the so-called 'mirror wall' at Sigiriya. The wall is situated along a staircase that leads the visitors to the famous frescos of female figures that are attached to the Western face of the huge natural rock (*c.* 200 m high). Similar to the palace on the top of the rock, these drawings and the highly polished plastered wall were probably created in the second half of the fifth century CE on behalf of the Sri Lankan King Kassapa. It is suggested that the place was abandoned rather early by the king and, subsequently, became a popular spot for visits. As such, Sigiriya might be one of the earliest attested tourist sites of South Asia. From the sixth century CE onwards, visitors left little poems in the Sinhalese language on this wall. The entire corpus of more or less complete and legible texts was first published by Paranavitana in two large volumes *Sigiri Graffiti* and contains 685 inscriptions, dating from the eighth to the tenth century CE.[48] There are many more incomplete texts or only names which were not included in this edition. According to Paranavitana, the period of inscribing seems to have already started in the fifth century CE (illegible inscriptions). In addition to the Sinhalese inscriptions, there are also texts in Sanskrit (some of them written in Nāgarī script) and Tamil. As Paranavitana remarks, 'the polished surface of the gallery wall looks as if it had been specially provided for visitors to indulge in this carving. Scribbling thereon can be done with much greater ease than on rock, using any sort of sharp-pointed implement [...]'.[49] The Sigiriya corpus seems to be unique in South Asian epigraphy, as a comprehensive presentation of a popular style of poetry written by people from different social strata, by both men and women. Beside

47 Hahn 2013.

48 Also see the publication by Priyanka (2010). Unfortunately, this new edition was not accessible to me.

49 Paranavitana 1956, vol. 1, vii.

the poetical qualities, it is the personal touch of these poems that makes them so exceptional. Most of the poems were apparently composed on the spot, under the impression of the frescos the visitors had just visited, for example: 'By means of the splendour of the mountain side, I saw the manner in which nymphs stood in heaven. My hand jumped up with the desire of grasping their girdle in dalliance'.[50]

In many cases, the visitors also identified themselves, among them people from a royal background, officials, merchants and a lot of Buddhist monks.[51] According to the inscriptions, they came from all over the island. Many poems describe the circumstances of their expedition to the rock. Not all the visitors were capable of expressing their emotions in poetical form. Budal, who wrote in prose, has become especially famous: 'I am Budal, I came in company and saw Sihigiri. Many people who saw (Sihigiri) have written verses. I therefore did not write one'.[52]

3.2.4 Case 4: Secondary inscriptions on Aśokan pillars

It is well-known that many of the Aśokan pillars were later used for secondary inscriptions, partly of an official or unofficial character. The majority of these pillars were erected in the vicinity of Buddhist sites, i.e. *stūpa*s or monasteries. As an integral and important part of these sites, most of them were protected from undesirable inscriptions for a long time. Accordingly, the beginning of graffiti on Aśokan pillars seems to coincide with the abandonment of the Buddhist institutions when only the pillars and the remains of the monuments attracted visitors. Due to their outstanding character, Aśokan pillars (and the Girnar rock) also attracted subsequent rulers to use them for their imperial edicts. Thus, the Gupta ruler Samudragupta (r. *c.* 335–375 CE) had his own inscription carved on the Allāhābād-Kauśāmbī pillar under the Aśokan edicts. Much later, the Mughal ruler Jahāngīr (r. 1605–1627 CE) added his own text, which was written in the middle of the text of the Aśokan edicts and partially destroyed it. The Delhi-Toprā pillar is secondarily inscribed with three texts by the Cāhamāna ruler Vīsaladeva (r. *c.* 1150–1164 CE). The Tughlaq ruler Fīrūz Shāh (r. 1351–1388 CE) was especially attracted by the pillars and removed some of them to other places in order to demonstrate his imperial power (e.g. Fatehābād-Hisār, Delhi-Toprā, Delhi-Mirāṭh[53]). One

50 No. 104; Paranavitana 1956, vol. 2, 64.

51 Paranavitana 1956, vol. 1, ccx–ccxv.

52 Paranavitana 1956, vol. 1, ccx.

53 See Flood 2003.

of these pillars has a long inscription praising this ruler (Fatehābād-Hisār). This Persian text covers almost the entire existing part of the pillar and has completely destroyed the original surface, which may have contained Aśokan edicts. Due to their official character, these secondary royal inscriptions can certainly not be regarded as graffiti.

However, most of the pillars also bear dozens, sometimes hundreds of smaller inscriptions and figures that were left by visitors. They are often carelessly executed, written one above the other, and are mostly rather short, containing usually not much more than the visitors' names and occasionally the date of their visit. Depending on the time of their creation and the origin of the visitors, they are written in a variety of Indian languages and scripts as well as Persian, Arabic and English. Among them, are numerous inscriptions in the so-called shell-script.

As usual for this kind of text, these secondary inscriptions have never been thoroughly studied. When exploring the ancient Aśokan epigraphs, most of the scholars limited themselves to merely pointing out the existence of these inscriptions, without always hiding their discontent about the behaviour of their authors and qualifying their texts as 'scribblings' or even 'rubbish'.[54] In a few cases, however, at least some of the inscriptions have been properly recorded.

The comprehensive documentation of *Aśokan Sites and Artefacts* by Harry Falk (2006) and Richard Salomon's documentation of shell-script texts (1980, 1986) allow us to present the following (preliminary and incomplete) survey on secondary inscriptions on Aśokan pillars and their contexts:

54 Cf. e.g. Cunningham 1877, 38: 'Above the Asoka edicts there is a mass of this modern scribbling equal size to the Samudra Gupta inscription. But besides this, the whole of the Asoka inscription is interlined with the same rubbish, which is continued below on all sides of the two shorter edicts, one of which has been half obliterated by the modern letters.'

Table 1: Survey of Aśokan pillars and their secondary inscriptions

Pillar	Aśokan inscriptions	Secondary official inscriptions	Pilgrims' and travellers' records	Shell inscriptions
Allāhābād	• Pillar Edicts 1–6 • 'Schism edict' • 'Queen's edict'	• Samudragupta inscript. (4th c. CE) - Fleet 1888, 1–7 • Jahāngīr inscription (17th c. CE) - Burt 1834, 107–108	• From the $3^{rd}/4^{th}$ century CE onwards - Burt 1834, 110–111 (no readings: refers to dates) - Prinsep 1837, 967 (on the basis of facsimiles published in this article, Plates LV and LVI) - Cunningham 1877, 38–39	Prinsep 1837, Plate LVI; Salomon 1980, 35
Ararāj	Pillar Edicts 1–6		• Only 'Reuben Burrow, 1792' - Cunningham 1871, 68	Salomon 1980, 24–25 (3 inscriptions); Falk 2006, 163, Fig. 3
Fatehābād-Hisār	• Chiselled out?	• Firūz Shāh inscription (14th c. CE) - Shokoohy 1988, 12–38	• From 4th century CE onwards - Cunningham 1875, 140–142, Plate XLI	
Kauśāmbī	• --		• From 4th century CE onwards - Cunningham 1871, 309–311 - Pargiter 1911–1912, Salomon 1998, 302–305	Salomon 1980, 16–17 (7 inscriptions); Falk 2006, 175, Fig. 2
Lumbinī	• Lumbinī inscript.		• 'Pilgrim marks' of uncertain dating • Invocation of Ripumalla (14th c.) - Mukherji 1901, 35 (no texts) - Führer 1897, 27 (no texts) - Weise 2013, 54 (with partial image)	

Pillar	Aśokan inscriptions	Secondary official inscriptions	Pilgrims' and travellers' records	Shell inscriptions
Mirāṭh (Delhi)	• Pillar edicts 1–6		• From 14th century CE onwards - Cunningham 1875, 144	Salomon 1980, 33 (1 inscription)
Nandangarh	• Pillar edicts 1–6		• From 16th century onwards, Nāgarī and Persian, English, including 'Rn Burrow 1792' - Cunningham 1871, 73 - Kureishi 1931, 10–11 - Falk 2006, 186, Fig. 9 • Drawings of birds - Falk 2006, 185, Fig. 3	Falk 2006, 186, Fig. 9
Niglīvā	• Niglīvā inscription		• Invocation of Ripumalla, (Śaka 1234 = 1312 CE) - Mukherji 1901, 30 (with wrong calculation of the date), Falk 2006, 188, Fig. 4 • Drawings of birds - Falk 2006, 189, Figs 9–11	
Rāmpūrvā	• Pillar Edicts 1–6		• Drawings of birds and a fish - Falk 2006, 196–197, Figs 5 and 7	
Sāñcī	• 'Schism edict'			Salomon 1980, 28 (2 inscriptions); Falk 2006, 203, Fig. 2
Saṅkisā	• Pillar not preserved, only capital			Salomon 1986, 137–138 (6 inscriptions)

Pillar	Aśokan inscriptions	Secondary official inscriptions	Pilgrims' and travellers' records	Shell inscriptions
Sārnāth	• 'Schism edict'	• Donative inscription (?), dated Aśvaghoṣa, year 40 (Kaniṣka era? = 167/168 CE) • Donative inscription (4th c. CE?) - Vogel 1905–1906, 171–172		
Toprā (Delhi)	• Pillar edicts 1–7	• 3 inscriptions of Cāhamāna Vīsaladeva (12th century) - Kielhorn 1890	• From 4th century CE onwards - Cunningham 1871 and 1875, 143–144 (Plate XLI) • Drawing of an elephant - Falk 2006, 217, Fig. 7	Salomon 1980, 30 (1 inscription)
Vesālī			• Indian (Nāgarī), Persian, and English graffiti, incl. 'Reuben Burrow, 1792' • Cunningham 1871, 61 (none of the Indian texts are older than 200–300 years)	Salomon 1980, 21–22 (5 inscriptions); Falk 2006, 222

Although this survey must remain incomplete and lacks proper documentation and edition of most of the texts, some preliminary conclusions seem possible. It can generally be said that, of course, the presence of graffiti bears witness to different aspects of the history of the individual pillars and their architectural contexts: the accessibility of the pillar, its position (standing, lying on the ground), status and religious interpretation, and the function and character of the surrounding space.

It becomes clear that not all the pillars were used for informal records from an early period onwards. This can be explained by either their rather remote location or their protection through the institution to which it belonged (in most cases, Buddhist monasteries). One of the best documented pillars is the Allāhābād pillar, which shall serve here an example (Fig. 8).

Unfortunately, no attempt has ever been made to produce a systematic and complete documentation of the informal secondary texts on the Allāhābād pillar.

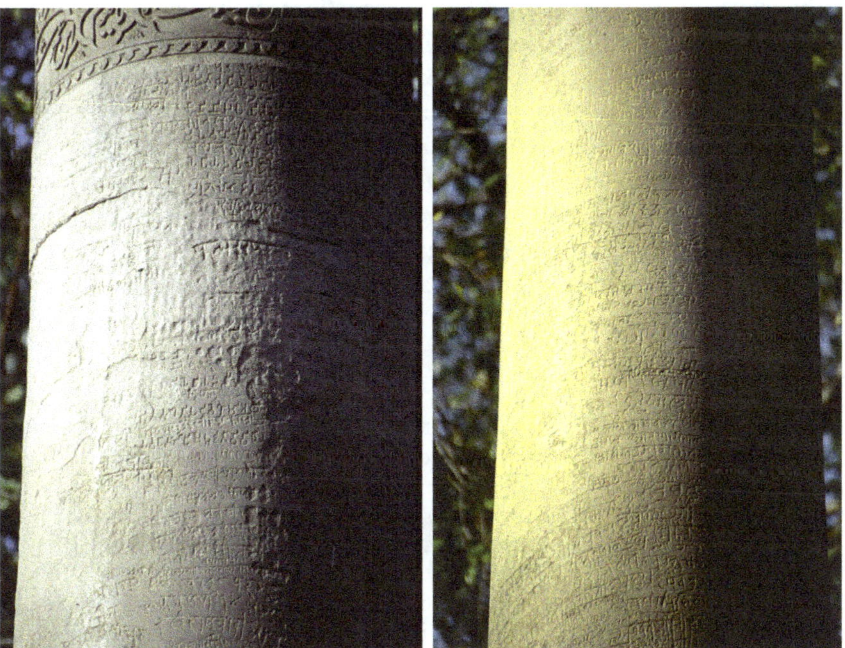

Figs 8–9: The Allāhābād pillar covered with graffiti; on Fig. 8 (left) the inscription of Jahāngīr on the top; below remains of the Aśokan edicts with interlinear graffiti; photographs courtesy Harry Falk.

Neither the facsimiles of the early nineteenth century, the rubbings presented by Hultzsch (1925) nor modern photographs present the complete picture.[55] Judging by the Aśokan 'Schism edict' that addresses the officials of Kauśāmbī, the pillar was probably originally erected at Kauśāmbī. The date of its relocation to Allāhābād near the conflux of the Ganga and Yamuna, the sacred Prayāg, is controversially discussed, but it is not impossible that the Gupta ruler Samudragupta already had the pillar shifted.[56] The best description of the graffiti was provided by James Prinsep (1799–1840), the decipherer of the Brāhmī script and pioneer of Indian epigraphy and palaeography. Prinsep published facsimiles of the Allāhābād pillar inscriptions in a little article of 1837, along with some readings of names from the interlinear inscriptions (Gopālaputra, Dhanara Singh, Dhamarāja) that 'may be taken as samples of the rest which it would be quite a waste of time to examine'.[57] He gives some more readings of surrounding inscriptions, mainly in order to show that they were executed while the pillar was lying on the ground. The drawn facsimiles published alongside Prinsep's text that give an impression of the shape and types of these secondary inscriptions are, however, of special interest. According to their palaeography, some of them are clearly written in an early type of Brāhmī, probably prior to Samudragupta's inscription (Fig. 10).

According to the inscriptions written vertically on the pillar, it was no longer standing at the time of these early inscriptions.[58] This could indicate that it was Samudragupta who restored the prestige of the pillar by re-erecting and inscribing it. As Prinsep has already rightly observed, after the re-erection of the pillar and the official inscription of Samudragupta, there was a considerable gap in the graffiti activities which were taken up again only in the thirteenth century CE.[59]

55 This situation has already been criticized – without showing any consequences – by Krishnaswamy and Ghosh 1935, 703: 'It is unfortunate that the scribblings on the pillar have not been considered worthy of attention. They ought to be re-studied from the original and will certainly yield more definite material for the study of the history of the pillar.'

56 See Krishnaswamy and Ghosh 1935, who also consider the possibility that Aśoka had already placed the pillar in its present position, which seems to me, however, less likely.

57 Prinsep 1837, 967.

58 Cf. Prinsep 1837, 968: 'Now it would have been exceedingly inconvenient if not impossible to have cut the name, No. 10, up and down at right angles to the other writing while the pillar was erect, to say nothing of the place being out of reach, unless a scaffold were erected on purpose, which would hardly be the case since the object of an ambitious visitor would be defeated by placing his name out of sight and in an unreadable position'.

59 The dates of these inscriptions start according to Cunningham (1877, 38–39) in the year Vikrama 1297 = 1250 CE. Cunningham concludes that the pillar was 'out of the reach of pilgrims' scribbling from the time of the Guptas until that of early Musalmân kings of Delhi' (Cunningham 1877, 39).

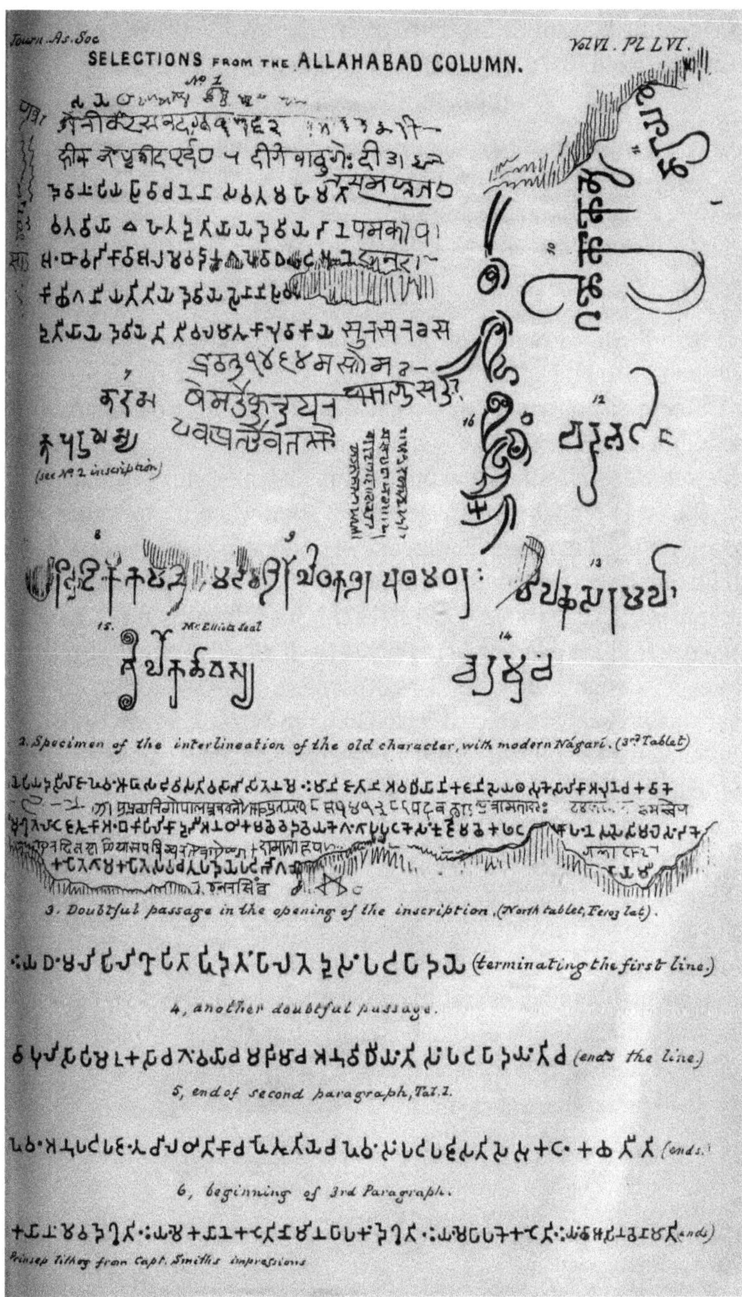

Fig. 10: Facsimile drawings of some graffiti from the Allāhābād pillar; after Prinsep 1837, Plate 56.

Cunningham identified the following dated inscriptions (without giving their exact location and texts) in 1877:

- Seven texts: (Vikrama) Saṃvat 1297–1398 (1250–1341 CE)
- Five texts: (Vikrama) Saṃvat 1464–1495 (1407–1438 CE)
- Twelve texts: (Vikrama) Saṃvat 1501–1584 (1444–1527 CE)
- Three texts: (Vikrama) Saṃvat 1632–1640 (1575–1583 CE)
- Three texts: (Vikrama) Saṃvat 1864 (1807 CE)[60]

Most of the dated records give dates in the month of Māgha (November-December). According to Krishnaswamy and Ghosh, this date points to the prescribed period of pilgrimages to Prayāg.[61] Although Cunningham did not indicate the exact location of these inscriptions, Prinsep's description helps to distinguish different phases of the pillar's history.

The earliest thirteenth century graffiti point again to the lying position of the pillar.[62] The pillar was probably re-erected again soon when visitors started to use the Aśokan text itself to make interlinear inscriptions in between the Aśokan lines.[63] And, finally, it was apparently again lying when one of the favourites of the Moghul emperor Akbar (ruled 1556–1605 CE), his minister and court poet Birbal, commemorated his pilgrimage to Prayāg (*tīrth rāj prayāg ke jātrā*) on the pillar in the year (Vikrama) Saṃvat 1632 = 1575 CE.[64]

The pillar was probably re-erected in 1605 by the Moghul emperor Jahāngīr who commissioned the last official record written on the pillar, completely ignoring the preceding inscriptions and placing his text just in the middle of the Aśokan pillar edicts.

From this time on, the pillar seems to have been protected from inscriptions again until General Kyd had it pulled down in 1804.[65] Consequently, the next datable graffiti (according to the data available) are from the beginning of the nineteenth century CE.

The extremely high number of graffiti on the Allāhābād pillar is perhaps best explained by its location at one of the most sacred and most visited places of Hinduism. If the pillar had indeed been moved to its present location earlier by

---

60 Cunningham 1877, 38–39.

61 Krishnaswamy and Ghosh 1935, 703.

62 Prinsep 1837, 968: 'these occupy one side of the shaft, or that which was uppermost when the pillar was in a prostrate position'.

63 Prinsep 1837, 967. For identified dates (the earliest 1319 CE) in the interlinear graffiti, see Krishnaswamy and Ghosh 1935, 702.

64 Cunningham 1877, 39.

65 Falk 2006, 159.

Samudragupta (as suggested by Krishnaswamy and Ghosh 1938), it had already lost its connection to a Buddhist site at a fairly early period. Although it was not constantly well maintained, the pillar's location at the important *prayāga* pilgrimage site ensured a constant influx of visitors who left their names and other small texts.

Other pillars were much less visited. As in the case of the Allāhābād pillar, the graffiti activity at most of these sites begins when the pillars were no longer integrated into a protective Buddhist environment.[66] Thus, the small texts sometimes give an indication of the religious reinterpretation of the sites and pillars.

Two longer texts are inscribed on the Kauśāmbī pillar (Fig. 11), for example, that refer to different ways of perception.[67] A verse inscription from the seventh/eighth century CE states:

> The man, who fixes his look on this very tall pillar, preserves great fortitude when the planets are adverse: delivered from sin, he purifies his kindred and proceeds without doubt to Indra's world.[68]

The second text, an inscription from a family of goldsmiths and dated to 1565 CE, begins with an invocation to Bhairava[69] and indicates a fairly common association of pillars with the god Śiva and his erect penis (*liṅga*).

The graffiti on the pillars in Niglīvā and Lumbinī[70] in the north, in present-day Nepal, seem to attest to the re-enactment of these sites as Buddhist pilgrimage places. The texts referring to the king Ripumalla (early fourteenth century CE)

---

66 The Sarnath pillar bears two additional texts of the Kuṣāṇa and Gupta periods which cannot be characterised as graffiti but most probably as donative inscriptions (Vogel 1905–1906, 171–172). Both of them use the term *parigraha* 'possession' that points to their donative character.

67 According to Falk (2006, 175), the earliest inscriptions on this pillar belong to the Gupta period. I was unable to get access to any images of these texts or publications that would mention their contents.

68 Pargiter 1911–1912, 89. *ya īkṣate stambham idam sutuṅgaṃ grahārucau pāti naras sudhīrmaṃ (= sudhīryaṃ) punāti gottraṃ sa vimuktapāpaḥ prayāti cāśaṃśayam indralokaṃ* (Pargiter 1911–1912, 88, without editorial signs).

69 Pargiter 1911–1912, 89–92, re-edited by Salomon 1998, 302–305.

70 Führer (1897, 27) describes the pillar as 'being covered with many records of pilgrims' visits, one of which was incised about A. D. 700'. Cf. Falk 1998, 13, n. 41, where Bühler uses the same words, but gives 800 CE as the year. Apparently, rubbings of these modern graffiti had been made before the pillar was completely unearthed. Since they were not of great antiquity, the pillar was quickly disregarded as unimportant (Cf. Falk 1998, 14). The whereabouts of these rubbings are unknown to me.

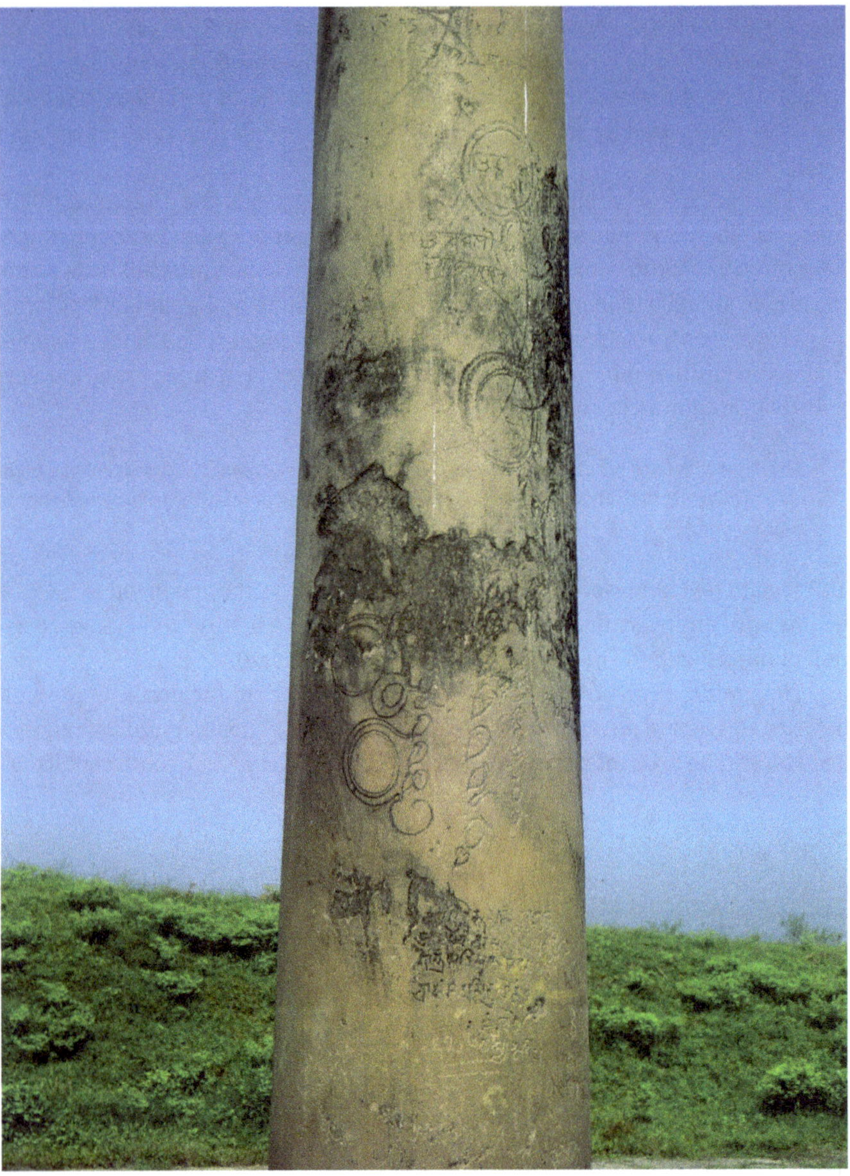

Fig. 11: Kauśāmbī pillar with Brāhmī and shell-script graffiti, the verse inscription on the lower part; photograph courtesy Harry Falk.

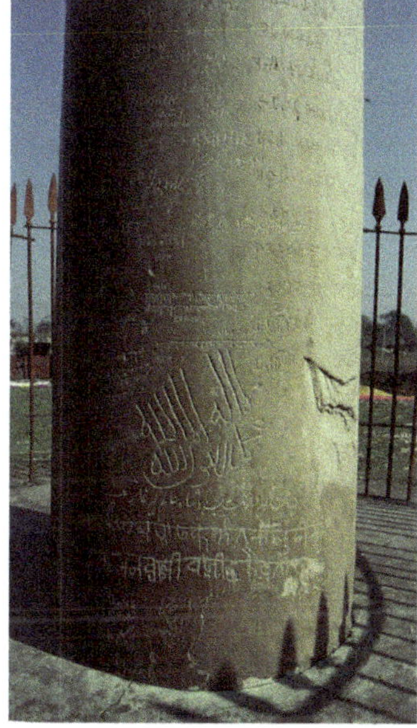
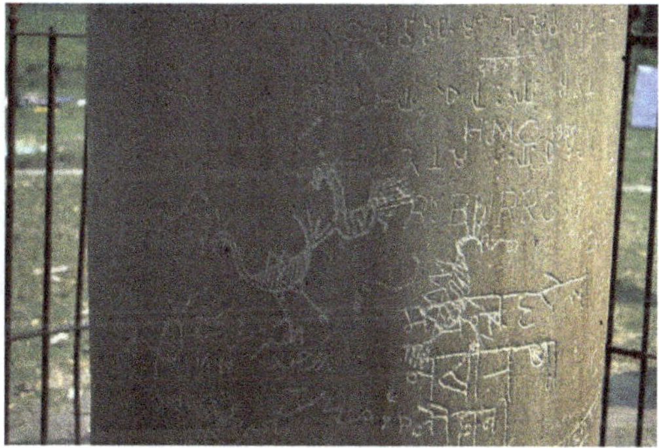

Figs 12–13: Graffiti in different scripts and languages on the Nandangarh pillar, including those of Reuben Burrow, dated 1792, the police sub-inspectors P. Sinha and S. L. Husain, dated 1898 and (19)00, respectively, and the Arabic graffiti and drawings dated H. 1071 (= 1660/1661 ce); photographs courtesy Harry Falk.

are particularly noteworthy here.[71] They represent a formula that is also attested on numerous Buddhist bronzes and *thangkas*: *śrī-ripumallaś ciraṃ jayatu* 'May śrī Ripumalla be victorious for a long time'.[72]

Graffiti on Aśokan pillars shed light on the history of the sites well into colonial times. The most remarkable British graffiti are those by Reuben Burrow,[73] who left his name and the date 1792 at Nandangarh, Ararāj and Vesālī, apparently shortly before his death on 7 June 1792, in the town of Buxor (Bihar). The Nandangarh pillar (Figs 12–13) contains many additional graffiti and was evidently

71 For the Buddhist king Ripumalla, and inscriptions referring to him, see Andolfatto 2021. The dates of his inscriptions range from 1312 to 1314 CE.

72 Lumbinī: '(o)n the uppermost portion on the eastern side of the Ashoka Pillar' (Weise 2013, 54), preceded by the Tibetan prayer *oṃ maṇipadme hūṃ* (in the same script) and concluded by the name of Ripumalla's son, Saṃgrāmamalla. Niglīva: '(b)etween 8′ 6″ and 9′ 7″ [= c. 260 – 290 cm] below the top' (Mukherji 1901, 30), preceded by the Tibetan prayer *oṃ maṇipadme hūṃ* (in Tibetan script) and concluded by the date (Śaka) 1234 (1312 CE), cf. the image in Falk 2006, 188, Fig. 4.

73 For a short biography of this mathematician who came to India in 1782, see Stephen 1886.

also popular among the local police officers. At least two sub-inspectors (S.I.) left their names here: *P. Sinha S.I. Police Louria*, dated 31 May 1898, and *S.L. Hosain, Ex.S.I.*, dated 24 December (19)00. An Arabic graffito, which was apparently inscribed together with a drawing of a Mughal nobleman (to the right of the Arabic inscriptions), is of special interest. Below the Muslim *šahāda* prayer we find the date formula:

محیی الدین محمد اورنگزیب بادشاه عالمگیر غازی سن ۱۰۷۱

Muḥyī ad-Dīn Muḥammad Aurangzīb Bādšāh ʿĀlamgīr ḫāzī sana 1071 (= 1660-61 CE)

4 Some preliminary conclusions and further perspectives for the study of Indian graffiti

Based on the somewhat arbitrary use of the term 'graffiti' in Indian epigraphy, we suggest avoiding this term for the categories of inscribed pottery and for non-alphabetic signs. According to the refined definition proposed above, they do not have most of the primary characteristics of a graffito. Although in many cases they are personal, they can hardly be described as the result of an accidental or immediate personal decision. The fact that they are inscribed on vessels does not mean that this surface was not intended for writing. Their content and function clearly link the inscriptions to these objects, therefore, we must consider these surfaces as intended for writing.

Instead, the term should be reserved for texts that are referred to by Salomon as 'pilgrims' and travellers' records'. Most of the texts and drawings of this category seem to be based on an individual initiative (cf. above 'accidental, personal, spontaneous, arbitrary, or immediate production'). They occur on surfaces that were not especially assigned to them. Most of them are of a secondary character, i.e. they were added to already existing inscriptions or drawings. Clusters of graffiti share other similarities, due to their common character: they are often written in cursive scripts, comprise inscriptions in different scripts and languages, and are found on places of religious significance.

However, as our four case studies show, the character of these texts is rather diverse. Although most of them share the features mentioned above, they must also be clearly distinguished from each other.

The differences concern mainly the following features:

- location (landscape, building, relation to pilgrimage routes),
- techniques (scratching, chiselling, drawing, bruising),

- script types (formal/cursive),
- literary form (short/long inscription, prose/verse),
- religious or personal character (religious invocation or name), and
- primary and secondary character (initiation of writing/image making, addition to existent writings or images).

It is not always possible to draw clear lines and clearly attach a single label to the texts and drawings. Names left at a religious site are personal but clearly a religious dimension is included in this action.[74] A cluster of graffiti in a previously uninscribed place can be considered in its entirety as an initial act of writing, but this is strictly speaking only true for the first graffito at the respective site. Each graffito or group of graffiti we have examined reflects this multidimensional aspect. Even the rather generic characterisation of 'informal texts' is not without contradictions: many of the little texts share certain formal features and indicate that they followed certain formal rules. In some cases, even their accidental or immediate character is not always evident. As we have seen, only some of the Upper Indus Valley inscriptions seems to fulfil this condition. It is, therefore, questionable if we should consider all of the Upper Indus Valley inscriptions as graffiti in the sense suggested here. The same restriction applies to the numerous Buddhist images found along the trade routes. As many of the accompanying inscriptions show, they are not the result of a spontaneous or personal production, but rather objects commissioned by influential local agents.

In this paper, I have mainly discussed texts, although images often accompany these texts or even stand alone. Most of the images bear a religious – or at least auspicious – meaning (see Hoq above). Others elude a clear interpretation (e.g. the birds on some of the Aśokan pillars). Further research is needed in order to understand the function and types of these images and their relationship to their spatial and inscriptional environment, which is beyond the scope of the present paper.

The future study of Indian graffiti should take into account the diversity of these objects – but a priority task is to document the existing sites, to make them accessible for thorough palaeographic and philological analysis, which can help to turn them into valuable historical sources. Remarkably, the most valuable source for such an endeavour is generally not found in recent scholarship, but in the reports of the pioneers of Indian epigraphy and archaeology, in particular James Prinsep and Alexander Cunningham (1814–1893). Although both scholars were not very appreciative of the presence of graffiti on historical sites, they

74 Compare with the early Buddhist donative inscriptions, for which see Schopen 1996 (reproduced in Schopen 2004, 382–394).

almost never failed to mention them and often described them (frequently accompanied by drawings of the inscriptions). A thorough reading of Prinsep's notes and articles, and Cunningham's Reports for the Archaeological Survey of India can help (re)discover many forgotten or neglected graffiti sites.

A more recent source is available with Richard Salomon's invaluable documentation of sites that yield shell-script inscriptions. The presence of this type of inscription can serve as an important indicator for other types of graffiti. Consequently, many of the sites documented and described by Salomon in his research on shell-script texts also yield inscriptions in other scripts, including numerous 'pilgrims' and travellers' records'. Among them are also painted inscriptions, usually in combination with other paintings that are often (but probably incorrectly) characterised as prehistoric paintings.[75] Among the 67 sites documented by Salomon, at least 19 (with the exception of the Aśokan pillars) are reported to yield other types of graffiti, most of them undocumented and unpublished. The most important of them include the Buddhist monastic complex of Salihundam (Andhra Pradesh), where dozens of inscriptions are found on the pavement,[76] the Khapra Kodiya cave at Junagadh (Gujarat),[77] the Durgā Kho cave at Chunar (Mirzapur district, Uttar Pradesh)[78] and especially Muṇḍeśvarī (Kaimur district, Bihar).[79]

It is to be hoped that the growing awareness of graffiti in all their varieties will also reach the field of Indian epigraphy. Studying these types of texts and

75 Ahmedpur ki Pahadia, Vidisha district, Madhya Pradesh (Salomon 1986, 113–114), Bairagarh, Sehore district, Madhya Pradesh (Salomon 1986, 118–119), Makoria, Raisen district, Madhya Pradesh (Salomon 1986, 129). Salomon (1986, 119, n. 11) also refers to shell-script inscriptions at the famous rock-painting site of Bhimbetka, Raisen district, Madhya Pradesh.

76 Salomon 1980, 14–15 ; cf. ARIE 1954–55, 31–32, nos 44–65 ; Subrahmanyam 1964, 122–123.

77 Salomon 1980, 5–6. Cf. Burgess (1876, 145–147): 'many scribblings on the pillars and walls'. Burgess provides some drawings of four undeciphered Indian (Brāhmī) and one Persian inscription (apparently dated to Hijra 700), and remarks that 'there were inscriptions, only six years ago, in the old Pali character; Colonel Tod also distinctly states so. But now they have entirely disappeared with the chambers in which they were: the forms of the letters alone would have helped us to assign an age to these works; but, unless copies are to be found among Dr. Bhau Dâji's papers, there is probably no record left of these inscriptions. Let us hope there are, and that they will be given to the world in time to be of some use!' (Burgess 1876, 147). Unfortunately, Burgess' wish was never fulfilled, but when visiting the site in February 2016, I was able to see many inscriptions on the site which wait for a proper documentation, a task that will need professional equipment, such as spotlights and scaffolding, and a lot of patience, since the texts are very faintly visible and often written one above the other.

78 Salomon 1980, 30–31. Some of the numerous graffiti at this site were described and depicted as drawings in Cunningham 1880, 126–127, Plate XXXII; 1885, 128–129.

79 See above n. 25.

images is not always easy, as they are often in a poor state of preservation and sometimes difficult to access. Moreover, most of the texts are short and the amount of information in a single inscription is limited. Graffiti reveal their historical meaning mainly when looked at from different perspectives, taking into account the full set of data available – their language and palaeography, (textual and spatial) relationship to each other, to other (non-graffiti) texts, and to their architectural and broader environment.

When graffiti are studied in this way, they can help us to better understand the history of religious and non-religious sites, identify social networks, and assess the role of individuals and communities in different historical periods. Graffiti can help to give a voice to historical agents who are otherwise almost invisible for us – should we even say: graffiti make the subaltern speak?

Abbreviation

ARIE: *Annual Report on Indian Epigraphy. Archaeological Survey of India.*

References

Andolfatto, David C. (2021), 'Ripu Malla, a Buddhist Emperor from Western Nepal', *Orientations*, 52: 69–76.

Baird, J.A. and Claire Taylor (eds) (2011), *Ancient Graffiti in Context*, New York: Routledge.

Bandini-König, Ditte (ed.) (1999), *Die Felsbildstation Hodar* (Materialien zur Archäologie der Nordgebiete Pakistans, 3), Mainz: Philipp von Zabern.

Bandini-König, Ditte (ed.) (2003), *Die Felsbildstation Thalpan: I. Kataloge Chilas-Brücke und Thalpan (Steine 1–30)* (Materialien zur Archäologie der Nordgebiete Pakistans, 6), Mainz: Philipp von Zabern.

Bandini-König, Ditte (ed.) (2005), *Die Felsbildstation Thalpan: II. Katalog Thalpan (Steine 31–195)* (Materialien zur Archäologie der Nordgebiete Pakistans, 7), Mainz: Philipp von Zabern.

Bandini-König, Ditte (ed.) (2007), *Die Felsbildstation Thalpan: III. Katalog Thalpan (Steine 196–450)* (Materialien zur Archäologie der Nordgebiete Pakistans, 8), Mainz: Philipp von Zabern.

Bandini-König, Ditte (ed.) (2009), *Die Felsbildstation Thalpan: IV. Katalog Thalpan (Steine 451–811)* (Materialien zur Archäologie der Nordgebiete Pakistans, 9), Mainz: Philipp von Zabern.

Bandini-König, Ditte (ed.) (2011), *Die Felsbildstation Thalpan: V. Kataloge Ziyarat, Thakot, Khomar Das, Gichoi Das, Dardarbati Das* (Materialien zur Archäologie der Nordgebiete Pakistans, 10), Darmstadt: Philipp von Zabern.

Bandini-König, Ditte (ed.) (2013), *Die Felsbildstation Thalpan: VI. Kataloge Ba Das, Ba Das Ost, Gali, Gukona, Mostar Nala, Ke Ges, Ame Ges und Drang Das* (Materialien zur Archäologie der Nordgebiete Pakistans, 11), Darmstadt: Philipp von Zabern.

Bandini-König, Ditte and Oskar von Hinüber (eds) (2001), *Die Felsbildstationen Shing Nala und Gichi Nala* (Materialien zur Archäologie der Nordgebiete Pakistans, 4), Mainz: Philipp von Zabern.

Bemmann, Martin (ed.) (2005), *Die Felsbildstation Dadam Das* (Materialien zur Archäologie der Nordgebiete Pakistans, 5), Mainz: Philipp von Zabern.

Bemmann, Martin and Ditte König (eds) (1994), *Die Felsbildstation Oshibat* (Materialien zur Archäologie der Nordgebiete Pakistans, 1), Mainz: Philipp von Zabern.

Bonmann, Svenja, Jakob Halfmann, Natalie Korobzow and Bobomullo Bobomulloev (2023), 'A Partial Decipherment of the Unknown Kushan Script', *Transactions of the Philological Society*, 121: 293–329 <doi.org/10.1111/1467-968X.12269>.

Burgess, James (1876), *Report on the Antiquities of Kâṭhiâwâḍ and Kacch, Being the Result of the Second Season's Operation of the Archaeological Survey of Western India, 1874–75*, London: India Museum.

Burt, Thomas Seymour (1834), 'A Description, with Drawings, of the Ancient Stone Pillar at Allahabad Called Bhim Sén's Gadá or Club, with Accompanying Copies of Four Inscriptions Engraved in Different Characters upon Its Surface', *Journal of the Asiatic Society of Bengal*, 3: 105–113.

Chhabra, Bahadur Chand (1953–1954), 'Devaprayag Brahmi Inscriptions', *Epigraphia Indica*, 30: 133–134.

Cunningham, Alexander (1871), *Four Reports Made during the Years 1862–63–64–65* (Archaeological Survey of India, Reports, 1), Simla: Government Central Press.

Cunningham, Alexander (1875), *Report for the Year 1872–73* (Archaeological Survey of India, Reports, 5), Calcutta: Office of the Superintendent of Government Printing.

Cunningham, Alexander (1877), *Inscriptions of Asoka* (Corpus Inscriptionum Indicarum, 1), Calcutta: Office of the Superintendent of Government Printing.

Cunningham, Alexander (1880), *Report of Tours in the Gangetic Provinces from Badaon to Bihar in 1875–76 and 1877–78* (Archaeological Survey of India, Reports, 11) [repr. New Delhi: Archaeological Survey of India, 2000].

Cunningham, Alexander (1885), *Reports of a Tour in Bundelkhand and Rewa in 1884–84; and of a Tour in Rewa, Bundelkhand, Malwa, and Gwalior, in 1884–85* (Archaeological Survey of India, Reports, 2) [repr. New Delhi: Archaeological Survey of India, 2000].

Falk, Harry (1991), 'Zur Geschichte von Lumbinī', *Acta Orientalia*, 52: 70–90.

Falk, Harry (1998), *The Discovery of Lumbinī* (Lumbini International Research Institute, Occasional Papers, 1), Lumbini: Lumbini International Research Institute [translation of Falk 1991].

Falk, Harry (2000), 'Protective Inscriptions on Buddhist Monastic Implements', in Christine Chojnacki, Jens Hartmann and Volker M Tschannerl (eds), *Vividharatnakaraṇḍaka: Festgabe für Adelheid Mette* (Indica et Tibetica: Monographien zu den Sprachen und Kulturen des indo-tibetischen Kulturraumes, 37), Swisttal-Odendorf: Indica et Tibetica, 251–257.

Falk, Harry (2006), *Aśokan Sites and Artefacts: A Source-Book with Bibliography* (Monographien zur indischen Archäologie, Kunst und Philologie, 18), Mainz: Philipp von Zabern.

Falk, Harry (2014), 'Owners' Graffiti on Pottery from Tissamaharama', *Zeitschrift für Archäologie außereuropäischer Kulturen*, 6: 45–94.

Falk, Harry (2020–2021), 'Revision of Kharoṣṭhī Inscriptions in the Light of New Material', *Bulletin of the Asia Institute*, 30: 113–142.

Fleet, John Faithful (1888), *Inscriptions of the Early Gupta Kings and Their Successors* (Corpus Inscriptionum Indicarum, 3), Calcutta: Superintendent of Government Printing, India.

Flood, Finbarr B. (2003), 'Pillars, Palimpsests, and Princely Practices: Translating the Past in Sultanate Delhi', *Res: Anthropology and Aesthetics*, 43: 95–116.

Führer, A. (1897), *Antiquities of Buddha Sakyamuni's Birth-Place in the Nepalese Tarai* (Archaeological Survey of India, New Imperial Series, 26; Archaeological Survey of Northern India, 6), Allahabad: Government Press, N.W.P. and Oudh [repr. Varanasi: Indological Book House 1972].

Fussman, Gérard (2011), *Monuments bouddhiques de Termez, I : Catalogue des inscriptions sur poteries* (Publications de l'Institut de civilisation indienne, 79), Paris: Collège de France.

Fussman, Gérard and Ditte König (eds) (1997), *Die Felsbildstation Shatial* (Materialien zur Archäologie der Nordgebiete Pakistans, 2), Mainz: Philipp von Zabern.

Hahn, Johannes (2013), 'Graffiti', in Roger S. Bagnall, Kai Brodersen, Craige B. Champion, Andrew Erskine and Sabine R. Huebner (eds), *The Encyclopedia of Ancient History*, Oxford: Blackwell, 2974–2975.

Hultzsch, Eugen (1925), *Inscriptions of Aśoka: New Edition* (Corpus Inscriptionum Indicarum, 1), Oxford: Clarendon Press.

Jettmar, Karl, Ditte König and Volker Thewalt (eds) (1989), *Antiquities of Northern Pakistan: Reports and Studies, Vol. 1. Rock Inscriptions in the Indus Valley*, Mainz: Verlag Philipp von Zabern.

Keegan, Peter (2014), *Graffiti in Antiquity*, New York: Routledge.

Kielhorn, Franz (1890), 'Delhi Siwalik Pillar Inscriptions of Visaladeva: The Vikrama Year 1220', *The Indian Antiquary*, 19: 215–219.

Krishnaswamy Rao Sahib, C. S. and Amalananda Ghosh (1935), 'A Note on the Allahabad Pillar of Aśoka', *The Journal of the Royal Asiatic Society of Great Britain and Ireland*, 4: 697–706.

Kureishi, Maulvi Muhammad Hamid (1931), *List of Ancient Monuments Protected under Act VII of 1904 in the Province of Bihar and Orissa* (Archaeological Survey of India, New Imperial Series, 51), Calcutta: Government of India Central Publication Branch.

Lohmann, Polly (ed.) (2018), *Historische Graffiti als Quellen: Methoden und Perspektiven eines Jungen Forschungsbereichs*, Stuttgart: Franz Steiner.

Mukherji, Purna Chandra (1901), *A Report on a Tour of Exploration of the Antiquities of Kapilavastu, Tarai of Nepal during February and March, 1899* (Archaeological Survey of India, New Imperial Series, 26/1), Calcutta: Office of the Superintendent of Government Printing.

Neelis, Jason (2011), *Early Buddhist Transmission and Trade Networks: Mobility and Exchange within and beyond the Northwestern Borderlands of South Asia* (Dynamics in the History of Religion, 2), Leiden: Brill.

Neuss, Jürgen (2003), 'The Temple of Muṇḍeśvarī: Reconsidering the Evidence', *Berliner Indologische Studien*, 15–16–17: 531–585.

Paranavitana, S. (1956), *Sigiri Graffiti: Being Sinhalese Verses of the Eighth, Ninth and Tenth Centuries*, 2 vols, London: Oxford University Press.

Pargiter, F.E. (1911–1912), 'Two Records on the Pillar at Kosam', *Epigraphia Indica*, 11: 87–92.

Prinsep, James (1837), 'Note on the Facsimiles of the Various Inscriptions on the Ancient Column at Allahabad, Retaken by Captain Edward Smith, Engineers', *Journal of the Asiatic Society of Bengal*, 6: 963–980.

Priyanka, Benille (2010), *Recently Deciphered Records from the Mirror Wall at Sigiriya, 7th to 13th Centuries*, Colombo: Godage International Publishers.

Ragazzoli, Chloé, Ömür Harmanşah, Chiara Salvador and Elizabeth Frood (eds) (2018), *Scribbling through History: Graffiti, Places and People from Antiquity to Modernity*, London: Bloomsbury.

Rajan, K. (2015), *Early Writing System: A Journey from Graffiti to Brāhmī*, Madurai: Pandya Nadu Centre for Historical Research.

Ray, Himanshu Prabha (1987), 'Inscribed Potsherds: A Study', *Indica*, 24: 1–14.

Salomon, Richard (1976), 'New Inscriptions from the Muṇḍeśvarī Temple', *Journal of the Bihar Research Society*, 62: 104–108.

Salomon, Richard (1980), *Shell Inscriptions*, Calcutta: Centre for Advanced Study in Ancient Indian History and Culture, Calcutta University.

Salomon, Richard (1983), 'More New Inscriptions from Mundesvari', in Dineshchandra Sicar and Bratindra Nath Mukherjee (eds), *Sri Dinesacandrika, Studies in Indology: Shri D.C. Sircar Festschrift*, Delhi: Sundeep Prakashan, 73–78.

Salomon, Richard (1986), 'New Śaṅkhalipi (Shell Character) Inscriptions', *Studien zur Indologie und Iranistik*, 11–12: 109–152.

Salomon, Richard (1998), *Indian Epigraphy: A Guide to the Study of Inscriptions in Sanskrit, Prakrit, and the Other Indo-Aryan Languages (South Asia Research)*, New York: Oxford University Press.

Salomon, Richard (2002), 'A Jar with a Kharoṣṭhī Inscription', in Jens Braarvig (ed.), *Buddhist Manuscripts, Volume II* (Manuscripts in the Schøyen Collection, III), Oslo: Hermes Academic Publishing, 351–355.

Schopen, Gregory (1996), 'What's in a Name: The Religious Function of the Early Donative Inscriptions', in Vidya Dehejia (ed.), *Unseen Presence: The Buddha and Sanchi*, Bombay: Marg, 58–73.

Schopen, Gregory (2004), *Buddhist Monks and Business Matters: Still More Papers on Monastic Buddhism in India* (Studies in the Buddhist Traditions), Honolulu: University of Hawai'i Press.

Shokoohy, Mehrdad (1988), *Haryana I: The Column of Fīrūz Shāh and Other Islamic Inscriptions from the District of Hisar* (Corpus Inscriptionum Iranicarum, Part IV, Persian Inscriptions Down to the Early Safavid Period, Vol. 47, India: State of Haryana), London: School of Oriental and African Studies.

Sircar, Dinesh Chandra (1961–1962), 'Some Inscriptions from U.P.', *Epigraphia Indica*, 34: 243–254.

Stephen, Leslie (1886), 'Burrow, Reuben', in Leslie Stephen (ed.), *Dictionary of National Biography, Volume VII*, New York: Macmillan and Co., 448–449.

Strauch, Ingo (ed.) (2012), *Foreign Sailors on Socotra: The Inscriptions and Drawings from the Cave Hoq* (Vergleichende Studien zu Antike und Orient, 3), Bremen: Hempen Verlag.

Strauch, Ingo (2019), 'Buddhism in the West? Buddhist Indian Sailors on Socotra (Yemen) and the Role of Trade Contacts in the Spread of Buddhism', in Birgit Kellner (ed.), *Buddhism and the Dynamics of Transculturality: New Approaches* (Religion and Society, 64), Berlin: De Gruyter, 15–51.

Strauch, Ingo (forthcoming), 'Inscribed Pots and Potsherds from Āndhradeśa in the Context of Early Buddhist Archaeology', in Vincent Tournier, Akira Shimada and Arlo Griffiths (eds), *Early Āndhradeśa: Towards a Grounded History* (Gonda Indological Studies), Leiden and Boston: Brill.

Subrahmanyam, R. (1964), *Salihundam, a Buddhist Site in Andhra Pradesh* (Archaeological Series, 17), Hyderabad: Government of Andhra Pradesh.

Vogel, J. Ph. (1905–1906), 'Epigraphical Discoveries at Sarnath', *Epigraphia Indica*, 8: 166–179.
von Hinüber, Oskar (1989a), 'Brāhmī Inscriptions on the History and Culture of the Upper Indus Valley', in Jettmar, König and Thewalt 1989, 41–71.
von Hinüber, Oskar (1989b), 'Buddhistische Inschriften aus dem Tal des Oberen Indus (Inschriften Nr. 68–109)', in Jettmar, König and Thewalt 1989, 72–106.
Weise, Kati (2013), *The Sacred Garden of Lumbini: Perceptions of Buddha's Birthplace*, Paris: United Nations Educational, Scientific and Cultural Organization.

Carlo G. Cereti

Graffiti in Middle Iranian: Some Preliminary Notes

Abstract: This article aims to present a limited selection of Middle Iranian graffiti while proposing a definition of the term 'graffito' in the Iranian area. Middle Iranian languages were spoken over a vast region that stretches from Mesopotamia to Central Asia. Traditionally, scholars in our field consider the Middle Iranian period to cover the fourth century BCE to the end of the first millennium CE. The number of known written artefacts dating from this period has progressively increased and today we possess a sizeable epigraphic corpus, of which languages such as Middle Persian, Parthian and Sogdian take the lion's share. Here the author presents a selection of written artefacts that, on material and linguistic grounds, seem to better fit the idea of 'graffito', and briefly focuses on a few drawings scratched into palace walls in ancient Persepolis. Furthermore, the article aims at contributing to the growing debate on graffiti across different traditions, while remaining well aware that the definition of 'graffiti' in the Iranian area is still an open question and requires further discussion to establish a shared classification.

1 Introduction

The objective of this article is to present a limited selection of graffiti written in Middle Iranian languages over a vast area ranging from Mesopotamia to Central Asia, thus contributing to the discussion on the use of graffiti in the Iranian-speaking region. Middle Iranian languages were spoken over a period ranging from the fourth century BCE to the end of the first millennium CE and have left us a sizeable epigraphic corpus.[1] The definition of 'graffiti' in the Iranian area is still an open question, because this term has been used to define inscriptions and drawings that differ much from one another. On the one hand, many of the surviving Middle Iranian inscriptions were written or commissioned by persons of limited means, therefore being poorly written, painted or scratched on objects, walls or stone. However, some of the examples presented in this paper – though corresponding to the definition of graffiti from the point of view of the technique

1 On pre-Islamic Iranian epigraphic literature, see most recently Huyse 2009.

https://doi.org/10.1515/9783111326306-011

used – were commissioned by persons of high social standing. Therefore, an effort should be made to reach a comprehensive definition, including material properties, commissioning and content. As we shall see, graffiti, though often extremely concise, allow a privileged view into the life and beliefs of the people who wrote them, since the majority of these texts and drawings are devoid of the social and political constrictions typical of 'official' inscriptions and reliefs that are meant to convey a clear political message.

According to Peter Keegan, graffiti are 'one of the most visible (then) and least studied (now) methods of communicating thoughts and feelings in antiquity',[2] this being all the more true for the Iranian world. Not that graffiti have not been studied, since each of the ones that I will present here has been published to a high academic standard; rather, no theoretical study has yet been devoted to this specific means of communication. In fact, in our field, the very definition of what one should consider to be a 'graffito' is still unclear. Shall we rely on content, on realia, on a mixture of the two? Should we consider Prince Waxšahr's ownership inscription a 'graffito' on account of its material properties, or not? The famous figural graffiti realized by pre-Sasanian dynasts in Persepolis were certainly scratched into the walls of ancient Achaemenian palaces, but they were by no means illicit, being commissioned by the ruling elite (see further section 3). Whichever the choice, the considerable number of unofficial inscriptions known to the present day show that literacy, or at least some form of specialized literacy, must have been relatively widespread in the late antique and medieval Iranian world. In fact, in the first millennium of the Common Era, Iranian peoples wrote extensively, as is witnessed by the surviving inscriptions, religious traditions and remaining secular documents, however limited. Though less has survived than one may expect, the number of known Middle Iranian inscriptions is constantly on the rise. Several surviving inscriptions should be considered graffiti if one follows modern definitions such as that found in *Merriam-Webster Dictionary* ('usually unauthorized writing or drawing on a public surface')[3] or the *Concise Oxford English Dictionary* ('unauthorized writing or drawings on a surface in a public place')[4]. As a matter of fact, the great majority of Middle Iranian non-official inscriptions may be classified under the general heading of 'graffiti' at least from a technical point of view, since they were poorly inscribed in public spaces. However, in the given context, the notion of 'authorized' or 'licit' differs much from

2 Keegan 2014, xii.

3 'Graffiti', *Merriam-Webster.com Dictionary*, <https://www.merriam-webster.com/dictionary/graffiti> (accessed on 19 April 2023).

4 Stevenson and Waite 2011, 611.

today's definition. The graffiti found in Southern Khorasan and those discovered while building the Karakorum Highway in northern Pakistan (on both see section 2) were not officially authorized according to modern standards, but no one would consider them to be illicit when they were written. In fact, the graffiti carved by cultivated travellers at Persepolis and Bisotun until the early twentieth century show that the modern stigma against graffiti being written in public spaces is a recent development. In early Islamic times, a considerable number of Middle Persian funerary inscriptions were carved or scratched in far-away places escaping central control. Certainly, these were not authorized by any authority, but should one consider them 'illicit' because they were written by Zoroastrians? And what about the Middle Persian Kamfiruz inscription,[5] written in Middle Persian, but carrying a final line in Arabic showing that the deceased was probably a Muslim?

These and other questions can only be answered once a comprehensive survey of pictorial and inscriptional graffiti has been carried out, a task that long overshoots the limits of this paper. However, in the coming pages I shall try to introduce a limited selection of graffiti that may offer the interested reader some food for thought.

2 Middle Iranian graffiti

2.1 The beginnings

The more ancient attested Middle Iranian texts can be dated to a period bridging the late second and early first century BCE. While ostraca and Arameo-Iranian texts should not concern us here, inscriptions on silver vessels may at a stretch be considered graffiti, though they do not respect all criteria of the genre.[6] Inscriptions on vessels are attested throughout the Old and Middle Iranian periods and should be studied on their own. However, some are more important than others for understanding the development of script and language; therefore, the earliest text that I shall briefly present here is an inscription published on a silver bowl with gold inlay in the centre. The inscription runs along the outside of the

5 Asadi and Cereti 2018, 95–97.

6 On the evolution of Middle Iranian scripts from Aramaic, the fundamental work is still Henning 1958, 58–72; see further Skjærvø 1995 and 1996 as well as Huyse 2009, 84–86. On ostraca, see Huyse 2009, 102–105 with further bibliography; the vast majority of Parthian ostraca discovered at Nisa were published by Diakonov and Livshits (1976–2001), while a large collection of Middle Persian ostraca was published by Weber 1992.

rim and should probably be dated to the second half of the first century BCE (see Fig.1). It was studied by P. O. Skjærvø, who read it as follows:

> ʾrtḥštr MLKʾ AḤʾyn dʾrynkn BRH dʾryn MLKʾ šʾtḥw ZNH YNGDWN zl KSP s-20-20-10 wḥwḥštr BRBYTʾ NPŠH
>
> Of the brothers of King Ardaxšahr (II), the Dārid, son of King Dārāyān (II)! This bowl of *hammered gold-and-silver (weighs) 50 staters. Property of Prince Waxšahr.[7]

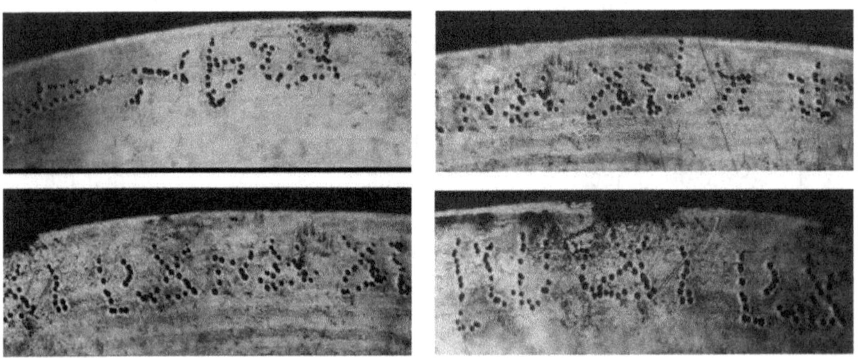

Fig. 1: Detail of the beginning of the inscription on the rim of the cup; after Skjærvø 1997, 96; courtesy of Prods Oktor Skjærvø and Carol Bromberg.

From a technical point of view, the inscription has been engraved using the pointillé technique, the letters being composed of a row of dots hammered into the metal. The alphabet used by the author of the ownership inscription closely resembles that attested on the coins of Dārāyān II, who likely reigned *c.* 50 BCE. Notwithstanding formal aspects that suggest classifying this inscription and similar ones under the wide umbrella of the genre we are here discussing, I believe that from the point of view of their content and commissioning, inscriptions on precious objects should not be considered to be graffiti tout court, but rather assigned to a related and very specific subgroup of texts.

7 The inscription was first published in Skjærvø 1997. My translation follows Skjærvø 1997, 11 with the improvements suggested by Sims-Williams 2021, 614–616. It only differs in the interpretation of dʾrynkn, which in my opinion could be the name of the dynasty. As rightly underlined by Sims-Williams 2021, 616, AḤʾyn is a problematic form, which he interprets as oblique plural ‘of the brothers’, against Skjærvø’s ‘our brother’. Semantics would here require rather the oblique singular ‘of the brother’ i.e. ‘belonging to the brother of…’.

2.2 Middle Persian and Parthian graffiti at Dura Europos, third century CE

Much later are the Middle Persian and Parthian graffiti and dipinti dating to the third century CE found at Dura Europos, which clearly belong to the genre.[8] Dura Europos was an important city and emporium founded under the Seleucids in 303 BCE, which flourished in the Parthian period and was destroyed by the Sasanian Šābuhr I in 256 CE. It was a multicultural urban centre that knew different dominations throughout its history, therefore it is no surprise that different religious cults are attested.[9] In the synagogue, we count twelve dipinti in ink written in Middle Persian, three Parthian graffiti and one long Middle Persian graffito on the north jamb of the main door. One Parthian and five Middle Persian dipinti were found in the House of Frescos. Two Parthian graffiti were discovered in the temple of Zeus Megistos at Dura Europos, one preserving a date that Henning has interpreted as being Seleucid or Seleucid Babylonian: 'ŠNT 522 YRḤ' ʾdʾr sḥt 11 pty ḥwnn' ('Jahr 522, Monat Addār, am elften des Morgens'),[10] respectively corresponding to March 221 or 212 CE according to the chosen era.[11] I will not discuss these materials further here, being convinced that they deserve to be studied as part of the complex archaeological and epigraphical context of Dura Europos in order to understand the relationship of each graffito or dipinto to the building in which it was found, and to the other texts and monuments discovered in the town.

2.3 Middle Persian inscriptions dating to the late Sasanian or early Islamic period

Switching now to a much later period, the majority of these texts likely date to the sixth to eighth centuries CE. Sasanian and early Islamic inscriptions written in cursive Middle Persian represent a large corpus that deserves to be further investigated in order to understand whether some or all these inscriptions should be classified as graffiti – a task that cannot be carried out here for lack of space. A considerable number of late Middle Persian inscriptions were written in the early

8 See Frye 1968 and the review article Brunner 1972. For a reassessment of the Iranian inscriptions in Dura Europos, see Grenet 1988.

9 See Leriche 1997 and MacKenzie 1997, the latter more specifically on the inscriptions.

10 In English: 'Year 522, month Addār, on the eleventh in the morning'.

11 Henning 1958, 41–42. Most Iranian documents from Dura Europos have been published in Frye 1968. However, he mentions but does not reproduce this graffito, which was originally published in Altheim and Stiehl 1953, 310, Figs 2–3.

Islamic centuries, the youngest ones dating to the early eleventh century CE. At this stage, Zoroastrian communities, though still numerically relevant, were confronted with a new political and social reality, having lost the power deriving from a century-long alliance with the throne. Known Middle Persian private inscriptions dating to the Sasanian and early Islamic periods have been assembled and discussed by Cyrus Nasrollahzadeh in a valuable work that opens doors to further research.[12] No doubt, some of these inscriptions should be considered to be graffiti, since they were commissioned and realized by commoners, without any specific authorization, by scratching into rocks in remote places. Others, more formal, cannot be considered to belong to this genre. A clear example of such are the funerary inscriptions recently discovered on the cliff of Kuh-e Hossein, not far from Naqsh-e Rostam.[13] In 2012, the French Archaeological Mission discovered a group of four finished and two unfinished niches at the base of a ca. 100 m cliff on the Kuh-e Hossein, about 3 km east-northeast of the monumental complex of Naqsh-e Rostam, across the plain from the historical city of Estakhr. These niches are accompanied by nine inscriptions of varying lengths, some indicating that the niches were Zoroastrian dakhmas hosting the bones of the deceased. The technique used here is quite similar to that attested for the Upper Indus graffiti, inscriptions being 'sgraffiate' into the rock's outer patina. Though no inscription of this group bears a date, chances are that the funerary area where these graffiti were found dates to the early Islamic era, when Zoroastrian communities of the era performed rituals for their deceased in far-away areas so as not to provoke the harsh reaction of the new Muslim overlords. One of the inscriptions belonging to this group reads (Fig. 2):

> ZNH dḥmkyḥ ḥwrdt-gwšnsp Y
> wyḥ'wḥrmzddt NPŠH ('Y)T
> wḥšt(') p'ḥlwm
> bḥl YḤWWN't

> This is the own dakhma (*daxma*) of Hordād-Gušnasp (son) of Weh-Ohrmazd-dād; may paradise be his best lot.[14]

12 Nasrollahzadeh 1398 SH.

13 See further Cereti and Gondet 2015.

14 Cereti and Gondet 2015, 386 and 388, Fig. 10. For a different reading see Nasrollahzadeh 1398 SH, vol. 1, 169–170.

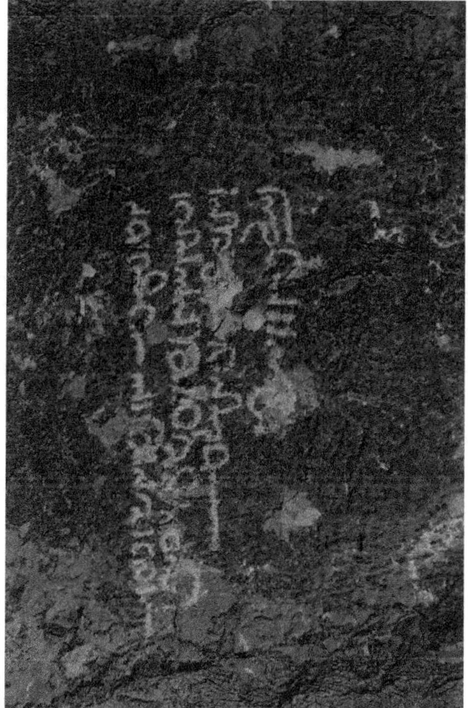

Fig. 2: Kuh-e Hossein, inscription no. 9; after Cereti and Gondet 2005, 388, Fig. 10; reproduced with permission.

2.3.1 Two corpora of rock-cut graffiti

It is now time to focus on two areas that have preserved significant corpora of graffiti: Southern Khorasan in Iran and the Upper Indus region in Pakistan. The present-day administrative region of Southern Khorasan in the Islamic Republic of Iran covers an area where Western Iranian languages were spoken in pre-Islamic times. In fact, the presence of such a concentration of Parthian graffiti in the area shows the survival of a living tradition of the North-Western Iranian tongue that had been the language spoken in the Arsacid courts, a tradition that survived not only in official usage – i.e., the trilingual or bilingual inscriptions of the early Sasanian kings – but also in day-to-day usage. Further east, in present-day Pakistan, the clusters of graffiti found in the Upper Indus region demonstrate the presence of lively Iranian (mainly Sogdian) merchant communities in the Indo-Iranian border regions.

These two graffiti corpora have many similarities between them. Both groups consist of pictorial and textual graffiti scratched into cliffs, rocks and stones; both contexts present collections of texts and drawings that were scratched into stones by commoners and not due to the will of the court. The first group includes graffiti found in two separate valleys near Birjand, in Southern Khorasan, that may well be connected with each other; the second group, much larger in size, includes the graffiti written in Middle Iranian languages, mainly Sogdian, but also Bactrian, Parthian and Middle Persian, which were discovered at different sites in the Upper Indus area of northern Pakistan. The Upper Indus graffiti were published by Nicholas Sims-Williams in 1989 in a magnificent two-volume set, the *Corpus Inscriptionum Iranicarum*, complete with a very good set of photographs.[15] On the contrary, the South Khorasan inscriptions have been studied in a number of different publications, the great majority published in Iran, and still lack complete and reliable documentation.[16] These two complexes constitute, in my opinion, the two most important areas for the study of graffiti in the pre-Islamic Iranian world, showing that graffiti were common both in eastern and western Iran, and attested in several Middle Iranian languages. It is not easy to date the different corpora mentioned in this paragraph. Excluding the texts in Persian and Arabic found at Lakh Mazar, which may be much more recent, Middle Iranian graffiti should be dated between the third and seventh century CE.

2.3.2 Southern Khorasan near Birjand, present-day Iran

Two very important sites bearing Middle Iranian graffiti are found in Southern Khorasan, not far from each other. Lakh Mazar (Lāẖ Māzar) hosts numerous graffiti written in Parthian, Middle Persian, New Persian and Arabic. The texts found at Kal Jangal (Kāl-e Jangāl) are in Parthian. As a matter of fact, Kal Jangal and Lakh Mazar both feature figurative and textual graffiti, which may point to their having one and the same group of writers, as recently suggested by Rasul Bashash Khanzaq (Bašāš-Kanzaq), who identifies the family name Wīštīwēn at both sites. However, his interpretation of the inscriptions as belonging to a group of Mazdakites that found refuge in this area of South Khorasan, known as Kuhestān,

15 Sims-Williams 1989b.

16 See *infra*. For an assessment of the main publications on the subject, see recently Pourshariati and Alimoradi 2022.

needs further proof.[17] A recent article by Parvaneh Pourshariati and Pooriya Alimoradi has reassessed the evidence, and the authors have done valuable work on the inscriptions, particularly by bringing together information often published in volumes that are not easily accessible. Nevertheless, some aspects of their paper demand further discussion, specifically the religious interpretation of the texts and symbols found at these sites, which, according to Pourshariati and Alimoradi's argument, should be assigned to an aristocratic Parthian household worshipping Mithra.

Several carvings were discovered at Kal Jangal, near Birjand, at different stages.[18] The most impressive of these is a drawing measuring 164 × 123 cm, presenting a well-drawn if somewhat disproportionate picture of a man dressed in Parthian clothes fighting a large feline (Fig. 3), which is accompanied by a two-line inscription. The text reads 'gry'rtḥštr nḥwdr W ḥštrp' (Prefect and satrap of Gar-Ardašir) and may lack the first line, possibly carrying the name of the character depicted on the rock.[19] This graffito was dated by Henning[20] to the early years of the Sasanian dynasty. The argument used by the German scholar is disputable, since it was based mainly on the occurrence of the toponym Gari Artaxšaθr/Gar-Ardašir, containing the name of the first sovereign of the first king of this line, as well as on the style of drawing, which has few if any parallels.

Moreover, the man's profile faces right, as Arsacid sovereigns do on their coins, while Sasanian kings face left. In fact, these drawings were probably influenced by the Parthian tradition, though an early Sasanian date should by no means be excluded.[21] Moreover, Rasul Bashahsh has been able to identify a very similar iconography on a seal originally published by Ernst Herzfeld. The seal

17 See Bašāš-Kanzaq 1379 SH, 1382 SH and 1394 SH; Bašāš-Kanzaq and Soltāni 1387 SH. Though not impossible, we have no proof to say that when Kawād was chased from the throne by angered nobles who sided with his brother, a group of Mazdakites took refuge in the Reč mountains, nor do the graffiti present evidence pointing in this direction. Remarkably, however, according to the foundation story narrated in the *Qesse-ye Sanjān* and in the *Qesse-ye Zartoštiān-e Hendustān*, after the Islamic conquest of Iran and before migrating to India, the Zoroastrian communities that were later known as Parsis took refuge in a 'Kuhestān', which may be identified with the Kuhestān of Khorasan; see further Cereti 1991, 36 and 94 and Williams 2009, 74–75.

18 On the graffiti found at Kal Jangal and Lakh Mazar, see most recently Pourshariati and Alimoradi 2022, presenting an up-to-date and very detailed report of the *status quaestionis* as well as several innovative suggestions.

19 Following Henning 1958, 42. For a different and to my mind less convincing translation, see Pourshariati and Alimoradi 2022, 339.

20 Henning 1953, 134–135. This graffito is part of a larger group preliminarily studied in Rezāi and Kiyā 1320 YZ.

21 See Bašāš-Kanzaq and Soltāni 1387 SH, 50 for a bird's-eye view of earlier studies.

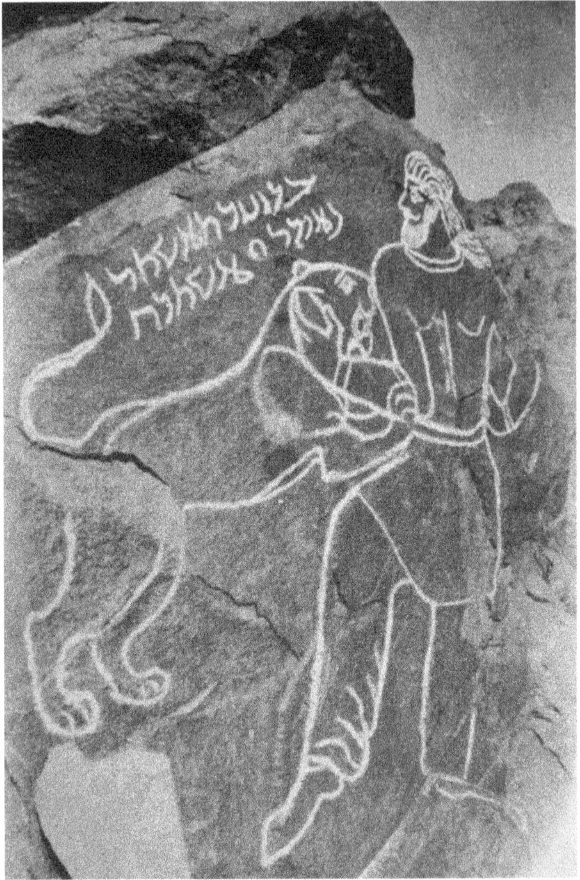

Fig. 3: Graffito from Kal Jangal: after Henning 1977, Plate XXVII; reproduced with permission.

depicts a man fighting a lion and carries a short Middle Persian inscription, suggesting it dates to the Sasanian period (Fig. 4).[22] This combination of drawing and inscription should, in my opinion, definitely be considered a graffito, and indeed a remarkable one on account of the quality of both handwriting and drawing. A number of other graffiti were discovered in the valley of Kal Jangal, some already known to Jamal Rezai (Rezāi) and Sadeq Kia (Kiyā), others first presented and

22 Bašāš-Kanzaq and Soltāni 1387 SH, 74; Herzfeld 1941, Plate CXXXI.

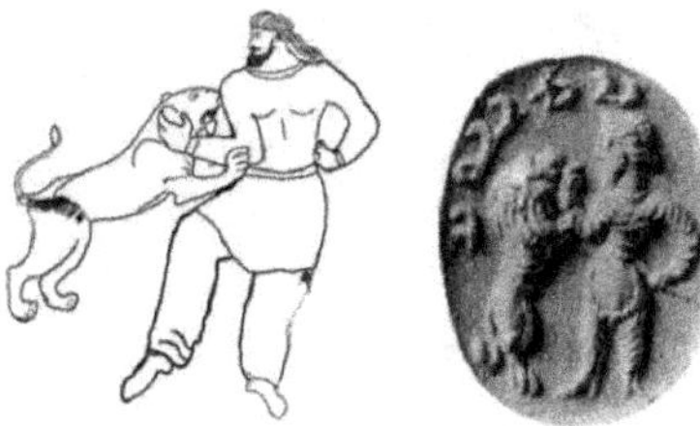

Fig. 4: Rock drawing from Kal Jangal with seal impression for comparison; after Bašāš-Kanzaq and Soltāni 1387 SH, 74, Fig. 12; courtesy of Meysam Labāf-Ḫāniki and Rajab'Ali Labāf-Ḫāniki.

studied by Bashash.[23] A second relevant graffito shows a male bust looking to the right, accompanied by a Parthian inscription that may be read 'wyštywyny l'šty(gw)', thus providing a parallel with the inscriptions found in Lakh Mazar.[24] The agnatic name wyštwyny /Wīštīwēn/, admitting that this be the correct reading, also occurs in other Kal Jangal inscriptions, most clearly on graffito no. 2, found on a rock carrying three different texts (Fig. 5).[25] Here lines 1 and 2 may be read 'mtrwk ZY wyštywynyn' '/Mihrōk čē Wīštīwēnīn/'.[26] Other inscriptions were read by Rasul Bashash, but the available photos do not allow us to check the readings put forth by the Iranian scholar.[27] The presence of the agnatic name Wīštīwēn connects these graffiti with a second group of texts found in the mountain range of Kuh-e Reč, this being the name of the westernmost ridge of the Kuh-e Bāqrān range in Southern Khorasan.

The complex of Lakh Mazar was discovered in the month of Ordibehešt 1371 (April–May 1992) in the village of Kuč, twenty-nine kilometres south-east of Birjand, by an archaeological team led by Rajabʿ Ali Labbaf-Khaniki (Labāf-Ḫāniki).

23 Rezāi and Kiyā 1320 YZ document five rocks into which graffiti were carved; according to Henning 1953, 133, they can be summed up as follows: '(a) A rock-drawing of a man and a lion, accompanied by a Parthian inscription [...] (b) A rock-drawing of a male bust [...] with damaged Parthian inscription [...] (c) Fragments of seven further inscriptions, all apparently in Parthian'. Further material is presented in Bašāš-Kanzaq 1379 SH, 1382 SH and 1394 SH as well as Bašāš-Kanzaq and Soltāni 1387 SH, showing that the site should be further investigated.

24 See Bašāš-Kanzaq and Soltāni 1387 SH, 54–55 for photos and commentary. However, the reading of the second word is far from certain. This inscription was known to Henning, who suggested a reading wyšt'ny k'štyr(wk), comparing the first word to the proper name 'Hystanes | Histanes | Bisthanes' (Henning 1953, 133 n. 2).

25 See Bašāš-Kanzaq and Soltāni 1387 SH, 58–59.

26 On -*īn*, see Durkin-Meisterernst 2014, 197–203.

27 See Bašāš-Kanzaq and Soltāni 1387 SH, 55–58 for the suggestions put forth by the Iranian scholar.

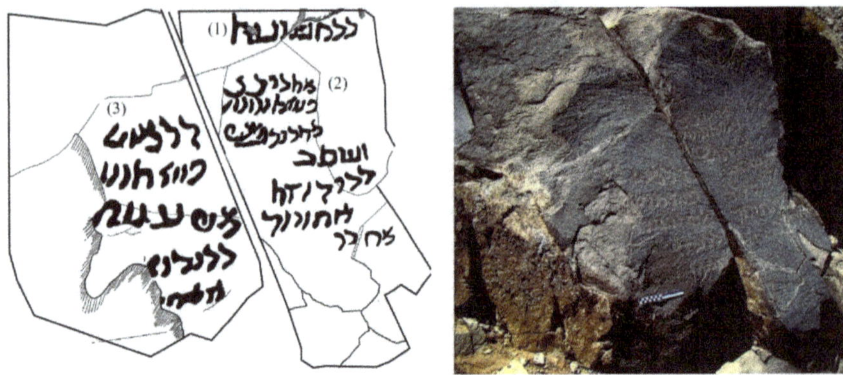

Fig. 5: Graffiti from Kal Jangal; photograph and drawing after Bašāš-Kanzaq and Soltāni 1387 SH, 58, Fig. 7; courtesy of Meysam Labāf-Ḫāniki and Rajab'Ali Labāf-Ḫāniki.

According to the report, the stone cliff known as Lakh Mazar carries 22 human and 33 animal figures, 22 vegetable motifs, 35 symbols, 4 calligraphies, 81 Parthian and Middle Persian inscriptions, 34 Arabic and 8 Persian inscriptions and 68 other drawings.[28] This shows that the site was in use over a long period of time, at least from the Sasanian to the Islamic period.[29] Remarkably, the graffiti found at Lakh Mazar on a 5 × 5 m rock slab are much smaller than the ones found at Kal Jangal, the former having letters measuring an average of 1 × 1 cm compared to the 5 × 5 cm of the latter site.[30] The historical context of these texts and drawings has been understood differently by the diverse authors that have written about Lakh Mazar. According to Rasul Bashash, the graffiti witness the existence of a community of Mazdakites who went into hiding after King Kawād had gone into exile.[31] To the contrary, Livshits has labelled the inscriptions as being written by 'Parthians joking',[32] while Parvaneh Pourshariati believes that these texts may provide evidence for Mithra worship in the area.[33] Pourshariati and Pooriya Alimoradi

28 Labāf-Ḫāniki and Bašāš-Kanzaq 1373 SH, 38.

29 See further Labāf-Ḫāniki and Bašāš-Kanzaq 1373 SH, 23–38, though many of the drawings are difficult to date.

30 Bašāš-Kanzaq 1379 SH, 98; Pourshariati and Alimoradi 2022, 336.

31 See Labāf-Ḫāniki and Bašāš-Kanzaq 1373 SH, 72–74. Bashash also believes that the Parthian texts may bear witness to the performance of the coming-of-age ceremony that the Parsis call Navjot(e).

32 Livshits 2002.

33 Pourshariati and Alimoradi 2022.

conveniently summarize the history of research on this monument in a recent article.[34] Remarkably, most authors agree in dating these graffiti to the Sasanian period and if one were to accept Bashash's suggestion, these Parthian texts may date to the late fifth or early sixth century CE. Such a late dating would show that the Parthian alphabet was current in eastern Iran until the end of Sasanian dominion, in a version still close to the one attested in Sasanian royal inscriptions. These texts were written by members of the Wīštīwēn family and vary from very simple writings – similar to the ones found in other Iranian and non-Iranian contexts, such as the Upper Indus graffiti, Pompei or any of the many Middle Eastern towns that were inhabited by diversified populations in antiquity – to slightly more complex ones that, content-wise, bring to mind modern graffiti.

Simple texts may include a personal name followed by a patronymic (Fig. 6):

> pyrwc ZY wyštywynyn
> wrḥr'm ZY wyštywynyn
> Pērōz of (the) Wīštīwēn – Wahrām of (the) Wīštīwēn

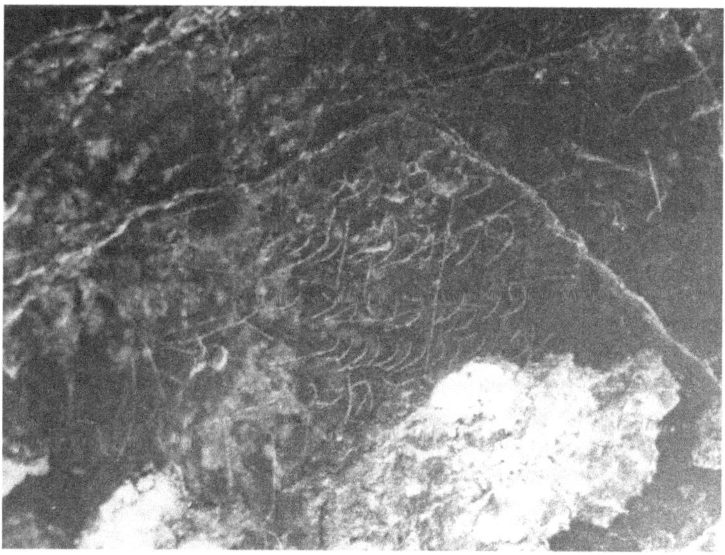

Fig. 6: Graffito from Lakh Mazar; after Labāf-Ḫāniki and Bašāš-Kanzaq 1373 SH, 59; courtesy of Meysam Labāf-Ḫāniki and Rajab'Ali Labāf-Ḫāniki.

34 Pourshariati and Alimoradi 2022, 331–332.

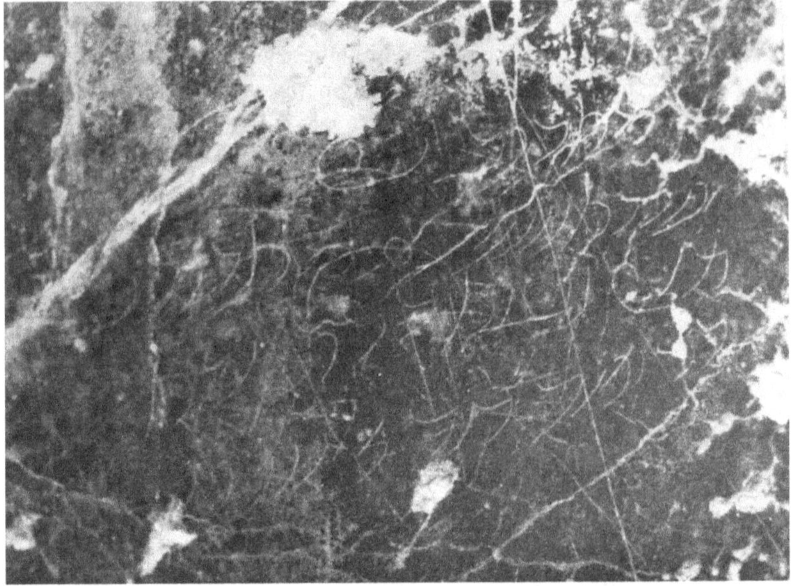

Fig. 7: Graffito from Lakh Mazar; after Labāf-Ḫāniki and Bašāš-Kanzaq 1373 SH, 63; courtesy of Meysam Labāf-Ḫāniki and Rajab'Ali Labāf-Ḫāniki.

More complex is a text exalting the capacities of another member of the Wīštīwēn family in acting as a guide (Fig. 7):[35]

> mtrwb[n] ZY
> wyštywynyn W mtrwbn[w]
> MNW n'yt drwdšt
> (W *dryst) sr ḤWYt
> Mihrbān of (the) Wīštīwēn. Mehrbān, he whom he leads, reaches the end (of the trip) sound and well.

A third inscription provides an interesting insight into the daily life of the persons who wrote these texts (Fig. 8). It has been interpreted in different ways by Bashash

35 On this graffito, see the different interpretations found in Labāf-Ḫāniki and Bašāš-Kanzaq 1373 SH, 63; Livshits 2002, 27–34; Pourshariati and Alimoradi 2022, 338. Here I suggest that we have a hendyadys construction joining the synonyms Pth. *druwišt* and Middle Persian *drīst*. However, reading dryst requires emending. Another very similar inscription is reported by Labāf-Ḫāniki and Bašāš-Kanzaq 1373 SH, 61 and commented on by the other authors; in my opinion, it should be read: mtrwb[n ZY wyš]tywynyn MNW n'yt drwdšt s[...]. Here I share Livshits's (2002, 35 n. 18) comments on the untenability of the last words as reported by Bashash.

and Livshits, Alimoradi's translation being closer to the one proposed by the former author.

> ʾrtḥštr
> ḥwtwy pty
> ḤMR ʾyysyt
> pty ḤMR MH
> ʾnywš
> Lord Ardaxšir comes forth in wine, in the wine of oblivion.

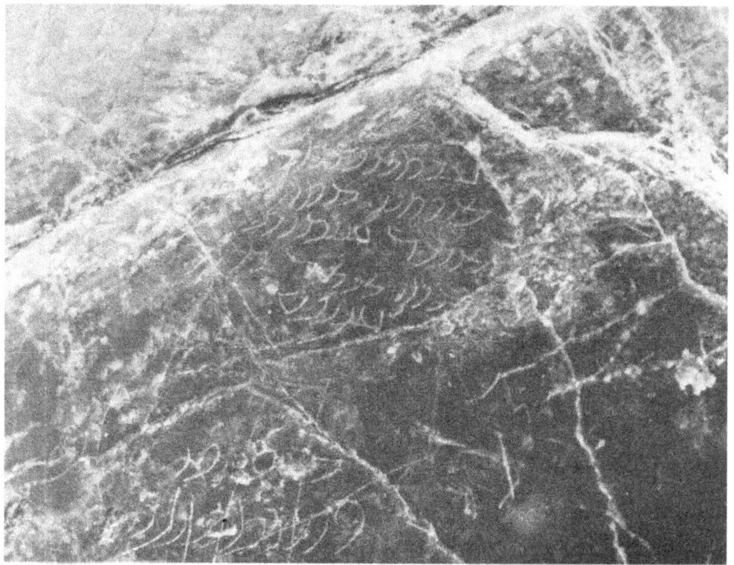

Fig. 8: Graffito from Lakh Mazar; after Labāf-Ḫāniki and Bašāš-Kanzaq 1373 SH, 58; courtesy of Meysam Labāf-Ḫāniki and Rajab'Ali Labāf-Ḫāniki.

Livshits translates the text: 'Lord Ardaxšīr comes upon a donkey, the donkey which is out of his mind (lit. "which is mad")'. His rendering is based on the assumption that here the heterogram 'ḤMR' does not render Pth. *maδ*, as common in the Nisa ostraca, but rather the almost homograph Pth 'ḤMR[ʾ], MP ḤMRʾʾ attested once in the Paikuli inscription.[36]

---

36 Paikuli inscription § 58, Pth. 25, MP 28, Skjærvø 1983a, 54 and 1983b, 93. Livshits (2002, 35 n. 20) suggests the existence of two homographic heterograms in Parthian, one deriving from Aramaic *ḥámar* 'wine' and the other from Aramaic *ḥęmắr* 'donkey, ass'. However, the Paikuli

The informal and relaxed mood revealed by this text is confirmed by other graffiti, such as the following one (Fig. 9):

(*ptkr) ZNH kyrt
wyštyw[y]n mtrwbnw ʾrtḥ[štr]
W MNW p[ty] ZNH *ptkr ḤMR
ʾKLW W šʾt [...] ʾKLW
wyštywyn [...]
Mihrbān (and) Ardaxšir Wīštīwēn made this drawing. Whoever drinks wine on this drawing and happily drinks [...], Wīštīwēn [...].

The reading and interpretation of the word that I have tentatively read '*ptkr' are extremely doubtful. Livshits[37] suggests reading 'ḥršk' (bear), while Bashash[38] and Alimoradi[39] prefer to read 'prsb' (beam). Unfortunately, the available photographs do not allow for a better reading.

I believe that the overall frame of mind betrayed by these graffiti is closer to that suggested by Livshits than to what either Bashash or Pourshariati have put forth, though I do not share all the philological choices made by Livshits. The general mood revealed by these texts is one of merrymaking and hilarity, while there is no evidence to suggest that the inscriptions belong to a specific religious community. On the contrary, I believe that Wīštīwēn stands a good chance of being a (pro-)patronymic defining the agnatic group responsible – should the suggested readings be correct – for both the graffiti found at Kal Jangal and those of Lakh Mazar. The presence of these inscriptions and drawings in the region of Birjand raises a number of questions that require more research and better documentation. Why were these graffiti carved and who carved them? Were they written by members of the local society or by a group of exiles hiding away because of their religious beliefs? What is their age? What can they tell us about the continuing use of the Parthian alphabet in eastern Iran? Only further field research and a full documentation of both the pictorial and inscriptional graffiti will allow scholars to answer these questions.

evidence does not confirm this. The MP form of the heterogram for *xar* 'donkey' is ḤMRʾ and Parthian probably used the same. The last letter of the Parthian heterogram occurs in a block that was not available to Humbach and Skjærvø, but has now been recovered by MAIKI (Missione Archeologica Italiana nel Kurdistan Iracheno). Unfortunately, the beginning of the first line of block e11 is not entirely readable, though the surviving traces are compatible with the presence of a [-ʿ], which would disprove Livshits's hypothesis.

37 Livshits 2002, 34.

38 Labāf-Ḫāniki and Bašāš-Kanzaq 1373 SH, 62.

39 Pourshariati and Alimoradi 2022, 338.

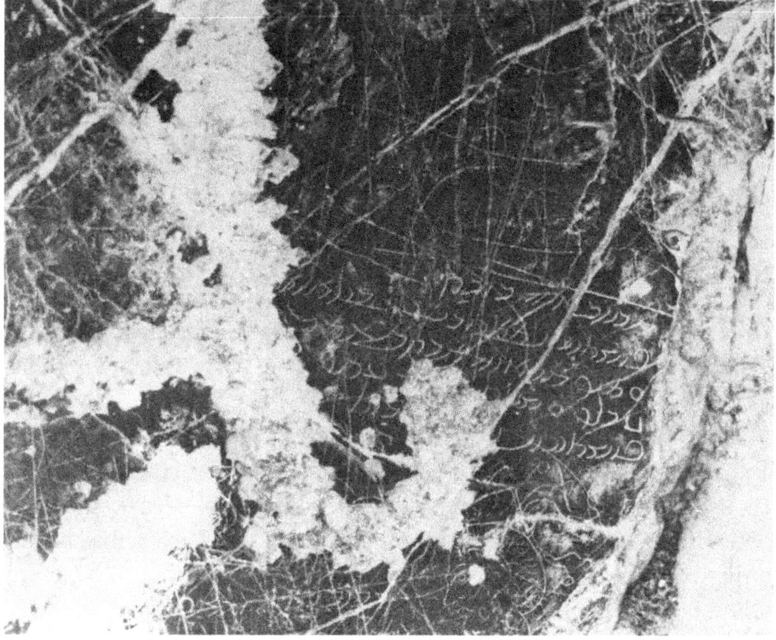

Fig. 9: Graffito from Lakh Mazar; after Labāf-Ḫāniki and Bašāš-Kanzaq 1373 SH, 62; courtesy of Meysam Labāf-Ḫāniki and Rajab'Ali Labāf-Ḫāniki.

Whoever wrote the graffiti in Southern Khorasan had a good command of both script and language, coupled with excellent drawing skills. Moreover, the physical dimensions of these graffiti, which were simply scratched into the rock's surface, were small in Lakh Mazar, and larger, but not monumental, in Kal Jangal; the fact that they are not found on long-distance communication routes, but rather on roads of regional importance all testify to the fact that the texts and drawings were made (or commissioned) by the local population. Should they date to the Sasanian period, as suggested by the similarity of the script to that attested on Sasanian royal inscriptions and some stylistic traits of the drawings,[40] these graffiti would point to the existence of a fine level of literacy in Parthian among inhabitants of the region until a relatively late period. Moreover, the wide variety of scripts and styles attested shows that these graffiti were engraved over a long period of time. Finally, the subject matter of the Parthian graffiti allows us a

40 See Callieri 2006, 141, who suggests that on account of their similarity to busts attested on Hephtalite gems, some of the drawings found at Lakh Mazar could date to the fifth century CE.

welcome insight into the habits of commoners of the era, showing what their day-to-day behaviours were, what clothes they wore, what symbols they used.

2.3.3 Graffiti in the Upper Indus valley (Karakoum Highway, present-day Pakistan)

Further east, on the upper course of the Indus River, in present-day northern Pakistan, travellers and merchants roaming this important communication artery left us a treasure house of graffiti written in many different languages. The majority of these graffiti were written in Indian scripts, but a compact group of Iranian texts also exists.

In 1979, once the Karakorum Highway was completed, Karl Jettmar and Ahmad H. Dani began a survey in the Upper Indus area that led to the documentation of thousands of petroglyphs and inscriptions on both sides of the river, mainly between the village of Shatial and the town of Chilas, as well as further north, in the Hunza region, where the sacred rock of Haldaikish is to be found. The existence of a vast number of graffiti had been known for decades and a few of them had already been studied by Aurel Stein in 1944, but it was only the opening of the Karakorum Highway that made this project feasible.[41]

In addition to texts written in Brāhmī, Kharoṣṭhī, Chinese and other scripts and languages, more than 600 Middle Iranian inscriptions, 410 of which are still readable, were discovered and documented. Two of these inscriptions are written in Parthian, two in Middle Persian and ten in Bactrian; the others are all in Sogdian.[42]

From a chronological point of view, one can only remark that the script is closer to that attested by the Ancient Letters (early fourth century CE) than to the style attested by the Mt. Mugh documents (early eighth century). Considering also Sims-Williams's remarks on the attested personal names, which verify the presence of western personal names pointing to the Sasanian period, it is likely that

41 See Jettmar 1989, xi–lvii for a detailed introduction to the project and to earlier studies. In our context, his discussion of the terms used to define the Upper Indus petroglyphs (*sgraffiti*, *graffiti*) as well as his technical observations on the means used to inscribe them into the rocks are very interesting (Jettmar 1989, xv–xviii). In my opinion, on semantic, social and material grounds, these petroglyphs fully correspond to the modern (and classical) definition of graffiti.

42 See Sims-Williams 1989b, I, 8. The Iranian inscriptions were published in 1989 by Nicholas Sims-Williams in a magnificent two-volume set, the *Corpus Inscriptionum Iranicarum*. See volume 1, 8–9 for a short introduction.

these graffiti were mostly realized between the fourth and sixth century CE.[43] More than nine-tenths of all Sogdian graffiti have been found at Shatial I, a phenomenon that warrants explanation. Jettmar believes that this concentration may depend on the presence of a border or emporium in Shatial:

> A disturbing question is still open: Several hundred Iranian inscriptions (surely more than 90% of those known from Northern Pakistan) are concentrated in the western wing of the site Shatial Bridge, on rocks spread over a steep slope, leading down to the left bank of the Indus. They are intermingled with many Brahmi inscriptions, together with some other scripts and languages.
> The eastern wing of the site, however, now called Shatial II or Shatial East, has almost exclusively Brahmi inscriptions (an isolated Sogdian palaeograph was recently observed). Here, stupa-carvings are most numerous. We are definitely in another cultural setting. There is no reasonable chance of getting an explanation of the difference between eastern and western wing by chronology; for they are contemporary or at least overlapping. And what was the reason that Sogdian inscriptions are rare in most of the other sites in the Indus valley east of Shatial Bridge?
> [...] Should the site Shatial Bridge not be explained as an emporium, situated on the fringe of the territory normally permitted to Sogdian caravans? Was it the place where the traders exchanged their goods against Indian exports brought by partners from Gandhara, Taxila and Urasa? Maybe one of the Chinese inscriptions refers to this situation. One word might be translated as 'mountain pass' but also as 'transition' or 'boundary' – as I was informed by H. FRANKE and D. SECKEL.
> In this interpretation one problem remains, i.e. that all inscriptions – Sogdian as well as those in Brahmi – are situated on the southern bank of the Indus.
> The river below the inscriptions is not broad – but swift, even raging. Travellers [sic] using skin rafts crossed the Indus a few miles upstream – at the mouth of the Harban valley. There it was even possible to bring horses to the opposite embankment by using flat barges (as it was in 1955, when I myself had to cross there). The problem can be solved by assuming that the Indus could be crossed near Shatial by a bridge, broad enough and solidly constructed so that it could be used by riders and pack-animals. Such bridges must have existed in the heyday of the Trans-Karakorum Traffic System (5th–8th century A.D.). A bridge connecting the banks of the Gilgit river, over a distance of an arrow-shot and suitable for cavalry is mentioned in a Chinese report. [...] Such a laborious construction was certainly well guarded.

43 Jettmar (1989, xliii) summarizes the different positions as follows: 'LIVSIC dated the earliest inscriptions within the 3rd to 4th centuries A.D., others between the 5th to 8th centuries; but in some cases even the 9th century would be acceptable to him. HUMBACH assumed that at least a part of the Sogdian inscriptions are contemporary with Sanskrit inscriptions of the 5th and 6th centuries A.D. The rest might be earlier, nearer to the famous Sogdian "Ancient Letters", which were found in or near watchtowers of the "Tun-huang Limes" by Aurel STEIN. SIMS-WILLIAMS insists that the "Ancient Letters" were correctly attributed by HENNING to the beginning of the 4th century (312/313 A.D.). The date proposed by J. HARMATTA (1979: 164), at the end of the 2nd century A.D., is rejected by him'. See further Sims-Williams 1989a, 133–134, who also argues that the presence of numerous West Iranian personal names points to the Sasanian period.

> Accordingly, I concluded that the power controlling the access from the northern side, protecting the Sogdian merchants, had a fortified bridgehead on the southern bank. So I named a suitable place overlooking the site Shatial I and easy to defend 'Shatial Fort'. In the meantime, Dr THEWALT found the remains of stone walls closing the gaps between the natural barriers – so my prediction was justified [...].[44]

Personal names attested in the inscriptions show that the Sogdians and other Iranians who traded at Shatial still followed the old ways, worshipping their ancient divinities.[45] The discovery of drawings of fire altars in the area points in this same direction.[46]

The majority of Sogdian graffiti are simple in structure. Some mention only the name of the person writing, such as no. 1 'nnyprn'; many also contain the name of the father, such as no. 23 'p'p'k ZK kwš''n BRY' (Pābag the son of Kušān).[47] Remarkably, feminine names are also attested, though rarely:

no. 371 xnsc | δwyt'kkh | cyn'nch
'Chinanch (the) daughter of Khansach'[48]

However, more complex texts are also attested, such as the following:

no. 92 βrzyr'k | 'β(y)'mnβntk ZKy | m'ymrγc | BRYN
'Varzirak (and) Avyaman-vandak the sons of Maymarghch'. (Fig. 10)

44 Jettmar 1989, xliv–xlvi.
45 Sims-Williams 1989a, 134–136.
46 See further Jettmar (1989, xlviii–xlix): 'Among the rock-carvings observed in Shatial Fort we find the impressive representation of a fire-altar, rather low and broad, with two horns and a central funnel-shaped spout. The shape is similar, but not identical, with that seen on coins of the Iranian Huns [...]. There, such compact fire-altars are flanked by two attendants. Below, we see two wheels connected by a curved line like a pair of spectacles upside down. The name of the ruler mentioned on the front-side of such coins was Narendra or Narana. GÖBL is convinced that such coins belong to a relatively late period in the history of the Hunnic tribes in India, between 570/80–600 A.D. Then, he concludes, defeated in the plains and even losing their grip on Kashmir, they returned via present-day Afghanistan to their northern starting position. Maybe the occurrence of the typical fire-altar at Shatial Fort means that the Hephthalite rulers who had formerly controlled the bridgehead were now replaced by "White Huns" (Chionites) who had their base in the south. This would explain an inscription in Brahmi observed near the fire-altar'.
47 Sims-Williams 1989b, I, 13 and 14, respectively.
48 Sims-Williams 1989b, I, 29 and II, 31. Sims-Williams remarks on the fact that here the name of the father precedes that of the daughter, perhaps out of respect. However, in another occurrence of a feminine name, this is not the case: no. 18 **sn'xr'mh | ZKh pry-•δ•••h |γ'th** 'Sanakhram the (daughter) of Fri- ... (the **γ'th**)'. See Sims-Williams 1989b, I, 13 and II, 31.

no. 304 cwz'kk | ZK wn'ynk BRY | 'ḤRZY šy | 'Ḥ(Y) š'ns 'BY | wkw(r) βγ'
'Chuzakk the son of Wanenak (came here) (?), and his brother Shans (and his) father (and) the heads (?) of the family'.[49] (Fig. 11)

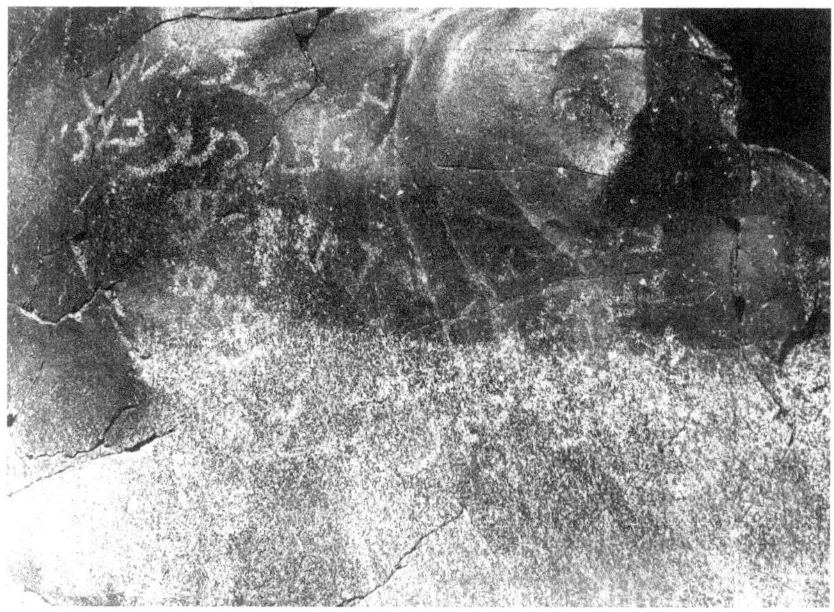

Fig. 10: Upper Indus graffito no. 92; after Sims-Williams 1989b, Plate 35a; courtesy of Nicholas Sims-Williams and *Corpus Inscriptionum Iranicarum*.

The longest of Sogdian inscriptions attested at Shatial attests the existence of a shrine in the area and reports the name of either the temple itself or the divine being worshipped (Fig. 12):[50]

no. 254 nnyβntk | ZK nrsβ| ''γt-kym | kw 10 'ḤRZY | MN k'rt | βyncytk | y'n pt'|yst 't | xrβntn | twxtr | pr'ys'n | rty ZKw | 'ḤY pr | šyr wyn|'n 'M wyš'
(I,) Nanai-vandak the (son) of Narisaf, has come (here) on (the) ten(th day) and asked a boon from the spirit of the sacred place K'rt that ... I may arrive (home?) more quickly and see (my) brother in good (health) with joy.[51]

49 Sims-Williams 1989b, I, 26 and II, 33.
50 Sims-Williams 1989a, 133: 'Here the word *k'rt-* appears to be a name, either of the *βyn-* "sacred place" (presumably the Shatial site) or of its "spirit"'.
51 Sims-Williams 1989b, I, 23 and II, 33.

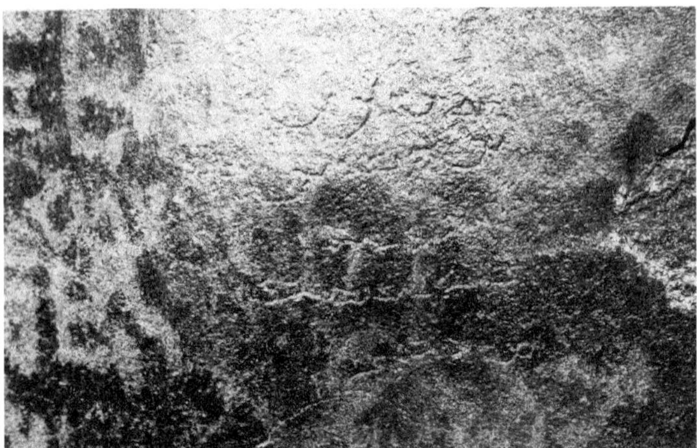

Fig. 11: Upper Indus graffito no. 304; after Sims-Williams 1989b, Plate 131b; courtesy of Nicholas Sims-Williams and *Corpus Inscriptionum Iranicarum*.

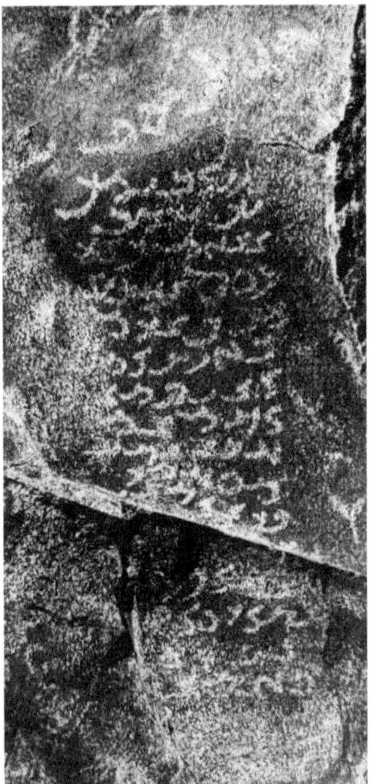

Fig. 12: Upper Indus Graffito no. 254; after Sims-Williams 1989b, Plate 111a; courtesy of Nicholas Sims-Williams and *Corpus Inscriptionum Iranicarum*.

Other than Sogdian, the Upper Indus corpus also contains two inscriptions in Middle Persian, two in Parthian and twelve in Bactrian. All these inscriptions are very short and often incomplete. The two more interesting ones are no. 410, in Parthian: 'wryḥrn | šḥypwḥrn' (Wahrām son of Šābuhr), featuring the Middle Persian forms of these names, which were also the names of two sovereigns of the Sasanian dynasty;[52] and no. 52, in Bactrian: ναμω βοτο 'homage to the Buddha', attesting a religious belief that, though rare among Iranians, was widespread among those who wrote in Brāhmī in the same area.[53]

3 Pictorial graffiti

Before reaching the end of this paper, a few words about pictorial graffiti are in order. As we have seen, drawings were common both at the sites found in Southern Khorasan and among the Upper Indus material.[54] However, the graffiti found on the walls of the Achaemenian palaces of Persepolis are of the utmost importance, both because of the significance they had in the development of Sasanian art and on account of their historical meaning, since they show that the sub-Arsacid kings of Fars thought of themselves as being the heirs to the Achaemenians, or at least as the heirs of the by then mythical kings who had built the palaces of Persepolis (Fig. 13).[55]

These beautiful miniature drawings have been known to scholars since 1928, when Roland de Mecquenem and Alotte de la Fuye discovered the first graffiti during the French missions to the site. Later, they were studied with innovative insights by Ernst Herzfeld, Taghi Asefi, Ali Sami and Peter Calmeyer.[56] In the 1990s,

52 Cf. Sims-Williams 1989b, I, 31 and II, 27.

53 Cf. Sims-Williams 1989b, I, 15 and II, 27.

54 See, among others, graffito no. 99 (Plate 39a, Sims-Williams 1989, I, 16), where the two words δ(s) nnyβntk are separated by the image of a stupa (?), a rare example attesting a combination of a Buddhist image and a Sogdian inscription.

55 Callieri (2006, 139) correctly remarks that the inscription written by Šābuhr Sagānšāh on a door jamb to the south of the Tacara shows that the Sasanian nobility considered Persepolis to be an important part of their heritage, just as the Fratarakas and the King of Persis had done in earlier times, concluding, '[t]he act of incising (and painting) on the walls of these ancient monuments would therefore represent an homage to the ancestors, and at the same time a mark of ownership of the ruins and a way to point out the continuity between those kings of the mythical past and the kings of the present time'.

56 Razmjou 2005, 317, with earlier bibliography.

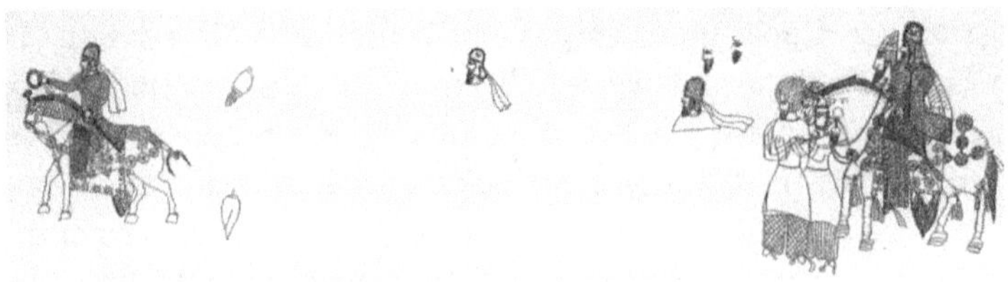

Fig. 13: Reconstruction of the pictorial graffiti from Persepolis; after Calmeyer 1976, Plate 3; reproduced with permission.

Sharokh Razmjou carried out on-site research to spot and document existing graffiti, and in 2000, he published a first short notice introducing a few inscriptional graffiti that he had discovered.[57] Thereafter, in 2005, he introduced the corpus of graffiti, including a number of new findings in an important contribution published in a volume dedicated to Herzfeld's contribution to Near Eastern studies.[58] One year later, and independently, Pierfrancesco Callieri published a similarly influential article studying six of the Persepolis graffiti, which he correctly assigns to the 'sub Arsacid dynasty of the Kings of Fars'.[59] The themes found in these drawings can be compared to some of the pictorial graffiti found at Dura Europos,[60] but the quality of the incision is much higher, showing that they were commissioned by members of the upper class. This is clear when one compares the graffiti of a mounted armoured lancer found at Dura[61] with the superb drawing of a king on horseback found on the wall of the Harem.[62] On account of the quality of these incisions and of the places where they were carved, I share the opinion of Callieri, who suggests:

> Herzfeld's observations on the connection of these graffiti with painting seems particularly fitting also. When visiting the site of Persepolis some years ago, the present author was impressed by the fact that the signs incised on the stone are so thin, that the motifs are barely visible, only with a grazing light. Therefore, it is likely that the graffiti were originally painted with colour, and that the incisions were only the preliminary phase of the painting. Indeed, if we examine the whole of Graffito no. 2, we can really consider the possibility that the minor figures, or better the figures of which only parts are represented in the different

57 Razmjou 1379 SH.

58 Razmjou 2005. In this paper, Razmjou also reports that, according to James Russels, five of the inscriptions were written in Hebrew (Razmjou 2005, 324).

59 Callieri 2006, 138.

60 On which see Goldman 1999.

61 See Goldman 1999, 33–34 and Figs 14a–b, and Wójcikowski 2013.

62 Razmjou 2005, 339, Fig. 11.

> modern drawings, are not parts of an unfinished scene (Calmeyer 1976: 65), but may represent engraved patches of a larger scene which were originally painted. If we try to complete all the engraved figures with painted ones, now vanished, we have the representation of a procession, in which mounted princely figures line up with their horses each guided by two standing figures [...].[63]

Regardless of whether we call them graffiti or not, the fact that these drawings were commissioned by members of the higher nobility, probably by members of the local ruling house, shows that the practice of engraving pictorial scenes on walls was not limited to the lower classes, a phenomenon that seems to be attested also in other cultural contexts.

4 Concluding remarks

To conclude, the groups of graffiti discussed in this paper only cover part of the corpus dating to the Middle Iranian period; further research is needed to highlight the different contexts in which graffiti, both pictorial and inscriptional, were made in the Iranian expanse. However, the evidence presented here aims at providing an initial framework to propose a shared definition of this genre in the Iranian context. Interestingly, the main known corpora of graffiti, both from inner and outer Iran, show many similar characteristics that are common to what we know from the Classical world and other contexts.

From the point of view of content, we have seen that most of the inscriptional graffiti are very short and provide limited information. However, the study of personal names attested in graffiti, the presence of theonyms, the combination of drawing and inscription, and the few longer texts can allow for novel insights into the day-to-day lives of commoners and nobility in the given period and geographical setting.

Finally, graffiti cannot be studied without taking into account the archaeological context of their finding, as well as the social structure of the societies that produced them. Therefore, I believe that we should develop a sort of 'landscape epigraphy' to better understand these texts and drawings and the reasons that led individuals, groups or communities to engrave them in specific public and private places. To me, 'landscape epigraphy' means an effort to understand the written text – in its different expressions – in context, that is in its relation to the

63 Callieri 2006, 140, an idea shared also by Razmjou 2005, 320, though the latter refers to drawings datable to the Achaemenian period.

archaeological site and landscape, as well as an expression of a living, if historical, population that behaves according to social patterns, religious beliefs, ideas and aspirations, in addition to being moved by economic needs.

References

Altheim, Frantz and Ruth Stiehl (1953), 'Pahlawīk und Pārsīk', *La Parola del Passato*, 8: 307–317.

Asadi, Ali and Carlo G. Cereti (2018), 'Two New Pahlavi Inscriptions from Fars Province, Iran', in Maria Vittoria Fontana (ed.), *Istakhr (Iran) 2011–2016: Historical and Archaeological Essays* (Quaderni di Vicino Oriente, 13-2018), Rome: Sapienza–Università di Roma, 87–106.

Baird, Jennifer A. (2018), 'In Small Scratches Forgotten: New Perspectives on Graffiti from Ancient Dura-Europos', *Tijdschrift voor Geschiedenis*, 131/1: 17–33.

Bašāš-Kanzaq, Rasul (1379 SH) [2000], 'Qerā'at-e katibehā-ye Kāl Jangāl-e Ḫusf va riše-ye nāmhā-ye Ḫusf va Birjand', *Ḫorāsān-pažui*, 3/1: 97–110.

Bašāš-Kanzaq, Rasul (1382 SH) [2003], 'Katibe-ye tāze-yāft be ḫaṭṭ-e partī dar Ḫusf', *Nāme-ye pažuhešgāh-e mirās-e farhangi*, 5: 53–56.

Bašāš-Kanzaq, Rasul (1394 SH) [2015], 'Katibehā-ye Ḫusf va Lāḫ Mazār 'jok-gōyi-ye pārthā' yā katibehā-ye 'dorost dinān-e salṭanat-e Qobād?', in *Dovomīn hamāyeš-e melli-ye bāstānšenāsi-ye Īrān*, Tehran: Pažuhešgāh-e Mirās-e Farhangi, 1–13.

Bašāš-Kanzaq, Rasul and Mojtaba Soltāni (1387 SH) [2008], 'Katibehā va sang-negārehā-ye Kāl Jangāl-e Ḫusf, Ḫorāsān-e Junubi, (Moʿarafi-ye dādehā va barrasi-ye nazārat)', *Dāneš-e bumi-ye aqvām*, 1: 47–79.

Brunner, Cristopher J. (1972), 'The Iranian Epigraphic Remains from Dura Europos', *Journal of the American Oriental Society*, 92/4: 492–497.

Callieri, Pierfrancesco (2006), 'At the Roots of the Sasanian Royal Imagery: The Persepolis Graffiti', in Matteo Compareti, Paola Raffetta and Gianroberto Scarcia (eds), *Ērān ud Anērān: Studies Presented to Boris Il'ič Maršak on the Occasion of His 70th Birthday*, Venice: Libreria Editrice Cafoscarina, 129–148.

Calmeyer, Peter (1976), 'Zur Genese altiranischer Motive: V. Synarchie', *Archäologische Mitteilungen aus Iran N.F.*, 9: 63–95.

Cereti, Carlo G. (1991), *An 18th Century Account of Parsi History: The Qesse-ye Zartoštiān-e Hendustān. Text, Translation and Commentary* (Etnolinguistica dell'area iranica, 3), Naples: Istituto Universitario Orientale.

Cereti, Carlo G., and Sebastien Gondet (2015), 'The Funerary Landscape Between Naqš-e Rostam and Estaḫr (Persepolis Region): Discovery of a New Group of Late Sasanian Inscribed Rock-Cut Niches', *Iranica Antiqua*, 50: 367–403.

Diakonov, Igor Mikhailovich and Vladimir Aronovich Livshits (1976–2001), *Inscriptions of the Seleucid and Parthian Periods and of Eastern Iran and Central Asia (1976–1980)* (Corpus Inscriptionum Iranicarum, Part, II, Vol. II: Parthian Economic Documents from Nisa [Parfyanskie khozyaystvenïe dokumentï iz Nisï]), London: Corpus Inscriptionum Iranicarum.

Durkin-Meisterernst, Desmond (2014), *Grammatik des Westmitteliranischen (Partisch und Mittelpersisch)*, Vienna: Verlag der Österreichischen Akademie der Wissenschaften.

Frye, Richard N. (1968), *The Parthian and Middle Iranian Inscriptions of Dura-Europos* (Corpus Inscriptionum Iranicarum, Part III: Pahlavi Inscriptions, Vol. III: Dura-Europos, Portfolio I: Plates i-xxxiv), London: Percy Lund, Humphries.

Gignoux, Philippe (1975), 'Coupes inscrites de la collection Mohsen Foroughi', in Jacques Duchesne-Guillemin (ed.), *Monumentum H. S. Nyberg I* (Acta Iranica, 4), Tehran/Liège/Leiden: E. J. Brill – Bibliothèque Pahlavi, 269–276.

Goldman, Bernard (1999), 'Pictorial Graffiti of Dura-Europos', *Parthica–Incontri di culture nel mondo antico*, 1: 19–106.

Grenet, Frantz (1988), 'Les Sassanides à Dura Europos (253 ap. J.-C.): réexamen du matériel épigraphique iranien du site', in Pierre-Louis Gatier, Bruno Helly and Jean-Paul Rey-Coquais (eds), *Géographie historique au Proche-Orient (Syrie, Phénicie, Arabie, grecques, romaines, byzantines): actes de la table ronde de Valbonne, 16–18 septembre 1985*, Paris: CNRS Editions, 133–158.

Henning, Walter Bruno (1953), 'A New Parthian Inscription', *Journal of the Royal Asiatic Society*, 3–4: 132–136.

Henning, Walter Bruno (1958), 'Mitteliranisch', in Bertold Spuler and Hermann Kees (eds), *Handbuch der Orientalistik: I, 4. Iranistik 1, Linguistik*, Leiden: Brill.

Henning, Walter Bruno (1977), *Selected Papers*, 2 vols (Acta Iranica, 14–15), Leiden: Brill.

Herzfeld, Ernst Emil (1941), *Iran in the Ancient East*, London: Oxford University Press.

Humbach, Helmut (1980), 'Die sogdischen Inschriftenfunde vom oberen Indus (Pakistan)', *Beiträge zur allgemeinen und vergleichenden Archäologie*, 2: 201–228.

Huyse, Philip (2009), 'Inscriptional Literature in Old and Middle Iranian Languages', in Ronald E. Emmerick and Maria Macuch (eds), *The Literature of Pre-Islamic Iran: Companion Volume I to A History of Persian Literature* (A History of Persian Literature 17), London and New York: I. B. Tauris, 72–115.

Jettmar, Karl (ed.) (1989), *Antiquities of Northern Pakistan: Reports and Studies 1. Rock Inscriptions in the Indus Valley*, Mainz: Philipp von Zabern.

Keegan, Paul (2014), *Graffiti in Antiquity*, Abingdon: Routledge.

Labāf-Ḫāniki, Rajabʿali and Rasul Bašāš-Kanzaq (1373 SH) [1994], *Sang-negāre-ye Lāḫ Mazār – Birjand* (Selsele-ye maqālāt-e pažuheši, 1), Tehran: Sāzemān-e Mirās-e Farhangi-ye Kešvar.

Leriche, Pierre (1997), 'Dura Europos I: Archaeology and History', in Ehsan Yarshater (ed.), *Encyclopaedia Iranica* 7, Costa Mesa, CA: Mazda Publishers, 589–593.

Livshits, Vladimir Aronovich (2002), 'Parthians Joking', *Manuscripta Orientalia: International Journal for Oriental Manuscript Research*, 8/1: 27–35.

MacKenzie, David Neil (1997), 'Dura Europos II: Inscriptions', in Ehsan Yarshater (ed.), *Encyclopaedia Iranica 7*, Costa Mesa, CA: Mazda Publishers, 593–594.

Nasrollahzadeh, Cyrus (1398 SH) [2019], *Katibehā-ye ḫosusi-ye fārsi-ye miyāne sāsāni va pasāsāsāni (gurnevešte, yādbudi)/Middle Persian Private Inscriptions in the Sasanian and Post-Sasanian Period (Funerary and Memorial Inscriptions)*, 2 vols, Tehran: Institute for Humanities and Cultural Studies.

Pourshariati, Parvaneh and Pooriya Alimoradi (2022), 'Mehr Worship in Lākh Māzar', in Amin Shayeste Doust (ed.), *Dādestān ī Dēnīg: Festschrift for Mahmoud Jaafari-Dehaghi*, Tehran: Farhang Moasser Publishers, 331–353.

Razmju, Shāhroḫ (1379 SH) [2000], 'Katibehā-ye Now-yāfte-ye Taḫt-e Jamšid', *Majale-ye bāstan-šenāsi va tariḫ*, 13/1: 92–93.

Razmjou, Shahrokh (2005), 'Ernst Herzfeld and the Study of the Persepolis Graffiti', in Ann C. Gunter and Stefan R. Hauser (eds), *Ernst Herzfeld and the Development of Near Eastern Studies 1900–1950*, Leiden: Brill, 316–341.

Rezāi, Jamal and Sadeq Kiyā (1320 YZ) [1952], 'Gozāreš-e neveštehā va paykarhā-ye kāl-e jangāl', *Erānkuda*, 14: 1–14.

Sims-Williams, Nicholas (1989a), 'The Sogdian Inscriptions of the Upper Indus: A Preliminary Report', in Karl Jettmar (ed.), *Antiquities of Northern Pakistan: Reports and Studies 1. Rock Inscriptions in the Indus Valley*, Mainz: Philipp von Zabern, 131–137.

Sims-Williams, Nicholas (1989b), *Sogdian and Other Iranian Inscriptions of the Upper Indus*, 2 vols (Corpus Inscriptionum Iranicarum, Part II, Vol. III), London: School of Oriental and African Studies.

Sims-Williams, Nicholas (2021), 'Another Pre-Sasanian Middle Persian Inscription', *Journal of the Royal Asiatic Society*, 31/3: 609–616.

Skjærvø, Prods Oktor (1983a), *The Sassanian Inscription of Paikuli, Part 3.1: Restored Text and Translation*, Wiesbaden: Reichert.

Skjærvø, Prods Oktor (1983b), *The Sassanian Inscription of Paikuli, Part 3.2: Commentary*, Wiesbaden: Reichert.

Skjærvø, Prods Oktor (1995), 'Aramaic in Iran', *ARAM*, 6: 283–318.

Skjærvø, Prods Oktor (1996), 'Iranian Alphabets Derived from Aramaic', in Peter T. Daniels and William Bright (eds), *The World's Writing Systems*, New York: Oxford University Press, 515–535.

Skjærvø, Prods Oktor (1997), 'The Joy of the Cup: A Pre-Sasanian Middle Persian Inscription on a Silver Bowl', *Bulletin of the Asia Institute*, 11: 93–104.

Stein, M. Aurel (1944), 'Archaeological Notes from the Hindukush Region', *Journal of the Royal Asiatic Society of Britain and North Ireland*, 1: 5–24.

Stevenson, Angus and Maurice Waite (eds) (2011), *Concise Oxford English Dictionary*, 12th edn, Oxford: Oxford University Press.

Weber, Dieter (1992), *Pahlavi Papyri, Pergamente und Ostraca: Textband* (Corpus Inscriptionum Iranicarum, Part III: Pahlavi Inscriptions, Vols. IV–V: Ostraca and Papyri, Texts I), London: School of Oriental and African Studies.

Williams, Alan (2009), *The Zoroastrian Myth of Migration from Iran and Settlement in the Indian Diaspora: Text, Translation and Analysis of the 16th Century Qeṣṣe-ye Sanjān. 'The Story of Sanjan'*, Leiden: Brill.

Wójcikowski, Robert S. (2013), 'The Graffito from Dura-Europos: Hybrid Armor in Parthian-Sasanian Iran', *Anabasis*, 4: 233–248.

Michael C.A. Macdonald

Voices in the Wilderness: Some Unexpected Uses of Graffiti

Abstract: In this paper I discuss the wide range of personal inscriptions found in the deserts of North Arabia: tags, graffiti, 'public notices', what I have called 'personal records', and 'prayers'. There is inevitably an overlap between some of these categories, for instance a tag (a personal name) may be followed by a prayer ('Personal Name and O Divine Name grant security'), or may be contained within a prayer ('O Divine Name help Personal Name'). I then go on to describe and discuss some of the more unexpected types of personal inscriptions found in these deserts. Among these are the uses of literacy by members of non-literate societies of nomads, the 'swapping' of scripts and languages by nomads and people from settled societies, and conquerors – and even kings – carving graffiti and tags in the scripts and languages of the peoples they have conquered.*

1 Introduction

I would suggest defining graffiti as 'the expression of personal thoughts in a public place'. Thus, it seems to me that there is a difference between a graffito and a 'public notice' (whether personal or official) such as 'Demo 2 o'clock Tuesday' sprayed on a wall in Oxford or the election posters and announcements of entertainments painted on the walls of Pompeii.[1] There is also a difference between a graffito and a 'tag' or signature: that is, simply carving one's name with or without a conventional addition such as 'was here' or *šlm* ('may he be safe and sound') in Nabataean, or a pious word or a symbol such as a cross, or a date (see below). Unlike a tag or signature, a graffito does not need to betray the identity of the author. It can be in the form of an anonymous statement such as 'You might at least TRY!',[2] and, of course, graffiti can also be pictures, drawn either for their own

* Unless otherwise stated, all inscriptions mentioned can be found under the sigla cited here in the Online Corpus of the Inscriptions of Ancient North Arabia (OCIANA <krc.orient.ox.ac.uk/ociana/>).

1 See, for instance, Franklin 1991, 84–85.

2 This appeared on a wall in Hampstead, London, in the 1960s.

https://doi.org/10.1515/9783111326306-012

sake or with a message, such as a huge drawing of an elongated dinosaur, I once saw, running the entire length of a long wall in Oxford with 'Remember me!' written above the tip of its tail!

We tend to associate written (as opposed to pictorial) graffiti with urban landscapes in 'literate societies'. I would define a 'literate society' as one in which reading and writing have become essential to its functioning, either throughout the society (as, for example, in the modern West) or in certain vital aspects, such as the bureaucracy, economic and commercial activities, or religious life.[3] Thus, in this sense a society can be literate even when the majority of its population cannot read or write, as in mediaeval Europe or Mycenaean Greece.

By contrast, I would regard as 'non-literate' or 'oral', a society in which literacy is not essential to its vital operations.[4] Instead, memory and oral communication perform the functions which reading and writing provide within a literate society. Prehistoric and – until very recently – most nomadic societies as well as those of speakers of the modern South Arabian languages such as Mehri and Soqotri, were 'non-literate' in this sense.[5] But just as it is possible to have large numbers of illiterates in a 'literate society', so it is also possible to have many people who can read and write in a 'non-literate society', without this changing its fundamentally oral nature.

2 Literacy in a non-literate society

A remarkable case of non-literate societies with large numbers of people who could read and write was that of the ancient nomads of Arabia in what is now the area between southern Syria and the northern borders of Yemen. We know this because they left tens of thousands of tags and graffiti on the rocks of the desert. We do not know how these nomads became literate or why literacy spread to such a large number of individuals. I have suggested elsewhere[6] that on a visit to an

3 See Macdonald 2005, 49–50.

4 Thus, I distinguish between '*il*literates' who are those members of a literate society who cannot read and write, and '*non*-literates' who are members of a society where reading and writing are not essential to its functioning.

5 It should be noted, however, that the mobile phone has now introduced literacy into these societies and individuals text in their own (previously unwritten) languages, using the Arabic script.

6 See Macdonald 2005, 74–81; 2018, 67–68. I should emphasize that this is only one possible explanation for the introduction and spread of literacy among these nomads and, of course, there may well be others.

oasis, one or more nomads may have seen merchants or other people writing and, out of curiosity (an important survival skill for those who live in the desert), asked to be taught to write. With the excellent memories of the non-literate, they would have picked it up very quickly[7] and when they went back to the desert, they would have shown their new skill to their friends and relatives. Writing would then have spread among the nomads, without any formal teaching[8] because, in such a society, literacy was of no practical use, quite apart from the fact that the only freely available surfaces to 'write' on were desert rocks. As I have pointed out elsewhere, this is how, until recently, the Tifinagh script spread among the non-literate Tuareg nomads of North-West Africa, even when paper and other writing materials were available.[9] This is because, in both cases, the societies had always been 'non-literate' and clearly people in a non-literate society have a quite different attitude to record and communication from those born into a literate one.

Those of us in literate societies today are – often unconsciously – obsessed with the written word. We regard something that is written down as more trustworthy than 'hearsay', and this is surely why 'fake news', conspiracy theories, etc. are so successful when they appear in *written* media. Of course, intelligent persons will make judgements as to whether a written statement is or is not true but, I would suggest, what is written is still given more respect than the spoken word.[10] In a non-literate society, this prejudice in favour of written material does not exist, and the judgement as to whether a statement is or is not true depends on the perceived character of the person saying it.[11]

Similarly, in such a society you accept that the description of 'historical events' will no doubt differ depending on whom you ask.[12] This is something which it is extremely difficult for us to grasp, but it is vital that we try to do so if we are to understand the attitudes to writing of people in a non-literate society. The idea of fixed and enduring accuracy which we in literate societies crave and often associate with the written more than the spoken word, obviously does not exist in non-literate societies. Thus, history, when told by someone in such a society, is not required or expected to be an accurate recitation of past events but a lesson from the past which is relevant to the present situation. Moreover, genealogy is

---

7 See Macdonald 2005, 78–79, 96–97 for modern examples of this.

8 See Sections 3 and 5 below.

9 See Macdonald 2005, 61–63.

10 As the expression 'Can I have that in writing?' suggests.

11 In mediaeval England, where the majority of the population was illiterate, a man's sworn spoken testimony was considered far more reliable than a written document which could easily be forged, see Clanchy 1993, 77, and Macdonald 2005, 62–64.

12 Cf. Lancaster 1981, 120.

necessarily fluid in its upper reaches and changes in order to explain present circumstances.[13] To write it down would fix it and so limit its uses. Poetry and stories are not written down but are kept in people's memories and so are different each time they are recited – not simply through minor lapses of memory but because the performer adapts them to each particular audience – and this brings them freshness and renewed vigour.[14] In all these, it is the *present* which is important and what has been done or composed in the past is there to bring pleasure in present circumstances or to help explain them.

In a non-literate society, if you are happy or unhappy, you talk to friends or family members or the deities. Carving your troubles and prayers on a rock when there is no one around to talk to can be a substitute, as we might write in a diary or on Facebook. However, the vast majority of these texts by nomads on desert rocks do not express such things and are either just tags, or tags with prayers, or simply record features of their authors' daily lives and, if they have a prayer at all, use the conventional request for security (*s¹lm*, cf. Nabataean *šlm* which accompanies virtually every Nabataean tag). So, it seems likely that the impetus for carving most of them was to pass the time. This does not mean that they are in any sense frivolous. One can, of course, write serious things as well as trivia when passing the time, as all who have taken long train journeys know.

3 The scripts

The scripts used by these nomads were members of what is called today the South Semitic script-family.[15] In antiquity, this family of scripts was used only in the Arabian Peninsula with a northern extension into what is now Jordan and southern Syria and a western extension into Ethiopia. Within this 'extended Arabian Peninsula', various versions of the script developed. Thus, in ancient South Arabia, a very beautiful form known as the *musnad* was developed for formal inscriptions and this script was used to express the languages of each of the four principal kingdoms in official inscriptions. Naturally, it was also used for tags and

13 Cf. Lancaster 1981, 151–154 on the purpose of genealogy in non-literate tribal societies.

14 See for instance Galand-Pernet 1998, 1–4, 27–43.

15 The South Semitic script-family developed in parallel to the Phoenico-Aramaic one (from which all but one of the traditional modern alphabets are descended) and its only modern descendant is the script used to write Gəʿəz, Amharic and some other Ethiopic Semitic languages. For a description see Sass 2005, 96–132 and Macdonald 2008, 207–210.

graffiti, since these are almost always carved in formal letter-shapes.[16] However, alongside the *musnad*, a 'minuscule' script called the *zabūr* developed which was used for carving more ephemeral documents such as letters, memoranda, legal documents, lists, etc. on palm-leaf stalks or sticks.[17] In the north-west of the Peninsula, the oases of Taymāʾ, Dadan (modern al-ʿUlā) and Dūmah (modern Dūmat al-Ǧandal, al-Ǧawf) each had its own version of the South Semitic script, and, as we have seen, the nomads from southern Syria to the borders of Yemen also had many varieties of it which they used to carve tags and graffiti wherever there were desert rocks to carve on.[18]

There is one group of these desert tags and graffiti[19] which is particularly interesting. They are mainly found in the deserts of broken-up lava-flows in southern Syria, north-eastern Jordan, and northern Saudi Arabia. They are in a script called by modern scholars 'Safaitic'. Several features of the script and its orthography tell us that it was not habitually used for writing in ink on soft materials.[20] For a start, Safaitic texts can run in any direction: left-to-right, right-to-left, up, down, wandering all over a rock face, and round and round in circles, wherever it was most comfortable or convenient for the author to carve! This also meant that no letter is dependent on its stance for its interpretation, i.e. whatever its stance, no letter is ever upside-down or back-to-front.[21] There are no spaces between

16 As J. Ryckmans pointed out many years ago (Ryckmans 1993, 30), carved graffiti in the Roman script are almost always in upper case (i.e. formal script) letters. It is interesting that the use of spray-paint to write graffiti has introduced a somewhat greater, though by no means complete, use of lower case letters in graffiti. See also Macdonald 2005, 75–76.

17 See Stein 2005, 2010, and 2023.

18 See Macdonald 2000, 28–48.

19 This is a distinction made by myself and other modern 'readers' of these texts. The authors were, of course, entirely unaware of it and so it did not affect the distribution or placement of tags and graffiti.

20 See above for the lack of incentive to use literacy for practical purposes in an oral society. In addition, as I have explained elsewhere, before paper and mobile phones, there were no portable materials for nomads to write on. Papyrus outside Egypt was expensive, they had more urgent things to do with the leather from their animals, they had no palm-leaf stalks as were used in ancient South Arabia, and they would have had few, if any, potsherds (the common writing surface in the settled lands), since they would have carried little or no pottery because it gets broken when one lives in a stony environment and is constantly on the move. Therefore, even though a script became available in their society, there was no incentive to replace memory and speech by writing in everyday life (see Macdonald 2005, 71).

21 Some letters with curves, like those representing *b*, *m*, *r*, etc. usually have the curve open in the direction in which the text is running, but there are examples where this is not so and, importantly, the change of stance does not change the interpretation of the letter as, for instance,

words or joins between letters. This contrasts with the script of a settled, literate society such as the Nabataeans whose form of the Aramaic script developed through writing in ink. Thus, it has a fixed direction because it is very difficult to cut a pen nib which can write in more than one direction; the forms of the letters and the joins between them develop for ease and speed of writing in ink; the end of a word can be indicated either by a special final shape of its last letter and/or by a space between it and the next word. These are all things which you need when writing a text in ink for someone else to read easily. In Nabataean these forms of the script were all carried over from writing in ink into carving inscriptions, graffiti, and tags. They are not things which would develop naturally in a script that was only used for carving on stone and where helping a reader was of no concern to the author.[22] Indeed, a script used only for carving on stone has no particular internal pressure to change.[23]

Similarly, the orthography of the script lacks any of the features which help the reader, such as vowels or diphthongs, or spaces between words or word-dividers, or final forms of letters to show where a word ends. The script is purely consonantal and its orthography has developed purely for the convenience of the carver. He or she knew what they were writing and since, as I have suggested, they were carving purely for the pleasure or relief it gave them, there was no necessity to make it comprehensible to someone else. This is important because, unlike much urban graffiti, they were clearly carving for themselves, usually on one rock amongst billions of others, rather than for an audience of any sort. The fact that quite often we find a sort of 'graffiti companionship' with a number of texts squeezed onto the same or adjoining stones, or that occasionally others came across a single graffito, read it, and recorded that they had found it, does not seem to have affected the original carvers in any way (see below). Their graffiti are records of personal emotions and experiences, like pages from tens of thousands of diaries, rather than outbursts like 'Romans go home'!

in the Roman script a *b* back-to-front would be a *d*, or *b* upside down would be a *p*, and this reversed would be a *q*, etc.

22 See below on whether there is evidence that the 'The Safaitic inscriptions were meant to be read by passersby' (Al-Jallad and Jaworska 2019, 17).

23 Changes in formal scripts used for carving on stone are either driven by changes in fashion (as in Ancient South Arabian) or by changes which have developed through writing in ink (as in Nabataean).

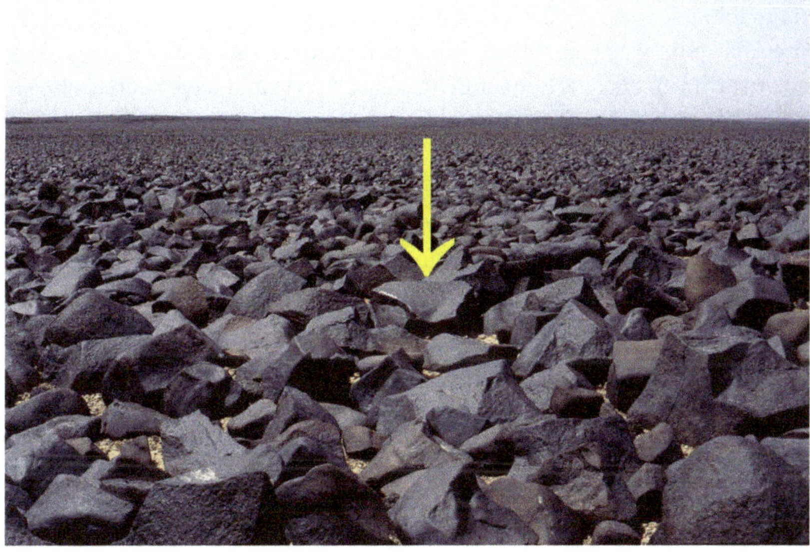

Fig. 1: The *ḥarrah* or basalt desert with an arrow indicating one Safaitic graffito among huge numbers of uninscribed rocks; photograph © M.C.A. Macdonald.

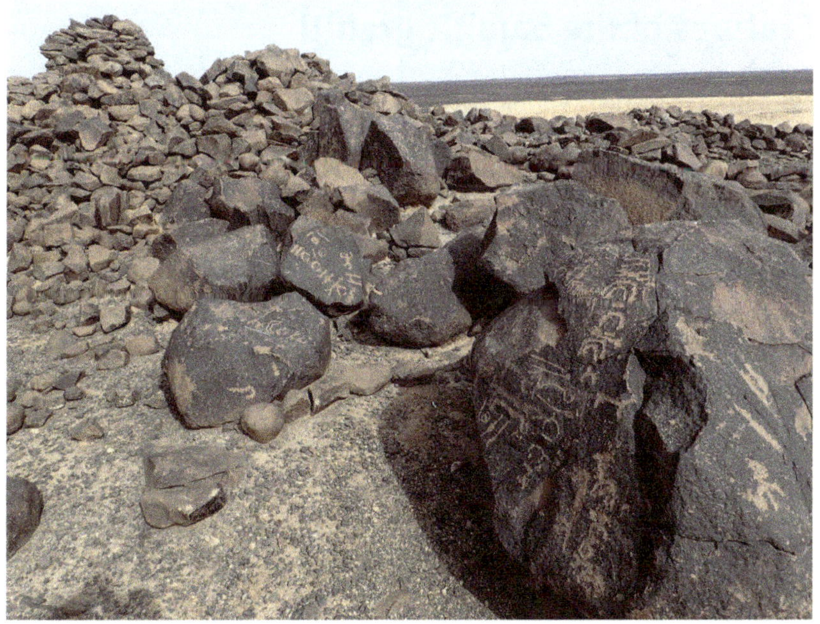

Fig. 2: 'Graffiti companionship' at a cairn in the *ḥarrah*; photograph © M.C.A. Macdonald.

Given the limited, and very personal, use of literacy within this society, and the fact that the script was completely different from the Greek and Aramaic of the settled areas in what is now Syria and Jordan and so would have been useless in obtaining jobs there, learning to read and write would have had no practical value and there would have been no point in any formal schooling. Indeed, we have clear evidence that the skill was passed on *in*formally from one person to another because there are several examples of the Safaitic alphabet carved on rocks and, in each case, the letters are in a different order and none of these orders bears any relation to the two traditional alphabetic orders of the Phoenico-Aramaic alphabet (the *abgad*, our ABC) or the South Semitic alphabet family (known as *hlḥm* after its first four letters), from which the Safaitic alphabet was descended. Formal teaching inevitably uses a fixed order because it is easier to teach and to memorize by rote. But when you do not even know that there *is* a 'right' order for the letters and you have an excellent memory you just teach or learn them in any order you like. In most of these cases, the authors have tried to group the letters according to their shapes, roughly grouping those with straight lines, those consisting of circles, and those consisting of squiggles, etc., perhaps for mnemonic purposes.

4 Features of the Safaitic graffiti

My colleague, Chiara della Puppa, has recently made a very detailed study of the different varieties of the Safaitic script and has suggested a chronological development by linking different forms of the script to different levels in the genealogies of one of the major confederations of these nomads.[24] This is extremely interesting, but there is one problem. Because no vowels or doubled consonants are shown in the Safaitic script and Semitic names often have the same consonantal structure and differ from each other only in the vocalization or doubling of medial consonants – thus ʿ-B-D covers ʿabd, ʿubayd, ʿabbād, etc. – it is impossible to be certain that genealogies of only two generations consisting of names with the same consonantal structure refer to the same persons. Thus, the sequence *ʿbd bn s¹lm* could represent someone called "ʿābid son of Sālim' or someone completely different called "ʿabd son of Salīm', with numerous other permutations. In addition, we know from graffiti which give long genealogies that the same sequence of names (e.g. *ʿbd bn slm*) can occur more than once at different points in a

24 Della Puppa 2022.

genealogy, and that the practice of paponomy (naming a son after his grandfather) is also common and so one can get sequences of *ʿbd bn slm bn ʿbd bn slm* etc. Thus, while Chiara della Puppa's palaeographical study of the different varieties of Safaitic script is extremely interesting, I would suggest taking very seriously her words of caution about the genealogical trees she has built up (inevitably) largely from two-name sequences.[25]

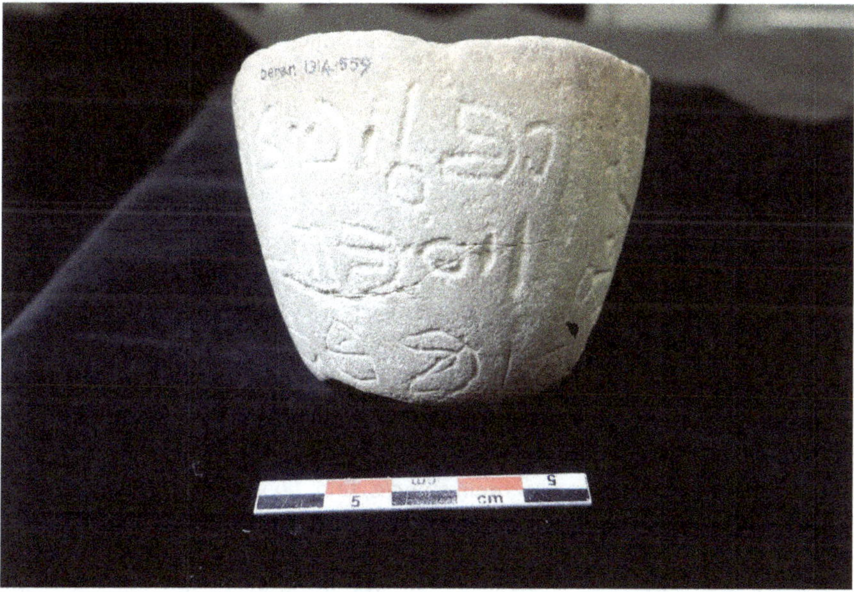

Fig. 3: A beaker with three Safaitic inscriptions bought in Darʿā, southern Syria, and given to the Ashmolean Museum (reg. no. 1914.559) in 1914 by T.E. Lawrence and Sir Leonard Woolley. To be published in Macdonald (forthcoming a); photograph © M.C.A. Macdonald.

The deserts in which these graffiti are found could only have sustained relatively small populations at any one time and yet these small populations carved tens of thousands of tags and graffiti on the rocks within a period of some 400–500 years.[26] So, we have a non-literate society which would have relied on memory and

25 Della Puppa 2022, 84, particularly note 260.

26 Safaitic inscriptions are thought to have been carved very roughly between the first century BCE and the fourth century CE, though the evidence is extremely sparse. Most of the very few inscriptions which can be given absolute dates are in the first and second centuries CE.

word-of-mouth for record and communication, but in which practically everyone seems to have been able to read and write.

We have graffiti by women as well as men, though perhaps inevitably, given the dangers from wild carnivores and enemies, there are far fewer on rocks far out in the desert. However, it seems that some women did go out with the flocks and herds – as indeed Bedouin women still do today – and carved their graffiti. These are very similar to those carved by the men, though occasionally one is brought up short by a very personal statement such as 'she was having her period' (WH 2814). There are also graffiti carved on limestone bowls, beakers (Fig. 3) and tripod platters[27] of which a number are by women.[28] The much smaller number of texts by women does not necessarily mean that fewer women than men could read and write, simply that the opportunities to do so were probably more restricted for women than for men.

So what did these ancient nomads do with their literacy? They passed the time, usually while they were out alone with the flocks and herds, carving tags – i.e. their names and genealogies of different lengths, sometimes with their affiliation to a lineage group. Many then developed the tag into a graffito by saying what they were doing, or had been doing, or were feeling, the people they were missing, sometimes their relations with the Romans, the Nabataeans, or with other nomadic groups, news or gossip from the desert or the settled areas, etc. They would very often end with a prayer, almost always for security (*s^1lm*, see above) but also for a change of circumstances, rain, booty if they were going on a raid, revenge, a reunion with loved ones, and much more. Others would make a drawing, often with extraordinary skill, and sign it. Interestingly, they would often sign it in a way which, to our eyes, disfigures the drawing, but this apparently did not matter to them. It is also very curious that when a drawing portrays both animals and humans the artist mentions only the animal(s) in the text. Occasionally, two or more people would claim the same drawing, either mischievously or because they had each contributed to it.

27 Unfortunately, none of these vessels has been found in a scientific excavation and all have been bought on the antiquities market. So it is impossible to know whether their use was domestic or ritual. A large number of the graffiti on them record that the author was 'longing for' someone. See a catalogue of these in Macdonald (forthcoming a).

28 Just under 25% of the texts on these vessels are clearly by women, as opposed to just under 48% which are clearly by men. Unfortunately, the gender of the remaining 27% is unknown and so there may in fact have been more texts by women than we can identify.

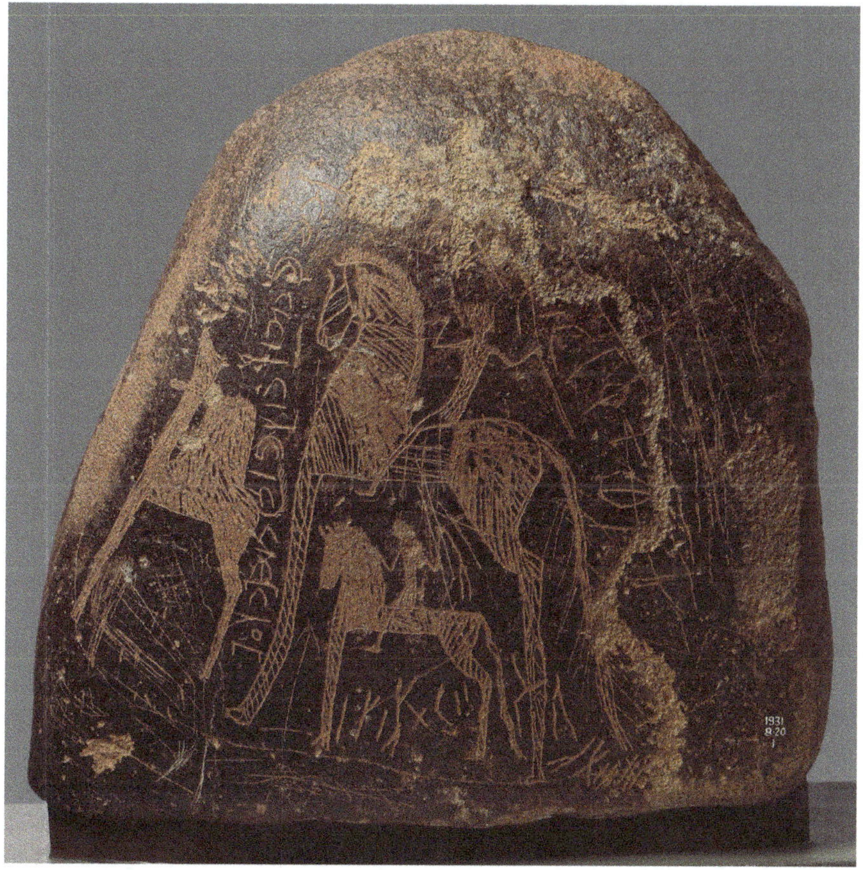

Fig. 4: A drawing of two men riding equine hybrids (see Macdonald 2019, 157–165) raiding a camel; British Museum reg. 122182; photograph © M.C.A. Macdonald.

5 Structure and purpose of the Safaitic graffiti

Most Safaitic graffiti usually have the structure: name ± genealogy – narrative – prayer. If we try to put ourselves in the position of someone watching over the animals pasturing and deciding to pass the time by carving on a rock, the most obvious thing to carve is one's name. In a genealogically based society without surnames, one identifies oneself not simply by one's personal name but also that of one's father and by as many further steps up the family-tree as necessary, according to the circumstances. When passing the time by carving one's tag, this usually means as many ancestors as the author could remember or could be bothered to carve. So we need to bear in mind that in these particular circumstances carving a long genealogy is not so much a question of making oneself more recognizable – usually the first two or three generations would be adequate in an area where he/she was known – as the satisfaction of an excellent memory providing plenty to do to stave off boredom.[29]

However, we need to remember that the vast majority of these texts are carved on single rocks among billions of others (see Fig. 1) and so it was unlikely that the author was expecting, let alone intending, anyone to read his or her graffito. Of course, as mentioned above, there are certain places where large numbers of these graffiti have built up – usually hilltops with an excellent view over a valley or the surrounding countryside which are ideal for watching the animals pasture or keeping watch for enemies or game. There are also cairns which mark the graves of particularly beloved people (see Fig. 2). At such places, a writer could be pretty sure that his or her tag or graffito would be read. But these places account for only a minority of the texts.[30]

Moreover, wherever they were carved, these tags and graffiti are entirely self-centred and in no way address, or even assume, a reader. This is an important point, because my friend and colleague Ahmad Al-Jallad has put forward the view that 'the Safaitic inscriptions were meant to be read by passersby'.[31] He bases this on a single Safaitic text (RSIS 126), out of the more than 36,000 in OCIANA in which blessings are invoked on *ḏ qrʾ h-ktb* 'on whoever reads the writing', and backs it up by his interpretation of the verb *dʿy* in another 64 Safaitic texts (i.e. 0.18% of those in OCIANA). It is indeed difficult to work out exactly what *dʿy* means in the context in which it is contrasted with obliterating the text. The basic meaning of Arabic *daʿā* (Dʿ W) is to 'seek, ask'. I can find no basis for a stretch of this to mean 'to read' (whether aloud, as was very common in antiquity,[32] or to

29 It is worth noting that of the Safaitic inscriptions in OCIANA (accessed 27 July 2023) just over 49% have only two-generation genealogies (i.e. the author and his/her father), while just under 21% have three, and the percentage decreases dramatically as the number of generations increases, with only one text with 20 generations.

30 It should, however, be noted that these are the places which have attracted many epigraphic surveys because it is easier to go from hilltop to hilltop or from cairn to cairn than to search systematically the general spread of basalt stones and boulders between them. So a disproportionate number of *recorded* inscriptions have been found at these places. See Macdonald and Al-Manaser 2019, 209–219.

31 Al-Jallad and Jaworska 2019, 17 and s.v. *dʿy*.

32 See Macdonald 2005, 64–68, 94–95, especially n. 156. Note that, on the two occasions – one Safaitic (RSIS 126) and one Hismaic (MNM b 6) – when an author wants to bless someone who

oneself). In the past, this word has been interpreted as 'to leave [the inscription] intact' which is what seems to be required by the context, which is always within a blessing in contrast to a curse on those who would damage the inscription. The problem is that there is no etymological justification for such an interpretation. A similar situation exists with a much more common word in Safaitic, *ḫrṣ*, which the contexts require to mean 'keep watch, be looking out for [in both senses]'. For many decades, therefore, it has simply been translated as the context seems to require, despite the lack of an etymological basis.[33] I would suggest that, for the time being, we need to do the same with *dʿy* and translate it as the context appears to require ('to leave [an inscription] unharmed') until such time as a convincing etymology can be suggested.

To return to Ahmad Al-Jallad's claim that 'the Safaitic inscriptions were meant to be read by passersby', I would suggest that we have no evidence to support this assumption. It is worth noting that of the more than 36,000 Safaitic inscriptions in OCIANA only 2% record finding another's inscription.[34] Moreover, even if one were to accept Al-Jallad's interpretation of *dʿy* – which, as I have said, occurs in only 0.18% of the Safaitic texts in OCIANA – it cannot be used as a basis for such a statement. For it surely stands to reason that, in a non-literate society, if you want to communicate with one person you talk to them or, if you want to talk to a group, you make a speech. The one thing you do not do is to carve a personal statement on one rock among billions of others and expect it to be read. In a non-literate society, communication is fundamentally oral and it does not occur to men or women to communicate by writing,[35] even if they know a script, and certainly not to do so on a rock in the middle of the desert. The idea of writing in public without caring whether or not it is read is hard to understand for those

---

reads his text, they use the verb *qrʾ* with the basic meaning of 'to read aloud, to recite'. The Hismaic script is another South Semitic script used mainly by nomads in southern Jordan and northwest Saudi Arabia.

33 The etymology proposed in Al-Jallad and Jaworska 2019 s.v. *ḫrṣ* is very ingenious but, for me at least, strains credulity.

34 One of those who reviewed this paper pointed out that this percentage represented '550 [actually 720] texts', which was still quite a number. However, one should remember that we think the Safaitic texts were carved between the first century BCE and the fourth century CE and so 550 (or 720) texts over at least 400–500 years would only be between 1.4 and 1.8 such texts per year.

35 The one possible exception is the writing of secret small, encoded, love notes in the Tifinagh by young people among the Tuareg (see Aghali-Zakara and Drouin 1973–1979, 285 and Macdonald 2005, 57), but this is the very opposite of carving an inscription on a rock. So far in Safaitic, only one 'conversational' exchange is known and that is where author A says he built an enclosure. Then author B comes along and says *he* built it. A then says that B is a liar and B then says it is A who is the liar. See della Puppa 2022, 23.

of us who live in literate, urban societies where writing is almost always for communication or record and where public statements (nowadays on social media as well as on walls) are felt to have failed if they are not read and reacted to.

However, when you leave even just your name at a place you are leaving something of yourself, even if you just carved it to pass the time. So, if someone deliberately obliterates it or alters the carving, it is an insult or an aggressive act towards you. It is not surprising therefore that the authors of these tags and graffiti heaped curses on anyone who might do so (Fig. 6). After all, they were not in a hurry and so had plenty of time to warn off 'epigraphic aggressors'!

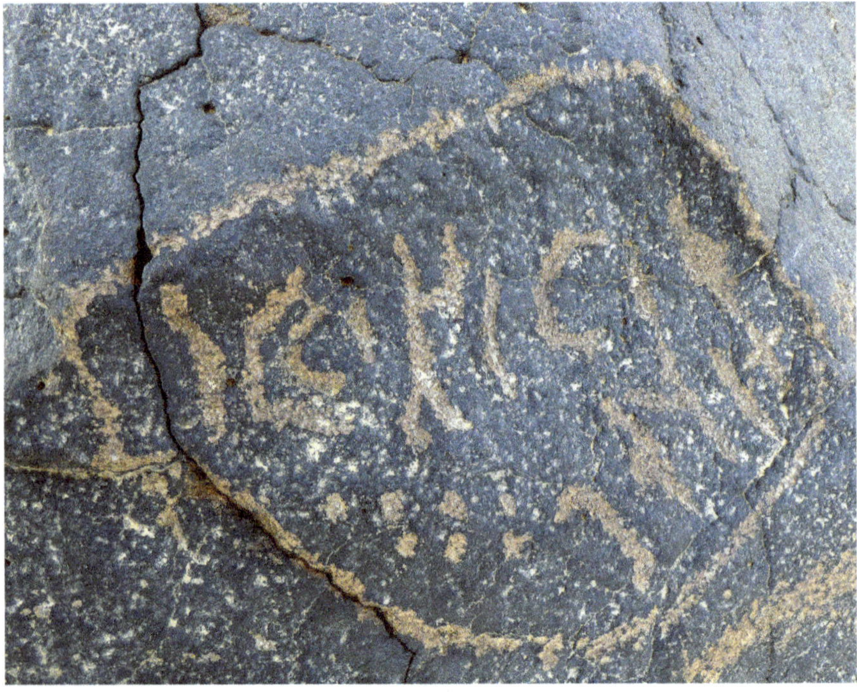

Fig. 5: A Safaitic tag which says 'Mnʾl son of Qtl was here' with the apotropaic seven dots which accompany many Safaitic tags and graffiti; WH 1797; photograph © OCIANA.

Thus, in disagreeing with Al-Jallad, I am *not* saying that the authors did not *want* their tags and graffiti to be read by others. Clearly, in this case they would not have carved them in a public place. I am simply saying that they did not carve them *in order for them to be read by passersby* (which is what Al-Jallad's statement implies). I would suggest that the authors carved them for their own satisfaction

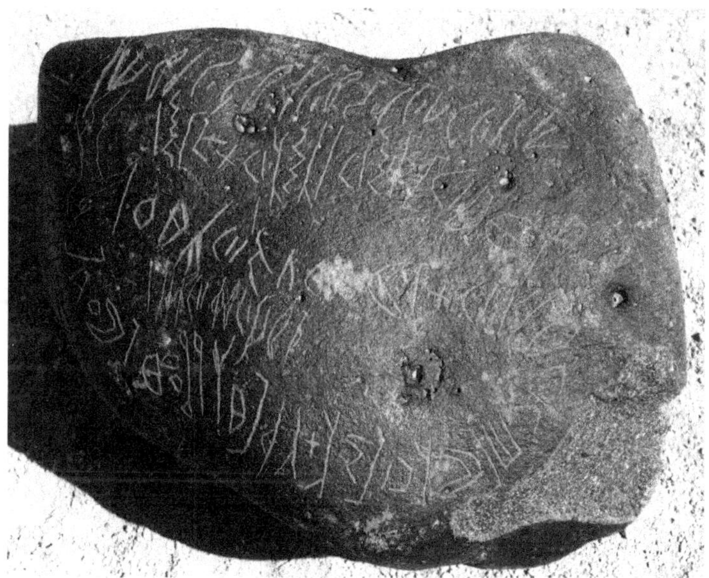

Fig. 6: A Safaitic tag with a curse: ‘ʿwḏ son of Nks¹ son of [ʿ]mrt son of Ḫrg son of Bḥrmh son of Rfʾt was here and O Yṯʿ [a deity] blind whoever scratches out [the inscription]’. AbSWS 14; photograph © OCIANA.

and/or relief and were not concerned if anyone read them but did not want anyone to destroy them.

To return to the ‘structure’ of the graffiti. Tags are, of course, far more common than graffiti in these deserts. But in a great many cases the writers had more to say and described their activities and/or their feelings and in this they were, from our point-of-view, remarkably frank. They describe how they have lost friend after friend, are hungry, lonely, frightened, suffering from drought and famine, missing and/or grieving for family members or friends (often long lists of them), and much else.

Occasionally, they date their graffiti, usually by events known to them but which we cannot recognize, such as ‘the year the king died’, without saying which one, or the year of an inter-tribal war, or the year someone was killed, etc. – another example of the writer knowing what he/she meant and so not needing to explain since they were not writing in order to be read. Birthing the goats seems to have been a very important annual event since it is more regularly dated than any other activity.[36] This practice of dating their graffiti is also reminiscent of a diary entry. Of course, there are also both ancient and modern tags which are dated, but these tend to be markers that the author was in such-and-such a place on this date, and are different from these graffiti which are describing events in the authors' lives.

As we have seen, their descriptions of emotions and events often lead to prayers addressed to a variety of deities almost always for security – the most important thing in the open desert, but also a convention as mentioned above – and, less often but still frequently, for a wide variety of other things.

Ahmad Al-Jallad has suggested that the order: 'name, narrative, prayer' must have been taught at the same time as a man or woman (or, more likely, a boy or girl) learnt to write.[37] However, this seems to me most unlikely.[38] Why would anyone try to impose this or any other structure when teaching a companion the alphabet, especially when literacy seems to have been passed on informally and the graffiti (in which we find this structure) seem only to have been carved as a pastime (if, of course, I am correct in this assumption)? We need to remember that this division of the structure ('name, narrative, prayer') is one made by modern scholars[39] and did not exist for the authors, who were simply writing or reading a graffito. Moreover, the order: 'name, narrative, prayer' is a perfectly understandable mental progression when someone is carving a graffito to pass the time. The tag, or signature, is the most basic form of linguistic (as opposed to pictorial) graffito. It is the one thing any literate person can write or carve without having to think about what to say. If, while doing that – and, as I have said, carving on basalt can take quite a lot of time and effort – thoughts occur to you and you still

36 In Safaitic, OCIANA (accessed 27 July 2023) has 54 references to the birthing of goats, six to that of sheep, and sixteen where no animal is specified. There are no references to the birthing of camels, probably because camels usually calve in the winter and since camel calves are rather delicate compared to ovicaprids, this may have taken place further south in the Nafūd sand desert which, then as now, was less cold (Lancaster and Lancaster 1999, 234).

37 Al-Jallad 2015, 3: 'most of the [Safaitic] inscriptions are highly formulaic. Their uniform structure suggests that writers would have learned a set of compositional and thematic formulae along with the script itself – in other words, one did not simply learn *how* to write, but *what* to write as well' [Italics in the original]. See also Al-Jallad and Jaworska 2019, 8.

38 It seems to me highly likely that, like the Tifanagh script among the Tuareg, the Safaitic script was generally passed on from one to another by children in games, see Macdonald 2005, 57. For the informal transmission of the Safaitic script, see Macdonald 2005, 75–76, 81–87, and see above on the transmission of the alphabet.

39 This order was recognized and labelled *Superscriptio, Narratio, Invocatio* by Knauf 1980, 173, n. 42 and these labels were later used by Sima (1999, 49) to analyse the Dadanitic *ẓll*-texts which are formal inscriptions, not graffiti, but also have this structure.

have the time and motivation, you carve them when you have finished your name. These thoughts may often – but by no means always – produce the need to pray for security and other forms of help.[40] Moreover, while carving, an author's mind can race away with other thoughts, so that by the time he/she carves the prayer it may be for something quite different from what he/she has carved in the narrative, and by the time they had finished the prayer, they often had another 'narrative' thought and so added that, and then possibly another prayer, with the result that these graffiti can record a kind of 'stream of consciousness': a succession of apparently unconnected thoughts, sometimes alternating with prayers.

Thus for instance,

1. (CSNS 410)

[Name]	*l bnʿtm bn qymt bn ʿḏr bn ḏl bn ʾs^{1}*
	By Bnʿtm son of Qymt son of ʿḏr son of Ḏl son of ʾs^{1}
[Narrative 1]	*w bny ʿl ʿd ḏ ʾl tm*
	and he built [a burial cairn] for ʿd of the lineage of Tm
[Narrative 2]	*w ḥll*
	and he camped [here]
[Prayer]	*f h lt w ds^{2}r s^{1}lm w qbll*
	so O Lt and Ds^{2}r [grant] security and a reunion with loved ones
[Narrative 3]	*w ʿty [?] mʿ ʾl-h*
	and he rebelled together with his lineage group
[Narrative 4]	*w wgm ʿl fṣʾl w ʿl ġṯ*
	and he grieved for Fṣʾl and for Ġṯ

2. (KRS 1422)

[Name]	*l ʾḥrb bn ġs^{1}m bn ʾḥrb bn ms^{1}k bn ẓʿn bn s^{2}rb*
	By ʾḥrb son of Ġs^{1}m son of ʾḥrb son of Ms^{1}k son of Ẓʿn son of S^{2}rb
[Narrative 1]	*w rʿy h-ʾbl bql*
	and he pastured the camels on spring herbage
[Prayer 1]	*f h lt s^{1}lm*
	so O Lt [grant] security
[Narrative 2]	*w ts^{2}wq ʾl ʾs^{2}yʿ-h*
	and he missed his companions
[Prayer 2]	*h lt qbll*
	O Lt may they be reunited
[Prayer 3]	*w h rḍy ʿwr ḏ yʿwr h-tll*
	and O Rḍy blind whoever scratches out these words

Of course, there are variations. When someone just wants to express a prayer, they do so without first carving their name and a narrative. For example,

---

40 It should be remembered that only a minority of Safaitic graffiti contain prayers.

3. (C 5278) Name only:
h rḍw s¹ʿd rb bn ndʾ
O Rḍw help Rb son of Ndʾ

There are also many which have just name and narrative or just name and prayer.

4. (Ruben 1) Name and narrative:
l ddb bn qtl bn {l}km bn qtl w wgm ʿl ʾḫ-h w ʿl ʿm w ʿl nz{m} w ʿl yʿl w ḥll
By Dbb son of Qtl son of {Lkm} son of Qtl and he grieved for his brother and for ʿm and for {Nzm} and for Yʿl and he camped [here]

5. (WH 3736.1) Name and prayer:
l mlkt bn s¹rk bn ʾṣhb w h rḍw s¹ʿd-h m-s²nʾ ġnmt m-rhy w nbṭ w ḥwlt
By Mlkt son of S¹rk son of ʾṣhb and, O Rḍw, help him against enemies through spoil from Rhy and the Nabataeans and Ḥwlt

Ahmad Al-Jallad has even found a parallel to the frequent attempts in the graffiti at Pompeii to quote the first line of the *Aeneid*: *arma virumque cano, Troiae qui primus ab oris*, and other poems.[41] This is a Safaitic graffito which consists of name and narrative followed by a quotation from a poem or war chant which would, of course, have been known in oral not written form.[42] Thus, as one would expect, we find considerable flexibility, when desired, in the order in which things were set down even though the 'logical' order described above is the most common.

The texts carved in the Nabataean cities of Petra and Hegrā (modern Madāʾin Ṣāliḥ in north-west Saudi Arabia) as well as in the desert, usually just register the presence of the author: i.e. name + patronym, occasionally profession, and a symbolic apotropaic word or sign.[43]

6. UjadhNab 361
dkyr šly br ʾbgr b-ṭb
Šly son of ʾbgr may he be remembered in well-being

7. UjadhNab 97
tymʾlḥwr br qwpʾ ḥnṭʾ dkyr b-ṭb
Tymʾl-ḥwr son of Qwpʾ the embalmer may he be remembered in well-being

---

41 See Benefiel 2018, 111–114. The comparison with Pompeii is mine, not Al-Jallad's.
42 Al-Jallad 2017. Writing this in a graffito was not of course the same as making a permanent record of the poem, simply adding a quotation as one might in speech.
43 See Macdonald 2018, 73–78 and above.

Similarly, in the oasis of Dadan (modern al-ʿUlā in north-west Saudi Arabia), authors often placed at the beginning and/or end of tags the letter *ḏ*, being the first consonant in the name *ḏ-ġbt* the principal deity of the oasis. Almost never do the Nabataean (or indeed the Dadanitic) tags or graffiti tell us what the author was doing, let alone what he/she was thinking or feeling. Very occasionally, they make a wish without even giving their name,[44] as in one on the road between Petra and Ḥegrā.

8. UjadhNab 199:[45]
šlm kl gbr dy ʾzl l-ḥgrʾ w kl gml
May any man who went to Ḥegrā and any camel be safe.

But otherwise, they are simply markers that the author had been there or occasional prayers.

9. UjadhNab 345[46]
šmʿt l-{ʾ}dyw br {ṣ}brh ʾlʿzy
May [the goddess] al-ʿuzzā listen to {ʾdyw} son of {Ṣbrh}

Among the nomads, of course, the situation was quite different. Even when they were travelling – for instance on the annual migration to the inner desert – it was usually with their flocks and herds and so they would have needed to stop and pasture on the way and they would have had plenty of time to carve graffiti. Thus, because literacy was very widespread among the nomads and so many of them expressed their thoughts, experiences, and ideas on permanent surfaces, we know much about their way-of-life, society, religion, and relations with other nomads and with the settled peoples of the area, something which we almost entirely lack for the country folk and townspeople. This is because the latter, even if they were literate, did not have the opportunity of enforced solitary idleness and were not surrounded by an inexhaustible supply of permanent surfaces on which to carve.[47] If they carved or painted on wall plaster (as many people did in

---

44 See Macdonald 2018, 75–77. For a fascinating discussion of the more than 900 Nabataean and Developing Arabic tags and graffiti recorded on the Darb al-Bakra (the ancient road between Ḥegrā and Petra) in north-west Saudi Arabia, see Nehmé 2018, 25–103.

45 Nehmé 2018, 152–153, and see the same formula in UJadhNab 5, p. 131, where the author does give his name: *May any man who went to Ḥegrā and any camel be safe. And may Gdyw son of Gb---- son of Ḥyw be safe.*

46 Nehmé 2018, 169.

47 It is interesting that of the approximately 400 Safaitic inscriptions which Hussein Zeinaddin (2000 = ZeGA) recorded on the eastern side of Jabal al-ʿArab (an area populated mainly by farmers), the vast majority, including those by people who claimed to be from villages such as Šaʿf

Pompeii) it has long since disappeared in Arabia and the Levant. There is nothing in the cities of this area to compare with the riches of the tags and graffiti on the walls in Pompeii which have been protected by the nature of the city's destruction. Curiously enough, writers of Safaitic also contributed to these, carving eleven tags among the hundreds of Latin and Greek ones in the plaster of a passage in Pompeii![48]

Although the nomads wrote frankly about their feelings, they do not seem to have worried that what they wrote might be read by others, for the situations and emotions they describe are not dishonourable and so do not shame the author.[49] Moreover, we should try to imagine a society in which extended families share one or more tents, where there is no privacy and everyone knows everyone else's business. In a society like this, carving the equivalent of 'diary entries' on rocks, where they may or may not be read by others, is no great problem, as long as it does not dishonour you.

6 Tags and graffiti by settled oasis-dwellers and their 'visitors'

It is interesting to contrast this attitude with that of urban writers in the deserts around the oasis of Taymāʾ, in north-west Arabia. Here, we find the very interesting phenomenon of foreigners writing graffiti in the *local* language, or in a vehicular language,[50] presumably to ensure that the local people could read them, or perhaps to show off their knowledge of the language and script? Of many examples, two groups are particularly interesting. In 552 BC, Nabonidus, the last king of Babylon, swept through what is now Jordan and north-west Arabia, killing the rulers of the oases of Taymāʾ and Dadan, and conquering four other important oases on the trade routes bringing frankincense and other aromatics from Yemen

(ZeGA 6), were in areas of pasture or villages on the desert's edge, not in the towns or ploughed fields, where the stones had either been removed or had never been (Zeinaddin 2000, 268–271).

48 See Calzini Gysens 1990 = CGSP 1–9.

49 It is interesting, for instance, that unlike the Hismaic graffiti, very few Safaitic graffiti mention sex (only 14 out of the more than 36,000 in OCIANA accessed 27 July 2023).

50 I use this calque of French *langue véhiculaire* instead of *lingua franca* since the latter is actually the name of a particular language used by merchants and others in the Mediterranean in the late Middle Ages and Early Modern periods and it is therefore technically incorrect to use it to mean simply 'any common language'.

to Mesopotamia, the Levant, Egypt and the Mediterranean.[51] He then settled in Taymāʾ for ten years of his seventeen-year reign. He brought with him his court and his administration, the vehicular language of which was Imperial Aramaic, and we have several graffiti in the desert near Taymāʾ in Imperial Aramaic by his officials, one of whom, from his name *šmʿn*, was almost certainly Jewish.[52]

However, at least two other of Nabonidus' officials also carved graffiti – or had them carved for them – but these are in the local Taymanitic language and script (Figs 7–8).[53] Either these officials were interpreters whom Nabonidus had brought with him from Babylon, or they had their graffiti carved for them by a Taymanite with the clear intention that they should be read by the locals. Their names certainly suggest that they were not Taymanites working for Nabonidus.[54]

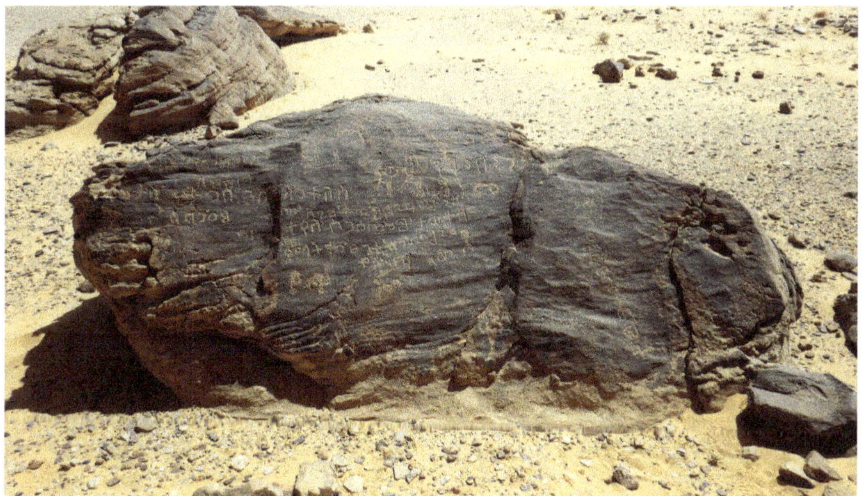

Fig. 7: A graffito in Taymanitic (Hayajneh 2001, no. 1) by one of Nabonidus king of Babylon's officials at an outcrop called al-Mushamrakhah, in the desert *c.* 18 kms south-south-west of Taymāʾ: 'I am Mrdn, companion of Nabonidus king of Babylon. I came with the Rbsrs (military commander) in order to deploy cavalry in pursuing the Lʿq nomads'; photograph © M.C.A. Macdonald.

51 See Beaulieu 1989, 149–185.

52 These inscriptions are published in Macdonald (forthcoming b).

53 See Hayajneh 2001; Müller and Saʿīd 2002. On the Taymanitic language and script see Kootstra 2016.

54 See the discussion in Hayajneh 2001, 89–92, but on his assumption that Taymanitic language is 'very close to Arabic' (Hayajneh 2001, 91) see now Kootstra 2016, 107.

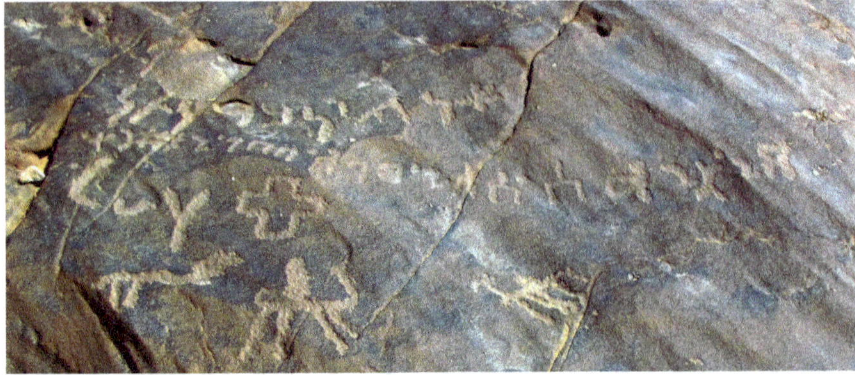

Fig. 8: A graffito in Taymanitic (Hayajneh 2001, no. 4; see Macdonald forthcoming b) by another Babylonian official on an outcrop *c.* 16 kms south of Taymā᾿: 'I am ᾿nds[1], court official of the king of Babylon. I kept guard'. Note, above it, the graffito in Aramaic probably by one of his colleagues (Hayajneh 2001, no. 5); photograph © M.C.A. Macdonald.

It is highly unusual for a conqueror to produce a personal graffito in the language and script of the conquered people. For these are not propaganda notices or official announcements, they are simply personal graffiti.

After Nabonidus' ten-year sojourn in Taymā᾿, writing in the local Taymanitic language and script seems to have been gradually replaced first by Imperial Aramaic and then by a local derivative which I have called 'Taymā᾿ Aramaic'.[55] At some stage between the fifth and fourth centuries BCE, Taymā᾿ came to be ruled by the kings of Liḥyān based at the rival oasis of Dadan (modern al-ʿUlā). The people of Liḥyān had their own language and script (Dadanitic) in which they produced large numbers of official inscriptions, as well as personal tags and graffiti in and around Dadan. Yet all the inscriptions in Taymā᾿ which mention kings of Liḥyān are in the local Taymā᾿ Aramaic language and script and not a single one is in Dadanitic. Thus, the conquerors appear to have chosen to communicate with the conquered in the language of the conquered (or at least in a vehicular language) rather than making them learn the conqueror's own tongue and script.

55 See Macdonald 2020, 111.

7 Tags in Aramaic

While this was probably sensible for formal inscriptions, it does not explain why on desert rocks tens of kilometres from Taymāʾ, we find four tags by two kings of Liḥyān[56] which are also in Aramaic and not in Dadanitic, their own language and script (Fig. 9).

These simply say:

1. *mšʿwdw mlk lḥyn ktb dnh*
   Masʿūdū king of Liḥyān wrote this (JSNab 334)[57]
2. *mšʿwdw mlk lḥyn*
   Masʿūdū king of Liḥyān (JSNab 337)
3. *mšʿwdw mlk*
   Masʿūdū king .... (ELHT site 26)[58]
4. *šhrw mlk lḥyn šlm*
   May Šahrū king of Liḥyān be safe and sound (Al-Theeb 1435 AH, 34–45, 'Nabataean' no.1)

This is all the more curious because, in contrast to the Taymanites, the population of Dadan does not seem to have embraced Aramaic following Nabonidus' conquest, and very few Aramaic inscriptions have been found there from before its absorption into the Nabataean empire.[59] Not only is it extraordinary to find tags by kings – and in this case conquering kings – but it seems that, like the officials of Nabonidus, these kings of a rival oasis who were presumably ruling Taymāʾ wanted their simple tags to be readable by the local people, and indeed an international audience. One is tempted to ask why would a king carve a tag on a desert rock and why would he do so in a foreign language? After all, there is

56 One of these is by a king of Liḥyān called S²hr (no. 4 above, on whom see Macdonald 2020, 119) and three by Mašʿūdū (nos 1–3 above). Note that until recently no formal public inscriptions mentioning this latter king had been found and this led Caskel (1954, 42) to suggest that he was a 'Schadenkönig' or pretender. However, a formal Aramaic inscription dated to the third year of Mašʿūdū king of Liḥyān has now been found in Taymāʾ, see Macdonald and Al-Najem (forthcoming), TM.TAr.004.

57 'JSNab' is the siglum for Nabataean, and in this case local Aramaic, inscriptions published in Jaussen and Savignac 1909–1922.

58 'ELHT' is the Saudi-British-German 'Epigraphy and Landscape in the Hinterland of Taymāʾ project', the discoveries of which are being prepared for publication.

59 At least this is the case at present. However, it is said that a very large number of previously unknown inscriptions in many scripts have been recorded at al-ʿUlā during the Royal Commission on AlUla's work there and are awaiting publication. These may radically change the situation.

also at least one tag in Dadanitic by a commoner on one of these rock faces.[60] Could Aramaic have had a similar status at the Lihyanite court as French did among the upper classes in pre-revolutionary Russia? I suspect not, but we must await the publication of the newly found inscriptions from al-ʿUlā. More puzzling, however, is why some of Nabonidus' officials carved, or had carved for them, graffiti in the local language, Taymanitic, also in the middle of the desert. In both cases we have no firm answers.

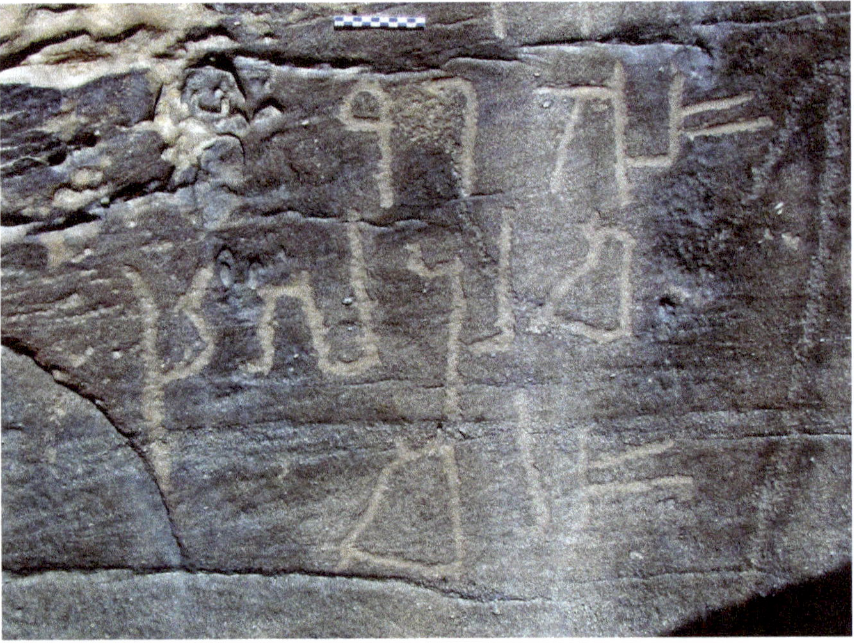

Fig. 9: A graffito in 'Taymāʾ Aramaic' by Šahrū king of Liḥyān at Sarmadā in the desert some 38 kms south-west of Taymāʾ. (Al-Theeb 1435 AH, 34–45, 'Nabataean' no.1); photograph © M.C.A. Macdonald.

Yet, even in this there is a parallel with tags in the basalt desert by people using the Safaitic script. There are five in Safaitic by people who describe themselves as Nabataeans[61] (whose written language was Aramaic) and one in Safaitic and two in the Hismaic script by people who describe themselves as members of the

60 This is ELHT Sarmadā Dad. 1.
61 See CSNS 661, RMenv.C 1 and 2, BES18 4, NEH 13.

Ḥwlt tribe from north-west Arabia,[62] which is otherwise known in the graffiti as a marauding enemy making persistent attacks on the tribes in the *ḥarrah* (basalt desert).[63] Finally, there is a Safaitic graffito by someone who calls himself 'Gaius of the lineage group of Rome' (*gyṣ ḏ ʾl rm*), though since it is among other Safaitic graffiti which refer to serving in a regular (probably Roman) army, I suspect that this may be a nomad who has adopted a Roman name (for whatever reason) or may even have been given Roman citizenship after long service in an auxiliary unit.[64]

8 Conclusion

There were no doubt perfectly reasonable explanations for these apparent anomalies which, of course, are only 'anomalies' to us. Obviously, when carving or writing a graffito, anyone can choose to use any script they know, and their reasons for choosing a particular one are entirely personal and beyond our reach. However, these 'surprises' are a reminder to us that any collection of tags and/or graffiti is only a 'corpus' from the point-of-view of the collector, whereas to the authors each text was a unique personal statement with a vast personal background of character and individual history, of which we are sadly ignorant.

62 The Safaitic tag is C 3787+3788 (= LP 87), and the Hismaic are Lemaire-Macdonald 5, and one as yet unpublished (see Macdonald 2005, addendum to p. 308, n. 34).

63 There is also one Safaitic graffito (KRS 30) which Ahmad Al-Jallad recognized as being by someone who claims to come from the oasis of Dūmah in north-west Arabia. Unfortunately, it is undatable and it is impossible to know whether the Dumaitic script was still in use at the time it was written. Certainly, there are many Safaitic and 'Mixed Safaitic-Hismaic' tags and graffiti in the area around Dūmah (see Norris 2018, 75, Fig. 3, 79–87).

64 See Lavan 2019 on the award of Roman citizenship to veterans of *auxilia* (raised from the populations of the Provinces) after service usually of twenty-five or twenty-six years. A less likely explanation could be that this Gaius lived after the *Constitutio Antoniana*, Caracalla's grant of Roman citizenship to all free men in the empire in AD 212, but if so, he must have had some closer connection with the Roman provincial administration than his fellows for him to identify himself by it. Ahmad Al-Jallad has a different explanation for this graffito, assuming that the author was indeed a Roman, not a nomad, and that the text was carved for him by the author of two of the other texts in the group (Al-Jallad et al. 2020, 358–359, Al-Jallad 2022, 23). Note, also, that Al-Jallad read the passage after *ḏ ʾl rm* differently in each article. In 2020, 357 he read it as *h-dr m-dr{b}* 'at this place from [the] {road}', and in 2022, 23 as *h-dr m-dr{b} ṣʿrl* 'from [the] road of Ṣʿrl'. I read this passage as *h-dr m-dr ʾʿrl* 'was here from his station at ʾʿrl [an as yet unidentified place]'.

References

Aghali-Zakara, Mohammed and Jeanine Drouin (1973–1979), 'Recherches sur les Tifinagh', *Comptes rendus du Groupe linguistique d'études chamito-sémitiques*, 18–23: 245–272, 279–292.

Al-Jallad, Ahmad (2015), *An Outline of the Grammar of the Safaitic Inscriptions* (Studies in Semitic Languages and Linguistics, 80), Leiden: Brill.

Al-Jallad, Ahmad (2017), 'Pre-Islamic 'Ḥamāsah' Verses from North-Eastern Jordan: A New Safaitic Poetic Text from Marabb al-Shurfā', with Further Remarks on the ʿĒn ʿAvdat Inscription and KRS 2453', *Proceedings of the Seminar for Arabian Studies*, 47: 117–128.

Al-Jallad, Ahmad (2022), 'The Inscription of Ẓāʿen Son of Keḥsemān and Knowledge of Greek among the Nomads East of the Ḥawrān', *Adumatu*, 45: 23–28.

Al-Jallad, Ahmad and Karolina Jaworska (2019), *A Dictionary of the Safaitic Inscriptions* (Studies in Semitic Languages and Linguistics, 98), Leiden: Brill.

Al-Jallad, Ahmad, Zeyad Al-Salameen, Yunus Shdeifat and Rafe Harahsheh (2020), 'Gaius the Roman and the Kawnites: Inscriptional Evidence for Roman Auxiliary Units Raised from the Nomads of the *Ḥarrah*', in Peter M. M. G. Akkermans (ed.), *Landscapes of Survival: The Archaeology and Epigraphy of Jordan's North-Eastern Dessert and Beyond*, Leiden: Sidestone, 355–361.

Al-Theeb [Al-Ḏīyīb], Sulaymān (1435 AH) [2014], *Nuqūš mawqiʿ sarmadā muḥāfaẓat taymāʾ* (Dirāsāt āṯāriyyah, 12), Al-Riyāḍ: Al-ǧamʿīyah al-saʿūdiyyah li-l-dirāsāt al-aṯariyyah.

Beaulieu, Paul-Alain (1989), *The Reign of Nabonidus King of Babylon 553–534 B.C.* (Yale Near Eastern Researches, 10), New Haven, CT: Yale University Press.

Benefiel, Rebecca R. (2018), 'Gladiators, Greetings and Poetry: Graffiti in First Century Pompeii', in Ragazzoli et al. (2018), 101–116, 200–202 (notes), 220–223 (bibliography).

Calzini Gysens, Jacqueline (1990), 'Safaitic Graffiti from Pompeii', *Proceedings of the Seminar for Arabian Studies*, 20: 1–7.

Caskel, Werner (1954), *Lihyan und Lihyanisch* (Arbeitsgemeinschaft für Forschung des Landes Nordrhein-Westfalen, Geisteswissenschaften, 4), Cologne: Westdeutscher Verlag.

Clanchy, Michael Thomas (1993), *From Memory to Written Record: England 1066–1307*, (2nd edn), Oxford: Blackwell.

Della Puppa, Chiara (2022), *The Safaitic Scripts: Palaeography of an Ancient Nomadic Writing Culture*, PhD thesis, University of Leiden, <hdl.handle.net/1887/3283744> (accessed 25 April 2022).

Franklin, James L. (1991), 'Literacy and the Parietal Inscriptions of Pompeii', in John H. Humphrey (ed.), *Literacy in the Roman World* (Journal of Roman Archaeology, Supplementary Series, 3), Ann Arbor, MI: University of Michigan, 77–98.

Galand-Pernet, Paulette (1998), *Littératures berbères: Des voix, des lettres*, Paris: Presses Universitaires de France.

Hayajneh, Hani (2001), 'First Evidence of Nabonidus in the Ancient North Arabian Inscriptions from the Region of Taymāʾ', *Proceedings of the Seminar for Arabian Studies*, 31: 81–95.

Jaussen, Antonin and Raphael Savignac (1909–1922), *Mission archéologique en Arabie*, 5 vols. (Publications de la Société Française des Fouilles Archéologiques, 2), Paris: Leroux/Geuthner.

Knauf, Ernst A. (1980), 'Eine Gruppe safaitischer Inschriften aus der Ḥesmā', *Zeitschrift des Deutschen Palästina-Vereins*, 98: 169–173, Plates 11–13.

Kootstra, Fokelien (2016), 'The Language of the Taymanitic Inscriptions & Its Classification', *Arabian Epigraphic Notes*, 2: 67–140.

Lancaster, William (1981), *The Rwala Bedouin Today*, Cambridge: Cambridge University Press.

Lancaster, William and Fidelity Lancaster (1999), *People, Land and Water in the Arab Middle East: Environments and Landscapes in the Bilâd ash-Shâm* (Studies in Environmental Anthropology, 2), Amsterdam: Harwood.

Lavan, M. P. (2019), 'The Army and the Spread of Roman Citizenship', *Journal of Roman Studies*, 109: 27–69.

Macdonald, Michael C.A. (2000), 'Reflections on the Linguistic Map of Pre-Islamic Arabia', *Arabian Archaeology and Epigraphy*, 11: 28–79 [reprinted with addenda and corrigenda in Macdonald 2009]

Macdonald, Michael C.A. (2005), 'Literacy in an Oral Environment', in Piotr Bienkowski, Christopher B. Mee and Elizabeth A. Slater (eds), *Writing and Ancient Near Eastern Society: Papers in Honour of Alan R. Millard* (Library of Hebrew Bible/Old Testament Studies, 426), New York: T. & T. Clark, 49–118 [reprinted with addenda and corrigenda in Macdonald 2009].

Macdonald, Michael C.A. (2008), 'The Phoenix of Phoinikēia: Alphabetic Reincarnation in Arabia', in John Baines, John Bennet and Stephen Houston (eds), *The Disappearance of Writing Systems: Perspectives on Literacy and Communication*, London: Equinox, 207–229.

Macdonald, Michael C.A. (2009), *Literacy and Identity in Pre-Islamic Arabia* (Variorum Collected Studies, 906), Farnham: Ashgate.

Macdonald, Michael C.A. (2018), 'Tweets from Antiquity: Literacy, Graffiti, and Their Uses in the Towns and Deserts of Ancient Arabia', in Ragazzoli et al. (2018), 65–81, 199–200 (endnotes), 215–217 (bibliography).

Macdonald, Michael C.A. (2019), 'Horses, Asses, Hybrids, and Their Use as Revealed in the Ancient Rock Art of the Syro-Arabian Desert', in Peter Raulwing, Katheryn M. Linduff and Joost H. Crouwel (eds), *Equids and Wheeled Vehicles in the Ancient World: Essays in Memory of Mary A. Littauer* (BAR International Series, 2923), Oxford: BAR.

Macdonald, Michael C.A. (ed.) (2020), *Taymāʾ II: Catalogue of the Inscriptions Discovered in the Saudi-German Excavations at Taymāʾ 2004–2015*, Oxford: Archaeopress.

Macdonald, Michael C.A. (forthcoming a), 'A Preliminary Catalogue of Stone Vessels with Safaitic, Hismaic, and Nabataean Inscriptions'.

Macdonald, Michael C.A. (forthcoming b), 'Babel around Taymāʾ and Dūmat', in Iwona Gajda and Françoise Briqel-Chatonnet (eds), *Arabie – Arabies: Volume offert à Christian Julien Robin par ses collègues, ses élèves et ses amis* (Orientalia Lovaniensia Analecta), Louvain: Peeters.

Macdonald, Michael C.A. and Ali Al-Manaser (2019), 'Recording Graffiti in the Black Desert: Past, Present, and Future', *Journal of Eastern Mediterranean Archaeology and Heritage Studies*, 7: 205–222.

Macdonald, Michael C.A. and Mohammed Al-Najem (eds) (forthcoming), *Catalogue of the Inscriptions in the Taymāʾ Museum and Other Collections*, Oxford: Archaeopress.

Müller, Walter W. and Saʿīd F. Al-Saʿīd (2002), 'Der babylonische König Nabonid in taymanischen Inschriften', in Norbert Nebes (ed.), *Neue Beiträge zur Semitistik* (Jenaer Beiträge zum Vorderen Orient, 5), Wiesbaden: Harrassowitz, 105–122.

Nehmé, Laïla (ed.) (2018), *The Darb al-Bakrah: A Caravan Route in North-West Arabia Discovered by Ali I. al-Ghabban; Catalogue of the Inscriptions*, (Series of Archaeological Refereed Studies, 50), Riyadh: Saudi Commission for Tourism and National Heritage.

Norris, Jérôme (2018), 'A Survey of the Ancient North Arabian Inscriptions from the Dūmat Al-Jandal Area (Saudi Arabia)', in Michael C.A. Macdonald (ed.), *Languages, Scripts and Their Uses in Ancient North Arabia* (Supplement to volume 48 [2018] of the Proceedings of the Seminar for Arabian Studies), Oxford: Archaeopress, 71–93.

Ragazzoli, Chloé, Ömür Harmanşah, Chiara Salvador and Elizabeth Frood (eds) (2018), *Scribbling through History: Graffiti, Places and People from Antiquity to Modernity*, London: Bloomsbury Academic.

Ryckmans, Jacques (1993), 'Pétioles de palmes et bâtonnets inscrits: un type nouveau de documents du Yémen antique', *Bulletin de la classe des lettres et des sciences morales et politiques de l'Académie royale de Belgique*, 4: 15–32.

Sass, Benjamin (2005), *The Alphabet at the Turn of the Millennium: The West Semitic Alphabet ca. 1150–850 BCE; The Antiquity of the Arabian, Greek and Phrygian Alphabets*, (Tel Aviv Occasional Publications, 4), Tel Aviv: Emery and Claire Yass Publications in Archaeology.

Sima, Alexander (1999), *Die lihyanischen Inschriften von al-ʿUḏayb (Saudi-Arabien)* (Epigraphische Forschungen auf der Arabischen Halbinsel, 1), Rahden/Westfalen: Leidorf.

Stein, Peter (2005), 'The Ancient South Arabian Minuscule Inscriptions on Wood: A New Genre of Pre-Islamic Epigraphy', *Jaarbericht van het Vooraziatisch-Egyptisch Genootschap 'Ex Oriente Lux'*, 39: 181–199.

Stein, Peter (2010), *Die altsüdarabischen Minuskelinschriften auf Holzstäbchen aus der Bayerischen Staatsbibliothek in München, vol. 1: Die Inschriften der mittel- und spätsabäischen Periode* (Epigraphische Forschungen auf der Arabischen Halbinsel, 5). Tübingen: Wasmuth.

Stein, Peter (2023), *Die altsüdarabischen Minuskelinschriften auf Holzstäbchen aus der Bayerischen Staatsbibliothek in München, vol. 2: Die altsabäischen und minäischen Inschriften* (Epigraphische Forschungen auf der Arabischen Halbinsel, 10). Wiesbaden: Reichert.

Zeinaddin, Hussein (2000), 'Safaitische Inschriften aus dem Ǧabal al-ʿArab', *Damaszener Mitteilungen*, 12: 265–289, Plates 58–69.

Mia Trentin

Medieval and Early Modern Graffiti in Eastern Mediterranean: A New Methodological Approach

Abstract: In the last decades, an increasing number of studies on medieval and early modern graffiti has consolidated the importance of this medium in collecting new details about the practices and socio-cultural aspects of writing and communication. On the other hand, it has also highlighted methodological gaps deriving from the lack of a uniform and inclusive approach in the relevant fields. This paper identifies these gaps and illustrates how they have been addressed by specific research projects carried out at the Cyprus Institute's Science and Technology in Archaeology and Culture Research Center (STARC). The ongoing work of these projects entails a specific methodological approach for documenting, analysing, and interpreting graffiti in the Eastern Mediterranean between the Middle Ages and the early modern period. Moreover, the approach intends to support and promote the study of historic graffiti as an independent discipline, not depending solely on palaeography, epigraphy, or archaeology, but joining them in the analysis of graffiti material.

1 Introduction

The present contribution aims to address methodological issues in the study of graffiti as identified and faced by the GRAFMEDIA and DIGIGRAF research projects, both based at the Cyprus Institute's Science and Technology in Archaeology and Culture Research Center (STARC), which address Eastern Mediterranean graffiti between the Middle Ages and the early modern period.[1]

1 GRAFMEDIA (GRAFfiti-MEDiterranean DIAlogue: Visual and Verbal Communication in the Medieval and Early Modern Adriatic and Eastern Mediterranean) was a Marie Skłodowska-Curie Action (MSCA) project that ran from January 2019 to October 2021; it was funded by the European Regional Development Fund and the Republic of Cyprus through the Research and Innovation Foundation (project identifier POST-DOC/0916/0010). The project investigated medieval and early modern mobility in the Eastern Mediterranean by focusing on the graffiti heritage of Cyprus, providing new and original data on cultural exchange through informal writings.

https://doi.org/10.1515/9783111326306-013

Faced with the need to tackle the multifaceted graffiti material of the island of Cyprus, part of this research has been dedicated to developing new strategies to address methodological gaps in the study of graffiti. As described below (Part 2), to this day, the field is still fragmented across various disciplines, such as archaeology, palaeography, epigraphy, and art history. Each scholar, in fact, approaches graffiti based on his specific research interests and expertise. What is missing – and what this contribution aims to promote – is a tailored graffiti methodology capable of aggregating elements of other disciplines that may be functional to graffiti analysis. In this way, the multiform (textual and pictorial) graffiti material can be analysed in a more inclusive way, without prioritizing one form or type to the detriment of others (e.g. texts to the detriment of drawings; ship graffiti to the detriment of texts or other drawings).

The present contribution retraces the steps that have led to this new, more inclusive approach, overcoming the identified methodological gaps and producing data based on the FAIR Data Principles (Findable, Accessible, Interoperable, and Reusable).[2] The first step in this research focused on defining graffiti (Section 2) based on its origins and development to date. What emerged was a strong link between graffiti and epigraphs, yet also their distinctness. Another concern that surfaced, however, was the difficulty of elaborating a definition that could circumscribe such an enduring and heterogeneous phenomenon, extending from prehistoric times until today.[3] Given the impossibility of reaching a satisfactory definition, the STARC projects have taken another path: describing rather than defining (Section 4).

At this point, different approaches to studying Eastern Mediterranean graffiti were surveyed to review how they had faced the sheer graphic variety of the material (Section 3). The panorama that emerged showed both the strengths and the weaknesses of the approaches considered, highlighting how the absence of a specific methodology posed substantial limitations to the discipline. Once identified, these issues – such as the overall discontinuity of approaches to the study

DIGIGRAF (DIGItizing GRAFfiti: Methodology Definition for the Study of Cypriot Historic Graffiti) is an Excellence Hubs project (duration: April 2022 to September 2023) co-financed by the Republic of Cyprus and the European Regional Development Fund (ERDF), in the frame of the Operational Programme "ΘΑλΕΙΑ" 2021–2027 (project identifier EXCELLENCE/0421/0540). It aims to establish relevant advances in graffiti studies by developing a well-defined and tested methodology at both local and international levels. Moreover, DIGIGRAF will define best practices for the documentation and study of Cypriot graffiti for local authorities and stakeholders to adopt for the preservation and promotion of the island's graffiti heritage.

2 Wilkinson et al. 2016.

3 Lovata and Olton 2015, 17–18; Lohmann 2020.

of graffiti or the arbitrary selection of material based on the researcher's interests and expertise – were addressed through a theoretical approach, identifying the three constitutive elements of graffiti: form, content, and space.[4] Afterwards, practical tools, such as formal classification and data structure for cataloguing graffiti, were developed to fill the identified gaps (Section 4). This process, presented and discussed below, offers a further contribution: a different approach to this field of study that can stimulate the discussion and elaboration of a specific methodology for the analysis of graffiti.

2 Between East and West: The term 'graffiti' in the study of medieval and early modern Europe and the Eastern Mediterranean

The study of historic graffiti in Europe is traditionally associated with discovering the Roman cities of Herculaneum and Pompeii, whose private and public buildings disclosed a lively graphic archive scratched and traced onto walls. The amount and variety of this graphic material aroused the interest and curiosity of various scholars. In 1841, the archaeologist, linguist and numismatist Francesco Maria Avellino became the first scholar to offer an overview of the phenomenon and its inscriptions,[5] having immediately appreciated the value of graffiti as an informal and non-mediated mode of expression, capable of offering a glimpse into the daily life of the city. His work includes both inscriptions and drawings without privileging text over image,[6] as would later happen due to the inclusion of textual graffiti within epigraphic studies.[7] However, a much more detailed study is that of Raffaele Garrucci, a decade later, which presents a different, text-oriented approach. Despite his intention to write a palaeographic work, he found himself dealing with epigraphy.[8] Garrucci is considered to have consolidated the category of 'graffiti' precisely for his description of the phenomenon, its origin and characteristics in this work. The lexical change between the first (1854) and second (1856) editions of Garrucci's work on Pompeian graffiti is worthy of note. In the title of the first edition, he uses the expression 'inscriptions gravées au

4 Trentin 2021.
5 Avellino 1841.
6 Garrucci 1856, 2.
7 Trentin 2021, 6–9.
8 Garrucci 1856, 6–7.

trait', while only in the second does the word 'graffiti' appear, with the subtitle 'inscriptions et gravures'. The distinction between 'inscriptions' and 'gravures' underlines the presence of traced and scratched or carved inscriptions, observed by the author during his site surveys, and the hand-traced reproduction of these materials. He also collected a selection of ancient written sources to illustrate that writing on walls in ancient times was a common practice that did not arouse disapproval.[9] Thus, within archaeology and epigraphy, the term 'graffiti' emerged in a neutral sense with reference to the material nature of inscriptions: that is, scratched on a surface.

Yet, just as Garrucci was paving the way for the formal study of historical graffiti in Italy, Gustave Flaubert, while travelling in the East in this same period, complained of his contemporaries' graffiti disfiguring the most famous and important monuments of Egypt.[10]

Garrucci and Flaubert express how graffiti was suspended between the two sometimes contradictory attitudes towards cultural heritage that was taking place in the mid-nineteenth century in Europe:[11] on the one hand, the in-depth study of every aspect of monuments considered as bearers of historical and cultural value, including graffiti, and on the other, criticism towards any possible intervention – therefore also graffiti and even restorations[12] – that may harm or damage this heritage. After all, both consider the same object – graffiti – yet in antithetical ways. In the first case, graffiti are seen as a precious source, providing original information on the everyday life, writing practices, and customs and habits of ordinary people, not otherwise attested in traditional sources.[13] In the second case, graffiti are seen as the result of a practice – that of commemorating a visit – that is self-referential and celebratory, made by 'imbeciles'[14] who do not recognize the monument's value and deface it. Nevertheless, these same imbeciles mentioned by Flaubert left behind what is now considered a precious source for recreating the history of Grand Tours to the Middle East and the perception and use of antiquities between the eighteenth and nineteenth centuries.[15]

---

9 Garrucci 1954, 1–2.
10 Champion 2017, 18–19.
11 Ashworth 2011.
12 An emblematic example of the conservatism of this period is the work of Alvise Pietro Zorzi (1877), who gave voice to criticism of the invasive restoration interventions taking place at the Basilica of San Marco in Venice (1865–1875), strongly contested by intellectuals of the time.
13 Garrucci 1854, 3–4. A detailed description of attitudes and approaches towards graffiti in history is presented in Sarti 2020.
14 Champion 2017, 18, n. 26.
15 Goyon 1944; Dord-Crouslé 2011; Van Belle and Brun 2020.

Since then, these two attitudes have characterized the development of graffiti studies, animating the debate over the legality of graffiti and questioning their possible historical and socio-cultural value by interpreting graffiti *tout court* as illegal and sometimes vandalistic.[16] This discussion is also stimulated by the inevitable but biased reading of the phenomenon in the past, namely on the basis of contemporary graffiti practices. Despite being the natural evolution of this phenomenon,[17] present-day graffiti and street art offer a starting point for reflecting on the contemporary dynamics that produce them – not for providing models or interpretations of the phenomenon that can then be extrapolated to the past. The latter risks flattening a complex and enduring phenomenon without taking into account the differences in geographical, historical, and socio-cultural context of which graffiti are an expression.[18] The extensive history of graffiti practices, which have accompanied human evolution from prehistoric times until today, and the multiform, multifunctional, and multimodal nature of graffiti have challenged scholars aiming to elaborate an inclusive and exhaustive definition of graffiti material.

One of the most debated aspects of this definition is the boundary between graffiti and inscriptions. In Europe, the study of graffiti was born of epigraphy and archaeology, and has a solid textual orientation with the inclusion of graffiti within the main epigraphic corpora of the classical (*Inscriptiones Graecae* and *Corpus Inscriptionum Latinarum*)[19] and medieval periods (*Corpus des Inscriptions de la France Médiévale*, *Deutsche Inschriften*, and *Inscriptiones Medii Aevii Italiae*). Although the epigraphic tools allow for a detailed analysis of textual graffiti, they have shown two fundamental limitations over the years: the impossibility of describing non-textual material with the same degree of accuracy and the difficulty of conveying the peculiarities and differences of graffiti compared to traditional epigraphic material.

These two aspects are in fact linked. Textual graffiti themselves are already a borderline material within the epigraphic landscape.[20] Aspects such as the planning of the epigraphic text and the inscription's public character still animate the epigraphic discussion today, mostly when considering graffiti in the debate. If we add to this the consistent presence of pictorial (not textual) material – which, in

16 Champion 2017; Ritsema van Eck 2018.
17 Lovata and Olton 2015, 11–16.
18 Trentin 2021, 280–282.
19 Lohmann 2020, 43–44.
20 Panciera 2012, 4, 9; Felle 2017, 599–600; Felle 2020; Trentin and Felicetti 2023.

medieval and early modern Europe, constitutes 80% of the total[21] – such an exclusively text-oriented approach is unable to convey a complete and inclusive picture of the phenomenon.

If we move to the Eastern Mediterranean, the relationship between graffiti and epigraphy follows the same dynamic but in a different landscape. Insofar as we may observe from the published material, context plays a fundamental role in distinguishing between the two graphic forms. While in the European context, graffiti and epigraphs are mainly linked with urban and anthropic spaces, in the Eastern Mediterranean, the natural landscape emerges as a relevant setting for graffiti and epigraphs.[22] The routes across the desert, connecting religious sites (like the monasteries of Egypt and Sinai)[23] with administrative ones (such as the castles of the Jordanian desert),[24] collect a multilingual and multiform graffiti heritage, a precious source for understanding itineraries and shedding light on the socio-cultural and economic situation of the people who followed those routes.

In this context, a distinction between graffiti and inscriptions or epigraphs is offered by Frédéric Imbert in his *Corpus des inscriptions arabes du Jordanie du nord*:

> Un graffito, par définition, est une inscription gravée à la hâte sur un mur, un rocher ou un support de ce type. Tout graffito est donc une inscription, mais le contraire est rarement vrai. Certains gravures dites 'graffiti', délicatement et soigneusement exécutées, n'ont pas pu être faites à la hâte et relèvent de la même intention esthétique qu'une inscription. [...] Le contenu et le formulaire des textes nous aident à différencier une inscription d'un graffito [...]. Les graffiti sont l'expression écrite d'une volonté personnelle, et non officielle, du graveur de laisser une marque de son passage.[25]

Imbert's approach is in line with what is presented in other corpora and collections of Arabic epigraphy[26] in differentiating graffiti from inscriptions on the basis of their publicity, the form of the text, and the intimacy of their writing.

21 For example graffiti in Northern Italy in Trentin 2011, 152–215.
22 Stone 1992a, 1992b, 1993.
23 Meinardus 1996; Kraack 1997.
24 Imbert 1996.
25 Imbert 1996, 495–496. 'A graffito, by definition, is an inscription hastily engraved on a wall, rock or similar support. Any graffito is therefore an inscription, but the opposite is rarely true. Some so-called "graffiti" engravings, delicately and carefully executed, could not have been done hastily and have the same aesthetic intention as an inscription. [...] The content and the form of the texts help us to differentiate an inscription from a graffito [...]. The graffiti are the written expression of a personal, and unofficial, desire of the engraver to leave a mark of his passage' (translation mine).
26 Imbert 2018.

Much more common in the epigraphic studies of this area is the distinction between graffiti and rock inscriptions. The addition of the attribute 'rock' underlines the critical role played by the natural landscape – basaltic rocks of the desert and mountain formations – as a support for textual writing in the area. Though the distinction between the two types of inscriptions is often clear, at other times the differences are much more subtle and present borderline or doubtful cases. In contexts such as those described by Michael Stone for the Sinai Peninsula, the difference between graffiti and rock inscriptions may be difficult to establish. The discriminating aspects certainly include both formal ones, e.g. the letter tracing and the writer's graphic knowledge, as well as the type of text, e.g. single names, formulae, and textual quotations. Yet it is not clear whether the author[27] makes any distinction between graffiti and inscriptions in terms of writing techniques (e.g. incised, scratched, punched, painted, produced in relief), as Imbert does in his definition. Once again, we are faced with contexts and materials that make it challenging to develop a clear definition distinguishing graffiti from inscriptions. If we leave aside the strictly text-oriented epigraphic perspective to consider graffiti material in its integrity – textual and pictorial – proposing a definition becomes even more complex.

In recent years, the flourishing of more inclusive, interdisciplinary studies on graffiti, considering textual and pictorial forms without distinction, has fuelled the debate and the search for a shared definition of graffiti. Many attempts have been made, but have not yet been entirely satisfactory, as they fail to encompass all the elements necessary for a complete and exhaustive definition. Further, different approaches yield different definitions that, without a specific, standard methodology for graffiti studies, integrate pieces without ever reaching a holistic concept, which perhaps remains a utopia. Like any discipline, graffiti studies has attempted to define its object of study, but in this case, the absence of a specific methodology for the analysis of graffiti material prevents its elaboration. This is due to the fact that, as scholars, we are trying to define an object – graffiti – without yet having the tools to describe it.[28] To better understand the difficulties and challenges of defining graffiti, it is useful to consider the different approaches to graffiti material as an essential point of reflection on the discipline's current state. Towards this end, the area of the Eastern Mediterranean between the Middle Ages and the early modern period offers considerable food for thought on the current state of graffiti studies and possible future steps.

27 Stone 1992a, 10.
28 Trentin 2021, 6–12.

3 Graffiti in the medieval and early modern Mediterranean: An overview

The Eastern Mediterranean has always been a very active and lively area from many points of view thanks to its strategic position as a crossroads between East and West, collecting, merging, and redeploying socio-cultural elements, political experiences, and economic interests. From the tenth century, the area passed from the Byzantine Empire and different caliphates to the Crusader kingdoms. It then saw the gradual expansion of the Ottoman Empire from the fourteenth century to its seventeenth-century peak. In the meantime, the Byzantine Empire declined until its fall with the conquest of Constantinople in 1453. As a commercial and economic crossroads between East and West, the area has always hosted merchants of different origins who settled there, enriching the local socio-cultural and economic milieux. Religions flourished, with Jerusalem at the centre of three main cults: Judaism, Christianity, and Islam.[29]

This lively and intercultural context is reflected in the area's graffiti, scratched onto urban buildings or secluded in the desert, on basalt rocks along caravan routes and on the Sinai mountains. Texts in different alphabets and languages, marks, drawings, and symbols record the relationship between humans and space, offering an original glimpse of everyday life.

The following overview is intended to illustrate selected and representative projects and studies that have focused on the documentation and analysis of graffiti in this area over the last fifty years. The collection is therefore not intended to be exhaustive and does not include all contributions on the subject. Rather, attention has been paid to identifying different approaches that can serve to map the potential and limits of the current state of the art. The selection has favoured corpora, large collections or studies that analyse specific types of graffiti (e.g. inscriptions and coats of arms of the European nobility, ship graffiti, Islamic inscriptions) to offer a more complete panorama both from a typological and methodological point of view.[30]

---

29 Abulafia 2011, 241–523.

30 The works considered here, in chronological order, are: Meinardus 1966; Stone 1992a, 1992b and 1993; Imbert 1996; Kraack 1997; Kawatoko et al. 2006; Demesticha et al. 2017; and Langaron 2018.

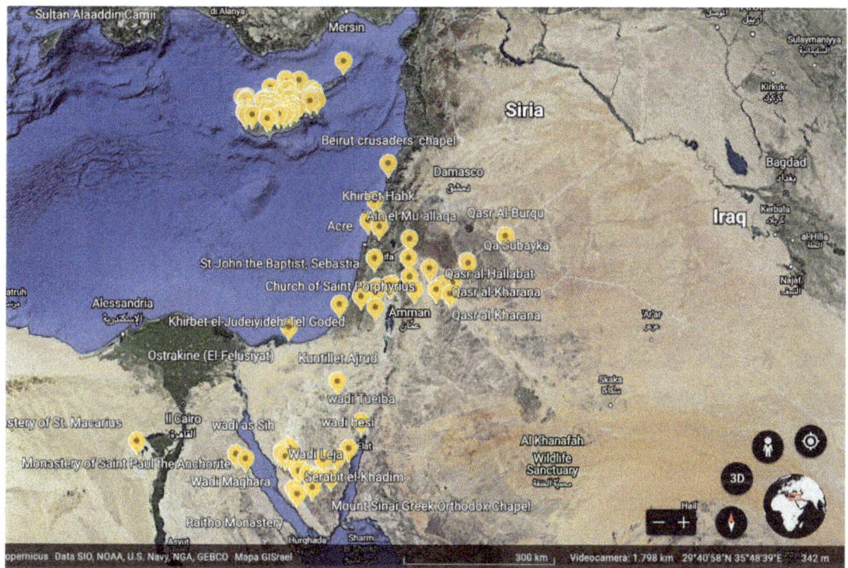

Fig. 1: Mapping of Eastern Mediterranean graffiti sites considered.

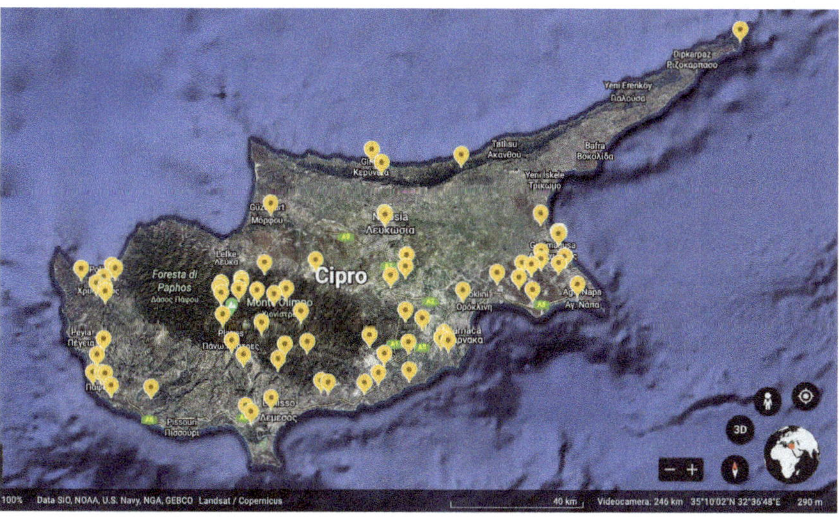

Fig. 2: Mapping of Cypriot graffiti sites.

As a starting point, all the sites considered have been geolocated to illustrate their distribution (Fig. 1). For Cyprus, the mapped sites include the 44 analysed by the KARABOI project[31] and those identified so far within the STARC projects, for a total of 85 landmarks (Fig. 2).

The most frequently investigated areas are the Sinai Peninsula, Israel and Syria, and Northern Jordan, as the map reveals. Graffiti are present in urban and natural areas, with most of the sites located in the desert, either on rocks or isolated castles, offering insight into the different landscapes that characterize the Eastern Mediterranean.

3.1 The Sinai Peninsula and eastern coast of Egypt

In the Sinai Peninsula, graffiti are primarily distributed throughout the natural landscape, on rocks along the valleys and routes leading to Saint Catherine's Monastery, the area's primary destination. In the contributions under study, graffiti have been recorded at only three sites: the monasteries of Saint Catherine, Saint Anthony, and Saint Paul the Anchorite. The first is located in the southeast of the peninsula, while the other two are on the eastern coast of Egypt, facing Sinai (Fig. 3).

The graffiti in this area have been collected and studied in the contributions of Otto Meinardus (1966), Michael Stone (1992a–b; 1993), Detlev Kraack (1997), Mutsuo Kawatoko (2006), and Anna Langaron (2018). Meinardus and Kraack focus on the specific graffiti typologies of Latin inscriptions and heraldry. While Meinardus has collected medieval Latin graffiti and some coats of arms from the above-mentioned three monasteries, Kraack has employed the same material in his extensive analysis of Western nobility across Europe and the Eastern Mediterranean between the fourteenth and sixteenth centuries. His main goal was to collect evidence of a practice in vogue among the nobility – that of marking the places where they lodged or passed through with their identity mark (coat of arms) or name – and to study the evolution of this phenomenon, which progressed from leaving their mark on wooden tablets and paper to tracing or scratching it directly onto walls. Therefore, the graffiti he published represent a selection of the existing material functional to his study. In his catalogue, graffiti

31 The project KARABOI: Ship Graffiti on the Medieval and Post-Medieval Monuments of Cyprus: Mapping, Documentation and Digitisation (2014–2016) was coordinated by Stella Demesticha (Archaeological Research Unit, University of Cyprus) and funded by the Leventis Foundation Committee and the University of Cyprus. The project conducted an extensive survey on the island, collecting and studying Cypriot ship graffiti.

are divided by site; inscriptions are transcribed and analysed; and heraldry is identified where possible.

Meinardus, too, makes a selection, considering only the material clearly related to the movement of Western visitors and pilgrims. His contribution collects inscriptions commemorating the visits of nobles and clerks in the form of personal names, sometimes with the date of the visit, on different parts of the buildings. The material is presented in narrative form, with comments on the inscriptions. However, he does not consider or mention any other types of graffiti, suggesting no other evidence. Nevertheless, the images published at the end of the text show a different picture.[32] The Latin graffiti analysed in Meinardus' work are surrounded by many other Arab and Greek inscriptions, which are not documented nor even mentioned in the text.

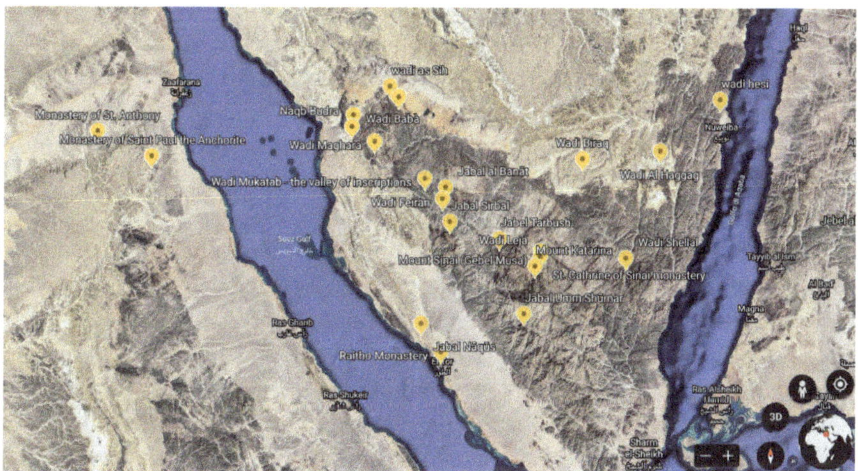

Fig. 3: Mapping of Sinai graffiti sites considered.

A more complete picture of the Saint Catherine graffiti is presented by Michael Stone and his Rock Inscriptions and Graffiti project. In the seventies, Michael Stone began collecting Armenian inscriptions on the Sinai Peninsula. While documenting Armenian graffiti on monasteries, caves, and rocks, he noticed the rich heritage of the other texts and drawings preserved and decided to record as much as possible. In the following decades, his survey and graffiti documentation

32 Meinardus 1966, Plate XXXVI.

extended to the Holy Land's main Christian shrines. He organized his collection in a simple database, which he began sharing online in the nineties.[33] The repository allows for a basic search and access to the 8,500 graffiti he has recorded. For each site, graffiti are documented and corresponding pictures provided, along with the author's notes (providing graffiti ID numbers) and a short descriptive text (see Figs 5a and 5b). To facilitate the database search – which is not so straightforward – Stone published three volumes detailing the surveyed sites with a description of the general characteristics of graffiti. This database represents the only extensive graffiti documentation so far available for this area, with the merit of including all the material Stone has discovered, with no selection criteria (e.g. kind of writing, chronology, graffiti type). Stone realized the importance of documenting all the graffiti, even in languages he didn't know or when the inscription was no longer readable due to its poor state of preservation. Only a small part of the material has been published, namely the Armenian inscriptions of Sinai and the Greek inscriptions from Wadi al Haggag.[34]

A different approach and research interest characterizes a Japanese project on Islamic rock inscriptions that focused on Islamic written evidence using a palaeographic approach. In 2006, the project published a corpus[35] that includes, among others, the sites of Jabal Naqus, Wadi Mokhatab – also called the 'valley of inscriptions' due to its abundance of graffiti (more than 1700 texts) – and Wadi Al Haggag. Headed by Mutsuo Kawatoko, the team collected ancient and medieval inscriptions up to the eleventh century, focusing their attention on the Arabic ones. Nevertheless, the expedition observed and noted the presence of Greek, Latin, Hebrew, Coptic, Syriac, and Georgian inscriptions, crosses, and petroglyphs. Beyond offering information about knowledge of writing, its use, and its evolution in the area, the palaeography of the inscriptions has also been considered a 'marker' for tracing mobility in the Sinai Peninsula between the ancient and medieval periods. Moreover, the documentation and study of the Arabic inscriptions are part of a broader programme of investigations in Egypt aiming to retrace material and socio-cultural exchanges characterizing the area where 'the European, Asian and African continents converge'.[36]

---

33 <http://rockinscriptions.huji.ac.il> (accessed on 9 December 2022).

34 Stone 1982.

35 Kawatoko et al. 2006.

36 Kavatoko 2005, 844.

3.2 The coast of Israel and Lebanon and the north of Jordan

Moving to the north, two other areas have been investigated: the first is the coastal region, with its Crusader castles and pilgrimage sites, and the second is inland, in the northern part of Jordan, with its majestic desert castles and other desert sites (Fig. 4).

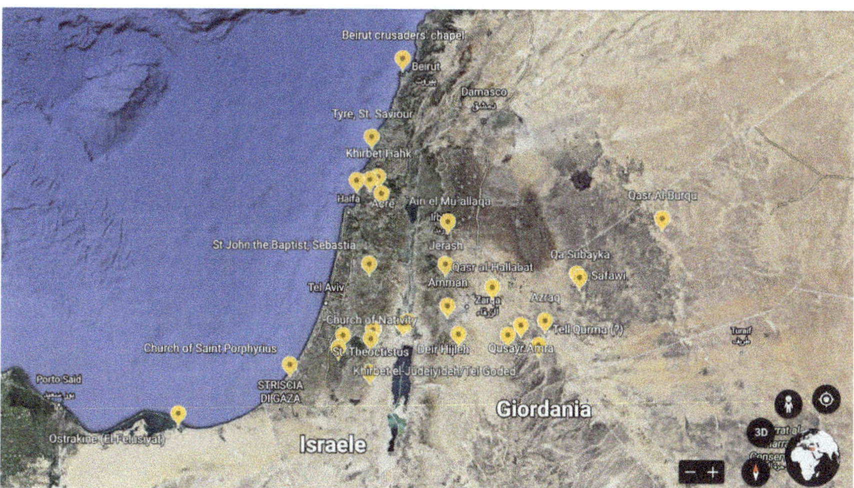

Fig. 4: Mapping of coastal and desert sites considered.

3.2.1 The coast of Israel and Lebanon

The graffiti at the coastal sites of Israel and Lebanon have been investigated in the above-mentioned works by Michael Stone and Detlev Kraack. Denys Pringle mentions a few other sites preserving graffiti in his work on the churches of the Crusader kingdoms.[37] In his detailed catalogue of religious buildings, the monument descriptions include bibliographical information and occasionally short descriptions of graffiti (e.g. the alphabet in the case of textual graffiti; the presence of crosses and other drawings). Although Pringle's research focuses on buildings, the mention of graffiti is noteworthy. The information on graffiti has been mainly collected through bibliographic references, but in some cases is the

37 Pringle 1993.

result of on-site inspections and observation. The recorded material is not the result of a selection, at least not a conscious one.

View Media #974

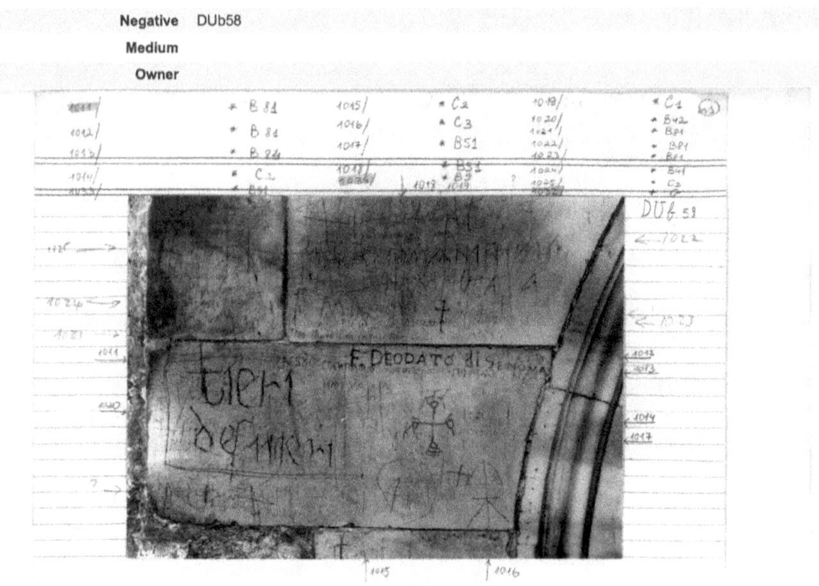

Fig. 5a: Rock Inscriptions Project online database; picture locating the graffiti through their ID in the Basilica of the Nativity (Media #974, Inscriptions from 1011 to 1020); © Rock Inscriptions Project.

Related Inscriptions

Number	Type	Site
1011	Russian inscription	south door to crypt, Church of the Nativity
1012	Russian inscription	south door to crypt, Church of the Nativity
1013	Italian inscription	south door to crypt, Church of the Nativity
1014	crosses alone	south door to crypt, Church of the Nativity
1015	crosses alone	south door to crypt, Church of the Nativity
1016	encircled crosses	south door to crypt, Church of the Nativity
1017	Armenian inscription	south door to crypt, Church of the Nativity
1018	Armenian inscription	Church of the Holy Sepulchre
1019	crosses with inscription	south door to crypt, Church of the Nativity
1020	Latin inscription	south door to crypt, Church of the Nativity

Fig. 5b: List of corresponding graffiti in the database; © Rock Inscriptions Project.

INSCRIPTIONS 89

Inscription 1012
Site Church of the Nativity, south door to crypt, #258
Technique incised
Condition fair
Content Russian inscription
Limitation *Tentative decipherment only*
Access DUb58 (photograph, M. Stone)

Inscription 1013
Site Church of the Nativity, south door to crypt, #258
Technique incised
Condition good
Content Italian inscription
Limitation *Tentative decipherment only*
Access DUb58 (photograph, M. Stone)

Inscription 1014
Site Church of the Nativity, south door to crypt, #258
Technique incised
Condition good
Content crosses alone
Access DUb58 (photograph, M. Stone)

Inscription 1015
Site Church of the Nativity, south door to crypt, #258
Technique incised
Condition fair
Content crosses alone
Access DUb58 (photograph, M. Stone)

Inscription 1016
Site Church of the Nativity, south door to crypt, #258
Technique incised
Condition fair
Content encircled crosses
Access DUb58 (photograph, M. Stone)

Inscription 1017
Site Church of the Nativity, south door to crypt, #258
Technique incised
Condition fair

Inscription 1019
Site Church of the Nativity, south door to crypt, #258
Technique incised
Condition fair
Content crosses with inscription
Access DUb58 (photograph, M. Stone)

Inscription 1020
Site Church of the Nativity, south door to crypt, #258
Technique incised
Condition fair
Dimensions 35 x 19 cm.
Content Latin inscription
Limitation *Tentative decipherment only*
Access DUb58 (photograph, M. Stone)

Inscription 1021
Site Church of the Nativity, south door to crypt, #258
Dating 1666
Technique incised
Condition fair
Content Russian inscription
Limitation *Tentative decipherment only*
Access DUb58 (photograph, M. Stone)

Inscription 1022
Site Church of the Nativity, south door to crypt, #258
Technique incised
Condition fair
Content Russian inscription
Limitation *Tentative decipherment only*
Access DUb58 (photograph, M. Stone)

Inscription 1023
Site Church of the Nativity, south door to crypt, #258
Technique incised
Condition poor
Content Russian inscription
Limitation *Tentative decipherment only*
Access DUb58 (photograph, M. Stone)

Inscription 1024

Fig. 5c: Print catalogue entries; © Rock Inscriptions Project.

The most inclusive and complete collection of graffiti in the coastal area has been provided by Michael Stone,[38] who offers the best insight into the forms and distribution of this graffiti thanks to his extensive documentation. By cross-referencing the Rock Inscriptions Project website with the printed volumes, one may find basic information about an individual inscription, know its location, and see its relation to other graffiti nearby. We may take an example from the Basilica of the Nativity in Bethlehem (Fig. 5): the picture on the project website (Fig. 5a) shows a scanned card file with a photograph of a marble slab covered with Latin, Russian, and Armenian inscriptions. Around the photograph, Stone's handwritten notes may be

38 Stone 1992a, 89.

discerned, indicating each graffito ID. The scan is linked to an online list of 'related inscriptions' (Fig. 5b), where each ID number corresponds to a single graffito. At this point, further information can be found in the printed volumes, in this case, vol. 1 (Fig. 5c). The graffito ID can easily be found in the catalogue, followed by basic details: site, technique, condition, content and accessibility (photo IDs).

Michael Stone's photographic collection, database, and published catalogue are valuable and essential sources for undertaking more in-depth studies in this area, as the author hopes in the presentation of this project.[39] Stone's approach offers a complete documentation of the material and its cataloguing, albeit in a synthetic and elementary form, wherever possible. In his project, he does not make a selection based on his research interests or his knowledge, but, understanding the fragility of graffiti, documents and catalogues as much as possible to preserve this heritage and offer a tool to undertake more detailed studies.

Unfortunately, the Rock Inscriptions Project suffered from the limitations imposed by analogue photography, the only kind available during the period of the project. This affected not only the documentation of individual graffiti but, above all, the reconstruction of their position and distribution within each building. Although Stone's catalogue reports the location of graffiti and inscriptions as accurately as possible, the lack of a complete overview makes it more challenging to investigate the relationship between graffiti and their space, one of the fundamental elements to be considered in their analysis.[40]

Finally, a survey of the study of graffiti in this area must mention the ongoing ERC project GRAPH-EAST, led by Estelle Ingrand-Varenne.[41] GRAPH-EAST, launched in October 2020, focuses on epigraphic evidence of the Latin alphabet in the Eastern Mediterranean (seventh to sixteenth century), including graffiti. The project investigates the presence, function, and reception of texts in the Latin alphabet. Moreover, it aims to integrate different kinds of inscriptions, including textual graffiti, and to analyse them in a heuristic way as part of a wider panorama of written practices. From the technological point of view, GRAPH-EAST will implement a specific database for inscriptions in the Latin alphabet based on the FAIR guidelines.[42] Despite the relevance and innovation of the research framework, in terms of graffiti, the approach is selective, focused on Western evidence: textual graffiti in the Latin alphabet and coats of arms. Even so, the general approach and the comparative analysis of sites in different regions of the Eastern

39 Stone 1992a, 9.

40 Trentin 2021, 18–20.

41 <https://grapheast.hypotheses.org/about> (accessed on 9 December 2022).

42 <https://grapheast.hypotheses.org/259> (accessed on 9 December 2022).

Mediterranean will help to shed light on the practices of writing in the Latin alphabet on various levels and to enrich our knowledge of the multicultural interaction of the area.

3.2.2 Northern Jordan

Graffiti from Northern Jordan have been included in Frédéric Imbert's corpus of Arabic inscriptions,[43] with the aim of providing insights on writing practices, traditions, knowledge and literacy, and the use of writing along desert routes and on desert castles. He takes a palaeographic approach to surveying and documenting epigraphs and graffiti in Arabic, focusing on both the methodological and analytical aspects of the task. Starting from an epigraphic approach, Imbert has contributed to creating a model for the cataloguing and editing of Arabic inscriptions that includes their formal and contextual aspects, while proposing a standardization of the epigraphic terms and concepts used in Arabic studies.[44]

Graffiti predominate within the epigraphic material analysed in this collection. Of the 192 inscriptions, 120 are graffiti dated between the eighth and fourteenth centuries. Most of these (78 out of 120) are traced on rocks, with invocations outnumbering commemorative inscriptions. The remaining 42 are located on castles and palaces, onto which the graffiti has not only been scratched but also traced in ink, with invocations again prevailing over commemorative inscriptions. Most of the graffiti date to the ninth century, and their number gradually decreases until the fourteenth century.[45]

The cataloguing is very detailed. Each graffito has a photographic reproduction and a hand copy (included in the appendix), and its material (support, location, number of lines, state of conservation, measures) and formal (style of writing, dating, and palaeographic comment) properties are described, with bibliographical references to previous editions. The text is transcribed, translated, and annotated. Considering digital tools were not available at that time, the context is described and documented with the best tools of that period: areal maps, building plans, and height measurements for the buildings' outer and inner walls help the reader reconstruct the visual context and the graffiti's distribution. However, it is not clear whether there are other graffiti, either textual or pictorial,

43 Imbert 1996.
44 Imbert 1996, 10–12.
45 Imbert 1996, 495–503.

alongside those in Arabic. In very few cases, some pictorial graffiti are visible next to the inscriptions.[46]

Overall, Imbert's work has contributed to shedding light on various elements of writing in everyday life and the social and cultural implications of Arabic writing, its evolution, and its diffusion. The detailed analysis of the inscriptions and their territorial as well as historical and social contextualization have allowed us to understand aspects of mobility in and the traditions and customs of this desert area.[47] Even from a methodological point of view, despite the coexistence of inscriptions and graffiti in the corpus, it does not appear to favour the former. On the other hand, the material in this case is homogeneous: it is only Arabic texts. Graffiti and inscriptions coexist harmoniously within the collection, helping to give a more articulated image of the use of writing in public and private spheres. The lack of other – primarily pictorial – forms of graffiti makes this possible.

3.3 The Cypriot experience: The KARABOI project

Between 2014 and 2016, Stella Demesticha coordinated the KARABOI project,[48] focusing on the ship graffiti of Cyprus. The project had a twofold aim: to develop a methodology for cataloguing and studying ship graffiti using digital tools, and to investigate Cypriot maritime culture from a different point of view, namely a bottom-up perspective. During the surveys, ship graffiti were located in 44 buildings and monuments, for a total of 233 examples. Digital tools for site documentation (e.g. 3D models of buildings and graffiti; RTI documentation)[49] and data management (a specific database) were specifically developed and employed to better study and analyse the material and its context. Thanks to the project's multidisciplinary team, the data could be analysed and interpreted in depth, recovering information not otherwise recorded by traditional sources, to enhance our knowledge of maritime activity.[50] Moreover, the project carried out the first

---

46 Imbert 1996, Plate 156 (Byzantine cross); Plate 248 (pentalpha); Plate 308 (four-legged animal); Plate 315 (camel).

47 Imbert 2013.

48 The project was coordinated by Stella Demesticha of the Archaeological Research Unit, University of Cyprus, and funded by the Leventis Foundation Committee and the University of Cyprus.

49 Reflectance Transformation Imaging (RTI) is a computational photographic method developed to capture surface shape and colour and to use interactive lightening to reveal details difficult to see with the naked eye <https://culturalheritageimaging.org/What_We_Offer/Downloads/> (accessed on 9 December 2022).

50 Demesticha et al. 2017.

extensive graffiti survey of its kind, offering the possibility to approach the context from both the micro and macro scale.[51] Although the project was a significant step forward in both the methodology and understanding of ship graffiti on the island of Cyprus, it also highlighted how the sectoral analysis of a specific type of graffiti conveys only a partial and fragmentary image of the phenomenon.

Most of the sites where ship graffiti were recorded also preserve other types of graffiti, such as Latin and Greek inscriptions and a wide variety of pictorial graffiti. The observation and relationship of ship graffiti and other types of graffiti helped to better frame the presence and distribution of the different ship graffiti and to gain deeper insight into their context, history, and reception by visitors across the centuries.[52]

3.4 One object, different approaches: Methodological issues in graffiti analysis

This overview, encompassing the main projects and studies on medieval and early modern graffiti in the Eastern Mediterranean over the last fifty years, offers examples of the state of graffiti studies, especially its potential and limits. These initiatives demonstrate the relevance of graffiti as an original source for the study of the socio-cultural and economic life of the past, illuminating aspects from mobility to written communication, the history of writing and writing practices in everyday life, and the perception of space and human interaction with it. On the other hand, their different, targeted approaches often fail to present a complete picture of the phenomenon, hence the difficulty – illustrated in the initial part of this contribution – of finding a shared definition for the term 'graffiti'.

What emerges from this overview is the generally selective approach to the material and the fragmentation of the analyses due to the lack of a specific methodology. Most of the above-mentioned projects are based on the researchers' specific interests and expertise, which motivates their selection of graffiti material. The main focus has tended to be textual graffiti, specifically in contexts preserving texts in different languages and alphabets, with the selection further narrowed based on the researchers' expertise. When the focus has been on pictorial graffiti (e.g. ship graffiti), textual graffiti and other pictorial typologies have often been considered only marginally. On the other hand, the lack of a specific methodology for the analysis of the graffiti leads to the presence of different

51 Demesticha et al. 2017, 247–253.
52 Demesticha et al. 2017, 374–375.

approaches corresponding to different cataloguing/descriptive practices, which may be efficient for describing the selected data but not the whole material.

These concerns relate mainly to the nature of graffiti, which includes both textual and pictorial forms. When textual inscriptions and graffiti are analysed together, as in Imbert's study, the epigraphic methodology is effective. However, the same methodology would not be suitable for a corpus of both textual and pictorial graffiti, as it has been specially tailored to textual material alone. Text and image are different – not so much in their form, but in the processes of reading and understanding required to decode them. Text conveys content through linguistic coding, while images rely on pictorial codification. The two graphic forms and their histories have been studied independently due to the development of two disciplines: rock art and epigraphy.[53] Thanks to their well-established traditions, the two disciplines have proved their descriptive and analytical efficiency. What is now missing is a new methodology that can benefit from both sources of expertise, merging the analytical methods of epigraphy for texts and those of rock art for images to create a methodology specific to graffiti.

Such a methodology should be able to catalogue and analyse textual and pictorial graffiti on the same level, without privileging one form to the detriment of the other, allowing for a more inclusive approach. In this, Michael Stone's initiative demonstrates the importance of documenting all the material and describing it preliminarily with basic descriptors to instil numerical and typological consistency. Such tools allow scholars access to the material, facilitate its exchange, and foster debate on the topic, aspects that form the basis of scientific research.

4 The GRAFMEDIA and DIGIGRAF projects: An attempt at a graffiti workflow and data structuring scheme

4.1 Describing rather than defining

The above-mentioned issues were the focal point of GRAFMEDIA's and DIGIGRAF's theoretical considerations, aimed at defining a specific methodology based on standards combined with the creation of digital tools for the documentation and visualization of graffiti and their context. Cyprus preserves a rich and

53 Trentin 2021, 3–12.

varied graffiti heritage, a result of the lively interaction of locals and visitors with the natural and anthropic landscape. Texts in different languages and alphabets, symbols, and drawings offered challenging and stimulating material on which to develop and test such a methodology.

In its initial phase, the project necessarily had to deal with the definition of graffiti. As described in the first part of this paper, at the moment, an exhaustive and shared definition is not available. Therefore, another path was taken: that of describing graffiti rather than defining it. The description elaborated in this context is the following: Graffiti are graphic (textual and pictorial) media displayed on natural and anthropic spaces or objects, on surfaces not intended for writing.

This means that, from an archaeological point of view, graffiti exist at an interface, in an invisible layer that records human interaction with natural or anthropic spaces or objects. The concept of 'interface' is fundamental to appreciating the temporal gap between the creation of the support and the making of the graffiti. In this sense, graffiti, more than written artefacts, are material traces of immaterial practices, something in between tangible and intangible artefacts. They record an interaction rather than being an integral part of an object.

The following step was to create a specific methodology – as described above, one that is able to embrace such a multiform material and consider textual and pictorial forms on the same level, without favouring one form to the detriment of others. Towards this end, five operations have been identified as necessary for the creation of a specific methodology for graffiti based on structured data, descriptive standards, and guidelines:

- definition of the constitutive elements of graffiti and their semantic relations (4.2);
- definition of a workflow (4.3);
- definition of guidelines for the documentation of graffiti and their context, testing different techniques and establishing the most appropriate solution for each case (4.4);
- definition of cataloguing records based on standards (thesauri) for a uniform description (4.5–4.6); and
- creation of a graffiti data structure based on semantic description (ontology) (4.7).

4.2 The constitutive elements of graffiti: Form, content and space

To better describe the phenomenon of graffiti, with a focus on its mechanism of communication and graphic expression, semantic and semiotic studies have served as a reference point. In particular, Ogden and Richards' semiotic triangle, elaborating the constitutive elements of communication and their mutual relations, was the reference point for identifying the constitutive elements of graffiti: form, content, and space (Fig. 6).[54]

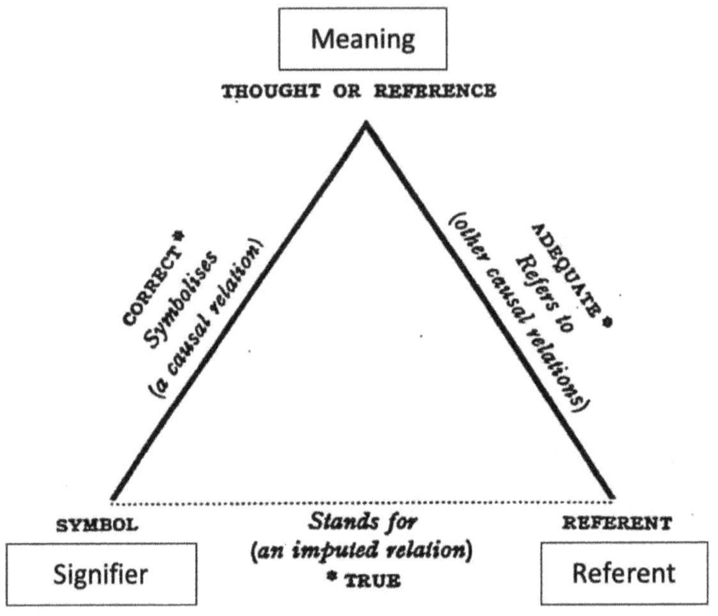

Fig. 6: The semiotic triangle (Odgen and Richards, 1923) as adapted in Trentin 2021, Fig. 2.

'Form' entails the graphic aspect of the graffiti – textual or pictorial. Developing a framework for treating these forms on the same level is fundamental to the analysis of graffiti, which should be approached as a single graphical system, without privileging textual graffiti over pictorial ones. The form of graffiti is always a result of a semiotic communicative choice by the creator, who either selects language as the medium (textual graffiti) or represents the concepts without linguistic mediation (pictorial graffiti). Clarifying the different communication mechanisms underlying the two systems also helps define the graffiti creation process. The two graphical systems offer various possibilities: if writing is more universal – as text transmits organized content through language – drawing can be more effective in expressing abstract and complex concepts, and faster due to

54 Trentin 2021. For the semiotic triangle, see Ogden and Richards 1923.

its use of symbols.[55] This point of view casts doubt on the equation of pictorial graffiti with the activity of illiterates who use drawing due to their low or absent literacy.[56] The form, therefore, assumes an essential role in the study of informal everyday communication, allowing us to observe the variety of solutions adopted to convey content.

The second element is the content of graffiti.[57] Thanks to semiotics, it is possible to establish and clarify the relationship between content and form.[58] A graffito is an entity composed of one or more graphic elements on the expressive level (signifier, i.e. the form) and one or more elements on the level of content (meaning, i.e. the content) (Fig. 6). The union of the two puts the graffito sign in a non-univocal relationship with its content: a shape can correspond to different content, and vice versa. A boat, for example, can correspond to different contents, representing a workplace for a sailor, a means of transport for a traveller, a gift for a worshipper, and an element of the landscape for an inhabitant of the coast: one form, different contents. In the same way, the same content can be expressed in various forms, as in Kraack's study, where the European nobles represented themselves through various graphic forms, such as texts with their names, coats of arms, and other identity signs. Form and content are the expression of the referent, i.e. the object – real or abstract. However, as underlined by Umberto Eco, the referent should not be considered a specific and universal object, but as cultural content.[59] This step is fundamental, as it explains how a sign is linked to the society that produces it through specific cultural content. Outside of this socio-cultural context, the sign can take on different meanings or even be meaningless, as the cultural meanings that originated it and gave it meaning may have changed or been lost.[60] The more culturally distant a society is in space and time, the more complex the reconstruction of the referents will be. This explains the difficulty in 'reading' some forms of graffiti (e.g. depictions of lightning or nine men's morris)[61] whose diffusion across Europe attests to the persistence of certain signs that, rather than representing a single vector of content have different referents depending on the specific socio-cultural context in which they were used.

55 Morin et al. 2020.
56 Fleming 2020, 32; Sarti 2020, 16.
57 Trentin 2021, 16–18.
58 Eco 2016, 17.
59 Eco 2016, 95.
60 Eco 2016, 15; Morin et al. 2020, 736–739.
61 Trentin 2021, 17–18.

The third constitutive element identified is space.[62] In recent years, graffiti studies have emphasized context as an essential element in the study and interpretation of graffiti.[63] While this is certainly the case, the notion of context entails interpretative elements that need to be sifted out, at least in the initial part of the analysis that must document and describe the object of study in an objective way. Space, therefore, represents the physical and material aspects of the context, which, combined with interpretations of the socio-cultural, historical, and economic reality, defines the full context. Replacing the notion of context with that of space in the description of graffiti creates a more precise and objective way to highlight how in the analysis and interpretation phase, context (physical space plus socio-cultural and functional elements) plays a primary role in understanding graffiti's functions. Consider, for example, how a name traced on a church wall takes on different functions based on its position, according to a 'sacred hierarchy'.[64]

The endless variations and associations within these elements define the function of every single graffito. Moreover, by combining the elements of form, content, and space, it is possible to describe and analyse, case by case, in a precise and objective way, the mechanism of communication used and the spatial interaction that will lead to a definitive interpretation of graffiti's functions.

4.3 The workflow

The theoretical definition of the elements of graffiti and its mechanism of communication has been translated into a practical approach through an operational workflow (Fig. 7). This is divided into three phases: documentation, analysis, and interpretation. For each phase, the individual graffito and the support, monument, or site are considered separately. The first phase focuses on testing and defining the best solutions for the high-quality, reliable, and transparent documentation of each graffito and their site (4.4). The second phase deals with the analysis, therefore with the definition of analytical models suitable to describe and practically catalogue the graffiti and sites or buildings (4.6). This operation presupposes the existence of cataloguing standards to guarantee quality data creation. The choice of the STARC graffiti projects has been to follow the FAIR

62 Trentin 2021, 18–20.

63 Baird and Taylor 2011; Lovata and Olton 2015; Dirven and van Gelder 2018, 11.

64 Plesch 2002; Yasin 2015; Ritsema and van Eck 2018; Trentin et al. 2023, Appendix A.

Data Principles and their guidelines for creating Findable, Accessible, Interoperable, and Reusable data (4.5). Once collected and analysed, data can be interpreted based on different combinations of the three constitutive elements identified above: form, content, and space. Moreover, to keep track of all the steps, defining and describing each part of the process and sharing this knowledge, a specific ontology has been developed (4.7). An ontology is a formal description of knowledge concerning a specific domain. By defining the concepts and their relationships in a semantic way, complex processes can be addressed and described in order to share knowledge and obtain a deeper and more structured view of the domain.

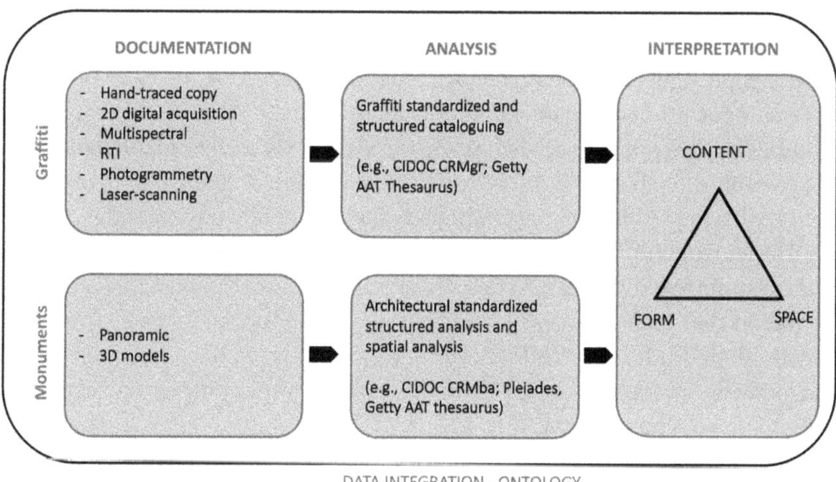

Fig. 7: Graffiti workflow as developed within the STARC projects.

4.4 Graffiti and space documentation

The first part of the workflow deals with the documentation that focuses on a graffito and its site or monument. Among scholars, graffiti documentation is known to be particularly difficult due to the very nature of the material, drawn with makeshift tools on surfaces not intended for writing. Garrucci himself has stressed the material difficulties of the documentation, summarizing the main issues:

> Presque toutes les inscriptions reproduites dans ce recueil ont été calquées de ma main ; je le dis pour qu'on sache que je m'en fais garant. Lorsque je les ai seulement dessinées, j'ai soin d'en avertir. L'exécution d'un pareil projet offrait des difficultés qu'on appréciera

> difficilement si on ne l'a expérimenté soi même. Il faut bien des fois chercher sous le papier des traits qui se dérobent ; le moindre souffle peut obliger à recommencer un calque ; le plus grand jour peut même devenir un embarras, parce qu'une demie-ombre est quelquefois bien plus favorable. Sur la muraille même, l'enduit modifié par le temps peut altérer les traits anciens, et rendre la lecture douteuse.[65]

Before the advent of digital photography, graffiti was mainly documented through manual copies with frottage or hand-tracing.[66] The two techniques create copies that are not always sufficient for reading and studying the inscriptions. Frottage, in fact, while producing a sort of cast of the graffiti, cannot be precise and misses its most subtle features. Furthermore, disruptive elements, such as irregular surfaces, could impede this method and make it unsuitable. Frottage, then, is not adapted to documenting graffiti traced with pigment. Hand-copying, on the other hand, is based solely on the surveyor's experience and skills, so different people may produce copies with different details.[67]

Analogue photography guarantees a more objective documentation, but unfortunately, these images also do not always allow for a clear reading of graffiti due to requiring specific lighting conditions. Michael Stone's photographic archive, collected in his Rock Inscriptions Project, is an illustration of this.[68]

The advent and rapid development of digital photography have solved many of these problems over the past few decades. First, it has enabled low-cost documentation that has exponentially increased graffiti documentation, and consequently their study. New technologies and applications have been developed, and today we have a wide range of options capable of guaranteeing objective and high-quality documentation.[69]

The various techniques used in the study of graffiti today will not be treated here. In the context of a broader methodological approach, one factor that must

65 Garrucci 1854, avertissement. 'Almost all the inscriptions reproduced in this collection have been traced by my [own] hand; I say this so to state that I vouch for them. When I have only sketched them, I make a note of this. Undertaking such a project posed difficulties that one can hardly appreciate without experiencing it oneself. Many times you have to look under the paper for features that may have slipped away; the slightest breath can force you to start the copy over again; the brightest daylight can even become a trouble, because half shade is sometimes much more favourable. On the wall itself, the surface, modified by time, can alter the old features, and make the reading doubtful' (translation mine).

66 Valente and Brazzetti 2020, 2.

67 Valente and Brazzetti 2020, Fig. 1.

68 <http://rockinscriptions.huji.ac.il> (accessed on 9 December 2022).

69 For a complete and detailed description and critical discussion concerning the state of the art of ancient graffiti documentation see Valente and Brazzetti 2020.

instead be considered is the creation of good practices and guidelines that follow the principles of FAIRness, also with respect to documentation.

The graffiti's documentation must reflect the data structure previously defined and be able to record the material aspects of the graffiti, its form and support, which in the case of graffiti is not only the surface that bears the graffiti, but the whole natural or anthropogenic structure (e.g. isolated rocks or buildings). This is the reason why the workflow entails two levels: a specific one linked to each graffito and a more general one documenting the support, considered as a whole. The support documentation is essential, as it records one of the three constituent elements of graffiti: space. Space is the element that contributes to assigning a function to graffiti during the interpretation phase. As noted above, the space concerns the specific position (e.g. at a certain height on a particular wall) and the graffito position in relation to the structure (e.g. in which part of the building).

The guidelines and good practices must therefore be thought of as a tool that guarantees the quality and reliability of the collected data through the definition of specific workflows and standards, and must guide the creation of a documentation framework. For each context – as is already being done in graffiti studies – the different documentation possibilities (e.g. 3D models with photogrammetry or laser scanning, panoramic pictures) should be weighed based on the characteristics of the site, the needs of the project, and the available resources.

4.5 Graffiti as complex data managed with the FAIR approach

The second step of the workflow concerns the data describing the graffiti and the site or monument. The structuring of these data has been defined based on the theoretical description of the three constituent elements of graffiti – form, content, and space. On a practical level, it translates to a complex set of variants that combine differently case by case, graffito by graffito. These variants, their relationships, and their various combinations can be defined and approached as complex data, not in the most common sense of denoting a high number of single records, but in the more theoretical sense of comprising different formats and natures (e.g. texts, pictures, 3D models, analytical data). Therefore, the aggregation of these complex data needs to be addressed with a multidisciplinary approach that can manage the various challenges of graffiti data,[70] such as:

70 Gattiglia 2015, 117.

- a high number of inscriptions;[71]
- the presence of both textual and pictorial forms with their specific descriptions and specific approaches (e.g. epigraphy for textual graffiti, nautical archaeology for ship graffiti, art history for figurative graffiti);
- the presence of various visual data as the result of the different techniques used for the specific graffiti documentation (e.g. photogrammetry, RTI, 3D scanning, multispectral imaging) based on specific characteristics (scratched or painted);
- site documentation and visualization to record the graffiti location and distribution (e.g. 3D models, panoramic imaging, GIS);
- the existing bibliography; and
- the existing non-digital documentation (e.g. analogue pictures, hand-tracings).

Therefore, the method does not exclusively pertain to collecting the descriptive elements of graffiti and their context, but also includes all the processes of documentation, cataloguing, archiving, structuring, management, formatting, and processing to which the data are subjected – hence the need to establish not only a cataloguing methodology, but a structured workflow that guarantees the reliability of all the data processes on a qualitative and operational level.[72]

To deal with the complexity and magnitude of the Cypriot graffiti corpus, the FAIR Data Principles were identified as the most fitting solution. The FAIR Data Principles promote the creation of Findable, Accessible, Interoperable, and Reproducible data based on standards and guidelines that guarantee data quality and reliability and facilitate their interoperability, exchange, retrieval, and dissemination. The growing adoption of the FAIR Data Principles in research – encouraged by the European Union through the work of All European Academies (ALLEA)[73] and increasingly widespread in the cultural heritage sector, including galleries, libraries, archives, and museums ('GLAMs') – confirms their efficiency in addressing and fulfilling diverse needs.

4.6 Cataloguing records and standards for graffiti

One of the basic requirements for the creation of FAIR data is the presence of standards. In the field of epigraphy, descriptive standards are well established

71 Matthew Champion, director of the Norfolk Medieval Graffiti Survey, estimates the number of graffiti collected in Norfolk County at more than 65,000 items (personal communication with the author, 2021); meanwhile, a single site, such as the Basilica of San Marco in Venice, may preserve more than 2,500 graffiti (result of a preliminary survey by the author).

72 Djindjian 2020, 210–213.

73 As noted in a 2020 report of the All European Academies (ALLEA) Working Group E-Humanities.

thanks to the guidelines of the Leiden Conventions (1931)[74] and their digital adaptation, the EpiDoc system.[75]

Once again, epigraphic methodology offers an excellent starting point for developing more inclusive tools, capable of cataloguing not only textual graffiti but also pictorial ones.

As part of STARC's research on graffiti, these epigraphic standards have been maintained for cataloguing texts, while other descriptors have been incorporated for the remaining material. The records generated follow the data structure described in the ontology, and standardized definitions from various thesauri have been combined to guarantee a standard description in terms of the FAIR principles.

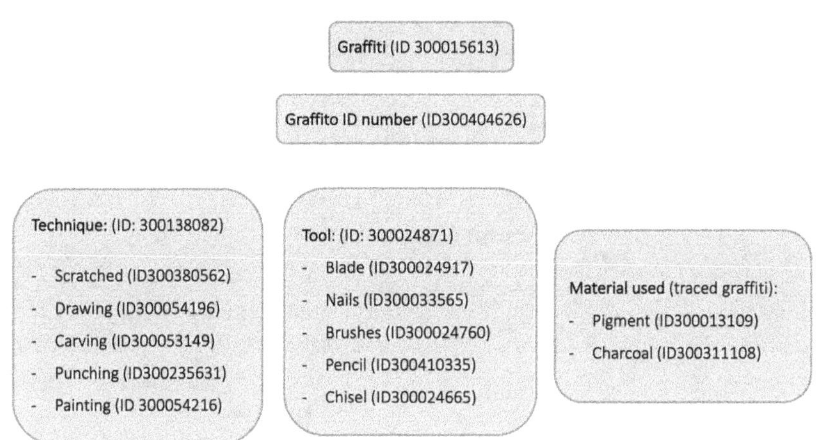

Fig. 8: Examples of graffiti material descriptors.

To illustrate the structuring procedure, Fig. 8 lists some of the descriptors that define the technique and the materials or tools used to create the graffiti.[76] The reference thesaurus is the Getty Art and Architecture Thesaurus (AAT).[77] When a descriptor has a corresponding entry in the AAT, it is indicated in brackets, which facilitates the identification and characterization of the different items in a standardized format.

74 Van Groningen 1932; Wilcken 1932.

75 <https://epidoc.stoa.org/gl/latest/> (accessed on 9 December 2022).

76 The descriptors used for the context cataloging are based on the works of Brogiolo 1988 and Parenti 2002.

77 <https://www.getty.edu/research/tools/vocabularies/aat/> (accessed on 9 December 2022).

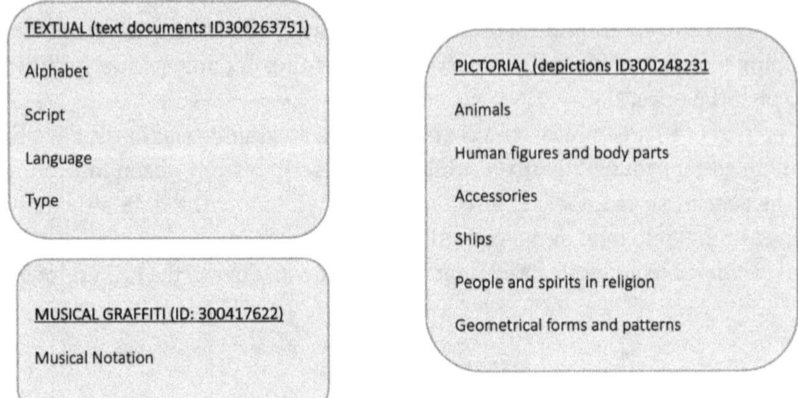

Fig. 9a: Examples of graffiti classes and subclasses as defined within the STARC projects.

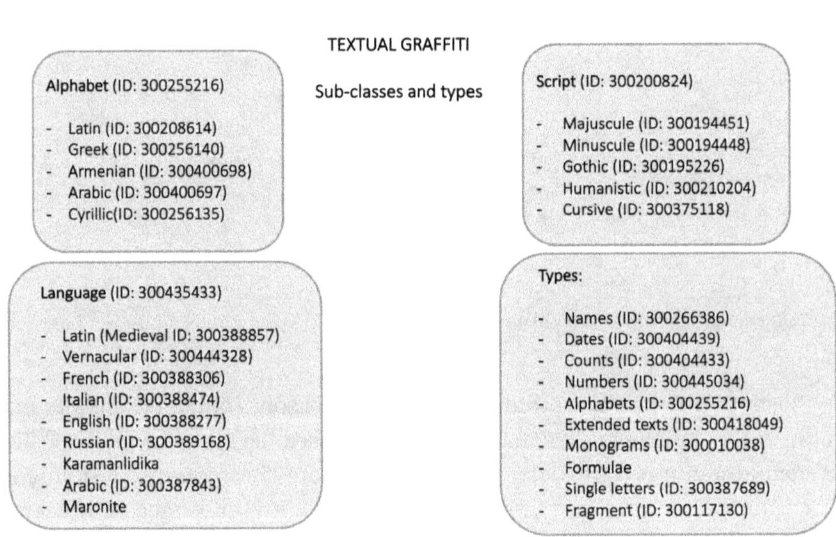

Fig. 9b: Textual graffiti subclasses and types.

GEOMETRICAL FORMS AND PATTERNS

- Cross (ID30235443)
- Compass drawn designs
- Triangles (ID300009806)
- Arboriform
- Mandorla (ID300375683)
- Ladders
- Meshes
- Nine men morris
- Lightening
- Butterfly
- Stars (motifs ID300009811)
- Group of vertical lines
- Groups of horizontal lines
- Zig-zag (ID: 300165028)
- Rectangles with internal partition
- Meshes with inscribed points
- Square with inscribed X

Fig. 9c: Geometrical form and pattern of subclass types.

In Fig. 9a, the graffiti classification is presented, defined on the basis of the Cypriot material. The classes identified are divided into textual and pictorial graffiti and musical notation. They have been defined through a formal approach that focuses on the form, not the content or function of graffiti. Each class has subclasses, and each subclass has types structured in a hierarchical way. The class of textual graffiti, for instance, has the subclasses of alphabet, script, and language (Fig. 9a). Each subclass has types to allow a more detailed and in-depth description, as shown in Fig. 9b, with the subclasses and types of textual graffiti. All classes, subclasses, and types have been mapped onto the AAT in order to guarantee the standardization of the descriptors. Nevertheless, some types do not find a match in the AAT and may be problematic. This is the case, for example, of the group 'geometrical forms and patterns', a subclass of pictorial graffiti (Fig. 9c), where types such as ladders, meshes, and lightning do not have a Getty AAT ID. These forms, in fact, have been named based on their similarity to an object or its stylization. The term 'lightning', for example, defines vertical zigzag lines reminiscent of the stylization of a lightning bolt, which are reported for the first time in Matthew Champion's graffiti typologies, as developed within the Norfolk Medieval Graffiti Survey project (NMGS).[78] Some of these forms are rarely

78 <http://www.medieval-graffiti.co.uk>. The graffiti types developed by the NMGS are outlined at <http://www.medieval-graffiti.co.uk/graffiti%20types4.pdf> (accessed on 9 December 2022).

documented precisely because they are not among the most popular graphic motifs and have so far been the object of marginal attention; therefore, their name is still subject to each researcher's creativity. The comparison with thesauri and descriptive standards is helpful in the sense of stimulating dialogue and encouraging the definition of aspects not yet adequately addressed. The creation of a common language, as we find in the field of epigraphy, is fundamental to the identification, documentation, and analysis of all graffiti forms, aiming to offer more inclusiveness and completeness in this field of study. Moreover, the lack of a shared and standardized lexicon prevents the exchange of data between researchers, slowing down the progress of research.

4.7 Graffiti: An ontological approach

A last endeavour towards the creation of FAIR data was the definition of a specific ontology to ensure data sharing, interoperability, and reuse. An ontology is a formal description of knowledge structured through the semantic definition of sets of concepts and their mutual relations. The structure of the ontology allows us to better manage the data. As indicated in the workflow schema (Fig. 7), the ontology is the tool that links all parts of the process and unites them semantically, creating a structure of knowledge for the specific field of graffiti. As will be seen in greater detail below, the ontological description offers the possibility of penetrating deeply into the description of various aspects of a phenomenon, linking them together by creating an organic, inclusive, transparent, and standardized description. Being a theoretical, ontological description, the advantage is that each element is described and considered on a theoretical level capable of overcoming the limitations often imposed by its real manifestations. In the specific case of graffiti, for example, the ontology has made it possible to create a description of graffiti as a graphic expression – textual or pictorial – and to insert it within a space that is also described and treated in the same way. In this way, focusing on the theoretical definition, it was possible to create a system applicable to all physical evidence, and therefore to any form of graffiti in any context.

In our case, the ontology has been fundamental to describing the communication mechanism behind the creation of graffiti, overcoming the methodological imbalance existing between textual graffiti – approached with epigraphic tools – and pictorial ones, so heterogeneous and different from texts that their integration seems impossible. The ontological model selected as most fitting was the CIDOC

Conceptual Reference Model. The CIDOC CRM is a Conceptual Reference Model[79] capable of structuring an object's implicit and explicit elements by identifying and defining the entities and relations that characterize it. The analysis of the different approaches and methodologies used in the study of graffiti so far, as presented in the first part of this contribution, allowed for the identification of the three constitutive elements of graffiti, as described above: form, content, and space.

This step was crucial in making explicit the two different communication mechanisms underlying graffiti, which are expressed formally through texts and images. To clarify the distinction between formal and interpretative aspects and graffiti analysis, the ontology has been divided into three levels: physical, symbolic, and conceptual (Fig. 10).[80] In this way, it was possible to include textual and pictorial forms in the first level (both as graphic evidence), focusing only on the description of their form and their material characteristics (e.g. technique, the tool used) and, in the case of traced graffiti, the material employed. The second level defines the relations between the forms (symbolic object–symbol) and the content (expression–meaning) attributed to the graffiti by observation. The third level, the conceptual one, indicates the relation of the two previous entities to the object (information object–referent) to which the graffiti refers. If we consider, for example, a simple coat of arms (only the shield with shield elements inside), on the first level we will consider the material elements of the graffito, such as the making technique (traced or scratched) and the tools used for its realization. The second level will consider the form, describing all the elements present, such as the shield and each shield element (e.g. animals, flowers, crosses). On the third level, the coat of arms, considered as a composition of single elements, will be associated with its content: an expression of the identity of a noble family or individual.

This specific ontology for graffiti was developed based on the ontology for epigraphic texts elaborated by Achille Felicetti and Francesca Murano,[81] using more general categories (superclasses) to allow for the necessary inclusion of non-textual material. In the case of pictorial graffiti, a more general extension will be used,[82] while in the case of texts, the specific extension for epigraphic

79 <https://www.cidoc-crm.org> (accessed on 9 December 2022).

80 The diagram reflects the concept based on which the graffiti ontology was developed. A detailed description, with the CIDOC CRM standard and a specific graffiti extension, is available in Trentin and Felicetti 2023.

81 Felicetti et al. 2015; Felicetti and Murano 2017.

82 The ontology for graffiti has introduced the specific new extension CRMgr (Conceptual Reference Model for graffiti). Once finalised, the new extension will be presented for discussion and validation by the CIDOC CRM committee.

materials will be applied.[83] As it has developed, the graffiti ontology has maintained and clarified the unbreakable link between graffiti and epigraphy, and manages to guarantee a level of inclusiveness that, until now, the epigraphic methodology was unable to provide by itself.

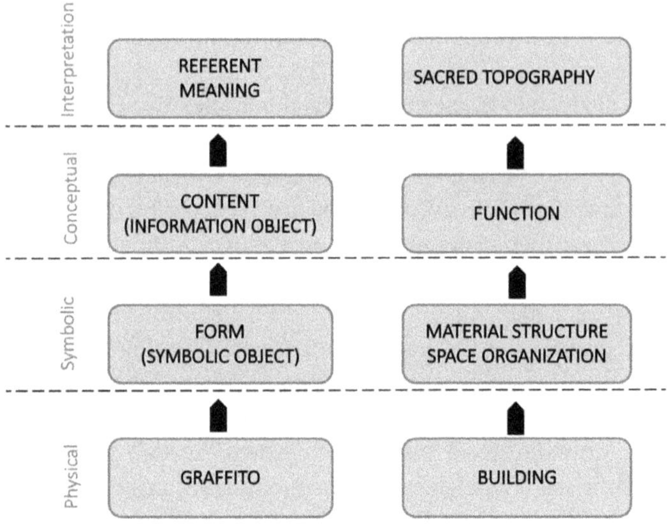

Fig. 10: Diagram of graffiti ontology.

Finally, space must be dedicated to the elements of form and content. This part, still under discussion, has been developed thanks to the specific extension for building archaeology.[84] In this case, too, the building that supports the graffiti is analysed on three levels: physical, functional, and conceptual. The first level identifies the structure based on its material dimensions, and in terms of individual parts. The second level determines the building units' physical and space-time relations. The third describes their use and functions.

If we consider, for example, a church, the first level defines the object as a building. The second level identifies its various parts and their components (e.g. the wall structures, the architectural elements, the liturgical furnishings, the

83 This is the CRMtx (Conceptual Reference Model for Texts) developed by Felicetti and Murano (2015 and 2017).

84 This is the CRMba extension (Conceptual Reference Model for building archaeology) developed by Ronzino et al. 2016 (<https://www.cidoc-crm.org/crmba/>; accessed on 9 December 2022).

coverings). On the third level, the spaces and their characteristics are defined by the functions they had to perform (e.g. the nave to host the public, the altar for the liturgy). This last level in the analysis of a church maps the sacred topography, which associates a physical space with its liturgical function, defining a sort of hierarchy.

The upper level constitutes the final stage of the analysis: interpretation. This is the meeting point of the individual analyses of form, content, and space as just described. The distinction and description of the various steps are useful in the final interpretation phase, allowing one to analyse the material first from a formal and conceptual point of view before reaching a final interpretation.

In addition to the part presented here, the ontology that is being developed also includes a part relating to documentation and data collection, as outlined in the CIDOC CRM model for heritage science documentation.[85] This part will cover the first step of the workflow, dealing with the ontological description of the documentation processes of individual graffiti and monuments using different technologies, such as photogrammetry, 3D scanning, RTI, and multispectral imaging.

5 Conclusions

> Conta ciò che si può contare, misura ciò che è misurabile e rendi misurabile ciò che non lo è.
> (Count what can be counted, measure what is measurable, and make measurable what is not.)
> – Galileo Galilei[86]

This quote from Galileo Galilei summarizes the purpose of the research on historic graffiti that STARC has been developing over the last five years. As discussed in the first part, historic graffiti has always been a challenging topic. Although the study of this field dates back to the nineteenth century, the debate over this graphic evidence has only recently flourished. It now highlights graffiti's potential to provide original information about the past, mostly about the everyday life of ordinary people, their thoughts and feelings, interaction with and perception of the landscapes.

In the Eastern Mediterranean, graffiti reflect the multicultural environment and exchanges between different cultures and traditions along the pilgrimage and economic routes connecting cities and religious sites across the sea and deserts. To collect the traces and stories recorded on the walls and rocks of the area,

85 Niccolucci and Felicetti 2018.

86 Dominici and Amagliani 2018, 83.

scholars have approached graffiti in various ways, adding relevant information on literacy, writing practices, visual culture, rituals, and traditions to the historical and socio-cultural context. The panorama shown in the first part of the paper is rich and complex, challenging to capture in a single definition, as widely discussed.

Thus, STARC has addressed graffiti differently by describing the phenomenon as it emerges from the Cypriot material: describing in order to measure, as Galileo has argued. Thanks to the support of digital technologies and the contributions of digital humanities, Cypriot graffiti heritage has been tackled with a theoretical approach. This innovative method has focused on creating tools for data 'measurability'. Contrary to the previous approaches, STARC investigated the communication mechanisms that lead to graffiti production instead of interpreting the graphic material to understand it. Hence, we identify the three constituent elements of graffiti: form, content, and space. By defining this 'triad' and their mutual relations, it was possible to describe the communication mechanism that underlies expression through graffiti. In practice, this innovative approach resulted in an operating model developed through a workflow in which the documentation and analysis phases follow the FAIR principles. As a fundamental requirement of scientific analysis, quality data creation is based on verification, exchange, and interoperability standards. This work provided the basis for developing a comprehensive database, currently in the testing phase. The DIGIGRAF database allows for the documentation and analysis of graffiti within its context, integrating textual and pictorial graffiti within the same system for the first time. The online publication and open access to the database are scheduled for the end of 2023. The data structure, which includes the classes, subclasses, and types of graffiti identified for the Cypriot context, will be published together with the platform.

However, this achievement is not the final goal, but only a milestone. As argued in this contribution, the study of historical graffiti requires a specific methodology of analysis, inclusive and shared, eventually allowing for the examination of graffiti of different forms and contexts. On the one hand, this approach will facilitate and encourage the exchange and sharing of data, a fundamental part of advancing any discipline or form of knowledge. On the other hand, the study of historical graffiti is foreseen as a centralized field of investigation fuelled by an interdisciplinary approach arising from more than one research group. The DIGIGRAF database will encourage this debate and offer a structured starting point for further developments. Thanks to the collaboration of researchers engaged in historical graffiti studies, it may be possible to 'make measurable' what, for now, is only partially so.

Abbreviations

AAT = Art and Architecture Thesaurus
CIDOC CRM = CIDOC Conceptual Reference Model
DIGIGRAF = DIGItizing GRAFfiti: Methodology Definition for the Study of Cypriot Historic Graffiti
FAIR = Findable, Accessible, Interoperable, Reusable
GRAFMEDIA = GRAFfiti Mediterranean DIAlogue
NMGS = Norfolk Medieval Graffiti Survey
STARC = Science and Technology in Archaeology and Culture Research Center

References

Abulafia, David (2011), *The Great Sea: A Human History of the Mediterranean*, Oxford: Oxford University Press.

All European Academies (ALLEA) Working Group E-Humanities (2020), 'Sustainable and FAIR Data Sharing in the Humanities Report, February 2020' <https://www.ria.ie/sites/default/files/allea_sustainable_and_fair_data_sharing_in_the_humanities_2020_0.pdf> (accessed on 9 December 2022).

Ashworth, Gregory (2011), 'Preservation, Conservation and Heritage: Approaches to the Past in the Present through the Built Environment', *Asian Anthropology*, 10: 1–18.

Avellino, Francesco Maria (1841), *Osservazioni sopra alcune iscrizioni e disegni graffiti sulle mura di Pompei*, Naples: Stamperia Reale.

Baird, Jennifer A. and Claire Taylor (eds) (2011), *Ancient Graffiti in Context*, New York: Routledge.

Brogiolo, Gian Pietro (1988), *Archeologia dell'edilizia storica*, Como: New Press.

Champion, Matthew John (2017), 'The Priest, the Prostitute, and the Slander on the Walls: Shifting Perceptions Towards Historic Graffiti', *Peregrinations: Journal of Medieval Art and Architecture*, 6: 5–37.

Demesticha, Stella, Katerina Delouca, Mia Gaia Trentin, Nikolas Bakirtzis and Andonis Neophytou (2017), 'Seamen on Land? A Preliminary Analysis of Medieval Ship Graffiti on Cyprus', *International Journal of Nautical Archaeology*, 46: 346–381.

Dirven, Lucinda and Maartje van Gelder (2018), 'Inleiding: Graffiti van de oudheid tot heden', *Tijdschrift voor Geschiedenis*, 131/1: 1–15.

Djindjian, François (2020), 'Big Data and Archaeology', *Humanities, Arts and Society*, 1: 208–217.

Dominici, Martina and Olga Amagliani (eds) (2018), *Il libro della scienza*, Milan: Gribaudo.

Dord-Crouslé, Stéphanie (2011), 'Inscrire la mémoire de soi dans les lieux visités: pratique et réception des graffitis par les voyageurs du XIXe siècle', in Sarga Moussa and Sylvain Venayre (eds), *Le voyage et la mémoire au XIXe siècle*, Grane: Créaphis Éditions, 321–337.

Eco, Umberto (2016), *Trattato di Semiotica Generale*, Milan: La Nave di Teseo [1st edn: Milano: Bompiani, 1975].

Felicetti, Achille and Francesca Murano (2017), 'Scripta manent: A CIDOC CRM Semiotic Reading of Ancient Texts', *International Journal on Digital Libraries*, 18/4: 263–270.

Felicetti, Achille, Francesca Murano, Paola Ronzino and Franco Niccolucci (2015), 'CIDOC CRM and Epigraphy: A Hermeneutic Challenge', in Paola Ronzino and Franco Niccolucci (eds), *Extending, Mapping and Focusing the CIDOC CRM: Proceedings of CRMEX 2015* <https://www.semanticscholar.org/paper/CIDOC-CRM-and-Epigraphy%3A-a-Hermeneutic-Challenge-Felicetti-Murano/5ac4f10e5f824bb35ede6af40ee36489408017ca> (accessed on 9 December 2022).

Felle, Enrico Antonio (2017), 'Casi di epigrafi "non esposte": alcune considerazioni', *Studi Medievali*, 58/2: 579–606.

Felle, Enrico Antonio (2020), 'Scritture esposte e graffiti: alcune note di riflessione', in Ferraiuolo Daniele (ed.), *La dimensione spaziale della scrittura esposta in età medievale. Discipline a confronto (Napoli, 14–16 dicembre 2020)* (Quaderni delle IMAI, 1), Spoleto: Fondazione CISAM, 1–14.

Fleming, Juliet (2020), 'Graffiti Futures', *Journal of Early Modern Studies*, 9: 29–36.

Garrucci, Raffaele (1854), *Inscriptions gravées au trait sur les murs de Pompei*, Brussels: J. B. De Mortier.

Garrucci, Raffaele (1856), *Graffiti de Pompei: inscriptions et gravures tracées au stylet*, Paris: Benjamin Duprat.

Gattiglia, Gabriele (2015), 'Think Big about Data: Archaeology and the Big Data Challenge', *Archäologische Informationen*, 38: 113–124.

Goyon, Georges (1944), *Les inscriptions et graffiti des voyageurs sur la Grande Pyramide*, Cairo: Publications spéciales de la Société Royale de Géographie.

Imbert, Fréderic (1996), *Corpus des inscriptions arabes de Jordanie du Nord*, PhD thesis, 3 vols, University of Provence.

Imbert, Fréderic (2013), 'Le Coran des pierres: statistiques épigraphiques et premières analyses', in Azaiez Mehdi and Mervin Sabrina (eds), *Le Coran: Nouvelles approches*, Paris: CNRS Editions, 99–124.

Imbert, Fréderic (2018), 'Un siècle d'épigraphie arabe et islamique en Jordanie', *TOPOÏ*, 22: 347–368.

Kawatoko, Mutsuo (2005), 'Multi-Disciplinary Approaches to the Islamic Period in Egypt and the Red Sea Coast', *Antiquity*, 79/306: 844–857.

Kawatoko, Mutsuo, Risa Tokunaga and Masato Lizuka (2006), *Ancient and Islamic Rock Inscriptions of South Sinai*, Tokyo: Middle Eastern Culture Center in Japan. Research Institute for Languages and Cultures of Asia and Africa, Tokyo University of Foreign Studies.

Kraack, Detlev (1997), *Monumentale Zeugnisse der spätmittelalterlichen Adelsreise: Inschriften und Graffiti des 14.–16. Jahrhunderts*, Göttingen: Vandenhoeck und Ruprecht.

Lagaron, Anna (2018), 'Le christianisme oriental au sud du Sinaï vu au prisme des graffiti arabo-chrétiens (IX–XIe siècle)', *Annales islamologiques*, 52: 81–106.

Lohmann, Polly (2020), 'Historical Graffiti: The State of the Art', *Journal of Medieval and Early Modern Studies*, 9: 37–56.

Lovata, Troy R. and Elisabeth Olton (eds) (2015), *Understanding Graffiti: Multidisciplinary Studies from Prehistory to the Present*, London: Routledge.

Meinardus, Otto (1966), 'The Mediaeval Graffiti in the Monasteries of SS. Antony and Paul', *Studia Orientalia Christiana*, 11: 513–527.

Morin, Olivier, Kelly Piers and James Winters (2020), 'Writing, Graphic Codes, and Asynchronous Communication', *Topic in Cognitive Science*, 12: 727–743.

Niccolucci, Franco and Achille Felicetti (2018), 'A CIDOC CRM-Based Model for the Documentation of Heritage Sciences', in Alonzo C. Addison and Harold Thwaites (eds), *3rd Digital*

Heritage International Congress (DigitalHERITAGE) Held Jointly with 2018 24th International Conference on Virtual Systems & Multimedia (VSMM 2018), San Francisco, CA, 1–6 <doi: 10.1109/DigitalHeritage.2018.8810109> (accessed on 14 March 2023).

Ogden, Charles K. and Ivor A. Richards (1923), *The Meaning of Meaning: A Study of the Influence of Language upon Thought and of the Science of Symbolism*, London: Kegan Paul, Trench, Trubner.

Panciera, Silvio (2012), 'What Is an Inscription? Problems of Definition and Identity of an Historical Source', *Zeitschrift für Papyrologie und Epigraphik*, 183: 1–10.

Parenti, Roberto (2002), 'Dalla stratigrafia all'archeologia dell'architettura: alcune recenti esperienze del laboratorio senese', *Arqueología De La Arquitectura*, 1: 73–82.

Plesch, Veronique (2002), 'Graffiti and Ritualization: San Sebastiano at Arborio', in Joëlle Rollo-Koster (ed.), *Medieval and Early Modern Rituals: Formalized Behaviour in Europe, China and Japan*, Leiden: Brill, 127–146.

Pringle, Denys (1993), *The Churches of the Crusader Kingdom of Jerusalem*, 4 vols, Cambridge: Cambridge University Press.

Ritsema van Eck, Marianne (2018), 'Graffiti in Medieval and Early Modern Religious Spaces: Illicit or Accepted Practice? The Case of the Sacro Monte at Varallo', *Tijdschrift voor Geschiedenis*, 131/1: 51–72.

Ronzino, Paola, Franco Niccolucci, Achille Felicetti and Martin Doerr (2016), 'CRMBA a CRM Extension for the Documentation of Standing Buildings', *International Journal of Digital Libraries*, 17: 71–78.

Sarti, Raffaella (2020), 'Editorial', *Journal of Early Modern Studies*, 9: 7–26.

Stone, Michael E. (1982), *The Armenian Inscriptions from the Sinai with Appendixes on the Georgian and Latin Inscriptions by M. van Esbroeck and W. Adler* (Harvard Armenian Texts and Studies, 6), Cambridge: Harvard University Press.

Stone, Michael E. (1992a), *Rock Inscriptions and Graffiti Project*, vol. 1 (SBL Resources for Biblical Study), Atlanta: Scholars Press.

Stone, Michael E. (1992b), *Rock Inscriptions and Graffiti Project*, vol. 2 (SBL Resources for Biblical Study), Atlanta: Scholars Press.

Stone, Michael E. (1993), *Rock Inscriptions and Graffiti Project*, vol. 3 (SBL Resources for Biblical Study), Atlanta: Scholars Press.

Trentin, Mia Gaia (2011), *I graffiti come fonte per la storia delle pratiche religiose medievali*, PhD thesis, University of Venice Ca' Foscari <http://hdl.handle.net/10579/1079> (accessed on 9 December 2022).

Trentin, Mia Gaia (2021), 'Form, Content, and Space: Methodological Challenges in the Study of Medieval and Early Modern European Graffiti', *Papers from the Institute of Archaeology*, 30/1: 1–25 <doi.org/10.14324/111.444.2041- 9015.1283> (accessed on 9 December 2022).

Trentin, Mia Gaia and Achille Felicetti (2023), 'Between Written and Visual Communication: CIDOC CRM Ontology for Medieval and Early Modern European Graffiti', *Journal on Computing and Cultural Heritage,* <doi.org/10.1145/3589230>.

Trentin, Mia Gaia, Doron Altaratz, Moshe Caine, Amit Re'em, Andrea Tinazzo and Svetlana Gasanova (2023), 'Historic Graffiti as a Visual Medium for the Sustainable Development of the Underground Built Heritage', *Sustainability*, 15/15: 11697 <doi.org/10.3390/su151511697>.

Valente, Riccardo and Luigi Barazzetti (2020). 'Methods for Ancient Wall Graffiti Documentation: Overview and Applications', *Journal of Archaeological Science: Reports*, 34: 102616 <doi.org/10.1016/j.jasrep.2020.102616> (accessed on 9 December 2022).

Van Belle, Jean Louis and Anne Sophie Brun (2020), *Le graffiti-signature: reflet d'histoire*, Brussels: Safran.

Van Groningen, Bernard A. (1932), 'Projet d'unification des systèmes de signes critiques', *Chronique d'Égypte*, 7: 262–269.

Wilcken, Ulrich (1932), 'Das Leydener Klammersystem', *Archiv für Papyrusforschung*, 10: 211–212.

Wilkinson, Mark, et al. (2016), 'The FAIR Guiding Principles for Scientific Data Management and Stewardship', *Scientific Data*, 3: 160018 <doi.org/10.1038/sdata.2016.18> (accessed on 3 April 2023).

Yasin, Anne Marie (2015), 'Prayers on Site: The Materiality of Devotional Graffiti and the Production of Early Christian Sacred Space', in Anthony Eastmond (ed.), *Viewing Inscriptions in the Late Antique and Medieval World*, New York: Cambridge University Press, 36–60.

Zorzi, Pietro Alvise (1877), *Osservazioni intorno ai ristauri interni ed esterni della Basilica di San Marco*, Venice: s.n.

Europe

Rebecca R. Benefiel, Holly M. Sypniewski

Documenting Ancient Graffiti: Text, Image, Support and Access

Abstract: This chapter discusses how the method for documenting ancient graffiti, including both what to document and how, has changed over the centuries. With a focus on the inscriptions of first century Pompeii, we stress that graffiti are epigraphic artefacts, thus requiring both epigraphic and archaeological consideration. We present a historical overview explaining how graffiti have been documented, from early publications in the nineteenth century to technological innovations in the twenty-first. We then discuss the aims, methods and results of the Ancient Graffiti Project, a current project to document graffiti and a public-facing scholarly resource. Based on a decade of epigraphic research and archaeological fieldwork, AGP offers a digital platform and tools to support a richer understanding of ancient graffiti from the early Roman Empire in their archaeological context.

1 Introduction

In 2018, new excavations conducted by the Archaeological Park of Pompeii yielded a treasure trove of discoveries: a remarkable fresco of the mythological subject of Leda and the swan, a *thermopolium*, or snack bar, still containing food residue and animal bones, and a handwritten inscription, or graffito (Fig. 1).[1] It was the announcement about the graffito that generated headlines in major news outlets, such as CNN and The Guardian.[2] The graffito, written in charcoal, an easily perishable material, contained a date in October and so was brought into the active debate about whether the eruption of Mt. Vesuvius occurred in late summer or later fall of 79 CE. The graffito reached such a wide audience and so

1 The press releases for each have been archived on the website of the Archaeological Park of Pompeii (http://pompeiisites.org/).

2 Mezzofiore 2018 ('Pompeii's Charcoal Graffiti May Rewrite History'); AFP in Rome 2018 ('Archaeological Find Changes Date of Pompeii's Destruction'). Other headlines included 'Graffiti in Pompeii Set to Rewrite History Books" (*The Week UK*) and 'A Newly Discovered Piece of Graffiti Has Changed the History of Pompeii as We Know It' (*Lonely Planet*).

https://doi.org/10.1515/9783111326306-014

quickly because it was shared by Massimo Osanna, Director of the Archaeological Park – on Instagram. This was a very twenty-first century mode for sharing an epigraphic discovery.

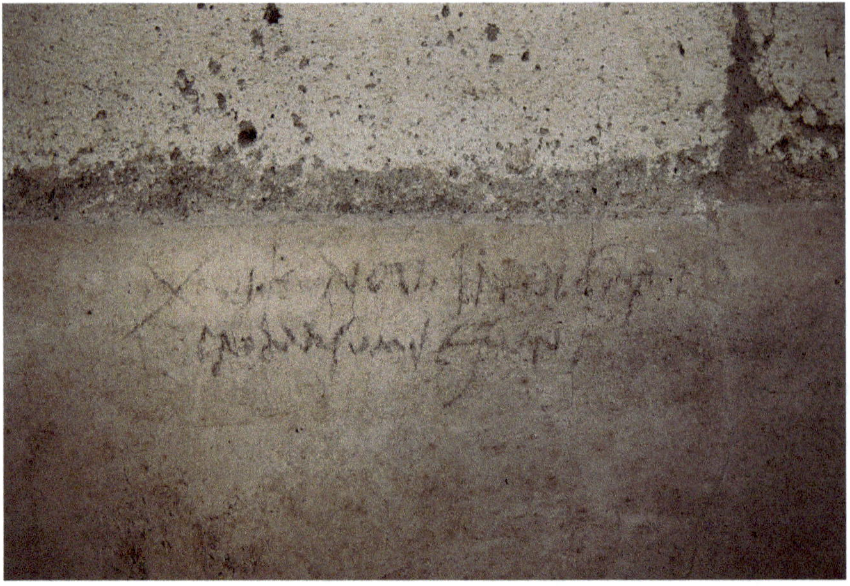

Fig. 1: Graffito in charcoal from Regio V, Pompeii; photograph kindly provided by the Parco Archeologico di Pompei, Archivio fotografico. Su concessione del Ministero della Cultura - Parco Archeologico di Pompei. Reproduction expressly prohibited.

The global attention that this charcoal graffito generated can be compared with another discovery in Pompeii that similarly exploded in international news outlets nearly one hundred years earlier: the SATOR square (Fig. 2). Written in five lines, with a single word of five letters on each line, and arranged into a 5×5 grid, the graffito was called a magic square since it can be read from left to right, right to left, vertically up or down and the text will be the same:[3]

3 *CIL* IV 8623. See the entry EDR073638 in the Epigraphic Database Roma (www.edr-edr.it), by Holly Sypniewski, for full text and copious bibliography on the inscription. The standard reference for Latin inscriptions is the *Corpus Inscriptionum Latinarum*, (abbreviated *CIL*, followed by the appropriate volume number) an immense, international project begun in the mid-nineteenth century, and which continues today, to edit and publish all Latin inscriptions from antiquity. It continues under the auspices of the Berlin-Brandenburgische Akademie der Wissenschaften (cil.bbaw.de).

ROTAS
OPERA
TENET
AREPO
SATOR

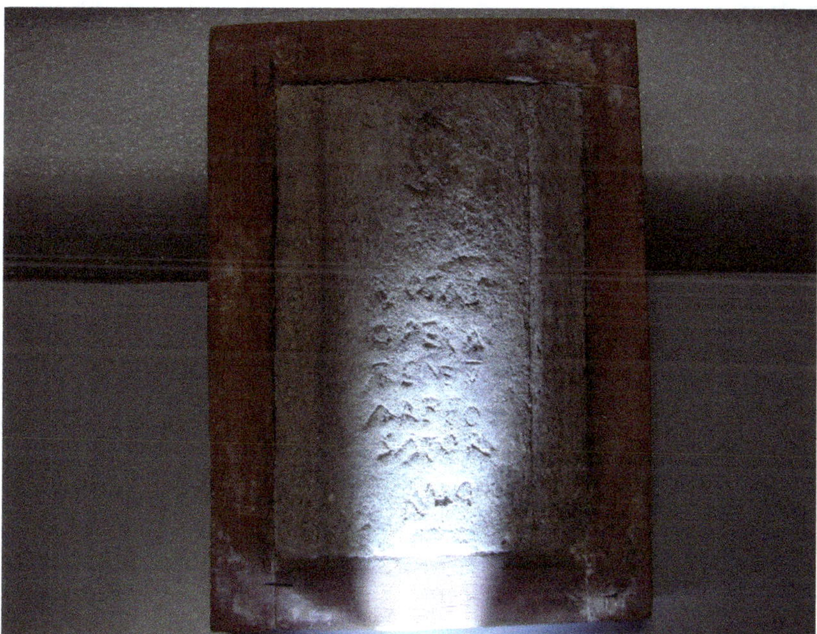

Fig. 2: Plaster cast of the SATOR square graffito (CIL IV 8623), storerooms of the Parco Archeologico di Pompei, inv. 20565. Su concessione del Ministero della Cultura - Parco Archeologico di Pompei. Reproduction expressly prohibited.

The inscription is an intriguing example of wordplay, but its fame resulted from the fact that two early twentieth century scholars independently rearranged the letters to spell out *Pater Noster* (mostly, only a few extra letters had to be explained) and it was thence connected with early (encoded or hidden) Christianity. Pompeii is not the only place this word square was found, and, in fact, this was not the only example inscribed in Pompeii.[4] The SATOR square pattern has also

4 *CIL* IV 8123 (inscribed in the House of Paquius Proculus at Pompeii). The text is also represented in the fresco depicting the riot in Pompeii as painted on the facade of the Praedia of Julia Felix. See Benefiel 2012, 68 and O'Donald 2018, 87–89.

been found in Dura Europos and in medieval contexts. The first century destruction of Pompeii, however, creates doubts that this inscription derived from a Christian context. It is more likely one of a number of word squares that were popular in antiquity across the Mediterranean. Another example of this trend, also found at Pompeii, presented a 4×4 word square:[5]

ROMA
OLIM
MILO
AMOR

In this instance, the writer frames the square with the palindrome ROMA / AMOR (Rome / Love), a favorite bit of wordplay also found in literary texts.

The potential mystery behind the SATOR square, however, created sustained interest in the graffito.[6] When it became clear that the first-century plaster on which the graffito had been inscribed was suffering damage and wear and tear, that portion of the column was excised and removed to the storerooms of Pompeii for safekeeping. Recognizing the value of the inscription, a modern plaster cast was also created. The original plaster that held the graffito has now crumbled into small pieces, but the plaster cast provides a facsimile of the original.[7] Fortunately, the inscription was also photographed in 1964, and the resulting image reveals that the SATOR square was one among a handful of inscribed messages on this column.[8]

These two examples demonstrate the ability Pompeian graffiti have to captivate the public despite their brief nature. Their stories also hint at the challenges involved in documenting, preserving and publishing ancient graffiti as they have been discovered over the past two centuries. The charcoal graffito revealed in the most recent excavations has so far been left in situ in the atrium in Regio V where

5 *CIL* IV 8297.

6 The 2020 science fiction film, *Tenet*, directed by Christopher Nolan, took inspiration from this pattern. *Sator* and *Arepo* are names of characters in the film, while *Rotas* is the name of the security company. In an article in *Digital Spy*, Ian Sandwell, explains that even *opera* made it into the movie as the setting for the opening scene (Ian Sandwell, 'Tenet Has a Link to an Ancient Unsolved Puzzle (Because of Course It Does). Oh Nolan…', <https://www.digitalspy.com/movies/a33885154/tenet-sator-square-link-explained/>, posted on 2 September 2020 (accessed on 21 September 2022). Articles and websites are still being created to explain this mysterious graffito. A google search for 'SATOR square' in June 2022 returns 855,000 results.

7 It is difficult to cast in plaster the small, thin incisions of ancient graffiti; the replica offers the size and scale and a rough image of the original graffito.

8 Varone (2012, vol. I, 144) reproduces the photograph.

it was found. Charcoal, however, is an incredibly delicate medium: it can be easily erased with a brush of the hand. It *can* survive, but only if it is protected from the elements and from any accidental contact. The SATOR square graffito, on the other hand, demonstrates that even when thoughtful steps are taken to protect and preserve an ancient graffito, such as removal from a public space to a protected context, the two-thousand-year-old plaster that holds these writings is only so strong. At some point, its lifespan is finite.

We might guess that documenting ancient graffiti would be a simple matter of photography. However, photography was not broadly available when ancient graffiti were first recognized and collected. Secondly, once photography was employed more widely, it was not applied to graffiti.[9] Thirdly, even when the value of obtaining illustration of graffiti is clear, graffiti are not easy to photograph. They are small, often discreet, and there is little contrast to render marks visible or clear in a photograph. Add to this the massive corpus of graffiti from the region affected by the eruption of Mt. Vesuvius, the long span of nearly two centuries that Pompeian graffiti have been known, and the concomitant changes in method during the many generations of this span. There has, therefore, been no clearly evident route forward to document ancient graffiti.

This chapter on documenting ancient graffiti is grounded in our experience in long-standing projects, the Herculaneum Graffiti Project and the Ancient Graffiti Project. It is also informed by Rebecca Benefiel's work as contributing scholar in charge of publishing the graffiti from the imperial villa at Oplontis and as a supervisor for the Epigraphic Database Roma. Studying and publishing ancient graffiti for various projects has shown us that the process of documenting ancient graffiti does not have a standard set of guidelines. Each site will hold its own challenges. This chapter offers both a retrospective for how graffiti have been documented over the centuries and as a model of how our nearly decade-long project has sought to overcome the obstacles our material involves.

In this chapter, we will discuss the need, potential methods and the process of documenting ancient graffiti, especially within the context of what we have learned over the past decade in building The Ancient Graffiti Project. Our work focuses on ancient graffiti in the sites destroyed by the volcanic eruption of Mt. Vesuvius in 79 CE. The immediate and overwhelming destruction of the eruption preserved the plaster and wall coverings of entire cities to an extent that is unparalleled elsewhere. The Vesuvian area has yielded thousands of ancient graffiti. In addition to documenting many of these inscriptions, we have built an

9 The earliest publication that provides more than a few photographs of Pompeian graffiti is that of Varone 2012.

open-access digital platform that presents ancient graffiti to the public and that provides critical editions and a suite of digital tools for scholars to study ancient graffiti in context.[10]

2 Ancient graffiti as epigraphic artefacts

Silvio Panciera, esteemed professor of Latin epigraphy at La Sapienza University of Rome, would instruct his students: In order to be a good epigrapher, one must be a philologist, an ancient historian, an archaeologist, a palaeographer, in sum, a Classicist conversant in the many sub-disciplines of Classics.[11] The same is true for studying ancient graffiti. There was a time when these handwritten inscriptions were treated simply as texts – and limited texts at that; but graffiti have physical characteristics in addition to textual content. To neglect or ignore their physicality is to miss all the other ways ancient graffiti communicate to their reader. How large was an inscription? How deeply incised was it? What style of lettering? Where on the wall was it inscribed? Did the writer take into account aspects of the physical environment, for example, decoration, lighting sources, or the presence of other writings? What was the visual impact upon the reader or the passerby? In order to understand the message, the author's intent and the audience for an ancient graffito, a scholar must engage with its content, as well as its historical background, topographical and archaeological context, handwriting, physical appearance and more. Graffiti represent both text and object. A graffito is manually created in a physical environment and becomes part of that environment, at least for some period of time. Ancient graffiti are therefore best considered epigraphic artefacts, an approach that acknowledges and addresses both their epigraphic and archaeological nature.

Furthermore, it is crucial to note that, as artefacts, ancient graffiti often exist under precarious circumstances: they are inscribed on fragile, perishable material; they are routinely exposed to atmospheric elements and the general public; and, because of their integration into building surfaces, they are seldom removed

10 www.ancientgraffiti.org.

11 Benefiel had the good fortune to study at La Sapienza under both Professor Silvio Panciera and Professor Silvia Orlandi thanks to a Rotary Foundation Scholarship. The leadership and impact of both scholars on the field of Latin epigraphy cannot be stressed enough. Panciera's publications reflect his approach, cf. Panciera et al. 2006. The massive three-volume compilation of his writings (Panciera 2006) demonstrates his productive and broad approach to the field. Panciera 2012 is also fundamental.

to climate-controlled environments. Given these vulnerabilities, it is fundamentally important to document ancient graffiti as thoroughly as possible.

First, a word about the term *graffiti*. It was coined in the mid-nineteenth century to describe small scratched writings that were being found in excavations of Roman ruins in Pompeii and Rome. The word began as an adjective used to describe scratched drawings and inscriptions, then by the end of the nineteenth century had evolved to become a noun for these scratched inscriptions in anglophone scholarship.[12] During the course of the second half of the twentieth century, the term *graffiti*, at least for English speakers, expanded to mean any informal writing on a wall.

Pompeii is the site most closely associated with ancient graffiti. Destroyed by the eruption of Mt. Vesuvius in 79 CE, the city of Pompeii was buried to a depth of up to 6m, covered by light lapilli and volcanic debris, which preserved the wall-plaster of virtually every building in the town. That wall-plaster held painted wall-inscriptions (*dipinti*) advertising gladiatorial games and candidates for local elections; it also held thousands of individual, casual messages written by members of the general population.

Most of these handwritten inscriptions were created by means of a sharp implement, such as a stylus or fibula, which was used to lightly scratch marks, words or images, into the wall-plaster. Other material could be used to create handwritten inscriptions too. Chalk, charcoal, rocks and gypsum are among the materials noted sporadically by excavators.[13] Those materials are easily erased when brushed against or exposed to rain, and so it is difficult to estimate how frequently these might have appeared on the city's walls. Thousands of scratched graffiti of Pompeii, however, reveal that the practice of writing on the city walls was popular indeed.[14]

Significant quantities of ancient graffiti have been recovered from other sites also destroyed by Mt. Vesuvius. Herculaneum, Stabiae, Oplontis and the

12 Avellino 1841 ('Osservazioni sopra alcune iscrizioni e disegni graffiti sulle mura di Pompei'); Mau (1899, 481) had to explain the term to his readers: 'The graffiti… compris[e] about three thousand examples, or one half the entire number [of wall-inscriptions uncovered at that time]; the name is Italian, being derived from a verb meaning "to scratch."' Italian scholarship still observes the difference between graffiti (scratched wall-inscriptions) and dipinti (painted wall-inscriptions) while English speakers use the word 'graffiti' now to refer to essentially any writing on a wall.

13 Cf. Benefiel 2021, esp. 5–6, and DiBiasie-Sammons 2022.

14 Benefiel and her team have edited more than 1800 scratched wall-inscriptions from Pompeii thus far for the Epigraphic Database Roma (www.edr-edr.it), and more than 2500 ancient graffiti altogether from Pompeii and other sites around Mt. Vesuvius.

suburban, maritime and rustic villas of the *ager Pompeianus* have all yielded ancient graffiti.[15] The practice was likely common elsewhere in the ancient world as well. The sites of Dura Europos, Ephesus and Delos have yielded large numbers of ancient graffiti.[16] Elsewhere, chance finds suggest that ancient graffiti tend to turn up anywhere wall-plaster from the Roman Empire was somehow preserved.[17]

3 Documenting ancient graffiti: Historical overview

As we discuss the topic of documenting ancient graffiti, we will be writing from the perspective of the early Roman Empire, and in particular central Italy of the first century CE, for several reasons. That area has yielded the largest corpus of graffiti from the ancient world; Pompeian material has had a significant impact on ancient graffiti studies as a result of the abundance of material belonging to a clearly defined time and place; and, finally, that area has been the center of our work for the past decade. To provide an overview that encompasses the past two centuries, we will highlight four moments that have been fundamental to the process of documenting ancient graffiti:

- the mid-nineteenth century and discovery of Pompeian graffiti
- the late-nineteenth century and publication of Pompeian graffiti
- the end of the twentieth century and expanded views on ancient graffiti
- the early twenty-first century and technological innovations for ancient graffiti

3.1 The mid-nineteenth century and discovery of ancient graffiti

The site of Pompeii was explored already in the eighteenth century, while systematic excavations began in the nineteenth century. Excavations moved swiftly and uncovered massive amounts of material (architecture, mosaics, frescoes,

15 E.g. Herculaneum: Benefiel and Sypniewski 2018; Stabiae: Varone 2020; Oplontis: Benefiel and DiBiasie-Sammons 2019.

16 Cf. Dura Europos: Stern 2012; Baird 2016; Ephesus: Taeuber 2014 and 2016; Delos: Zarmakoupi 2016.

17 E.g. Stern 2018; Buonopane 2012; Molle 2012; Gregori and Massaro 2005; Solin and Itkonen-Kaila 1966. Rock-cut inscriptions are receiving more attention too, cf. Macdonald and Al-Manaser 2019.

artefacts). It was toward the middle of the century that ancient graffiti were recognized and received scholarly attention. At this point, documentation took the form of essays incorporating examples of graffiti.

Christopher Wordsworth, nephew of the poet William Wordsworth and eventual bishop of the Anglican church, visited the excavations and in 1837 published a small, 33-page book that took the form of a letter to a friend (addressed only as P.).[18] In it, he highlighted the graffiti that charmed him most, from quotations of the poets Vergil, Ovid and Propertius, to a graffito that gave a consular date. Only a few years later, F. M. Avellino, a leading Italian archaeologist of the period,[19] published his remarks to the Reale Accademia Ercolanese about ancient graffiti, a short essay in which he discussed drawings of gladiators, inscriptions on building facades applauding decisions of the emperor and others.[20] In 1841, the same year in which he published his essay, Avellino was responsible for the decision to excise nineteen very large panels of plaster from the walls of Pompeii's basilica, mount them on large wooden frames for support and transfer them for safekeeping to the National Archaeological Museum in Naples, where numerous panels of Pompeian painting had also been transferred for storage or to be put on display.[21]

The earliest organized documentation was Raffaele Garrucci's *Graffiti de Pompéi: Inscriptions et gravures tracées au stylet recueillies et interprétées*, which was already in its second edition in 1856. Rather than a continuous essay, Garrucci organized his 46-page narrative into six chapters, one of which focused on letter forms where he provided examples of the various formats each letter might have. His further innovation was to present graffiti as groups in thirty-two 'planches' (or plates) and to provide (limited) discussion.[22] The graffiti themselves were not numbered, nor was their location or provenance recorded. Systematic

---

18 Wordsworth 1837.

19 García y García 1998, 140: 'Dal 1839 al 1850 [Avellino] occupa anche la carica di massima responsibilità nel campo dell'Archeologia e Belle Arti, cioè la direzione del Real Museo Borbonico e la Soprintendenza dei R. Scavi di Antichità del Regno'.

20 Avellino 1841. This was 36 pages long.

21 Cf. *CIL* IV, p. 113: *[inscriptiones], quae in undeviginti tectorii tabulis... e basilica... excisae, ligneisque formis inclusae in museum Neapolitanum translatae sunt.* ('...[the inscriptions] were excised from the basilica in nineteen panels of plaster, transferred onto wooden backings and moved to the museum in Naples').

22 There was some categorization to the arrangement into plates. Planche I presented examples of the alphabet, while planche VII presented inscriptions using primarily vertical strokes. The explanatory chapters and commentary explaining each inscription made this a volume of 102 pages. The plates presented line-drawings of the graffiti at the end of the volume.

documentation of that kind would eventually come later with the *Corpus Inscriptionum Latinarum.*

3.2 The late-nineteenth century and publication of Pompeian graffiti

Later in the nineteenth century, the value of Pompeian wall-inscriptions had come into focus and Pompeii came to be incorporated into the *Corpus Inscriptionum Latinarum*. The *Corpus Inscriptionum Latinarum* began under the direction of Theodor Mommsen in the mid-nineteenth century – and work on it continues to this day – as a large-scale, international, collaborative venture to document and record Latin inscriptions from across the ancient world.[23] The project was divided into volumes that were each dedicated to a different geographical area (e.g. vol. II: *Inscriptiones Hispaniae*, vol. III: *Inscriptiones Asiae*, vol V: *Inscriptiones Galliae Cisalpinae*, vol. VI: *Inscriptiones Urbis Romae*).[24] Volume IV of the *Corpus Inscriptionum Latinarum* (*CIL*) was distinctive in that, rather than documenting inscriptions on stone or marble, it was devoted to wall-inscriptions that were being found in large numbers in Pompeii and surrounding areas. The initial publication of *CIL* IV appeared in 1871 and contained over 3200 inscriptions, both painted wall-inscriptions (*tituli picti*) and scratched wall-inscriptions or graffiti (*graphio inscripta*).[25] The overwhelming majority of these inscriptions came from the site of Pompeii, where a far greater area had been excavated. The title of *CIL* vol. IV was, in fact, *Inscriptiones Parietariae Pompeianae* (*'Pompeian Wall-Inscriptions'*). A subtitle followed in a smaller font: *Herculanenses, Stabianae*. In reality, the subtitle was forward-looking rather than representative at similar levels; a small number of wall-inscriptions had been recorded at

23 As the *CIL* continues to grow and additional supplements to its volumes appear in print, it also now has a website that includes a digital database. For more information, see: https://cil.bbaw.de/. From the sub-page 'History of the CIL': 'Today, the *CIL* counts 17 volumes in folio format in about 80 parts, containing almost 200,000 inscriptions' (accessed on 21 September 2022).
24 *CIL* vol. I is the only volume dedicated to a particular time period: *Inscriptiones Latinae antiquissimae ad C. Caesaris mortem.*
25 *CIL* (vol. IV, p. 76) explains this second category (graffiti) as follows: *Posterior huius voluminis pars inscriptiones parietarias continet eas, quae graphii sive stili aut alius cuiuslibet rei cuspide incisae vel potius scariphatae sunt...* ('The latter part of this volume contains those wall-inscriptions which were inscribed or rather scratched with the point of a writing instrument, stylus, or some other thing').

Herculaneum, but difficult excavation conditions there had resulted in activity shifting to Pompeii.

As excavations have proceeded over the past 150 years, so has publication of new inscriptions. *CIL* IV now includes four weighty supplements. (The graffiti of Herculaneum appear in Supplement III.)[26] The most recent supplement contains new inscriptions, updated readings of previously published texts and bibliography of recent scholarship. Publication in *CIL* remains the standard reference for Pompeian graffiti. When using it, a scholar must be aware that early entries might be substantially improved in later *addenda et corrigenda* sections and that the system of addresses was changed after the publication of the first section (*CIL* IV 1–3255). Nonetheless, the *CIL* framework provides a solid base for documentation with sequential entries arranged topographically, each providing text, editor, apparatus and occasionally a line-drawing. The value of *CIL* IV endures.

3.3 The end of the twentieth century and expanded views on ancient graffiti

Documentation of ancient graffiti underwent a significant expansion at the turn of the millennium with the publication of two important studies of graffiti that have become reference works and have influenced much subsequent work: Antonio Varone's publication of the ancient graffiti within the Villa S. Marco in Castellamare di Stabia (ancient Stabiae) and Martin Langner's catalogue and analysis of figural graffiti from across the ancient world.[27]

Antonio Varone made fundamental decisions that expanded the way we think about and study ancient graffiti. The most significant documentation decision was to organize the graffiti he cataloged into three categories: verbal, figural and numerical. This decision made explicit that he was documenting all purposefully scratched inscriptions in the large, opulent suburban villa in the elite area of Stabiae. The earlier focus of documentation that had highlighted text first and foremost was diffused in Varone's study, as he represented text (verbal), along with everything else that had been inscribed on the wall (figural, numerical). His catalogue, for example, includes a number of tally marks, a series of Roman numerals that may have been used to keep track of quantities. Such non-textual, yet clearly functional writing tends not to appear in the early sections of *CIL* IV.

26 Supplementum III appeared in fascicles (published 1952–1971) and Supplementum IV, pars I and pars II have appeared recently (2011 and 2020), with pars III forthcoming.

27 Varone 1999 (within Alix Barbet's comprehensive study of the villa); Langner 2001.

Varone's full documentation and publication of the totality of ancient graffiti in the villa validated the inclusion of non-textual graffiti and offered the first comprehensive look at the classification types of ancient graffiti.[28]

Varone also included three appendices at the end of his publication, one of which listed the presence of graffiti by room, highlighting the importance of location.[29] He further provided details about the precise location of graffiti, e.g. distance from the corner of the room or a doorway, so that the graffiti could be found and checked by others. With each of these decisions, Varone's work stressed the importance of documenting all graffiti and underscored the benefits of subsequent verification.

Martin Langner has had a similarly large influence on ancient graffiti studies, particularly for the acknowledgment and value he gave to figural graffiti or hand-sketched graffiti drawings (*antike Graffitizeichnungen*).[30] His mission was to comb previous publications to collect all graffiti drawings and build a corpus of figural graffiti from ancient sites across the Mediterranean. He also documented the previously unpublished figural graffiti that he discovered. The breadth of his catalogue illustrated that figural graffiti were not just a sporadic occurrence, as one might have guessed from the manner in which they tended to be documented in *CIL* IV, i.e. when they appeared in conjunction with or close to text. Rather, figural graffiti were significant and worth documenting in their own right. He arranged the figural graffiti by subject matter, so a scholar could compare the format of gladiators drawn in Pompeii with those in Aphrodisias or Lyon, or the style of birds sketched in Dura Europos with those found at Rome.[31] His other major contribution was to include a CD-Rom with a FileMakerPro database program along with the monograph. The CD held sets of information for each graffito that would have been too unwieldy to include in a print publication. This was the first

28 This inclusive strategy was subsequently applied to the elite House of Maius Castricius in Pompeii. The *editio princeps* had documented thirty textual inscriptions (Giordano 1966, nos 18–47). Heikki Solin's subsequent evaluation of the residence documented additional graffiti that had either not been identified or had been ignored by Giordano, for a new total of 45 ancient graffiti (Solin 1975, nos 18–50 and 57–70, now numerical graffiti included). Reassessment of the residence a generation later revealed still additional graffiti for a total of 74 handwritten inscriptions (Benefiel 2010a, nos 1–74). It is clear, then, that focusing on only textual graffiti presents only a portion of the full epigraphic record. Graffiti in the small building to the north were also documented by Solin (1975, nos 51–56) and Benefiel (2010a, nos 75–85).

29 Varone 1999, 361. The graffiti of the villa also belonged to different time periods (Roman, Bourbon and uncertain) and this criterion was articulated in the charts as well.

30 Langner 2001. Articles by Chaniotis (2011) and Benefiel and Sypniewski (2016), e.g., demonstrate the impact of Varone and Langner's works.

31 Cf. Langner 2001, nos 769–916 (gladiators), nos 1634–1747 (birds).

large dataset of ancient graffiti where information was available in a format beyond the print publication.

3.4 The early twenty-first century and technological innovations

The early twenty-first century has brought technological innovations in the fields of photography, web-based publication and computational and digital processes. For the field of ancient graffiti, digital photography has become vitally important, and the expansive framework of digital publication has meant that more can be shared with scholars and the public than ever before. To give one example for archaeology at the site of Pompeii, an immense photographic campaign that lasted more than a decade resulted in the 11-volume work, *Pompei: Pitture e Mosaici*, published by the Istituto della Enciclopedia Italiana (1990–2003). This beautifully illustrated work documented all wall-painting and mosaics that remained extant, with excellent floorplans and essays to introduce each building, followed by essential bibliography. This series remains a fundamental reference work. A decade later, an online resource took photographic publication even further with the creation of Pompeii in Pictures (pompeiiinpictures.com). This site presents a spatially-organized photographic collection that has grown to be very comprehensive. Smaller buildings and those without painting or mosaics that were not included in *PPM* can now be found among the pages of photographs on Pompeii in Pictures. The number of images the website holds is extensive and the collection grows every year. Every building in Pompeii has been the subject of photographic documentation, and the website now includes photographs as well for the nearby major sites of Herculaneum, Stabiae and Oplontis; the villas of Gragnano, Boscoreale, Boscotrecase; the site of S. Maria Capua Vetere and more.

Greater access to photographic documentation for ancient inscriptions has also been a huge benefit that came about as a result of Antonio Varone's tenure as Director of the Scavi di Pompeii. In conjunction with the director of Pompeii's photographic archive, Greta Stefani, Varone published the archives' historical photographs of Pompeii's painted wall-inscriptions.[32] He also oversaw a decade-long,

32 Varone and Stefani 2009 (painted inscriptions from Pompeii). The photographic archive contained images of large-scale painted inscriptions that were visible in photographs of building facades.

large-scale photographic campaign to document Pompeian graffiti – the first of its kind.[33]

The spatial turn also reached ancient graffiti studies with new approaches that sought to reintegrate ancient graffiti into their archaeological or geographical context, and publications also began to highlight graffiti in dialogue with each other and with their surroundings.[34]

3.5 New technologies, new approaches

Within the last decade, technology has also driven new innovation for the documentation and study of graffiti.[35] Laser scanning, photogrammetry and reflectance transformation imaging (RTI) represent three major technological advances applied to ancient graffiti.[36] Laser scanning, or 3D scanning, represented a huge step forward in documenting large spaces. While capturing the architecture and decoration of an entire room or area, laser scanning can also reveal markings that may not be immediately visible to the naked eye.[37] As early as 2003, a feasibility study was conducted in Pompeii wherein 3D scanning was used to document the graffiti of the Lupanar, or purpose-built brothel.[38] Technology changes rapidly, however, and now photogrammetry and RTI have eclipsed laser scanning as the technology of preference. These documentation techniques are also being used for conservation.[39] While photogrammetry has been used in archaeology for a generation, the development of Structure from Motion, increasingly powerful computational algorithms, and more open source options has led to photogrammetry

33 The two volumes published as the result of this campaign (Varone 2012, 2 vols) are the first systematic photographic documentation for Pompeian graffiti.

34 Benefiel 2010b (GIS and Pompeian graffiti); Benefiel 2010a and 2011 (Graffiti in dialogue); Baird and Taylor 2011 (Graffiti in context); Lohmann 2017 (Graffiti als Interaktionsform).

35 For an excellent summary regarding the application of new technologies for the documentation of ancient graffiti, see Valente and Barazzetti 2020. Cf. also Valente et al. 2019. Parker and Rollston 2019 have recently discussed the incorporation of digital drawing tools for the field of Northwest Semitic epigraphy.

36 The study of papyri in recent years has involved still others, including multi-spectral imaging, CT scanning, x-ray fluorescence for ink analysis and x-ray phase contrast tomography. For an overview, see Marchant 2018. Cf. also Mocella et al. 2015; Parker et al. 2019 and Stabile et al. 2021.

37 Cf. Tenschert et al. 2020; Valente and Oreni 2017.

38 Balzani et al. 2004. See also Varone 2008.

39 Cf. the work at El-Kurru in Sudan (Davis et al. 2018).

being increasingly adopted over the past decade.[40] Photogrammetry is now used at archaeological sites across the globe.[41] Likewise, RTI has become a common strategy for documenting ancient inscriptions, especially since it can be conducted in the field with little specialized equipment (digital camera, spheres and computer).[42] The computational photography of RTI then allows a user to manipulate the image by rotating the light source and changing color saturation to highlight surface texture and thereby illuminate markings from different angles. Our project chose several locations in the site of Herculaneum where we employed RTI to document and evaluate ancient graffiti (Fig. 3).[43] Technology is driving innovation in the study of ancient graffiti and the field is expanding rapidly. Numerous publications have appeared in just the past few years and there are no signs of slowing down. Many can be found in specialized conference proceedings as well as in the *Journal of Archaeological Science: Reports*.[44]

Scholars recognize that this is a time of innovation and explosive growth. In this regard, Andreau and Serrano have declared, 'These are new times for epigraphic research', and Helmke and collaborators underscore that 'Continued collaboration between researchers and digital humanities facilities will enhance dialogue and serve as the basis for the implementation of new methods in the study of more extensive material, inevitably yielding additional research synergies and discoveries in the future'.[45] Exploring new technologies for documenting graffiti will remain an important facet of epigraphic projects for the foreseeable future.

---

40 See Valente and Barazzetti 2020 for a thorough overview and case studies of what photogrammetry can offer. Their article also presents a retrospective regarding previous contact-based methods of documentation of graffiti (tracing, rubbings, etc.). As early as 1982, the journal *World Archaeology* was already highlighting the technique of photogrammetry in multiple articles (vol. 14, issue 2).

41 E.g. the basilica of San Marco in Venice (Abate and Trentin 2019); graffiti at Mayan sites in modern Belize (Helmke et al. 2022) and Elkab in upper Egypt (Prada and Wordsworth 2018). This last article tackles the challenges of changes in epigraphic standards for Greco-Roman graffiti in Egypt, another area with a long history of documentation for ancient graffiti.

42 Cf. Kleinitz 2012; Gill 2018, Bosco and Minucci 2020, Solem and Nau 2020.

43 DiBiasie-Sammons 2018 (RTI process) and Frampton 2019 (analysis of graffiti in the so-called College of Augustales).

44 Recent publications in this journal about the documentation of ancient graffiti include Palomar-Vazquez et al. 2017; DiBiasie-Sammons 2018; Valente and Barrazzatti 2020; Lech et al. 2021. This journal also contains numerous articles devoted to the study of rock art.

45 Andreau and Serrano 2019; Helmke et al. 2022.

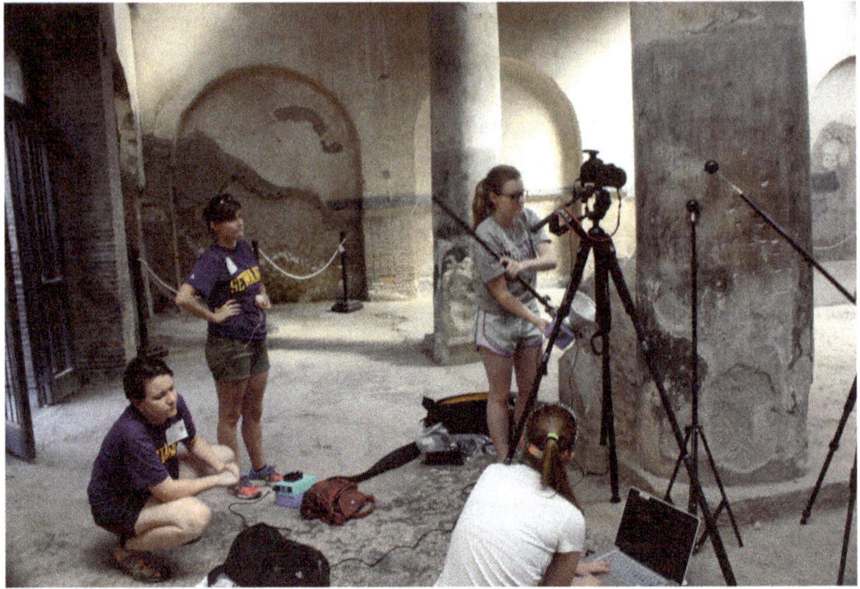

Fig. 3: Part of the AGP team setting up for RTI in Herculaneum with our RTI specialist, Jacqueline DiBiasie-Sammons (left) and undergraduate assistants.

4 The Ancient Graffiti Project

This historical overview of documentation brings us to The Ancient Graffiti Project (AGP), which we began nearly a decade ago. The Ancient Graffiti Project provides direct access to ancient graffiti as well as digital resources that support a richer understanding of handwritten inscriptions from the early Roman Empire in their archaeological context at our open-access website: http://ancientgraffiti.org. AGP has been developed: 1) to provide a scholarly resource for the study of graffiti by providing accurate, comprehensive and up-to-date critical editions of each inscription; 2) to lower the barriers to the study of ancient graffiti for scholars, teachers and the interested public; and 3) to facilitate new avenues of research through the provision of digital tools, a user-friendly interface and a digital resource that is interoperable and integrated within leading digital humanities initiatives. It is the result of a decade of epigraphic research, archaeological fieldwork and development of a digital platform to make graffiti publicly available, and it continues to grow.

Epigraphy has been at the forefront of digital humanities for the past generation, with large-scale international, collaborative projects to create digital databases of inscriptions in place and underway already in the 1990s.[46] The sheer volume of Latin epigraphy – hundreds of thousands of ancient inscriptions – led to the decision to divide responsibility for the ancient world among four large projects: inscriptions of the Italian peninsula to the Epigraphic Database Roma (www.edr-edr.it), the Roman provinces to the Epigraphic Database Heidelberg (www.uni-heidelberg.de/institute/sonst/adw/edh/indexe.html), the Iberian peninsula to Hispania Epigraphica (eda-bea.es) and the Christian inscriptions of Rome (third to eighth centuries) to the Epigraphic Database Bari (www.edb.uniba.it).

The concept and design for the Ancient Graffiti Project arose from our team's work with the Epigraphic Database Roma (EDR). EDR was organized around a collaborative framework, with teams responsible for inscriptions from different geographical areas in Italy (http://www.edr-edr.it/it/strutt_it.php). Rebecca Benefiel was appointed the EDR supervisor responsible for the handwritten wall-inscriptions of Campania. She began editing the ancient graffiti of Pompeii and contributing inscriptions to EDR in 2012. As Benefiel and her team moved forward, it became clear that these ancient graffiti along with their well-preserved archaeological context offered further information that was not generally applicable for most inscriptions on stone. Benefiel began to consider how the unique characteristics of ancient graffiti could be documented and highlighted. With the addition of Sara Sprenkle as Technical Director in 2013 and Holly Sypniewski as Assistant Director in 2015, we designed and began to build a project that would work in conjunction with EDR and that would also provide direct access to the corpus of handwritten inscriptions.[47]

The documentation method of the Ancient Graffiti Project has been shaped to meet two primary goals: preparing the digital editions and updates to publish ancient graffiti for the Epigraphic Database Roma (EDR)[48] and producing our own geo-referenced database of graffiti enhanced by additional, graffiti-specific contextual data on AGP. We present here discussions of our methods for editing, fieldwork and platform design.

46 For a summary to that point and a look to the future, see Cayless et al. 2009. Cf. also Bodel 2012 and Orlandi 2016.

47 Benefiel and Sprenkle 2014 (for prototype and initial steps of the project).

48 Publication of the work of EDR teams is presented in the series *Italia Epigrafica Digitale*. For the work of our team, see Benefiel et al. 2017b and Benefiel and Sypniewski 2020.

4.1 Our method, part I: Documentation and editing

As described above, more than a hundred years of discussion and editions of Pompeian graffiti exist. It is our responsibility to bring this collective body of data up to date by applying current conventions, assembling bibliography and reevaluating the readings and presentation of inscriptions in earlier publications.[49] Updating is only part of the process, though, since we recognize the value of, and therefore document, additional characteristics of ancient graffiti that were not recorded previously. We also integrate graffiti that did not appear in *CIL* because they were published subsequently or were not initially valued as part of the epigraphic record. In part I, we discuss our work documenting ancient graffiti on the basis of previously published information; in part II, we explain how we conduct fieldwork to document graffiti when they survive.

The first step is to reconcile previous editions and apply current epigraphic conventions to edit each graffito. In contrast to inscriptions on stone or marble, ancient graffiti regularly require the employ of multiple conventions, punctuation that is used to indicate information about the support (if, for example, an inscription is broken or abraded), the legibility of an inscription, or where the text requires editorial explanation (e.g. in the case of abbreviation or non-standard spelling). An inscription on stone might require one or two of these editorial explanations every so often, while ancient graffiti might need three or more types of intervention for a single inscription.

The early volumes of *CIL* IV were published before adoption of the Leiden system, the first standard set of epigraphic conventions to be adopted for papyri and inscriptions.[50] Epigraphic conventions have shifted more than once over the past century and the varied nature of the publication of Campanian graffiti has meant that very different conventions are used across the corpus of over 7,000 inscriptions. For example, the lacunae in inscriptions where letters are lost have been treated differently—with an ellipsis, slashes, or even just spaces in the text—as have non-standard spellings and abbreviations, all of which are frequently found among ancient graffiti. The following examples demonstrate how ancient graffiti were presented in the first volume of *CIL* IV.

49 This includes revised readings that were published subsequent to *CIL* IV.
50 The Leiden system was updated in the later twentieth century and current conventions are often called Leiden+ or termed the Krummery-Panciera system. See Krummery and Panciera 1980. The Krummery-Panciera system provides a basis for EpiDoc, see https://epidoc.stoa. org/gl/latest/app-epi-krummreypanciera.html.

In this example (Fig. 4), low dots were used to show damage and inclined letters denoted uncertain readings. It is unclear if the dots denote a specific number of missing letters or just that some text has been lost. No comment is supplied to explain the form HIRE, written for *ire* (the standard form of the verb). Elsewhere in *CIL*, low dots and slashes (/////) are used to denote damage or loss of text, sometimes both within a single inscription. A reader is left to guess what the difference between the two notations might be. The editors of *CIL* were trying to represent the inscription as faithfully as possible when a reading or meaning was not immediately understood. However, the meaning behind the conventions used are not transparent to the reader.

1227 in columna angulari ordinum orientalis et meridionalis.

VENIMVS
H*AC*V..II
.. V*NO*
MAGIS
HIRE · VT
LICEAT
NOSTROS
VISERE
RO*M*ΛL*A*RES

Fig. 4: *CIL* IV 1227.

For our edition of this inscription on AGP (Fig. 5), we bring together the improvements to the reading that have been made since its publication as *CIL* IV 1227, we apply current standards and we offer explanation for all the epigraphic conventions that are applied to the inscription. We present the text as follows:[51]

51 EDR151415 (Sypniewski). The text was improved in *CIL* IV at three separate points: cf. Addenda p. 205, p. 463 and p. 704. Further bibliography is also provided at our entry in EDR.

Venimus
hục̣ [c]u[pi]ḍi
[m]uḷṭọ
magis
hire (:ire) ⟨:cupimus⟩ · ut
liceat
nostros
visere,
Roṃa, Lạres.

Hide Epigraphic Convention Key

Epigraphic Convention Key

Symbol	Meaning
[abc]	Letters once present, now missing due to damage to the surface or support
ạḅ	Characters damaged or unclear that would be unintelligible without context
(:abc)	Gives standard spelling to explain non-standard text in an inscription (used by EDR and AGP)
⟨:abc⟩	Explanation of editor, either subaudible word or regarding the layout of the text, e.g. ⟨:col. I⟩ (used by EDR and AGP)

Full List of Conventions ➜

Fig. 5: AGP editorial conventions.

Previous readings are preserved in the critical apparatus of the inscription. Our transcription reveals the poetic nature of the message, as we include modern punctuation for the vocative case of *Roma*, while also clarifying with underdots and brackets how much damage the inscription has suffered. Our transcription also makes clear what the ancient writer wrote, particularly if he or she used non-standard forms. Epigraphic conventions often 'correct' ancient 'errors' or misspellings.[52] We instead present – without intervention – what was written by

52 A superfluous letter would be bracketed off with braces, e.g. {h}ire, while an omitted letter could be included within angle brackets, e.g. Cresce<n>s, the aim being to forefront the 'corrected'

the ancient writer, and then subsequently explain the standard form, e.g. *hire (:ire)*, above. The epigraphic key that explains the significance of the brackets, underdots and other punctuation can be displayed or hidden by the user. Including such a key along with the inscription was a design decision to make our work accessible to a wider audience of professionals and interested non-experts.

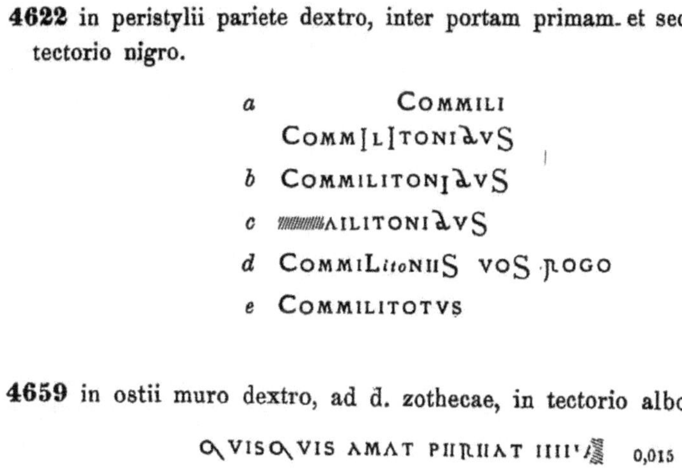

4622 in peristylii pariete dextro, inter portam primam et secundam, in tectorio nigro.

a COMMILI
COMM[L]TONIbVS
b COMMILITONIbVS
c AILITONIbVS
d COMMILitoNIIS VOS ROGO
e COMMILITOTVS

4659 in ostii muro dextro, ad d. zothecae, in tectorio albo.

QVISQVIS AMAT PIIRIIAT IIII 0,015

Fig. 6: Examples of epigraphic conventions in CIL vol. IV, supp. 2.

In *CIL* IV, Supplementum II (published 1909), the editors continued their aim to represent graffiti as they appeared, as best as they could without the benefit of images. To do this, they utilized a mix of different fonts, with conventional letter shapes and some custom letter shapes designed to reflect the appearance of Roman handwriting. In the examples above (Fig. 6), the form of the letter B in the word *commilitionibus* is represented as it was written on the wall-plaster.[53] Scratches still denote damage to the plaster, and the loss of letters that can be restored are inserted in lower case lettering. In *CIL* IV 4659 (Fig. 6), the letter A

form or what was intended. Graffiti, however, are far less consistent than inscriptions on stone, and so would require significantly more of these interventions. We chose to simplify and forefront what was actually written.

53 The letter B written in this inscription did not resemble our capital letter B, which is also found on the walls of Pompeii, but something closer to a lowercase 'd'. Latin at this time did not have strictly delineated capital and lowercase versions.

is represented without a crossbar to indicate that it was written thus.[54] The letter E is represented as it was sometimes handwritten in graffiti and on wax tablets, as two parallel vertical lines, or II.[55] This letter form is notoriously problematic for those who have not worked extensively with *CIL* IV, and often leads to confused readings.[56]

Our documentation also includes integration of all graffiti into the record, as we follow the examples of Antonio Varone and Martin Langner, discussed above. We create individual entries for figural or numerical graffiti that were not included in *CIL* or whose presence was mentioned briefly in a headnote or apparatus for another inscription. We have described elsewhere our decision-making process for publishing hand-sketched images individually or as groupings.[57] Sometimes figural graffiti are related to nearby text, and the figural and textual inscription should be treated together in one epigraphic entry. Spatial proximity, however, does not always (and, in fact, does not often) mean association, and when messages and images are unrelated, we publish them separately and then create the association by means of hyperlinks in the critical apparatus.

Figural graffiti, furthermore, had been described by a variety of terms that were not consistent across editors. A drawing of a head might be called any of the following Latin terms: *caput*, *facies*, *protome*, or *herma*.[58] We therefore created controlled vocabularies aligned with the Getty vocabularies for art and architecture and standardized our descriptions, so that a drawing of a human head is described as *caput hominis*.[59] Figural graffiti are described within the text field, via verbal notation set within punctuation that denotes them as sketches ((:*caput hominis*)). We also provide an English translation of the Latin description for each figural graffito, so that searching is possible in either language.[60] Finally, we illustrate figural graffiti whenever possible with accompanying photos or line-drawings.

54 This letter form should not be confused with a Greek lambda.

55 This letter is also written as a capital E, and both letter forms can appear in the same inscription and even in the same word.

56 The word *pereat*, for example, as written in 4659, should never be presented as *piiriiat*, but mistakes like this understandably occur in transcriptions when scholars have little experience with ancient graffiti.

57 Benefiel and Sypniewski 2016.

58 Some editors such as Matteo Della Corte seem to have developed their own guidelines for the features they used to identify the subject matter of graffiti drawings, but the practices across various editors ranged widely.

59 Previous descriptions are preserved in the apparatus.

60 We further make our data available for download, with results returned in EpiDoc format including descriptions of figural graffiti in Latin and English.

Our critical edition also includes a detailed bibliography and a critical apparatus that we write for each inscription. The bibliography summarizes the publication history for each graffito, including published editions that preceded the publication of *CIL*, as well as interpretive scholarship that discusses the graffito. In the apparatus, we include variant readings, editorial explanations, and we add the following information when applicable:[61]

- detailed measurements for the size of a graffito. The *CIL* will sometimes include length and letter height.
- notes on the appearance of a graffito, including discussion of palaeography.
- explanations of non-standard spellings. Rather than 'correcting' a text, we present the text as it was written by the ancient individual; then we provide what a reader would expect as the standard form, e.g. *Cresces (:Crescens)* or *cinedus (:cinaedus)*.
- brief discussion of status of preservation, including which, if any, letters have been lost since the initial publication.
- the condition of the wall plaster upon which it was written, if there is deterioration or abrasion that affect the visibility and legibility of the text.
- references to other inscriptions through hyperlinks, relevant for graffiti that are in close proximity or that share common elements such as themes, names, quotations from literature, or drawing subject.
- discussion of any elements of the inscription that are illegible. Due to deterioration and the fragility of plaster, it is not uncommon for parts of a graffito to be illegible.

Just as we reconcile previous and divergent conventions for editing, we also reconcile multiple systems for addresses of buildings and locations in Pompeii, so that each graffito we edit can be found using the current system of Pompeian addresses.[62] By reconciling and standardizing the locations of graffiti, we can then incorporate every inscription into a geo-referenced map of the site that is interactive and searchable. A scholar can begin research with the map and search for the graffiti in a particular location. Even if a scholar is searching for just a particular phrase, we always provide location information, so the archaeological context in which the inscription appeared is clear. The results page of any search includes a map of the site (of Herculaneum or Pompeii) highlighting the location of the graffito retrieved. Since the sites of Herculaneum and Pompeii are so well preserved that we can determine the type of space for each building, we also categorize each location into a building type that is a searchable category in the AGP database (e.g. house, sacred space, shop, workshop). These features were

61 Just as ancient graffiti themselves vary significantly in length and content, the same level of detail is not possible for every inscription. The apparatus for an inscription that remains extant will often have considerably more information than the apparatus for an inscription that is lost.
62 For more on the shifts in describing locations in Pompeii, see Benefiel et al. 2017b.

designed to facilitate research on graffiti: scholars can search for graffiti through their location by clicking on the interactive map, or they can use the filters to explore all the inscriptions in a particular type of building, such as taverns.

Ancient graffiti, brief and idiosyncratic, frequently are not immediately understandable. Since a primary goal of AGP is to bring ancient graffiti to a wider audience and make them more accessible, we offer a number of aids, which include translations into English and captions or brief summaries to inform a reader about the subject matter. In contributing entries to the Epigraphic Database Roma, we write in Latin to reach a global scholarly audience primarily of epigraphers. AGP is designed to be accessible for a more general academic audience, or the general public, to understand these inscriptions and their value.

4.2 Our method, part II: Documentation and fieldwork

We began with the task of editing inscriptions, updating and applying current epigraphic standards. When it became clear that it was time to commence fieldwork, a set of decisions had to be made about where to begin and what to prioritize. With several thousand graffiti to study, spread across the entire city of Pompeii and beyond, the many possibilities for where to start made strategic decision-making necessary.

We chose to begin not at Pompeii but with a survey of Herculaneum, a smaller site whose graffiti were barely known when compared to its larger, flashier neighbor of Pompeii. The site of Herculaneum consists of roughly five city-blocks, a fraction of the more than 100 city-blocks that have been excavated at Pompeii, but certainly not an insignificant area to assess and document. Each city-block of Herculaneum contains between 10 and 30 buildings, and more than 300 ancient graffiti had been documented across the entire city.

The goal of our first field season was a broad survey of ancient graffiti at Herculaneum.[63] Benefiel designed a two-week epigraphy summer school to be held on-site, since training is crucial for successful data collection. There was a huge response to the call for participants, and from the applicants we selected to participate thirty Classics faculty, postdocs, graduate and undergraduate students from six countries. We divided the group into five teams, with each team responsible for surveying an entire city-block over the course of the two weeks. We spent the morning surveying and documenting; the afternoons were devoted to instruction, guest lecturers and writing up notes from the morning. In the second week,

63 Benefiel et al. 2016.

we began site visits where each team would present their observations, finds and questions to the whole group. Our survey revealed greater numbers of ancient graffiti than we had expected still extant in Herculaneum and thus set the stage for further fieldwork at Herculaneum and eventually Pompeii.

Any project at its inception will face foundational questions: What should be documented, what not and why? How best to deal with contemporary graffiti – should they be documented in their entirety, or only selectively – and if so, based on which criteria? Each generation may adopt different ideas on what to document and what to leave aside. Our project has chosen not to document the modern graffiti that occur in certain areas of the archaeological site, unless these appear in direct contact with ancient graffiti. In that case, they will appear only in our photographic documentation (see Fig. 7); our line drawings (more on this, below), will display the ancient inscription alone to render it more clearly. The issue of contemporary graffiti does raise the importance of training.

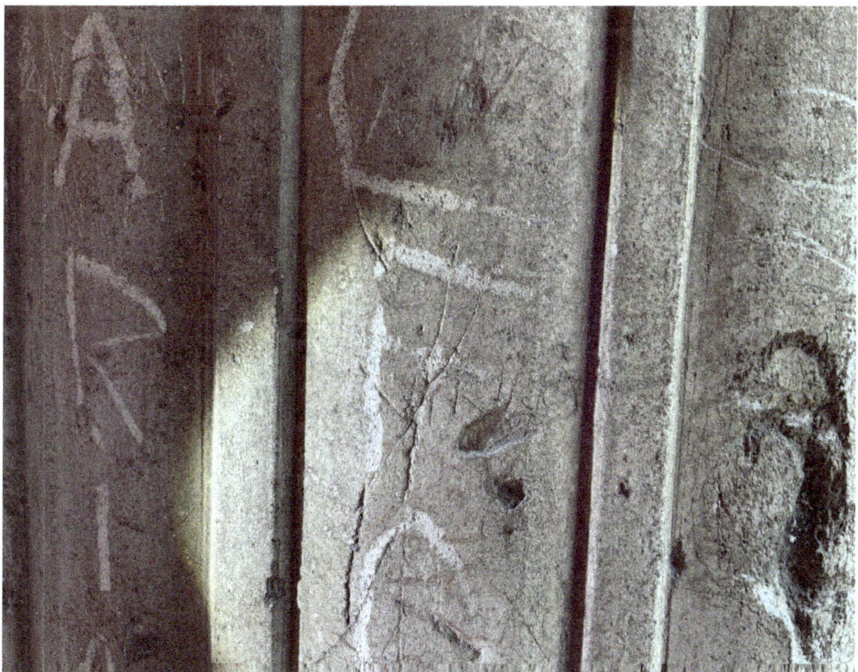

Fig. 7: Using raking light to illuminate *CIL* IV 8666b, the incised name *Virilio*, which has been obscured by modern graffiti, seen here in larger white lettering roughly gouged across the surface of a column in the Campus of Pompeii (II.7.1–10, column 74). Su concessione del Ministero della Cultura - Parco Archeologico di Pompei. Reproduction expressly prohibited.

Since our participants come from different universities and locations, we begin training our team before we arrive in the field by holding a series of virtual meetings. We provide introductions to the nature and format of ancient graffiti and to the main reference tools we use in the field. All team members study Roman handwriting, the variety of letter shapes used and the published inscriptions for each area where we will work. Because the script of ancient graffiti differs so dramatically from contemporary letter shapes of the Roman alphabet, this training is crucial for setting expectations and helping team members find graffiti in situ, where there are noticeable differences between physical graffiti and their published editions. During our training sessions, we also introduce a series of maps for the areas where we will work and we plan for documentation that is precise enough for a subsequent team to be able to locate our finds easily. That requires focused training on how to document precisely.

On day one in the field, we teach our team members how to distinguish ancient from modern graffiti. In the sites of Pompeii and Herculaneum, this is something easily taught with just a few examples. Ancient graffiti are generally small and discreet, rarely more than 1cm tall. Writers in the first century used very sharp implements, e.g. a metal stylus that made a thin incision into the plaster. Thus, ancient graffiti are usually very lightly incised into wall plaster with a slender *ductus*. As a result, they are often inconspicuous and difficult to notice. In contrast, visitors to the site today regretfully intent on leaving their own mark tend to use implements that are thicker and duller, such as pens or keys, and therefore often leave rough, jagged marks where the plaster breaks away in pieces. Modern visitors are also used to writing on a smooth horizontal surface, and their inexperience on a vertical surface results in a much larger size of letters. Finally, when a modern writer scratches into ancient plaster, the incision reveals a fresh white color below (Fig. 7). Ancient graffiti have a patina from years of exposure to the elements, and so the contrast seen with modern graffiti is often markedly different.

More difficult and exceedingly important is teaching our team members how to distinguish ancient graffiti from damage to the ancient wall surface. When the wall plaster is in good condition, finding graffiti can be challenging. When plaster has deteriorated, its top polished layers have worn away, or it has suffered damage in the form of chips, cracks, *lacunae* and breaks, finding and reading ancient graffiti requires immense patience and persistence. For all these reasons, we start by training participants to locate and identify ancient graffiti.

We then commence the documentation process by using decidedly low-tech methods: pencil, paper, measuring tapes and documentation forms which require team members to observe and record each inscription closely. We always

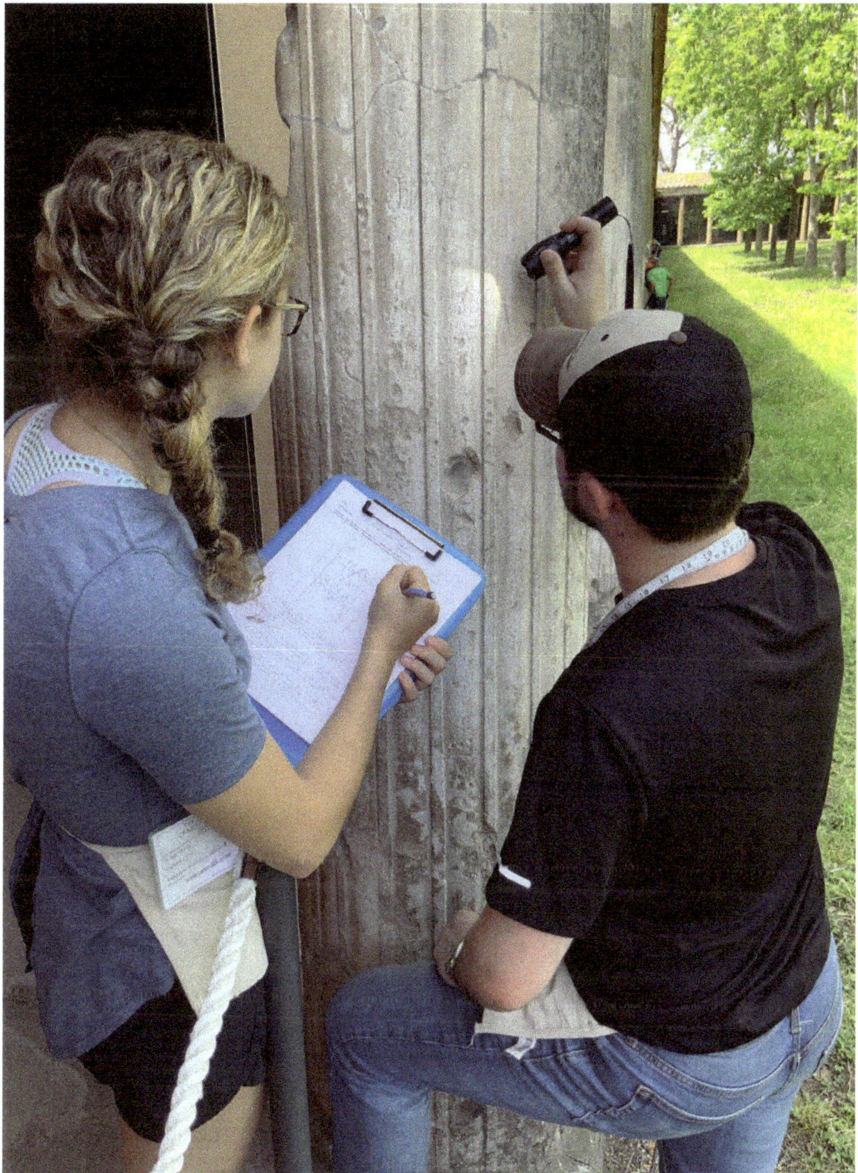

Fig. 8: AGP team members illuminate, document and discuss a graffito. Su concessione del Ministero della Cultura - Parco Archeologico di Pompei. Reproduction expressly prohibited.

work in small teams so that there are multiple eyes on each graffito and a team discussion of letter strokes, measurements and other contextual information. Because ancient graffiti are small and shallowly incised, we use LED panels and flashlights to provide raking light across the surface of each inscription. This method of lighting increases the surface contrast and illuminates small marks with greater visibility. We never document an inscription once: our team makes repeated visits at different times of day and during different natural lighting scenarios. An inscription that cannot be found in the bright Italian midday sunlight will often be more easily legible in the slanting light of the afternoon. Team members then discuss, record observations and sketch what they see (Fig. 8).

We next take a comprehensive set of measurements for each inscription, including height, length and letter-heights. The small size of ancient graffiti makes this challenging since we are often measuring to the nearest millimeter. The handwriting of ancient graffiti also means that each line, and often each letter, will vary in size. Many graffiti also include flourishes where an initial or final letter is inscribed with a longer down- or upstroke for aesthetic purposes. We therefore take a series of measurements that go beyond those that fit neatly into basic measurement fields. These additional measurements can help with research questions such as the height of each inscription from the ground, the distance from other graffiti on the same wall or some architectural feature or decorative elements of frescoes. As part of the documentation process, we have all team members note their observations about the location and environment of the graffito.

The major research products of our fieldwork are readings of inscriptions, measurements and images. Digital photography allows us to leave the field with thousands and even tens of thousands of images to then work with back at our home institutions. For our photography, we document each graffito at different times of the day and under different lighting scenarios. And just as we take a series of measurements, we take a series of photographs for broader measures: photographs with scale, without scale, and at different distances to record both text (or image) and context.

Even the best photographs, however, may not capture all of an ancient graffito or may not render it easily legible. All of our field documentation is combined to create a series of images that we incorporate into a photo gallery on the Ancient Graffiti Project (Fig. 9). Creating an image gallery for each inscription is time-intensive as each step requires several iterations to ensure that we are representing the graffito as accurately as possible. We begin by reviewing all the photographs taken since it is very difficult to capture all the letters equally well in a single photograph, particularly for a longer message or one inscribed on a curved column. We frequently reference our field notes as well as the sketches made in the field.

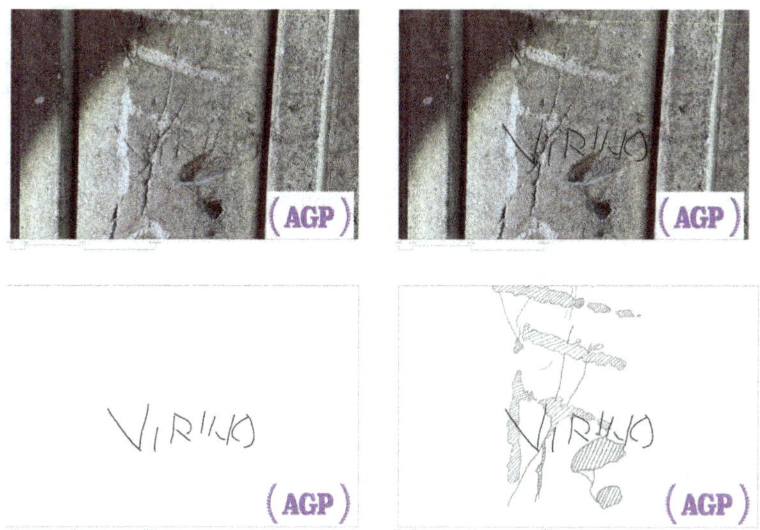

Fig. 9: The gallery of images for *CIL* IV 8666b: photograph (top left), enhanced photo (top right), line drawing (bottom left), line drawing with damage (bottom right). These line drawings were created by Gracie Singleton, a student research assistant at Millsaps College.

The final task in our documentation process is creating line-drawings that are integral to the full series of illustrations for ancient graffiti that still survive. These illustrations are displayed as a series of thumbnails on the AGP results page and then in a larger format on the individual graffito page. We use Archisketch, an architectural sketching app, with an iPad and Apple pencil to create our series of images. Archisketch allows us to add layers and draw over photographs and features a scale, which we set based on our measurements and which we can export with each image layer to provide a visual reference for understanding the size of the inscription. We begin by selecting the photograph whose lighting best illuminates the whole inscription and use that photo as the base for the series, keeping the zoom level consistent so that the size and appearance of the inscription remains the same throughout the series of images. The image series begins with the photograph of the inscription. Next we present the same photograph overlaid with a line-drawing of the graffito in black to render the ancient markings more legible. Third, we remove the photograph and present just the line-drawing of the graffito. In the fourth image, we display the line drawing and damage to the wall surface. The damage is drawn in a different color, so that the viewer can better distinguish between the intentional marks of the ancient graffito and other marks on the wall, such as surface abrasions, loss of plaster and modern graffiti, which can impede understanding. The individual graffito page displays the first image at a larger size, with the image gallery below. A user can click among the series of images in the gallery, which then makes that image the largest on display. With the series of images set at the same scale, a user can then toggle between images in order to compare the photograph, photograph with overlay and line-drawings. The ancient markings become easier to identify in the base photograph once a viewer knows where to look and what to look for. The full series then displays the objective (photograph) and the subjective (line-drawing) so that a viewer may make his or her own judgment.

All images are stored on the server of the Epigraphic Database Roma, which has a Memorandum of Understanding with the Italian Ministry of Culture for displaying images of cultural heritage. The images on AGP each point to the originals stored in EDR. A user may click the largest image on the photo gallery to go to the original photo at EDR and view it at high resolution.

Our practices have evolved over the field seasons. An initial field season will require flexibility and adapting to find the best methodology and process. For our first season, for example, we linked the iPad of each team to sync to each other and quickly realized that plan resulted in overwriting uploaded images. In subsequent seasons, we elevated one person to manage documentation and gave stronger roles to team leaders. We started a check in and out system not only for cameras and iPads so that photos were downloaded on a daily basis, but also for our paper forms, so that they could be reviewed each evening by team leaders and project supervisors. Our documentation forms were also enhanced with new fields to capture more contextual data about each inscription.

Technology also requires adjustments from one field season to the next. For example, photographs taken with new devices are now stored in HEIC formats, which are not as widely accepted as the JPEGs that were produced previously. The software and applications a project uses may also change over time or be superseded by a better resource. We have used two different architectural drawing applications over the past eight years. In certain years, one was more advantageous than the other; more recently, Archisketch issued updates that made it our application of preference. Other changes will come with new versions of computer equipment, such as the newest version of Apple's pencil, which is now pressure-sensitive and creates a thicker line the harder one presses on the iPad. We wished to avoid such output when creating our line-drawings and so to ensure consistency we disabled this feature. For our project, RTI was used for our fieldwork in Herculaneum. In Pompeii, however, our RTI specialist, Jackie DiBiasie-Sammons, chose to use neutral density filters for photographing the graffiti in the theater corridor. These worked well for a location that was often in sunny conditions, and provided results as useful as RTI but created in a fraction of the time.

4.3 Making ancient graffiti accessible

The final step to documenting ancient graffiti consists of sharing the results and making one's documentation public. Traditionally, results were shared in print publications and large folio publications were the primary research product.[64] Now that born-digital projects are proliferating, and many journals and volumes have adopted digital formats, a much wider variety of venues exists for publishing data related to documentation. Earlier projects were sometimes closed or subscription based, but open access has been widely adopted as part of the growth of digital humanities. Since our primary mission has been to make ancient graffiti more accessible, we have built a digital platform and have designed AGP to be fully open access; in addition, user search results can be downloaded in EpiDoc, JSON, or CSV formats.[65]

Since we are based at smaller institutions, we do not have the support of a department or center of digital humanities within our university. The architecture of AGP is therefore built on well-supported, freely available tools. Our technical director of AGP is a professor of computer science and our tools are developed and tested by students in advanced software engineering courses and as summer research experiences. We store our data in a PostgreSQL database and leverage Elasticsearch for fast indexing and searching of the data. Information about the properties and streets in our maps (e.g., name and geographic location) are stored in CSV and GeoJSON files. The Web application's backend is built using JavaEE technology and Spring MVC. Bringing together the geographic location and graffiti data, the application generates interactive maps, which are implemented using Leaflet (https://leafletjs.com/), an open-source JavaScript library, and which are used to enable searching and to visualize results. By leveraging Leaflet as well as the open-source CSS framework Bootstrap (https://getbootstrap.com/), our user interface is responsive to a variety of devices and mobile-friendly. The front end provides users with access to the graffiti and location data in human-readable (HTML) and machine-readable (e.g., JSON,

64 For Pompeian graffiti, initial publication in a journal was customarily followed by publication in the *Corpus Inscriptionum Latinarum*, vol. IV.

65 For more about the design decisions behind AGP, see Benefiel et al. 2017a.

EpiDoc and CSV) forms. Finally, our source code is freely available on Github at: https://github.com/AncientGraffitiProject.

Maintaining AGP's responsiveness and ease of use requires recurring reflection on how a variety of users (e.g., scholars, teachers, students) use the application and then implementing solutions that will best satisfy all users. We have enhanced AGP with new features in response to user feedback. This has included creating the following tools: an epigraphic key which can be turned on and off depending on the user's needs, a collection of featured graffiti with accompanying teaching resources and a standardized reference list of property names and addresses for both Pompeii and Herculaneum. The featured graffiti are listed as a top level menu option since they provide an easy point of entry to the collection. Lesson plans and activities for teachers and the reference list of properties are available under the Resources tab at the top of the page (Fig. 10). Finally, a digital tool needs continuous monitoring and maintenance. Software patches to address security vulnerabilities need to be applied whenever they are identified.

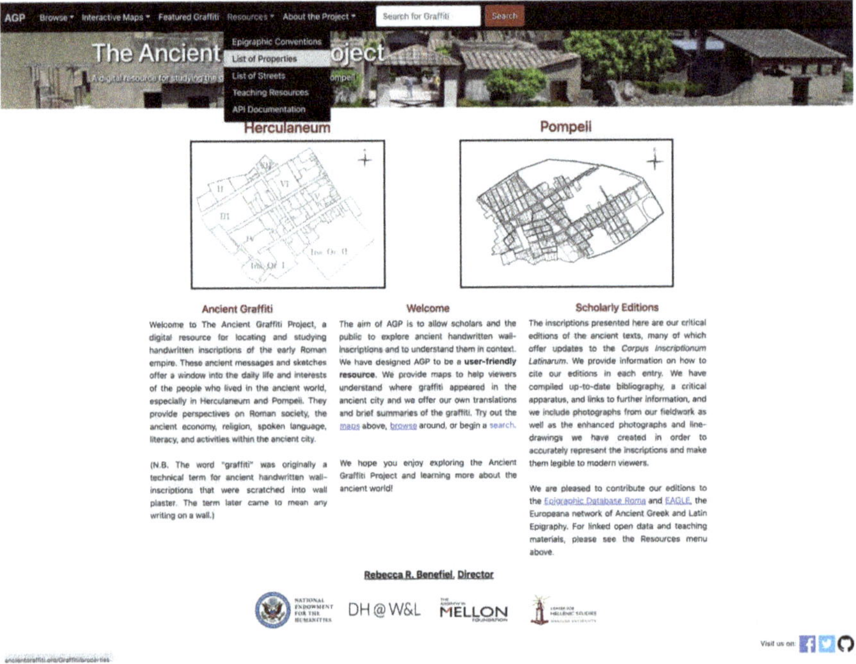

Fig. 10: Homepage of the Ancient Graffiti Project (ancientgraffiti.org).

Digital publication requires standardization and shared standards. For epigraphy, EpiDoc is the mark-up system that provides a common digital language among projects, and is based on TEI XML encoding. A tireless group of scholars have publicized and promoted EpiDoc for Latin and Greek epigraphy over the past two decades, and have educated those in the field by hosting several workshops in different countries each year.[66] Our use of EpiDoc allows our project to be flexible and compatible with other publications and projects.

We designed AGP to be an extensible platform that allows the incorporation of handwritten inscriptions from other sites as well. The Ancient Graffiti Project began by hosting ancient graffiti of Pompeii and Herculaneum as its primary locations, but now features ancient graffiti of Smyrna (modern Izmir, Türkiye) as well. This expansion resulted from working in collaboration with Roger Bagnall and the Institute for the Study of the Ancient World (ISAW) at New York University. The graffiti discovered within the substructures of the basilica at Smyrna in 2003 had been documented and published in a traditional print publication.[67] Behind that print publication, however, the digital files and metadata created for each graffito existed in EpiDoc which allowed us to harmonize that data and bring the graffiti of Smyrna into AGP. Additionally, we will soon be incorporating the ancient graffiti of Stabiae. These graffiti were comprehensively published in 2020 by Antonio Varone, a scholar with deep knowledge of graffiti and using up-to-date methods.[68] It requires significantly fewer resources to collaborate and incorporate a newly published dataset that has shared standards and common vocabulary than it does to take legacy data and metadata and update it.

Digital projects do require staff and support to be sustained. Unlike print publications, whose products take a final, permanent form, digital projects can be further updated, edited, altered and expanded. They can also disappear. Funding schemes mean that certain projects will be supported for a specific duration, will create their research outcome and will conclude. Other projects will have a longer lifespan by finding additional means of support. The main requirements for an ongoing project are a commitment from staff and a host institution.[69]

66 EpiDoc guidelines are housed here: https://epidoc.stoa.org/gl/latest/. Workshops are announced at http://currentepigraphy.org and have resumed again after the pandemic, with a workshop in Cyprus held in May 2022. Training videos are also available on YouTube on the Sunoikisis Digital Classics channel.

67 Bagnall et al. 2016.

68 Varone 2020.

69 Washington & Lee University provides the server for the Ancient Graffiti Project. Institutions may set up projects differently. A digital project might be housed within a department, a center, or within the resources of a library.

In the field of Latin epigraphy, strong initiatives continue to support collaboration and growth of projects. The Digital Classicist wiki provides a clearinghouse listing digital projects and tools of relevance to classicists.[70] As a member partner, AGP contributed data, translations and controlled vocabularies to EAGLE (the Europeana network of Ancient Greek and Latin Epigraphy). EAGLE was a European Commission-funded best practice network, which created a single portal and search mechanism for more than thirty individual epigraphy projects.[71] AGP is also a partner member of Epigraphy.info, a collaborative environment for digital epigraphy. Epigraphy.info and IDEA, the International Digital Epigraphy Association, have assumed the mantle of digital epigraphy leadership and continue the push to create and refine advanced methodologies and refine vocabularies and ontologies.

5 Concluding remarks

Even with two centuries of study and documentation, ancient graffiti continue to hold great potential, with much still to be explored. Our process for documenting ancient graffiti has evolved through our efforts to establish an infrastructure for fieldwork and a framework for presenting our research to a wide audience with varying degrees of expertise. In order to build a team with the skill set to work with these complicated, idiosyncratic inscriptions, Benefiel first offered an epigraphic summer school, whose aim was a preliminary survey of which ancient graffiti were still extant in Herculaneum, as described above. We were fortunate to have the support of Harvard University's Center for Hellenic Studies in Washington DC subsequently where we hosted a week-long workshop instructing graduate students, postdoctoral scholars and faculty how to study, analyze and edit Greek graffiti from Herculaneum and Pompeii. Through these events and the field seasons following, we grew a team with experience and a base of knowledge about ancient graffiti. The publications that have grown out of our work together display a broad range of material still to be studied and analyzed. These include, among others, studies that explore the identity of a building in Herculaneum, the variety of women's names among graffiti, explanation of an idiom about vegetables and a cluster of Safaitic graffiti likely left by Roman soldiers originally from

70 https://wiki.digitalclassicist.org/Category:Projects (accessed on 12 January 2023). The Ancient Graffiti Project is one of many epigraphic projects listed here.

71 https://www.eagle-network.eu/ (accessed on 12 January 2023).

the East.[72] As our work has developed, scholars using it have discovered new lines of inquiry into graffiti. In this way, documentation of ancient graffiti can serve as the cornerstone for new epigraphic scholarship.

To conclude, we offer the following recommendations from the perspective of a team that has nearly a decade of experience creating, designing and growing a digital epigraphic project dedicated to ancient graffiti.

- Think about the uniqueness of your material. Graffiti can be much more than text, or even geo-located inscribed content. What should be documented? What can be documented?
- Adopt disciplinary standards, contribute to controlled vocabularies or ontologies if you can. That will allow you to create consistency within your project and to ensure easier integration of your data with other projects.
- Collaborate with larger projects, if possible, to be integrated into networks of knowledge. It is important to avoid silos of data. Link to other projects and resources when possible.
- Consider long term sustainability. Build infrastructure that will allow you to maintain a site and tools within it. A university may provide server space but consider how to ensure the resources will be maintained through administrative and institutional changes.
- User-friendly is best. Consider the range of users who may be interested in your material and develop, if possible, ways to present the material appropriate to different audiences.

Acknowledgements

We would like to express our thanks to Francesco Sirano, Director of the Archaeological Park of Herculaneum, and Massimo Osanna, former Director of the Archaeological Park of Pompeii, for the opportunity to study and document the ancient graffiti in both sites. Our thanks go also to the National Endowment for the Humanities for supporting our work.

Abbreviations

CIL = *Corpus Inscriptionum Latinarum*

CIL IV: *Inscriptiones parietariae Pompeianae Herculanenses Stabianae* (1871), Carl Zangemeister and Richard Schöne (eds). Berlin.

72 Frampton 2019: so-called College of the Augustales in Herculaneum; Zimmermann Damer 2021: women's names; Cheung 2021: the idiom 'born between a beet and a cabbage'; Helms 2021: Safaitic graffiti. Cf. also DiBiasie-Sammons and Sypniewski 2019: using archival material; Benefiel and Sypniewski 2018: Greek graffiti in Herculaneum.

Supplementi pars I: Tabulae ceratae Pompeiis repertae (1898), Carl Zangemeister (ed).
Supplementi pars II: Inscriptiones parietariae et vasorum fictilium (1909), August Mau (ed).
Supplementi pars III: Inscriptiones Pompeianae Herculanenses parietariae et vasorum fictilium (1952–1970), Matteo della Corte and Pio Ciprotti (eds).
Supplementi pars IV. Inscriptiones parietariae Pompeianae:
Fasc. I (2011), Volker Weber, Antonio Varone, Roberta Marchionni and Jana Kepartová (eds).
Fasc. II (2020), Heikki Solin, Antonio Varone and Peter Kruschwitz (eds).

References

Abate, Dante and Mia Trentin (2019), 'Hidden Graffiti Identification on Marble Surfaces through Photogrammetry and Remote Sensing Techniques', *The International Archives of Photogrammetry, Remote Sensing and Spatial Information Sciences*, 42: 1–8.

AFP in Rome (2018), 'Archaeological Find Changes Date of Pompeii's Destruction', *The Guardian*, 16 October 2018, <https://www.theguardian.com/world/2018/oct/16/archeological-find-changes-date-of-pompeiis-destruction> (accessed on 12 January 2023).

Andreau, Javier and Pablo Serrano (2019), 'Contributions of the Digital Photogrammetry and 3D Modelling of Roman Inscriptions to the Reading of Damaged *tituli*: An Example from the Hispania Tarraconensis (Castiliscar, Saragossa)', *Digital Applications in Archaeology and Cultural Heritage*, 12 <doi.org/10.1016/j.daach.2019.e00091>.

Avellino, Francesco (1841), *Osservazioni sopra Alcune Iscrizioni e Disegni Graffiti sulle Mura di Pompei* (Memorie della Reale Accademia Ercolanese, 5), Napoli: Stamperia Reale.

Bagnall, Roger, Roberta Casagrande-Kim and Cumhur Tanriver (2016), *Graffiti from the Basilica in the Agora of Smyrna*, New York: Institute for the Study of the Ancient World and the New York University Press.

Baird, Jennifer A. (2016), 'Private Graffiti? Scratching the Walls of the Houses at Dura-Europos', in Rebecca R. Benefiel and Peter Keegan (eds), *Inscriptions in the Private Sphere in the Greco-Roman World*, Leiden: Brill, 11–31.

Baird, Jennifer A. and Claire Taylor (eds) (2011), *Ancient Graffiti in Context*, New York: Routledge.

Balzani, Marcello, Marco Calliei, Matteo Fabbri, Andrea Fasano, Claudio Montani, Paolo Pingi, Nicola Santopuoli, Roberto Scopigno, Frederico Uccelli and Antonio Varone (2004), 'Digital Representation and Multimodal Presentation of Archeological Graffiti at Pompei', in Kevin Cain, Yiorgos Chrysanthou, Franco Niccolucci and Neil Silberman (eds), *VAST 2004: The 5th International Symposium on Virtual Reality, Archaeology and Cultural Heritage* <doi:10.2312/VAST/VAST04/093-103>.

Benefiel, Rebecca R. (2010a), 'Dialogues of Ancient Graffiti in the House of Maius Castricius in Pompeii', *American Journal of Archaeology*, 114/1: 59–101.

Benefiel, Rebecca R. (2010b), 'Rome in Pompeii: Wall Inscriptions and GIS', in Francisca Feraudi-Gruénais (ed.), *Latin on Stone: Epigraphic Research and Electronic Archives*, Lanham, MD: Rowman & Littlefield, 45–75.

Benefiel, Rebecca R. (2011), 'Dialogues of Graffiti in the House of the Four Styles at Pompeii (Casa dei Quattro Stili, 1.8.17, 11)', in Baird and Taylor (2011), 20–48.

Benefiel, Rebecca R. (2012), 'Magic Squares, Alphabet Jumbles, Riddles and More: The Culture of Word-Games among the Graffiti of Pompeii', in Jan Kwapisz, David Petrain and Mikolaj Szymanski (eds), *The Muse at Play: Riddles and Wordplay in Greek and Latin Poetry*, Berlin: De Gruyter, 65–79.

Benefiel, Rebecca R. (2021), 'Graffiti in Religious Spaces in First-Century Pompeii: *Lararia*, Neighborhood Shrines, and Graffiti in the Early Roman Empire', in Antonio E. Felle and Bryan Ward-Perkins (eds), *Cultic Graffiti in the Late Antique Mediterranean and Beyond*, Turnhout: Brepols, 1–16.

Benefiel, Rebecca R. with Jacqueline F. DiBiasie Sammons (2019), 'The Scope and Typology of the Graffiti at Oplontis', in John Clarke, Stefano De Caro and Michael Thomas (eds), *Villa A ('of Poppaea') at Oplontis*, vol. 2, New York: American Council of Learned Societies, 2002–2050 <http://hdl.handle.net/2027/heb.90048.0002.001>.

Benefiel, Rebecca R. and Sara Sprenkle (2014), 'The Herculaneum Graffiti Project', in Tom Elliott, Sebastian Heath and John Muccigrosso (eds), *Current Practice in Linked Open Data for the Ancient World* (ISAW Papers, 7) <http://dlib.nyu.edu/awdl/isaw/isaw-papers/7/benefiel-sprenkle/>.

Benefiel, Rebecca R. and Holly M. Sypniewski (2016), 'Images and Text on the Walls of Herculaneum: Designing the Ancient Graffiti Project', in Antonio Felle and Anita Rocco (eds), *Off the Beaten Track: Epigraphy at the Borders: Proceedings of 6th EAGLE International Event (24–25 September 2015, Bari, Italy)*, Oxford: Archaeopress 26–45.

Benefiel, Rebecca R., Jacqueline DiBiasie and Holly M. Sypniewski (2016), 'The Herculaneum Graffiti Project: Initial Field Season, 2014', *FOLD&R Italia*, 361 <https://www.fastionline.org/docs/FOLDER-it-2016-361.pdf>.

Benefiel, Rebecca R., Sara Sprenkle, Holly M. Sypniewski and Jamie White (2017a), 'The Ancient Graffiti Project: Geo-Spatial Visualization and Search Tools for Ancient Handwritten Inscriptions', *DATeCH2017: Proceedings of the 2nd International Conference on Digital Access to Textual Cultural Heritage*, New York: Association for Computing Machinery, 163–168 <doi.org/10.1145/3078081.3078104>.

Benefiel, Rebecca R., Holly M. Sypniewski, Kyle Helms and Erika Zimmerman Damer (2017b), 'Regio I, Latium et Campania: Fascicolo III, Pompeii et Herculaneum: Graffiti', *Italia Epigrafica Digitale*, II.3 <https://ojs.uniroma1.it/index.php/ied/issue/view/1169>.

Benefiel, Rebecca R. and Holly M. Sypniewski (2018), 'The Greek Graffiti of Herculaneum', *American Journal of Archaeology*, 122/2: 209–244.

Benefiel, Rebecca R. and Holly M. Sypniewski (2020), 'Regio I, Latium et Campania: Fascicolo V, Pompeii: Tituli scariphati', *Italia Epigrafica Digitale*, 1/2.5 <https://rosa.uniroma1.it/rosa03/italia_epigrafica_digitale/issue/view/IED%20II%2C%202.5>.

Bodel, John (2012), 'Latin Epigraphy and the IT Revolution', in John Davies and John Wilkes (eds), *Epigraphy and the Historical Sciences* (Proceedings of the British Academy, 177), Oxford: Oxford University Press, 275–296.

Bosco, Angela and Eleonora Minucci (2020), 'Rendering RTI ed editing d'immagine per elaborazioni SfM: Confronto tra tecniche e strumenti di visualizzazione per la documentazione di graffiti in contesto archeologico', *Newsletter di Archeologia CISA*, 11: 43–66.

Buonopane, Alfredo (2012), 'Un'officina epigrafica e una "minuta" nel laboratorio di un marmorarius a Ostia?', in Angela Donati and Gabriella Poma (eds), *L'officina epigrafica romana: in ricordo di Giancarlo Susini*, Faenza: Fratelli Lega, 201–206.

Cayless, Hugh, Charlotte Roueché, Tom Elliot and Gabriel Bodard (2009), 'Changing the Center of Gravity: Transforming Classical Studies through Cyberinfrastructure', *Digital*

Humanities Quarterly, 3/1 <http://www.digitalhumanities.org/dhq/vol/3/1/000030/000030.html>.

Chaniotis, Angelos (2011), 'Graffiti in Aphrodisias: Images—Texts—Contexts', in Baird and Taylor (2011), 191–208.

Cheung, Caroline (2021), 'Born Roman Between a Beet and Cabbage', *American Journal of Philology*, 142/4: 659–697.

Davis, Suzanne L., Caroline Roberts and Janelle Batkin-Hall (2018), 'A Comprehensive Approach to Conservation of Ancient Graffiti at El Kurru, Sudan', *Journal of the American Institute for Conservation*, 57/1–2: 1–18.

DiBiasie-Sammons, Jacqueline F. (2018), 'Application of Reflectance Transformation Imaging (RTI) to the Study of Ancient Graffiti from Herculaneum, Italy', *Journal of Archaeological Science: Reports*, 17: 184–194.

DiBiasie-Sammons, Jacqueline F. (2022), 'Qui carbone rudi putrique creta scribit: The Charcoal Graffiti of Herculaneum', *American Journal of Archaeology*, 126/3: 385–410.

DiBiasie-Sammons, Jacqueline F. and Holly M. Sypniewski (2019), 'Hyacinthus and His Verginia in Herculaneum: A New Reading of CIL IV.10525 Using Archival Research and Digital Documentation', *Zeitschrift für Papyrologie und Epigraphik*, 210: 251–262.

Frampton, Stephanie (2019), 'Graffiti in the So-Called College of Augustales at Herculaneum (Insula VI 21, 24)', in Carlos F. Noreña and Nikolaos Papazarkadas (eds), *From Document to History: Epigraphic Insights into the Greco-Roman World*, Leiden: Brill, 165–178.

García y García, Laurentino (1998), *Nova bibliotheca pompeiana. 250 anni di bibliografia archeologica*, Rome: Scienze e Lettere.

Gill, Rachel (2018), 'Reflectance Transformation Imaging: Documenting Graffiti in the Maya Lowlands', Master's thesis, University of Central Florida <https://stars.library.ucf.edu/etd/5762/>.

Giordano, Carlo (1966), 'Le iscrizioni della Casa di M. Fabio Rufo', *Rendiconti della Accademia di archeologia, lettere e belle arti, Napoli*, 41: 73–89.

Gregori, Gian Luca and Matteo Massaro (2005), 'Brescia, domus delle fontane: i graffiti del "passaggio del kantharos"', *Epigraphica*, 67: 129–157.

Helmke, Christophe, Cristian Bercu, Iulian Drug, Aleksandr Jakovlev, Lars Kjær, Pavel Saulins and Sergei Vepretskii (2022), 'All That is Old is New Again: Epigraphic Applications of Photogrammetry in Ancient Mesoamerica', *Digital Applications in Archaeology and Cultural Heritage*, 25 <doi.org/10.1016/j.daach.2022.e00214>.

Helms, Kyle (2021), 'Pompeii's Safaitic Graffiti', *The Journal of Roman Studies*, 111: 203–214.

Kleinitz, Cornelia (2012), 'Reflectance Transformation Imaging (RTI) in der Bestandsdokumentation der Sekundärbilder und-inschriften von Musawwarat es Sufra im Rahmen des Musawwarat Graffiti Project', *Der Antike Sudan. Mitteilungen der Sudanarchäologischen Gesellschaft zu Berlin*, 23: 7–20.

Krummery, Hans and Silvio Panciera (1980), 'Criteri di edizione e segni diacritici', *Tituli*, 2: 205–215.

Langner, Martin (2001), *Antike Graffitizeichnungen: Motive, Gestaltung und Bedeutung*, Wiesbaden: Ludwig Reichert.

Lech, Paweł, Marcin Matera and Piotr Zakrzewski (2021), 'Using Reflectance Transformation Imaging (RTI) to Document Ancient Amphora Stamps from Tanais, Russia. Reflections on First Approach to Their Digitalisation', *Journal of Archaeological Science: Reports*, 36 <https://doi.org/10.1016/j.jasrep.2021.102839>.

Lohmann, Polly (2017), *Graffiti als Interaktionsform. Geritzte Inschriften in den Wohnhäusern Pompejis*, Berlin: De Gruyter.

Mau, August (1899), *Pompeii: Its Life and Art*, New York: MacMillan.

Macdonald, Michael C.A. and Ali Al-Manaser (2019), 'Recording Graffiti in the Black Desert: Past, Present, and Future', *Journal of Eastern Mediterranean Archaeology and Heritage Studies*, 7/2: 205–222.

Marchant, Jo (2018), 'Buried by the Ash of Vesuvius, These Scrolls Are Being Read for the First Time in Millennia', *Smithsonian Magazine*, July/August <https://www.smithsonianmag.com/history/buried-ash-vesuvius-scrolls-are-being-read-new-xray-technique-180969358/> (accessed on 12 January 2023).

Mezzofiore, Gianluca (2018), 'Pompeii's Charcoal Graffiti May Rewrite History', *CNN*, 17 October 2018, <https://www.cnn.com/style/article/pompeii-eruption-inscription-date-intl/index.html> (accessed on 12 January 2023).

Mocella, Vito, Emmanuel Brun, Claudio Ferrero and Daniel Delattre (2015), 'Revealing Letters in Rolled Herculaneum Papyri by X-ray Phase-contrast Imaging', *Nature Communications*, 6/5895 <doi.org/10.1038/ncomms6895>.

Molle, Carlo (2012), '*Hic hospitati sunt homi(nes)*: Graffiti parietali antichi a Villa Adriana (Tibur)', *Sylloge Epigraphica Barcinonensis*, 10: 389–404.

O'Donald, Megan (2018), 'The ROTAS "Wheel": Form and Content in a Pompeian Graffito', *Zeitschrift für Papyrologie und Epigraphik*, 205: 77–91.

Orlandi, Silvia (2016), 'EAGLE: From the Birth of an Idea to the Realization of a Project', *Forma Urbis International*, 1: 10–13.

Palomar-Vazquez, Jesus, Sergio Baselga, María-José Viñals-Blasco, Carles García-Sales and Ignacio Sancho-Espinós (2017), 'Application of a Combination of Digital Image Processing and 3D Visualization of Graffiti in Heritage Conservation', *Journal of Archaeological Science: Reports*, 12: 32–42.

Panciera, Silvio (2006), *Epigrafi, epigrafia, epigrafisti: scritti vari editi e inediti (1956–2005)*, Rome: Quasar.

Panciera, Silvio (2012), 'What is an Inscription? Problems of Definition and Identity of an Historical Source', *Zeitschrift für Papyrologie und Epigraphik*, 183: 1–10.

Panciera, Silvio, Werner Eck, Daniele Manacorda and Carlo Tedeschi (2006), 'Il monumento iscritto come punto d'incontro tra epigrafia, archeologia, paleografia e storia', *Scienze dell' Antichità*, 13: 583–660.

Parker, Heather Dana Davis and Christopher Rollston (2019), 'Teaching Epigraphy in the Digital Age', in David Hamidović, Claire Clivaz and Sarah Bowen Savant (eds), *Ancient Manuscripts in Digital Culture: Visualisation, Data Mining, Communication*, Leiden: Brill, 189–216.

Parker, Clifford Seth, Stephen Parsons, Jack Bandy, Christy Chapman, Frederik Coppens and William Brent Seales (2019), 'From Invisibility to Readability: Recovering the Ink of Herculaneum', *PLoS ONE*, 14/5 <doi.org/10.1371/journal.pone.0215775>.

Prada, Luigi and Paul D. Wordsworth (2018), 'Evolving Epigraphic Standards in the Field: Documenting Late Period and Graeco-Roman Egyptian Graffiti through Photogrammetry at Elkab', in Francisca A.J. Hoogendijk and Steffie van Gompel (eds), *The Materiality of Texts from Ancient Egypt: New Approaches to the Study of Textual Material from the Early Pharaonic to the Late Antique Period*, Leiden: Brill, 76–93.

Solem, Dag-Øyvind and Erich Nau (2020), 'Two New Ways of Documenting Miniature Incisions Using a Combination of Image-Based Modelling and Reflectance Transformation Imaging', *Remote Sensing*, 12/10: 1626 <doi.org/10.3390/rs12101626>.

Solin, Heikki (1975), 'Die Wandinschriften im sog. Haus des M. Fabius Rufus', in Bernard Andreae and Helumt Kyrieleis (eds), *Neue Forschungen in Pompeji und den anderen vom Vesuvausbruch 79 n. Ch. verschütteten Städten*, Recklinghausen: Bongers, 243–266.

Solin, Heikki and Marja Itkonen-Kaila (1966), *Graffiti del Palatino: I. Paedagogium*, Helsinki: Institutum Romanum Finlandiae.

Stabile, Sara, Francesa Palermo, Inna Bukreeva, Daniela Mele, Vincenzo Formoso, Roberto Bartolini and Alessia Cedola (2021), 'A Computational Platform for the Virtual Unfolding of Herculaneum Papyri', *Scientific Reports*, 11/1695 <doi.org/10.1038/s41598-020-80458-z>.

Stern, Karen (2012), 'Tagging Sacred Space in the Dura-Europos Synagogue', *Journal of Roman Archaeology*, 25: 171–194.

Stern, Karen (2018), *Writing on the Wall: Graffiti and the Forgotten Jews of Antiquity*, Princeton: Princeton University Press.

Taeuber, Hans (2014), 'Graffiti und Steininschriften', in Hilke Thür and Elisabeth Rathmayr (eds), *Hanghaus 2 in Ephesos: Die Wohneinheit 6: Baubefund, Ausstattung, Funde*, Vienna: Verlag der Österreichischen Akademie der Wissenschaften, 331–344.

Taeuber, Hans (2016), 'Graffiti und Inschriften', in Elisabeth Rathmayr (ed.), *Hanghaus 2 in Ephesos: Die Wohnheit 7: Baubefund, Ausstattung, Funde*, Vienna: Verlag der Österreichischen Akademie der Wissenschaften, 233–258.

Tenschert, Ruth, Max Rahrig, Rainer Drewello and Sebastian Kempgen (2020), 'Scratches? Scribbles? Scripture! Revealing the Unseen–3D Scanning of Glagolitic Graffiti of the 10th Century at the Monastery of St. Naum', *Proceedings of the 23rd International Conference on Cultural Heritage and New Technologies 2018* <https://archiv.chnt.at/wp-content/uploads/eBook_CHNT23_Tenschert.pdf>.

Valente, Riccardo, Luigi Barazzetti, Mattia Previtali and Fabio Roncoroni (2019), 'Considerations on the Use of Digital Tools for Documenting Ancient Wall Graffiti', *The International Archives of the Photogrammetry, Remote Sensing and Spatial Information Sciences*, XLII-2/W9: 731–737 <doi.org/10.5194/isprs-archives-XLII-2-W9-731-2019>.

Valente, Riccardo and Luigi Barazzetti (2020), 'Methods for Ancient Wall Graffiti Documentation: Overview and Applications', *Journal of Archaeological Science: Reports*, 34/A <doi.org/10.1016/j.jasrep.2020.102616>.

Valente, Riccardo and Daniela Oreni (2017), 'Survey and Drawings for the Study and Enhancement of Ancient Wall Graffiti: The Case of the Baptistery of Castiglione Olona', *Designarecon*, 10/19 <https://disegnarecon.univaq.it/ojs/index.php/disegnarecon/article/view/277>.

Varone, Antonio (1999), 'I Graffiti', in Alix Barbet (ed.), *La Villa San Marco a Stabia*, Naples: École Française de Rome, 345–362.

Varone, Antonio (2008), 'Inseguendo un'utopia. L'apporto delle nuove tecnologie informatiche alla lettura "obiettiva" delle iscrizioni parietali', in Olof Brandt (ed.), *Unexpected Voices: The Graffiti in the Cryptoporticus of the Horti Sallustiani and Papers from a Conference on Graffiti at the Swedish Institute in Rome, 7 March 2003*, Stockholm: Svenska Institutet i Rom, 125–135.

Varone, Antonio (2012), *Titulorum graphio exaratorum qui in C.I.L. vol. IV collecti sunt*, 2 vols, Rome: L'Erma di Bretschneider.

Varone, Antonio (2020), *Iscrizioni parietali di Stabiae*, Rome: L'Erma di Bretschneider.

Varone, Antonio and Grete Stefani (2009), *Titulorum pictorum Pompeianorum qui in CIL vol. IV collecti sunt: imagines*, Rome: L'Erma di Bretschneider.
Wordsworth, Christopher (1837), *Inscriptiones Pompeianae; or, Specimens and Facsimiles of Ancient Inscriptions Discovered on the Walls of Buildings at Pompeii*, London: John Murray.
Zarmakoupi, Mantha (2016), 'The Spatial Environment of Inscriptions and Graffiti in Domestic Spaces: The Case of Delos', in Rebecca R. Benefiel and Peter Keegan (eds), *Inscriptions in the Private Sphere in the Greco-Roman World*, Leiden: Brill, 50–79.
Zimmermann Damer, Erika (2021), 'What's in a Name? Mapping Women's Names from the Graffiti of Herculaneum and Pompeii', in Brenda Longfellow and Molly Swetnam-Burland (eds), *Women's Lives, Women's Voices: Roman Material Culture and Female Agency in the Bay of Naples*, Austin: University of Texas Press, 151–173.

Anne Vieth

Curating Graffiti: The Exhibition *WÄNDE | WALLS* in the Kunstmuseum Stuttgart

Abstract: This paper gives an insight into my curatorial experiences regarding the comprehensive exhibition *WÄNDE | WALLS*, which for the first time took the wall in its diversity of meanings as the starting point for an exhibition. In addition to the theoretical considerations and concepts, I report on the discussion with the sprayers, who exhibited that graffiti is a unique and thoroughly ambivalent art form. The project traced the artistic examination of the spatial boundary of walls at three central locations in Stuttgart. While wall works were realised in the interior at the Kunstmuseum, the focus at the StadtPalais – Museum für Stuttgart and Stuttgart's central station was on graffiti as an artform, which dealt with the design of walls in public spaces. The exhibition *Graffiti in the City* (*Graffiti im Kessel*, StadtPalais) provided a comprehensive overview of the history of graffiti in Stuttgart, based on photographic and archive material. The impact of graffiti in public spaces could be experienced in the Bonatzbau, the main building of Stuttgart's central station. More than seventy artists from the Stuttgart sprayer scene transformed the interior of the historic hall into a huge temporary graffiti gallery, the ~~*Secret*~~ *Walls Gallery*. It became clear within the multi-perspective project that in addition to its visual manifestation, graffiti is also a socio-cultural phenomenon with its own mechanisms, rules, intentions and slang. It is an art form that has a decisive influence on public space and, thus, on our everyday culture. Graffiti is a global, universal and historically evolved phenomenon which needs to be researched, exhibited and communicated.

1 Introduction

In addition to its visual manifestation, graffiti is a socio-cultural phenomenon with its own mechanisms, rules, intentions and slang. The motivations of graffiti artists are just as diverse as the works of art themselves. It is, on the one hand, the thrill of the illegal act or the desire to mark one's territory; on the other hand, graffiti is usually based on an urge to create. It is about finding one's own style,

https://doi.org/10.1515/9783111326306-015

improving with each piece and gaining the recognition of other graffiti artists, as well as the attention of the public.

As curator of the Kunstmuseum Stuttgart, I was able to implement a cross-disciplinary and cross-institutional exhibition project in Stuttgart in 2020. The pivotal point of the project *WÄNDE | WALLS* was the wall as an aesthetic element and the question of how artists reflect its different levels of meaning.[1] At first glance, walls are architectural elements that form rooms. Walls separate interior and exterior spaces from each other or structure the interior of a room. In their vertical orientation, they are directly in the human field of vision and, thus, shape our spatial perception more clearly than the floor and ceiling. Their significance, however, goes far beyond this basic function: walls are a symbol and expression of manifold demarcations. They have always stood for the protection of the individual, but they can also lock up and deny access. They are, thus, ambiguous boundaries.

Graffiti was an important component of the project, as the wall plays a crucial role in this art form. This article reflects a number of experiences from curatorial practice which illustrate that graffiti is a subcultural artistic form of expression whose presentation in institutional exhibition contexts requires specific approaches.

The following text (as well as the exhibition project presented here) refers to the term graffiti as a subcultural form of expression. Graffiti, understood as codified visualization of a name, increasingly supplemented by figurative elements, emerged in the mid-1960s in Philadelphia, USA, where the first graffiti-writings – usually the names of graffiti artists – were sprayed onto the sides of buildings and city walls. Since then, writers have left their pseudonyms and crew names with markers and spray cans, literally inscribing themselves in space and time. The techniques, motifs and intentions of graffiti artists are now very diverse and differentiated. The boundaries between the terms graffiti and street art, for example, are fluid, a clear definition seems difficult and not very purposeful. In the case of the exhibition project, two things were significant for the fruitful examination of graffiti: the artistic examination of the wall in the public outdoor space (due to the overarching exhibition theme) and the interest in graffiti as a social phenomenon.

1 *WÄNDE | WALLS* (25 September 2020 – 30 May 2021) at the Kunstmuseum Stuttgart. For further information and images, see: <https://www.kunstmuseum-stuttgart.de/en/exhibitions/wande-walls> (accessed on 31 October 2021).

2 The exhibition project *WÄNDE | WALLS*

Three venues were involved in the large-scale exhibition project *WÄNDE | WALLS*:

1. the Kunstmuseum Stuttgart;
2. the StadtPalais – Museum für Stuttgart;
3. the historic hall of the central station in Stuttgart (the so-called Bonatzbau).[2]

While wall works were realised in the interior at the Kunstmuseum, the focus at the StadtPalais – Museum für Stuttgart and the Bonatzbau was on graffiti as an artform, which deals primarily with the design of walls in public spaces (Figs 1–3). The thematic frame of the exhibitions at all three venues was the artistic examination of the spatial boundary of the wall. When the project was conceived, it was not yet

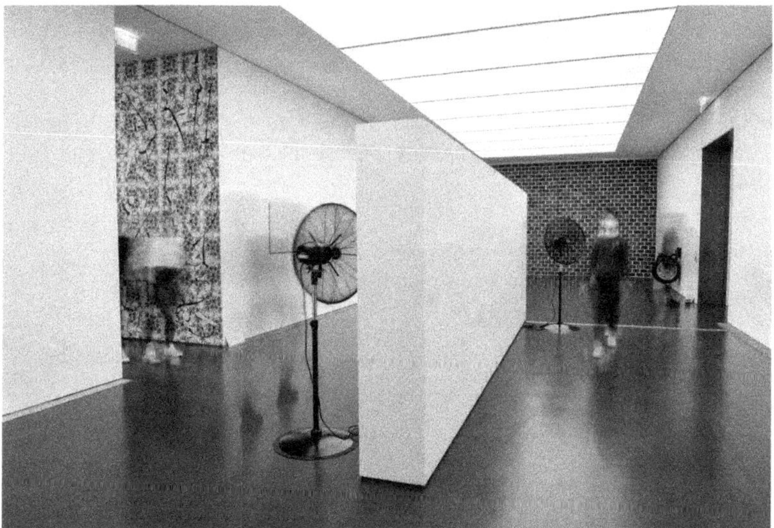

Fig. 1: *WÄNDE | WALLS* – Kunstmuseum Stuttgart, 2020; works by Bruce Nauman, Michael Sailstorfer, Thomas Schütte, Parastou Forouhar; © Kunstmuseum Stuttgart 2020 and VG Bild-Kunst, Bonn 2023 for Bruce Nauman, Michael Sailstorfer, Thomas Schütte; photograph: Gerald Ulmann; reproduced with permission. Creative Commons license terms for re-use do not apply to this image. Further permission may be required from the rights holder.

2 A photo documentation contains impressions of all three venues and is available under: https://www.kunstmuseum-stuttgart.de/en/exhibitions/wande-walls#toc-brochure (accessed on 31 October 2021).

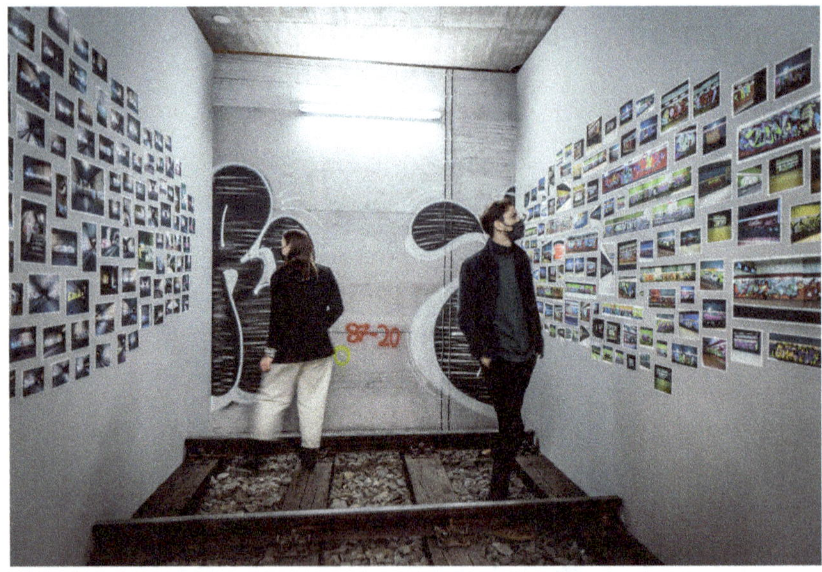

Fig. 2: Graffiti im Kessel – StadtPalais – Museum für Stuttgart, 2020; © Kunstmuseum Stuttgart, StadtPalais – Museum für Stuttgart 2020; photograph Gerald Ulmann; reproduced with permission.

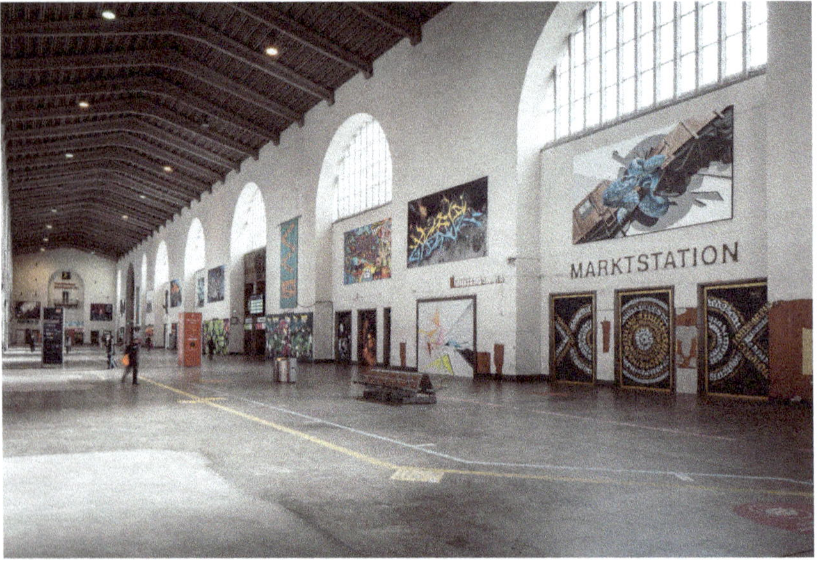

Fig. 3: *~~Secret~~ Walls Gallery* – Bonatzbau Hauptbahnhof Stuttgart, 2020; © Kunstmuseum Stuttgart 2020; photograph Gerald Ulmann; reproduced with permission.

possible to anticipate how the significance of one's own four walls, as well as walls in outdoor spaces as a part of public life, would change in 2020 due to the Corona pandemic. Lockdown, working from home and home schooling, along with other precautionary measures, especially in enclosed spaces, have influenced our perception of spaces. The ambivalent nature of walls – protecting us, while, at the same time, isolating us – is something we have all experienced first-hand. This sensitivity to the symbolic meaning of the wall beyond its pure function as a building element was the common ground of the project.

The exhibition *WÄNDE | WALLS* took the wall in its diversity of meanings as the starting point for an exhibition. The focus was not on wall paintings or the history of wall-bound work in the visual arts. Instead, the exhibition brought together works of art that understand the wall as a cultural product and inquire into its properties as an artistic medium. Artists began to use walls as space-filling image carriers early on. A new approach to the wall emerged in the course of the twentieth century; since then, it has no longer been designed essentially from a decorative point of view – that is to say, to embellish existing architecture. Rather, the wall has come to the fore as an independent object of space to be analysed. Many artists, in interaction with the increasing awareness of spatial and contextual issues in the 1960s, have ascribed an aesthetic value to the wall.[3] The exhibition at the Kunstmuseum provided an overview of reflective work with the wall including selected works by, for example, Sol LeWitt, Yoko Ono, Bruce Nauman and Monica Bonvicini, from the period of 1966 to 2020.

A central and conceptually relevant distinction in the project was the separation between interior and exterior space, namely, between walls that define an interior space and those room boundaries that determine the exterior. There is a clear difference whether an artist works on a wall indoors or outdoors. The two divergent contexts entail specific requirements, be it regarding the production and reception conditions as well as concerning the symbolic meaning of the wall surface. The exhibition at the Kunstmuseum was, therefore, deliberately limited to the theme of interior walls and, even more precisely, to the white wall of the exhibition space in the thematic and complex framework of the 'White Cube'.[4]

3 Vieth 2014.

4 O'Doherty 1976a, 1976b and 1976c. Walls are always associated with specific architectural concepts. In the case of the exhibition and the art business, one of the predominant models is known as the 'white cube'. What is meant by this is the white, empty exhibition space that began to manifest itself in modernism and is still considered the standard for the presentation of modern and contemporary art. It is characterised by uniform floor coverings, homogeneous light, no visible technical elements when possible, and – as a key feature – the white, immaculate walls on or in front of which the works of art are displayed at a suitable distance from one another. This creates

However, it was essential for the overall exhibition project to engage with the wall in the outdoor space as well as outside the institutional exhibition space. Graffiti, as an art form that deals particularly with wall surfaces in public spaces, was the obvious and, above all, most challenging art for this undertaking.

Graffiti in the origin horizon of style-writing spilled over from the United States into Europe in the 1980s as a subculture within the framework of hip hop culture: Amsterdam, Paris and Munich were initially the metropoles with the most noticeable influences from New York. Graffiti culture eventually reached Stuttgart, via Munich and Basel, in the late 1980s.[5] The exhibition *Graffiti im Kessel* at the StadtPalais – Museum für Stuttgart shed light on the development of graffiti on various walls in Stuttgart from the 1990s till 2020 with a focus on twelve relevant 'spots'. The starting point was visual material documenting sites such as different *Halls of Fame*, or the entrance to the central station, as well as urban graffiti phenomena such as *street bombing* and *murals*. The history of graffiti in Stuttgart was sketched out based on roughly 2,000 photographs, which were contextualized in the exhibition by their localisation and chronology (Figs 4–6).[6]

The photographic documents revealed that the writers encountered different conditions at the respective locations, which are reflected in the design of their images. They leave their messages on many walls of different types and sizes, ranging from abutments and bridge piers, to concrete and limestone walls, as well as noise barriers and façades. The photographs illustrate to the same extent how individual prominent locations have changed under the influence of a dynamic graffiti culture as well as the broader changes of urban planning. Graffiti document and shape the history of public spaces. The walls are the underlying support of the styles and pieces, thus, play a decisive role in this process. Walls in outdoor spaces go far beyond their visible function of demarcation and protection. They shape the cityscape, and their surfaces especially can serve as vehicles of communication, and carriers of both commercial and individual messages. Politics, the economy and culture, as well as subcultures that are not institutionally justified, assert their rights to parts of such outdoor wall faces. In order to counteract the autocracy of capital-strong players, many graffiti artists lay claim

the illusion of a neutral space in which the works of art can unfold their effect independently of their surroundings and undisturbed by the reality of the external environment.

5 Wurster and Babusch 2005.

6 The exhibition was curated by Elisabeth Kuon and Studio Vierkant from Stuttgart, a young, multidisciplinary design studio that works at the interface between design, graffiti and mural design. These connoisseurs of the graffiti scene and the graffiti history of Stuttgart were the exhibition designers.

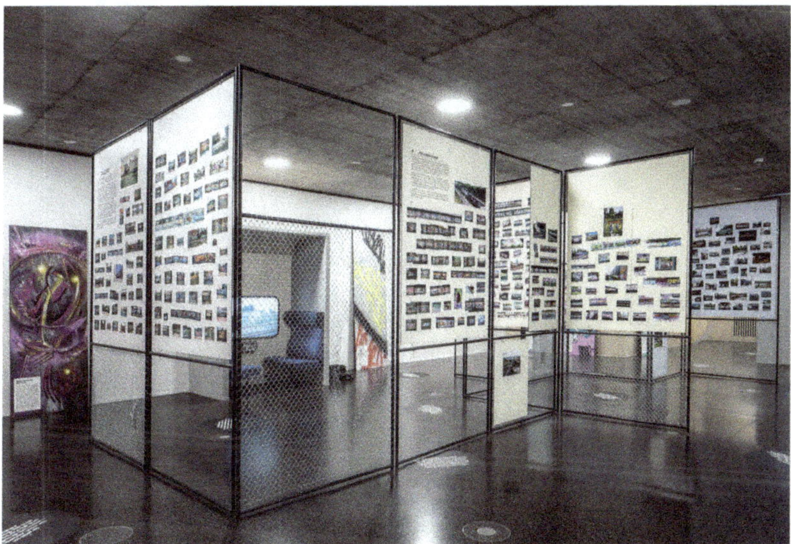

Fig. 4: Graffiti im Kessel – StadtPalais – Museum für Stuttgart, 2020; © Kunstmuseum Stuttgart, StadtPalais – Museum für Stuttgart 2020; photograph Gerald Ulmann; reproduced with permission.

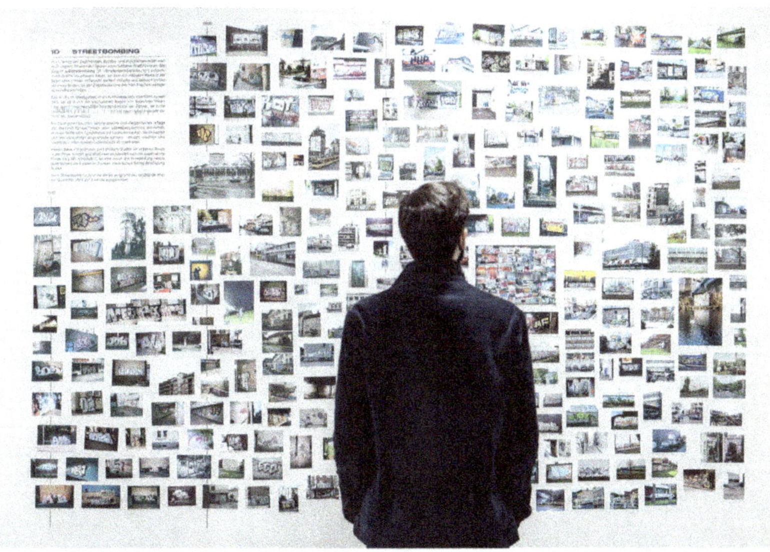

Fig. 5: Graffiti im Kessel – StadtPalais – Museum für Stuttgart, 2020; © Kunstmuseum Stuttgart, StadtPalais – Museum für Stuttgart 2020; photograph Gerald Ulmann; reproduced with permission.

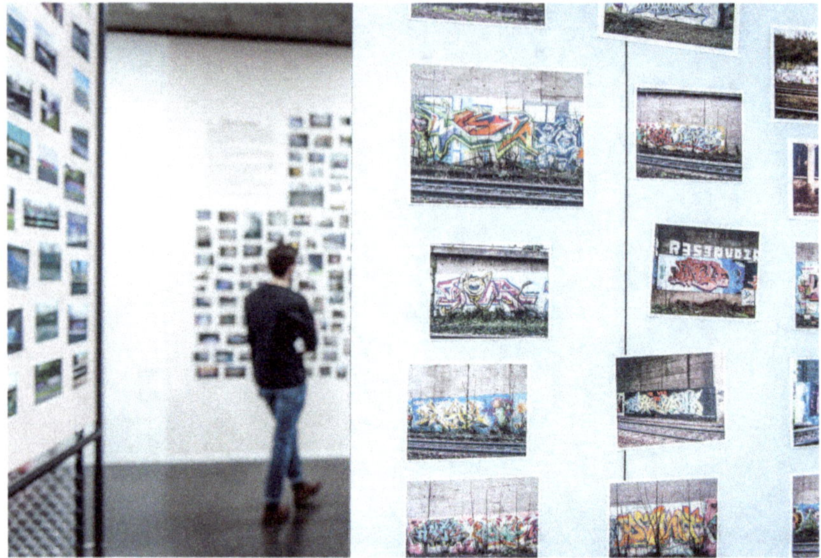

Fig. 6: Graffiti im Kessel – StadtPalais – Museum für Stuttgart, 2020; © Kunstmuseum Stuttgart, StadtPalais – Museum für Stuttgart 2020; photograph Gerald Ulmann; reproduced with permission.

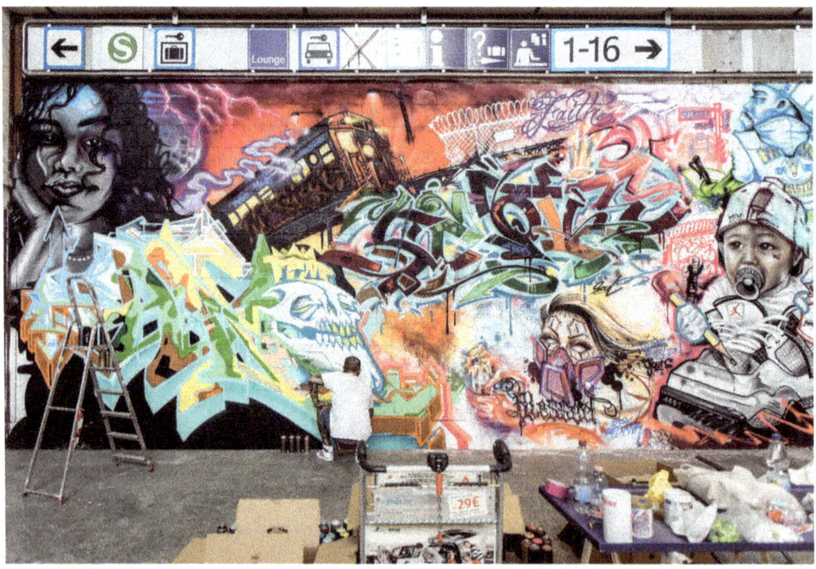

Fig. 7: *~~Secret~~ Walls Gallery* – Bonatzbau Hauptbahnhof Stuttgart, 2020; © Kunstmuseum Stuttgart 2020; photograph Gerald Ulmann; reproduced with permission.

to the public space for their art and their messages. With this anarchic gesture, the artists appropriate the public space, which is, in principle, accessible to everyone. This is and can be criticised as action itself. At the same time, these graffiti draw attention to the fact that there is little transparency or even say in the occupation and design of this public space.

3 The ~~Secret~~ *Walls Gallery* at the Central Station in Stuttgart

The public and discursive potential of graffiti became most evident at the third exhibition site of *WÄNDE | WALLS*. More than 70 artists from the Stuttgart graffiti scene transformed the interior of the historic hall of the central station into a huge temporary graffiti gallery, the ~~*Secret*~~ *Walls Gallery*. The artists worked on-site during the month of August 2020, providing insights into their creative work (Figs 7–8). In addition to the stylistic diversity of graffiti, its historical development in Stuttgart was reflected in more than 50 works. This collaboration between the Kunstmuseum Stuttgart and Deutsche Bahn transformed the Bonatzbau into a lively artistic production site before its extensive renovation.[7] The graffiti and the space influenced each other as the entrance hall was a permeable space that was neither indoor nor outdoor: a completely new atmosphere was created in the station for the more than 300,000 daily passers-by.

The artists, some of whom work alone and some in crews, worked on over 50 different areas in the Bonatz building. Pieces were carried out both on wall surfaces and canvases that are inserted into the existing architecture, for example, where large-format advertisements were once displayed. The graffiti works appropriated a room in its entirety. A kind of *graffiti cathedral* was created, strongly influenced by the hall architecture of the building (Figs 9–10). The building was previously used for consumption and a quick walk through. Suddenly, people stopped, lingered in front of the works of art, and observed the artists. They walked from piece to piece, many of them started talking with the artists. A

7 The Bonatzbau, which serves as the entrance hall to Stuttgart's main train station, is being remodelled as part of the station's redesign. All stores and information desks had already been dismantled at the time of the action. Train traffic on the adjacent tracks had not been suspended, so there was a lively through-traffic in the hall. The conversion of the Bonatzbau is part of the 'Stuttgart 21' transport and urban development project for the reorganisation of the Stuttgart rail junction. The project will see the construction of eleven new, mostly underground lines, as well as four new passenger stations, including a new main station.

fundamental impulse of graffiti emerged in this *in-situ* project: the public space is understood as a common good that offers space for diverse forms of design and creativity and enables alternative perspectives of the living space. Graffiti has established itself as an art form, often on the border of illegality and vandalism, that is now enjoying tolerance and approval within large sections of the population. It has become an indispensable part of public space, especially due to the increasing number of legal places of activity. The reactions of passers-by in the Bonatz building made this obvious. There was mostly positive, even enthusiastic feedback. The people recognised the creative work of the artists, came back regularly and watched the place change.

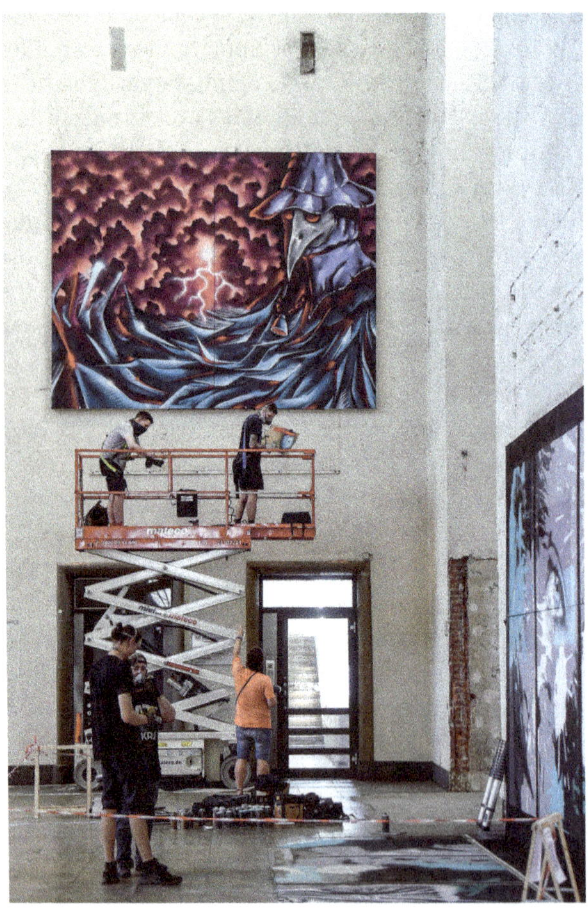

Fig. 8: *~~Secret~~ Walls Gallery* – Bonatzbau Hauptbahnhof Stuttgart, 2020; © Kunstmuseum Stuttgart 2020; photograph Gerald Ulmann; reproduced with permission.

It became clear that the barriers to the reception of graffiti are low-threshold and significantly lower than with many other art forms. This was not only due to the publicly accessible location. Presentations of graffiti in museum or exhibition institutions also show a different audience dynamic. A lot of people feel some form of relationship to graffiti as part of the living environment, a creative form of expression for numerous young people and a *smearing* that still stirs many tempers. Even if only a few laypeople can actually decipher the elaborated styles, this rarely-prevents them from evaluating a piece of graffiti. We are used to graffiti from everyday life. Another factor is the popularity that the graffiti aesthetic has achieved in recent years, especially in youth and popular culture.

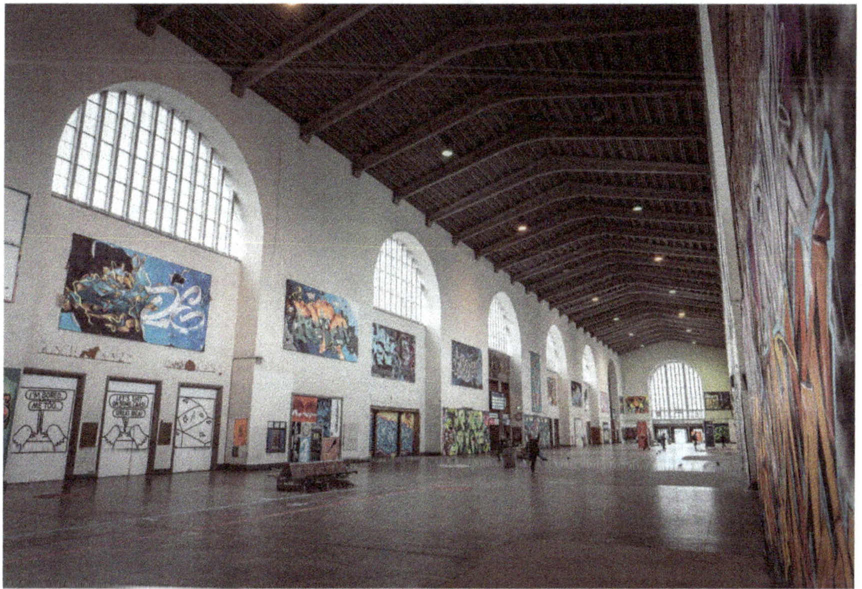

Fig. 9: ~~*Secret*~~ *Walls Gallery* – Bonatzbau Hauptbahnhof Stuttgart, 2020; © Kunstmuseum Stuttgart 2020; photograph Gerald Ulmann; reproduced with permission.

This popularity opens up new possibilities for the graffiti culture, a clearer visibility, a new kind of discourse – but this is also associated with far-reaching changes. This *opening up* of the graffiti amounts to a sell-out for many graffiti artists. The collaboration between established or commercial institutions and the graffiti culture is a problematic process for those who value the illegal moment of spraying as a genuine characteristic and see its softening as a loss of authenticity. This was also a frequent point of criticism of the ~~*Secret*~~ *Walls Gallery*, in which not only a museum, but also the Deutsche Bahn acted as a partner. A corporation that, ironically, deals with fighting and cleaning graffiti on trains every day. This point of discussion led to Deutsche Bahn being accused of using the *~~Secret~~ Walls Gallery* as a whitewashing campaign.[8] There were a number of writers who turned down the offer of participation in the project. They perceived it as a co-optation by the Deutsche Bahn and the art business.

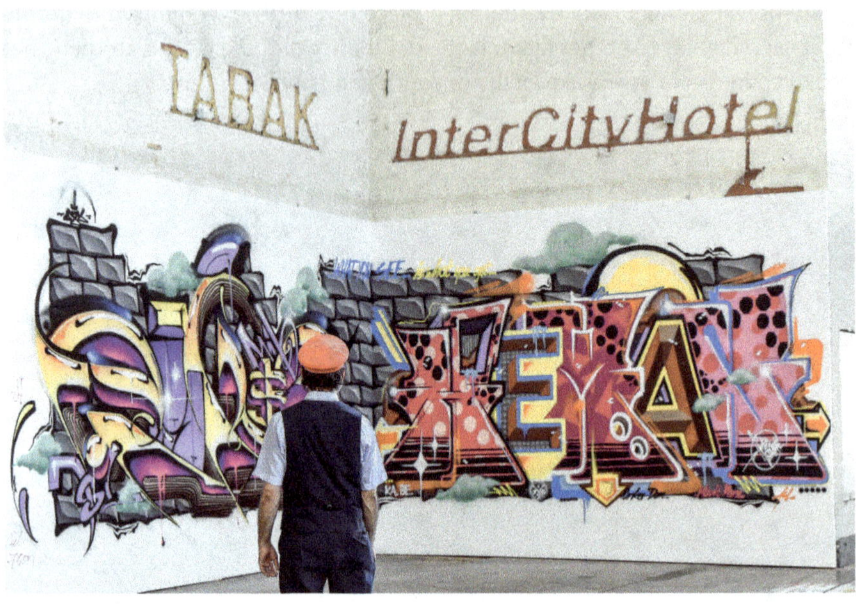

Fig. 10: *~~Secret~~ Walls Gallery* – Bonatzbau Hauptbahnhof Stuttgart, 2020; © Kunstmuseum Stuttgart 2020; photograph Gerald Ulmann; reproduced with permission.

This decision reflects the great diversity in the self-image of graffiti artists. Some absolutely denied the concept of the artist and the notion of art, while others saw the opening up of graffiti regarding the art business as the decisive step for the future of this art form. The question of *museumization* or *institutionalisation* of graffiti goes back to the first exhibitions in New York galleries in the 1980s.

8 It should be noted that Deutsche Bahn can already look back on a number of collaborations with graffiti artists in the Stuttgart region. Wall areas in and around train stations are regularly assigned as legal commissioned work. Nevertheless, this will not put a stop to painting on trains.

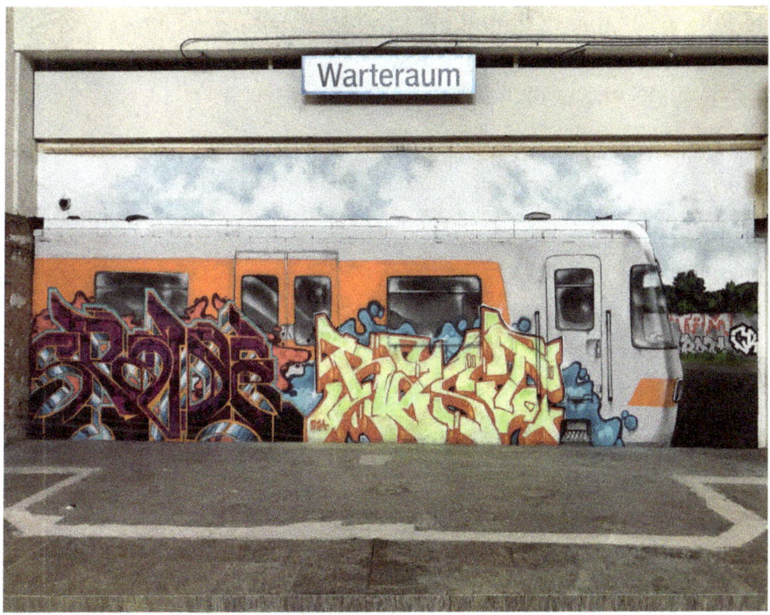

Fig. 11: *Train* by Rust53 and Spade, *~~Secret~~ Walls Gallery* – Bonatzbau Hauptbahnhof Stuttgart, 2020; © Kunstmuseum Stuttgart 2020; photograph Andrea Welz; reproduced with permission.

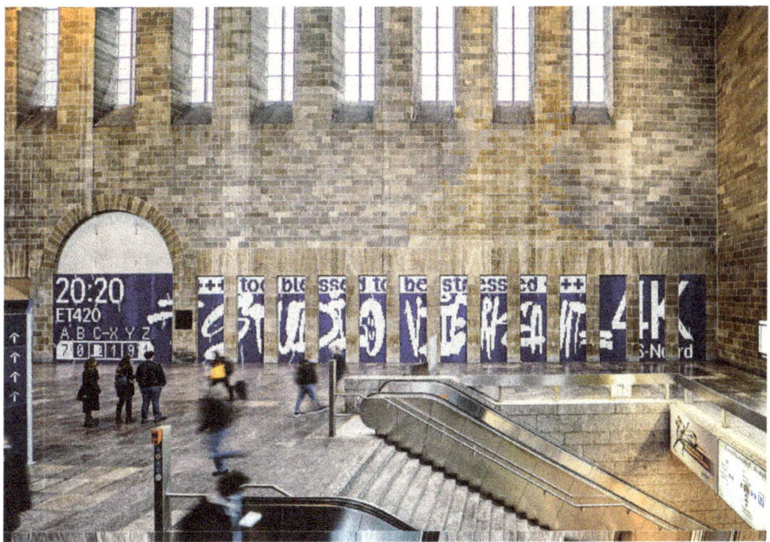

Fig. 12: *too blessed to be stressed* by Studio Vierkant, *~~Secret~~ Walls Gallery* – Bonatzbau Hauptbahnhof Stuttgart, 2020; © Kunstmuseum Stuttgart 2020; photograph Studio Vierkant; reproduced with permission.

Since then, the credibility of graffiti and, in the meantime, of street art in the framework of exhibitions has been discussed with very different attitudes. Javier Abarca, for example, argues in his article 'Curating Street Art':

> From the smallest tag or sticker to the biggest roller piece, the artwork is not so much about what is being written, painted or pasted, but about where, when, how and why this appears. The visual element added to the context can be understood as an excuse to trigger a game of choosing spots and working with them – playing with existing forms, colors, textures, meanings, connotations and history, playing with scale, distance, visibility, intimacy, surprise and risk, among other factors. The core of the artistic process deals with exploring the landscape, discovering and adapting to different contexts, and thus giving shape to a particular understanding of the built environment [...]. When intervening in public space the artist faces a whole scenario full of superimposed shapes, messages and connotations, and tries to take these into account while adding a new element that plays with them. Therefore, to simply reproduce the images of graffiti or street art on a canvas and in a white cube has never been a successful approach to art making.[9]

The author describes an artistic way of working that reflects the respective site of attachment in detail and, thus, the place of action. Art-historical discourse refers to this as a site-specific method. I share the opinion that graffiti is an art form that is fundamentally related to the performance site. This is a particular strength of graffiti that is lost in a mere transfer of graffiti onto a canvas which is installed on a gallery wall. From a curatorial point of view, this special feature of graffiti was taken into account by creating a work and exhibition situation in public space in the *~~Secret~~ Walls Gallery* that comes close to the original conditions of graffiti. On the part of the artists, there were some contributions that got involved in this situation and worked in a reflective way with the site. Some examples were the work in the form of a (sprayed) train entering the waiting hall by the artists Rust53 and Spade (Fig. 11) or the piece *too blessed to be stressed* by the Studio Vierkant (Fig. 12), which acts as an advertisement at a former advertising site. A central point of discussion is and will remain the question of context transfer. What happens to graffiti when it wanders from the outside space into an exhibition gallery? To what extent does such a shift need to be reflected by the artists, curators and customers, bearing in mind the media specifics of graffiti?

9 Abarca 2017, 112–113.

4 Graffiti – an institution of its own

Curating graffiti, as in many other areas of contemporary exhibition practice, requires a multi-perspective and collaborative method.[10] It is absolutely necessary to work with insiders of the scene for projects such as the ~~Secret~~ *Walls Gallery* and *Graffiti im Kessel*. It is a thoroughly hermetic scene, not in the sense of uncooperative, but rather cautious. Because no matter how much graffiti has arrived in the mainstream, the majority of works are unlawful from a legal point of view. Graffiti that is not commissioned or carried out with permission on so-called 'legal walls' is a crime and the creators can be prosecuted. From a curatorial point of view, this fact also required a number of precautions and considerations when preparing the exhibition, which are rather unusual in conventional exhibition business. We paid close attention to the anonymity of those involved. We only named the artists or authors at their request in both *Graffiti in the Kessel* and the Bonatzbau. There is no work list for the ~~Secret~~ *Walls Gallery*, and no official assignment of work and name. Of course, a lot of pieces are signed and the styles can be recognised, but there were no labels of the works or any sort of lists with authors' names. This may sound like paranoia, but photos and works in the train station could serve as evidence for potential lawsuits. It was important for us that the writers were not endangered due to their participation in the *WÄNDE | WALLS* project.

The first contact with the Stuttgart graffiti artists was through some insiders, who thoroughly explained the project. The graffiti artist Moritz Vachenauer played a particularly important role for the ~~Secret~~ *Walls Gallery*. He acted as curator, contact person and interface to the Kunstmuseum. Together with him we developed a number of criteria that can be summarised as: reference to Stuttgart, relevance for the development of graffiti in Stuttgart, visibility in Stuttgart; depicting the stylistic diversity of graffiti and the different time phases since the 1980s. These selection criteria also provide an answer to a frequently asked, quite critical question: why more than a few well-known graffiti artists have worked on the station concourse, especially regarding this unique space. The answer is simple: The project was about graffiti walls as part of an urban society, and when the option of the station hall opened up, it was clear that this central location for Stuttgart's urban development should be available to the Stuttgart graffiti scene.

10 Mayr 2020.

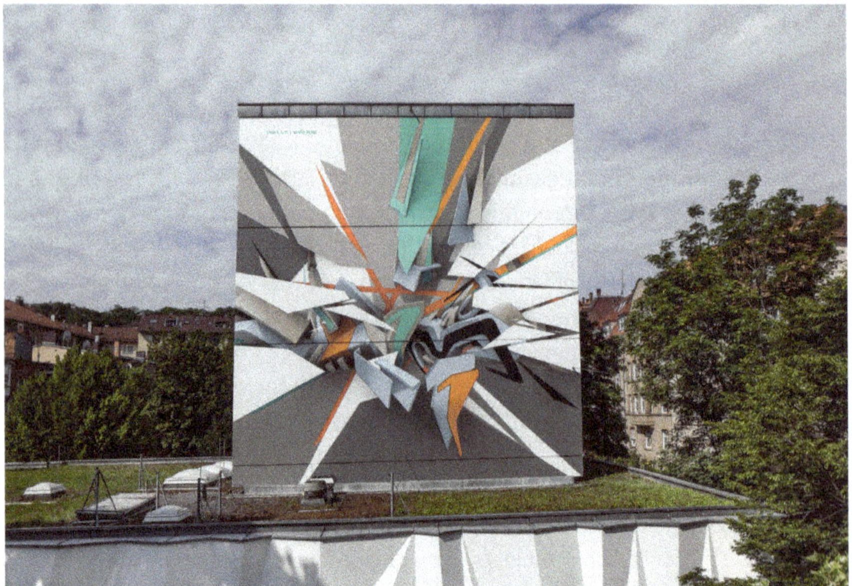

Fig. 13: Façade DAIM (Mirko Reisser), Eberhard-Ludwigs-Gymnasium Stuttgart, 2021; © Kunstmuseum Stuttgart 2020 and VG Bild-Kunst, Bonn 2023; photograph Gerald Ulmann; reproduced with permission.

A further aspect came into play here, which is addressed in some scholarly approaches to graffiti and street art: the performativity of graffiti, its status as an act integrally located in the city, inherently in and of urban space.[11] The opportunity to watch the artists relevant to Stuttgart graffiti at work brought to light the performative moment of this art form and led to a real exchange and dialogue between artists and audience. A strong identification with what was happening and what was seen could be observed on both sides. This special potential of graffiti was also evident in the final project of *WÄNDE | WALLS*: the Hamburg based artist Mirko Reisser, alias DAIM, realised a huge wall piece at a Stuttgart high school (Figs 13–14). His style was already known in the city because he designed the glass front on the Kunstmuseum Stuttgart with a spectacular *3D-Style*, which announced the exhibition project and seemed to make the façade of the Kunstmuseum burst open (Fig. 15). The work served as a link between the three exhibition venues. At the end of the exhibition, the façade design disappeared. One of the main impulses of graffiti, however, is to set a lasting symbol that is visible

11 See for example Schacter 2014.

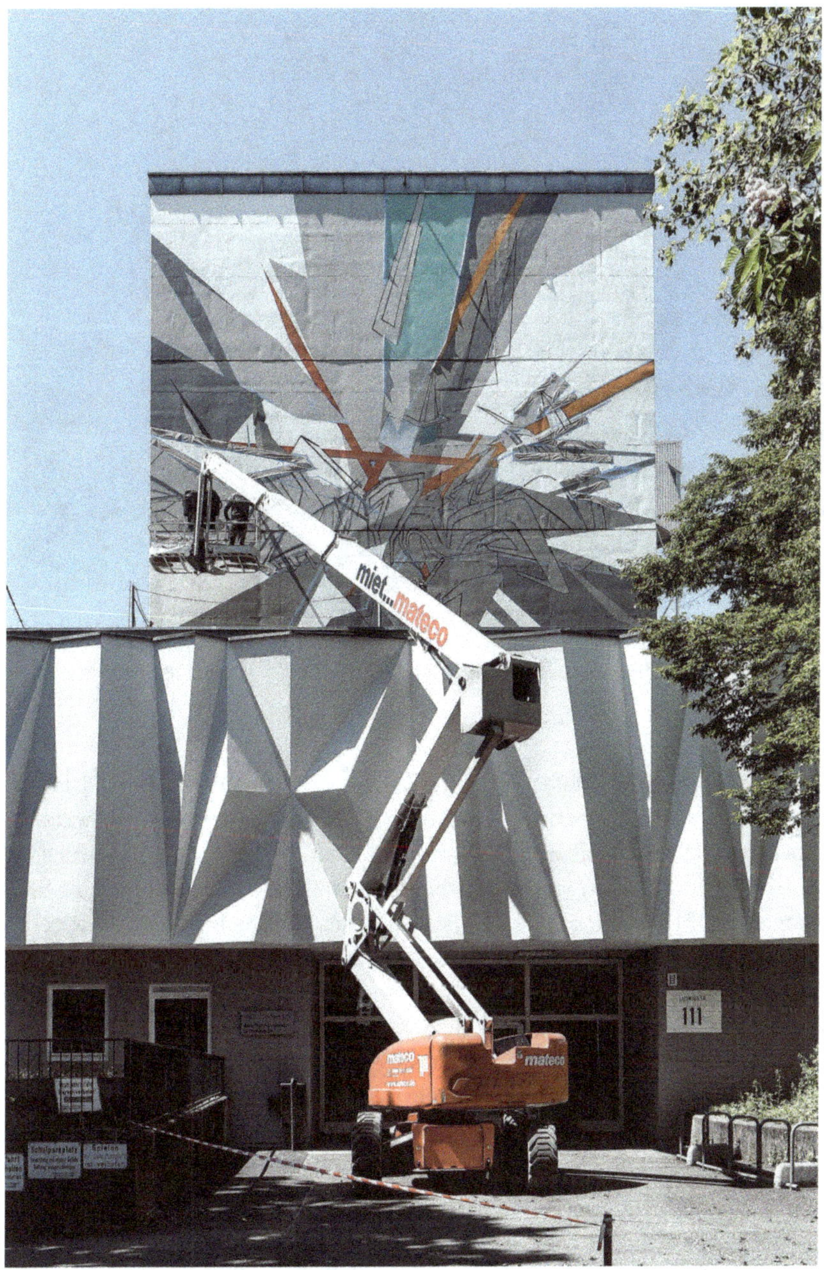

Fig. 14: Façade DAIM (Mirko Reisser), Eberhard-Ludwigs-Gymnasium Stuttgart, 2021; © Kunstmuseum Stuttgart 2020 and VG Bild-Kunst, Bonn 2023; photograph Gerald Ulmann; reproduced with permission.

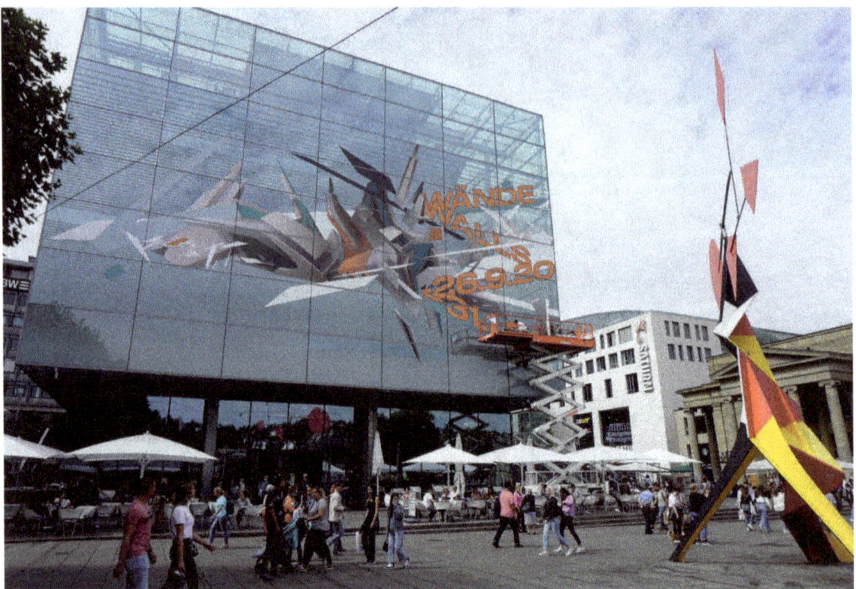

Fig. 15: Façade by DAIM (Mirko Reisser), Kunstmuseum Stuttgart, 2020; © Kunstmuseum Stuttgart 2020 and VG Bild-Kunst, Bonn 2023; photograph Gerald Ulmann; reproduced with permission.

to as many people as possible. Fortunately, the Eberhard-Ludwigs-Gymnasium in Stuttgart-West made a prominent, well over 100 square metre area of the school façade available, on which Mirko Reisser created an explosive and colourful style that is typical for him. In contrast to other cities in Germany, the number of commissioned graffiti in Stuttgart is still manageable, but one increasingly encounters artistically painted house facades, transformer stations, subway stations, bus stops and bridge piers, whose mostly dreary appearance is changed by the graffiti. In this way, graffiti inscribes itself permanently in public space. The dialogue with the residents is of great importance in this process and very often leads to a mutual exchange about living together, and the appearance and common design of the living space. In the case of the DAIM façade, the students spoke of a clear upgrade of their school. The work of art increased identification with the institution accompanied by a project on graffiti in art class, an interview with the artist and a film documenting the creation.

This leads to another important issue when it comes to curating graffiti: documentation is essential because graffiti is usually an ephemeral work. In the case of not institutionally anchored graffiti, the artists choose whether they want to record their work. Yet, the documentation of a curated project is the responsibility of the organiser. In the case of the *~~Secret~~ Walls Gallery*, a professional photographer took photos several times during the production period. These were incorporated into the photo documentation mentioned that was published regarding the overall project. In addition, a short film was produced that also captures impressions from the Bonatz building in the medium of moving images.[12] However, this material is not yet optimal for professional project archiving. This would have meant that each work is recorded successively in the creation process, the surrounding context is captured in several photos and different perspectives of the work that exist on-site – because the writers pay particular attention to this when designing the work. Graffiti is primarily created according to the rules of visibility. It is, therefore, also important to record in the documentation for whose reception the work was developed – for driving in the S-Bahn or car, for those waiting at the stop or for the pedestrians in the streets. Numerous archiving measures have been initiated by the artists themselves in the area of graffiti and street art, for example, in the Back Jumps exhibitions[13] or the book and exhibition *Eine Stadt wird bunt*,[14] which focuses on the history of Hamburg graffiti. Here, too, it is obvious that graffiti and street art are more than just the hobby of wild youngsters. It is an art form that has a decisive influence on public space and, thus, on our everyday culture. Graffiti, as a global, universal and historically evolved phenomenon, needs to be researched, exhibited, communicated and, most importantly, provided with the financial resources necessary to do so.

Acknowledgements

A number of artists whose work was displayed at the ~~Secret~~ Walls Gallery at Bonatzbau Hauptbahnhof Stuttgart chose to stay anonymous. Some of their work is captured on photographs accompanying this chapter. The author wishes to acknowledge their creative work that made the exhibition possible.

12 KunstmuseumStuttgart, 'Review: Secret Walls Gallery' [Video], <https://www.youtube.com/watch?v=ZF1phInbjg4>, posted on 15 January 2021 (accessed on 31 October 2021).

13 See the website 'Backjumps – urbane Kommunikation und Ästhetik', <http://theliveissue.com/> (accessed on 31 October 2021).

14 *EINE STADT WIRD BUNT. Hamburg Graffiti History 1980–1999*, exhibition at the Museum für Hamburgische Geschichte (2 November 2022–31 July 2023), <https://einestadtwirdbunt.de/> (accessed on 31 October 2021); Nebel et al. 2021.

References

Abarca, Javier (2017), 'Curating Street Art', *Street Art and Urban Creativity*, 3/2: 112–118.
Mayr, Helen-Sophie (2020), *Curating the Subversive: Illegal Graffiti in Urban Space on the Example of Berlin and How to Approach It Curatorially*, PhD thesis, Stockholm University.
Nebel, Oliver 'Davis', Frank Petering, Mirko Reisser and Andreas 'Cario' Timm (eds) (2021), *Eine Stadt wird bunt: Hamburg Graffiti History 1980–1999*, Hamburg: Double-H.
O'Doherty, Brian (1976a), 'Inside the White Cube: Notes on the Gallery Space, Part I', *Artforum*, 14/7: 24–30.
O'Doherty, Brian (1976b), 'Inside the White Cube, Part II: The Eye and the Spectator', *Artforum*, 14/8: 26–34.
O'Doherty, Brian (1976c),'Inside the White Cube, Part III: Context as Content', *Artforum*, 15/3: 38–44.
Schacter, Rafael (2014), *Order and Ornament: Graffiti, Street Art and the Parergon*, London: Routledge.
Vieth, Anne (2014), *Addicted to Walls: Zeitgenössische Wandarbeiten im Ausstellungsraum*, Munich: Schreiber.
Wurster, Kim 'Uran' and 'Dingo' Babusch (2005), *Sprüher im Rudel: Eine Dokumentation der Stuttgarter Graffitiszene*, Stuttgart: Dingo Grafix.

Contributors

Alexander Araya López is a Marie Skłodowska-Curie Actions (MSCA) postdoctoral fellow at the University of Potsdam with the project PROTEST-AIRT, which explores the emergence of social movements campaigning against global air transport. His first MSCA fellowship was granted for the project RIGHTS UP, hosted at Ca' Foscari University of Venice, during which he studied social movements campaigning against mass tourism in Europe. He concluded his PhD in Sociology in 2014 at the Institute for Latin American Studies of the Free University of Berlin. His research interests include radical activism, civil and democratic disobedience, spatial politics, and media representations of acts of dissent.

Rebecca Benefiel is Abigail Grigsby Urquhart Professor of Classics at Washington & Lee University in Lexington, VA. Her research focuses on Latin epigraphy and Roman social history. She is Director of the Ancient Graffiti Project, a supervisor for the Epigraphic Database Roma, and a past president of the American Society of Greek and Latin Epigraphy. She has co-edited *Inscriptions in the Private Sphere in the Greco-Roman World* (Brill, 2016), *Inscriptions and the Epigraphic Habit* (Brill, 2023), and is co-editing the *Oxford Handbook to Pompeii* (Oxford, in preparation).

Nadine Bregler is a research associate at the CSMC (Centre for the Study of Manuscript Cultures), Universität Hamburg. Her research interests include Medieval Chinese history and literature, and particularly the reasons for the various combinations of Chinese literary texts in Dunhuang manuscripts.

Carlo Giovanni Cereti's early research focused on the history of the Zoroastrian Parsi community in India. Over time, his main research field shifted to Middle Iranian languages and literatures, and more specifically to the study of Zoroastrian literature. His interest in Zoroastrianism has led him to prepare critical editions of Middle Persian texts, such as the Zand ī Wahman Yasn and many chapters of the Bundahišn, as well as a work synthesising Pahlavi literature. From 2006 onwards, he has worked intensively on epigraphic Middle Persian, with a focus on Narseh's Paikuli inscription. He is Principal Investigator of several research projects.

Sanja Ewald studied cultural anthropology, art history, and modern German literature in Hamburg from 2004 to 2013. After holding roles as a lecturer in cultural anthropology and research assistant to the equal opportunities officer, she started her PhD at the Cluster of Excellence 'Understanding Written Artefacts' at the CSMC with a thesis on style writing in Hamburg in the 1980s and 1990s. Her research focuses on the writing process of the modern graffiti form and its constantly changing materiality.

Michael C. A. Macdonald is an honorary fellow of Wolfson College, University of Oxford, and a fellow of the British Academy. For the last forty-five years, he has worked on the languages, scripts, and inscriptions of Syria, Jordan, and Arabia as well as literacy in the ancient Near East, the prehistory of the Arabic language, and the origins of the Arabic script, rock art, and the history of the nomads of the Near East up to the revelation of Islam. He has led numerous epigraphic surveys in Syria, Jordan, and Saudi Arabia.

Seth M. Markle is Associate Professor of History and International Studies at Trinity College, Hartford, CT, where his research and teaching focuses on political movements, diaspora identity formation, and hip-hop culture in Africa and the African diaspora. He is the author of *A Motorcycle on Hell Run: Tanzania, Black Power, and the Uncertain Future of Pan-Africanism, 1964–1974* (Michigan State University Press, 2017) and "The Hip Hop DJ as Black Archaeologist: Madlib's Beat Konducta in Africa and the Politics of Memory." He received his BA in Africana Studies from Tufts University (2000), Medford, MA, and PhD in History from New York University (2011).

Leah Mascia is a postdoctoral researcher in Egyptology and Coptology at the Cluster of Excellence 'Understanding Written Artefacts' at the CSMC. She is an archaeologist and epigraphist member of the Archaeological Mission of the University of Barcelona working at the archaeological site of Oxyrhynchus (Egypt) and of the Archaeological Mission of the University of Urbino, Italy, investigating ancient Cyrene (Libya). She specialises in the study of written artefacts associated with religion, mortuary practices, and magic in Greco-Roman and Late Antique Egypt.

Matsui Dai obtained his PhD from Osaka University (1999). His main research interest is the history of Central Asia under the rule of the Turkic Uyghurs (during the tenth to twelfth centuries) and the Mongols (during the thirteenth and fourteenth centuries). He has also engaged in producing philological editions of the Old Uyghur and Mongolian texts retrieved from East Turkestan (present-day Xinjiang) and Dunhuang. He is a professor at the Graduate School of Humanities of Osaka University.

Ann Lauren Osthof studied ancient history and classical archaeology at the University of Tübingen, Germany, and Trinity College, Dublin. Her interest in graffiti stems from her current interdisciplinary dissertation project 'Immersive City Scripts: Inscriptions and the Construction of Social Spaces in Miletus (Asia Minor)', which is situated at the Cluster of Excellence 'Understanding Written Artefacts' at the CSMC.

Malena Ratzke studied German studies and art history, and her research interests combine speech, script, and image in Medieval and Early Modern European culture. Apart from graffiti as written artefacts, she is interested in the materiality and hermeneutics of illustrated devotional manuscripts. She has worked on Medieval and Early Modern book culture with a focus on intermediality and on premodern political culture, narrative, drama, and poetry. After posts and fellowships at the universities of Hamburg, Leipzig, and Oxford, she currently works as Research Associate at Friedrich Schiller University Jena.

Mirko Reisser has been an active graffiti writer since 1989. He studied liberal arts in Lucerne from 1996 to 1998. He has realised numerous projects in Germany, Switzerland, and other countries under the pseudonym DAIM and is involved in various exhibitions as an artist as well as a curator and publisher of graffiti books, such as the recently published volume *Eine Stadt wird bunt: Hamburg Graffiti History 1980–1999* (Double-H, 2022).

Ondřej Škrabal is a postdoctoral researcher and spokesperson of the research group 'Situating Graffiti' at the Cluster of Excellence 'Understanding Written Artefacts' at the CSMC. A historian of ancient China, his current research focuses on the sociocultural, political, and technological underpinnings of epigraphic and manuscript practices, the provenance and craftsmanship of premodern bronze art, and the social history of graffiti in East Asia. He is the co-editor of the *Handbook of Epigraphic Cultures* (De Gruyter, forthcoming 2024).

Ingo Strauch is Professor of Sanskrit and Buddhist Studies at the University of Lausanne. His research interests concern early Buddhist manuscripts and Indian epigraphy. He published the volume *Foreign Sailors on Socotra: The Inscriptions and Drawings from the Cave Hoq* (Hempen) in 2012, which contains a significant corpus of Indian and other graffiti from the early centuries of our era.

Holly M. Sypniewski is Professor of History at Clarkson University, NY. She is the Assistant Director of the Ancient Graffiti Project and a lead editor for the Epigraphic Database Roma. Her current research projects include studies of the Campus ad Amphitheatrum (II.7.1-10) in Pompeii, the Suburban Baths of Herculaneum, and the documentation methods of the epigrapher Matteo Della Corte.

Mia Gaia Trentin is an associate research scientist at the Science and Technology in Archaeology and Culture Research Center at the Cyprus Institute, Nicosia. She has followed an interdisciplinary curriculum, including archaeology (BA), cultural heritage studies (MA), and social history (PhD), that reflects her interests and research approach. In 2017, she joined the Cyprus Institute, focusing on digital humanities. Her current research addresses Medieval and post-Medieval graffiti with a digital humanities approach that supports the analysis of different contexts, such as pilgrimage sites and routes and anthropic (urban) and natural landscapes.

Minna Valjakka is Associate Professor of Art History at the University of Helsinki. Through her long-term and locally embedded interdisciplinary research in East and Southeast Asian cities, she examines how artistic and creative practices interact with current global conditions, how they reformulate public spaces and spheres, and how they provoke new formulations of civil society. She has published in a wide range of journals, including *Cultural Studies*, *City*, *Culture and Society*, and *China Information*.

Ursula Verhoeven has been Professor of Egyptology at the Johannes Gutenberg University of Mainz since 1998 and an ordinary member of the Academy of Sciences and Literature Mainz since 2011. Her research interests lie in Egyptian papyrology, Book of the Dead manuscripts, literary and religious texts, and hieratic visitor inscriptions. From 2005 to 2019, she was co-leader of a fieldwork project in the necropolis of Asyut. In 2015, she initiated the long-term project 'Altägyptische Kursivschriften' at the Mainz academy, developing a digital palaeography of hieratic and cursive hieroglyphs.

Anne Vieth has been a curator at the Kunstmuseum Stuttgart since 2017. She studied art history, German philology, and Spanish literature in Hamburg and wrote her doctoral dissertation on contemporary wall works in the exhibition space. She began her curatorial career at the Kunsthalle Mannheim, and worked at the Staatliche Kunstsammlungen in Dresden from 2014 to 2016. Her research focuses on classical modernism and contemporary art. At the Kunstmuseum Stuttgart, she is in charge of the Otto Dix collection, the Fritz Winter collection, and the collection of works from 1945 onwards.

Jarosław Źrałka is Associate Professor of Archaeology at the Jagiellonian University, Kraków. Working as an archaeologist in Central America for more than ten years, he specialises in Mesoamerican archaeology with a particular focus on the ancient Maya. Since 2006, he has been co-directing the Nakum Archaeological Project at the Maya site of Nakum, in north-eastern Guatemala. He is currently conducting a project in the Guatemalan Highlands aimed at the conservation of colonial wall paintings from the town of Chajul (Quiché department). His monographs include *Terminal Classic Occupation in the Maya Sites Located in the Area of Triangulo Park, Peten, Guatemala* (Jagiellonian University Press, 2008) and *Pre-Columbian Maya Graffiti: Context, Dating and Function* (Wydawnictwo Alter, 2014).

Index

Within this index, headings are arranged in a word-by-word order. The index aims to assist the reader in finding names and terms of interest, rather than creating a concordance, which is why terms that appear too frequently (e.g. 'inscription'), and would therefore be impractical as index headings, are omitted.

Imre Galambos

2008 Olympic Games (Beijing) 235, 257
2Pac 82
50 Cent 82
AAT *see* Art and Architecture Thesaurus
Abarca, Javier 34, 480
Abusir 59
Abydos 50, 56
accessibility *see also* FAIR Data Principles; visibility
– of data 30–32, 319, 335, 445
– of graffiti 66, 87, 398, 448, 455, 475
– of sites 29, 311, 477
Achaemenians 17, 328, 349, 351 n. 63
Adityazen 177 n. 8, 182–183, 186, 195
advertisement 12, 20, 147, 246–248, 475, 480
– banners/posters 19, 243
Aegean Sea 21
Africa 33, 77, 83, 94, 97, 394; *see also* South Africa
– North-West 357
– sub-Saharan 6 n. 10
African Americans 78, 81, 83, 88, 96
African Diaspora 79
African Socialism 79, 81, 88
AGP *see* Ancient Graffiti Project
AIDS 82, 88
Ailton dos Santos 164
Akbar, Moghul emperor 314
Aksumite 297
Al-Jallad, Ahmad 366–368, 370, 372, 379
Alimoradi, Pooriya 335, 338, 341–342
All European Academies (ALLEA) 410
Allāhābād pillar 306, 308, 311–315
alliterative poems 180–181, 195, 199
alphabet 330, 390, 395, 401, 403, 413, 433 n. 22
– Latin/Roman 271, 398–399, 450
– Parthian 339, 342
– Phoenico-Aramaic 358 n. 15, 362
– Safaitic 362, 370 n. 38
– teaching 370
alphabetic writing 253, 289, 358 n. 15, 362; *see also* non-alphabetic signs
Amitāyus/Amitābha 196
Amsterdam 472
amulets 20–21
Amun-Ra 1
Anatolia 174
Ancient Graffiti Project (AGP) 31, 429, 440–444, 447–448, 451–458
Ancient Letters (Sogdian) 344–345
Āndhradeśa 292
Andrews, George 111–112
Angkor Wat 5
anonymity 277, 248–249, 256–257
– and illegality 82, 235 n. 5, 246, 272, 481
anthropology 4–5, 18 n. 47, 66, 79
Anuradhapura 288–289
Aphrodisias 436
Arabia 356, 374; *see also* Saudi Arabia
– North 32, 355, 374, 379
– South Arabia 358–359
Arabian Peninsula 358
Arabic graffiti/inscriptions 23–24, 329, 356 n. 5, 373 n. 44
– Egypt 52, 394
– India 307, 317–318

https://doi.org/10.1515/9783111326306-017

– Lakh Mazar 334, 338
– Northern Jordan 399–400
Arabic script 23–24, 307, 356 n. 6
Aramaic graffiti 52, 376–378
Aramaic script 329 n. 6, 358 n. 15, 360, 362, 376
Arameo-Iranian texts 329
Araya López, Alexander 27 n. 90, 32–33
Archaeological Survey of India 320
Archisketch 453, 454
Architectural Graffiti and the Maya Elite 111
architectural space 18–19, 225 n. 52
architecture 16, 84, 417, 446, 471, 475
– Buddhist 221 n. 32, 293, 299, 311, 321
– Egyptian 60, 66
– Maya 25, 110–119 *passim*, 123, 127, 131, 135–136
– at Pompeii 432, 438
Armenian inscriptions 393–394, 397
Arsacid courts/kings 17, 333, 335, 349–350
Art and Architecture Thesaurus (AAT) 30, 411, 413
artistic self-expression *see* self-expression
Arusha 89, 94–95
Äsän-Qutluy 200, 202
Asefi, Taghi 349
Aśokan pillar edicts 306–312, 314, 317, 319–320
astronomical notation 114, 125
Asyut 14, 47–48, 54–56, 59, 65, 69–71
– Project 62–63, 69–70
Athens 27
Athribis 19
Austin, Joe 148
Australia 25 n. 80, 27, 253
authorship 110, 116
Avalokieśvara 196
Avellino, Francesco Maria 385, 433
Awe, Jamie 113
Babylon 374–376
Bactrian (language) 297, 301, 334, 344, 349
Bagamoyo 94
Baghdad 23
Bagnall, Roger 457
Banganarti *see* Upper Church of Banganarti
Banksy 150
Basel 162, 472
Bashash, Rasul 334, 337–340, 342
Basquiat, Jean-Michel 84
bathroom graffiti 248; *see also* latrinalia
Bedouins 11, 364
Beihai 244
Beijing 204 n. 91, 236, 244, 252–254
– 2008 Olympics 235, 257
Belize 109, 113, 127, 439 n. 41
Belo Horizonte 149, 162, 164
Benefiel, Rebecca 6, 20, 31, 429–431, 441, 448, 458
Bešbalïq (Beiting 北庭) 176, 183, 205
Bethlehem 397
– Basilica of the Nativity 396–397
Bezeklik Cave 178–179, 181
Bhuilī 294
Bieber, Justin 162
big-character posters (*dazibao*) 243–244
Biggie 82, 85 n. 21
Bihar 295, 317, 320
bihua *see* murals
bilingual graffiti 180, 183–184, 186, 248, 333
Birbal 314
Birjand 334–335, 337, 342
Bisotun 329
blank spaces 217–219, 225–226, 230
BnF *see* Bibliothèque nationale de France
Bogotá 162
bombing/bombs 11–12, 254, 472; *see also* murals
Bonvicini, Monica 471
boredom 32, 111, 185, 203–204, 230, 366
Brāhmī script 344–346, 349
– India 288–295 *passim*, 301, 303, 312, 316, 320 n. 77
– Xinjiang and Gansu 182–183, 185–186
Brazil 144, 148–152, 154–155, 159, 161–162
Bregler, Nadine 14, 16
British Council 85
Broken Windows theory 155

the Bronx 78, 83–84
Brown, Kathryn 113
brushes 155, 238–239, 241–243, 245–246, 257
Brussels 84–85
Buddha 194, 197, 199, 221, 302, 304
– and the Monkey King 1, 3
– paying respect to 200, 224, 349
– Śākyamuni 195, 199 n. 79, 298, 304
Burrow, Reuben 317
Byzantine Empire 390
Byzantine period 21
Cabrini, Roberto 155
Cahal Pech 125
Calakmul 109, 121, 128
Calendar Round dates 125–126
calendrical notation 114, 126
Callieri, Pierfrancesco 349–350
Calmeyer, Peter 349
Čambalïq 205, 207
Campania 129, 441–442
Cao Yuanzhong 219 n. 25, 221
capitalism 79, 81, 145
Catacomb of Commodilla 19
Cataract, Aswan 52, 61
Catholic church 155
Cave of Elijah 21
caves 111, 235, 241, 276, 294, 320, 393
– in Central Asia 14, 16, 32, 174–209 *passim*, 216–230 *passim*
– at Socotra 296–299
CCM (Chama Cha Mapinduzi) 88, 91, 99
Central Asia 173–208 *passim*, 327
ceramics, inscriptions on 14, 19 n. 55, 113, 119, 294
Cereti, Carlo Giovanni 13, 17, 26
Chalfant, Henry 282
chalk 10–11, 288, 296, 431
Chama cha Demokrasi na Maendeleo (CHADEMA) 88
Chama Cha Mapinduzi (CCM) 88, 91, 99
Champion, Matthew 16, 25, 30, 34, 410 n. 71, 414
Chan, Brian 249
Chilas 302–304, 344
Chinese graffiti/inscriptions 175, 177, 216, 344–345
– bilingual 180, 184
Chinese manuscripts 14, 198–199, 203–204, 217–220, 222, 224–230
Choque Cultural gallery 159
Christian graffiti 20, 134, 393–394, 428, 441
– by Uyghurs 190–191, 193, 199, 203
Christianity 191 n. 54, 193 n. 56, 390, 427
chronology 19 n. 55, 56, 182 n. 27, 344–345, 362, 394, 472; *see also* dating graffiti/inscriptions
Church of the East 175, 189, 191, 193 n. 56
Church of the Holy Sepulchre 21–22
Cidade Escola Aprendiz 157
CIDOC Conceptual Reference Model 415–417
civil disobedience *see* disobedience
clan marks 289
Classic of Filial Piety (*Xiaojing* 孝經) 226, 228
Classics 25, 66, 430, 448
climate change 88, 166
CNN 425
coats of arms 390, 392, 398, 415
'Coco-Colonization' 83
Colombia 152, 162
colonialism 83, 111, 127, 317
colophons
– Chinese 219 n. 23, 221–224, 228, 230
– Old Uyghur 181, 194, 198–199, 208
commercialization 79, 81, 159, 165
Concise Oxford English Dictionary 328
Conexão Repórter TV show 155
conservation 399, 438
Constantinople 390
Cooper, Martha 282
Copan (Honduras) 124, 127
Coptic graffiti 19–20, 52, 72, 394
Corpus Inscriptionum Iranicarum 334, 344 n. 42, 347–348
Corpus Inscriptionum Latinarum 25 n. 81, 387, 426 n. 3, 434, 455 n. 64
corrections, scribal 72, 219, 444
Costa Rica 148, 156 n. 44
counter-aesthetics 147; *see also* public aesthetics

counterculture 147–148
counterpublics 146, 153
COVID-19 pandemic 11 n. 22, 93, 166
criminality 79, 94, 102, 146, 155, 157
– connotations of 10 n. 21, 151, 155, 165, 234, 259
criminalization 79, 94, 249
criminogenic discourse 149, 155, 165
criminological verstehen 146
Crusader kingdoms 390, 395
cultic spaces 4, 14–16, 19, 21
cultural heritage 16, 161, 260, 386, 410, 454
– China 7, 240–242, 250
cultural identity *see* identity
cultural memory 19–20, 48
Cultural Revolution 244
cuneiform script 23–24
Cunningham, Alexander 312 n. 59, 314, 319–320
cursive script 238 n. 11, 288, 297, 318–319, 331
– Egyptian 51, 65, 70
Cyprus 383–384, 391–392, 400–402, 410, 413, 418, 457 n. 66
– Science and Technology in Archaeology and Culture Research Center (STARC), The Cyprus Institute 383–384, 392, 406–407, 411–412, 417–418
Dadan (oasis) 359, 370 n. 39, 373–374, 376–378
Dahshur 59
DAIM *see* Reisser, Mirko
damage 208, 386, 428, 450, 453; *see also* deterioration
– curse against 367
– representing 67, 443–445
Daozhen (monk) 222, 230
Dar es Salaam 77, 80–103 *passim*
Dārāyān II 330
Darius I 52
dating graffiti/inscriptions 71, 110, 125, 186, 223, 334–335, 369–370; *see also* chronology
dazibao (big-character posters) 243–244
de Laguna Haviland, Anita 111
deejaying 78, 81, 83
defacement, graffiti as 1, 242, 248, 386
Deir el-Bahari 51, 59, 64
Deir el-Medina 55, 57
Delhi-Toprā pillar 306, 309–310
Delos 432
Demesticha, Stella 392 n. 31, 400
Democracy Wall movement 244
Demolition: Forbidden City 252
demotic script 51–52, 57, 72
Den Doncker, Alexis 60
desecration 2, 61 n. 43, 111
deterioration 80, 447, 450; *see also* damage
Deutsche Bahn 475, 478
Devaprayāg 295
*dhāraṇī*s 228, 304
dharma 198–199
diagrammatic graffiti 22, 25
diasporic publics 146, 153
DiBiasie-Sammons, Jacqueline 440, 454
DIGIGRAF 383–384, 402, 418–419
digital humanities 26, 418, 439–441, 455
digital photography 28, 67, 283, 408, 437, 452
digital storage 29–30, 282–283, 454–455
dipinti 288, 331, 431
– in Egypt 49, 54–56, 59–60, 62, 64–65, 69–73
direction of writing 51, 226 n. 60, 359, 360
disenfranchisement 79, 81, 146, 153
dishu (water calligraphy) 23, 244–245, 259
disobedience 153, 166, 249
divination 227, 237
Dixon, Neil 113
Do More Together 101
documentaries 91, 149, 152–153, 159, 162–163, 166
'documenters' vs. 'interpreters' 9–10, 26–28, 32
donations 177, 193, 202–203, 207, 294, 304
donative inscriptions 292–294, 298, 304, 310, 315 n. 66, 319; *see also* donor inscriptions

Dong-Qianfodong (Eastern Thousand-Buddha Caves) 200–202
Dongola 20
donor inscriptions 177–179; *see also* donative inscriptions
Dowson, Thomas 111
drugs 93, 97–98, 147, 153, 155, 157
Dudbridge, Glen 241–242
Dunhuang 14, 16, 32, 174–208 *passim*, 216–230 *passim*
Dura Europos 18, 21, 331, 350, 432, 436
– SATOR square pattern 428
Durgā Kho cave 320
Dzibanche 109
EAGLE (Europeana network of Ancient Greek and Latin Epigraphy) 458
East Asia 5–6, 236
East Side Boys 100
East Turkestan 174 n. 2, 184–186, 205, 207–208
Eco, Umberto 405
economy 56, 81–82, 472
EDR *see* Epigraphic Database Roma
Egyptian Ministry for Antiquities 67
Egyptology 25, 60, 65
Eighteenth Dynasty (Egypt) 54, 60
El Castillo complex 113
El Chilonche 115
El Peru 121
El Salvador 109
Elephantine Island 58
Elkab 62–63, 439 n. 41
England 25, 357 n. 11; *see also* United Kingdom
Ephesus 18 n. 48, 432
EpiDoc 30, 411, 442 n. 50, 446 n. 60, 455–457
Epigraphic Database Bari 441
Epigraphic Database Heidelberg 441
Epigraphic Database Roma (EDR) 426 n. 3, 429, 431 n. 14, 441, 448, 454
erasure of graffiti 49
Estakhr 332
Ethiopia 18 n. 47, 358
ethnicity 145, 182, 258; *see also* race
ethnography 33, 78, 80; *see also* oral history
– of buildings/spaces 165
Eurasia 173–175, 204, 208
European Union 410
evanescent calligraphy *see* water calligraphy
Ewald, Sanja 23, 33
Facebook 92, 97, 358
facsimiles 67–68, 70–73, 179, 308, 312–313, 428
fading of graffiti 67, 86, 88, 208–209, 230
FAIR Data Principles 384, 398, 406–411, 414, 418; *see also* accessibility
Falk, Harry 289, 292–293, 307–311, 315–317
Family Tree 250–251
Fars 17, 349–350
Fash, William and Barbara 127
Fashion Moda 84
Felicetti, Achille 416
Feliu, Núria 112
Felle, Antonio E. 25
Felsbilder und Inschriften am Karakorum-Highway 301
Ferrell, Jeff 146, 152
Fīrūz Shāh 306, 308
Fitzmaurice, Rosamund 113
Flaubert, Gustave 386
Florida, South 162
Folha de São Paulo 148, 151, 158–160, 163, 166; *see also* São Paulo
footprints 4, 57–58, 298–299
Franco, Sérgio Miguel 148
Frankfurt 279
Frederick, Ursula 27
French Archaeological Mission 332
frescoes 19 n. 54, 235, 305–306, 452
– House of 331
– Pompeii 425, 427 n. 4, 432
frottage 408
Fujian Province 207
Futura 2000 84
Fuye, Alotte de la 349
Galilei, Galileo 417–418
Gandhara 301, 345
Gangsta One 82

Gansu 2 n. 4, 174–175, 186, 196, 205–206, 208
- cave temples 180, 183, 186, 188, 192, 201–202, 206
Gaochang (*Qočo*) 174, 205
Garrucci, Raffaele 385–386, 407, 433
gender 79, 97, 145, 164, 248, 259
genealogies 49, 357, 362–366
Georgian inscriptions 394
German Turfan expeditions 182
Germany 33, 274, 276, 484
Gervers, Eva 60
Ghosh, Amalananda 314–315
Giza 59
Global North 11, 79
Global South 5
globalization 79, 82–83
Goffman, Erving 145
Graf, Ann 31
graffiti companionships 7–8, 360–361
GRAFMEDIA 383, 402
GRAPH-EAST 398
Great Wall of China 7, 28, 248
Greece 125, 356
Greek graffiti/inscriptions 52, 288–289, 297, 374, 393–394, 401, 458–459
Guatemala 109, 111–112, 127
Guazhou 181, 183, 188–189, 192–193, 200–202, 206
Gülden, Svenja 54, 69, 71
Habermas, Jürgen 146
Haldaikish, rock of 344
Hamburg
- Altona Museum 280
- graffiti artist 31, 33, 482
- graffiti scene 267–269, 271, 273, 275–276, 278, 281, 485
- University of 6 n. 11, 15 n. 38, 33–34
Han dynasty (China) *see* Later Han dynasty
Hargrove, Charles (Kool Koor) 83–85, 94
Haring, Keith 84
Harrist, Robert 240, 242
Harvard University 458
- Center for Hellenic Studies 458
Harvey, David 145
Hathor (goddess) 54
Hatnub, quarry of 52–53, 65
Haviland, William 111
Hebei Province 205
Hegrā 372–373; *see also* Petra
Heidelberg Academy 301
Henning, Walter Bruno 329 n. 6, 331, 335, 337 n. 24, 345 n. 43
heraldic graffiti 25, 392–393
Herculaneum 431, 439–440, 448–449, 454, 458, 459 n. 72
- Graffiti Project 429
- and Pompeii 385, 435, 437, 447, 450, 456–458
Hermes, Bernard 112
Hernandez-Llach, Israel 'Reefa' 162
Herzfeld, Ernst 335, 349–350
hieratic script 51–55, 57, 65, 68, 70, 72
Hinduism 302 n. 39, 314
von Hinüber, Oskar 303
hip hop *see also* rap music
- culture 80, 85, 92–93, 95, 472
- graffiti 12 n. 26, 77–87, 92–103, 147–157 *passim*, 253, 257–258
- movement 78–79, 97, 103, 157
- music 12 n. 26, 277, 280
Hispania Epigraphica 441
HIV/AIDS epidemic 82, 88; *see also* medical-epidemiological discourse
hobo graffiti 234
Hohhot 181, 184–185, 190–191, 195, 200, 207
- ruled by Önggüd tribe 193 n. 56
Holmul 134
Holy Land 394; *see also* Jerusalem
Honduras 109, 127
Hong Kong 11–12, 249, 254
Hoq cave 296–297, 301, 303–304, 319
House of Frescos 331
House of Nebuchelus 18
human sacrifices 116–117, 119–120, 127, 129, 131, 134
Huntley, Katherine 129
Hutson, Scott 131
iconicity of script 23
iconography 26, 110, 116, 335
identity 19, 174 n. 2, 234, 355, 458
- community 78, 91–92, 103, 258

- cultural 239, 250
- inscriptions 176–177, 179–180
- marks/signs 392, 405, 415
Iezzi, Adriana 258
illegibility 221, 289–290, 294, 305, 447; *see also* legibility
Imbert, Frédéric 388–389, 399–400, 402
Imperial Aramaic 375–376
imprinting *see* printing
Indo-Iranians 173, 333
Informationssystem Graffiti in Deutschland (INGRID) 31
infra-red photographs 67
Ingrand-Varenne, Estelle 398
Inner Mongolia 181, 185, 190–191, 205
inscribed landscapes 239
Instagram 23 n. 78, 165, 426
intention 81, 102, 234–250 *passim*, 261, 388, 467–468
interdisciplinarity 8, 26–27, 30–31, 79, 389, 419
'interpreters' vs. 'documenters' 9–10, 16, 26–28, 32
Iran 26, 205 n. 98, 333–335, 339, 342, 351
Iraq 23–24
Islam 174, 193, 329, 331–333, 338, 390
- history 66
- Nation of 83
Islamic inscriptions 331, 390, 394
Israel 21, 392, 395
Istituto della Enciclopedia Italiana 437
Italian Ministry of Culture 454
Italy 21 n. 70, 129, 151, 288 n. 21, 386, 432, 441
Jabal Naqus 394
Jāgeśvar 290, 295
Jahāngīr, Mughal ruler 306, 308, 311, 314
Japan 174
*Jātaka*s 302
Jay Z 82
Jerusalem 21–22, 390; *see also* Holy Land
Jettmar, Karl 344–346
Jiangsu Province 207
Jordan 11, 374, 388
- literacy 358–359, 362, 367 n. 32, 399
- Northern 392, 395, 399
Journal of Archaeological Science: Reports 439
Journey to the West 1, 3
Judaism 390
Kal Jangal 334–338, 342–343
Kalasinga 78, 85–86, 94–95, 97
Kamfiruz inscription 329
Kampen, Michael 111
Kang Youwei 238
Kara Tepa 292
KARABOI project 392, 400
Karakorum Highway 288, 291, 294, 301, 304
- building of 329, 344
Karnak 57–58
Kassab, Gilberto (Mayor) 159–160
Kassapa, king 305
Kauśāmbī pillar 306, 308, 312, 315–316
Kawatoko, Mutsuo 392, 394
Keegan, Peter 328
Kemyt 56
Khapra Kodiya, Junagadh 320
Kharoṣṭhī script 289 n. 4, 301, 344
Khonsu Temple 57–58
Kienitz, Sabine 14–15
Kiswahili language 81–82, 85, 88, 91, 97, 100
Kitsudō Kōichi 182–183, 186 n. 45
Kool Koor (Charles Hargrove) 83–85, 94
Kraack, Detlev 392, 395, 405
Krishnaswamy, Rao Sahib 314–315
Kuala Lumpur 24, 254
Kuh-e Bāqrān 337
Kuh-e Hossein 332–333
Kuh-e Reč 337
Kunming 254–256
Kwanyin Clan 258
La Blanca 115, 133–134
La Nación 148, 151, 156 n. 44
La Sapienza University of Rome 430
Labbaf-Khaniki, Rajab'Ali 337
Lakh Mazar 334–335, 337–343
landscape epigraphy 351, 387
landscape painting 258
Langaron, Anna 392
Langner, Martin 435–436, 446
laser scanning 409, 438

Later Han dynasty (China) 23 n. 45, 237–238
Latin alphabet *see* alphabet
Latin America 32–32, 148
latrinalia 7, 11, 234; *see also* bathroom graffiti
layout 20, 70, 72
Lebanon 395
Lefebvre, Henri 145
legibility 289–290, 294, 305, 442, 447, 452–453; *see also* illegibility; visibility
– in Dunhuang caves 221–222
– low priority of 270
Leiden Conventions 30, 411, 442
the Levant 374–375
Lewis-Williams, David 111
LeWitt, Sol 471
Li Hua 257
Li Zhengyu 216
Libyan Desert 57
Liḥyān, kings of 376–378
literacy 7, 88, 125, 399, 405, 418
– in the Iranian world 328, 343
– in non-literate societies 32, 356–373 *passim*
literate societies 4, 356–357, 360, 368
Livshits, Vladimir Aronovich 338, 341–342
Local Fanatics 78, 85–87, 91, 93–94, 97 n. 44, 99, 101 n. 53
London, Institute of Archaeology, University College London 113
Longxing Monastery 224
Los Angeles, Venice Beach 280
love tags 13
Löw, Martina 145
Lucian 27
Lumbinī 308, 315, 317 n. 72
Luxor Temple 1–2
Lyon 436
Macao 249
Macdonald, Michael 7, 13, 32
Magufuli, John 91
Mahāyāna Buddhism 195–196, 203
Maitreya 178 n. 8, 186, 194, 196, 198
Manhattan 84, 143
Manichaeism 173, 175, 178–179, 203 n. 86
Mañjuśrī Bodhisattva 178 n. 8, 195–196, 201, 207
Mao Zedong 240, 243
marginalization 78, 81, 83, 146, 153
Markle, Seth 31, 33
Martini, Stella 150
materiality 30, 236, 239, 245, 259, 261
Matsui Dai 14, 32, 216
Maue, Dieter 182
Maya Graffiti International Database 112
Mayan civilisation 18, 109, 115, 135–136
Mazdakites 334–335, 338
McCurdy, Leah 113
MCing 83
Mecquenem, Roland de 349
medical-epidemiological discourse 152–153, 155, 165; *see also* HIV/AIDS epidemic
Medinet Habu 56
meditation 198, 200 n. 82
Mediterranean 5, 20–21, 125, 374–375, 428, 436
– Eastern 26, 383–385, 388–392, 398–399, 401, 418
Medy 78, 85–86, 88–89, 93–94, 96, 99–100
Meeting of Styles (Asia) 254–257
Mehri language 356
Meidum 59
Meinardus, Otto 392–393
Mejah 78, 81–86, 91, 99, 100 n. 51
Mercado, Jorge 162
meritorious deeds 177, 188, 194, 197, 219 n. 23; *see also* transfer of merit
Merriam-Webster Dictionary 328
Mesoamerica 5, 21, 113, 125, 132, 136; *see also* Maya
– deity 119
– game 116, 125, 128, 135
Mesopotamia 327, 375
Mexico 109–110
Miami 162
Middle Ages 19, 57, 374 n. 50, 383, 389
Middle Egypt 19, 59

Middle Iranian languages 26, 327, 333–334
Middle Persian graffiti/inscriptions 13, 329–338 *passim*, 344, 349; *see also* Persian graffiti/inscriptions
Miletus 29
Mira 19
Mithra 335, 338
Mixteca-Puebla style 132–133, 135
Mkapa, Benjamin 83
mnemonic lines 226–230
Moganshan Road, Shanghai 253
Mogao cave temples 174, 184, 196, 200, 216–230 *passim*
Mommsen, Theodor 434
Mongol empire 174, 186, 204; *see also* Yuan dynasty
Mongol period 181, 184, 186–187, 191, 200, 203–205, 208
Mongolian graffiti/inscriptions 175, 180, 187–189, 199
Mongolian Plateau 173
Monkey King 1–4
Montana spray cans 85–87
Moriyasu Takao 179
mosaics 432, 437
Mount Tai 239–240
Mt. Mugh documents 344
multigraphic graffiti 6, 8, 22–23, 32, 52
multilingual graffiti 8, 207, 388
multimodality of graffiti 23, 387
multispectral imaging 410, 417, 438 n. 36
Muṇḍeśvarī 295
Munich 279–280, 472
muralism 147, 156, 234
murals 82, 234–235, 257, 472; *see also* bombing/bombs
- Buddhist 209, 216, 220
- WCT 87–88, 90–91, 98, 100
Murano, Francesca 416
Museum of Fine Arts, Houston 251–252
Museum of Islamic Art, Berlin 24
Muslims 88, 174 n. 2, 193, 318, 329, 332
Mwanza 86, 94
Nabataean graffiti 355, 358, 360, 373, 377–378
Nabataeans 360, 364, 372, 377–378
Nabonidus, king 374–378
Nafasi Art Space 93, 99 n. 47, 102
Nāgarī script 305, 309–310
Nairobi 96
Nakas, Ioannis 113
Nakum 112–113, 116, 118–119, 121–124, 126, 128, 131–135
Nandangarh pillar 309, 317
Nanjing 1
Naqsh-e Rostam 332
Naranjo 121, 134
Nasrollahzadeh, Cyrus 332
National Archaeological Museum, Naples 433
Nauman, Bruce 469, 471
Navrátilová, Hana 58
Nepal 315
Nestorian Christians 175
New Kingdom, Egypt 55, 59–60, 65, 72
New York 96, 143, 148, 150, 250, 282, 478
- contemporary graffiti 11–13
- hip hop 78, 95, 267
- -inspired graffiti 13, 23, 472
Institute for the Study of the Ancient World (ISAW) 457
- Metropolitan Museum of Art 48, 50–51, 64
- subway 267, 270
The New York Times 143
New York University 457
newsworthiness 150
NGOs 82, 87, 92, 100, 103, 147, 156
Niglīvā 309, 315, 317 n. 72
Nikitin, Alexander B. 13
Nina (Nina Pandolfo) 157
Nineteenth and Twentieth Dynasties (Egypt) 57
Ningxia 180, 205
NMGS *see* Norfolk Medieval Graffiti Survey
nobility 349, 351, 390, 392–393, 405, 415
nomads 356–359, 362, 364, 367 n. 32, 373–375, 379; *see also* non-literate societies
- Uyghur 173
non-alphabetic signs 287–289, 293, 318; *see also* alphabetic writing

non-literate societies 356–358, 363, 367; see also nomads
Nondédéo, Philippe 131
Norfolk Medieval Graffiti Survey (NMGS) 25, 30–31, 410 n. 71, 414
North Arabia 32, 355
Nubia *see* Sudan
Nunca (Francisco Rodrigues da Silva) 157
Nyerere, Julius 88
Oaxaca 148
Obama, Barack 88
OCIANA 355, 366–367, 370 n. 36, 374 n. 49
offering 60, 187, 193, 199–200, 203
– formulas 52, 56, 72
Olko, Justyna 112
Olympic Games (Beijing 2008) 235, 257
Önggüd tribe 191, 193 n. 56
Online Corpus of the Inscriptions of Ancient North Arabia *see* OCIANA
Oplontis 429, 431, 437
oral history 27, 80; *see also* ethnography
Osanna, Massimo 426
OSGEMEOS (Otavio Pandolfo and Gustavo Pandolfo) 150–151, 157, 161
Osthof, Ann Lauren 29
ostraca 55–56, 71–72, 329, 341; *see also* potsherds
overpainting of graffiti 49
Ovid 433
ownership inscriptions/marks 13 n. 29, 225 n. 52, 289–293, 328, 330, 349 n. 55
Oxford 355–356
– Ashmolean Museum 363
Pakistan 26, 287 n. 1, 301, 329, 333–334, 344–345; *see also* Upper Indus Valley
palanquins 116, 119–121, 124, 127
Palenque 132, 134
palettes 48, 51
Palmyra 21
pan-Africanism 88
Panciera, Silvio 430
Pandolfo, Nina (Nina) 157
panoramic imaging 409–410
papyrus 18, 48, 51, 55–56, 71, 359 n. 20
Paranavitana, Senarath 291, 305
Paris 11 n. 22, 280, 472
– Bibliothèque nationale de France (BnF) 217, 219–220, 227–229
Parke, Elizabeth 246
Parkinson, John 146
Parthian graffiti/inscriptions 329, 331, 333–335, 337–339, 341–344, 349
patolli (game) 18, 116, 125, 127–128, 135
Patrois, Julie 131
Peden, Alexander 60
Pelliot, Paul 179 n. 13, 184
Persepolis 17, 327–329, 349–350
Persian graffiti/inscriptions 193, 307, 309–310, 320 n. 77, 338; *see also* Middle Persian graffiti/inscriptions
Petra 372–373; *see also* Hegrā
petroglyphs 11, 301, 344, 394
'Phags-pa script 182, 186, 188
Philadelphia 11, 96, 468
Phoenico-Aramaic script 358 n. 15, 362
photogrammetry 67, 409–410, 417, 438–439
piety graffiti 16, 49, 54, 60, 65, 178
pilgrim graffiti/inscriptions 4, 21–22, 280; *see also* tourist graffiti; visitors' graffiti
– Chinese 2 n. 4, 220–221, 239
– in India 288–290, 294–295, 308–310, 315, 318, 320
– Uyghur 32, 177–209 *passim*, 216
Pivetta da Mota, Caroline 150, 156
pixação 13, 147–166 *passim*; *see also* tagging
pixadores 149–156, 161–162, 164
Pixadores de Elite 162
Pixo (documentary) 152–153, 162–163
Plumber King 11–12
poetic graffiti 14, 199
poetry 305–306, 358
– Chinese 238, 240–241, 246, 248, 258
police 28, 94, 166, 317–318; *see also* social repression
– abuse/violence 90–91, 143, 152–153, 161–164
political graffiti 11–12, 145, 147–148, 165–166, 276

– and illegality 153–155, 157 n. 46, 161
Polo, Marco 193 n. 56, 203, 205 n. 98
Pompeii 17, 18 n. 46, 20, 21 n. 62, 65, 259, 339, 355, 372, 374, 385, 425–438, 441–442, 445 n. 53, 447–451, 454–458
– Archaeological Park of 425–426
Pompei: Pitture e Mosaici 437
Porció, Tibor 14, 181, 186, 194–195, 207
Portuguese 149, 153
possession inscriptions 292–294
potsherds 18, 56, 288–290, 292–293, 359 n. 20; *see also* ostraca
potter's marks 289
pottery 14, 19 n. 55, 134, 288–290, 292, 294, 318
Pourshariati, Parvaneh 335, 338, 342
Powers, Stephen 27, 31
Prayāg 312, 314
prayers 18, 21, 318, 358, 364–365, 370–373
– Buddhist 239, 317 n. 72
– Christian 21, 134, 190–191
– Maya 134
preservation of graffiti 28 n. 94, 33, 208, 267, 398, 428
– best practices for 384 n. 1
– as digital data/photographs 29, 80, 282
– through removal 429
– as rubbings 215
– *in situ* 5, 216
– state of 30, 73, 122, 321, 394, 447
Pringle, Denys 395
Prinsep, James 312, 314, 319–320
printing 110, 114–116, 240, 243
– woodblock 3, 204, 207
prisoners 117, 129
prisons 11 n. 22, 25 n. 80, 83
privacy 7, 248, 374
Propertius 433
public aesthetics 16, 143, 145, 147; *see also* counter-aesthetics
public calligraphy (*tizi*) 23, 238, 240, 243, 245–246
public sphere 144, 165, 238
punctate graffiti 113–114
punctuation 30, 442, 444–446
punishment 144, 153–155, 161–162, 165–166; *see also* removal
della Puppa, Chiara 362–363
pyramids 116, 119, 123, 128–129, 135
Qočo (Gaochang) 174, 205
Quixote Spray Arte 157
race 78, 145, 164; *see also* ethnicity
Ragazzoli, Chloé 59, 62
Rajan, K. 289
rap music 88, 92–93, 99; *see also* hip hop
rapping 78, 81–83
Razmjou, Sharokh 350
Reflectance Transformation Imaging *see* RTI
Reisser, Mirko (DAIM) 23, 31, 33, 267–283
removal of graffiti 17, 28, 157, 159, 161; *see also* punishment
– cost of 143
– for protection 66, 428–430
resistance 79, 145, 234, 248–249
Rhapsody on the Swallow (*Yanzi fu*) 228
Rio Bec 113, 118, 123, 128, 130–132
Rio de Janeiro 149
Ripumalla, king 308–309, 315, 317
rock inscriptions 389, 394
– Egyptian 49, 52, 56, 62–63, 65, 72
Rock Inscriptions Project 393, 396–398, 408
Rodney, Walter 88
Rogers, Janine 14
Roman Empire 21, 379, 432, 440–441
Roman script/handwriting 359–360, 445, 450
Romans 24, 288–289, 364, 385, 431–432, 458
Rome 19, 431, 436, 441
– ancient 21, 125, 276, 379
– La Sapienza University of 430
RTI (Reflectance Transformation Imaging) 400, 410, 417, 438–440, 454, 455
rubbings 215, 240, 312, 315 n. 70, 439 n. 40
Russia 378
Russian Academy of Sciences 198–199, 203

Rust53 479–480
S. Maria Capua Vetere 437
Šābuhr I 331
sacrifices *see* human sacrifices
Sadiq, Osama 23–24
Safaitic graffiti/inscriptions 32, 359–363, 365–374, 378–379, 458
Saint Anthony, monastery of 392
Saint Catherine's Monastery 392
Saint Paul the Anchorite, monastery of 392
Śākyamuni *see* Buddha
Salihundam (Andhra Pradesh) 292, 320
Salomon, Richard 288–291, 294–295, 307, 318, 320
Salvador, Chiara 66
Sami, Ali 349
Samudragupta's inscription 306, 308, 312, 315
sanctioned graffiti 63, 77, 87, 156; *see also* unsanctioned graffiti
Sanskrit 292, 295 n. 23, 299, 304–305, 345 n. 43
– Xinjiang and Gansu 175, 182–183, 185 n. 43
São Paulo 149, 155, 158–159, 161, 163–164; *see also Folha de São Paulo*
– Biennial 150, 154, 156, 159, 161
Saqqara 59, 66
Sasanian graffiti/inscriptions 13, 17, 331–339 *passim*, 343–345, 349
SATOR square 20, 426–429
Saudi Arabia 359, 367 n. 32, 372–373; *see also* Arabia
school curriculum 14, 55
scribal corrections 72, 219, 444
secondary epigraphy/graffiti 8, 60, 62, 110, 115, 306–312, 318–319
Sela-One 82–83
Seleucid 331
self-expression 93, 234, 238
semiotics 17 n. 45, 22, 239, 243, 403–405
Sennett, Richard 144
sexual symbols 116, 125
Shang dynasty (China) 237
Shanghai 236, 247, 253–254
Shanxi Province 207
Shatial 301–302, 304, 344–347
shell-script (*śaṅkhalipi*) 209, 295, 307–310, 316, 320
ship graffiti 5, 384, 390, 392 n. 31, 400–401, 410
Sigiri Graffiti 291, 305
Sigiriya 289 n. 4, 291, 305
signatures 49, 59–60, 85, 248, 268, 355, 370
Silk Road 173–174, 207
silver vessels, inscriptions on 13, 329–330
Sims-Williams, Nicholas 334, 344–348
Sinai 388–390, 392–394
Singgim 195
Sinhalese inscriptions 305
Śiva 315
Six Dynasties (China) 238, 241
Skjærvø, Prods Oktor 330, 342 n. 36
slave trade 83
Smith, Nick 249
Smyrna 457
social calligraphy 243, 250
social justice 83, 162
social media 88, 149, 165, 244, 368
social repression 79, 90; *see also* police
social sciences 233
Socialism *see* African Socialism
sociology 4–5, 33, 66, 79, 145
Socotra 296
Sogdian graffiti/inscriptions 301 n. 37, 334, 344–347, 349
Sogdians 301, 333, 346
Song dynasty (China) 204 n. 91, 215 n. 1, 240–241
Soqotri language 356
The Source magazine 83
South Africa 25 n. 80, 82–83; *see also* Africa
South Arabia 358–359
South Arabian languages 297, 356, 360 n. 23
South Bronx 78, 84
South Semitic script-family 358–359, 362, 367 n. 32
Southeast Asia 6 n. 10, 236

Southern Khorasan 26, 329, 333–335, 337, 343, 349
Spade 479–480
spatial politics 144, 161, 165, 249
spray cans 78–95 *passim*, 155, 161, 257, 277–278, 468
– Montana 85–86, 87
Sprenkle, Sara 441
squeezes 66, 73, 360
Sri Lanka 287 n. 1, 289, 291
– King Kassapa 305
St Petersburg 178, 198–199, 203
– State Hermitage Museum 178, 198 n. 73
Stabiae 431–432, 435, 437, 457
StadtPalais – Museum für Stuttgart 469–470, 472–474
STARC (Science and Technology in Archaeology and Culture Research Center) 383–384, 392, 406–407, 411–412, 417–418
Staring, Nico 60, 63, 65
Stein, Aurel 344–345
stigma 145, 329
stone inscriptions 238–240, 242
Stone, Michael 389, 392–395, 397
storage *see* digital storage
Strauch, Ingo 14
street calligraphy *see* water calligraphy
street propaganda 147
Studio Vierkant 472 n. 6, 479–480
Stuttgart 31, 33, 468–470, 472–479, 481–484
– Bonatzbau 469–470, 474–479, 481
stylus 431, 434 n. 25, 450
subaltern publics 146–147, 153, 321
Sudan 15, 20, 438 n. 39
surveillance of public spaces 246, 248, 250, 254
sutras 32, 239
Suzhou 196, 205, 207 n. 102
Switzerland 84
Sypniewski, Holly 20, 31, 441
Syria 356, 358–359, 362–363, 392
Syriac language/script 182, 189–191, 199, 394
Syros Island 21
tabula ansata 20–21
Tag Master Killers 84
tagging 82–83, 87, 95, 143, 147–166 *passim*, 253; *see also pixação*
Taki 183 (Demetrius) 143
Tamil Nadu 292–293
Tang dynasty (China) 173, 215 n. 2, 238, 241
Tangut language 175, 180, 183, 195 n. 66, 207 n. 100
Tanguts 199, 205–206
Tanzania 77–85, 87–90, 92, 94–97, 99–101, 103
– Wachata Crew 31, 33, 77–78, 80–83, 85–103
Tarkasnawa 19
Taweza 99, 101
Taymāʾ (oasis) 359, 374–378
Taymanitic graffiti 375–378
Thalpan 301 n. 35, 304
Theban Desert Road Survey 57
Thebes 65
– Western 55, 57, 59
Thousand Character Classic (*Qianziwen*) 228
throw-ups 11–12, 82, 84
Tianshan Mountains 173
Tibetan language/script 175, 182, 184–186, 203, 216, 301, 317 n. 72
tibishi (verses on walls) 241–242
Tifinagh script 357, 367 n. 35
Tikal kingdom 109, 111, 117–121, 123–126, 128, 131–134
Tikal Project 111
timing (explanatory inscriptions) 177, (inscribed names) 240
Tissamaharama 289–290, 293
Tocharian language 175, 182–184, 186, 197
Tocharians 173, 185, 207
Tonkiss, Fran 149
torture, scenes of 117, 119–120
tourism 1, 3, 7, 99, 166
tourist graffiti 11, 65, 181, 248, 305; *see also* pilgrim graffiti; visitors' graffiti
Toyoq 182, 197–200, 203
transfer of merit 178, 187, 194; *see also* meritorious deeds

travellers' graffiti *see* visitors' graffiti
Trentin, Mia 6, 9, 26, 31
Trik, Helen 111
Tuareg nomads 357, 367 n. 35, 370 n. 38
Turfan 14, 32, 174–208 *passim*
Türkiye 19, 29, 457
Twenty-First Dynasty (Egypt) 57
Twitter 165
Umbrella Movement 249
underemployment 81, 90, 98
United Arab Emirates 87
United Kingdom 22, 31; *see also* England
United States 94, 152, 162, 253, 472; *see also* USA
University of Dar es Salaam 82, 88
University of Pennsylvania Museum 111
University of Valencia 112
unsanctioned graffiti 10, 86, 94; *see also* sanctioned graffiti
Unut, goddess 53
Upper Church of Banganarti 20
Upper Egypt 62, 439 n. 41
Upper Indus Valley inscriptions 26, 288–289, 301, 319, 332–349 *passim*; *see also* Pakistan
urban graffiti 242, 275, 360, 472
urbanization 79, 243, 246
USA 268, 274, 468; *see also* United States
Uttar Pradesh 294, 320
Uyghur script 173 n. 1, 175, 179, 182, 189
Vachenauer, Moritz 481
Valencia 112
Valjakka, Minna 23
Valley of the Kings 57
value discourse 156–157, 165–166
Varone, Antonio 435–437, 446, 457
Vergil 433
Verhoeven, Ursula 6, 8, 14
verses on walls (*tibishi*) 241–242
Vesuvius, Mt. 425, 429, 431
Vieth, Anne 31, 33
Vīsaladeva, Cāhamāna ruler 306, 310
visibility 61 n. 43, 66–69, 243, 447, 480–482, 485; *see also* accessibility; legibility
– potential for 87, 277, 477
visitors' graffiti *see also* pilgrim graffiti; tourist graffiti
– Chinese 177, 179, 220–221
– Egyptian 4, 54, 58–60, 62, 65, 72
– Old Uyghur 14, 205
VisualGlyph 70
votive inscriptions 5, 13 n. 30, 18–22, 60, 69, 222
Vulture Rock 62–63
Wachata Crew (WCT) 31, 33, 77–78, 80–82, 84–103
Wadi al Haggag 394
Wadi el-Hol 54
Wadi Mokhatab 394
Wadi Rum Reserve, Jordan 11
Wall Lords Asia 254–256
wall paintings 66, 235, 288, 437, 471
– Buddhist 175 n. 4, 177–179, 201, 216
Wang, Dan 248
Wang Liping 216
Wang, Meiqin 257
WaPi (Words and Pictures) 85
Ward-Perkins, Bryan 25
water calligraphy (*dishu*) 23, 244–245, 259
Watkins, Tia 113
wax tablets 288, 446; *see also* writing tablets
Waxšahr, Prince 328, 330
WCT *see* Wachata Crew
West Uyghur kingdom 173, 176–178, 183
White Pagoda 185, 190–191, 207
Women Xpress 96–97
Wordsworth, Christopher 433
Wordsworth, William 433
writing tablets 48, 51, 56, 392; *see also* wax tablets
written artefact 6–8, 13, 17–32 *passim*, 403
Wu Hung 253
Wuhan 254, 256–257
Wutaishan (Mt. Wutai) 188, 205
Xinjiang 173–186 *passim*, 197–198, 203, 208, 301
Xunantunich (Belize) 113, 126–127, 134
Yaxha (Guatemala) 119, 127–130, 133
Yemen 287 n. 1, 356, 359, 374

Yen, Yuehping 239, 243–245
Yongchang 189, 205
YouTube 27, 97, 457 n. 66
Yuan dynasty (China) 181, 184, 186–187, 202, 204–205, 207; *see also* Mongol empire
Yulin caves 179, 183–199 *passim*, 203, 205–206
Zaki 82
Zeitlin, Judith 241–242
Zeus Megistos, temple of 331
Zhang Dali 252–253
Zhang, Gehao 257
Zhang, Hong 249
Zhang Huan 250–251
Zhang Yingrun 221–224, 229–230
Zhejiang Province 207
Zhending 205, 207 n. 100
Zieme, Peter 181
Zito, Angela 245
zones of tolerance 147, 157
Zoroastrians 329, 332, 335 n. 17
Źrałka, Jarosław 18, 25

www.ingramcontent.com/pod-product-compliance
Lightning Source LLC
LaVergne TN
LVHW010851110826
845149LV00005B/1382

* 9 7 8 3 1 1 2 2 1 5 4 7 0 *